Clinical Psychology

Clinical Psychology: An Introduction is for students studying clinical psychology as part of an undergraduate programme in psychology, nursing, sociology or social and behavioural sciences. Undergraduate students who wish to know if postgraduate study in clinical psychology would be of interest to them will find this book particularly useful.

The book will inform students about

- the profession of clinical psychology
- how to get onto a clinical psychology postgraduate training programme
- the way clinical psychologists work with children, adolescents and adults with common psychological problems
- the main models of practice used by clinical psychologists, and
- the scientific evidence for the effectiveness of psychological interventions.

There is a focus on both clinical case studies and relevant research, and the book includes summaries, revision questions, advice on further reading and a glossary of key terms, all of which make it an excellent, student-friendly introduction to an exceptionally interesting subject.

Alan Carr is director of clinical psychology training at University College Dublin and has a clinical practice at the Clanwilliam Institute, Dublin. He has produced over 20 volumes and 200 papers and presentations in the areas of clinical psychology, family therapy and positive psychology. His books include the *Handbook of Child and Adolescent Clinical Psychology*, the *Handbook of Adult Clinical Psychology*, the *Handbook of Intellectual Disability and Clinical Psychology Practice*, and *What Works with Children, Adolescents and Adults? A Review of Research on the Effectiveness of Psychotherapy and Positive Psychology*. He has worked in the fields of clinical psychology and family therapy in the UK, Ireland and Canada.

Clinical Psychology

An Introduction

Alan Carr

Routledge
Taylor & Francis Group

LONDON AND NEW YORK

First published 2012
by Routledge
27 Church Road, Hove, East Sussex BN3 2FA

Simultaneously published in the USA and Canada
by Routledge
711 Third Avenue, New York NY 10017

Routledge is an imprint of the Taylor & Francis Group, an Informa business

British Library Cataloguing in Publication Data
A catalogue record for this book is available from the British Library

Library of Congress Cataloging in Publication Data
Carr, Alan, 1957–
    Clinical psychology : an introduction / Alan Carr.
        p. cm.
    Includes bibliographical references.
    ISBN 978-0-415-68396-8 (hardback)—ISBN 978-0-415-68397-5 (paperback)
    1. Clinical psychology—Textbooks. I. Title.
    RC467.C35 2012
    616.89—dc23   2011038606

ISBN: 978-0-415-68396-8 (hbk)
ISBN: 978-0-415-68397-5 (pbk)
ISBN: 978-0-203-09763-2 (ebk)

Typeset in Arial MT and Frutiger by RefineCatch Limited, Bungay, Suffolk
Paperback cover design by Andrew Ward

Contents

List of figures

List of tables

Preface

This book will help you find out about the profession of clinical psychology, how to get a place on a training programme, what it's like to work as a clinical psychologist, and the theoretical and scientific basis for clinical psychology. The first chapter answers the questions: 'What is it like working as a clinical psychologist?' and 'How do I get a place on a training programme?' It provides an overview of the profession and academic discipline of clinical psychology. There is a discussion of the many settings in which clinical psychologists work, the wide range of topics researched in this field, and advice on how to obtain a place on a postgraduate clinical psychology professional training programme in the UK and Ireland. Reference will be made to training in the US and Australia.

Chapters 2–8 cover common psychological problems of childhood, adolescence and adulthood. In Chapter 2 on childhood problems, conduct disorder, oppositional defiant disorder and ADHD are discussed. Chapters 3 and 4 deal with eating disorders and drug abuse, which are common difficulties in adolescence. Anxiety, depression, schizophrenia and personality disorders are considered in Chapters 5–8. In these chapters on specific disorders, case examples are given along with relevant theory and research on the diagnosis, classification, epidemiology, course, assessment and treatment of these conditions. Controversies relevant to each condition are addressed.

In all of these chapters a description of the principal clinical features of a disorder or group of disorders is given, with illustrative clinical examples. Formulations and treatment plans, based on best practice principles, are included where appropriate. This shows how clinical psychologists approach common psychological problems in routine practice. Epidemiological information on the prevalence, patterns of comorbidity and outcome for each disorder is given. This is followed by theoretical explanations from neurobiological and psychological perspectives. Where appropriate, psychological explanations from psychodynamic, cognitive-behavioural and family systems perspectives are given. Reference is made to empirical research relevant to each theoretical perspective and to research on the effectiveness of various treatments. However, this is not intended as a textbook for clinical practice, so insufficient information is given for such purposes.

Virtually all of the assertions made about the psychological problems in Chapters 2–8 require qualification as to the limits of their reliability and validity. However, I have not peppered the text with statements of qualification, since this would detract from the clarity of the prose. In adopting this style, there is a risk that readers may get the impression that there is considerable consensus within the field about most key issues and that most empirical findings are unquestionably reliable and valid. To guard against this risk, in Chapters 2–8, a section on important controversies about the clinical problems considered in each chapter are included. Each chapter opens with learning objectives and concludes with a summary and recommendations for further reading.

An attempt has been made throughout the text to take account of two widely used classification systems for psychological problems: the fifth chapter of the World Health Organization's (1992) *International Classification of Diseases – Tenth Edition* (ICD-10) and the American Psychiatric Association's (2000) *Diagnostic and Statistical Manual of Mental Disorders – Fourth Edition Text revision* (DSM-IV-TR). In DSM-IV-TR and ICD-10 there are slight differences in terminology and diagnostic criteria. There are, in addition, differences in the way disorders are clustered and subclassified. Also, in routine clinical practice and in the scientific literature, in some instances the terminology used differs from that in ICD-10 and DSM-IV-TR. Care has been taken throughout the text to employ those terms that have widest usage in the clinical field and to clarify terminological ambiguity, where appropriate, without inundating the reader with multiple terms and criteria for each condition.

Chapter 9 deals with models that inform clinical psychology research and practice. The biological, psychodynamic, cognitive-behavioural and family systems models are considered in detail with reference to their assumptions, their contributions to our understanding and treatment of psychological problems, and their limitations. Other perspectives are also mentioned, including humanistic–client-centred tradition, personal construct psychology and the positive psychology. This chapter provides an opportunity to reconsider the material in the body of the text from a critical standpoint and to question the limits of the knowledge claims made throughout the text. I was tempted to place this chapter after Chapter 2, but my undergraduate students at UCD have told me that reviewing models of practice is a more productive learning experience after topics contained in the main body of the text have been covered.

In the final chapter, evidence for the effectiveness of psychological interventions is summarized. Evidence-based practice is now embraced by clinical psychologists around the world. This chapter underlines the importance of evidence-based practice within clinical psychology, and the centrality of a scientific perspective to ethical practice.

Because this text was written with brevity as a central feature, inevitably it is not comprehensive in its coverage. Many important topics often covered in larger introductory clinical psychology texts have not been addressed in this book and these deserve mention, if only to alert you to their existence and importance. They include: intellectual disability; language delay; specific learning disabilities; pervasive developmental disorders; psychological problems of old age, particularly dementia; psychological problems secondary to medical conditions such as heart disease or epilepsy; neuropsychological problems; somatoform disorders such as conversion hysteria; dissociative disorders such as dissociative amnesia; factitious disorders; sexual and gender identity disorders; paraphilias such as pedophilia; sleep disorders such as insomnia; impulse control disorders such as kleptomania; and adjustment disorders which are transient responses to acute stresses.

In writing this text I have tried to show, as simply as possible, that understanding psychological problems in a rigorous clinical and scientific way is a complex matter.

If you read this book with a view to deciding on whether or not to become a clinical psychologist, I hope that it helps you make up your mind.

Alan Carr, July 2011

Acknowledgements

Throughout *Clinical Psychology* the following are widely taken into account:

Diagnostic and Statistical Manual of Mental Disorders, fourth edition, text revision (copyright © 2000) American Psychiatric Association, reprinted with permission.

The ICD-10 Classification of Mental and Behavioural Disorders World Health Organization (1992), copyright © World Health Organization 1992, reprinted with permission.

What is clinical psychology?

1

Learning objectives

After studying this chapter you will be able to:

- outline the basic aspects of the profession of clinical psychology
- give an account of the main features of professional clinical psychology training
- plan your career so as to maximize your chances of getting a place on a clinical psychology programme
- explain the difference between clinical psychology, other applied psychology specialties and related mental health professions
- give a balanced view on the pros and cons of clinical psychology as a prospective career.

Introduction

This chapter will give an overview of the profession and discipline of clinical psychology. There will be a description of clinical psychology training. The selection procedures used by clinical psychology training programmes in the UK and Ireland will be discussed, and there will be guidance on how to get a place on a clinical psychology programme. A brief account will be given of clinical psychology training in the US and elsewhere. The factors that distinguish clinical psychology from other types of applied psychology and other mental health professions will be discussed. The chapter will close with a consideration of the pros and cons of clinical psychology as a career.

The profession and scientific discipline of clinical psychology

Clinical psychology is both a health care profession (like medicine, surgery or social work), and a health-related scientific discipline (like physiology or sociology).

The profession

The profession of clinical psychology involves using clinical judgement to apply knowledge from the scientific discipline of clinical psychology in clinical practice with clients and patients. Clinical practice refers to the assessment, treatment and prevention of psychological problems in a range of populations. For example, assessing a boy who is failing in school and defiant with parents and teachers; helping a woman with depression regulate her mood more effectively; or helping the family of a person whose psychotic symptoms have been reduced through using medication to develop a supportive style to prevent relapse.

Clinical judgement is developed through supervised clinical practice while undertaking professional training, and during post-qualification clinical experience. Psychologists who have worked with a wide variety of cases over an extended time period have a broader experiential base on which to draw when making clinical decisions than their less experienced colleagues. Scientific knowledge about clinical psychology is developed through initial academic training, ongoing continuing professional development (CPD) and research. Throughout their careers clinical psychologists keep up to date with recent developments through CPD and must show evidence of this periodically to retain practising certificates.

The scientific discipline

Within the scientific discipline of clinical psychology, research is conducted to find out about how best to understand, assess, treat and prevent psychological problems, and also to find out how widespread psychological problems are. The results of clinical psychology research provide information for planning services for whole populations, and evaluating and treating individual cases in an evidence-based way. For example, the results of epidemiological research indicate that depression and anxiety are the most common problems that need to be addressed by clinical psychologists in outpatient adult mental health services (Carr & McNulty, 2006). The results of research on intelligence testing show that people with IQs below 50 require considerable support in community settings to be able to sustain a reasonable quality of life (Carr et al., 2007). Psychotherapy research shows that family therapy is more effective than individual therapy in the treatment of anorexia nervosa in young adolescent girls (Carr, 2009a).

TABLE 1.1
Main elements of clinical psychologists' roles

- Direct work with clients, patients, service users
- Indirect work
- Administration and management
- Research
- Continuing professional development

Clinical psychologists' roles

The main elements of clinical psychologists roles are listed in Table 1.1. Clinical psychologists' jobs typically involve both direct and indirect work with clients, patients or service users. (Throughout this book the terms client, patient and service user will be employed interchangeably, as there is not currently a consensus on the most appropriate term to use.) Clinical psychologists' jobs also involve administration or management, research, and continuing professional development (CPD) (Carr, 2000; Hall & Llewelyn, 2006). Beinart et al.'s (2009) *Clinical Psychology in Practice* gives many detailed example of clinical psychologists' roles from a UK perspective.

Direct work

With direct work, clinical psychologists meet with clients, patients or service users, and in some instances with their families. In these meetings they assess psychological problems and provide psychological interventions. Assessments may include interviews, psychological testing and observation. For most cases, psychologists interview clients (and in some instances members of their families) to find out about the history of the presenting problem, previous attempts to resolve the problem, the person's personal and family history and any other relevant details. In some cases psychologists administer tests to assess patient's intelligence, memory, personality, psychopathology, family relationships and other aspects of their functioning. The main benefit of psychological tests is that they measure constructs in a reliable and valid way, and yield scores that can be interpreted within the context of population norms. For example if a person returns an IQ score of 100, the norms indicate that this person is more intelligent than 50% of people of the same age within the normal population. With regard to intervention, the media typically associate individual psychotherapy with the practice of clinical psychology. However, clinical psychologists use many other interventions such as parent training to equip parents with skills to manage their children's problems, training in meditation to help people regulate depressed mood or impulsivity, and family psychoeducation to help families provide a supportive environment for family members with psychosis. Psychological interventions may be offered to individuals, groups with similar sorts of problems, couples and families. Increasingly clinical psychologists are supplementing direct face-to-face work with clients with bibliotherapy and computer-based interventions (Carr, 2009a). With bibliotherapy patients are invited to read specific self-help books that address their main presenting problems. For example, a person with panic disorder could be given a book that outlines how to manage panic attacks using evidence-based procedures. There are a growing number of computer-based interventions, but the best validated are structured cognitive behavioural programmes for managing depression. With these programmes clients work though a series of web-based mood management exercises over period of weeks.

Indirect work

With regard to indirect work, psychologists provide training, clinical supervision and consultation to colleagues in psychology, psychotherapy, social work, child care, medicine, nursing and other disciplines to empower them to provide services to patients. This is referred to as indirect work because psychologists influence patients indirectly through the actions of their colleagues. In the area of training, clinical psychologists may offer lectures or skills building programmes on particular topics relevant to specific groups, for example teaching foster parents about the psychology of attachment. In the area of clinical supervision, most senior psychologists in public health services provide placements of supervised clinical practice to clinical psychologists in training to help them develop the technical and self-reflective skills to practise professionally. Technical skills refer to those procedures used to evaluate and treat clients. Self-reflective skills refer to the capacity to monitor accurately the interactions between oneself, clients and colleagues, and the impact of these interactions on oneself. With regard to consultation, clinical psychologists may advise others how best to manage clients with specific problems. For example, in an intellectual disability service where a client engages in repeated challenging behaviour (such as aggression or self-harm), a clinical psychologist may advise staff in the service how to manage this on the basis of a thorough functional analysis. This type of assessment is used to establish the function of the challenging behaviour (for example, communicating to staff that they are stressed or bored) by carefully observing, recording and analysing the antecedents and consequences of the challenging behaviour.

Administration and management

Most clinical psychologists manage waiting lists, set appointment schedules, document clinical sessions by writing reports, and communicate with colleagues through correspondence, phone calls and meetings. As psychologists gain increasing managerial responsibility, they not only fulfil these functions for their own clinical work, but also support their more junior staff in doing so. Psychologists with managerial responsibilities also contribute to policy development and service planning for clinical psychology services, and in some instances for wider multidisciplinary teams in which clinical psychologists are involved.

Research

Clinical psychologists conduct a range of different types of research. They conduct literature searches to find out about recent developments in assessment and treatment, so that their practice with clients is informed by up-to-date research findings. Periodically they conduct service-based research projects to answer specific questions such as 'What are the profiles and outcomes of referrals over a one-year period?' or 'What are the main reasons clients give for dropping out of therapy?' Large specialist psychology services within university-affiliated agencies may have broad ongoing research programmes on specific themes such as eating disorders, drug abuse or attention deficit hyperactivity disorder (ADHD). Postgraduates on clinical psychology training programmes may conduct their doctoral research theses within these research programmes. In services without such research programmes, but which provide placements of supervised clinical practice, psychologists in clinical training may initiate smaller research projects to address questions of concern to the service, themselves and their university-based academic supervisors.

Continuing professional development

Clinical psychologists devote a proportion of their time each year to CPD. This is a requirement for remaining a registered practitioner. CPD includes regular participation in clinical supervision and journal clubs; attendance at professional short courses and conferences; and enrolment in advanced specialist training programmes, for example in psychotherapy or neuropsychology.

Populations and work settings

Clinical psychologists provide services to a wide range of people with diverse difficulties in an array of different work settings, as outlined in Table 1.2 (Carr, 2000; Hall & Llewelyn, 2006; Beinart et al., 2009).

Populations and problems

Clinical psychologists work with people across the life-span including children, adolescents, adults and older adults. They provide services to people with psychological disorders, intellectual and physical disabilities and psychological difficulties secondary to physical illnesses such as HIV/AIDS, heart disease or cancer. They also work with people experiencing significant stress associated with major life transitions and challenges such as infertility, child bearing, adoption, fostering, marital discord and bereavement.

Work settings

Clinical psychologists work in a wide variety of settings including primary care, community mental health teams, general and specialist adult and paediatric hospitals, disability services, services for older adults,

TABLE 1.2
Populations, problems and work settings

Populations	Children
	Adolescents
	Adults
	Older adults
Problems	Mental health problems
	Adjustment of physical health problems
	Intellectual disability
	Physical disability
	Adjustment to major life transitions
Work settings	Primary care
	Community mental health teams
	Hospitals
	Disability services
	Older adult services
	Family services (e.g. fostering, adoption)
	Specialist services (e.g. addiction, chronic pain)

prisons, fostering and adoption services and hospices. They also work in a wide variety of specialist services for people with specific difficulties such as addiction, eating disorders, aggression, sexual offending, chronic pain and head injury. Most clinical psychologists in the UK and Ireland work mainly within the public health service, although some work in private practice. The following statements are first-hand accounts of a typical day's work of psychologists working in a number of different settings.

Child and adolescent mental health

Martin, a clinical psychologist working on a child and adolescent mental health team, offered the following brief description of a typical day.

> Today I saw two families in the morning; went to a case conference after lunch; made some calls to clients and colleagues after 4pm; and (finally) finished a report that I'd been working on for 2 weeks. The first family I saw this morning was a case of school refusal or separation anxiety. The little fellow was 8 and very anxious. So were his parents. We've met for three sessions, and worked today on the final elements of a return to school plan. The second case was a review of long-term client. This is a 16-year-old girl who came to our service first because she was cutting herself. I've seen her for nearly 2 years and she is doing much better now. This afternoon the case conference was about a chaotic family, where there are major child protection concerns. The report I finished was an assessment of need report on a 7-year-old boy with ADHD.

The child and adolescent mental health curriculum for the UCD clinical psychology programme is contained in the *Handbook of Child and Adolescent Clinical Psychology* (Carr, 2006a).

Adult mental health

Rose is a clinical psychologist working on a community adult mental health team. She gave this account of one day in her working life.

> On Wednesday myself and Paul, my clinical psychology trainee, had our anxiety management group for people with panic disorder. This was fairly demanding. There are 10 patients in the group and we were on session 6 of a 12 week CBT programme. A lot of unexpected issues came up, around abuse one of the group members had experienced, that we had to deal with. Afterwards at lunch I debriefed Paul, who found the group heavy going. After lunch, we ran our 'hearing voices' group for people with psychosis. This was a lower key affair. A few issues came up around medication and compliance, so after the group I phoned Seamus, the psychiatrist to discuss the meds issue. I picked up my son, Ruan, from the childminder's at 5. What a day!

The adult mental health curriculum for the UCD clinical psychology programme is contained in *Handbook of Adult Clinical Psychology* (Carr & McNulty, 2006).

Older adults

Fintan works for a specialist older adult service attached to a large general hospital. Here is how he described a day at this service.

> On Thursday morning we had a team meeting at 9. The psychiatrist, social worker, physiotherapist and occupational therapist were there and the secretary for the unit. A lot of the meeting was about discharge planning for patients who were about to leave hospital. We also reviewed follow-up support plans for some cases where there were snags in the support plans that needed to be ironed out. Between 11 and 1 the social worker, Sue, and I ran our reminiscence group for older adults recovering form depression. We had a journal club at lunch time where our team discussed two really interesting papers on cognitive rehabilitation for older adults with dementia. In the afternoon I did an assessment with a 75-year-old woman. The main issue was whether she had dementia or depression. I scored the tests and drafted the report. Just as I was leaving at 6, one of the nurses on the ward called to ask about a patient whose relatives were visiting and wanted some information, so I didn't leave work till nearly 7. It was a long day.

The older adult mental health curriculum for the UCD clinical psychology programme is contained in *Handbook of the Clinical Psychology of Ageing* (Woods & Clare, 2008).

Intellectual disability service

Karen is a clinical psychologist working in a community based early intervention intellectual disability service. Here is what she had to say about her day.

Monday is always a strange sort of day. I don't start till 12 but go through till 8pm because we run our parent training programme on Monday evenings from 6 to 8. This went very well yesterday. We have six mums and four dads in the group. We have been doing behavioural parent training with them. They are beginning to 'get it'. I like when it clicks and they 'get it'. They also find the support they get from each other very useful too. I think the younger parents in the group felt very isolated, and like they were the only ones with parenting issues. But now they have other people to talk to about the same stuff they are facing. Before the group session, I did a home visit at 12 with a single mother who was having a crisis with managing her son's challenging behaviour. She was very distressed, so I stayed quite a while and didn't make it to the centre till 3. Most of the afternoon was spent preparing for the evening group session with the social worker who runs the group with me and doing routine phone calls and reports.

The intellectual disability curriculum for the UCD clinical psychology programme is contained in *Handbook of Intellectual Disability and Clinical Psychology Practice* (Carr et al., 2007).

Hospital clinical neuropsychology service

Morgan, a clinical psychologist working with a neuropsychology service in a busy university hospital, gave this account.

First thing on Friday our team met to review referrals which had come in on Thursday afternoon (mainly from the neurological wards). I got two cases. One was a 63-year-old woman who had had a stroke. I had to do a preliminary assessment of her neuropsychological functioning to get a baseline. The second case was a man in his late 20s who had been in a road traffic accident and had a closed head injury. I plan to do periodic follow-up assessments of both of these cases to monitor their recovery. It took all day to do these two assessments, score tests, phone relatives and get their views, write up reports and discuss them with the relevant neurologists. I'll be following up both of them next week and meeting with the families and patients to talk about how to manage things after discharge.

Lezak et al.'s (2004) *Neuropsychological Assessment* is a widely used neuropsychology text on many clinical psychology programmes.

Specialist family therapy service

I run a family therapy clinic on Thursday evenings at the Clanwilliam Institute in Dublin. Here is what happened last Thursday.

There was a request from a couple for an emergency appointment, so I saw them first at 5pm. The husband has bipolar disorder, which is moderately well controlled with medication. I've been seeing the couple for a long time for relapse prevention therapy. When this couple came to me first the husband was being hospitalized five times a year. This has reduced significantly in the past few years. The main issue on Thursday was helping the couple handle the husband's sudden dip in mood without hospitalization. The next clients were a couple who are working on addressing trauma-related issues. The woman is a courageous survivor of long-term child sexual abuse, who is using couples therapy to find ways to expand her constricted lifestyle and deal with trauma-related flashbacks. The last family I saw on Thursday night included a 9-year-old girl who has difficulty controlling her temper. This leads to major problems at home and in school. This little girl was a neglected and abused Vietnamese orphan when her parents adopted her 7 years ago. She has always had significant behaviour problems, and I have been working long-term with this family to help them address these.

The family therapy curriculum for the UCD clinical psychology programme is contained in *Family Therapy: Concepts, Process and Practice* (Carr, 2006b).

Clinical psychology training

The central objective of clinical psychology programmes is to train candidates to a level that will enable them to work safely, competently and ethically as basic grade clinical psychologists and to provide a foundation for later specialization through CPD. Clinical psychology graduates are able to provide clinical services to a wide range of client groups, use their academic knowledge to solve clinical problems, provide consultancy and teaching services to colleagues and clients and use their research skills to address relevant questions in a scientific way.

Currently in the UK and Ireland professional clinical psychology training programmes are 3 year doctorates and are variously called D Clin Psych, Clin Psy D, and D Psych Sc (Clin Psych). In 2011 there were 30 such programmes in Britain (including England, Scotland and Wales) and five in Ireland (including Northern Ireland). The UK programmes are listed on the website for Clearing House for Postgraduate Courses in Clinical Psychology. The Irish programmes are in UCD, Trinity College Dublin (TCD), the National University of Ireland Galway (NUIG), the University of Limerick (UL) and Queen's University Belfast (QUB). Web addresses for the clearing house and the Irish universities are included at the end of the chapter. All of these programmes are accredited by professional associations: the British Psychological Society (BPsS) or the Psychological Society of Ireland (PsSI). Since the end of the first decade of the 21st century they have been approved by statutory registration bodies. These are the Health Professions Council (HPC) in the UK and the Health and Social Care Professional Council (HSCPC) in Ireland. Effectively the BPsS and PsSI regulate the content of courses, and the HPC and HSCPC approve such courses and provide statutory registration for their graduates.

The roles for which clinical psychologists are trained are conceptualized by different programmes in different ways. The most common orientations are the scientist-practitioner and the practitioner-scholar (McFall, 2006). With the scientist-practitioner model, there is a strong emphasis on training psychologists in research skills so that they can both generate scientific knowledge and apply scientific knowledge in clinical practice. With the practitioner-scholar model, the emphasis is predominantly on clinical practice, and on training psychologists to inform their clinical work with scholarly knowledge of the relevant scientific literature. Most UK and Irish courses tend more towards the scientist-practitioner than the practitioner-scholar model.

The role of the clinical psychologist has also been conceptualized as that of a reflective practitioner (Scaife, 2010); that is, as a professional who enhances their practice by sensitively reflecting on the way in which personal psychological strengths and vulnerabilities impinge on skilled clinical practice. Reflective practice is enhanced through engaging in experiential personal and professional processes such as personal psychotherapy and process-oriented supervision. Reflective practice is increasingly receiving greater emphasis on UK and Irish clinical psychology training programmes (Hughes & Youngson, 2009). For example, at UCD it is mandatory for postgraduates to engage in personal psychotherapy during their training.

In the UK and Ireland each clinical psychology programme is run by a partnership involving a university and a public health service unit. The university provides the academic and research foundation for the course; the health service unit provides the clinical practice foundation for the course and placements of supervised clinical practice. These doctoral programmes in clinical psychology have three main elements: (1) academic course work, (2) placements of supervised clinical practice, and (3) research requirements. A summary of these components is given in Table 1.3.

Academic coursework

Academic coursework covers theory, research and practice-related material essential for developing competencies required to practise as a

TABLE 1.3
Components of professional clinical psychology training programmes

Research	Doctoral thesis on major research project
	Small-scale service-based research project
	Coursework or research design, methods and statistics
Academic course work	Children and adolescents
	Adults and older adults
	Intellectual disability
	Assessment and intervention competencies
Clinical placements	Range of populations (child, adult, older adult, disability, specialties)
	Range of competencies (assessment, intervention, training)
	Quality control (placement contract and monitoring)
	Regular supervision (observe and be observed)

clinical psychologist. These competencies include the ability to assess and formulate psychological problems using relevant psychological methods and theories; treat psychological problems using evidence-based interventions and evaluate the effectiveness of treatment; and work within psychology services, multidisciplinary teams, and wider health service and multiagency contexts using appropriate communication and organizational skills. Within academic courses on clinical psychology programmes, these issues are covered with reference to psychological disorders and problems typical in the fields of child and adolescent mental health, adult and older adult mental health, intellectual and physical disability, and neuropsychological problems. A range of teaching formats are used including lectures, video-modelling, role-playing, video feedback, discussion groups, and problem-based learning.

Placements of supervised clinical practice

On doctoral programmes in clinical psychology, most of the time is spent on placements of supervised clinical practice. For example, on the UCD clinical psychology training programme, each year there are two 4.5 month placements of supervised clinical practice. This is significantly longer that the two 6 week periods devoted to academic coursework. Placements occur in a range of services including primary care, secondary and tertiary services; adult mental health services; child and adolescent mental health services; intellectual disability services; services for older adults; neuropsychology services; paediatric services; and various specialist adult health services such as cardiology and oncology. In the UK and Ireland, clinical psychology training programmes provide supervisors with ongoing training and CPD to ensure that they develop strong supervision skills (Fleming & Steen, 2004; Milne, 2009).

Placement contracts

At the outset of each clinical placement, contracts are formed between postgraduates and clinical supervisors specifying the overall placement goals. These goals refer to competencies to be developed, the kinds of assessment and treatment procedures to be learned, the types of cases to be seen and other types of professional skills to be developed. These placement contracts are based on the minimum experience requirements listed in the course logbook, the learning opportunities available on the placement, the unique skills of clinical supervisors, and the unique clinical interests of postgraduates. Over the course of placements, postgraduates and supervisors work together to ensure that these goals are reached.

Supervision and quality control

On most clinical psychology programmes the supervision and quality control procedures described below are used to facilitate the development of clinical competence. Postgraduates on clinical placements receive a minimum of an hour's supervision per week, and the ratio of postgraduates to supervisors is never greater than 2:1. 'Observe and be observed' is a central training process on clinical psychology placements. That is, postgraduates develop clinical competencies by observing their supervisors' clinical practices, and also by having their supervisors observe their clinical practice and give feedback on this. Video or audio recording of clinical sessions may be used to facilitate this 'observe and be observed' training process. In an Irish study, Hughes and Byrne (2011) identified the 'observe and be observed' aspect of supervision as that most valued by clinical psychology postgraduates. Progress on clinical placements is monitored through placement visits made by members of the course team. These visits are made towards the middle and end of clinical placements. Mid-placement visits offer an opportunity to monitor progress and resolve any teething difficulties that have arisen. End-of-placement visits provide a context for evaluating whether postgraduates pass or fail placements and for identifying areas for competency development in future placements.

Research requirements

On UK and Irish programmes, clinical psychologists are trained to be competent in research as well as clinical practice. All clinical psychology programmes provide training in research design, methods and statistics, and require postgraduates to complete small-scale service-based research and a major doctoral research thesis. On the UCD clinical psychology programme, postgraduates have regular research seminars over the 3 years of the programme and complete small quantitative and qualitative service-based research projects, in addition to a major doctoral research project. A day a week over the 3 years of the programme is set aside for research, as well as 2 weeks' study leave per year.

Assessment

A range of procedures is used for assessment on doctoral programmes in clinical psychology. Academic coursework may be assessed by exams or continuing assessment assignments such as essays or clinical case studies. Placements are assessed by end-of-placement competency ratings. Research competence is usually assessed by the submission and oral defence of a doctoral thesis with an internal and external examiner at the end of the programme.

Getting a place on a clinical psychology programme

Admission information for UK clinical psychology training programmes is available on the website of the Clearing House for Postgraduate Courses in Clinical Psychology. For Irish programmes, details are given at the websites for UCD, TCD, NUIG, UL and QUB. Web addresses for these universities and the clearing house are given at the end of the chapter. The intake for most doctoral programmes in clinical psychology in the UK and Ireland varies from about eight to 42 candidates, with most courses having annual intakes. In 2010 there were just over 600 places on UK courses and just under 50 on Irish courses. Between 2005 and 2010 about 20–30% of applicants were offered places on doctoral programmes in clinical psychology in the UK and Ireland. Entry requirements for all of these courses are a 2.1 honours degree or higher diploma in psychology recognized by the BPsS or PsSI as conferring graduate basis for registration, and about a year's relevant clinical experience.

Planning to get onto a clinical psychology programme

Because entry to doctoral programmes in clinical psychology in the UK and Ireland is highly competitive, it is useful to develop a strategy to maximize your chances of getting a place. Guidance on applying for UK and Irish clinical psychology programmes is given in Knight (2002), O'Shea and Byrne (2010), Papworth (2004, 2007) and Roth (1998). Most course selection teams judge suitability on the basis of academic and clinical criteria. Your strategy should take account of this, and balance your efforts so that you do well academically but also make time to get relevant clinical experience. A summary of items to consider when building your profile for admission to clinical psychology training is given in Table 1.4.

Studies of successful entrants to UK and Irish clinical psychology programmes have reached a number of important conclusions (Clare, 1995; O'Shea & Byrne, 2011a; Phillips et al., 2004; Scior et al., 2007). With regard to the academic domain, candidates with better secondary school results, higher undergraduate grades, master's and PhD degrees, more favourable academic references and greater research achievements and publications are more likely to be admitted to clinical psychology programmes. Those with first class undergraduate degrees and master's degrees are admitted to clinical programmes at a younger age. In the clinical domain, candidates who have acquired basic clinical skills by working in a variety of assistant psychologist or research assistant posts, and have more favourable clinical references, are more likely to obtain a clinical psychology programme training place.

TABLE 1.4
Building your profile for admission to clinical psychology training

Academic and research competence	Honours undergraduate degree in psychology
	Postgraduate degree in area relevant to clinical psychology
	Short courses relevant to clinical psychology
	Other qualifications relevant to clinical psychology
	Experience doing clinical research
	Theses, publications and presentations
Clinical competence	Relevant clinical experience
	Basic clinical skills

Academic qualifications

Academic suitability for doctoral programmes in clinical psychology is assessed by taking account of performance in high school and on undergraduate degree programmes; completion of postgraduate degrees in psychology, short courses relevant to clinical psychology, and other non-psychological qualifications; and research achievements and publications.

Undergraduate degree

While a 2.1 honours degree is the minimum academic requirement for entry to a clinical psychology programme, many successful candidates exceed this minimum standard. Some have first class honours undergraduate degrees. Many have master's degrees. Some have PhDs. In planning your strategy, provided it does not tax your personal resources too much and leave little time and energy for relevant clinical experience, it's a reasonable strategy to aim for a first class honours undergraduate degree. However, if things do not go well for you in your undergraduate programme and you get a 2.2, this does not prevent you from entering the profession. Some clinical psychology programmes will accept applications from candidates with a 2.2 honours degree or higher diploma in psychology provided they also have a master's or PhD degree.

Master's programmes

There are a number of types of master's degree in psychology that enhance chances of gaining a place on a clinical psychology programme. These include master's by research on a clinical topic, master's in applied psychology (with a clinical emphasis), master's in neuropsychology or neuroscience, master's in developmental psychology, master's in health psychology, master's in counselling psychology, master's in psychotherapy or counselling and master's in applied behaviour analysis. All master's programmes that include advanced research and statistics coursework and a minor or major thesis conducted on a clinical topic enhance your profile because they give you advanced research skills and may give you clinical interviewing skills if you collect interview data from people with psychological problems for your thesis.

Master's programmes in applied psychology (that include coursework on psychopathology and related topics), neuropsychology or neuroscience, health psychology, disability, and developmental psychology are a useful preparation for clinical psychology because they provide a grounding in academic areas relevant to the practice of clinical psychology. Insofar as neuropsychology programmes include skills training in administering and interpreting psychological tests, they are an academic route to acquiring relevant clinical experience. Master's programmes in psychotherapy, counselling and applied behaviour analysis may also help you acquire relevant clinical experience and basic clinical skills if they include placements of supervised clinical practice.

From this, it is clear that there is no single best master's programme to opt for as a stepping stone to obtaining a place on a clinical psychology programme. You will maximize your chances of gaining a place if you take account of your overall profile (including academic and clinical suitability) when choosing a master's programme. For example, if you have acquired a lot of relevant clinical experience, but limited research experience, then it might improve your profile to opt for a master's programme with a strong academic and research orientation rather than a clinical practice orientation.

PhDs

PhDs in psychology can enhance chances of admission to a clinical psychology programme, especially if the research is conducted on a clinical topic, involves interviewing or assessing people with psycho-logical problems, and if the work is conducted within a health service setting. All of these factors make the process of conducting a PhD a relevant clinical experience. At UCD my colleagues and I have super-vised PhD candidates who did their theses in psycho-oncology, the psy-chology of sex-offenders, neuropsychology and the psychology of eating disorders. All obtained places on clinical psychology programmes on the grounds that their PhD research provided them with both rele-vant clinical experience and research skills. If you want to undertake a PhD as a stepping stone to getting onto a clinical psychology training programme, make sure at the outset that your research project will involve significant contact with people with psychological problems, and be conducted within a public health service context, or a context that has much in common with the public health service. PhDs conducted in university laboratories with non-clinical participants or animals are not a useful preparation for clinical psychology training.

Short courses

Diploma and certificate courses, CPD short courses and workshops and attendance at psychology conferences that facilitate the develop-ment of clinical skills for understanding, assessing and treating psycho-logical problems are taken into account by many selection panels in judging academic suitability for clinical psychology programmes. If you want to enhance your chances of getting a place on a clinical psychol-ogy programme, consider taking a diploma or certificate course in basic assessment or counselling skills and regularly attend CPD short courses and conferences to develop your clinical skills. Such courses are adver-tised in the BPsS magazine, *The Psychologist*, and the PsSI magazine, *The Irish Psychologist*.

Non-psychology qualifications

For mature students who have come to psychology (possibly through the higher diploma in psychology route) after a career in nursing, counselling, social work, occupational therapy, speech and language therapy or teaching, some selection panels will take account of your prior qualifications in assessing your suitability for clinical psychology training. In filling out your application form, be sure to include these prior relevant qualifications and to state the academic and clinical skills you acquired from them relevant to engaging in clinical psychology training.

Research competence

One aspect of academic suitability for a clinical psychology programme is research competence. In rating research competence, selection panels take account of research and statistics skills; participation in clinical research projects; publication of research presentations, reports and articles; and relevant qualifications such as diplomas or certificates in specific research methods, statistics or data analysis. Research competence may be assessed by taking account of the highest research thesis completed (e.g. undergraduate thesis, master's thesis or PhD), involvement in other research projects (e.g. conducting clinical audits or working as a research assistant on a big project), and the number of conference presentations, research reports and academic publications. To enhance your chances of being rated well for research competence, present the results of your undergraduate and postgraduate theses, and any other research projects in which you have been involved at academic conferences, and publish them as reports or academic journal articles. List these presentations and publications in your application form chronologically in the style used in BPsS, PsSI or American Psychological Association (APA) journals.

Relevant clinical experience

Relevant experience includes part-time or full-time, voluntary or paid clinical or research work, involving interaction with patients, clients or service users in health service settings. The sorts of work experience that count as relevant experience are discussed in Knight (2002) and Williams (2001). Working as an assistant psychologist in a clinical psychology service, a psychology research assistant on a major clinical project, or conducting a master's or PhD postgraduate research degree that involves extensive interaction with people with psychological problems are all types of relevant experience frequently reported by successful applicants to clinical psychology programmes (O'Shea & Byrne, 2011a, 2011b; Phillips et al., 2004; Scior et al., 2007). Work as a therapist within the IAPT (Improving Access to Psychological Therapies) programme in the UK, a clinical associate in applied psychology (or associate psychologist) in the UK, or a psychometrist in the US is a very good way to acquire relevant clinical experience. The weblink for IAPT is given at the end of the chapter.

Other ways to acquire relevant clinical experience are to work as a care worker (with children, older adults or people with disabilities), a nursing assistant, a psychiatric day centre assistant, a support worker for people with mental health problems or disabilities, an applied behavioural analysis (ABA) tutor with children with autism spectrum disorders, a special educational needs assistant for children with psychological problems, a volunteer with a development agency that offers health or educational services in underdeveloped countries, a children's summer camp counsellor, or a mental health helpline worker. Work that is supervised by a clinical psychologist and is conducted within a psychology service or within a public health service multidisciplinary team is often judged by selection panels to prepare people better for clinical psychology training than work conducted in other settings.

Some UK programmes require applicants to have gained their relevant experience within the NHS. Check if this is a requirement for your preferred courses, and plan your relevant experience to take account of this requirement. If relevant experience is not supervised by a clinical psychologist, then it will enhance your chances of getting a place on a clinical programme if you arrange regular supervision from a clinical psychologist who will give you a reference when you apply for a place on a clinical psychology programme and comment on the clinical skills you have acquired during your relevant experience.

Relevant experience is an entry requirement for clinical psychology training programmes because it familiarizes candidates with the sorts of setting in which clinical psychologists work, their roles, the types of people with whom they work and also because it equips candidates with basic clinical skills. These include skills for interacting with clients with psychological problems, and skills for working in a psychology service or on a multidisciplinary team in a health service organization. During relevant clinical experience you may gain interviewing skills; skills for administering and interpreting psychological tests; skills for engaging clients in therapy; specific therapeutic procedures for treating clients with particular psychological problems such as anxiety, depression, autism, or ADHD; teamwork skills; report writing skills and so forth.

Clinical suitability is assessed by clinical psychology course selection panels with reference to the way in which candidates have made use of the opportunities available to them to engage in relevant clinical experiences. This means that candidates with more experience are not always rated as more suitable. The key issue is how candidates have used the opportunities available to them. For example, young candidates who have had less time to acquire relevant experience than older candidates, but who have used the time available to them during their undergraduate and postgraduate years to maximize their clinical skills, may be rated as more suitable than older candidates who have used the time available to them to acquire relevant clinical experience less efficiently.

From the foregoing, it is clear that it is never too early to start acquiring relevant experience. If you have not already done so, now is a good time to start. When filling out an application form for clinical psychology training it is vital to list both the relevant clinical experience jobs you have done and the skills you have acquired while doing those jobs.

Finding relevant clinical experience is challenging. Some jobs are advertised in the *Psychologist* and *Irish Psychologist*. Others are advertised in national newspapers such as the *Guardian* or the *Irish Times*. The Psyclick website (listed at the end of the chapter) contains links to many websites where 'relevant experience jobs' may be advertised. A good source of information on relevant experience for Irish candidates is the assistant psychologist Ireland Google group (listed at the end of the chapter). Many people get relevant clinical experience by sending their CVs to clinical psychologists or managers of relevant agencies. If you do this, make it clear that you wish to acquire relevant experience to increase your suitability for clinical psychology training and are available for voluntary or paid work, and are prepared to be flexible and fit in with the overall needs of the service. The key thing is to convey that you are prepared to make a contribution to the service in return for the opportunity to acquire relevant experience.

The process of acquiring psychology assistant or research assistant posts, or other good relevant experience positions, is highly competitive. Your chances of being successful in job competitions for relevant experience will be enhanced if you have a master's degree, so it may speed up your acquisition of relevant experience if you obtain a master's degree as soon as possible after your primary degree.

There is a danger of viewing the process of obtaining a portfolio of academic, research and clinical requirements to get onto a clinical psychology programme as having value only insofar as it makes you eligible for selection onto a clinical course. This may not be the most useful way to think about it. A postgraduate on the UCD clinical psychology programme who gave feedback on this chapter remarked, 'I wonder also if it is worth discouraging people who want to get onto clinical programmes from thinking of clinical experience like a means to an end, and encourage them to conceptualize it as part of the process of getting on training, yes, but also as a valuable journey!'

The application process

To get a place on a clinical psychology programme it is essential to manage the application process well. This includes completing the application form and submitting it prior to application deadlines; arranging references; attending interviews; engaging in assessment exercises; accepting negative feedback; and reapplying if you do not get a place first time round.

Application forms

Begin the application process well in advance of application deadlines. This will give you time to refine your application, obtain supporting documents and invite referees to write your references. The clearing house deadline, which is posted on the clearing house website, is usually at the end of November or in early December. For Irish courses, deadlines are posted on college websites, but they are usually in the winter months (December–February). Relevant web addresses are given at the end of this chapter. Download application forms and write answers to questions in the application form in a Word document. Read and edit your answers until you have produced your best draft. Ask a recent successful applicant to a clinical psychology course for feedback on this draft, and use their comments to refine your application. Then submit your final 'polished version' through the electronic application process or in hardcopy, as directed in the application guidelines.

When completing application forms give concise accurate information about your secondary school exam results, university degree results, other relevant qualifications, publications and details of relevant clinical and research experience jobs. For master's degrees give the type of master's degree (by thesis only, applied psychology, health psychology, etc.) and your mark (e.g. 70%). This is important to include if the degree was awarded on a pass/fail basis, since some selection panels will take high marks on a master's degree into account in judging suitability. If the master's degree included a placement of supervised clinical practice, note this on the form (e.g. MSc, Counselling Psychology, 65%, containing a 100 hour placement of supervised clinical practice). When listing theses, reports, presentations and publications, use the format in BPsS, PsSI or APA academic journals. For relevant clinical or research experiences, give the name of the job, the employer, and the main duties, the dates of employment, the number of hours per week, and whether the job was voluntary or paid. Keep these descriptions concise.

Most application forms include a section where there is an opportunity to indicate other relevant life experiences such as world travel or past career (for mature applicants); to reflect on the clinical and personal skills you have acquired from graduate degrees, relevant clinical and research experiences and other life experiences; and to make a personal statement about your own evaluation of your suitability for clinical psychology training. There are usually word limits for these sections, so it is useful to draft, edit and redraft these statements a few times until you get them right. One way to go about this is to list the skills you have developed, and for each skill state how your qualifications and experiences have helped you develop it. Another approach to state the skills that each of your main qualifications or experiences helped you develop. In writing a personal statement it is important to show why you consider that your skills and personal qualities make you ready to train as a clinical psychologist in the public health services. To write a credible statement of this type, it is important to convey that you know about the roles clinical psychologists fulfil within the UK National Health Service (NHS) or the Irish Health Service Executive (HSE).

Supporting documents

When planning your application strategy, leave lots of time to obtain supporting documents that must accompany your application. If your primary degree is from a non-UK university and you apply to UK courses through the clearing house, you will be required to submit a letter from the BPS indicating that your degree confers graduate basis for membership. If you are applying to Irish universities you may be asked to submit university transcripts for your primary degree, so you will need to request these from your alma mater.

Arranging references

The clearing house and most clinical psychology courses require one academic reference and one reference from a clinical psychologist or clinical manager who supervised your relevant clinical experience. Invite referees who know you fairly well; are familiar with your work and so can accurately comment on your skills, personal qualities and suitability for clinical psychology training; and are willing to write a reference by the deadline date. As a courtesy, when inviting referees to write you a reference, send them an up-to-date copy of your CV. Unless there are no other options, do not invite colleagues to be referees if they have close personal connections to you (e.g. family members or business partners).

Short listing

Clinical psychology courses establish selection panels to shortlist applicants for interview. These panels typically include a group of staff with a range of academic and clinical expertise. Panels read and rate large numbers of application forms during the short-listing process; make collective judgements about the suitability of candidates for clinical psychology training; and select the most suitable for interview. While applying for clinical psychology training is stressful for applicants, short listing is very demanding for selection panel members, and this is worth keeping in mind when writing your application. The easier you make it for selection panel members to read and rate your application, the better. Our experience at UCD last year gives an idea of how demanding short listing is. Each member of our panel read and rated over 160 applications. This took a number of days. They rated responses to all questions on application forms using objective criteria, and then summarized these into an overall score reflecting academic and clinical suitability. In an all-day panel meeting, ratings of panel members were aggregated, rank ordered, and approximately 40 applicants were selected and invited to interviews.

Some courses are experimenting with using writing assignments to assist with the short-listing process. For example, the UK Lancaster course has published a report on its use of written assignments in short listing and shown that these assignments predict academic performance on clinical psychology programmes (Hemmings & Simpson, 2008). Lancaster's written task was adapted from one designed by the University of Surrey, and applicants were invited to complete the task on a computer. The task involved reading five abstracts, synthesising them into a 250-word summary that answered a specific question, answering a number of short statistical and methodological questions about the studies described in the abstracts, and completing the assignment within an hour. Applicants' answers were rated for writing skills, critical thinking skills and methodology skills. If you apply for courses with these types of short-listing tasks, it may be useful to speak to successful applicants about them and practise similar sorts of task before completing the actual short-listing task.

Interviews

There is considerable variability in the types of interview and assessment exercise used on the 35+ clinical psychology programmes in the UK and Ireland (Hemmings & Simpson, 2008; O'Shea & Byrne, 2011b; Phillips et al., 2001; Roth & Leiper, 1995). Find out the format and duration of the interview and assessment exercises that will be used on the courses for which you are shortlisted from their websites, and also from previous successful applicants. All courses have selection interviews in which candidates are asked about material relevant to their academic and clinical suitability. In some courses there are separate academic and clinical interviews, while in others both areas are covered in one interview.

In preparing for these interviews, it is useful to list the main points you want to make, and then illustrate each of these points with examples from your academic career and relevant clinical experience. The kinds of point that it is useful to make are that you know how to do research (and can illustrate this by describing one of your research projects), that you have basic clinical skills (and can illustrate these by describing some clinical work you have done), and that you can work on a team (and can illustrate this by describing some of your team work). It is also useful to be able to show that you know about the roles of clinical psychologists within the public health service and about recent relevant policy documents. You can find these on the NHS or HSE websites, which are listed at the end of the chapter.

It may also be worth mentioning that you have interests and hobbies that allow you to maintain a degree of work–leisure balance in your life, and that if you are offered a place on a course you intend to continue these interests and hobbies to help you manage stress.

Most candidates find it helpful to rehearse their interviews with previously successful applicants. When rehearsing for interviews, aim to make your points and illustrate them with relevant examples in a succinct way. It is also useful to prepare an opening statement that gives your interviewers an overview of your career to date, and a closing statement that summarizes the key points you made in your interview. In doing this preparation and rehearsal, do not assume that your interviewers will remember all of the detail in your application form. Most interviewers on selection panels are on 'information overload' having read 150+ applications during short listing and then interviewed a number of candidates. It becomes difficult for panel members to remember 'who did what'. Your task is to make your points and illustrate them with examples from your experience in a clear, engaging and memorable way.

Selection interviews are stressful. Stress reduces our capacity to focus on the concerns of others. It narrows our attention so that we tend to focus on our own well-being, our own survival in the face of threat, and our primary 'emotional concerns'. In selection interviews common emotional concerns are 'I hope I'm doing OK here', 'I really want a place on the programme', 'I'll be disappointed if I don't get on', 'I hope I'm not making a mess of this', and so forth. This stress-induced focus on the self is compounded by exposure to 'pop-psychology' advice to use self-focused stress management techniques during interviews. For example, some pop-psychologists advise that you periodically ask yourself 'How am I doing?', tell yourself mentally that you are doing OK, tell yourself to stay calm, take deep breaths, relax your muscles, etc. There are two problems with this. First, it is a waste of your cognitive capacity. In selection interviews you should be using all your cognitive capacity to listen to questions, give clear answers and make your points. It is a waste of cognitive capacity to engage in an inner dialogue. When people 'go blank' in an interview it is usually because they have overloaded their cognitive capacity by trying simultaneously to engage in the interview and engage in an inner dialogue. Second, when candidates engage in inner dialogues during interviews and tell themselves to calm down etc., to interviewers they appear to be disengaged from the interview process. For these reasons, it is best not to use any of these strategies.

The most efficient interview stress management strategy is to focus on addressing the interviewing panel's agenda. In selection interviews there are two parallel agendas. Your 'emotional agenda' is that you want to get a place on a training programme because it's what you've always wanted, because it's what you deserve after all your hard work, and because you would be very disappointed if you didn't get a place. The panel's agenda is different. They are not overly concerned about what you always wanted, what you deserve or how disappointed you will be if you don't get a place. They want to know if you have the qualifications, skills and potential to be a really good clinical psychology trainee, compared to other applicants, or whether you will be the sort of trainee who 'doesn't have what it takes to get the job done and go the distance'.

If this is their agenda, then a very useful approach is to put your own agenda to one side, and prioritize the panel's agenda during your interview preparation and during the interview itself. That is, in preparing all the points you want to make, and in making your points in the interview, frame what you say in terms of the panel's agenda, not your own 'emotional agenda'. This is very difficult to do when the possibility of failure is so high. Under stress we all tend to prioritize our own agendas rather than those of others. However, if you prepare with the panel's agenda in mind, then in the interview you will be better able to show the panel how your qualifications and relevant experiences have given you the skills and personal qualities necessary for training as a clinical psychologist.

 You should try to show the panel, through the way you talk about your past achievements, that in the future, if you get a place on the course you will be the sort of trainee who will work hard, be reliable, do good academic work, do rigorous research in a clinically sensitive way, work with clients in a respectful way that is informed by psychological science, and fit in with course staff and clinical teams. If you prepare for your interview with the panel's agenda in mind, then in the interview itself you will be more likely to show the panel that you have the profile and potential to be a good clinical psychology trainee.

When you attend a selection interview, listen carefully to the questions you are asked. Answer these specific questions, and then expand your answers to include relevant points that you have prepared prior to the interview. You will probably be asked about the clinical and research experiences and skills you have developed, and you will have prepared points you want to make in these areas, so building them into your answers will not be too challenging. You may also be asked hypothetical 'problem solving' or 'competency testing' questions during the interview, for which you are unlikely to have a prepared answer. In these questions the panel may ask you how you would manage a specific clinical or research problem. Listen to these questions very carefully. Reflect for a moment or two, and then give your answer in a step-by-step manner, so the panel can hear how you reason, make decisions and solve problems. Panels ask these sorts of question because they are interested in how you think and make judgements, not because they want to see if you can come up with the right answer.

Towards the end of the interview, you may be asked if there is anything you would like to add or ask. The most useful thing to do at this point is to mentally go down your checklist of prepared points you wanted to make in the interview, make any points you have not already made, and briefly summarize how you think your qualifications and relevant experiences have given you the basic academic, research and clinical skills required to undertake professional training in clinical psychology.

Some courses include various individual and group assessment exercises and psychological tests (Hemmings & Simpson, 2008; O'Shea & Byrne, 2011b; Phillips et al., 2001; Roth & Leiper, 1995). For example, to assess capacity for teamwork, some course selection panels invite groups of applicants to work as teams and solve specific problems. To assess basic clinical skills, some courses observe candidates conducting role-play interviews. To assess academic writing skills, some panels ask applicants to read an article and write an abstract, or to write an essay. To assess critical thinking skills, some courses ask applicants to read academic material and then answer a series of questions. To assess clinical judgement, some courses invite candidates to read case vignettes and answer questions about them. For the assessment of oral presentation skills, candidates may be invited to make a preliminary presentation of their career to date and indicate how this has prepared them for clinical psychology training.

Personality and aptitude tests are used by some courses, usually to identify candidates with positive traits and rule out candidates with traits that would make them unsuitable for clinical psychology training. It's useful to get formal information on selection procedures from the courses for which you are applying and also to talk to previously successful applicants about their experiences of engaging in these procedures so that you will have a clear idea about what to expect. Practising writing abstracts, essays, giving presentations, interviewing and answering questions on academic material or case vignettes may improve your performance during the assessment tasks mentioned above.

Reapplying

Only 20–30% of candidates get places on clinical psychology courses, and a proportion of these are people who have been unsuccessful in previous years. O'Shea and Byrne (2011) in an Irish study of the 10 year period 2000–2009 found that the average successful applicant had previously made about three unsuccessful applications, and the range was 0–22! If you are not offered a place in a course, this does not necessarily mean that you will be judged to be unsuitable if you reapply. Rather, failure to be selected one year means that you were not as suitable as the candidates selected in that particular year. Enhance your portfolio of qualifications and relevant clinical and research experiences over the next year, and reapply. As your portfolio expands it becomes more likely that your application will be ranked highly enough, in comparison with other applicants, to be selected.

Professional society membership

If your career plan is to become a clinical psychologist and practise in the UK or Ireland, then join the BPsS and/or the PsSI sooner rather than later. Website addresses are given at the end of the chapter. The appointments sections of their monthly publications (the *Psychologist* and the *Irish Psychologist*) contain advertisements for psychology assistant and research assistant posts that may count as relevant clinical experience in your application for clinical psychology programmes. These publications will also contain articles on topics relevant to clinical psychology and help you develop an understanding of current professional issues. Some selection panels for clinical psychology training programmes rate candidates favourably if they have BPsS or PsSI membership, so you should mention your membership status on clinical psychology programme application forms.

Both the BPsS and the PsSI have Divisions of Clinical Psychology. It is useful to become an affiliate member of the clinical division of the BPsS because it publishes a monthly journal – *Clinical Psychology Forum* – that contains articles and information on the profession of clinical psychology and current issues of concern to the profession within the UK.

Training abroad

Apart from the UK and Ireland, there are well-developed doctoral clinical psychology training programmes in other English speaking countries including the US, Canada, South Africa and Australia. These may be of interest to you if decide to train abroad. If you return to the UK or Ireland to work as a psychologist you will be required to submit your clinical psychology qualification to the BPsS or PsSI for evaluation. If it is judged to be similar to a UK or Irish qualification you will receive a statement of equivalence. In some instances you may be required to complete an extra placement or some extra coursework or research to bring your qualification into line with UK and Irish standards. For example, when I moved to the UK from Canada (where I did a PhD in clinical psychology), to bring my qualification into line with its standards the BPsS required me to complete an intellectual disability placement in the NHS.

In 2010 in the US there were 232 clinical psychology training programmes accredited by the APA. Norcross et al. (2010) surveyed these programmes and what follows is based on this survey. In the US there are two main types of clinical psychology doctoral training programmes: the scientist-practitioner PhD, which places a strong emphasis on research, and the practitioner-scholar PsyD, which places greater emphasis on clinical practice. Both types of programme are of about 4 years' duration and include academic coursework and clinical practicums. However, on PhD programmes candidates are required to conduct a major research project and present it as a doctoral thesis, whereas on PsyD programmes postgraduates conduct a less extensive research project or a systematic literature review. Candidates must complete a one-year clinical internship and both national and state registration exams to become a registered practitioner in the US after graduating from a doctoral programme in clinical psychology. Most US clinical psychology training programmes focus on a much narrower range of problems and populations than UK or Irish training programmes. The broadest programmes focus on both child and adult mental health, but rarely on intellectual disability and older adulthood in the way that UK and Irish programmes do. Plante's (2009) *Contemporary Clinical Psychology* is a good undergraduate introduction to clinical psychology from a US perspective.

In Norcross et al.'s study, the mean undergraduate psychology degree grade point average for admission to US programmes was 3.6 and only 21% of entrants had master's degrees. Along with undergraduate psychology degree grades, the Graduate Record Examination (GRE) results are used to select people onto US clinical psychology programmes. There is a general GRE aptitude test and a specific GRE test in psychology. GREs can be taken anywhere in the world. The web address for the GRE is given at the end of the chapter and it contains information on the tests and test centres. Most people practise for the GRE general and psychology tests by taking preparation courses and using practice test books. Some of the most widely used preparation and practice test books are produced by Kaplan (2010a, 2010b), Barron (2009a, 2009b) and *Princeton Review* (2010a, 2010b). These are reissued every year, so the editions I have cited may be out of date when you read this. Web addresses for these three GRE preparation book publishers are given at the end of the chapter.

In Norcross et al.'s study, 17% of applicants to US doctoral programmes obtained places, and 57% of these were given full financial support by the courses that accepted them. They had their fees paid and were given a fellowship or teaching/research assistantship. Norcross et al. found that admission to university-based PhD clinical psychology programmes was far more competitive than admission to PsyD clinical psychology programmes based in non-university professional schools. Also, more university-based PhD programmes provided financial support than non-university PsyD programmes. Detailed guidance on gaining admission to doctoral clinical psychology programmes in the US is given in *Insider's Guide to Graduate Programs in Clinical and Counseling Psychology* (Sayette et al., 2010) and *Getting In: A Step-by-Step Plan for Gaining Admission to Graduate School in Psychology* (American Psychological Association, 2007). Canada's approach to training clinical psychologists is similar to that of the US, although its courses are accredited by the Canadian Psychological Association. Hunsley and Lee's (2009) *Introduction to Clinical Psychology* is a useful undergraduate overview of clinical psychology from a Canadian perspective.

In an Australian national survey Pachana et al. (2006) identified 34 universities or colleges that provided clinical psychology training. There were 30 master's programmes, 24 professional doctoral programmes similar to the US PsyD practitioner-scholar programmes and 16 PhD programmes similar to the US scientist-practitioner programmes. The admission requirement for these programmes was a 2.1 honours degree in psychology. One of the main differences between Australia and other jurisdictions is the relative lack of funding to support postgraduates during training. Page and Stritzke's (2006) *Clinical Psychology for Trainees* gives a good account of clinical psychology practice from an Australian perspective. In Australia, New Zealand and much of Europe, clinical psychologists can practise with master's or diploma level qualifications rather than a doctorate, so their doctoral programmes are not required to meet doctoral training standards set by accrediting bodies. Having said that, there are many exceptional doctoral clinical psychology training programmes in these jurisdictions.

Choosing courses

When deciding which courses to apply to, or which offers to accept if you are lucky enough to be offered places on more than one course, it's useful to base your decisions on your own clinical, academic and research criteria.

Select courses that provide training with a research or clinical emphasis that suits you. Some courses are strongly clinically oriented. Others are strongly research-oriented. Still others take a balanced approach, with equal emphasis on clinical and research competence.

Choose a course that trains postgraduates in a clinical approach that fits with your preferences. Some courses train postgraduates mainly in cognitive behaviour therapy. Others adopt psychodynamic, systemic or humanistic approaches (which are described in Chapter 9), while others encourage the use of multiple models. For example, at UCD we train postgraduates to adopt a systemic approach when working with children, adolescents and people with intellectual disabilities. In the field of adult mental health we teach basic cognitive behaviour therapy skills and basic psychodynamic therapy skills.

Choose courses where staff have research programmes that are of interest to you, so that you can conduct your doctoral thesis under their supervision. In applying for courses with a strong research orientation, particularly in the US, it is useful to correspond with potential research supervisors before you apply, indicating your interest in their work and your wish to work under their supervision. If, while planning and conducting your undergraduate research thesis, you correspond with an academic who is an expert on your topic to ask them for recent articles they have written or materials they have developed, they may look favourably on your application if you apply to their department for postgraduate clinical psychology training.

Clinical psychology and related professions

Clinical psychology can be distinguished from other types of applied psychology, notably counselling psychology, educational psychology, health psychology and forensic psychology. There is a significant overlap between the clinical practices and scientific foundations of these other applied psychology specialties. Practitioners in all of these specialties assess and treat clients; engage in research and evaluation; and conduct consultancy, supervision, administration and management. To train in any of these specialties, an honours undergraduate degree in psychology is a prerequisite. What distinguishes these specialties is (1) the extent to which they are embedded within national public service organizations, (2) the establishment of professional doctoral level training as the norm, (3) the practices they emphasize, (4) the populations they work with, and (5) the organizational contexts within which they are grounded.

Clinical psychology differs from other applied psychology specialties insofar as it is strongly embedded within the public health service in both the UK and Ireland. There are well-established partnerships between universities and public health services, supported by funding systems. Just as 'registrar' is an established grade within medicine, 'trainee clinical psychologist' is an established paid professional career grade within clinical psychology. In contrast, national funding systems for other applied psychology specialties have not been developed.

In both Ireland and the UK, the 3 year professional doctorate has been established as the required professional qualification in clinical psychology for far longer than in other applied psychology specialties. In other specialties, some universities still offer terminal master's level programmes and some professionals practise with master's level qualifications.

Clinical psychologists work with a very wide range of populations with diverse problems (described earlier in the chapter) and in the UK and Ireland are employed predominantly within the public health services. Other types of applied psychologist work with a narrower range of populations, and some work outside the public health service.

What follows is a thumbnail sketch of the other applied psychology specialties.

Educational psychology addresses learning problems, and social and emotional problems encountered by young people in educational settings. There is a strong emphasis within the profession on assessment of children's problems, recommending the provision of additional resources and developing programmes that teachers and parents can implement to deal with these difficulties. In the UK educational psychologists are employed by local education authorities, and in Ireland they are employed by the National Educational Psychology Service (NEPS). Educational psychologists work in schools, colleges, nurseries and special units. In North America educational psychology is referred to as school psychology.

Counselling psychology places a strong emphasis on psychotherapeutic processes in effecting change in people facing a range of normal life challenges as well as psychological disorders. The profession places a premium on the use of process-oriented supervision and self-reflective practices in training. Some counselling psychologists are employed in public health services. Others work in private companies and private practice.

Health psychology focuses on the application of psychology to help people change their lifestyles and prevent physical health problems. It is also concerned with treating psychological adjustment difficulties associated with health problems, medical conditions, chronic pain and disabilities. Health psychologists work in hospitals, universities and health research settings. In North America, health psychology is sometimes referred to as behavioural medicine, and health psychology applied to children is referred to as paediatric psychology.

Forensic psychology is concerned with applying psychology to criminal investigation, understanding psychological risk and protective factors associated with criminal behaviour, and the assessment and treatment of offending behaviour from a psychological perspective. In the UK forensic psychologists are mainly employed within the prison service. In Ireland a process for registering forensic psychologists has not been established, and the majority of psychologists working within Irish prisons are clinical or counselling psychologists.

Clinical psychologists may also be distinguished from the grades 'clinical associate in applied psychology' (or 'associate psychologist') in the UK and 'psychometrist' in the US and Canada. These grades are below the level of a qualified clinical psychologist and above that of psychology assistant. Duties of practitioners in these grades are similar though more circumscribed than those of a qualified clinical psychologist. Typically a master's degree in applied psychology is required for posts at these grades. Employment in these grades counts as relevant experience when making an application for a clinical psychology degree.

Clinical psychology may also be distinguished from other mental health professions including psychiatry, psychotherapy and counselling.

Psychiatry is a medical specialty concerned with the assessment and treatment of psychological disorders using a range of methods including physical or pharmacological treatments on one hand and psychological treatments on the other. To practise as a consultant psychiatrist, a medical degree and specialist postgraduate training in psychiatry are required. Psychiatry and psychiatry training are strongly embedded within public health services around the world.

Psychotherapy is a contractual process in which trained profession-als with expert knowledge of their discipline interact with clients to help them resolve psychological problems. There are many different schools of psychotherapy (e.g. psychoanalytic, cognitive-behavioural, humanis-tic and systemic). There are also many training routes for becoming a registered psychotherapist. Most involve acquiring a primary degree in a health profession (e.g. psychology, social work, nursing or medicine) and then completing a postgraduate professional psychotherapy train-ing programme. In the UK and Ireland the many diverse psychotherapy associations are united under the umbrellas of the UK Council for Psychotherapy and the Irish Council for Psychotherapy. Psychotherapy as an independent profession is not as well embedded within the public health service as clinical psychology, and there are far fewer jobs with the title 'psychotherapist'. However, many clinical psychologists spend a significant portion of their time in public health service jobs engaging clients in psychotherapy.

Counselling is similar to psychotherapy but training programmes usually focus on specific problems or client groups, for example drug and alcohol abuse, or career guidance. Psychotherapy training programmes cover a broader range of problems and client groups, but usually focus on a specific therapeutic approach, for example systemic, psychodynamic, humanistic, or cognitive behaviour therapy. In many instances, training for counselling is not as long or as extensive as that for psychotherapy.

Controversies

The history of clinical psychology in the UK, Ireland, the US, continental Europe, Australia and New Zealand is marked by controversy over the appropriate model for training clinical psychologists, the level to which they should be trained, and the roles they should adopt when qualified (Benjamin, 2005; Cheshire & Pilgrim, 2004; Hall & Llewelyn, 2006; Lunt, 2008; Pachana et al., 2008; Sammons et al., 2003). There has been controversy over whether the research-oriented scientist-practitioner, the practice-oriented practitioner-scholar, or the experientially oriented reflective-practitioner should be the core model for training. Currently the weight of opinion in the UK, Ireland and the US leans towards the scientist-practitioner model as the dominant approach. There has been controversy over whether registered clinical psychologists should be trained to the diploma or master's level, or to the doctorate level. Currently in the UK, Ireland and the US, doctoral level training has become the norm. However, in the UK and Ireland this is a relatively recent development, and in continental Europe and the antipodes master's and diploma level training models are prevalent.

There has been controversy over whether clinical psychologists should engage in assessment only, or assessment and treatment. Historically clinical psychologists' roles mainly involved psychometric assessment. In the latter half of the last century this changed, and psychological therapy became a central part of psychologists' roles.

More recently, there has been controversy over whether clinical psychologists should have the right to prescribe psychotropic medication, with strong arguments on both sides. Currently in some US jurisdictions clinical psychologists have acquired prescribing rights, but this trend has not had a major impact in the UK or Ireland.

There is agreement among clinical psychologists that service-users should contribute to clinical psychology training and service development, but divergent opinions about how best to facilitate their involvement. Clinical psychology has traditionally focused on psychological disorders and disability. The positive psychology movement has challenged this and proposed that the focus of our work shift from deficits to strengths and resilience (Carr, 2011).

Pros and cons of selecting clinical psychology as a career

The down side

On the down side, it can take 8–10 years to become a qualified clinical psychologist after graduating from secondary school. This time includes 3–4 years completing an honours undergraduate programme; 1–3 years obtaining relevant clinical experience (including a relevant master's degree in some cases); and 3 years completing a professional doctorate in clinical psychology. Another major problem is the competition for places on clinical psychology doctoral programmes. In the UK and Ireland during the period 2005–2010, only 20–30% of applicants secured places. So the chances of getting a place on a programme are approximately between 1 in 3 and 1 in 5. A third drawback to choosing clinical psychology as a career is that doctoral programmes are exceptionally demanding. When you are training as a clinical psychologist, there is limited room for much else in your life. A final problem with clinical psychology as a career is that for qualified practitioners, issues to do with staffing, resources, waiting lists, administrative procedures, interprofessional rivalry and so forth can be stressful. Dealing with these organizational and administrative issues within the public health service over an extended time period in both the UK and Ireland can be very challenging, and can wear you down.

Positive features

There are many pluses to clinical psychology as a career. In the UK and Ireland, the public health service sponsors candidates with primary degrees in psychology on doctoral programmes to train as clinical psychologists, paying them a salary at the trainee clinical psychologist grade. (There is a loose parallel here with medicine, where candidates with primary degrees in medicine are employed as non-consultant hospital doctors during their specialist training in psychiatry, paediatrics and other fields of medicine.) In the UK and Ireland there are many job opportunities for clinical psychologists, and good career development prospects.

Clinical psychologists have the opportunity to make a real difference to a lot of people's lives. Over a career of 35–40 years a clinical psychologist may directly help (at a minimum) 1000 clients, and may indirectly help a lot more.

Clinical psychology is an exceptionally interesting job. The role of the clinical psychologist is complex, involving direct and indirect clinical work, consultation, training and supervision, research, administration and management. Over the course of a career there are opportunities to work in many different services with different client groups, and to progress from junior to senior career grades. For example, in my own career I have worked in addiction services, child and adolescent mental health, paediatric psychology, child protection, disability services, adult mental health and specialist family therapy services. I have worked in the public health service in Canada, the UK and Ireland; in private practice; and in universities. Finally, it is worth mentioning that clinical psychologists are reasonably well paid, although I have met very few clinical psychologists who were 'in it for the money'.

Summary

Clinical psychology is both a health care profession and a health-related scientific discipline.

The clinical psychologist's role has been conceptualized as that of a scientist-practitioner and a practitioner-scholar. Clinical psychologists' jobs typically involve direct work with clients, indirect work, administration or management, research, and continuing professional development. Clinical psychologists provide services to a wide range of people with diverse difficulties in an array of different work settings.

In the UK and Ireland professional clinical psychology training programmes are 3 year doctorates run by partnerships involving universities and public health service units. These programmes include course work, clinical placements and research. In the UK and Ireland there are about 35 clinical psychology programmes. Between 2005 and 2010 about 20–30% of applicants got places on these courses. Minimum entry requirements for clinical psychology training in the UK and Ireland are a 2.1 honours degree in psychology and about a year's relevant clinical experience. Because entry to programmes is very competitive, successful applicants typically exceed these minimum requirements.

Academic suitability for doctoral programmes in clinical psychology is assessed by taking account of performance in high school and on undergraduate degree programmes; completing postgraduate degrees in psychology, short courses relevant to clinical psychology, and other non-psychological qualifications; and research achievements. Clinical suitability is assessed with reference to the way in which candidates have made use of the opportunities available to them to engage in relevant clinical experiences and to acquire basic clinical skills. Finding relevant clinical experience is challenging and requires creativity and persistence in opportunity searching and professional networking. Getting a place on a clinical psychology programme involves completing the application form and submitting it prior to application deadlines; arranging references; attending interviews; completing assessment exercises; accepting negative feedback if unsuccessful and reapplying. If your career plan is to become a clinical psychologist and practise in the UK or Ireland, join the BPsS and/or the PsSI sooner rather than later, since their publications will keep you abreast of professional developments and relevant experience opportunities. Apart from the UK and Ireland, there are well-developed doctoral clinical psychology training programmes in other English speaking countries including the US, Canada and Australia.

Clinical psychology may be distinguished from other types of applied psychology, notably counselling psychology, educational psychology, health psychology, and forensic psychology. Clinical psychology may also be distinguished from other mental health professions including psychiatry, psychotherapy and counselling. There are pros and cons to choosing clinical psychology as a career. Training can take up to 10 years, programme entry is highly competitive, and working in the public health service can be stressful. However, for qualified psychologists there are many job opportunities, good career development prospects and the job is intrinsically very satisfying.

Questions

- What is clinical psychology?
- How are clinical psychologists trained?
- If you wished to train as a clinical psychologist, what steps would you like to take to increase your chances of getting a place on a professional training programme in clinical psychology?
- How does clinical psychology differ from other applied specialties, such as educational, counseling, health and forensic psychology, and from other professions such as psychiatry or psychotherapy?
- What are the advantages and disadvantages of choosing clinical psychology as a career?

- What is the most important thing you have learned from studying this chapter?

FURTHER READING

- Beinart, H., Kennedy, P. & Llewelyn, S. (2009). *Clinical psychology in practice.* London: British Psychological Society–Blackwell.
- Bennett, P. (2011). *Abnormal and clinical psychology: An introductory textbook* (third edition). Maidenhead: Open University Press.
- Davey, G. (2008). *Clinical psychology.* London: Hodder Education
- Knight, A. (2002). *How to become a clinical psychologist: Getting a foot in the door.* London: Routledge.

Major clinical psychology journals

- *Annual Review of Clinical Psychology*
- *British Journal of Clinical Psychology*
- *Clinical Psychology Review*
- *Clinical Psychology: Science and Practice*
- *Journal of Consulting and Clinical Psychology*

WEBSITES

Sites for relevant experience and general information

- Assistant Psychologists Ireland Google group: ap_ireland@googlegroups.com
- Psyclick website: www.psyclick.org.uk/

Sites for applying for clinical psychology courses

- Clearing House for Postgraduate Courses in Clinical Psychology: www.leeds.ac.uk/chpccp
- Hull University (which is not a member of the UK clearing house because the undergraduate psychology degree and postgraduate clinical degree programmes are integrated): www2.hull.ac.uk
- National University of Ireland Galway: www.nuigalway.ie
- Queen's University Belfast: www.qub.ac.uk
- Trinity College Dublin: www.tcd.ie
- University College Dublin: www.ucd.ie
- University of Limerick: www.ul.ie

Public health services

- Health Service Executive (Ireland):
  www.hse.ie
- Improving Access to Psychological Therapies:
  www.iapt.nhs.uk
- National Health Service (UK):
  www.nhs.uk

Psychological societies and professional associations

- American Psychological Association:
  www.apa.org
- American Psychological Association, Division 12, Society of Clinical Psychology:
  www.div12.org
- Australian Clinical Psychology Association:
  www.acpa.org.au
- Australian Psychological Society:
  www.psychology.org.au
- British Psychological Society:
  www.bps.org.uk
- British Psychological Society Division of Clinical Psychology:
  www.bps.org.uk/dcp
- Canadian Psychological Association:
  www.cpa.ca
- European Federation of Psychologists' Associations (EFPA):
  www.efpa.eu
- International Union of Psychological Science (IUPsyS):
  www.iupsys.org
- Irish Council for Psychotherapy:
  www.psychotherapy-ireland.com
- New Zealand Psychological Society:
  www.psychology.org.nz
- Psychological Society of Ireland:
  www.psihq.ie
- UK Council for Psychotherapy:
  www.psychotherapy.org.uk

Graduate Record Exam (GRE)

- Barron's GRE preparation:
  http://barronstestprep.com/gre
- Graduate record exam:
  www.ets.org/gre
- Kaplan GRE preparation:
  www.kaptest.com
- *Princeton Review* GRE preparation:
  www.princetonreview.com/grad/gre-test-preparation.aspx

Childhood behaviour disorders 2

Learning objectives

After studying this chapter you will be able to:

- list some of the main psychological disorders that occur in childhood
- give an account of the main clinical features of ADHD, oppositional defiant disorder and conduct disorder
- summarize the epidemiology of disruptive behaviour disorders
- outline the main biological and psychological theories of disruptive behaviour disorders
- name the main evidence-based approaches to assessment and treatment of disruptive behaviour disorders
- give a considered view on some of the main controversies surrounding the clinical psychology of childhood disorders.

Introduction

A wide variety of psychological problems may occur in childhood. These include problems that compromise children's capacities to learn and communicate such as intellectual disability, language delay, specific learning disabilities, and pervasive developmental disorders including autism spectrum disorders. Problems developing bowel and bladder control, and difficulties with feeding, sleeping and waking routines may also occur in childhood. Children and adolescents may develop neuro-psychological problems and adjustment difficulties secondary to conditions such as epilepsy or head injury. All of these difficulties are of concern to clinical psychologists (Carr, 2006a). However, in addition to these difficulties, two broad classes of conditions have been a focus for clinical psychologists who work with children and adolescents. These are disruptive behaviour disorders (such as attention deficit hyperactivity disorder (ADHD), oppositional defiant disorder and conduct disorder) and emotional disorders (such as anxiety and depression). Disruptive behaviour disorders are characterized principally by externalizing behaviour problems such as rule-breaking, defiance and aggression. In contrast, internalizing behaviour problems such as social withdrawal, tearfulness and avoidance are the main features of emotional disorders. Factor analyses of common childhood behaviour problems consistently identify internalizing and externalizing behaviour problems as the two main dimensions of childhood behavioural difficulties (Achenbach, 2009).

In Chapters 5 and 6 the emotional disorders – anxiety and depression – in children, adolescents and adults will be addressed. The central focus of the present chapter will be disruptive behaviour disorders. The diagnostic criteria for ADHD, oppositional defiant disorder and conduct disorder are given in Tables 2.1 and 2.2. It is noteworthy that all three of these conditions entail behaviour that is troublesome for others as well as for the child. In this chapter case examples of ADHD and conduct disorder will be given, along with an outline of the clinical features, epidemiology and theoretical explanations for these problems. Some comments will also be made on their assessment and treatment.

Attention deficit hyperactivity disorder

Attention deficit hyperactivity disorder, attention deficit disorder, hyper-kinetic disorder, hyperkinesis, minimal brain damage and minimal brain dysfunction are some of the terms used for a syndrome characterized by persistent overactivity, impulsivity and difficulties in sustaining attention (Barkley, 2005). Children with this profile were first described in modern medical literature by George Still in 1902. In this chapter preference will be given to the widely used term – attention deficit hyperactivity disorder or ADHD.

Case example of ADHD

Timmy, aged 6, was referred for assessment because his teachers found him unmanageable. He was unable to sit still in school and concentrate on his schoolwork. He left his chair frequently and ran around the classroom shouting. This was distracting for his teachers and classmates. Even with individual tuition he could not apply himself to his school work. He also had difficulties getting along with other children. They disliked him because he disrupted their games. He rarely waited for his turn and did not obey the rules. At home he was consistently disobedient and, according to his father, ran 'like a motorboat' from the time he got up until bedtime. He often climbed on furniture and routinely shouted rather than talked.

Family history

Timmy came from a well functioning family. His parents had a very stable and satisfying marriage and ran a successful business together. Their daughter, Amanda, was a well-adjusted and academically able 8-year-old. The parents were careful not to favour the daughter over her brother or to unduly punish Timmy for his constant disruption of his sister's activities. However, there was a growing tension between each of the parents and Timmy. While they were undoubtedly committed to him, they were also continually suppressing their growing irritation with his frenetic activity, disobedience, shouting and school problems. Within the wider family there were few resources that the parents could draw on to help them cope with Timmy. The grandparents, aunts and uncles lived abroad and so could not provide regular support for the parents. Furthermore, they were bewildered by Timmy's condition, found it very unpleasant and had gradually reduced their contact with Timmy's nuclear family since his birth.

Psychometric assessment and child interview

Psychometric evaluation showed that Timmy's overall IQ was within the normal range but he was highly distractible and had literacy and numeracy skills that were significantly below his overall ability level. Timmy perceived himself to be a failure. He believed that he could not do anything right at home or at school and he was sad that the other children did not want to play with him. He believed that his teacher disliked him and doubted his parents' love for him.

Developmental history

There were a number of noteworthy features in Timmy's developmental history. He had suffered anoxia at birth and febrile convulsions in infancy. He had also had episodes of projectile vomiting. His high activity level and demandingness had been present from birth. He displayed a difficult temperament, showing little regularity in feeding or sleeping; intense negative emotions to new stimuli; and was slow to soothe following intense display of negative emotion.

Formulation

Timmy was a 6-year-old boy with home- and school-based problems of hyperactivity, impulsivity and distractibility of sufficient severity to warrant a diagnosis of attention deficit hyperactivity disorder. The problems were longstanding, and there was no discrete factor that precipitated his condition. However, his entry into the school system precipitated the referral. Possible predisposing factors included anoxia

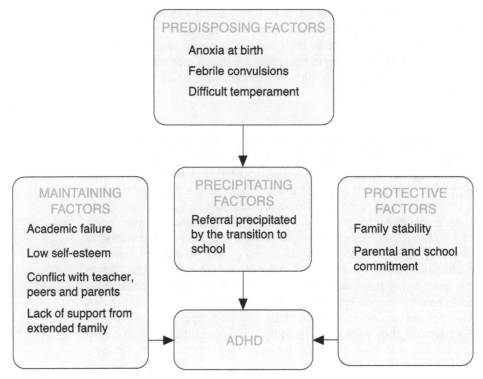

Figure 2.1 Formulation of a case of ADHD

at birth, subtle neurological damage due to febrile convulsions in infancy, and a difficult temperament.

In Timmy's case, ADHD had led to academic attainment difficulties, low self-esteem, conflict with his school teacher, peer relationship problems and tension within the family. This wider constellation of difficulties maintained and exacerbated his hyperactivity, impulsivity and distractibility. The absence of an extended family support system for the parents to help them deal with his difficulties was a possible maintaining factor. Important protective factors in this case were the commitment of Timmy's parents and teachers to resolving the problem and the stability of Timmy's nuclear family. This formulation is diagrammed in Figure 2.1.

Treatment

Treatment in this case involved both psychosocial and pharmacological intervention. The psychosocial intervention included parent and teacher education about ADHD, behavioural parent training, self-instructional training for the child, a classroom-based behavioural programme and provision of periodic relief care/holidays with specially trained foster parents. Timmy was also given stimulant therapy, specifically a twice-daily dose of methylphenidate (Ritalin). These interventions led to a significant improvement in his disruptive behaviour at home and school, his academic performance in school, and the quality of his relationships with his parents, teachers and friends.

Clinical features

ADHD has distinct clinical features in the domains of cognition, affect, behaviour, physical health and interpersonal adjustment. Timmy, in the case example, showed all of these. With respect to cognition, short attention span, distractibility and an inability to foresee the consequences of action are the main features. There is usually a poor internalization of the rules of social conduct, and in some instances low self-esteem may be present. With respect to affect, excitability associated with lack of impulse control is the dominant emotional state. This may be coupled with depressed mood associated with low self-esteem in some cases. With ADHD, the cardinal behavioural features are the high rate of activity, common comorbid aggressive antisocial behaviour, excessive risk-taking and poor school performance associated with inattention.

With respect to physical health in ADHD, in some instances food allergies may be present. Injuries or medical complications associated with antisocial behaviour such as fighting and drug abuse may also occur. Relationship difficulties with parents, teachers and peers are the principal interpersonal adjustment problems.

Difficulties with turn-taking in games due to impulsivity make children with ADHD poor playmates. The failure of children with ADHD to internalize rules of social conduct at home and to meet parental expectations for appropriate social and academic behaviour leads to conflictual parent–child relationships. In school, youngsters with ADHD pose classroom management problems for teachers and these children invariably have problems in benefiting from routine teaching and instructional methods. For these reasons, their relationships with teachers tend to be conflictual.

Currently the World Health Organization's (1992) International Classification of Diseases (ICD-10) criteria for hyperkinetic disorder, which are widely used in Europe, are stricter than those for ADHD in the American Psychiatric Association's (2000) *Diagnostic and Statistical Manual* (DSM-IV-TR), which are widely used in North America. Both sets of criteria are given in Table 2.1. The ICD criteria stipulate that the *actual symptoms* of inattention, hyperactivity and impulsivity must be present in two or more settings such as home and school for a positive diagnosis to be made. In contrast, the more lenient DSM criteria specify that only *impairment* in functioning arising from the symptoms, rather than the actual symptoms or inattention, hyperactivity and impulsivity, must be present in two or more settings for a positive diagnosis.

Epidemiology

In a review of 15 international epidemiological studies, Costello et al. (2004) found that the prevalence of ADHD ranged from 0.3% to 11.3%, with a median prevalence rate of 2.7%. The variability in rates may be due to the stringency of the diagnostic criteria applied and the demographic characteristics of the populations studied. Using stringent ICD-10 hyperkinetic disorder criteria demanding cross-situational stability of

TABLE 2.1
Diagnostic criteria for attention and hyperactivity syndromes in DSM-IV-TR and ICD-10

DSM-IV-TR: Attention deficit hyperactivity disorder	*ICD-10: Hyperkinetic disorder*
A. Either 1 or 2 1. Six or more of the following symptoms of inattention have persisted for at least 6 months to a degree that is maladaptive and inconsistent with developmental level. **Inattention** a. Often fails to give close attention to details or makes careless mistakes in schoolwork, work or other activities b. Often has difficulty sustaining attention in tasks or play activities c. Often does not seem to listen when spoken to directly d. Often does not follow through on instructions and fails to finish schoolwork, chores or work duties e. Often has difficulty organizing tasks and activities f. Often avoids or dislikes tasks that require sustained mental effort g. Often loses things necessary for tasks or activities h. Is often easily distracted by extraneous stimuli i. Is often forgetful in daily activities 2. Six or more of the following symptoms of **hyperactivity–impulsivity** have persisted for at least 6 months to a degree that is maladaptive and inconsistent with developmental level. **Hyperactivity** a. Often fidgets with hands or feet or squirms in seat b. Often leaves seat in classroom or in other situations in which remaining seated is expected c. Often runs about or climbs excessively in situations in which it is inappropriate d. Often has difficulty playing or engaging in leisure activities quietly e. Is often on the go or acts as if driven by a motor f. Often talks excessively **Impulsivity** g. Often blurts out answer before questions have been completed h. Often has difficulty awaiting turn i. Often interrupts or intrudes on others B. Some of these symptoms were present before the age of 7 years C. Some impairment from the symptoms is present in **two or more settings** (e.g. home and school) D. Clinically significant impairment in social, academic or occupational functioning E. Not due to another disorder Specify: Combined type if inattention and overactivity–impulsivity are present; Inattentive type if overactivity is absent; Hyperactive–impulsive type if inattentiveness is absent	The cardinal features are impaired attention and overactivity. Both are necessary for the diagnosis and should be evident in **more than one situation** (e.g. home or school). **Impaired attention** is manifested by prematurely breaking off from tasks and leaving activities unfinished. The children change frequently from one activity to another, seemingly losing interest in one task because they become diverted to another. These deficits in persistence and attention should be diagnosed only if they are excessive for the child's age and IQ. **Overactivity** implies excessive restlessness, especially in situations requiring relative calm. It may, depending on the situation, involve the child running and jumping around, getting up from a seat when he or she was supposed to remain seated, excessive talkativeness and noisiness, or fidgeting and wriggling. The standard for judgement should be that the activity is excessive in the context of what is expected in the situation and by comparison with other children of the same age and IQ. This behavioural feature is most evident in structured, organized situations that require a high degree of behavioural self-control. The characteristic behaviour problems should be of early onset (before the age of 6 years) and long duration. Associated features include disinhibition in social relationships, recklessness in situations involving some danger, impulsive flouting of social rules, learning disorders, and motor clumsiness. Specify: Hyperkinetic disorder with disturbance of activity and attention when antisocial features of conduct disorder are absent. Hyperkinetic conduct disorder when criteria for both conduct disorder and hyperkinetic disorder are met.

Note: Adapted from DSM-IV-TR (APA, 2000) and ICD-10 (WHO, 1992).

symptoms, a prevalence rate of 1% was obtained in a UK national epidemiological study (Meltzer et al., 2000).

The prevalence of ADHD varies with gender and age, and the occurrence of comorbid conditions is common (Brown, 2009; Carr, 2006a). ADHD is more prevalent in boys than in girls, and in preadolescents than in late adolescents. Comorbidity for conduct disorder and ADHD is about 20% in community populations and possibly double this figure in clinic populations. Comorbidity for emotional disorders, such as anxiety or depression, and ADHD is about 10% in community populations. In clinical populations the comorbidity rate may be twice this figure. Virtually all children with ADHD have attainment problems. However, comorbid severe specific learning difficulties have been estimated to occur in 10–25% of cases. A proportion of children with ADHD have comorbid developmental language delays, elimination problems and multiple tics or Tourette's disorder, although reliable epidemiological data are not available.

About a third of children with ADHD have a good prognosis, about a third have a moderate prognosis and a third have a poor prognosis (Faraone et al., 2006; Hinshaw, 1994). For two thirds of cases, the primary problems of inattention, impulsivity and hyperactivity persist into late adolescence and for some of these the primary symptoms persist into adulthood. Roughly a third develop significant antisocial behaviour problems in adolescence, including conduct disorder and substance abuse, and for most of this subgroup these problems persist into adulthood, leading to criminality. Occupational adjustment problems and suicide attempts occur in a small but significant minority of cases.

Etiological theories

Biological, cognitive-behavioural and family systems theories have been developed to explain the aetiology of ADHD.

Biological theories

Biological theories that focus on the role of genetic factors, structural brain abnormalities, neurotransmitter dysregulation, dietary factors and hypo-arousal have guided much research on the aetiology of ADHD.

Genetics

The genetic hypothesis proposes that ADHD symptomatology or a predisposition to hyperactivity is inherited by children who develop the condition. In support of this hypothesis, twin, adoption and family studies all show that rates of ADHD are higher in the biological relatives of children with ADHD than of those without the disorder (Taylor, 2008; Thapar & Scourfield, 2002; Thapar & Stergiakouli, 2008). Twin studies show that ADHD is 80% heritable, making it one of the most heritable psychological disorders. Twenty percent of the variance in ADHD symptomatology may be accounted for by environmental factors. The nature and extent of the contribution made by genetic and environmental factors varies from case to case. Extreme levels of the temperamental characteristic of overactivity, which is normally distributed within the population and polygenetically determined, probably interacts with environmental factors (either intrauterine or psychosocial) to give rise to the clinical syndrome of ADHD. It may be that in some cases, temperamentally overactive children sustain a prenatal or early childhood neurological insult and go on to develop ADHD, whereas others with an overactive temperament develop the syndrome following participation in ongoing non-optimal parent–child interactions.

Molecular genetic studies have found an association between ADHD and the dopamine transporter gene (DAT1) and the dopamine D4 receptor gene (DRD4). The search for these genes was informed by evidence for dysregulation of the dopamine system in the prefrontal region of the brain, associated with executive function in children with ADHD. For a small subgroup of children with ADHD, the syndrome appears to be caused by a genetic condition resulting in a generalized resistance to thyroid hormone (Hauser et al., 1993).

Organic deficits

Early work on ADHD was premised on the hypothesis that the syndrome reflected an organic deficit: probably some form of minimal brain damage (Strauss & Lehtinen, 1947). In support of this hypothesis, a number of factors that might be associated with brain damage or dysfunction during the prenatal or perinatal periods and in early childhood have been found to be more prevalent among youngsters with ADHD than normal controls. These include prenatal difficulties; maternal stress during pregnancy; maternal nicotine, alcohol, cocaine and anticonvulsant use during pregnancy; low foetal heart rate during delivery; small head circumference at birth; low birth weight; minor physical abnormalities; a high rate of diseases of infancy; lead poisoning and early neurological insult or severe head injury (Barkley, 2005; Taylor, 2008; Taylor & Rogers, 2005). It is important to point out that these factors which may be associated with, or contribute to, the development of an organic deficit are not unique to ADHD and also occur in youngsters with other disorders. Therefore they probably interact with other factors in contributing to the development of ADHD.

Neuroimaging studies have shown that ADHD is associated with a range of structural and functional neuroanatomical abnormalities (Shaw, 2010). The best established of these is lobar volume loss of around 3–4%, and abnormalities of the frontostriatal circuitry which underpins executive function (Makris et al., 2009). The frontostriatal circuitry of children with ADHD is less efficient than that of normal children and this may account for their executive function deficits, such as difficulties with planning and following through on tasks (mentioned below under psychological theories).

Neuroimaging studies have also found abnormalities in the cerebellum, which may underpin deficits in temporal information processing such as learning 'what to expect when', and in the parietal lobes, which may affect the capacity to attend to one stimulus without being distracted by another (Cherkasova & Hechtman, 2009). Ongoing research continues to identify other neural mechanisms associated with ADHD. Not all cases of ADHD show all abnormalities. It is likely that the symptom patterns of different subgroups of cases are associated with different neurophysiological abnormalities.

Neurotransmitter dysregulation

In 1937 Charles Bradley reported that Benzedrine – a stimulant – had a calming effect on the behaviour of hyperactive children. Subsequent research showed that methylphenidate, which is also a stimulant, and atomoxetine, a non-stimulant selective noradrenalin reuptake inhibitor, had similar affects (Taylor, 2008). Neurotransmitter dysregulation hypotheses have been proposed to explain the effects of these drugs on ADHD. These hypotheses attribute the symptoms of ADHD to abnormalities in neurotransmitter functioning at the synapses affected by medications that ameliorate the symptomatology of ADHD. Results of research in this field have converged on the view that a dysregulation of the dopaminergic system in the ventral tegmental areas of the brain and noradrenergic and adrenergic systems in the locus coeruleus may be present in ADHD (Solanto, 1998). Dexamphetamine and methylphenidate appear to improve functioning in people with ADHD by increasing extracellular dopamine, while atomoxetine has beneficial effects by increasing extracellular noradrenaline levels (Pliszka, 2007).

Controlled trials show that approximately 70% of children with ADHD respond to these medications (Hinshaw et al., 2007). Medicated children with ADHD show a reduction in symptomatology and an improvement in both academic and social functioning, although positive effects dissipate when medication ceases, if psychological interventions to improve symptom control have not been provided concurrently with medication. One of the most remarkable findings of the Multimodal Treatment study of ADHD (MTA) – the largest ever long-term controlled trial of stimulant medication for ADHD, involving over 500 cases – is that stimulant medication ceased to have a therapeutic effect after 3 years (Swanson & Volkow, 2009). It also led to a reduction in height gain of about 2 cm, and a reduction in weight gain of about 2 kg. Furthermore, it did not prevent adolescent substance misuse as expected. The MTA trial showed that tolerance to medication used to treat ADHD occurs and this medication has negative side-effects. These findings underline the importance of using medication to reduce ADHD symptoms to manageable levels for a time-limited period, while children and their parents engage in psychological interventions to develop skills to manage symptoms through psychological means.

Diet

The dietary hypothesis attributes the symptoms of ADHD to children's reaction to certain features of their daily diet. Originally Feingold (1975) argued that artificial food additives such as colourants accounted for a substantial proportion of ADHD symptomatology. However, controlled trials of additive-free diets did not support his position. Egger et al.

(1985) refined Feingold's original allergy theory and argued that particular children with ADHD may have unique allergy profiles and if their diet is modified so as to exclude the precise substances to which they are allergic, then their activity and attention problems may improve. Carefully controlled dietary studies have supported Egger's theory, showing that children with ADHD and food allergies can benefit from placement on a 'few foods' diet (Jacobson & Schardt, 1999; Stevenson, 2010). Results of controlled trials show that removal of food colours from the diet can have beneficial effects on the behaviour of children with and without ADHD, but evidence for the value of omega-3 supplementation in reducing hyperactivity is inconsistent (Stevenson, 2010).

Hypo-arousal

The hypo-arousal hypothesis explains hyperactivity and inattention as a failure to be sufficiently aroused by signal stimuli to attend to them and regulate activity levels. Psychophysiological studies in which arousal is assessed by electroencephalograph (EEG), skin conductance and heart rate recordings indicate that ADHD children show reduced psychophysiological responsiveness to novel stimuli with signal value (Rowe et al., 2005). The use of vivid stimuli in academic settings and highly salient and immediate reinforcers is implicated by the hypo-arousal hypothesis. Reward systems and operant programmes conforming to these specifications have been found to have significant short-term effects (Hinshaw et al., 2007). EEG neurofeedback to increase cortical arousal has been shown in preliminary trials to improve ADHD symptoms (Sherlin et al., 2010).

Cognitive-behavioural approaches

A number of theories that highlight the importance of deficits in specific cognitive or behavioural processes as the central factor underlying ADHD symptomatology have been proposed. Four of these will be mentioned below. All attempt to show how the overall syndrome of inattention, overactivity and impulsivity may be accounted for by a single underlying core deficit, be it one of the three core symptoms of ADHD or some other cognitive or behavioural process.

Inattention

The attentional deficit hypothesis proposes that problems with sustaining attention on a single task and screening out other distracting stimuli is the core difficulty that underpins the other symptoms of impulsivity and overactivity in ADHD (e.g. Douglas, 1983). That is, youngsters with ADHD at the outset of a task requiring attention will perform at a level equivalent to normal children but, over time, will show more errors that are directly attributable to the inability to sustain attention. This problem with sustaining attention leads them to change the focus of their attention frequently and is manifested at a behavioural level as excessive impulsivity and overactivity. On certain laboratory tasks children with ADHD show a gradual deterioration in sustained attention, as predicted by the inattention hypothesis. However, contrary to the inattention hypothesis, on other tasks they show immediate selective attention, like children without ADHD, and they also display overactivity while asleep (Barkley, 2003). These findings suggest that a deficit in the capacity for sustained attention alone cannot fully account for the ADHD syndrome.

Hyperactivity

The hyperactivity hypothesis argues that a problem with inhibiting motor activity is the core deficit that underpins the ADHD syndrome and can account for inattention and impulsivity (e.g. Schachar, 1991). There is a large body of evidence which shows that hyperactivity is unique as a symptom to children with ADHD compared to children with other psychological problems, and that hyperactivity as a construct correlates with many academic indices of attentional problems (Barkley, 2003).

Impulsivity

The impulsivity hypothesis proposes that a core problem in inhibiting cognitive and behavioural responses to specific stimuli leads to poor performance on tasks apparently requiring good attentional abilities and also to tasks requiring careful regulation of behaviour. Thus the central problem in ADHD, according to this hypothesis, is with cognitive and behavioural impulsivity (e.g., Nigg, 2001). According to this theory, with academic tasks requiring high levels of sustained attention, children with ADHD have problems using systematic cognitive problem-solving strategies because they are cognitively impulsive. Also, in both academic and social situations, children with ADHD engage in careless work practices in school and engage in socially inappropriate behaviour with peers, parents and teachers because they are behaviourally impulsive. There is some evidence to show that while children with ADHD may know and understand problem-solving skills and social skills, they fail to use them appropriately in academic and social situations (Barkley, 2003).

Executive function

Russell Barkley (2003, 2005) argues that the symptoms of ADHD (impulsivity, overactivity and inattention) reflect a central deficit in the core executive function of behavioural inhibition that is neurodevelopmental (rather than social) in origin. Children with deficits in behavioural inhibition cannot delay gratification, so as to reap better rewards later. This core deficit in behavioural inhibition is associated with, and reinforced by, secondary deficits in four other executive functions: (1) nonverbal working memory, (2) verbal working memory (or internalization of speech), (3) self-regulation of affect, arousal and motivation, and (4) verbal and behavioural creativity and fluency (or internalization of play). With poor verbal and non-verbal working memory, ADHD children cannot hold a picture of events in the mind, or obey a set of self-directed instructions so as to delay gratification or sustain planned sequences of goal-directed behaviour. With poor self-regulation of affect, arousal and motivation, ADHD children have difficulty in preventing strong emotional experiences and motives from interfering with planned goal-directed behaviour. With poor verbal and behavioural creativity and fluency, ADHD children have difficulty in developing, rehearsing and implementing creative plans to achieve novel goals.

The four secondary executive function deficits, according to Barkley, reflect failures to internalize and privatize functions that in early development were external features of the child's interactions with caregivers. In normal development the emergence of these four executive functions reflects a shift in the source of control of behaviour from external events to mental representations of events; from control by others to control by the self; and from immediate to delayed gratification. This complex and elaborate executive function hypothesis has to some degree supplanted earlier simpler psychological theories and is partially supported by a growing body of empirical evidence (Barkley, 2003, 2005; Nigg, 2005).

To compensate for deficits in attention, regulation of motor activity, impulsivity and executive function, various skills training programmes have been developed, largely within the cognitive-behavioural tradition. Self-instructional training for managing academic tasks and social skills training to manage relationship problems (particularly those involving peers) are the main types of training provided within these programmes. Because of the negligible impact that such programmes had when conducted in isolation, they are now offered as one element of a multimodal package involving stimulant medication, family intervention and school intervention (Hinshaw et al., 2007). Compensatory problem-solving and social skills training programmes can have optimum effect when offered after a consistent home- and school-based contingency management programme has been established and stimulant treatment is in progress.

Systemic theory

Family systems theories have focused largely on the role of the family system or the wider social context in the aetiology and maintenance of ADHD. Parental psychological problems such as depression, aggression or alcohol and substance misuse; exposure to severe marital discord or domestic violence; extreme abuse and neglect in infancy; and coercive parent–child interactions in childhood and adolescence have all been found to have associations with ADHD (Deault, 2010; Johnston & Mash, 2001; Taylor, 2008). With respect to the wider social system, the following factors have been found to be associated with ADHD: institutional upbringing, low socio-economic status, peer relationship problems, and relationship problems with school staff (Barclay, 2005; Taylor, 2008).

A problem with much of the research on psychosocial factors in the aetiology and maintenance of ADHD is the fact that in many cases comorbid conduct disorders are present and the risk factors that are identified, which bear a close resemblance to those identified for conduct disorders, may primarily be associated with the aetiology of conduct problems rather than ADHD. A second difficulty is untangling the causal chain, establishing which family and relationship difficulties precede the development of ADHD and are predisposing factors, and distinguishing these from relationship difficulties that evolve in response to ADHD and possibly maintain or exacerbate the condition. Results of longitudinal studies and family intervention studies suggest that chronic exposure to extremely adverse institutional or family environments early in life may heighten the risk of developing ADHD, and for children with predominantly biologically determined ADHD, improved parenting practices can affect the course of the disorder (Taylor, 2008).

Family-based interventions and multisystemic intervention programmes involving the child's wider social network have evolved from family systems theories of ADHD. These programmes focus on improving parenting skills and enhancing the child's relationships with members of the family and the wider network. Such programmes have been shown to have positive short-term effects on both symptomatology and social adjustment (Anastopoulos et al., 2005; Barkley et al., 1992; Young & Amarasinghe, 2010).

Assessment

Assessment and treatment of ADHD is usually carried out by multidisciplinary teams which include clinical psychologists, and colleagues from other disciplines such as psychiatry or paediatrics. Children with ADHD require assessment of their behaviour, abilities, and family and school situations. The revised Conners' Rating Scales (CRS-R, Conners, 1997) are widely used to assess ADHD behaviour. Conners' parent, teacher and self-report rating scales each contain almost 100 items and yield a range of scores on scales that assess aspects of ADHD and related difficulties. Computer scoring systems are available and normative data are used to interpret scores. To establish a DSM-IV-TR or ICD-10 diagnosis, a structured interview for parents and children may be administered, such as the attention and activity module of the Development and Well-Being Assessment (DAWBA, Goodman et al., 2000). Abilities may be assessed with intelligence tests such as the Wechsler Intelligence Scale for Children (WISC-IV, Wechsler, 2004a) for school-aged children and the Wechsler Preschool and Primary Scale of Intelligence (WPPSI-III, 2004b) for preschoolers. These tests yield full-scale IQs as well as scores for specific abilities that throw light on cognitive strengths and weaknesses.

Attainments may be assessed with tests such as the Wechsler Individual Achievement Test (WIAT-II, Wechsler, 2005), which assess reading, numerical and language attainments. Family and school situations may be assessed by conducting interviews with parents and school teachers about the young person's behaviour in these contexts. Assessment information is integrated into a formulation that is used for treatment planning as illustrated in the case study that opened the chapter. This should link predisposing, precipitating and maintaining factors to the child's presenting problems and specify protective factors that may be drawn on during treatment. A general clinical formulation model for ADHD is given in Figure 2.2.

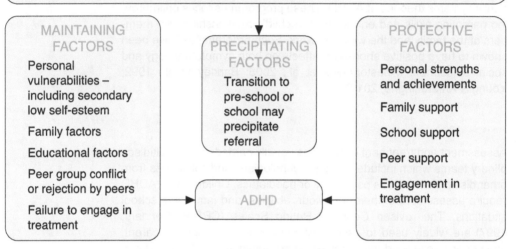

PREDISPOSING FACTORS

Any factor that impairs developing control of attention and activity

Personal vulnerabilities – Genetic vulnerability, prenatal & perinatal stresses, difficult temperament, executive function deficits

Family factors – Disorganization, parental maladjustment, parenting problems

Educational factors – Language delay, learning disability, school failure, lack of educational resources

Social factors – Institutional upbringing, low SES

MAINTAINING FACTORS

Personal vulnerabilities – including secondary low self-esteem

Family factors

Educational factors

Peer group conflict or rejection by peers

Failure to engage in treatment

PRECIPITATING FACTORS

Transition to pre-school or school may precipitate referral

ADHD

PROTECTIVE FACTORS

Personal strengths and achievements

Family support

School support

Peer support

Engagement in treatment

Figure 2.2 General formulation model for ADHD

Treatment

There is a growing consensus within the field that single factor theories are unlikely to be able to explain the complex and heterogeneous population of youngsters who qualify for a diagnosis of ADHD (Barkley, 2005). It is probable that a variety of biological and psychosocial factors interact in complex ways to give rise to the syndrome and that problems with a number of psychological processes particularly those involved in regulating both cognitive and motor responses underpin symptomatology. The symptomatology is probably partially maintained and exacerbated by problematic relationships within the family, the peer group and the school.

In view of this integrative formulation, it is not surprising that multi-modal treatment packages that include behavioural parent training, self-instructional and social skills training and school-based contingency management combined with stimulant therapy have been found to be most effective. International best practice guidelines recommend that multimodal programmes involving stimulant medication and behaviourally oriented family, school and individual psychological interventions should be offered to children with ADHD (American Academy of Child and Adolescent Psychiatry, 2007a; American Academy of Paediatrics, 2001; Consensus Development Panel, 2000; Kutcher et al., 2004, NICE, 2008a).

With behavioural parent training, parents are coached in how to consistently reinforce socially appropriate behaviour and extinguish inappropriate behaviour. School-based contingency management programmes extend this type of approach into the child's classroom environment. In self-instructional training, children with ADHD are coached in the use of self-instructions to regulate the way in which they deploy their attention and control their impulses. With stimulant therapy, children receive regular doses of methylphenidate which is available in a form that is taken twice or three times a day, or as a slow-release preparation taken only once a day. Psychological interventions collectively contribute to normalizing ADHD behaviour, largely by improving parenting practices and enhancing the way children with ADHD interact with their families and social networks, and pharmacological interventions reduce symptom intensity and so make it easier for parents and children to make these changes. However, as mentioned earlier, stimulant treatment loses its effectiveness after 3 years, so it is important that this 3 year window of opportunity be used to help children and parents develop ways to manage ADHD symptoms. Two promising innovations in child-focused psychological treatments of ADHD are the use of computer-based programmes to train children to enhance the functioning of working memory, and neurofeedback in which children modify the frequency, amplitude or other characteristics of their electroencephalogram (EEG) brain-wave patterns (Toplak et al., 2008).

Conduct disorder and oppositional defiant disorder

Conduct disorder refers to a pattern of persistent, serious, aggressive and destructive rule-breaking behaviour at home and within the wider community, while oppositional defiant disorder refers to a persistent pattern of oppositional and hostile behaviour confined to the home context (American Psychiatric Association, 2000a; World Health Organization, 1992). Diagnostic criteria for these two conditions are given in Table 2.2. Conduct problems constitute a third to a half of all clinic referrals, and chronic conduct problems are the single most costly disorder of adolescence for three reasons (Kazdin, 1995; Moffitt & Scott, 2008; Scott, 2009).

First, they are remarkably unresponsive to traditional individual approaches to treatment. Positive outcome rates for routine treatments range from 20% to 40%. Second, about 60% of adolescents with conduct problems have a poor prognosis. Adolescents with chronic conduct disorder turn to adult criminality and develop antisocial personality disorders, alcohol-related problems and a variety of psychological difficulties. They also have more problems with health, educational attainment, occupational adjustment, marital stability and social integration. The third reason for the high cost of conduct problems is the fact that they are intergenerationally transmitted. Adults with a history of conduct disorder rear children with a high prevalence of conduct difficulties.

TABLE 2.2
Diagnostic criteria for oppositional defiant disorder and conduct disorder in DSM-IV-TR and ICD-10

DSM-IV-TR	ICD-10
Oppositional defiant disorder A. A pattern of negativistic, hostile and defiant behaviour lasting at least 6 months, during which four or more of the following are present: 1. Often loses temper 2. Often argues with adults 3. Often actively defies or refuses to comply with adults' requests or rules 4. Often deliberately annoys people 5. Often blames others for his or her mistakes or misbehaviour 6. Is often touchy or easily annoyed by others 7. Is often angry or resentful 8. Is often spiteful or vindictive B. The disturbance in behaviour causes clinically significant impairment in social, academic or occupational functioning C. The behaviours do not occur exclusively during the course of a psychotic or a mood disorder D. Criteria are not met for conduct disorder or antisocial personality disorder.	The essential feature of this disorder is a pattern of persistently negativistic, hostile, defiant, provocative and disruptive behaviour which is clearly outside the normal range of behaviour for a child of the same age in the same sociocultural context and which does not include the more serious violations of the rights of others associated with conduct disorder. Children with this disorder tend frequently and actively to defy adult requests or rules and deliberately to annoy other people. Usually they tend to be angry, resentful, and easily annoyed by other people whom they blame for their own mistakes and difficulties. They generally have a low frustration tolerance and readily lose their temper. Typically their defiance has a provocative quality, so that they initiate confrontations and generally exhibit excessive levels of rudeness, uncooperativeness and resistance to authority. Frequently this behaviour is most evident in interactions with adults or peers whom the child knows well, and signs of the disorder may not be present during clinical interview. The key distinction from other types of conduct disorder is the absence of behaviour that violates the law and the basic rights of others such as theft, cruelty, bullying, assault and destructiveness.
Conduct disorder A. A repetitive and persistent pattern of behaviour in which the basic rights of others or major age-appropriate societal norms or rules are violated, as manifested by the presence of three or more of the following criteria in the past 12 months with at least one criterion present in the past 6 months. **Aggression to people and animals** 1. Often bullies, threatens or intimidates others 2. Often initiates physical fights 3. Has used a weapon that can cause serious physical harm to others 4. Has been physically cruel to people 5. Has been physically cruel to animals 6. Has stolen while confronting a victim 7. Has forced someone into sexual activity	Conduct disorders are characterized by a repetitive and persistent pattern of dissocial, aggressive, or defiant conduct. Such behaviour, when at its most extreme for the individual should amount to major violations of age-appropriate social expectations, and is therefore more severe than ordinary childish mischief or adolescent rebelliousness.

DSM-IV-TR	ICD-10
Destruction of property 8. Has deliberately engaged in firesetting 9. Has deliberately destroyed others' property	Examples of the behaviours on which the diagnosis is based include the following: excessive levels of fighting or bullying; cruelty to animals or other people; severe destructiveness to property; firesetting; steallng; repeated lying; truancy from school and running away from home; unusually frequent and severe temper tantrums; defiant provocative behaviour; and persistent and severe disobedience. Any one of these categories, if marked, is sufficient for the diagnosis, but isolated dissocial acts are not.
Deceitfulness or theft 10. Has broken into someone's house, building or car 11. Often lies to obtain goods or favours or avoid obligations 12. Has stolen items without confronting the victim	
Serious violation of rules 13. Often stays out late at night despite parental prohibitions (before 13 years of age) 14. Has run away from home overnight at least twice while living in parental home or once without returning for a lengthy period 15. Is often truant from school before the age of 13	
	Exclusion criteria include serious underlying conditions such as schizophrenia, hyperkinetic disorder or depression.
B. The disturbance in behaviour causes clinically significant impairment in social, academic or occupational functioning.	The diagnosis is not made unless the duration of the behaviour is 6 months or longer.
C. In those over 18 years, the criteria for antisocial personality disorder are not met.	Specify: CD confined to family context where the symptoms are confined to the home.
Specify childhood-onset (prior to 10 years) or adolescent onset. Specify severity (mild, moderate or severe)	Unsocialized CD where there is a pervasive abnormality in peer relationships. Socialized CD where the individual is well integrated into a peer group.

Note: Adapted from DSM-IV-TR (APA, 2000) and ICD-10 (WHO, 1992).

Case example of conduct disorder

Bill, aged 11, was referred by his social worker for treatment following an incident in which he had assaulted neighbours by climbing up onto the roof of his house and throwing rocks and stones at them. He also had a number of other problems according to the school headmaster, including academic underachievement, difficulty in maintaining friendships at school and repeated school absence. He smoked, occasionally drank alcohol, and stole money and goods from neighbours. His problems were longstanding but had intensified in the 6 months preceding the referral. At that time his father, Paul, was imprisoned for raping a young girl in the small rural village where the family lived.

Family history

Bill was one of five boys who lived with his mother, Rita, at the time of the referral. The family lived in relatively chaotic circumstances. Prior to Paul's imprisonment, the children's defiance and rule-breaking, particularly Bill's, was kept in check by their fear of physical punishment from their father. Since his imprisonment, there were few house rules and these were implemented inconsistently by Rita, so all of the children had conduct problems but Bill's were by far the worst.

Rita had developed intense coercive patterns of interaction with Bill and John (the second eldest). That is, she and the children engaged in escalating arguments, from which she typically withdrew when her sons became overly verbally or physically aggressive towards her. This coercive process of escalation and withdrawal led to Rita and her sons experiencing relief. The outcome of this was that the next time they engaged in conflict, they were likely to be even more abusive and aggressive to each other, since their expectations were that escalation would lead to withdrawal and relief.

In addition to the parent–child interaction difficulties, there were no routines to ensure that bills were paid, food was bought, washing was done, homework completed or regular meal and sleeping times observed. Rita supported the family with welfare payments and money earned illegally from farm-work. Despite the family chaos, she was very attached to her children and would sometimes take them to work with her rather than send them to school because she liked their company, and because they helped her to earn more money.

At the preliminary interview, Rita said that 'her nerves were in tatters'. She was attending a psychiatrist intermittently for treatment of depression with medication. She had a longstanding history of conduct and mood regulation problems, beginning early in adolescence. In particular she had had conflictual relationships with her mother and father, which were characterized by coercive cycles of interaction, similar to those in which she engaged with her sons. In school she had academic difficulties and peer relationship problems.

Rita had been ostracized by her own family when she married Paul, whom her parents saw as an unsuitable partner for her, since he had a number of convictions for theft and assault. Paul's family never accepted Rita, because they thought she had 'ideas above her station'. Rita's and Paul's parents were in regular conflict, and each family blamed the other for the chaotic situation in which Paul and Rita had found themselves. Rita was also ostracized by the village community in which she lived. The community blamed her for driving her husband to commit rape.

Paul, the father, also had longstanding difficulties. His conduct problems began in middle childhood. He was the eldest of four brothers, all of whom developed conduct problems, but his were by far the most severe. He had a history of becoming involved in aggressive exchanges that often escalated to violence. He and his mother had become involved in coercive patterns of interaction from his earliest years. He developed similar coercive patterns of interaction at school with his teachers, at work with various foremen and also in his relationship with Rita. He had a distant and detached relationship with his father.

Developmental history

From Bill's developmental history, it was clear that he was a child with a difficult temperament who did not develop sleeping and feeding routines easily and responded intensely and negatively to new situations. His language development had been delayed and he showed academic difficulties since his first years in school. On the positive side, Bill had a strong sense of family loyalty to his brothers and parents and did not want to see the family split up.

Psychometric assessment

From the Child Behaviour Checklists (CBCLs) completed by Rita, it was clear that Bill and his three brothers had clinically significant conduct problems and Bill's were by far the most extreme. A similar pattern emerged from behaviour checklists completed by the boys' teachers. A psychometric evaluation of Bill's abilities and attainments showed that he was of normal intelligence, but his attainments in reading, spelling and arithmetic fell below the 10th percentile. From his subtest profile on the psychometric instruments, it was concluded that the discrepancy between his attainment and abilities was accounted for by a specific learning disability – dyslexia.

School report

The headmaster at the school that Bill and his brothers attended confirmed that Bill had academic, conduct and attainment problems, but was committed to educating the boys and managing their conduct and attendance problems in a constructive way. The headmaster had a reputation (of which he was very proud) for being particularly skilled in managing children with behaviour problems.

Formulation

Bill was an 11-year-old boy with a persistent and broad pattern of conduct problems both within and outside the home, consistent with a diagnosis of conduct disorder. Bill's conduct problems had an insidious onset, beginning with wilfulness in early childhood and escalating as he developed. Thus there was no discrete precipitating factor to account for the onset of Bill's conduct disorder. However, the father's imprisonment 6 months prior the referral led to an intensification of Bill's conduct problems and precipitated the referral. Factors that predisposed Bill to develop conduct problems included a difficult temperament, a developmental language delay, dyslexia, exposure to paternal criminality, maternal depression and a disorganized family environment. The conduct problems were maintained at the time of the referral by engagement in coercive patterns of interaction with his mother and teachers; regular absences from school; rejection of Bill by peers at school; and isolation of his family by the extended family and the community. Protective factors in the case included the mother's wish to retain custody of the children rather than have them taken into foster care; Bill and his siblings' sense of family loyalty; and the school's commitment to retaining and dealing with Bill and his brothers rather than expelling them for truancy and misconduct. This formulation is diagrammed in Figure 2.3.

Treatment

The treatment plan in this case involved a multisystemic intervention programme. The mother was trained in behavioural parenting skills. A

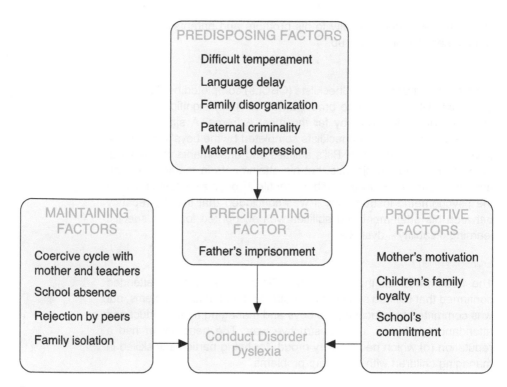

Figure 2.3 Formulation of a case of conduct disorder

series of meetings between the teacher, the mother and the social worker were convened to develop and implement a plan for regular school attendance. Occasional relief foster care was arranged for Bill and John (the second eldest) to reduce the stress on Rita. Social skills training was provided for Bill to help him deal with peer relationship problems.

There was some improvement in Bill's conduct problems, school attendance and academic performance. However, Bill continued to have residual conduct and academic problems throughout his adolescence. Coercive cycles of interaction between Bill and Rita, and family isolation and lack of support continued to be major factors maintaining Bill's difficulties. Rita required periodic crisis intervention and social work support throughout Bill's teenage years. Periodically, with social work assistance, Bill was placed for brief periods in voluntary care at Rita's request.

Clinical features

From Table 2.2 it may be seen that a distinction is made between oppositional defiant disorder and conduct disorder, with the former reflecting a less pervasive disturbance than the latter. In a proportion of cases oppositional defiant disorder is a developmental precursor of conduct disorder (Moffitt & Scott, 2008; Scott, 2009). The main behavioural feature of conduct disorder is a pervasive and persistent pattern of anti-social behaviour that extends beyond the family to the school and community; involves serious violations of rules; and is characterized by defiance of authority, aggression, destructiveness, deceitfulness and cruelty. Youngsters with conduct disorder show a limited internalization of social rules and norms and a hostile attributional bias. That is, the youngster interprets ambiguous social situations as threatening and responds with aggressive retaliative behaviour. Anger and irritability are the predominant mood states.

Problematic relationships with significant members of the child's network typify children with conduct disorder. Negative relationships with parents and teachers typically revolve around the youngster's defiant behaviour. Negative relationships with peers typically centre on aggression and bullying, which is guided by the hostile attributional bias with which conduct disordered youngsters construe many of their peer relationships. There may also be problematic relationships with members of the wider community if theft or vandalism has occurred. Multiagency involvement with juvenile justice or social work agencies is common. Also, because conduct disorder is associated with family disorganization, child abuse and neglect, parental criminality and parental psychological adjustment difficulties, professionals from child protection, adult mental health and justice systems may be involved.

Disruptive behaviour disorders follow three main developmental trajectories: life-course-persistent, adolescent limited, and childhood limited (Moffitt & Scott, 2008; Pardini et al., 2010). For about half of all children with childhood behavioural problems, their difficulties are limited to childhood or adolescence. The other half follow a life-course-persistent pathway and grow up to have antisocial personality disorders. The adolescent limited pathway is associated with deviant peer group membership. The life-course-persistent pathway is associated with a greater number of risk factors. Three classes of risk factors increase the probability that conduct problems in childhood or adolescence will escalate into later life difficulties. These are personal characteristics, parenting practices and family organization problems (McMahon et al., 2010; Moffitt & Scott, 2008; Scott, 2009).

Early onset, callous unemotional traits (absence of guilt, lack of empathy, shallow affect, and lack of concern about performance), difficult temperament, aggressiveness, impulsivity, inattention and educational difficulties are the main personal characteristics of children and adolescents that place them at risk for long-term conduct problems. Ineffective monitoring and supervision of youngsters, providing inconsistent consequences for rule violations, and failing to provide reinforcement for prosocial behaviour are the main problematic parenting practices that place children and adolescents at risk for the development of long-term antisocial behaviour patterns. The family organization problems associated with persistence of conduct problems into adulthood are parental conflict and violence, a high level of life stressors, a low level of social support, and parental psychological adjustment problems such as depression or substance abuse.

Epidemiology

In a review of 12 international epidemiological studies, Costello et al. (2004) found that the prevalence of conduct disorder ranged from 1.1% to 10.6%, with a median prevalence rate of 3.7%. The range for oppositional defiant disorder was 1.3–7.4% and the median prevalence rate also 3.7%. The variability in rates may be due to the diagnostic criteria applied (DSM or ICD) and the demographic characteristics of the populations studied. Using ICD criteria, a prevalence rate of 5.3% was obtained in a UK national epidemiological study (Meltzer et al., 2000). The prevalence of conduct disorder varies with gender and age, and the occurrence of comorbid conditions is common (Carr, 2006a). Conduct disorder is more prevalent in boys than in girls, with male/female ratios varying from 2:1 to 4:1. It is also more prevalent in adolescents than in children. The comorbidity rate for conduct disorder and ADHD in community populations is 23%. The comorbidity rates for conduct disorder and emotional disorders in community populations are 17% for major depression and 15% for anxiety disorders.

Etiological theories

Biological, psychodynamic, cognitive-behavioural and social systems theories have been proposed to explain the development of conduct problems and to inform their treatment. Since the distinction between oppositional defiant disorder and conduct disorder is a relatively recent development, most theories in this area have been developed with specific reference to conduct disorder but have obvious implications for oppositional defiant disorder, which is a developmental precursor of conduct disorder in many cases.

Biological theories

Biological theories have focused on the roles of genetic factors, neurobiological deficits, neurotransmitter dysregulation, neuroendocrine factors, arousal levels, temperament and neuropsychological deficits in the aetiology of conduct problems.

Genetics

There are many lines of research that focus on genetic and constitutional aspects of children with conduct disorder, and these are guided by the hypothesis that biological factors underpin antisocial behaviour. The predominance of males among youngsters with conduct disorders and the finding from a review of over 100 twin and adoption studies that antisocial behaviour is about 50% heritable point to a role for genetically transmitted constitutional factors in the aetiology of conduct disorders (Moffitt, 2005).

Current neuroscientific studies of conduct disorder aim to link specific genes with specific structural and functional brain abnormalities. At present a number of genes are being investigated. One of the most promising lines of research in this area has established a link between the monoamine oxidase A (MAOA) gene and conduct disorder in boys at risk of antisocial behaviour as a result of exposure to physical child abuse. In a meta-analysis of a series of studies, Kim-Cohen et al. (2006) found that physically abused children with the MAOA genotype conferring low levels of the MAOA enzyme, developed conduct disorder more often than abused children with a high-activity MAOA genotype. MAOA plays a key role regulating aggressive behaviour by selectively breaking down a number of neurotransmitters including serotonin, which has been found to be abnormally low in antisocial individuals. The MAOA gene has earned the nickname 'warrior gene' because of its link with aggression (McDermott et al., 2009). While specific genes, such as the MAOA gene, may contribute to the risk of antisocial behaviour, their contributions are probably quite small compared with the larger polygenetic effects of collections of genes on personal attributes such as temperament, executive function and verbal ability, all of which have strong associations with conduct disorder.

Neurobiological deficits

Neurobiological theories propose that antisocial, immoral and aggressive behaviour, typical of people with life-course-persistent disruptive behaviour disorders, is subserved by structural and functional brain abnormalities. In a wide-ranging review of evidence drawn mainly from studies of antisocial adults with histories of childhood conduct disorder, Raine and Yang (2006) concluded that antisocial behaviour is associated with structural and functional abnormalities of a number of brain regions including the prefrontal cortex, which subserves executive function and judgement, and the limbic system (including the amygdala, hippocampus and cingulate), which subserves learned emotional responses, particularly fear conditioning. People with antisocial personality disorder and psychopathy (who as children had disruptive behaviour disorders) have significantly reduced prefrontal lobe grey matter, reduced amygdala and hippocampus volume, and reduced activity in these areas compared with normal people. These abnormalities may be due to genetic factors or prenatal, perinatal or early childhood adversity (Moffitt, 2005; Taylor & Rogers, 2005).

Neurotransmitter dysregulation

Neurotransmitter dysregulation hypotheses propose that low levels of serotonin lead to aggression against others in the case of disruptive behaviour disorders (or the self in the case of depression) by enhancing sensitivity to stimuli that elicit aggression and reducing sensitivity to cues that signal punishment (Spoont, 1992). Studies of adults show that antisocial behaviour is associated with low levels of serotonin, but in studies of children the results are more mixed (van Goozen et al., 2007). However, medications that target serotonin, such as the selective serotonin reuptake inhibitors, do not modify aggression or antisocial behaviour in children or adults.

Neuroendocrine hypothesis

The hypothesis that antisocial behaviour is caused by androgens such as testosterone and dehydroepiandrosterone (DHEA) is premised on the fact that higher rates of both occur in males, and in animal studies a strong correlation has been found between aggression and testosterone levels. Research on adults has established a link between testosterone and violent crime, but studies of children and adolescents have yielded mixed results. In contrast, there is some evidence for higher levels of DHEA in children and adolescents with conduct disorder (van Goozen et al., 2007).

Hypo-arousal

In the most sophisticated version of the hypo-arousal hypothesis, Van Goozen et al. (2007, 2008) proposed that people who show marked aggression and antisocial behaviour do so because their stress response systems are underreactive, a neurobiological vulnerability that may arise from genetic factors or early adversity. This underreactivity accounts for fearless rule-breaking behaviour and risky sensation-seeking behaviour typical of young people with conduct disorder. In a previous version of this hypothesis, Raine (1996) proposed that because of their fearlessness, children with conduct disorder are insensitive to the negative consequences of antisocial behaviour, and so have difficulty learning and internalizing societal rules. Zuckerman (2007) argued that their low arousal levels lead them to become easily bored and they address this by engaging in risky, sensation-seeking behaviour. The hypo-arousal hypothesis is supported by a large body of evidence which shows that antisocial children and adults show low resting heart rate, skin conductance and cortisol levels, which are indices of hypoactivity within the autonomic nervous system and the hypothalamic–pituitary–adrenal (HPA) axis (Van Goozen et al., 2007, 2008).

There is also growing evidence that both genetic factors and adverse prenatal and early life environments may contribute to the development of underreactive stress response systems. The heritability of antisocial behaviour is well established (as noted above), and future research may indicate a mechanism that links specific genes to the stress response system. With regard to the prenatal environment, maternal smoking, drug and alcohol use, psychopathology and poor diet during pregnancy all compromise normal development of the central nervous system and may possibly compromise the development of the stress response system (Huizink et al., 2004). Stressful parenting environments in the early years associated with parental psychopathology, harsh, critical parenting, child abuse and neglect and domestic violence may adversely affect brain development and lead to an adaptive down-regulating of the stress response system to avoid the negative effects of chronic hyper-arousal (Dawson et al., 2000; Susman, 2006).

Treatment of conduct disorder based on the hypo-arousal hypothesis involves the use of highly structured and intensive learning situations to facilitate the internalization of social rules. The positive and negative reinforcers used must be highly valued and delivered immediately following responses. All rule infractions must lead to immediate withdrawal of desired stimuli. Rule-following should be immediately and intensely rewarded on a variable interval schedule, since this leads to learning that is maximally resistant to extinction. These treatment implications of arousal theory have been incorporated into the design of residential token economies for delinquent adolescents, behavioural parent training programmes, school-based behavioural programmes and treatment foster care (Carr, 2009a).

Temperament

The temperament hypothesis proposes that difficult temperament is a risk factor for disruptive behaviour disorders. Children with difficult temperaments, which are predominantly inherited, have difficulty establishing regular routines for eating, toileting and sleeping; tend to avoid new situations; and responded to change with intense negative emotions. Their temperamental style tends to elicit negative reactions from their parents, teachers and peers, to which they respond with defiance, aggression and other antisocial behaviour. The temperament hypothesis has been supported by many studies including Chess and Thomas's (1995) original New York longitudinal study (De Pauw & Mervielde, 2010).

There may appear to be an inconsistency between the hypo-arousal hypothesis and the temperament hypothesis, with the former proposing that antisocial behaviour is associated with low arousal and the latter with difficult temperament, possibly associated with high arousal in new situations. It may be that low arousal and difficult temperament are separate routes to antisocial behaviour or to different types of antisocial behaviour, with low arousal being associated with callous unemotional psychopathy and difficult temperament associated with aggressive behaviour. Lorber (2004) found support for this position in a meta-analysis of studies of heart rate and skin conductance resting levels and reactivity to various stimuli. All forms of antisocial behaviour were associated with low resting arousal levels, but individuals with aggressive conduct problems showed high reactivity, whereas those with callous unemotional psychopathic traits did not.

Neuropsychological deficits

The neuropsychological deficits hypothesis proposes that deficits in executive function and verbal reasoning underpin self-regulation difficulties that contribute to conduct problems. Executive function deficits limit the capacity to plan and follow through on prosocial courses of action, and so give rise to disruptive behaviour disorders. Children with verbal reasoning deficits may have difficulty remembering instructions, developing private speech to facilitate self-control, and using verbal strategies rather than aggression to resolve conflicts.

Executive function and verbal reasoning deficits may also account for academic underachievement typical of young people with conduct disorders, and this underachievement may lead to frustration and consequent aggressive behaviour. This position is supported by a substantial body of evidence that documents verbal reasoning and executive function deficits in children and teenagers with conduct problems, by studies that confirm a strong association between reading difficulties and conduct problems, and by studies which show that unsocialized conduct problems are associated with self-regulation problems (Moffitt & Scott, 2008; Nigg & Huang-Pollock, 2003; Teichner & Golden, 2000). Remedial interventions that facilitate the development of language and academic skills are the principal types of treatment deriving from this theory.

Psychodynamic theories

Classical psychoanalytic theory points to superego deficits and attachment theory to the role of insecure attachment in the development of conduct problems.

Psychoanalytic perspectives

Within psychoanalysis it is assumed that societal rules and expectations are internalized through identification with the parent of the same gender. This internalization is referred to as the superego. Aichorn (1935) argued that antisocial behaviour occurs because of impoverished superego functioning. The problems with superego functioning were thought to arise from either overindulgent parenting on one hand or punitive and neglectful parenting on the other. With overindulgent parenting, the child internalizes lax standards and so feels no guilt when breaking rules or behaving immorally. In such cases any apparently moral behaviour is a manipulative attempt to gratify some desire. With punitive or neglectful parenting, the child splits the experience of the parent into the *good caring parent* and the *bad punitive/neglectful parent* and internalizes both of these aspects of the parent quite separately with little integration. In dealing with parents, peers and authority figures, the child may be guided by either the internalization of the good parent or the internalization of the bad parent. Typically at any point in time such youngsters can clearly identify those members of their network who fall into the good and bad categories. They behave morally towards those for whom they experience a positive transference and view as good, and immorally to those towards whom they have a negative transference and view as bad.

Individual psychoanalytic psychotherapy has been used in the treatment of children and adolescents with conduct problems (e.g., Kernberg & Chazan, 1991). However, there are limits to the effectiveness of psychoanalytically based treatment for those with disruptive behaviour disorders (Fonagy & Target, 1994; Winkelmann et al., 2005). For example, in a naturalistic study, Fonagy and Target (1994) found that children with oppositional defiant disorder responded better than children with conduct disorder or ADHD.

Attachment

Bowlby (1944) pointed out that children who were separated from their primary caregivers for extended periods of time during their first months of life failed to develop secure attachments and so, in later life, did not have internal working models for secure trusting relationships. He referred to such children as displaying affectionless psychopathy. Since moral behaviour is premised on functional internal working models of how to conduct oneself in trusting relationships, such children behave immorally.

Later studies of children reared in intact families have established a link between attachment insecurity and behaviour problems (e.g., Moss et al., 2006). Treatment according to this position should aim to provide the child with a secure-attachment relationship or corrective emotional experience which will lead to the development of appropriate internal working models. These in turn will provide a basis for moral action. More secure attachment relationships may be facilitated within families of young people with disruptive behaviour disorders through parent training (Forgatch & Patterson, 2010; Webster-Stratton & Reid, 2010), family therapy (Carr, 2006b), multisystemic therapy (Henggeler & Schaeffer, 2010) and treatment foster care (Smith & Chamberlain, 2010), all of which are described later in this chapter.

Cognitive-behavioural theories

A range of theories of conduct problems have been developed within the broad cognitive behavioural tradition. Problems with social information processing and social skills deficits are the principal factors highlighted in cognitive theories. Social learning theories highlight the importance of modelling, and behavioural theories focus on the role of reinforcement contingencies in the maintenance of conduct problems.

Social information processing

Dodge and colleagues proposed that children with conduct disorders process social information in a different way to other children (Crick & Dodge, 1994). In ambiguous social situations their cognition is characterized by a hostile attributional bias. That is, children with conduct disorders attribute hostile intentions to others in social situations where the intentions of others are ambiguous. The aggressive behaviour of children with conduct disorders in such situations is, therefore, intended to be retaliatory. The aggression is viewed as unjustified by those against whom it is directed, and this leads to impaired relationships with peers and others in their social networks. The reactions of others to such apparently unjustified aggression provide confirmation for the aggressive child that others have hostile intentions, which justifies further retaliatory aggression. This social information procession theory of conduct disorder has been supported by extensive research (Dodge et al., 2006).

Dodge has embedded his social information processing theory within a more general model of the development of aggressive behaviour, in which he proposes that social information processing patterns are the proximal mechanism through which aggressive behaviour occurs

(Dodge, 2011; Dodge & Pettit, 2003). However, these patterns are sub-served by neural and psychophysiological processes and are acquired through genetic and environmental processes, especially in negative interaction with parents, teachers and peers.

Social skills deficits

The social skills deficit hypothesis is that conduct disorders involve inappropriate social behaviours, such as aggression or defiance, which have developed to compensate for social skills deficits. Research conducted to test this hypothesis has highlighted the social skills deficits of children with conduct disorders, and the value of training in social problem-solving in reducing antisocial behaviour (Losel & Beelmann, 2005). This position proposes that antisocial children lack the skills to generate alternative solutions to social problems such as dealing with an apparently hostile peer. They also lack the skills to implement solutions to social problems such as these, for example using humour or shared interests to reduce hostility.

Within the cognitive-behavioural tradition, group-based social skills programmes have been developed that aim to train youngsters in the social problem-solving skills they lack. A growing body of evidence shows that social problem-solving skills can reduce antisocial behaviour when offered alone (Lochman et al., 2010) or combined with parent training and other systemic interventions (Kazdin, 2010).

Modelling

Bandura and Walters (1959) proposed that aggression, characteristic of children and adolescents with conduct disorders, is learned through a process of imitation or modelling. Children subjected to harsh, critical parenting, neglect or physical abuse, or who witness domestic violence, become aggressive through a process of imitation. This position is sup-ported by a large body of evidence, particularly that which points to the intrafamilial transmission of aggressive behaviour associated with harsh, inconsistent parenting, child abuse and neglect, and exposure to domestic violence (Moffitt & Scott, 2008; Taylor & Rogers, 2005). According to modelling theory, treatment should aim to help parents, through parent training or family therapy, to model appropriate behav-iour for their children (Carr, 2006a; Forgatch & Patterson, 2010; Webster-Stratton & Reid, 2010) or provide alternative models of appro-priate behaviour in a residential or treatment foster care setting (Smith & Chamberlain, 2010).

Coercive family process

Patterson and his group proposed that children with conduct disorders learn their antisocial behaviours from involvement in coercive patterns of interaction with their parents, and these behaviours are then exhib-ited in school and community contexts (Forgatch & Patterson, 2010; Patterson, 1982). Marital discord, parental psychopathology, a variety of social and economic stressors and social isolation all contribute to the parents' use of a coercive parenting style. This style has three main features.

First, parents have few positive interactions with their children. Second, they punish children frequently, inconsistently and ineffectively. Third, the parents of children with conduct problems negatively reinforce antisocial behaviour by confronting or punishing the child briefly and then withdrawing the confrontation or punishment when the child escalates the antisocial behaviour, so that the child learns that escalation leads to parental withdrawal. By middle childhood children exposed to this parenting style have developed an aggressive relational style which leads to rejection by non-deviant peers. Such children, who often have comorbid specific learning difficulties, typically develop conflictual relationships with teachers and consequent attainment problems.

In adolescence, rejection by non-deviant peers and academic failure make socializing with a deviant, delinquent peer group an attractive option. Patterson's group have shown that this developmental trajectory is common among youngsters who first present with oppositional defiant disorder. The delinquency of adolescence is a staging post on the route to adult antisocial personality disorder, criminality, drug abuse and conflictual, violent and unstable marital and parental roles for more than half of all youngsters with conduct disorder (Farrington, 1995). Therapy for families with preadolescent children based on this model aims to help parents and children break coercive patterns of interaction and build positive relationships, but most importantly it helps parents develop skills for effectively disciplining their children. There is considerable evidence for the effectiveness of this type of behavioural parent training (Forgatch & Patterson, 2010).

Systems theory

Systems theories highlight the role of family systems and broader social systems in the aetiology and maintenance of conduct problems.

Family systems approaches

Within the family therapy tradition, a number of assumptions have been influential in offering a framework for understanding how conduct disorders are maintained by patterns of family interaction and how they may be resolved by intervening in these patterns (Carr, 2006b). According to family systems theory, families with youngsters who have conduct problems are more disorganized than other families. Rules, roles and routines are unclear, and parental supervision of children is deficient. Communication is problematic, unclear and confusing. There is also an absence of systematic family problem-solving skills.

The members of these families are more emotionally disengaged from each other in comparison with other families, and parent–child relationships may be lacking in warmth and empathy. In addition, families with youngsters who display conduct problems have difficulties maintaining clear, unambiguous intergenerational hierarchies and negotiating life-cycle transitions. With respect to ambiguous hierarchies, conduct problems are maintained if parents do not both agree on a basic set of rules of conduct for their children which they consistently enforce, with clear consequences for rule violations. With respect to lifecycle transitions, conduct problems are more likely to occur at transitional points in the life cycle, when there are changes in routines and a build-up of stress, such as starting primary school, moving to secondary school and entering adolescence, or leaving secondary school and entering adulthood.

Available evidence supports many of these assumptions of family system theory. Families of young people with disruptive behaviour disorders are more likely to be characterized by disorganization; harsh, critical and inconsistent parenting; lack of parental warmth; physical child abuse and neglect; parental criminality and psychopathology; marital discord; domestic violence; and many life stresses, notably poverty (Crosnoe & Cavanagh, 2010; Moffitt & Scott, 2008). Family therapy addresses disruptive behaviour disorders by helping families become more coherently organized, with better relationships, communication, problem solving, and fair, consistent parenting. There is good evidence for the effectiveness of family therapy in reducing adolescent antisocial behaviour (Carr, 2009b).

Sociological perspectives

A variety of sociological theories have posited a causal link between deviant antisocial behaviour and aspects of the wider socio-cultural context within which such behaviour occurs. Anomie theory is a commonly cited exemplar of this body of theories (Cloward & Ohlin, 1960). According to anomie theory, theft and related antisocial behaviours such as mugging and lying are illegitimate means used by members of a socially disadvantaged delinquent subculture to achieve material goals valued by mainstream culture. Anomie is the state of lawlessness and normlessness that characterizes such subcultures. In support of this position, there is good evidence for a link between antisocial behaviour and poverty (Moffitt & Scott, 2008), and that membership of deviant peer groups can facilitate antisocial behaviour (Dishion & Dodge, 2005). Treatment premised on this theory must provide delinquents and their peer groups with legitimate means to achieve societal goals. Remedial academic programmes, vocational training programmes, and treatment foster care are the main treatment approaches implicated by this theory. There is good evidence for the efficacy of treatment foster care (Smith & Chamberlain, 2010), and some evidence for the value of academic and vocational programmes in the rehabilitation of juvenile delinquents (Lipsey, 2009).

Multisystemic ecological theory

This position, proposed by Henggeler, entails the view that multiple systems (including the individual, the family, the school and the community) are involved in the genesis and maintenance of conduct problems, and consequently effective treatment must target multiple systems rather than any single system (Henggeler & Schaeffer, 2010). Bronfenbrenner's model of ecologically nested systems is the foundation for this theory (Bronfenbrenner & Morris, 2006). Conduct disorders, it is argued, are maintained by multiple factors in these multiple ecologically nested systems. Important individual factors include difficult temperament, early separation experiences, hostile attributional bias, poor social skills, difficulties learning prosocial behaviour from experience, and academic learning difficulties. Family factors include family disorganization, ambiguous family hierarchies, parent–child attachment difficulties, parenting and discipline problems, marital discord and difficulty negotiating family life-cycle transitions. School factors include patterns of interaction that maintain school-based discipline problems, attainment difficulties and lack of educational resources. Community factors include involvement with deviant peers, drug abuse and involvement in poorly co-ordinated multiagency networks.

Henggeler developed multisystemic therapy (MST) based on this ecological conceptualization of disruptive behaviour disorders. MST is a comprehensive empirically supported programme for antisocial young people and their families. For each case, treatment is individually tailored and based on a multisystem ecological assessment. Treatment packages include family therapy to reduce family disorganization, school-based interventions to deal with interactional patterns that maintain school-based conduct problems and underachievement, individual and group cognitive and social skills training, and peer-group-based interventions to enhance prosocial peer relationships and reduce involvement in deviant peer groups. Evidence from a series of trials supports the effectiveness of this approach (Henggeler & Schaeffer, 2010).

Assessment

Assessment and treatment of children with conduct disorders is usually carried out by multidisciplinary teams which include clinical psychologists and colleagues from other disciplines such as social work and psychiatry. Children's conduct problems require an assessment of their behaviour, abilities, and family and school situations. The Achenbach System of Empirically Based Assessment (ASEBA, Achenbach & Rescorla, 2000, 2001) and the Strengths and Difficulties Questionnaire (SDQ, Goodman, 2001) are widely used to assess conduct problems.

ASEBA parent, teacher and self-report rating scales contain over 100 items and yield a total problem score, scores for internalizing and externalizing behaviour problems, and scores in various problem areas including conduct problems. There are versions for school-aged children and preschoolers. Computer scoring systems are available and normative data are used to interpret scores. SDQ parent, teacher and self-report rating scales contain only 25 items and yield a total problem score, as well as scores for various problem areas, including conduct problems. There are also SDQ norms to facilitate interpretation. The brevity of the SDQ makes it very acceptable to parents and teachers.

To establish a DSM-IV-TR or ICD-10 diagnosis of oppositional defiant disorder or conduct disorder, a structured interview for parents and children may be administered, such as the troublesome behaviour module of the Development and Well-Being Assessment (DAWBA, Goodman et al., 2000). Abilities and achievements of children with conduct problems, as well as their family and school situations, are assessed in the same way as those of children with ADHD, mentioned earlier. Assessment information is integrated into a formulation that is used for treatment planning as illustrated in the case study of conduct disorder described earlier. This should link predisposing, precipitating and maintaining factors to the young person's behavioural problems and specify protective factors that may be drawn on during treatment. A general clinical formulation model for conduct disorder and oppositional defiant disorder is given in Figure 2.4.

Intervention

The material covered earlier in this chapter makes it clear that conduct problems are complex. Personal genetic, neurobiological and psycho-

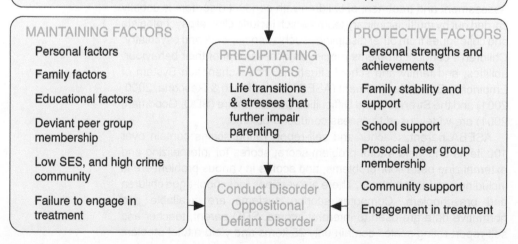

Figure 2.4 General formulation model for conduct disorder and oppositional defiant disorder

logical characteristics of children and adolescents, and psychosocial factors within the family and the wider system, may predispose young-sters to develop conduct problems. Once these develop, they may remain confined to the home in the case of oppositional defiant disorder or spread to the community in the case of conduct disorder. The degree to which conduct problems escalate depends on the degree to which there are problem-maintaining factors within the individual, family, school and peer group. Despite their complexity, conduct problems are not completely refractory to treatment. Available evidence from empiri-cal studies permits treatments of choice to be identified for preadoles-cent behaviour problems and more pervasive difficulties in adolescence.

For circumscribed conduct problems, typical of children with oppo-sitional defiant disorder, behavioural parent training is currently the treatment for which there is greatest empirical support. In a meta-analysis of over 70 studies, McCart et al. (2006) found that for children under 12, parent training programmes were significantly more effective than child-focused programmes. Behavioural parent training involves coaching parents to target and reinforce their children's prosocial behaviour while extinguishing their antisocial behaviour (Forgatch & Patterson, 2010; Webster-Stratton & Reid, 2010).

For pervasive conduct problems, typical of children with conduct disorder, family therapy, multisystemic therapy and treatment foster care are currently the treatments for which there is greatest empirical support (Carr, 2009b). Family therapy involves helping parents, adolescents and other family members develop patterns of interaction that promote prosocial behaviour, better communication and family problem-solving, and for conduct problems functional family therapy is one of the approaches with a particularly strong evidence base (Sexton & Alexander, 2003). Multisystemic therapy extends beyond the family and includes intervention in the school and peer group and also at the individual level, so that problem-maintaining factors in all of these systems are modified (Henggeler & Schaeffer, 2010). Multisystemic intervention may also involve addressing parents' personal difficulties such as depression or alcohol problems.

Where parents' personal difficulties are too severe to permit them to engage effectively in multisystemic treatment, treatment foster care is the intervention of choice (Smith & Chamberlain, 2010). Here, the conduct disordered youngster is placed with a specially trained foster family who work collaboratively with the child's natural parents in implementing a behavioural programme that allows the youngster to develop prosocial behaviour and disengage from patterns of antisocial behaviour.

With respect to service development, it may be most efficient to offer services for adolescent conduct disorder on a continuum of care (Carr, 2009a). Less severe cases may be offered family therapy. Moderately severe cases and those that do not respond to circumscribed family interventions may be offered multisystemic therapy. Extremely severe cases and those that are unresponsive to intensive multisystemic therapy may be offered treatment foster care. These conclusions are consistent with international best practice guidelines (American Academy of Child and Adolescent Psychiatry, 2007b; NICE, 2006a).

There are many other treatments for conduct disorders besides those highlighted in this chapter. Some are empirically untested so we do not know if they are effective. Some have been tested and found to be ineffective. And most importantly, there are those treatments that have been tested and found to be harmful. There is now considerable evidence that intervention programmes that bring youngsters with conduct disorders together in groups lead to an increase in conduct problems (Dishion & Dodge, 2005). This contamination process may occur because youngsters reinforce each other's deviant behaviour and share a commitment to a deviant set of values and ideology. The fact that interventions that aggregate conduct-disordered youngsters are harmful unfortunately has not had a major impact on policies for dealing with juvenile delinquents. Many delinquents are assessed and treated in group-based residential settings. Such policies exacerbate rather than ameliorate conduct problems.

Controversies

There are many controversies in the scientific study, assessment and treatment of psychological problems in children and adolescents.

Dimensions or categories

With regard to scientific study, there is controversy over whether children's abnormal behaviour is best conceptualized in dimensional or categorical terms. While the DSM and ICD diagnostic systems are clearly based on a categorical conceptualization of children's psychological difficulties, most empirical studies point to the validity of dimensional models. For example, factor analytic studies consistently show that common childhood difficulties fall on the two dimensions of internalizing and externalizing behaviour problems, which are normally distributed within the population (Achenbach, 2009).

Children with diagnoses of oppositional defiant disorder, conduct disorder and ADHD represent a subgroup of cases with extreme externalizing behaviour problems, while those with anxiety or depressive disorders have extreme internalizing behaviour problems (Carr, 2006a). Similarly, children with a diagnosis of intellectual disability fall at the lower end of the continuum of intelligence, a trait is normally distributed within the population (Carr et al., 2007). The dimensional approach is clearly more scientifically valid than a categorical approach, and has the potential to be less stigmatizing. On the other hand, categorical diagnoses such as ADHD create a focus for pressure groups whose interests are served by reifying psychological difficulties as 'psychiatric illnesses'.

Are psychological problems really 'psychiatric illnesses'?

This brings us on to the area of assessment, in which there is a controversy over whether ADHD, conduct disorder and other DSM and ICD diagnoses are 'real psychiatric illnesses', invalid fabrications, or spurious social constructions (Kutchins & Kirk,1999). Those who argue that they are invalid fabrications point to the evidence for the dimensionality of childhood psychological problems. Those who argue that they are spurious social constructions point to the interests that are served by defining them as 'real psychiatric illnesses'.

Parents, health and educational professionals, the pharmaceutical industry and society at large may all, in certain circumstances, derive benefits from conceptualizing children's psychological problems as 'real psychiatric illnesses'. For example, parents or schools may have difficulty meeting children's needs for intellectual stimulation, nurturance and clear limit-setting, and so children in their care become aggressive and disruptive. In response these parents or educational professionals may prefer children in their care to receive a diagnosis of ADHD and a prescription for stimulant therapy, rather than exploring ways to better meet the children's needs for intellectual stimulation, nurturance and clear limit-setting. In such instances pharmaceutical companies may support the diagnosis of ADHD, because they may stand to gain financially from offering a pharmacological treatment for behaviour problems.

Should treatment focus on the child or the context?

This brings us to controversies concerning the treatment of psychological problems in children and adolescents. If children's difficulties are conceptualized as individual 'psychiatric illnesses', there is a risk that the predominant focus for treatment will be on the individual child rather than on the broader social context within which the child lives. That is, the main emphasis will be on treating children's problems with medication and individual therapy to modify the 'illness inside the child', with less emphasis on addressing important risk factors within the child's family, school and wider social context.

In the cases of oppositional defiant disorder and conduct disorder this is particularly problematic, since the major risk factors that can effectively be addressed in treatment are social, through interventions such as parent training, family therapy, MST and treatment foster care. In the case of ADHD, the strong emphasis on medication is problematic because its effects are time limited to about 3 years (Swanson & Volkow, 2009). Also, stimulant medication may adversely affect growth and cardiovascular functioning and lead to a variety of somatic complaints including loss of appetite, headaches, insomnia and tics, which occur in 5–12% of cases (Breggin, 2001; Paykina et al., 2007; Rapport & Moffitt, 2002).

Summary

A wide variety of psychological problems may occur in childhood. This chapter focused on disruptive behaviour disorders, which include ADHD, oppositional defiant disorder and conduct disorder. ADHD is characterized by inattention, hyperactivity and impulsivity. The median prevalence rate for ADHD in international epidemiological studies is 2.7%. Comorbid developmental language delays, specific learning difficulties, elimination disorders, conduct disorders and emotional disorders are quite common. A poor outcome occurs for about a third of cases who typically have secondary conduct and academic problems.

ADHD is a one of the most heritable psychological disorders. Extreme levels of overactivity and executive function deficits, which are polygenetically determined, probably interact with environmental factors (either intrauterine or psychosocial) to give rise to the clinical syndrome of ADHD. Individuals with ADHD show structural and functional neuroanatomical abnormalities of the frontostriatal circuitry, which subserves executive function, and the cerebellum, which subserves temporal information processing. They also show a dysregulation of the dopamine and noradrenergic and adrenergic systems. Adjustment problems shown by youngsters with ADHD are in part maintained by problematic relationships within the family, school and peer group. Multimodal treatment includes behavioural parent training, school-based contingency management, self-regulation skills training, dietary control where food intolerance is present, and stimulant therapy. In addition assessment and treatment of comorbid problems may be required.

A distinction is made between oppositional defiant disorder and conduct disorder, with the former reflecting a less pervasive disturbance than the latter; the central feature of both is antisocial behaviour. The median prevalence rate for both oppositional defiant disorder and conduct disorder in international epidemiological studies is 3.7%. Children with conduct problems are a treatment priority because the outcome for more than half of these youngsters is very poor in terms of criminality and psychological adjustment. In the long term the cost to society of unsuccessfully treated conduct problems is enormous.

Comorbidity for conduct disorders and both ADHD and emotional problems such as anxiety and depression is very high, particularly in clinical populations. Three classes of risk factor increase the probability that conduct problems in childhood or adolescence will escalate into later life difficulties:

personal biological and psychological characteristics, problematic parenting practices, and family disorganization. Biological theories have focused on the roles of genetic factors, neurobiological deficits, neurotransmitter dysregulation, neuroendocrine factors, arousal levels, temperament, and neuropsychological deficits in the aetiology of conduct problems. Classical psychoanalytic theory points to superego deficits and attachment theory points to insecure attachment in the development of conduct disorders. Problems with social information processing and social skills deficits are the principal factors highlighted in cognitive theories of conduct problems.

Modelling and coercive family processes have been identified by social learning theory as central to the development and maintenance of conduct difficulties. Systems theories highlight the role of characteristics of family systems, broader social network systems and societal systems in the aetiology and maintenance of conduct problems, with oppositional defiant disorders in pre-adolescent children whose problems are confined to the home, behavioural parent training is the treatment of choice. With older children and adolescents who present with pervasive conduct problems, family therapy, multisystemic therapy and treatment foster care are currently the treatments for which there is greatest empirical support, and these may be offered on a continuum of care depending on problem severity.

There is controversy over whether children's abnormal behaviour is best conceptualized in dimensional or categorical terms. There is also controversy over whether DSM and ICD diagnoses are 'real psychiatric illnesses', invalid fabrications or spurious social constructions. Finally there is controversy over whether children's psychological problems are most usefully conceptualized as individual 'psychiatric illnesses' or as aspects of the broader social context within which the child lives.

Questions

- What are the main psychological disorders that occur in childhood?
- What are the main clinical features of ADHD, oppositional defiant disorder and conduct disorder?
- How prevalent are the disruptive behaviour disorders?
- What are the main biological and psychological theories of disruptive behaviour disorders and the main research findings relevant to these theories?
- What are the main evidence-based approaches to the assessment and treatment of disruptive behaviour disorders?
- Do you think it's useful to conceptualize children's behaviour problems as 'psychiatric illnesses'?

FURTHER READING

Professional

- Carr, A. (2006). *Handbook of child and adolescent clinical psychology: A contextual approach* (second edition). London: Routledge.
- Weisz, J. & Kazdin, A. (2010). *Evidence-based psychotherapies for children and adolescents* (second edition). New York: Guilford Press.

Self-help

- Barkley, R. (2000). *Taking charge of ADHD: the complete authoritative guide for parents* (revised edition). New York: Guilford.
- Forehand, R. & Long, N. (1996). *Parenting the strong-willed child: The clinically proven five week programme for parents of two to six year olds.* Chicago: Contemporary Books.
- Forgatch, M. & Patterson, G. (1989). *Parents and adolescents living together. Part 1. The basics.* Eugene, OR: Castalia.
- Forgatch, M. & Patterson, G. (1989). *Parents and adolescents living together. Part 2. Family problem solving.* Eugene, OR: Castalia.

WEBSITES

- AACAP (American Academy of Child and Adolescent Psychiatry) practice parameters for the treatment of ADHD, conduct disorder and oppositional defiant disorder:
  www.aacap.org/cs/root/member_information/practice_information/
  practice_parameters/practice_parameters
- Achenbach System of Empirically Based Assessment (ASEBA):
  www.aseba.org
- Incredible Years Programme:
  www.incredibleyears.com
- NICE (National Institute for Clinical Excellence) guidelines for treating ADHD:
  http://guidance.nice.org.uk/topic/mentalhealthbehavioural
- Parents Plus Programme:
  www.parentsplus.ie
- Parent–Child Interaction Therapy:
  http://pcit.phhp.ufl.edu
- Strengths and Difficulties Questionnaire (SDQ):
  www.sdqinfo.com

Eating disorders

3

Learning objectives

After studying this chapter you will be able to:

- give an account of the main clinical features of anorexia and bulimia nervosa
- summarize the epidemiology of eating disorders
- list the risk factors for eating disorders
- outline the main biological and psychological theories of eating disorders
- name the main evidence-based approaches to assessment and treatment of eating disorders.

Introduction

Anorexia nervosa and bulimia nervosa are the main eating disorders of concern in clinical psychology. They typically first occur during adolescence. In both conditions there is an overevaluation of body shape and weight, with self-worth being judged almost exclusively in terms of these personal attributes. With anorexia, the primary feature is the maintenance of a very low body weight, whereas with bulimia the main feature is a cycle of binge eating and self-induced vomiting or other extreme weight control measures including dieting, excessive exercise, and laxative use. Diagnostic criteria for these two eating disorders are given in Table 3.1.

Eating disorders are of concern because they are dangerous (Klump et al., 2009; Mitchell & Crow, 2010). In chronic cases they lead to many

TABLE 3.1
Diagnostic criteria for anorexia and bulimia nervosa

DSM-IV-TR	ICD-10
Anorexia nervosa	
A. Refusal to maintain body weight at or above a minimally normal weight for age and height (weight loss or failure to gain weight in a growth period leading to body weight less than 85% of that expected).	For a definitive diagnosis the following are required:
	A. Body weight is maintained at least 15% below that expected (either lost or never achieved) or a Quetelet's body mass index of 17. 5 or less (BMI = weight (kg)/(height (m)^2). Prepubertal patients may show failure to make the expected weight gain during the period of growth.
B. Intense fear of gaining weight or becoming fat even though underweight.	
C. Disturbance in the way in which one's body weight or shape is experienced, undue influence of body weight or shape on self-evaluation, or denial of seriousness of the current low body weight.	B. The weight loss is self-induced by the avoidance of fattening foods, self-induced vomiting, self-induced purging, excessive exercise, use of appetite suppressants or diuretics.
D. In postmenarcheal females, amenorrhea (the absence of at least three consecutive menstrual cycles).	C. There is a body image distortion in the form of a specific psychopathology whereby a dread of fatness persists as an intrusive, overvalued idea and the patient imposes a low weight threshold on himself or herself.
Specify restricting type or binge eating–purging type.	D. A widespread endocrine disorder involving the hypothalamic–pituitary–gonadal axis is manifest in women as amenorrhea and in men as a loss of sexual interest and potency. There may also be elevated levels of growth hormone, raised cortisol levels, changes in the peripheral metabolism of the thyroid hormone and abnormalities of insulin secretion.
	E. If the onset is prepubertal, the sequence of pubertal events is delayed or arrested (growth ceases; in girls breasts do not develop and there is a primary amenorrhea; in boys the genitals remain juvenile). With recovery, puberty is often completed normally but the menarche is late.
Bulimia nervosa	
A. Recurrent episodes of binge eating. An episode of binge eating is characterized by both of the following:	For a definitive diagnosis all of the following are required:
1. Eating in a discrete period of time (e.g. within a 2 hour period) an amount of food that is definitely larger than most people would eat during a similar period of time and under similar circumstances.	A. There is a persistent preoccupation with eating and an irresistible craving for food; the patient succumbs to episodes of overeating in which large amounts of food are consumed in short periods of time.
2. A sense of lack of control over eating during the episode (e.g. a feeling that one cannot stop eating or control what or how much one is eating).	B. The patient attempts to counteract the fattening effects of food by one or more of the following: self-induced vomiting; purgative abuse; alternating periods of starvation; use of drugs such as appetite suppressants, thyroid preparations or diuretics. When bulimia occurs in diabetic patients they may choose to neglect their insulin treatment.
B. Recurrent inappropriate compensatory behaviour in order to prevent weight gain, such as self-induced vomiting; misuse of laxatives, diuretics, enemas, or other medications; fasting or excessive exercise.	C. The psychopathology consists of a morbid dread of fatness and the patient sets herself or himself a sharply defined weight threshold, well below the premorbid weight that constitutes the optimum or healthy weight in the opinion of the physician. There is often but not always a history of an earlier episode of anorexia nervosa, the interval between the two disorders ranging from a few months to several years. This earlier episode may have been fully expressed or may have assumed minor cryptic form with a moderate loss of weight and/or a transient phase of amenorrhea.
C. The binge eating and inappropriate compensatory behaviours both occur, on average, at least twice a week for 3 months.	
D. Self-evaluation is unduly influenced by body shape and weight.	
E. The disturbance does not occur exclusively during episodes of anorexia nervosa.	
Specify purging or non-purging type.	

Note: Adapted from DSM-IV-TR (APA, 2000) and ICD-10 (WHO, 1992).

medical complications including growth retardation, osteoporosis, gastrointestinal bleeding, dehydration, electrolyte abnormalities and cardiac arrest. The mortality rate among women with anorexia is 12 times that of the normal population, and eating disorders are associated with a raised suicide risk. It is ironic in our western industrial culture, where food is plentiful, that self-starvation and a pattern of bingeing and purging are major problems affecting teenage girls.

In this chapter, after considering the classification, epidemiology and clinical features of eating disorders, a variety of theoretical explanations concerning their aetiology will be considered along with relevant empirical evidence. Some comments on assessment and treatment will also be made.

Case study of anorexia nervosa

Mar, a 14-year-old girl, was referred for treatment because her weight had fallen continuously since she was about 12 years old. When assessed she was 5 stone 11 pounds (37 kg) in weight and 5 feet 2 inches (1.57 m) tall. The normal weight range for a 14-year-old girl is 6 stone 8 pounds to 9 stone. Mar had a body mass index (BMI) of 15, which is at the first percentile and significantly below the normal range. BMI is an index of thinness which is calculated by dividing weight in kilograms by height in metres squared. The normal range for BMI is 18.5–24.9. Mar had amenorrhea, a highly restrictive eating pattern of 2 years' duration and a daily routine involving episodes of intensive exercise. She had gone through an episode of self-induced vomiting after mealtimes and occasional bingeing for about three months, but this had ceased a year previously.

Presentation

In the intake interview Mar expressed a fear of becoming fat and said she experienced her hips, buttocks, stomach and thighs to be considerably larger than their actual size. That is, she had a distorted body image, believing herself to be markedly larger than her actual size. She continually ruminated about food and the number of calories associated with each aspect of her diet. Her mood was generally low, and she had on occasion experienced suicidal thoughts, but had never had frank suicidal intentions. On the Eating Disorder Inventory (Garner, 2005), Mar obtained extreme scores on the drive for thinness, body dissatisfaction, ineffectiveness, perfectionism, and maturity fear subscales. Mar held a range of rigid beliefs about the importance of controlling her body shape.

Developmental history

Mar's personal developmental history was within normal limits. Her language and cognitive development had been advanced and Mar had always been in the top 10% of her class in school for academic subjects.

Within the family, she was described by her parents, Roddy and Maggie, as a model child. Mar had no previous behavioural or emotional problems. She had good peer relationships and a circle of about four to six good friends in her neighbourhood. The transition to secondary school had been uneventful, as had her menarche.

Mar continued to do as well in secondary school as she had in primary school, but towards the end of her first year she became despondent about her weight. As a young teenager she was, according to her mother, 'well built'. Mar began dieting shortly before her 13th birthday. She believed that she was not fitting in with her friends, who by now were going to discos and beginning to take an interest in boys. Her mother's view was that she had been hurt by some critical comments made by girls at her school about her weight.

History of the presenting problem

What began as normal dieting, which was supported wholeheartedly by her parents, gradually became more and more intense around the time that Bev, Mar's older sister, went to college and her younger brother Nick began school. Also, at that time there was increased conflict between Maggie and Seamus (Bev's father and Maggie's first husband). Most of the arguments were about financing Bev during her time at college. Maggie and Seamus had separated when Bev was young, and Bev had had little contact with her father since then. However, because of the family's limited financial resources, Maggie had asked Seamus to help with supporting Bev through college. It was about this issue that the conflict had arisen. Mar was a sensitive girl and worried about the effect of this conflict on her mother.

Shortly after she started dieting, Mar began to lose weight rapidly, and changed from being 'well built' to being quite slim. After about year of dieting (and a year before the intake interview), Roddy, quite by accident, had found Mar vomiting behind the toilet block when the family were on holiday on a campsite. Maggie and Roddy were shocked by this. They had seen programmes about bulimia on TV and knew that secretive vomiting was a sign of an eating disorder. Mar said she had a stomach upset, and denied that her vomiting was motivated by a fear of fatness.

After the holiday, she was taken to the family doctor by the parents for an assessment of her dieting and vomiting problems. The doctor said that Mar had a mild eating problem, but provided she stopped dieting all would be well. He saw her regularly over the course of the 12 months prior to a multidisciplinary assessment. During that period, he advised the parents to take a low-key approach and encouraged Mar to eat a healthy balanced diet and avoid bingeing and vomiting. He impressed on her the dangers of developing an electrolyte imbalance and cardiac problems if she persisted with the bulimic pattern. Mar stopped the bulimic pattern but continued with dieting. Her weight continued to fall drastically and her periods stopped about four months before the assessment.

Roddy and Maggie did not know what to do to stop this fanatical dieting, so they tried a few different things. Maggie, who loved to cook, made increasingly sumptuous meals to try to tempt Mar away from her diet. She took a softly-softly approach, never raising her voice and never being harsh or punitive. She looked to her mother, Mrs Fox, for support and gradually felt more and more guilt. She was convinced that the eating problem was a reflection on some mistake she had made as a parent, and ruminated about this and the effects on Mar of her conflict with Seamus. Roddy left the management of Mar's eating problem to Maggie, although occasionally he tried to convince Mar to eat. These conversations usually ended in a heated argument, with Roddy shouting at Mar and telling her she was breaking her mother's heart, and then storming out of the room.

Because Roddy's attempts to get Mar to eat had been stressful and unsuccessful, he had gradually stopped trying to encourage Mar to eat. Mealtimes had become a nightmare, according to Roddy. He said he now frequently played a round of golf after work and afterwards ate a bar-meal at the golf club with his brother Mel.

Family history

Mar lived with her mother, Maggie, her father, Roddy, and her younger brother, Nick, aged 7. Her older sister, Bev, aged 20, had moved out 2 years previously to go to college. Roddy's brother and three sisters and Maggie's two brothers were all married with children, none of whom had any significant psychological problems or eating disorders. Maggie's two brothers tended to deny the reality of Mar's problem or to say it was something she would grow out of. Roddy's brother saw Mar's behaviour as defiance that required strict discipline. Roddy's sisters thought that it was a personal problem and that she might be depressed about something.

Formulation

Mar was a 14-year-old girl who presented with anorexia nervosa and a history of bulimia, the onset of which was precipitated by Mar's entry into adolescence, critical comments made by peers about her weight and increased family stress. This stress was associated with her half-sister's move to college, conflict between her mother and her half-sister's father, and her younger brother's entry into primary school. Mar's personality profile and weight-related issues predisposed her to developing anorexia. She had a history of being 'well-built', was dissatisfied with her weight and in adolescence had dealt with this initially through dieting and later through a bulimic pattern of vomiting when she believed she had overeaten. Her attempts at weight control were excessive because of her personality profile. She was perfectionistic, but also believed herself to be ineffective and so strived excessively to achieve her ideal weight.

Mar's restrictive eating was maintained at an interpersonal level by the inconsistent way in which her parents managed her refusal to eat a

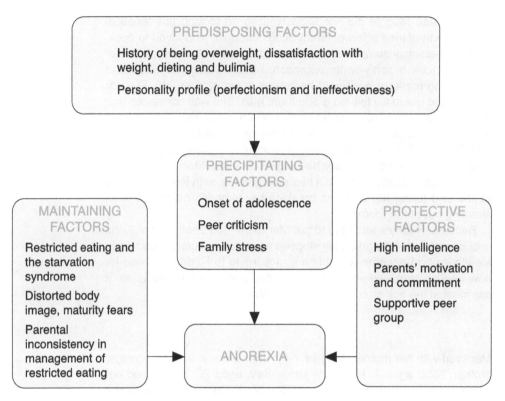

Figure 3.1 Formulation of a case of anorexia nervosa

normal diet and maintain a normal body weight. Mar's anorexia was maintained at an intrapsychic level by her distorted body image, maturity fears and need for control coupled with a sense of being powerless. It was also maintained by the rigid thinking, obsession with food and difficulty taking a normal perspective that accompanies the starvation process. Important protective factors were the parents' commitment to engaging in family treatment, the availability of Mar's supportive peer group, who wanted her to recover and rejoin them, and Mar's high intelligence. This formulation is diagrammed in Figure 3.1.

Treatment

Mar and her family participated in outpatient family therapy for 6 months. In the first stage Maggie and Roddy took responsibility for refeeding Mar and helping her attain a normal body weight. Once she attained a body weight in the normal range, she was encouraged to take control of her diet and weight. This was monitored by the therapy team on a weekly basis. Provided Mar did not fall below a BMI of 19, her parents agreed not to interfere in the self-management of her diet and weight.

In the middle phase of therapy the focus was on helping the family arrange for Mar to develop age-appropriate routines, pastimes and responsibilities with increasing autonomy and privacy. Mar rekindled her relationships with her friends, developed an interest in creative writing and began to go to dances and concerts, like a normal teenager. The final phase of therapy helped the family anticipate situations where relapses might occur and plan ways to manage such situations. Mar continued to maintain a normal body weight after treatment, but remained slim. She was very careful about her diet and exercise, so as to avoid becoming overweight.

Epidemiology, course and outcome

Anorexia nervosa and bulimia nervosa are most common among female adolescents and young women (Hoek, 2006; Keel, 2010). About 1–2% of the adolescent and young adult female population suffer from eating disorders. Anorexia is less common than bulimia. The average prevalence rates for anorexia nervosa and bulimia nervosa among young females are about 0.3–0.5% and 1–4% respectively. The onset for anorexia usually occurs in adolescence, and the peak age of onset for bulimia is in later adolescence or young adulthood. Community studies show that, contrary to earlier data from clinical studies, there is not a significant relationship between eating disorders and social class.

Since 1960 there has been an increase in the incidence of eating disorders in the UK and the USA, largely accounted for by increases in rates of bulimia rather than anorexia. Since the 1990s in the UK, rates of bulimia have begun to decline (Currin et al., 2005). While eating disorders may be more common in western industrialised countries, there is growing evidence of eating disorders in non-westernised cultures. In clinical rather than community populations, anorexia nervosa is commonly comorbid with mood and obsessive compulsive disorders, while bulimia nervosa is commonly comorbid with drug abuse and borderline personality disorder.

The outcome for eating disorders is poor for a significant minority of cases (Steinhausen, 2002; Stice, 2002), but can be improved with early intervention and evidence-based treatment (American Psychiatric Association, 2006; NICE, 2004a). For anorexia nervosa about half of all cases have a good outcome, a third have moderate outcome and a fifth have a poor outcome. At 20-year follow-up, the mortality rate is about 6% (with a range of 0–21% across studies). Starvation and suicide are the primary causes of death. A poor prognosis is associated with lower weight, a more chronic condition, the absence of a clear precipitating stressful life event, bulimic symptoms, comorbid obsessive compulsive disorder, problematic family relationships, dropping out of treatment and lower social class. For bulimia nervosa about half of all cases have a good outcome, a quarter have a moderate outcome and the remaining quarter have a poor outcome. A poor prognosis in bulimia is associated with later onset, a more chronic condition, more frequent bingeing and vomiting, greater body dissatisfaction, higher perfectionism, comorbid substance abuse, impulsive personality disorders, and lower social class.

Risk factors identified in an extensive review of longitudinal and cross-sectional studies for eating disorders are given in Table 3.2 (Jacobi et al., 2004).

TABLE 3.2
Risk factors for eating disorders

Risk factors common to anorexia and bulimia nervosa	Risk factors unique to anorexia nervosa	Risk factors unique to bulimia nervosa
Female	Preterm birth/Birth trauma	Childhood obesity
Adolescent	Infant feeding and sleep problems	Social phobia in adolescence
Genetic factors	High-concern parenting in early childhood	Parental criticism about weight, high expectations and low contact in adolescence
Pregnancy complications	Obsessionality (OCD, OCPD) in adolescence	Parental obesity in adolescence
Child sexual abuse	Perfectionism in adolescence	Parental depression, drug and alcohol abuse in adolescence
Physical neglect in childhood	Weight subculture (dancer, model, athlete)	
Gastrointestinal problems, picky eating and eating conflicts in childhood	Acculturation	
Childhood anxiety disorder		
Stressful life events in childhood and adolescence		
Weight concerns and dieting in adolescence		
Low social support in adolescence		
Low self-esteem		
Ineffectiveness		
Low interoception (difficulty interpreting internal gastrointestinal and emotional stimuli)		
Avoidant coping		

Note: Based on C. Jacobi, C. Hayward, M. de Zwaan, H. C. Kraemer, & W. S. Agras (2004). Coming to terms with risk factors for eating disorders: Application of risk terminology and suggestions for a general taxonomy. *Psychological Bulletin, 130,* 19–65.

Clinical features

Historically anorexia nervosa was first described in modern medical literature by Charles Lasègue in France in 1873 and by Sir William Gull in the UK in 1874, and it was Gull who first used the term 'anorexia nervosa'. Both Lasègue and Gull described anorexia as a condition characterized by emaciation, an inadequate and unhealthy pattern of eating, and an excessive concern with the control of body weight and shape. Attempts at subclassifying eating disorders led to the establishment of bulimia nervosa as a separate diagnosis from anorexia in 1979 by Gerard Russell in the UK. In the classification of eating disorders in both DSM-IV-TR (American Psychiatric Association, 2000) and ICD-10 (World Health Organization, 1992), this distinction between anorexia nervosa and bulimia nervosa is a central organizing principle, with the former being characterized primarily by weight loss and the latter by a cyclical pattern of bingeing and purging.

The distinction, while descriptively useful, does not take full account of variations in eating problems seen in clinical practice. Many anorexic clients present with bulimic symptoms and many bulimic clients develop anorexia. The DSM contains a category – eating disorders not otherwise specified – for the many 'mixed cases' seen in clinical practice that do not meet the criteria for either anorexia or bulimia.

Eating disorders are characterized by distinctive clinical features in the domains of behaviour, perception, cognition, emotion, social adjustment and physical health (Agras, 2010). At a behavioural level, restrictive eating is typical of anorexia. Clients report low calorific intake and eating low-calorie foods over a significant time period. They may cook for the family but not eat meals they prepare. Clients with anorexia present as thin or emaciated. They may wear baggy clothes to conceal the extent of their weight loss.

In contrast, clients with bulimia are typically of normal weight. A cycle of restrictive eating, bingeing and compensatory behaviours is typical of bulimia. These compensatory behaviours may include vomiting, using diuretics and laxatives or excessive exercising. Usually particular types of situation that are interpreted as threatening or stressful lead to a negative mood state and precipitate bouts of bingeing. Such situations include interpersonal conflicts, isolation, and small violations of a strict diet such as eating a square of chocolate. Bingeing may also arise from alcohol intoxication.

While bingeing brings immediate relief, it also leads to physical discomfort and to guilt for not adhering to a strict diet. Purging relieves both guilt and physical discomfort but may also induce shame and fear of negative consequences of the binge–purge cycle. Relatives who live with bulimic clients may describe specific routines they have developed to conceal their vomiting and excessive exercise, for example running the shower in the bathroom to mask the sound of them vomiting. In addition to abnormal eating patterns, clients with eating disorders – especially bulimia – may display a variety of self-destructive behaviours including self-injury, suicide attempts and drug abuse. These behaviours are often construed as self-punishments for not living up to perfectionistic standards or attempts to escape from conflicts associated with self-worth and individuation.

With respect to perception, in most clinical cases of eating disorder there is a distortion of body image. The client perceives the body or parts of the body such as the stomach, buttocks or thighs to be larger than they are. People with eating disorders may also have low interoception; that is, difficulty interpreting internal gastrointestinal and emotional stimuli. This makes it difficult for them to know when it's appropriate to start and stop eating, and how to interpret their feelings and emotions.

With respect to cognition, there is a preoccupation with food that is a consequence of dietary restraint. Low self-esteem and low self-efficacy are also common. Thus, many clients with eating disorders view themselves as worthless and powerless, and see achieving a slim body shape and low body weight through dietary restraint as the route to an increased sense of control over their lives and increased self-worth. This process is often compounded by perfectionist tendencies and a wish to attain exceptionally high standards. In bulimia, the repeated failure to sustain low-calorie intake leads to further self-criticism, and low self-esteem and also strengthens the belief in lack of control. In anorexia, starvation directly affects cognitive processes. There is an increasing rigidity and inflexibility in thinking style and a gradual reduction in the capacity to concentrate. In all eating disorders, there may be conflict concerning dependence and maturity. On one hand there may be a fear of maturity and independence; on the other there may be a wish to escape from parental control and the lack of autonomy and privacy that this entails.

With regard to emotional state, clients with eating disorders report an intense fear of fatness. In anorexia, low mood may arise from a failure to live up to perfectionist standards, and improvements in mood may occur when the urge to eat is resisted. In bulimia depressed or irritable mood may occur as a result of dietary restraint, or in response to life stresses. Such episodes of low mood lead to bingeing, which brings temporary relief. However, after binges, low mood may occur as a result of the sense of failure that this entails. Suicide attempts occur in up to 20% of patients with anorexia and 25% of those with bulimia (Franko & Keel, 2006). Suicidality in eating disorders is associated with depression, substance abuse, and a history of child physical and sexual abuse.

With respect to interpersonal adjustment, withdrawal from peer relationships, deterioration in family relationships, and poor educational or vocational performance may all occur as a result of eating problems.

The health complications of anorexia involve an endocrine disorder affecting the hypothalamic–pituitary–gonadal axis. This leads to amenorrhea; starvation symptomatology such as reduced metabolic rate, bradycardia, hypotension, hypothermia, and anaemia; lanugo hair on the back; delayed gastric emptying; electrolyte abnormalities; renal dysfunction; and zinc deficiency. In bulimia, erosion of dental enamel may occur due to vomiting. Lesions on the back of the dominant hand may develop if the hand is used to initiate vomiting. With both anorexia and bulimia a particularly serious concern is that the client may develop electrolyte abnormalities that may lead to a fatal arrhythmia.

Aetiological theories

Under normal circumstances hunger motivates people to eat until they have the experience of 'being full' and most of the time their weight is remarkably stable, as if homostatically governed. When people try to slim through restrained eating, they experience chronic hunger and negative affect, and become preoccupied with food. In response to these negative experiences, most people give up dieting and return to their usual eating habits and normal body weight. People who develop anorexia, however, redouble their efforts to maintain a pattern of restrained eating when they experience hunger, negative affect and intense food preoccupation. In contrast, people who develop bulimia engage in bingeing when the negative effects of restrained eating and life stresses make them feel bad, and later engage in compensatory purging. Biological, psychodynamic, cognitive-behavioural and systemic theories have been developed to explain the aetiology, course and treatment of eating disorders.

Biological theories

Hypotheses have been proposed to explain the role of a number of biological factors in the development and course of eating disorders. These have focused on genetics, mood dysregulation and starvation-related processes. Genetic and mood dysregulation hypotheses posit a role for each of these factors in the aetiology of eating disorders, while starvation theories are concerned primarily with the way in which the biological sequelae of self-starvation contribute to the maintenance of abnormal eating patterns.

Genetics

The genetic hypothesis proposes that a biological predisposition to eating disorders is genetically transmitted and that individuals with this predisposition when exposed to certain environmental conditions develop an eating disorder. Evidence from twin and family studies shows unequivocally that genetic predisposing factors contribute moderately to the aetiology of eating disorders, and that they are 50–83% heritable (Klump et al., 2009; Wade, 2010). Positive findings from candidate gene studies focusing on serotonin, dopamine and other neurotransmitter systems and on genes involved in body weight regulation have not been substantiated in meta-analyses (Scherag et al., 2010).

There is some evidence that appetite and satiety dysregulation renders people vulnerable to the development of eating disorders, and that this vulnerability may be polygenetically determined (Stice et al., 1999). Collier and Treasure (2004) propose that genetic factors contribute to temperamental dispositions that underpin the development of personality traits associated with eating disorders. These may be conceptualized as falling along a continuum from restrictive, anorexia-like disorders to disinhibited, bulimic-like disorders. The predisposing personality traits of perfectionism, harm avoidance and depression may place people at risk for developing both restrained, anorexic-like and disinhibited, bulimic-like eating disorders. Compulsivity and inflexibility may be the personality traits that place people at specific risk for developing restricting, anorexia-like disorders. Impulsivity and novelty seeking may be the personality traits that place people at specific risk for developing disinhibited, bulimia-like eating disorders. The assumption in this proposal is that the biological basis for each of these personality traits is polygenetically determined, and that through interaction with the environment the traits develop and predispose the person to developing an eating disorder.

Mood dysregulation

It has been proposed that eating disorders are an expression of an underlying mood disorder (Vögele & Gibson, 2010). Depression is often present in the family histories of people with eating disorders, along with other mood regulation difficulties such as substance abuse and borderline personality disorder. If anorexia and bulimia are fundamentally mood disorders, then a plausible hypothesis is that eating disorders arise from a dysregulation of the serotonergic neurotransmitter system in those centres of the brain that subserve mood. Considerable evidence suggests that abnormalities in the serotonergic neurotransmitter system contribute to dysregulation of mood as well as appetite and impulse control in eating disorders (Kaye, 2008).

The neurotransmitter dysregulation hypothesis has led to controlled trials of antidepressants for eating disorders, mainly conducted with young adults. Both selective serotonin re-uptake inhibitors (SSRIs) and tricyclic antidepressants (TCAs) have been found to lead to short-term improvements in bulimia, but have limited impact on anorexia nervosa (McElroy et al., 2010; Wilson & Fairburn, 2007).

Starvation

The starvation hypothesis proposes that eating disorders follow a chronic course because they are partly maintained by biological abnormalities and related alterations in psychological functioning caused by starvation. Evidence from studies of people with anorexia and bulimia and participants in starvation laboratory experiments show that the neuroendocrine abnormalities and changes in gastric functioning that arise from experimentally induced starvation are similar to those observed in patients with eating disorders (Frichter & Pirke, 1995; Singh, 2002). More pronounced changes occur in anorexia than in bulimia. Starvation-related neuroendocrine changes occur in the hypothalamic–pituitary–gonadal axis, which governs reproductive functioning. They also occur in the hypothalamic–pituitary–adrenal axis and the hypothalamic–pituitary–thyroid axis, which govern mood, appetite, arousal and other vegetative functions.

In addition, there is evidence that starvation leads to delayed gastric emptying and that this reduces hunger perception. Neuroimaging studies show that anorexia and bulimia lead to reduced cortical mass, with some degree of normalization after recovery (Kaye, 2008). One implication of starvation theories is that a distinction should be made between re-feeding programmes, which aim to reverse the starvation process by helping patients regain weight to render them accessible to psychological interventions, and later therapy in which the maintenance of normal body weight and eating patterns is the principal goal. This distinction is central to effective forms of therapy for anorexia.

Psychoanalytic theories

Psychoanalytic explanations of eating disorders focus on the role of intrapsychic factors in the genesis and maintenance of self-starvation.

Hilda Bruch (1973, 1978) argued that the psychodynamics that underpins anorexia arises from early childhood experiences. According to Bruch, the mothers of anorexic girls adopt a parenting style in which parental needs for control and compliance take primacy over the child's needs for self-expression and autonomy. The child has difficulty in learning how to interpret need-related internal physiological states and in developing a coherent sense of self separate from caregivers.

In adolescence the fear of fatness, obsession with food and guilt for eating are part of an attempt to manage a central conflict related to the attainment of autonomy and a coherent sense of self. The youngster experiences a fear of separation from parents and a fear of being overly controlled by the parents; a fear of maturation, sexuality, intimacy and independence; and a fear of having little control over the self or body size (as a symbol of self). This conflict about autonomy is characterized by low self-esteem coupled with perfectionistic strivings to improve the self.

There is ample evidence for distorted body image, low interoception, maturity fears, perfectionism, low self-esteem, the use of suppression as a coping strategy and low self-directedness among people with eating disorders (Aldeo et al., 2010; Cassin & von Ranson, 2005; Jacobi & Fittig, 2010; Jacobi et al., 2004). There is also some evidence for problematic parent–child relationships as precursors of eating disorders (Jacobi & Fittig, 2010; Jacobi et al., 2004; Striegel-Moore & Bulik, 2007). Over-concerned parenting in childhood is a risk factor for anorexia. Parental criticism about weight, high expectations and low contact with parents in adolescence are associated with bulimia.

Results of a small number of trials suggest that psychodynamic psychotherapy may be effective as a treatment for eating disorders in adults, but not adolescents (Thompson-Brenner et al., 2009). The Maudsley group in their controlled trials of psychodynamic psychotherapy with young adults, working within the context of Malan's (1995) psychodynamic therapy model, have found that a unique psychodynamic focal hypothesis may be formed for each patient and that Bruch's themes typically characterize these focal hypotheses. Psychoanalytic psychotherapy, as practised by the Maudsley group, aims to help the patient gain insight into the way in which the psychodynamics of past relationships with parents underpins the transference–countertransference, the patient–therapist relationship and the relationships that the patient has with other significant people in their life. In addition, psychoanalytic psychotherapy facilitates the patient's search for less destructive ways to assert autonomy from the parents and to develop a strong sense of personal identity.

Cognitive-behavioural theories

There are a number of cognitive-behaviour therapy (CBT) approaches to understanding and treating eating disorders (Wilson, 2010). A particularly well developed model has been proposed by the Oxford group led by Christopher Fairburn (2008). In this transdiagnostic model Fairburn proposed that the over-evaluation of shape and weight and their control is the core underlying cognitive cause of anorexia, bulimia and 'mixed' eating disorders. That is, people with eating disorders judge their self-worth in terms of their weight and shape and their capacity to control these, rather than in terms of the quality of their close relationships, their work performance or involvement in their pastimes. They hold beliefs such as 'I am only good if I am thin' or 'I can only be happy if I control my eating and weigh seven stone'. These belief systems motivate people with eating disorders to follow strict diets.

Those who develop anorexia are highly successful at dieting and develop very low body weight. This state gives rise to the starvation syndrome which involves a preoccupation with eating, a heightened sense of being full, rigid obsessionality and social withdrawal. These side-effects of the starvation process strengthen the core beliefs associated with over-evaluation of shape and weight. In this way people with anorexia become trapped in a vicious cycle whereby their over-evaluation of shape and weight is strengthened by the side-effects of starvation.

People who develop bulimia (like those with anorexia) also over-evaluate their shape and weight and engage in strict dieting. However, periodically, stressful life events lead to episodes of low mood, which they cope with by bingeing. This temporarily improves their mood, but afterwards they become self-critical for deviating from their strict diet, and compensate for their bingeing by vomiting, taking laxatives or exercising excessively. They then return to the practice of strict dieting, motivated by their over-evaluation of shape and weight. This continues until another stressful life event causes a drop in mood and a repetition of the binge–purge cycle. Fairburn's model is diagrammed in Figure 3.2.

Fairburn's (2008) model of CBT progresses through four stages over 20 sessions. In the first stage the therapist engages with the patient though bi-weekly sessions over a period of a month, conducts an assessment, collaboratively develops a formulation, provides psychoeducation about eating disorders and the CBT model, arranges regular 'in session weighing' and arranges for patients to start a pattern of regular eating. In the second stage appointments are held weekly, progress is reviewed, barriers to progress are identified, and the formulation is refined. In the third stage the repetitive cycles of cognition and behaviour that maintain the eating disorder are addressed. In the final stage, appointments are held fortnightly and the focus is on maintaining gains and planning for relapse prevention. Variations on this basic treatment model have been developed for patients with severe weight loss or complex personal and interpersonal problems, inpatients and younger patients, and for group therapy.

Many controlled trials have shown that about 50% of young adult patients with bulimia nervosa benefit from CBT (Wilson, 2010; Wilson & Fairburn, 2007). Few trials of CBT with anorexia have been conducted.

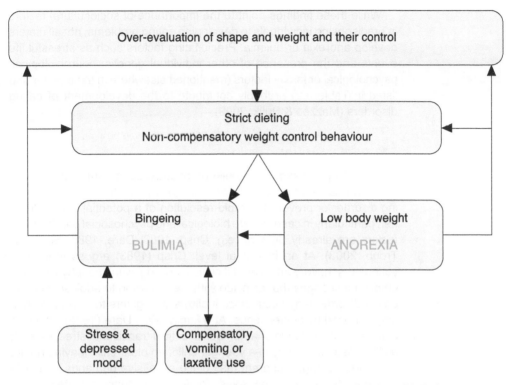

Figure 3.2 Fairburn's cognitive-behavioural model of eating disorders (adapted from C. Fairburn (2008). *Cognitive behaviour therapy and eating disorders.* London: Guilford)

Systemic theories

Systemic theories underline the role of contextual factors in the development and treatment of eating disorders. Sociocultural, developmental and family systems formulations fall into this broad domain.

Sociocultural factors

Sociocultural theories highlight the role of broad cultural factors such as the idealization of female thinness specific to particular societies, notably those prevalent in western industrialised nations, in predisposing individuals to developing eating disorders (Nasser & Katzman, 2003). Evidence supporting the sociocultural position allows the following conclusions to be drawn (Levine & Murnen, 2009; Levine & Smolak, 2010).

Epidemiological studies consistently show that eating disorders exist internationally but are more prevalent in western societies where food is plentiful, thinness is valued and dieting is promoted. Eating disorders are more prevalent among groups under greater social pressure to achieve the slim aesthetic ideal, such as dancers, models and athletes. Westernization, modernization and exposure to transnational mass media advocating the thin ideal are risk factors for eating disorders. The prevalence of eating disorders is higher in ethnic groups that move from a culture that does not idealize the thin female form to cultures that do.

While these findings point to the importance of sociocultural factors in predisposing individuals to developing eating problems, not all dieters develop anorexia or bulimia. Precipitating factors such as stressful life events and the presence of other individual genetic, neurobiological, psychological or family factors (mentioned elsewhere in the chapter and listed in Table 3.2) probably contribute to the development of eating disorders (Mazzeo & Bulik, 2009).

Life-cycle transitions and stress

It has been proposed that a build-up of stresses at particular points in the individual and family life cycles may precipitate the onset of an eating disorder or prevent the rapid resolution of a potential eating disorder, particularly in cases where biological and psychosocial predisposing factors are already present (e.g. Crisp, 1983; Dare, 1985; Serpell & Troup, 2003). At an individual level, Crisp (1983) argues that when youngsters have particular difficulties dealing with the physical and emotional changes that coincide with the transition to adolescence, an eating disorder may occur since it allows youngsters to avoid the challenges posed by adolescence. At a family level, Dare (1985) proposes that the co-occurrence of a number of critical transitional stresses such as the onset of puberty in a younger child, an older child leaving home, or the loss of a grandparent may place excessive demands on family members to develop new roles, routines and support systems. The development of an eating disorder provides families with a period of respite, where routines, roles and supports appropriate to a previous stage of the family life-cycle may continue to be used so that families may maintain the status quo rather than negotiating changes appropriate to the next stage of the life-cycle. Both of these theories are supported by evidence for the association between eating disorders and stressful life events in adolescence.

Serpell and Troup (2003) propose that childhood adversity (including neglect, sexual abuse and family conflict), helplessness, low self-esteem and rigid perfectionism predispose people to developing eating disorders. In response to sociocultural pressures for thinness, these four factors give rise to four intermediate predisposing factors: (1) dietary restraint, (2) low shape and weight-based self-esteem, (3) disgust at food and food-related body stimuli and (4) bodily shame. When stressful life events that involve managing complex interpersonal situations and relationships arise in people who have these vulnerability factors, an eating disorder may occur. This complex developmental theory is supported by evidence for a number of risk factors listed in Table 3.2.

Family systems approaches

Family systems theories of anorexia point to a number of organizational features that may be predisposing or maintaining factors for eating disorders (le Grange & Rienecke Hoste, 2010). For example, Minuchin et al.

(1978) characterized the families of teenagers with anorexia as enmeshed and rigid, with a strongly overprotective attitude to the child. He also argued that there was a lack of conflict resolution and an involvement of children in parental conflicts. Selvini Palazzoli (1988) pinpointed the following features as typical of the anorexic family: an ethic of self-sacrifice, limited parental leadership, blame-shifting since everything is done for the good of others, unclear communication and secret alliances between one parent and the anorexic child, and covert marital dissatisfaction.

Available empirical evidence indicates that there is not a single dysfunctional family constellation (a psychosomatic family) that causes anorexia and bulimia (Jacobi et al., 2004). Rather, a variety of patterns of family organization are associated with eating disorders. Families of youngsters with anorexia tend to be more controlled and organized, while families of bulimic adolescents tend to be more chaotic, conflicted and critical. These patterns of organization probably reflect families' attempts to cope with eating disorders.

A group at the Maudsley Hospital in London have developed an approach to family therapy for young teenagers with anorexia for which there is considerable empirical support. The model, which was manualized and popularized by James Lock (Lock et al., 2001), underlines the value of the family as a central treatment resource in facilitating recovery, rather than as an aetiological factor. The approach is premised on the idea that young teenagers with anorexia are regressed, and not capable of responsible autonomous eating. Rather than being in control of their eating, they are controlled by their eating disorder. That is, the starvation syndrome (mentioned in the section on CBT above) prevents the young person from recovering. It is because of this that parents play a central role in the recovery process. Therapists support parents in treating their adolescents as if they were younger children by refeeding them until a safe and stable weight has been achieved. At this point they may safely transfer responsibility for maintaining a healthy diet and weight to the adolescent.

Lock proposes that most children and teenagers can be treated effectively as outpatients, unless their low weight poses significant medical risks. Treatment typically spans about 20 sessions and lasts from 6 months to a year. In the first stage of therapy the therapist forms an alliance with the family, conducts a family assessment, offers psychoeducation about the risks associated with anorexia, sets up a routine for weighing the patient at the beginning of each session, and supports the parents in helping the young person to eat in the therapy session. In the second stage the aim is to help the parents gradually transfer responsibility for eating responsibly to the adolescent and explore the relationship between the anorexia and the adolescent's achievement of developmental tasks such as increasing autonomy within the family. In the final stage of treatment the emphasis is on consolidating the gains the parents and adolescent have made in managing the adolescent's growing autonomy, anticipating how the family will manage the adolescent's growing independence, and relapse anticipation and prevention.

Evidence from a series of trials shows that family therapy is effective with up to 90% of young adolescents with non-chronic anorexia (le Grange & Rienecke Hoste, 2010; Lock et al., 2001).

Interpersonal therapy

Interpersonal theory was developed by Harry Stack Sullivan (1953), who proposed that psychological problems are maintained by problematic current life relationships. From this theory interpersonal therapy (IPT) was developed as an effective treatment for depression. It was then adapted for bulimia in young adults and shown to be an effective treatment for this condition (Tanofsky-Kraff & Wilfley, 2010; Wilson & Fairburn, 2007).

In IPT for bulimia, it is assumed that one or more of four categories of interpersonal difficulties maintain the condition. These are: (1) grief following bereavement or other losses, (2) role disputes within important family or work relationships, (3) role transitions within the family or workplace, and (4) interpersonal deficits, such as problems in making and maintaining friendships. Interpersonal therapy alleviates bulimia by helping clients resolve problems in these areas that maintain their pattern of bingeing and purging.

IPT for bulimia involves three stages and spans 20 sessions conducted over a period of 4 to 5 months. In the first stage the client is engaged in treatment, current interpersonal problems are identified and a treatment contract is established. In the middle stage the core interpersonal problem that maintains the eating disorder is addressed. In the final stage gains made are consolidated and clients are helped to prepare to continue the work after termination of therapy.

Assessment

Assessment and treatment of eating disorders are usually carried out by multidisciplinary teams that include professionals from clinical psychology, psychiatry, psychiatric nursing, dietetics and other disciplines. Assessment covers the client's physical, nutritional and psychological state (Anderson & Murray, 2010; Katzman et al., 2010). With teenagers a family assessment is essential. With adults, interviews with involved family members are important.

Psychometric instruments that may be useful in the assessment of clients with eating disorder are the Eating Disorder Examination (EDE, Fairburn et al., 2008) and the Eating Disorder Inventory (EDI-3, Garner, 2005). The EDE, which is considered the diagnostic gold standard, is a detailed interview that allows DSM diagnoses of eating disorders to be made with high reliability. The EDI-3 is a comprehensive self-report psychological assessment instrument for assessing eating pathology and related psychological traits such as perfectionism and ineffectiveness. On the basis of the assessment a preliminary formulation may be drawn up. This should link predisposing, precipitating and maintaining factors to the abnormal eating pattern and specify protective factors that may be drawn on during treatment. A general clinical formulation model for eating disorders is given in Figure 3.3.

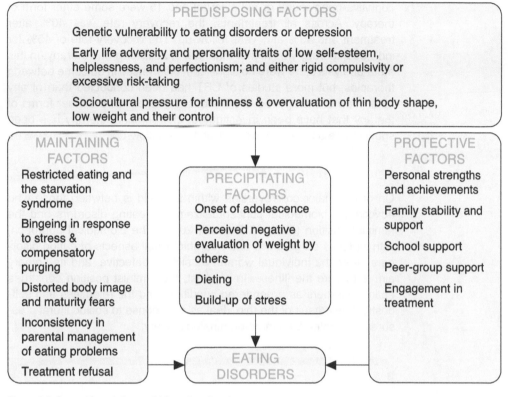

Figure 3.3 General formulation model for eating disorders

Intervention

Intervention for eating disorders is multidisciplinary. It includes management of the medical complications of eating disorders (Katzman et al., 2010) coupled with psychological intervention. There is strong evidence to support the effectiveness of family therapy for young teenagers with non-chronic anorexia nervosa and CBT for bulimia in young adults, following the models of these interventions outlined earlier in the chapter (Hay & Claudino, 2010; le Grange & Rienecke Hoste, 2010; Wilson, 2010). The use of these treatments for these populations is consistent with best practice guidelines (American Psychiatric Association, 2006; NICE, 2004a).

In a review of available evidence, Eisler (2005) concluded that after treatment, between a half and two-thirds of teenagers with anorexia achieve a healthy weight. At 6 months to 6 year follow-up, 60–90% have fully recovered and no more than 10–15% are seriously ill. Eisler also noted that the negligible relapse rate following family therapy is superior to the moderate outcomes for individually oriented therapies. It is also far superior to the high relapse rate following inpatient treatment, which is 25–30% following first admission, and 55–75% for second and further admissions.

Thompson-Brenner et al. (2003) conducted a meta-analysis of 26 studies involving 51 treatment conditions, of which 36 were cognitive-behavioural or behavioural and 15 were some other form of therapy. Across all treatments, the recovery rate was 40% after treatment and 43% at 1 year follow-up. The recovery rate of 45% for individual therapy was higher than that of 26% for group therapy. In this meta-analysis there were no significant differences in outcome between therapies, but more studies of CBT had been conducted than of any other form of therapy, so it is the best validated. Of the other forms of therapy that have been investigated, interpersonal therapy has been shown to be as effective as CBT at 1 year follow-up.

Controversies

On of the major controversies within the field is between those who advocate a biomedical conceptualization of eating disorders and the feminist position (Maine & Bunnell, 2010). The biomedical approach, with its focus on genetics and neurobiological aspects of eating disorders, sees the individual woman as sick or defective, and its primary aim is to cure the illness. In contrast, the feminist position construes eating disorders as a gendered condition, and the relentless and self-destructive pursuit of the thin ideal as a response to sociocultural pressures generated by a male-dominated society.

Summary

Anorexia nervosa and bulimia nervosa typically occur first during adolescence, principally among females. About 1–2% of the adolescent and young adult female population suffer from eating disorders. The average prevalence rates for anorexia nervosa and bulimia nervosa among young females are 0.3–0.5% and 1–4% respectively. In both conditions there is an overevaluation of body shape and weight.

With anorexia, the primary feature is the maintenance of a very low body weight; with bulimia a cycle of binge eating and purging is the distinctive feature. In most clinical cases of eating disorder there is a distortion of body image, depressed or irritable mood, and interpersonal adjustment problems. Eating disorders entail significant health complications.

The outcome for eating disorders is poor for a significant minority of cases. For anorexia nervosa about half of all cases have a good outcome, a third have a moderate outcome and a fifth have a poor outcome. At 20-year follow-up, the mortality rate is about 6%. For bulimia nervosa about half of all cases have a good outcome, a quarter have a moderate outcome and the remaining quarter have a poor outcome.

Biological theories point to the role of genetics, mood dysregulation and starvation-related processes in the aetiology and maintenance of eating disorders. Evidence from twin and family studies show unequivocally that genetic predisposing factors contribute moderately to the aetiology of eating disorders. Eating disorders have been conceptualized as mood disorders associated with dysregulation of the seratonergic system. Antidepressants have been found to lead to short-term improvements in bulimia, but have no impact on anorexia nervosa.

Starvation-related neuroendocrine changes occur In the hypothalamic–pituitary–gonadal axis, which governs reproductive functioning, and the hypothalamic–pituitary–adrenal axis and hypothalamic–pituitary–thyroid axis, which govern mood and appetite. The starvation syndrome maintains restricted eating. Bruch's psychoanalytic theory proposes that over-controlling parenting practices cause eating disorders and the related problems of distorted body image, maturity fears, perfectionistic strivings, low self-esteem and low self-efficacy.

There is some evidence that focal psychodynamic psychotherapy can lead to improvement for adults with anorexia, but not adolescents. Fairburn's transdiagnostic CBT model assumes that the over-evaluation of shape and weight and their control is the core underlying cognitive cause of anorexia, bulimia and 'mixed' eating disorders. About 50% of young adults with bulimia benefit from individual CBT. Few trials of CBT with people of any age with anorexia or with adolescents with any eating disorder have been conducted.

Social and family factors may play a role in the aetiology of anorexia. There is no single dysfunctional family constellation that causes eating disorders. The Maudsley approach to family therapy for adolescent eating disorders underlines the value of the family as a central treatment resource in facilitating recovery, rather than as an aetiological factor. Up to 90% of adolescents with non-chronic anorexia can benefit from this approach.

IPT assumes that eating disorders are maintained by interpersonal factors, notably grief, role disputes, role transitions and interpersonal deficits. IPT alleviates bulimia by helping clients resolve problems in these areas that maintain their pattern of bingeing and purging. IPT is as effective as CBT, but fewer validation studies have been conducted. Assessment and treatment of eating disorders is usually carried out by multidisciplinary teams, with an initial focus on weight restoration for anorexia and the development of a normal diet for bulimia. Once weight and diet have been normalized, the focus should shift to psychotherapy.

For young adolescents, family therapy is the treatment of choice; for adult bulimics, CBT is the best validated treatment. There is controversy over whether eating disorders are most usefully conceptualized as biologically based medical conditions or a gendered response to socio-cultural pressures for thinness.

Questions

- What are the main clinical features of anorexia nervosa and bulimia nervosa?
- How prevalent are eating disorders?
- What are the main biological and psychological theories of eating disorders and the main research findings relevant to these theories?
- What are the main evidence-based approaches to assessment and treatment of eating disorders?
- What are your views on the controversy concerning the biomedical and feminist views of eating disorders?

FURTHER READING

Professional

- Agras, W. (2010). *The Oxford handbook of eating disorders.* New York: Oxford University Press.
- Carr, A. (2006). *Handbook of child and adolescent clinical psychology* (second edition). London: Routledge (Chapter 17).
- Fairburn, C. (2008). *Cognitive behaviour therapy and eating disorders.* London: Guilford.
- Lock, J., Le Grange, D., Agras, W., & Dare, C. (2001). *Treatment manual for anorexia nervosa: A family based approach.* New York: Guilford.

Self-help

- Fairburn, C. (1995). *Overcoming binge eating.* London: Guilford.
- Lock, J. J. & Le Grange, D. (2004). *Help your teenager beat an eating disorder.* London: Brunner-Routledge.

WEBSITES

- Academy for Eating Disorders:
  www.aedweb.org
- APA (American Psychiatric Association) practice guidelines for treating eating disorders:
  www.guideline.gov/content.aspx?id=9318
- Beat (Beating Eating Disorders):
  http://www.b-eat.co.uk
- Eating Disorders Resources:
  http://edr.org.uk
- Eating Disorders Treatment:
  http://eating-disorder.com
- NICE (National Institute for Clinical Excellence) guidelines for treating eating disorders:
  http://guidance.nice.org.uk/topic/mentalhealthbehavioural

Drug misuse

4

Learning objectives

After studying this chapter you will be able to:

- distinguish between drug experimentation and harmful drug use
- name the main clinical features of drug dependence
- summarize the epidemiology of drug misuse
- list the risk factors for drug misuse
- outline the main biological, psychological and integrative theories of drug misuse
- name the main evidence-based approaches to assessment and treatment of drug misuse
- give a considered view on the pros and cons of harm reduction strategies for addressing drug misuse.

Introduction

Habitual drug misuse in adolescence is of particular concern to clinical psychologists because it may have a negative long-term effect on the adolescent and an intergenerational effect on their children (Crome et al., 2004; Heath et al., 2008; Kaminer & Winters, 2011). For the adolescent, habitual drug misuse may negatively affect mental and physical health, criminal and educational status, the establishment of autonomy from the family of origin and the development long-term intimate relationships. The children of teenagers who engage in chronic and harmful drug use may suffer from drug-related problems such as foetal alcohol syndrome, intrauterine addiction or HIV infection.

In this chapter, after considering the classification, epidemiology and clinical features of drug misuse, a variety of theoretical explanations concerning the aetiology and maintenance of these conditions will be considered along with relevant empirical evidence. Some comments on the assessment and treatment of drug use will be made and relevant controversies considered. Cases of drug misuse vary widely in their presentation. Below two examples of very different types of case are presented.

A case of harmful polydrug use

Carl, 18, and Betty, 19, referred themselves for treatment to an inner city drug clinic in a public health service. Both were polydrug users and had developed physiological dependence to opiates at the time of referral.

History of the presenting problem

They both had been using drugs since about the age of 10 years, beginning with cigarettes which they stole from their parents. They were part of a peer group involved in experimental drug use. At 12 they both began drinking alcohol. They stole beer from Carl's father and wine from a supermarket. They went on to experiment with benzodiazepines which they stole from Betty's mother, who had been prescribed these for anxiety and sleep problems by the family doctor. They then used cannabis, various solvents, and a variety of stimulants including amphetamines. They progressed to opiates about a year before they first attended the clinic. They had got to the stage where they could no longer finance their drug-taking habits and had a series of bad debts. They requested evaluation for placement on a methadone maintenance programme.

The couple lived together on welfare in a two-room apartment. They had financed their drug habits through theft and prostitution. They were part of a group of drug users who lived in Dublin's inner city. Their whole lifestyle centred around getting and using any drugs they could find, but mainly opiates.

Developmental and family history

Betty and Carl had known each other from childhood. Both had a history of academic and conduct problems at school. Their families were part of a community and so their parents knew each other and discussed Betty and Carl's relationship. When the young couple began living together about 6 months before the referral, their parents disapproved of this. However, in both of the families their mothers were very loyal to them and occasionally gave them financial assistance when it was clear that they were showing withdrawal symptoms and needed a fix.

Carl's grandfather lived with Carl's parents. Both he and Carl's father had a serious drink problem for which they had been unsuccessfully treated over many years. Carl had four siblings, all of whom had drug problems. Betty had three siblings, all but one of whom were using drugs. However, Carl and Betty had the most serious drug problems of the two families. They were both eldest children.

Formulation

Betty and Carl presented with habitual, harmful drug misuse and dependence. This had evolved gradually out of an earlier pattern of pre-adolescent experimental drug use, which may be viewed as a precipitating factor. Both Betty and Carl were predisposed to develop substance use problems because of their family role models, their academic difficulties, lack of career opportunities and other conduct problems. Their drug problems were maintained at a physiological level by dependence and the related fear of withdrawal.

At a psychosocial level their drug problems were maintained through involvement in a subculture and lifestyle that revolved around obtaining and using drugs to the exclusion of almost all other activities. The main protective factor was the couple's loyalty to each other, and their wish in the long term to have children. This formulation is diagrammed in Figure 4.1.

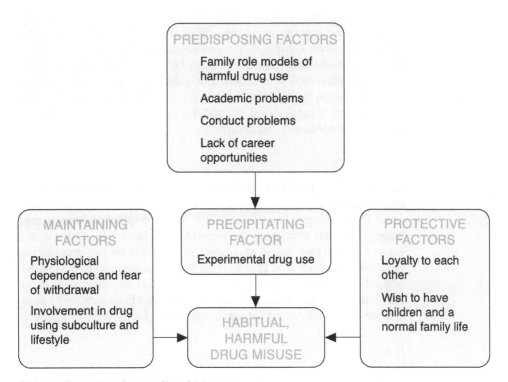

Figure 4.1 Formulation of a case of harmful drug use

Treatment

The initial treatment plan for Betty and Carl involved detoxification followed by either residential treatment in a therapeutic community or out-patient methadone maintenance. Betty and Carl completed detoxification and chose to enter the drug-free therapeutic community. However, they dropped out and relapsed after about 6 weeks. They returned to the inner-city clinic where they both commenced a methadone maintenance programme with adjunctive counselling.

Over a period of a couple of years they engaged in a cycle in which they periodically were detoxified, entered the therapeutic community, dropped out, relapsed and recommenced methadone maintenance with adjunctive counselling.

A case of early drug experimentation

Chas, aged 15, was referred for treatment to a private family therapy institute when his parents found that he had been smoking cannabis with his school friends at a party. He had smoked cannabis a couple of dozen times over a 6-month period and had also taken LSD once. His drug use occurred within the context of a peer group who were experimenting with a range of drugs, and who associated drug use with listening to and playing music.

Developmental history

Chas' developmental history was within normal limits. He was a fine student in the top stream of his school and had come second in his class in the Junior Certificate. He was an able sportsman, an avid chess player and musician. He loved to push himself to the limit in all of his leisure activities and was clearly a risk taker. He had excellent social skills and a wide circle of friends including a girlfriend with whom he had being having a relationship for about 4 months. He had particularly good relationships with his parents.

Family history

Neither of Chas' parents smoked or drank alcohol, and both were solicitors. They worked long hours, but on a matter of principle would not send Chas to boarding school (which was common practice among their peers), believing strongly in the importance of family life. There was a live-in nanny in their house who cared for Chas and his two younger sisters, Triona, aged 8, and Briony, aged 10. The parents were guilt-ridden when they brought the family for the intake interview. Both were of the view that Chas' drug misuse resulted from a failure to be sufficiently available for him during his adolescence due to their heavy work schedules.

Formulation

Chas presented with experimental rather than habitual drug use. The onset was precipitated by availability of cannabis. Chas was predisposed to become involved in experimental drug use because of his tendency for sensation seeking and risk taking. The drug use was maintained through involvement in a drug-using peer group. The principal protective factors were Chas' good premorbid adjustment and the supportiveness and stability of his family.

Treatment

In a series of family therapy sessions involving Chas and his parents, the risks of abusing various types of drug were discussed. Other recreational channels into which Chas could direct his energy were explored. As part of this process, Chas and his father arranged a weekend at an adventure sports centre in Donegal together. The parents were supported in setting strict limits on drug use while Chas lived in their house. In later sessions the focus moved to Chas' career plans.

Comparison of cases

These two cases are very different. The first is a chronic and complex case of habitual and harmful polydrug use and opiate dependence while the second involves only recreational or experimental use of cannabis. They differ along a number of dimensions including the pattern of drug-using behaviour, the types of drug used, the impact of the drugs used, the overall personal adjustment of the young people and the presence of other personal or family-based problems and protective factors.

Clearly drug misuse itself is not always a unidimensional problem. It may occur as part of a wider pattern of life difficulties. The definition and classification of drug misuse is therefore a complex challenge.

Classification, epidemiology, risk factors and protective factors

Within both DSM-IV-TR (American Psychiatric Association, 2000) and ICD-10 (World Health Organization, 1992) a distinction is made between drug dependence and harmful drug use. While substance abuse or harmful drug use refers to drug taking that leads to significant distress, health problems or impairment, drug dependence refers to those situations where there is a compulsive pattern of use involving physiological changes associated with tolerance and withdrawal. Diagnostic criteria for both conditions are given in Table 4.1.

Illegal drug use across the life span is common. In an Irish national survey of over 8,000 15–64 year olds conducted in 2002, the lifetime prevalence of illegal drug use was 19% (National Advisory Committee on Drugs and the Drug and Alcohol Information and Research Unit, 2004). In a UK national survey of over 9,000 11–15-year-olds conducted in 2001, the lifetime prevalence for illegal drug use was 29% (National Centre for Social Research and the National Foundation for Educational Research, 2002). In both surveys cannabis was the most commonly used drug and prevalence was higher among older male teenagers.

DSM-IV-TR	ICD-10

Substance abuse
A. A maladaptive pattern of substance use leading to clinically significant impairment or distress as manifested by one or more of the following occurring within a 12-month period:
  1. Recurrent substance abuse resulting in a failure to fulfil major obligations at work, school or home.
  2. Recurrent substance abuse in situations in which it is physically hazardous.
  3. Recurrent substance-related legal problems.
  4. Continued substance use despite having persistent or recurrent social or interpersonal problems caused by or exacerbated by the effects of the substance.
B. The symptoms have never met the criteria for substance dependence for this type of substance.
	Harmful use
	A pattern of psychoactive substance abuse that is causing harm to health. The damage may be physical (as in cases of hepatitis from the self-administration of injected drugs) or mental (e.g. episodes of depressive disorder secondary to heavy consumption of alcohol).
	
	The fact that pattern of use of a particular substance is disapproved of by a culture or may have led to socially negative consequences such as arrest or marital arguments is not in itself evidence of harmful use.

Substance dependence
A maladaptive pattern of substance abuse, leading to clinically significant impairment or distress, as manifested by three or more of the following occurring at any time in the same 12-month period:
1. Tolerance defined by either
  (a) a need for markedly increased amounts of the substance to achieve intoxication
  (b) markedly diminished effect with continued use of the same amount of the substance
2. Withdrawal as manifested by either of the following:
  (a) the characteristic withdrawal syndrome for the substance
  (b) the same substance is taken to relieve or avoid withdrawal symptoms
3. The substance is taken in larger amounts over a longer period than was intended.
4. There is a persistent desire or unsuccessful efforts to cut down or control substance use.
5. A great deal of time is spent in activities necessary to obtain the substance, use the substance or recover from its effects.
6. Important social, occupational or recreational activities are given up or reduced because of substance use.
7. The substance use is continued despite knowledge of having a persistent or recurrent physical or psychological problem that is likely to have been caused or exacerbated by the substance.
Specify with or without physiological dependence.
	Dependence syndrome
	A cluster of physiological, behavioural and cognitive phenomena in which the use of a substance or a class of substances takes on a much higher priority than other behaviours that once had greater value. Three or more of the following in a 12-month period:
	(a) A strong desire or sense of compulsion to take the substance.
	(b) Difficulty in controlling substance taking behaviour in terms of onset, termination or levels of use.
	(c) A physiological withdrawal state when substance use has ceased or been reduced as evidenced by: the characteristic withdrawal syndrome for the substance; use of the substance to avoid withdrawal symptoms.
	(c) Evidence of tolerance such that increased doses of the substance are required in order to achieve the effects originally produced by lower doses.
	(e) Progressive neglect of alternative pleasures or interests because of psychoactive substance use, increased amount of time necessary to obtain or take the substance or to recover from its effects.
	(f) Persisting with substance use despite clear evidence of overtly harmful consequences such as harm to the liver through excessive drinking, depressive mood states consequent to periods of heavy substance abuse, or drug-related impairment of cognitive functioning.

Note: Adapted from DSM-IV-TR (APA, 2000) and ICD-10 (WHO, 1992).

Experimentation with drugs in adolescence is common (Chung & Martin, 2011; Frischer et al., 2004; Griffin, 2010; Weinberg et al., 2002). Major US and UK surveys concur that by 19 years of age approximately three quarters of teenagers have drunk alcohol; about half have tried cigarettes and cannabis; and about a fifth have tried other street drugs such as solvents, stimulants, hallucinogens or opiates. Between 5% and 10% of teenagers under 19 have drug problems serious enough to require clinical intervention.

Drug use reaches its peak in the early 20s, and most young adults 'mature out' of substance use as they approach their 30s (Jochman & Fromme, 2010). This occurs partly because persistent drug use is incompatible with role changes such as employment, marriage and parenthood that occur in the 20s. Better outcomes occur in cases where there is no comorbid psychopathology; an easy temperament and low levels of sensation seeking and impulsivity; good social problem-solving skills; positive family and school relationships; a longer time in treatment; engagement in post-treatment aftercare; develop-ment of negative attitudes to drug use and positive health-oriented val-ues; and involvement with non-drug-using peers in the post-treatment period (Catalano et al., 2011; Chung & Martin, 2011; Jochman & Fromme, 2010).

About one third of adolescents who use drugs progress to chronic drug abuse or dependence (Catalano et al., 2011). Risk factors in multiple domains, listed in Table 4.2 are associated with the progression from experimental drug use to harmful abuse or dependence. The greater the number of risk factors, the higher the probability of developing serious drug problems.

Clinical features

In clinical practice psychologists take account of significant behavioural, physiological, affective, perceptual, cognitive and interpersonal features when assessing and treating cases of adolescent drug misuse (Heath et al., 2008; Kaminer & Winters, 2011; Scheier, 2010). These are sum-marized in Table 4.3.

Drug misuse is associated with a wide variety of behaviour patterns. These patterns may be described in terms of the age of onset, the duration and frequency of drug use, and the range and amount of substances used. Thus useful distinctions may be made between adolescents who began using drugs early or later in their development; between those who have recently begun experimenting with drugs and those who have a chronic history of drug misuse; between daily users, weekend users and occasional users; between those that confine their drug misuse to a limited range of substances such as alcohol and cannabis and those that use a wide range of substances; and between those who use a little and those who use a great deal of drugs.

Chronic and extensive daily polydrug misuse with an early onset is associated with more difficulties than experimental, occasional use of a limited number of drugs with a recent onset. The former usually entails

TABLE 4.2
Risk factors for adolescent drug use

Domain	Risk factor
Community	• Availability of drugs • Laws and norms favourable to drug use • Media portrayals of drug use • Transitions and mobility • High crime rate, low cohesion and community disorganization • Extreme economic deprivation
Family	• Parental drug use • Favourable parental attitudes to drug use • Poor parenting skills (lack of rules, consequences and supervision of children, and severe or inconsistent punishment) • Family conflict, child abuse and neglect, domestic violence
School	• Academic failure in late primary school • Lack of commitment to school
Peer group	• Involvement with friends who use drugs
Self	• Early and persistent antisocial behaviour • Early onset of drug use • Favourable attitude to drug use • Alienation and rebelliousness • Personality factors (sensation seeking, risk taking, impulsivity and low harm-avoidance)

Note: Adapted from R. F. Catalano, K. P. Haggerty, J. D. Hawkins, & J. Elgin (2011). Prevention of substance use and substance use disorders: Role of risk and protective factors. In Y. Kaminer & K. C. Winters (Eds.), *Clinical manual of adolescent substance abuse treatment* (pp. 30–31). Arlington, VA: American Psychiatric Publishing. At least two longitudinal studies have provided evidence for each risk factor.

a constricted drug-focused lifestyle and multiple associated physical and psychosocial problems, whereas the latter does not. A consistent finding is that only a minority of youngsters progress from experimental to habitual drug misuse and from the use of a single legal drug to multiple legal and illegal drugs. However, most polydrug misusers began with early use of 'gateway' drugs: nicotine, alcohol and cannabis.

Behavioural patterns of drug misuse evolve within specific contexts. Drug-using behaviour often comes to be associated with particular locations, times, modes of administering drugs, physiological and affective states, control beliefs and social situations. With recreational, experimental drug use, weekly oral drug taking at peer-group gatherings while in a positive mood state may occur and young people may have strong beliefs that they are in control of their drug-taking behaviour. With habitual drug use, solitary daily injections to prevent withdrawal and alleviate negative mood may occur. This type of drug use may be accompanied by strong feelings of being unable to control the frequency of drug use or to cut down on the amount taken.

Negative physiological features of drug use may be grouped into those associated with intoxication, those that follow intoxication, those associated with withdrawal following the development of dependence, and medical complications that arise from drug misuse. Stimulants

TABLE 4.3
Clinical features of drug use

Domain	Features
Behaviour	**Drug-using behaviour** • Age of onset • Duration and frequency of use • Range of substances and amount used • Change in pattern over time **Context of drug-using behaviour** • Solitary or social use • Locations and times of use • Modes of administering the drug (oral, nasal or injection) • Physiological state (when seeking excitement or during withdrawal) • Affective state (positive or negative) • Beliefs about ability to control drug use
Negative physiological effects	**Intoxication** • Physical problems due to hyper-arousal (e.g. arrhythmias or dehydration) • Physical problems due to hypo-arousal (e.g. stupor) **Following intoxication** • Exhaustion • Dehydration • Sleep and appetite disturbance • Sexual dysfunction **Withdrawal** • Nausea, vomiting, muscle aches and discomfort following opioid use • Sleep and appetite disturbance following stimulant use • Seizures following sedative use **Long-term medical complications** • Poisoning and overdose Infections including hepatitis and HIV • Liver and kidney damage
Negative emotional effects	**During intoxication** • Fear and anxiety due to unexpected effects of drugs (particularly hallucinogens) **Following intoxication and during withdrawal** • Depressed mood • Irritability and anger • Anxiety
Negative perceptual effects	**During intoxication** • Distressing hallucinations (with hallucinogens and some stimulants) **Following intoxication** • Brief flashbacks or protracted psychotic states (with hallucinogens and some stimulants)
Negative cognitive effects	• Impaired cognitive functioning • Declining academic performance
Negative effects on interpersonal adjustment	• Adolescent–parent conflict • Adolescent–teacher conflict • Induction into drug using peer subculture • Social isolation • Conflict with juvenile justice system • Conflict with heath care system

(such as amphetamines and cocaine) and hallucinogens (such as LSD) lead to physiological changes associated with increased arousal such as tachycardia and blood pressure changes. In cases of extreme intoxication cardiac arrhythmias and seizures may occur. On the other hand, extreme intoxication following the use of alcohol, sedatives, solvents and opioids leads to physiological changes associated with reduced arousal such as drowsiness, stupor and coma. Withdrawal from dependence-producing stimulants entails significant disruption of sleep and increased appetite. Withdrawal from sedatives and alcohol is particularly dangerous because, as part of a syndrome of autonomic hyperactivity, grand mal seizures may occur. Withdrawal from opioids leads to a syndrome characterized by nausea, vomiting, diarrhoea and muscle aches.

There are a wide variety of medical complications associated with drug misuse, ranging from injuries sustained while intoxicated, to liver or kidney damage due to the toxicity of substances abused, to infections including hepatitis and HIV arising from non-sterile injections. With all street drugs there is a risk of death by intentional or accidental overdose or poisoning due to impurities in the drug.

A central reason for many forms of drug use is to induce pharmaco-logically a pleasant affective state. It is therefore not surprising that for many drugs, including alcohol, stimulants, hallucinogens, and opioids, elation is a central feature of initial intoxication. With sedatives, in con-trast, intoxication leads to apathy. Many polydrug misusers refer to drugs by their primary mood-altering characteristics. Thus, a distinction is made between *uppers* and *downers*, and particular cocktails of drugs or sequences of drugs are used to regulate mood in particular ways.

Negative mood states typically follow intoxication, for most classes of drugs. This is particularly true for drugs such as opioids or cocaine that lead to tolerance and dependence. The intense negative mood states that characterize withdrawal syndromes associated with such addictive drugs motivate habitual drug misuse. The health problems, financial difficulties and psychosocial adjustment problems that evolve as part of habitual drug use may also contribute to frequent and intense negative mood states and paradoxically motivate drug users to use more drugs to improve their mood state. Negative mood states typically include some combination of depression, anxiety and anger.

At a perceptual level, some types of drugs, but particularly hallucino-gens, lead to pronounced abnormalities during intoxication and with-drawal. In the current decade, widely used hallucinogens include MDMA (known as *Ecstasy* or *E*) and LSD (known as *acid*). The hallucinations and perceptual distortions that occur during intoxication are not always experienced as pleasant. In some situations they lead to great distress. Brief flashbacks or enduring psychotic states that involve hallucinations and perceptual distortions may occur following intoxication and these invariably are experienced as distressing.

With respect to cognition, alcohol and most street drugs lead to impaired concentration, reasoning and judgement during intoxica-tion and withdrawal. Long-term regular drug misuse in many instances leads to chronic impaired cognitive functioning. The nature, extent and reversibility of this impairment vary depending on the pattern of drug misuse. With teenagers, the impaired cognitive functioning associated with regular drug use may lead to a decline in academic performance.

Drug use may have a negative impact on interpersonal adjustment. Within the family, drug use often leads to conflict or estrangement between adolescents and their parents. At school, drug use may lead to conflict between the adolescent and teachers both because of declining academic performance and because of antisocial behaviour such as theft or aggression associated with drug misuse. Young people who use drugs within a peer-group situation may become deeply involved in a drug-oriented subculture and break ties with peers who do not abuse drugs. Some teenagers develop a solitary drug-using pattern and become increasingly socially isolated as their drug using progresses.

Within the wider community, drug-related antisocial behaviour such as aggression, theft and selling drugs may bring youngsters into contact with the juvenile justice system. Drug-related health problems and drug dependency may bring them into contact with the health service. Conflict between drug users and health-care professionals may arise in situations where youngsters expect to be offered prescribed drugs (such as methadone) as a substitute for street drugs (such as heroin) and this does not occur.

Drug misuse often occurs with comorbid psychological problems including conduct disorder, ADHD, specific learning difficulties, mood disorders, anxiety disorders, schizophrenia and bulimia. In dual diagnosis cases, the relationship between these comorbid psychological problems and drug use is complex (Phillips et al., 2010). Any or all of them may precede drug use and contribute in some way to the development of drug-using behaviour. In addition, drug use may precipitate or maintain some of these other psychological problems. For example, the use of cannabis and hallucinogens may precipitate the onset of schizophrenia. Chronic polydrug misuse may lead to learning difficulties, and chronic alcohol use can lead to amnesic syndrome. Amphetamine usage may lead to anxiety problems. Drug dependence may lead to chronic conduct problems such as assault and theft. Negative drug-related experiences such as losses and drug-related accidents may lead to mood disorder, which in turn may lead to further drug use. Drug use is also an important risk factor for suicide in teenagers.

Theories

Some of the more clinically influential explanations for drug misuse will be presented below. These have been classified into five categories. Biological theories emphasize the role of genetic and physiological factors in harmful drug use and the disease-like nature of addiction. Intrapsychic deficit theories point to the importance of personal psychological vulnerabilities in the aetiology of drug misuse. Cognitive-behavioural theories underline the significance of conditioning and other learning processes in the genesis of drug problems. Systemic theories propose that drug use is strongly influenced by social factors within the family and community. Integrative theories draw on concepts from multiple domains to explain problematic drug use and inform treatment.

Biological theories

Biological formulations are concerned with the disease-like nature of drug addiction, the role of genetic and temperamental predisposing factors in rendering some adolescents vulnerable to drug misuse, and the centrality of neurobiological process to the maintenance of harmful drug use and addictive behaviour.

The disease model

The self-help organization Narcotics Anonymous (NA), which is modelled on Alcoholics Anonymous, takes the view that addiction is a disease that can only be managed, not cured (Narcotics Anonymous, 2008). Within NA it is assumed that this disease is characterized by abnormities of the central nervous system that give rise to uncontrollable urges, cravings and loss of control over drug-using behaviour. According to NA, complete abstinence and regular attendance at NA self-help meetings are essential for managing the disease of addiction. NA self-help meetings are convened and attended by other recovering drug users. Within these meetings a 12-step programme is pursued. The 12 steps of Narcotics Anonymous are set out in Table 4.4.

TABLE 4.4
The 12 steps of Narcotics Anonymous

Step	Principle
1	We admitted we were powerless over our addiction and that our lives had become unmanageable.
2	We came to believe that a power greater than ourselves could restore us to sanity.
3	We made a decision to turn our will and our lives over to God *as we understood Him.*
4	We made a searching and moral inventory of ourselves.
5	We admitted to God, to ourselves and to other human beings the exact nature of our wrongs.
6	We were entirely ready to have God remove all these defects of character.
7	We humbly asked Him to remove our shortcomings.
8	We made a list of all persons we had harmed, and became willing to make amends to them all.
9	We made direct amends to such people whenever possible, except when to do so would injure them or others.
10	We continued to take personal inventory and when we were wrong, promptly admitted it.
11	We sought through prayer and meditation to improve our conscious contact with God *as we understood Him*, praying only for knowledge of His will for the power to carry that out.
12	Having had a spiritual awakening as a result of these steps, we tried to carry this message to addicts, and to practise these principles in all our affairs.

Note: Adapted from Narcotics Anonymous (2008). *Narcotics Anonymous* (sixth edition). Chatsworth, CA: Narcotics Anonymous World Services (p. 17).

In NA meetings addicts invoke spiritual help to manage their addiction, and new members are teamed up with a sponsor to whom they can turn for support when they are tempted to relapse. The 12-step approach was developed in the US in 1935 by Bill Wilson, an alcoholic New York stockbroker and Dr Robert Smith, an alcoholic physician. Their approach and the international self-help organization – Alcoholics Anonymous – that they founded were based on their own experiences of recovery using principles of the Oxford Group, a non-denominational Christian organization (Jaffe & Kelly, 2011). NA derives from this movement.

Long-term, regular attendance at NA meetings is incorporated into some residential treatment programmes for adolescent drug users and is the mainstay of long-term aftercare in many such programmes. The Minnesota Model is a widely used example of this practice. It integrates the 12-step approach with group and family therapy (Winters et al., 2000). There is evidence from a few treatment outcome studies for the effectiveness of such programmes for adolescents recovering from drug dependence. Up to 53% of young people who participate in these programmes remain abstinent compared with 27% of those who do not (Jaffe & Kelly, 2011).

Evidence for a simple disease model as proposed by NA is lacking. Adolescents who use drugs are a heterogeneous group, only one third of whom go on to develop harmful drug use (Catalano et al., 2011). Multiple social, psychological and biological factors are implicated in the aetiology of ongoing harmful drug use within this subgroup. There is no evidence for an underlying unitary disease process. Also, the disease model cannot explain the fact that a proportion of very severe drug users mature out of their addiction in middle age (Jochman & Fromme, 2010).

Genetics

Genetic theories of drug misuse, which propose that vulnerability to addiction is inherited, are partly supported by the findings of twin, family and adoption studies (Hasin & Katz, 2010). These show that a predisposition to drug and alcohol misuse and dependence is moderately heritable, particularly in males, but that genetic influences on experimentation and recreational drug use are less pronounced. Over half of the variance in the genetic predisposition to drug, alcohol and nicotine abuse is shared, and not drug-specific.

However, genetic factors do influence individual differences in sensitivity to, and tolerance for, specific drugs. For example, some males are genetically predisposed to developing alcohol problems, and the characteristic that is transmitted may be a low physiological and subjective response to alcohol (Schuckit, 1994).

Temperament

The temperament hypothesis holds that youngsters who develop drug and alcohol problems do so because they have particular temperamental characteristics that are partially biologically determined, which predispose them to developing poor self-control. Thus, they are apt to engage in a range of risky behaviours including drug use. In support of this hypothesis, difficult temperament in early childhood, sensation-seeking, a low level of harm-avoidance and low self-control in adolescence have consistently been related to teenage drug use (Wills & Ainette, 2010). Youngsters with these temperamental characteristics engage in dangerous novel experiences and risky rule-breaking behaviour of which drug misuse is just one example. Related risky behaviours include driving fast cars or motor bikes, playing high-contact sports, fighting and theft.

Treatment programmes influenced by this position may aim to train youngsters in self-control skills so that they can regulate their tendencies to pursue novel and dangerous experiences including intoxication. Alternatively they may help these adolescents to refocus their energy into demanding and risky prosocial leisure or work activities. In some cases participation in group residential programmes where youngsters are challenged to take risks and master skills such as horse riding, sailing or mountain climbing may be effective, although this is still a controversial approach to treatment (Becker, 2010).

There is little evidence for the effectiveness of wilderness or adventure therapy as a treatment for adolescent drug use. It may be that such programmes lead to abstinence while young people are engaged in treatment, but the risk of relapse after treatment is high unless the wilderness experience is coupled with evidence-based individual or family interventions during and after the wilderness experience. A problem with wilderness therapy, common to all group-based approaches, is that it runs the risk of contagion effects, whereby groups of adolescent drug users on such programmes reinforce each other's positive attitudes to drugs (Dishion & Dodge, 2005).

Neurobiological perspectives

Neurobiological theories of drug use propose that two main systems are central to the development of harmful drug use and dependence (Hutchison, 2010). The first is the incentive motivation network or reward system, which includes the mesolymbic dopamine pathway involving the ventral tegmental area and the nucleus accumbens. The second is the control network or inhibitory system, which includes areas of the prefrontal cortex. These are illustrated in Figure 4.2.

The reward system motivates people to seek things essential for survival such as food, water and sexual mates. This is the system that is activated when positive reinforcement occurs (described below). The inhibitory system helps people consider the consequences of impulsively seeking these sorts of things without regard to possible dangers of doing so.

When adolescents repeatedly use drugs such as nicotine, alcohol, cocaine or heroin, the reward system of the brain that is normally activated to release dopamine by survival-relevant stimuli such as food, water and sexual mates is 'hijacked' into responding as if drugs were required for survival. With repeated use, drugs and cues associated with their use take on increasingly greater motivational significance – a

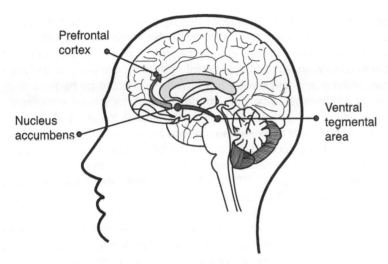

Figure 4.2 The reward system in the human brain. *Note:* The ventral tegmental area is connected to both the nucleus accumbens and the prefrontal cortex via the pathways in the diagram, and dopamine is the principal neurotransmitter involved in the reward system

process known as incentive sensitization – and drug use becomes compulsive. Eventually with chronic use of addictive drugs such as heroin or cocaine, people come to find drug use more rewarding than anything else, and other activities become far less rewarding. Through a combination of classical conditioning (described below) and incentive sensitization, intense motivation to use drugs – experienced as urges or cravings – comes to be activated by cues such as situations or people associated with drug use, and causes relapse even after long periods of abstinence. Loss of control over drug use is associated with greater activation of the brain's reward system relative to the control system when exposed to cues associated with drug use.

Adolescence is a critical period of addiction vulnerability due to the characteristics of the nervous system during this neurodevelopmental stage (Chambers et al., 2003). During adolescence there is a relative over-functioning of the incentive motivation network or reward system and under-functioning of the control network or inhibitory system. Adolescence is associated with increased impulsivity, risk-taking and novelty seeking, and with experiencing novel stimuli as more strongly reinforcing than in adulthood.

From an evolutionary perspective, this increased risk-taking and novelty-seeking may have been adaptive because it motivated adolescents to explore novel behaviours associated with adult roles. Unfortunately, this neurodevelopmental stage renders adolescents vulnerable to experimenting with drugs because drug taking is risky and provides novel experiences. It also renders adolescents vulnerable to addiction because the positive effects of drugs are experienced as more reinforcing than at other stages of the life cycle.

As adolescents mature into adulthood, the inhibitory system's effect on the reward system increases, and consequently risk-taking behaviour decreases. This process is facilitated by pruning of cortical synapses and increased myelination, particularly in the frontal and temporal lobes, which leads to an increase in the efficiency of neural circuitry between the inhibitory system and the reward system. There is some evidence that pruning and myelination are adversely affected by frequent drug use in adolescence, which in turn may account for greater vulnerability to addiction during the teenage years (Lubman & Yücel, 2008).

Neurobiological theories also propose that habitual drug use leads to long-term drug-induced changes in the brain's reward system (Shaham & Hope, 2005). This neuroadaptation accounts for the phenomena of tolerance, dependence, withdrawal, and the high rate of relapse among recovered addicts. With tolerance, a gradual increase in drug dosage is required for intoxication to occur. This increase in dosage in turn leads to physiological dependence and the related phenomenon of unpleasant or hazardous withdrawal symptoms when drug taking ceases abruptly. An attempt to avoid this withdrawal syndrome maintains further drug use. Extensive pharmacological evidence supports the hypothesis that for certain classes of drugs, tolerance, dependence and withdrawal occur. In particular these phenomena are associated with habitual use of alcohol, opioids, stimulants (such as cocaine) and sedatives, but not hallucinogens (such as cannabis, MDMA and LSD) (Kaminer & Marsch, 2011).

Neurobiological theories have led to the inclusion of detoxification in treatment programmes for adolescents who have developed dependence. These theories have also informed the development of pharmacological interventions such as methadone maintenance programmes (Kaminer & Marsch, 2011). In such programmes, youngsters who have developed opioid dependency are prescribed a daily dose of methadone as a substitute for street opioids. Methadone prevents withdrawal symptoms from occurring, but does not give the 'high' associated with heroin. People on methadone can function quite well socially and occupationally, and avoid the dangers of procuring and using street drugs. Methadone maintenance programmes typically include routine monitoring of drug use through urinalysis and adjunctive counselling. They are effective with a proportion of opioid-dependent adolescents.

Intrapsychic deficit theories

A number of theories account for drug misuse in terms of specific intrapsychic vulnerabilities and deficits. Among the more clinically influential are those that invoke personality traits, stress and coping processes, learning difficulties and the challenges of identity formation to explain the development of drug misuse.

Addictive personality

The idea that people are predisposed to develop drug problems or addiction because they have particular personality traits or attributes is often referred to as the addictive personality hypothesis. This is quite similar to the temperament hypothesis mentioned earlier, although the addictive personality hypothesis also assumes that environmental factors play a role in the development of personality.

There is some support for the addictive personality hypothesis. For example, a meta-analysis of data on personality traits of adult drug users showed that high levels of neuroticism and disinhibition and low levels of conscientiousness and agreeableness characterize adult substance use disorders (Kotov et al., 2010).

Stress and coping through self-medication

Stress and coping formulations propose that drugs are used to alleviate negative affective states, and specific drugs are chosen because of their unique effects. This theory is often referred to as the self-medication hypothesis (Grunberg et al., 2011; Khantzian, 2003). From this perspective drugs use is conceptualized as a strategy for coping with negative mood states or psychological disorders such as depression, posttraumatic stress disorder (PTSD) or psychosis that have arisen in response to a range of current or past adversities such as abuse, neglect, bereavement, armed combat or problematic parent–child relationships.

There are many versions of this broad hypothesis. For example, psychoanalytic theorists have argued that low levels of care and high levels of criticism from primary caregivers in early childhood may lead to insecure attachment, unmet dependency needs, harsh superego development and low-self esteem. Drugs are used, according to this formulation, to alleviate the negative mood states that arise from these detrimental formative experiences (Wieder & Kaplan, 1969). Another variant of this position proposes that where adolescents have suffered sexual abuse or exposure to other traumatic events, drugs may be used to deal with the symptoms of posttraumatic stress disorder or depression that have arisen from these adverse experiences. A third variant is that teenagers with a genetic vulnerability for psychosis may use drugs to cope with prodromal psychotic symptoms.

There is little doubt that in a proportion of cases adolescents use drugs to deal with stress, trauma and related psychopathology. In clinical samples between 70% and 80% of cases have comorbid substance use and other psychological disorders (Kaminer et al., 2011a). However, in many cases drug use is not preceded by stress or psychopathology. Rather stress and psychological difficulties arise as a result of harmful drug use. Where drug use occurs with comorbid psychological disorders such as PTSD, depression or psychosis, both the drug-use problem and the comorbid difficulties require treatment. There is no evidence to suggest that treating comorbid disorders alleviates drug misuse or addiction.

Learning difficulties

Another intrapsychic deficit that has been suggested to predispose youngsters to developing drug misuse is learning difficulties. According to this position, children who have learning difficulties and who experience academic failure at school do not develop a strong commitment to achieving academic goals and turn to drug use as an alternative lifestyle (Mason, 2010). Interventions that derive from this perspective aim to provide adolescents with a school curriculum appropriate to their ability levels and a participative ethos that includes teenagers and their parents in school activities so as to enhance commitment to academic goals (Griffin & Botvin, 2010).

Identity formation

Erik Erikson (1950, 1968) argued that the lack of an established identity during adolescence is a normative intrapsychic deficit and that participation in a drug-using subculture is one of a wide range of lifestyles that may be explored during the adolescent's search for adult identity and autonomy from parental control. Recent studies have shown that young people who consolidate their identities in early adulthood engage in less drug use and other risky behaviours than those who have difficulty with identity formation (e.g., Arnett, 2005; Schwartz et al., 2010).

Treatment programmes based on this position focus on facilitating individuation and developing alternatives to drug taking as a route to autonomy and identity formation. The treatment of chronic drug dependence in drug-free therapeutic communities such as Synanon, Daytop and Phoenix House in the US is consistent with this theoretical position (DeLeon, 2000). Therapeutic communities facilitate the development of drug-free lifestyles and identities by offering a context within which adolescent can engage in structured community living and therapeutic activities with ex-addicts who have successfully become drug-free. Research on therapeutic communities has shown that they can be effective for a proportion of young adult addicts who are motivated to engage in treatment (DeLeon, 2000; Smith et al., 2006). Therapeutic communities are probably not an appropriate intervention for young adolescents.

Cognitive-behavioural theories

Cognitive-behavioural theories focus on the role of classical and operant conditioning and cognitive processes in the maintenance of drug misuse.

Operant conditioning

Operant conditioning or instrumental learning theories propose that drug use is maintained initially by positive reinforcement associated with the mood-elevating effects of drugs and later, in the case of dependence-producing substances such as alcohol, cocaine or heroin, by negative reinforcement, where drug use prevents aversive withdrawal symptoms (e.g. O'Brien et al., 1992; Schulteis & Koob, 1996). Treatment programmes based on this formulation include initial detoxification so drugs lose their negative reinforcement value, and the provision of positive reinforcement for alternatives to drug-using behaviours.

The Adolescent Contingency Reinforcement Approach (A-CRA) is an evidence-based therapy in which operant conditioning is the central intervention (Dakof et al., 2011; Godley et al., 2006). With A-CRA, therapists work with adolescents and their parents, both alone and in conjoint sessions, to identify reinforcers or rewards that young people value and that will improve the quality of their lives, and reduce drug use. The process begins with a functional analysis of both drug using and prosocial behaviour to identify situations that trigger drug use and prosocial behaviours, and related reinforcers. Adolescents are helped to set goals and plan prosocial activities to improve their quality of life and, with their parents, arrangements are made for them to receive reinforcement for doing so. Adolescents and parents engage in communication, problem-solving, and relapse management skills training. Homework assignments are set and reviewed in all sessions, and drug use is monitored with regular urinalysis testing. A-CRA typically spans about 3 months of weekly sessions. In a series of trials A-CRA has been found to be effective for adolescents with a range of drug use problems (Waldron & Turner, 2008).

Classical conditioning

Wikler (1973) has offered an explanation of relapse following detoxification in people who have developed tolerance and dependence using a classical conditioning framework. According to this position, certain conditioned stimuli (CSs) or cues in the environments of drug users elicit withdrawal symptoms and craving (conditioned responses or CRs), because in the past these cues have been associated with withdrawal symptoms that are conceptualized as unconditioned stimuli (UCSs)

In cue exposure treatment, based on this formulation, exposure to withdrawal and craving eliciting cues (CSs) without engaging in drug taking leads to extinction of the CRs, particularly cravings. Adolescents enter situations that elicit craving, observe videotapes or audiotapes of such situations, or undergo imaginal exposure to such situations and concurrently use a variety of coping strategies to tolerate their discomfort and avoid drug-taking.

There is controversy about the effectiveness of cue exposure treatment, and few studies have evaluated it in the treatment of adolescent drug users (Conklin & Tiffany, 2002; Drummond et al., 1995).

Cognitive-behaviour therapy

Within cognitive-behaviour therapy (CBT) models, drug use is conceptualized as a set of learned behaviours and related cognitions (Kaminer et al., 2011b). Drug-use behaviours, and related urges, cravings, beliefs and expectations about the risks and benefits of drug use and the degree to which drug use can be controlled, are assumed to be learned through classical and operant conditioning as well as through cognitive learning processes.

Witkiewitz and Marlatt (2004) argue that in high-risk situations, drug users who have well-rehearsed coping strategies and use them effectively develop increased self-efficacy beliefs and a decreased probability of relapse. Those who have poor coping strategies are driven to relapse by their low self-efficacy beliefs in their capacity to avoid substance use and their expectations of a high from drug use. This leads to the abstinence violation effect (AVE), where guilt and a sense of loss of control predominate. With the AVE people may say to themselves, 'I've relapsed. I've let myself and my family down. I have no control over my drug taking. There is no point in trying to stop now.' This failure experience in turn leads to an increased probability of a minor slip becoming a major relapse.

CBT for drug use involves helping adolescents become motivated to reduce or stop drug use and develop and implement skills and coping strategies to avoid relapse. Motivational interviewing or motivational enhancement therapy is the main intervention used to facilitate engagement in treatment (Miller & Rollnick, 2002; Tevyaw & Monti, 2004). With motivational interviewing the psychologist invites the young person to describe their drug-using behaviour and consider the pros and cons of continued drug use; gives normative feedback on the effects of the young person's drug use and options for changing drug-using behaviour; invites the young person to make a decision about changing their drug use; and supports their self-efficacy beliefs about reducing drug use.

CBT programmes help young people set drug-reduction goals, identify situational cues that elicit urges or cravings to use drugs, and develop skills for drug refusal and strategies for coping with urges and cravings to use drugs in risky situations where they might relapse. In CBT programmes young people also develop skills for managing negative emotions including anger, anxiety and depression without recourse to drug use. Finally, CBT programmes help young people develop communication and problem-solving skills and use these to increase social support and develop a drug-free lifestyle.

Results from a series of controlled trials support the effectiveness of both individual and group-based CBT for adolescent drug use. Furthermore, contagion effects common in group treatment of antisocial youngsters have not been found in trials of CBT for adolescent drug misuse (Dishion & Dodge, 2005). Mindfulness-based meditation as a relapse prevention strategy has recently been incorporated into CBT for drug use (Zgierska et al., 2009).

Systemic theories

Systemic theories of drug misuse propose that family problems and challenges in the wider social system such as social disadvantage, deviant peer-group membership and drug availability are central to the aetiology of drug problems.

Family systems approaches

The ideas that adolescent drug misuse is caused or maintained by parental drug use, poor parenting skills and family disorganization are some of the more important family systems hypotheses. Empirical studies have established an association between each of these factors and adolescent drug use (Kliewer, 2010). In families where parents use drugs, adolescents may learn drug using behaviour patterns directly through a process of modelling. They may acquire positive attitudes to drugs through exposure to their parents' permissive attitudes. Furthermore, parents' drug-using behaviour may compromise their capacity to parent their adolescents adequately. If parents do not jointly establish clear rules prohibiting drug use and consistently apply clear consequences for violating these rules, then adolescent drug use is more likely to occur.

Parenting problems may occur within a broad pattern of family disorganization associated with adolescent drug use. The pattern may include parental psychological problems; lack of a clear parental alliance and clear intergenerational boundaries between adolescents and parents; poor family communication, problem-solving and conflict-resolution skills; extreme family enmeshment or disengagement; and difficulty addressing the family life-cycle transitions, especially that of facilitating adolescent autonomy. Within such disorganized families drug misuse may serve an organizing function, since it introduces certain predictable routines into family life and provides a focus for parental concern, which may increase family cohesion and prevent parental separation.

Multidimensional family therapy (MDFT, Liddle, 2010), functional family therapy (FFT, Waldron & Brody, 2010), brief strategic family therapy (BSFT, Robbins et al., 2010) and multisystemic therapy (MST, Henggeler & Schaeffer, 2010) are evidence-based approaches to treating adolescent drug misuse based on systemic theory (Waldron & Turner, 2008). All of these approaches involve working directly with adolescents and their parents to improve family functioning as an avenue to reducing adolescent drug misuse. Parents are helped to establish clear rules prohibiting drug use and consistently apply clear consequences for violating these rules.

These approaches also facilitate the development of positive family relationships and good family communication, problem-solving and conflict-resolution skills. There is a progression from initial engagement, to becoming drug-free, to addressing family issues associated with fostering adolescent development and autonomy, to disengagement, where the emphasis is on planning for relapse prevention. With these family-based approaches, treatment typically involves conjoint family sessions, separate sessions with adolescents and parents, and sessions with involved health, social service and juvenile justice professionals and school staff, as required. Evidence from controlled trials shows that evidence-based family-oriented approaches are very effective for adolescent drug-use problems (Waldron & Turner, 2008).

Extrafamilial social problems

Hypotheses about extrafamilial social problems propose that social disadvantage and deviant peer-group membership, as well as drug availability, cause and maintain drug misuse.

Social disadvantage

Social disadvantage theories argue that neighbourhoods character-ized by poverty, low socio-economic status, high population density and high crime rates create a context within which drug misuse can flourish. This is because drugs offer an escape from the multiple stresses associated with this type of social environment; they are avail-able in these environments; and they are socially sanctioned within a crime-oriented subculture (Catalano et al., 2011; Gardner et al., 2010). Social disadvantage theory entails the view that effective intervention programmes support families, enhance educational and vocational opportunities for young people, and strengthen communities. Evidence from prevention studies supports the effectiveness of parent training programmes during the prenatal, infancy, childhood and adolescent stages of the life cycle; school-based and after-school programmes that enhance social and academic competence; vocational programmes that create youth employment opportunities linked to ongoing educa-tion; and community-based programmes that strengthen community cohesion and reduce alcohol and drug availability to young people (Catalano et al., 2011).

Deviant peer-group membership

Problem-behaviour theory is an example of a formulation that links drug misuse to deviant peer-group membership. This theory pro-poses that drug use is one of a series of interrelated problem be-haviours, which reflect adherence to unconventional attitudes held by a deviant peer group (Catalano et al., 2011; Jessor & Jessor, 1977). Adolescents engage in these behaviours to obtain acceptance from their deviant peer group and for personal excitement. Young people are predisposed to developing problem behaviours if they are alien-ated from mainstream society. This may be reflected in their weak attachments to parents, their rejection of authority, their valuing independence more than academic achievement, and their lack of religiosity. A wealth of survey data supports this theory (Andrews & Hops, 2010).

Treatment programmes based on the hypothesis that deviant peer-group membership is central to adolescent drug abuse provide residen-tial peer-group-based treatment, within the context of a therapeutic community, where the rejection of drug use is part of the therapeutic community's subculture. Therapeutic communities as a treatment for drug use have been mentioned earlier, in the section on identify forma-tion, where it was noted that they can be effective for a proportion of young adult addicts, but may not be appropriate for young adolescents (DeLeon, 2000; Smith et al., 2006).

Availability

Hypotheses about availability suggest that lenient laws or inadequately enforced laws concerning teenage use of nicotine, alcohol and street drugs increase the probability of adolescent drug use. This type of theory has few treatment implications but suggests important avenues for prevention. Prevention programmes, according to this view, should promote stricter drug-related legislation, and the enforcement of laws affecting availability of drugs to teenagers. The availability hypotheses has largely been supported by empirical tests, and prevention programmes based on it have been moderately effective (Toumbourou et al., 2007).

Social norms

That social norms may contribute to the development of drug misuse is a widely held view. There is strong evidence from empirical studies for a causal link between exposure to favourable media attitudes to nicotine, alcohol and illicit drug use and drug-using behaviour (Nunez-Smith et al., 2010). One implication of this position is that the risks of drug use may be reduced by policies and legislation that prohibit positive media-based messages about nicotine, alcohol and drug use (Snyder & Nadorff, 2010).

Integrative theories

Two important integrative theories that draw on concepts from multiple domains are Prochaska and DiClemente's transtheoretical stages of change model (Prochaska et al., 1992) and West's (2006) synthetic model of motivation and addiction.

Transtheoretical stages of change model

From an analysis of 24 schools of psychotherapy, Prochaska and DiClemente identified five stages of therapeutic change which they labelled pre-contemplation, contemplation, preparation, action and maintenance (Prochaska et al., 1992). They also found, by surveying clients and therapists engaged in therapy, that specific techniques were maximally effective in helping clients make the transition from one stage of change to the next.

The techniques identified in this survey fall into the categories of support, belief exploration and consulting to behavioural change. In most schools of therapy there tends to be a progression from support, to belief-system exploration, to behavioural change consultation. Prochaska and DiClemente have applied their transtheoretical stages of change model and related interventions to the treatment of addictive behaviours including drug use (DiClemente, 2003). According to this model, in the pre-contemplation stage, the provision of support creates a climate within which adolescents may ventilate their feelings and express their views about their drug problems and life situation. Such support facilitates movement from the pre-contemplation to the contemplation stage.

Facilitating the exploration of beliefs about the pros and cons of modifying drug use, according to the model, may promote movement from the contemplation to the planning stage. In the transition from the planning to the action stage the most useful interventions are helping adolescents examine various action plans for reducing drug use, and facilitating the development of an emotional commitment to change. In moving from the action to the maintenance stage the focus is on helping adolescents integrate positive changes into their lives and avoidance or management of relapses.

Prochaska and DiClemente argue that five principal categories of factors are involved in symptom maintenance: situational maintaining factors, maladaptive cognitions, interpersonal conflicts, family conflicts and intrapsychic conflicts. These factors are hierarchically organized, with earlier factors being more responsive to change than later factors. Effective therapy follows one of three strategies once the person has passed through to the action stage. The first strategy is to target the situations that maintain drug use and only shift to the cognitive level or higher levels if no change occurs. The second strategy is to focus on the family systems level, which is the key level within the hierarchy typically involved in maintaining drug use. A third strategy is to target all levels, by, for example, offering individual work to alter maladaptive cognitions and intrapsychic conflicts associated with drug use; peer-group work and social skills training to target interpersonal conflicts or deviant peer-group membership; and family work to address family conflicts and drug misuse maintaining family interaction patterns.

The central prediction of this model is that stage-specific interventions will be more effective than those that are not stage-specific. Little research has been conducted to test this hypothesis with adolescent drug users, and results from studies of adults are mixed (West, 2006). However, the theory has been very influential clinically and has informed the development of procedures such as harm reduction (Marlatt & Witkiewitz, 2010) and motivational interviewing (Macgowan & Engle, 2010), where the aim is not to promote abstinence or reduction in drug use, but to prevent drug-related harm and facilitate movement towards planning and action stages. Needle exchanges and provision of safe injection sites are examples of harm-reduction interventions. Motivational interviewing has been described above in the section on CBT.

West's synthetic theory of motivation and addiction

Robert West (2006), a major critic of the stages of change model, proposed that addiction is not a matter of conscious choice and progression through invariant stages, but a reward-seeking behaviour over which a person has lost control. It arises from abnormalities in the motivational system, many of which are not conscious, or abnormalities in the physical and social environment that are conducive to prioritizing drug use. Abnormalities in the motivational system may be caused by drug use, for example withdrawal symptoms and the acquired drive to seek drugs to alleviate these, or they may be due to predisposing factors such as negative affectivity or impulsivity.

West explains drug addiction in terms of his synthetic theory of motivation, which is also referred to as PRIME theory. PRIME is an acronym for plans, responses, impulses and inhibitory forces (felt as urges), motives (felt as wants or needs) and evaluative beliefs. According to PRIME theory, adolescents' conscious plans and evaluations influence their drug use through motives, and motives influence drug use through impulses which are determined in large part by non-conscious processes. The motivational system that underpins drug use is influenced by past experiences through non-conscious processes such as habituation and sensitization, classical and operant conditioning, and conscious processes such as cognitive learning. However, it is also influenced by stimuli in the immediate internal and external environment. Therefore, an adolescent's motivation to use drugs is inherently unstable and changes from moment to moment.

Treatment based on this model capitalizes on the instability of the motivational system by bolstering the adolescent's motivation to exercise restraint or temporarily suppress the forces driving drug use and addressing relevant predisposing factors. This may be done by, for example, modifying relevant emotional or environmental factors such as negative mood states induced by stressful life events, drug availability, peer pressure to use drugs, or family disorganization. According to West's model, treatment sessions should be scheduled close together so that they have a cumulative effect in altering the adolescent's feelings, impulses and beliefs that motivate them to use drugs.

West's formulation integrates a vast body of animal and human research on the psychology, sociology and neurobiology of addiction, and offers an alternative to the oversimplified, but intuitively appealing, stages of change model described earlier. However, it has not yet led to the development of treatments for adolescent drug use.

Assessment

Assessment of adolescents with drug problems may be conducted by multidisciplinary teams that include clinical psychologists and medical staff, and should involve interviews with the adolescent and parents or carers. Brief questionnaires such as the Personal Experience Screening Questionnaire (PESQ, Winters, 1991) may be used to screen for drug use. Comprehensive questionnaires such as the Personal Experience Inventory (PEI, Winters & Henly, 1989) and comprehensive structured interviews such as the Global Appraisal of Individual Needs (GAIN, Dennis, 1998) may be used for a more thorough assessment of drug use severity and personal, family and school-related adjustment problems.

Physical examination and regular urinalysis may be included in the assessment of adolescents with drug problems. Physical examination facilitates the identification and treatment of drug-related physical

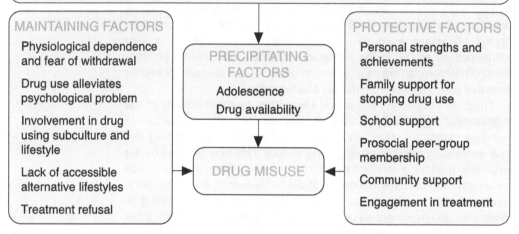

PREDISPOSING FACTORS

Personal factors – Genetic vulnerability to addiction, traits of impulsivity, risk taking and rebelliousness, and psychopathology, e.g., conduct disorder, ADHD, and mood or anxiety disorders

Family factors – Role models of harmful drug use, parental maladjustment, parenting problems, family disorganization, and family adversity

School factors – Learning disability, school failure, lack of educational resources, and lack of career opportunities

Social factors – Deviant peer-group membership; community, laws and media supportive of drug use

MAINTAINING FACTORS

Physiological dependence and fear of withdrawal

Drug use alleviates psychological problem

Involvement in drug using subculture and lifestyle

Lack of accessible alternative lifestyles

Treatment refusal

PRECIPITATING FACTORS

Adolescence

Drug availability

DRUG MISUSE

PROTECTIVE FACTORS

Personal strengths and achievements

Family support for stopping drug use

School support

Prosocial peer-group membership

Community support

Engagement in treatment

Figure 4.3 General formulation model for adolescent drug misuse

complications including hepatitis and HIV infection. Awareness of the extent of physical problems may motivate adolescents and their families to engage in treatment. Regular urinalysis provides reliable information on relapse, which is critical for effective treatment of habitual drug users. A formulation is drawn up that integrates assessment information; highlights predisposing, precipitating, maintaining and protective factors; and indicates whether the drug problem reflects transient experimentation or a more entrenched pattern of habitual drug misuse. This formulation is used to guide intervention. A general clinical formulation model for adolescent drug misuse is given in Figure 4.3.

Treatment

Treatment of adolescent drug use should aim to engage the adolescent and parents or carers in therapy, motivate them to use therapy to work towards reducing adolescent drug use, and address the young person's personal, family- and school-related difficulties. Reviews of treatment outcome studies show that family-oriented approaches such as MDFT, FFT, BSFT, MST and A-CRA, and individual approaches such as CBT, combined with motivational interviewing are effective interventions for adolescent drug use (Dakof et al., 2011;

Kaminer et al., 2011b; Waldron & Turner, 2008; Williams & Chang, 2000). Literature reviews consistently show that for adolescents living with their parents, evidence-based family-oriented treatment programmes are the treatment of choice for drug problems because they have the best outcome, involve the young person's family as a treatment resource, and modify family problems that may be maintaining adolescent drug use (e.g., Williams & Chang, 2000). Family-based approaches have been shown to be effective for engaging adolescent drug users and their networks in therapy, for reducing drug misuse, for improving associated behaviour problems, for improving overall family functioning and for preventing relapse.

Where there are significant obstacles to involving families in treatment, CBT combined with initial motivational interviewing is the intervention of choice. Motivational interviewing facilitates engagement in therapy and through CBT young people develop skills to reduce drug use, communicate, problem-solve and deal with relapses. Where adolescents have developed physiological dependence, psychological interventions may be combined with initial detoxification or with long-term pharmacological interventions such as methadone maintenance for opioid dependence (Kaminer & Marsch, 2011). For chronic drug problems with a high risk of relapse, long-term aftercare though regular attendance at 12-step NA meetings may prevent relapse (Jaffe & Kelly, 2011). This overall approach to treatment of adolescent drug use is consistent with international best practice guidelines (American Academy of Child and Adolescent Psychiatry, 2005; Department of Health 2007; NICE, 2008b).

Controversies

A central controversy in the field of adolescent drug use concerns the stability over time of the motivation to use drugs. In the stages of change model, Prochaska and DiClemente argue that motivation to cease drug use evolves through a series of relatively stable and sequential stages of change from pre-contemplation through contemplation, planning and action to maintenance (DiClemente, 2003; Proschaska et al., 1992).

In contrast, Robert West (2006) argues that motivation to cease drug use is inherently unstable. He has put forward the following arguments against the stages of change model. The precise boundaries of any of the stages of change are arbitrarily drawn in research studies; for example, a person is in the planning stage if their plans apply to the next 30 days. There is no evidence that stages are always stable and that progression through them is invariably orderly. There is also no evidence that drug users' attempts to quit are always guided by conscious, coherent plans, and much evidence that unconscious processes, classical and operant conditioning, erratic impulses, and highly specific environmental cues affect the development and cessation of drug use. In West's (2006) synthetic theory of addiction he proposes that abnormalities of the motivational system are central to addiction, that the motivational system is inherently unstable, and that important aspects of the motivation to use or abstain from drugs are governed by unconscious learning processes and impulses. According to West, interventions should not stimulate adolescents to think about what 'stage' they are in or be matched to such stages, but rather they should put maximum tolerable pressure on the young person to cease drug use.

A related controversy concerns harm-reduction programmes such as needle exchanges, safe injection sites, and the provision of free tests of the quality of MDMA sold at raves. Advocates of harm-reduction programmes argue that in the absence of highly effective treatments that all drug users and addicts are highly motivated to use, mortality or morbidity due to using street drugs of unknown quality under adverse conditions may be reduced by pragmatic and humane harm-reduction interventions (Marlatt & Witkiewitz, 2010). Critics of this approach argue that harm-reduction interventions send a message to adolescents that drug use is acceptable (Leshner, 2008).

Summary

Habitual drug misuse in adolescence is of particular concern to clinical psychologists because it may have a negative long-term effect on adolescents and an intergenerational effect on their children. A conservative estimate is that between 5% and 10% of teenagers under 19 have drug problems serious enough to require clinical intervention.

A distinction is made between drug dependence and drug misuse. While drug misuse refers to using drugs in such a way that the person is harmed, drug dependence refers to those situations where there is a compulsive pattern of use that may involve physiological changes that accompany the phenomena of tolerance and withdrawal. Drug misuse is associated with a wide variety of behaviour patterns which may be described in terms of the age of onset, the duration of drug misuse, the frequency of use, the range of substances used, and the amount used.

Physiological features of drug misuse may be grouped into those associated with intoxication, those that follow intoxication, those associated with withdrawal following the development of dependence, and medical complications that arise. At an affective level, negative mood states typically follow the euphoria of intoxication for most classes of drugs. At a perceptual level, some types of drug, but particularly hallucinogens, lead to pronounced abnormalities during intoxication and withdrawal. With respect to cognition, most street drugs lead to impaired concentration, reasoning and judgement during intoxication and withdrawal. Long-term regular drug misuse in many instances leads to impaired cognitive functioning. Drug misuse may have an impact on interpersonal adjustment leading to family, school and peer-group-based difficulties.

Drug misuse often occurs with comorbid psychological problems including conduct disorder, ADHD, specific learning difficulties, mood disorders, anxiety disorders, psychosis and bulimia. The relationship between these comorbid psychological problems and drug misuse is complex. Explanations for drug misuse focus on biological factors, Intrapsychic deficits, cognitive-behavioural learning processes, social factors and multiple factors from these four domains.

Biological formulations are concerned with the disease-like nature of drug addiction, the role of genetic and temperamental predisposing factors in rendering some adolescents vulnerable to drug misuse, and the centrality of neurobiological processes to the maintenance of harmful drug use and addictive behaviour. Biological theories have informed the development of pharmacological treatments for drug problems such as detoxification and methadone maintenance, and have been endorsed by the self-help movement Narcotics Anonymous to justify its claims that addiction is a medical disease.

With regard to theories that emphasize the role of intrapsychic vulnerabilities and deficits, among the more clinically influential are those that invoke personality traits, stress and coping processes, learning difficulties and the challenges of identity formation to explain the development of drug misuse. These perspectives have informed the development of a range of psychotherapeutic approaches to drug misuse including drug-free therapeutic communities. Cognitive-behavioural theories explain drug problems and their treatment in terms of classical and operant conditioning and various cognitive learning processes. CBT, motivational interviewing, contingency management and cue-exposure treatments for dug misuse developed within the cognitive-behavioural tradition.

Systemic theories of drug misuse propose that family problems and challenges in the wider social system, such as social disadvantage, deviant peer-group membership and drug availability are central to the aetiology of drug problems. Family therapy and community-oriented approaches to the prevention of drug use are based on systemic theories.

With regard to integrative theories, Prochaska and DiClemente propose that the motivation to cease drug use evolves through a series of sequential stages and effective intervention must be matched to the adolescent's readiness to change. In contrast, West's synthetic theory of addiction proposes that the motivational system is inherently unstable, and that effective interventions place maximum tolerable pressure on the young person to cease drug use.

The assessment of adolescents with drug problems should be multidisciplinary and involve both medical and psychological evaluation. Treatment of adolescent drug use should aim to engage the adolescent and parents or carers in therapy, motivate them to use therapy to work towards reducing adolescent drug use, and address the young person's personal, family- and school-related difficulties. Evidence-based family therapy is the treatment of choice for adolescent drug problems. There is controversy about the value of harm-reduction interventions for drug problems, with one group proposing that such interventions improve public health while another argues that they give adolescents the message that drug misuse is acceptable.

Questions

- What are the principal differences between drug experimentation and harmful drug use?
- What are the areas that need to be covered when offering a comprehensive description of the clinical features of an adolescent with drug problems?
- How prevalent is drug misuse?
- What are the main risk factors for drug misuse?
- What are the main biological, psychological and integrative theories of drug misuse and the main research findings relevant to these theories?
- What are the main evidence-based approaches to the assessment and treatment of drug misuse?
- Are harm-avoidance strategies for addressing drug misuse justified?
- Should parents be included in the treatment of adolescent drug problems?

FURTHER READING

Professional

- Carr, A. (2006). *Handbook of child and adolescent clinical psychology: A contextual approach* (second edition). London: Routledge (Chapter 16).
- Kaminer, Y. & Winters, K. (2011). *Clinical manual of adolescent substance abuse treatment.* Arlington, VA: American Psychiatric Publishing.
- Weisz, J. & Kazdin, A. (2010). *Evidence-based psychotherapies for children and adolescents* (second edition). New York: Guilford Press.

WEBSITES

- AACAP (American Academy of Child and Adolescent Psychiatry) practice parameters for the treatment of substance use disorders: www.aacap.org/cs/root/member_information/practice_information/practice_parameters/practice_parameters

- BSFT manual for Adolescent Drug misuse:
  http://archives.drugabuse.gov/txmanuals/bsft/bsftindex.html
- Chestnut Health Systems manuals for MDFT, CBT, A-CRA and GAIN are available:
  www.chestnut.org/LI/cyt/products
- Drugscope, UK:
  www.drugscope.org.uk
- Drug Treatment Centre Board, Ireland:
  www.addictionireland.ie
- GIlbert Botvin's Life Skills Training drug misuse prevention programme:
  www.lifeskillstraining.com
- Howard Liddle's Multidimensional Family Therapy (MDFT):
  www.miami.edu/ctrada
- Jim Alexander and Tom Sexton's Functional Family Therapy (FFT):
  www.fftinc.com
- José Szapocznik's Brief Strategic Family Therapy (BSFT):
  www.bsft.org
- Narcotics Anonymous:
  www.na.org
- National Institute on Drug Abuse, USA:
  www.nida.nih.gov
- National Treatment Agency for Substance Misuse, UK:
  www.nta.nhs.uk
- NICE (National Institute for Clinical Excellence) guidelines for treating drug misuse:
  http://guidance.nice.org.uk/Topic/MentalHealthBehavioural
- Scott Henggeler's Multisystemic Therapy (MST):
  http://mstservices.com
- Substance Abuse and Mental Health Services Administration, USA:
  www.samhsa.gov

5 Anxiety disorders

Introduction

While normal fear is adaptive and prevents people from entering threatening situations, with anxiety disorders people develop irrational fears of situations that do not threaten their survival (Antony & Stein, 2009a). They also develop non-adaptive behavioural patterns associated with avoidance of feared situations or experiences. For people with anxiety disorders, their fears are accompanied by intense physiological arousal shown by some or all of the following features: accelerated heart rate, sweating, trembling, sensations of shortness of breath or smothering, feelings of choking, chest pain, nausea, numbness or tingling, and chills or hot flushes. The person may also experience dizziness, derealization (feelings of unreality) or depersonalization (feelings of being detached from the self).

Within DSM-IV-TR (American Psychiatric Association, 2000) and ICD-10 (World Health Organization, 1992), distinctions are made between a variety of anxiety disorders based on the developmental timing of their emergence, the classes of stimuli that elicit the anxiety, the pervasiveness and topography of the anxiety response, and the role of clearly identifiable factors in the aetiology of the anxiety. The following are the principal anxiety disorders described in DSM-IV-TR and ICD-10.

- Separation anxiety
- Phobias
- Generalized anxiety disorder
- Panic disorder
- Posttraumatic stress disorder
- Obsessive compulsive disorder

Descriptions of these conditions and case examples are given below. This is followed by a consideration of the clinical features, epidemiology, risk factors, course, theoretical explanations, assessment and treatment of anxiety disorders.

Separation anxiety disorder

With separation anxiety disorder, which occurs most commonly in children, a recurrent and persistent fear is aroused when separation from parents or caregivers is anticipated (American Psychiatric Association, 2000; Furr et al., 2009; Pine & Klein, 2008; World Health Organization, 1992). Separation anxiety disorder is characterized by persistent, excessive worry about losing, or about possible harm befalling, a parent. In some instances nightmares about these issues may occur. Separation anxiety is also characterized by recurrent headaches, stomach-aches, nausea and vomiting. There may be a refusal to sleep without being near parents, and although not the only cause of school refusal, it is one of the most common causes.

Case example of separation anxiety

Barry, aged 11, was referred because he had not attended school for 2 months, following the Easter holidays in the year prior to his entry to secondary school. The family doctor could find no organic basis for the abdominal pain or headaches of which he periodically complained, particularly on the mornings when his mother asked him how his health was. Barry's friends visited him at weekends and he went cycling with them regularly. But on Monday mornings he was unable to get to school both because of the abdominal pains and also because of a sense of foreboding that something dangerous might happen to his mother. If forced to go to school, he would become tearful or aggressive.

Family history

While there was no serious threat to Barry's mother's health, she had a variety of complaints including rheumatism and epilepsy which compromised her sense of well-being. Her epilepsy was usually well controlled, but she had experienced a number of grand mal fits in the 6 months prior to Barry's referral. Barry was one of four children and all had histories of school refusal. Barry's three brothers aged 20, 25 and 30 all lived at home and had few friends or acquaintances. His eldest brother ran a computer software business from his bedroom. All of the boys had very close relationships with their mother and distant relationships with their father. The father, Martin, who was a healthy man, ran a grocery shop and worked long hours. He left early in the morning and returned late at night. He was very concerned for Barry's welfare and believed that his wife mollycoddled the boy. However, he was reluctant to challenge her because he did not want to upset her. The parents had a history of marital discord and over the year prior to the referral had strongly disagreed about how to handle Barry's separation anxiety.

Two of Barry's maternal uncles had psychological adjustment difficulties and both had been on medication, although details of their problems were unavailable. These uncles had lived at home with their mother until her death. They, Barry's mother and her sister Gina had very close relationships with their mother, Mary, but distant relationships with their father. Barry's mother's parents had also quarrelled about how best to manage the children, with Mary being lenient and her husband being strict. Thus, the pattern of relationships in Barry's mother's family of origin and Barry's family were very similar.

At school, Barry was very popular, particularly because he generously shared candy and sweets from his father's shop with his peers. He had complained of bullying once or twice and on one occasion said the gym teacher victimized him.

Psychometric assessment showed that Barry was of high average intelligence and his attainments in reading, spelling and arithmetic were consistent with his overall level of ability. His school reports were good and he was in the top third of his class with respect to ability.

Formulation

Barry presented with separation anxiety disorder and school refusal. Barry's anticipation of the transition to secondary school in the autumn and his awareness of his mother's worsening health may have precipitated the onset of these problems. Predisposing factors in this case include a possible genetic vulnerability to anxiety, a multigenerational history of mother–child over-involvement and the modelling experience of seeing his three brothers develop separation anxiety and subsequent school refusal.

The separation anxiety and school refusal were maintained by parental conflict about the management of these problems, the mother's over-concern and the father's limited involvement in the management of Barry's difficulties. They may also have been maintained by the availability of an active social life within the house involving frequent

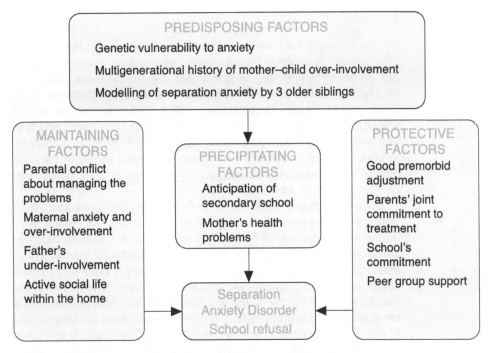

PREDISPOSING FACTORS

Genetic vulnerability to anxiety

Multigenerational history of mother–child over-involvement

Modelling of separation anxiety by 3 older siblings

MAINTAINING FACTORS

Parental conflict about managing the problems

Maternal anxiety and over-involvement

Father's under-involvement

Active social life within the home

PRECIPITATING FACTORS

Anticipation of secondary school

Mother's health problems

PROTECTIVE FACTORS

Good premorbid adjustment

Parents' joint commitment to treatment

School's commitment

Peer group support

Separation Anxiety Disorder School refusal

Figure 5.1 Formulation of a case of separation anxiety disorder

contact with his mother, three brothers and friends who regularly visited him.

Protective factors included Barry's good premorbid adjustment, the parents' commitment to become jointly involved in Barry's treatment, the school's commitment to help Barry overcome his school refusal, and Barry's membership of a supportive peer group, whose members wanted him to overcome his problems. This formulation is diagrammed in Figure 5.1.

Treatment

Treatment involved a series of family sessions and home–school liaison meetings of the parents and school staff. Martin, the father, agreed to drive Barry to school regularly for a month, and the school staff agreed for a teacher to meet Barry in the car park and bring him into the classroom, where he was to sit with two peers and work on a special project for 20 minutes before class started each day. Concurrently, weekly family sessions were held in which progress was assessed, a reward system for school attendance was set up, and the transition to secondary school was discussed.

Arrangements were also made for the mother to attend a series of consultations for her epilepsy, which became better controlled, and for Barry to be given some psychoeducation about his mother's seizure disorder, its treatment and prognosis. Barry returned to school and moved to secondary school in the autumn. His recovery, however, was incomplete and he later relapsed and required further treatment.

Phobias

Phobic anxiety is the intense fear that occurs when one is faced with an object, event or situation from a clearly defined class of stimuli which is out of proportion to the danger posed by the stimulus (American Psychiatric Association, 2000; Blackmore et al., 2009; Hofmann et al., 2009; World Health Organization, 1992). Exposure to the phobic stimulus, or anticipation of exposure, may lead to a panic attack in adults or to excessive crying, tantrums, freezing or clinging in children. In phobias there is persistent avoidance of phobic stimuli or they are endured with intense distress, and this interferes significantly with personal, social or academic functioning.

Specific phobias are subdivided in DSM-IV-TR into those associated with animals, injury (including injections), features of the natural environment (such as heights or thunder) and particular situations (such as elevators or flying). Specific phobias are distinguished from social phobias and agoraphobia. With social phobia, anxiety is aroused by social situations such as public speaking or eating in public, where there is the possibility of scrutiny by others and humiliation or embarrassment as a result of acting inappropriately. With agoraphobia there is a fear of public places, such as standing in a queue or travelling on public transport, and so these situations are avoided. Agoraphobia often occurs when panic attacks have spontaneously occurred in public places, and these places are avoided in case attacks recur. Panic attacks are discussed in more detail below.

Case example of a specific phobia

Nora, aged 9, was referred because of her fear of the dark. She wanted to go on a camping trip with the Brownies but was frightened because she would have to sleep in complete darkness. This was something she had never done. She always slept with the light on in her bedroom and with the door open and the landing light on. Her developmental history was within normal limits and she had never experienced a traumatic incident in the darkness. Her parents had tried to convince her to sleep with the light off, but she became so distressed on these occasions that they had stopped making such attempts and believed that she would eventually grow out of the darkness phobia.

Nora was an only child and there was no family history of anxiety disorders or adjustment problems, nor was there a developmental history of a particularly traumatic incident.

Treatment

This uncomplicated specific phobia was treated with *in vivo*, parent-assisted systematic desensitization. That is, with support from her parents, on successive nights Nora was helped to cope with sleeping in an increasingly darker bedroom at home. The level of illumination was decreased by leaving the light outside her room illuminated and gradually closing over the door further on successive nights. After a month of this treatment programme, Nora's darkness phobia had improved sufficiently for her to go camping and successfully sleep in a dark tent for three nights without experiencing undue anxiety.

Generalized anxiety disorder

When individuals experience generalized anxiety, they have an ongoing apprehension that misfortunes of various sorts will occur (American Psychiatric Association, 2000; Bitran et al., 2009; Hazlett-Stevens et al., 2009; World Health Organization, 1992). Their anxiety is not focused on one particular object or situation. There is also difficulty controlling the worrying process, and a belief that worrying is uncontrollable.

Generalized anxiety disorder is characterized by nervousness, restlessness, difficulty relaxing, feeling on edge, being easily fatigued, concentration difficulties, irritability, tearfulness, sleep disturbance and signs of autonomic overreactivity such as trembling, sweating, drymouth, light-headedness, palpitations, dizziness and stomach discomfort. DSM-IV-TR and ICD-10 require some but not all of these features to be present.

Case example of generalized anxiety disorder

Margie, aged 10, was referred because of excessive tearfulness in school which had been gradually worsening over a number of months. The tearfulness was unpredictable. She would often cry when spoken to by the teacher or while playing with her friends during break time. In the referral letter her family doctor described her as a worrier, like her mother.

Presentation

In the intake interview Margie said that she worried about many routine daily activities and responsibilities. She worried about doing poorly at school, that she had made mistakes which would later be discovered, that her friends wouldn't like her, that her parents would be disappointed with the way she did her household jobs, that she would be either too early or too late for the school bus, that there would be no room for her on the bus and that she would forget her schoolbooks. She worried about her health and had frequent stomach aches.

She also had wider ranging fears about the safety of her family. She worried that the house would be struck by lightening, that the river would break its banks and flood the low lying fens where she lived and her house would be washed away. She had concerns about the future and worried that she would fail her exams, be unable to find a satisfactory job, and would fail to find a marital partner or would marry an unsuitable person. She reported feeling continually restless and unable to relax.

Family history

Margie was the eldest of four children and the only girl in the family. The family was very close-knit. Both of the parents showed symptoms of anxiety in the intake interview and the mother had been treated with benzodiazepines for anxiety over a number of years. The parents regularly discussed their worries about their own health and safety and their own concerns about the uncertainty of the future.

The father, Oliver, worked with an insurance company, and frequently discussed at the family dinner table accidents and burglaries that had befallen his clients. Margie regularly participated in these conversations, being the eldest child. The parents' chief concern was about Margie's tearfulness, which they viewed as unusual. Her worries and fears they saw as quite legitimate. Margie had a couple of close friends with whom she played at the weekends, but she spent a lot of time in her parents' company.

Formulation

Margie presented with a generalized anxiety disorder. No clear-cut precipitating factor for the condition was apparent. It had gradually evolved over the course of Margie's development. However, the referral was precipitated by episodes of tearfulness at school. Predisposing factors in this case included a possible genetic vulnerability to anxiety and exposure to a family culture marked by a concern with safety and an over-sensitivity to danger. Ongoing involvement in parental conversations about potential threats to the well-being of family members possibly maintained the condition along with inadvertent reinforcement of Margie's tearfulness at school, where crying was responded to with considerable concern.

Protective factors in this case included good premorbid adjustment, particularly at school, the parents' and school's commitment to resolving the problem and the availability of peer-group support. This formulation is diagrammed in Figure 5.2.

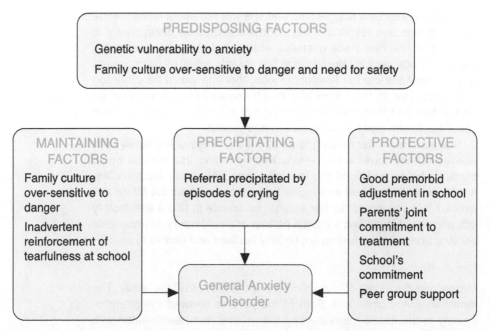

Figure 5.2 Formulation of a case of generalized anxiety disorder

Treatment

Treatment in this case involved family work focusing on helping Margie and her parents reduce the amount of time they spent talking about danger and threats to their health and safety, and increase the amount of time they spent engaged in activities and conversations focusing on Margie's strengths and capabilities. The parents were also helped to coach Margie in relaxation skills and mastery-oriented coping self-statements. Some reduction in anxiety and tearfulness occurred, and Margie showed some improvement in her adjustment in school.

Panic disorder

With panic disorder there are recurrent unexpected panic attacks; an ongoing primary fear of further attacks; and a secondary fear of losing control, going crazy, having a heart attack or dying (American Psychiatric Association, 2000; Ballenger, 2009; Hofmann et al., 2009; World Health Organization, 1992). Panic attacks are experienced as acute episodes of intense anxiety which reach a peak within 10 minutes. They are characterized by autonomic hyperarousal shown by some of the following: palpitations, sweating, trembling or shaking, shortness of breath, feelings of choking or smothering, chest pain or discomfort, nausea or abdominal distress, dizziness, chills or hot flushes, parasthesias, (numbness or tingling sensations), derealization (feelings of unreality) and depersonalization (feelings of being detached from oneself).

People with panic disorder come to perceive normal fluctuations in autonomic arousal as anxiety-provoking, since they believe that such fluctuations may signal the onset of a panic attack. During a panic attack there is typically an urge to escape from the situation in which the attack occurred and to avoid such situations in future. Panic attacks typically occur in public settings such as in queues or on public transport, and escaping from these situations usually alleviates acute autonomic arousal. Thus, secondary agoraphobia often develops whereby the person fears leaving the safety of the home in case a panic attack occurs in a public setting.

Case example of panic disorder

Sandra, a 15-year-old girl, was referred because of anxiety about sitting exams. She lived with her grandparents, Ruth and Josh. She slept and ate well and appeared to be happy. However, she would not leave the house to socialize or attend college. A tutor from the local technical college at which she was enrolled had regularly brought school work to her for about 9 months. The imminence of her GCSE state exams, which were due to be held at the college, precipitated the referral. She wanted to overcome her anxiety so that she could travel to college and sit her exams, which she had felt unable to complete the previous year due to anxiety.

History of the presenting problem

In a preliminary interview, conducted at her grandparents' house where she lived, Sandra described a fear of leaving the safety of her home and how the distress she experienced increased the further away from her home she travelled. The anxiety began during her mock O-Level school exams a year previously. She had a panic attack and left the exam hall. She ran to her grandparents' house after this incident and subsequent attempts to return to school led to further panic attacks. During the attacks she couldn't catch her breath and felt dizzy. She also felt as if she were out of her body (depersonalization) and as if the world was dream-like (derealization). She then feared she would die. The initial attack lasted no more than a few minutes. Subsequent attacks were similar to the first.

Her family and the college staff, after some preliminary ineffective attempts to help her get out and about, gave up trying. On many occasions, when she found herself any distance from the house, she would begin to panic and run back quickly. This led to the symptoms of panic abating. One staff member at the college visited her and taught her some relaxation exercises. He suggested she use these to help her cope with attempts to leave the house, but she found them of little benefit. Eventually she settled for a house-bound life.

On a couple of occasions, when she had sufficient courage to visit her friends, she had panic attacks. At these times she was frightened of accepting a cup of hot tea because she believed she might not be able to finish the tea without scalding herself, should she experience a panic attack and need to escape from the situation quickly. She said she would not like to offend her friends by not finishing her tea. Sandra was also frightened of going on buses or in cars on the motorway and of queuing at the bank. She worried that she might have a panic attack in these situations and not be able to get home safely.

Family history

Sandra's parents were divorced. Her father, Des, was a police officer in London and had separated from her mother, Lynn, when Sandra was 7 years old. Lynn lived near the grandparents, in a rural village about a 3-hour drive from London. Lynn cohabited with Jeff, whom she had met while hospitalized for depression. She had an extensive history of psychiatric treatment for anxiety and depression.

Sandra's mother and grandparents were preoccupied with physical illness and psychological problems, and regularly discussed threats to each other's well-being. They shared a view, based on Lynn's experiences, that psychological problems ran a chronic course and were unresponsive to psychological treatments, because they were due to biological factors.

There were a number of distinctive family relationships in this case. Sandra had very close relationships with her mother and grandparents. The mother and grandmother were involved in regular conflicts over the suitability of Jeff as a partner for Lynn. Sandra's brother, Paul, who attended university, visited her occasionally with his friends and she envied his lifestyle. He rarely joined in the conversations about illness at the grandparents' house. He was a drama enthusiast and Sandra would help him rehearse his lines when he visited. For Sandra, this was a welcome break from the regular conversation about ill-health at her grandparents' house. Sandra had four or five friends who lived locally, and two of these visited regularly.

Formulation

Sandra presented with panic disorder with agoraphobia, initially precipitated by participation in a school examination. The principal predisposing factors were a genetic vulnerability to anxiety from the mother's side of the family and a family culture that focused on illness, fear and danger. Multiple unsuccessful treatments and the experience of negative reinforcement afforded by escaping from threatening situations maintained the agoraphobic, avoidant behaviour. Other maintaining factors included the father's lack of involvement in attempts to help Sandra recover, combined with the grandparents' and mother's over-involvement with Sandra. This maintained Sandra's anxiety and prevented recovery because it led to her continued involvement in conversations about illness, fear and danger, and a pessimistic biomedical view of anxiety.

However, Sandra's good premorbid adjustment, her positive relationship with her brother who was a good role model for recovery, her two positive close peer relationships, and a desire for vocational progression were important protective factors in this case. The family and the school also were supportive of treatment that might help Sandra sit her exams. This formulation is diagrammed in Figure 5.3.

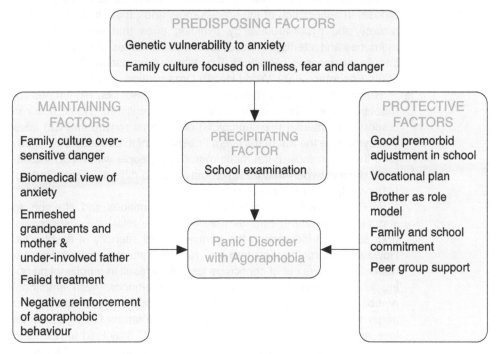

Figure 5.3 Formulation of a case of panic disorder with agoraphobia

Treatment

Treatment in this instance began with family work involving the grand-parents, the mother and, on a couple of occasions, the father, to reduce the amount of illness and anxiety-focused conversation to which Sandra was exposed and to challenge the beliefs that psychological problems were unresponsive to psychological treatments. This was followed with *in vivo* systematic desensitization coupled with a brief trial of clomi-parmine (Anafranil).

In vivo systematic desensitization involved Sandra being supported to make increasingly longer outings from her house, while concurrently using relaxation exercises to help her to manage the anxiety these out-ings evoked. Sandra could not tolerate the side-effects of clomiparmine, so the medication was discontinued. It was also arranged for her to sit exams at school in a private room. Following this, work placements at a crèche and at an old folks' home were arranged by the college staff. While Sandra made a good recovery, she suffered periodic relapses and re-referred herself for a number of further episodes of treatment over the following 2 years.

Posttraumatic stress disorder

Posttraumatic stress disorder (PTSD) occurs following a catastrophic trauma such as child abuse, rape, torture, a terrorist attack, armed combat, a natural or man-made disaster, or a serious accident that was perceived to be potentially life-threatening for oneself or others. PTSD is characterized by (1) recurrent intrusive traumatic memories; (2) intense anxiety in response to these memories and ongoing hyper-arousal in anticipation of their recurrence; and (3) attempts to regulate anxiety and hyper-arousal by avoiding cues that trigger traumatic memories and attempts to suppress these memories when they intrude into consciousness (American Psychiatric Association, 2000; Ehlers, 2009; Friedman, 2009; World Health Organization, 1992).

Recurrent, traumatic memories include flashbacks, nightmares, or repetitive trauma-themed play in the case of children. These occur in response to internal (psychological) or external (environmental) cues that symbolize the traumatic event or aspects of it. Because they antici-pate the recurrence of traumatic memories, people with PTSD experi-ence chronic hyper-arousal which may lead to difficulty concentrating, hyper-vigilance, irritability or sleep difficulties.

In PTSD, avoidance of trauma-related situations and attempts to suppress traumatic memories may initially be relatively unsuccessful and lead to an increase in the frequency and intensity of flashbacks. However, in chronic cases, frequent, recurrent attempts to keep trauma-related memories out of consciousness often result in emotional numb-ing and an inability to recall traumatic memories. With emotional numbing, not only are trauma-related emotions such as anxiety and anger excluded from consciousness, but also tender feelings such as love and joy are no longer experienced. PTSD may lead to restricted involvement in normal activities and a sense of foreshortened future.

Case example of PTSD

Margaret, a 25-year-old woman, was referred because of recurrent night-mares and erratic behaviour at work. She was employed as a cashier in a petrol station in a busy suburban area. On two occasions while she was at work, a man armed with a hypodermic syringe filled with blood, which he claimed was HIV-infected, had coerced her into handing over the con-tents of the cash register. She subsequently suffered from nightmares and daytime flashbacks. She also suffered from a high level of general-ized physiological arousal and was anxious and short-tempered at work.

She attempted to deal with the nightmares and flashbacks by putting them out of her mind and thinking about other things, but found that this was becoming less and less effective. When she became flooded with feelings of anxiety she would become inappropriately aggressive to customers at work and was frightened that she would lose her job because of this. At home her relationships with her mother and sisters had deteriorated.

Treatment

Treatment involved Margaret writing down accounts of her dreams and flashbacks and organizing these into a sequence from the least to the most threatening. She was also invited to alter the endings to these scenarios so that she emerged victorious rather than victimized at the conclusion of each of them. For example, in one scenario, rather than the aggressor successfully attacking her with the HIV-infected syringe, she imagined him shrinking to half his size and then she overpowered him easily.

In therapy sessions, Margaret was imaginally exposed to these scenarios, beginning with the least threatening and concluding with the most threatening, until she could vividly imagine each of them without being overwhelmed with anxiety. During the imaginal exposure ses-sions, she was helped to enter a state of deep relaxation and then listened to the account of the scenario that the psychologist read to her. She coped with the anxiety that listening to these traumatic scenes evoked by using relaxation and deep breathing exercises in which she had been coached, and also by concluding each imagined scenario by emerging victorious rather than victimized. Her symptoms abated over a 6-month period.

Obsessive compulsive disorder

Obsessive compulsive disorder (OCD) is a condition typically character-ized by distressing obsessions on one hand and compulsive rituals that reduce anxiety associated with obsessions on the other (American Psychiatric Association, 2000; Mathews, 2009; World Health Organiza-tion, 1992; Zohar et al., 2009). Obsessions are recurrent, persistent and stereotyped thoughts, images or impulses. They cause significant anxiety because they are experienced as involuntary, uncontrollable and senseless, and concern issues such as danger, violence and obscenity.

For example, there may be fears of contamination, of violently assaulting or raping others, or that a catastrophe may occur unless symmetry or order is maintained.

Compulsions are repetitive, ritualistic, stereotyped behaviours such as hand-washing, ordering and checking or mental acts such as praying, counting, or repeating words silently, which people feel compelled to perform to regulate anxiety caused by obsessions. Compulsions are either unrealistic ways to avert imagined dangers entailed by obsessions or are clearly excessive. They are not inherently enjoyable and are usually recognized as pointless, and repeated attempts are made to resist them.

Case example of obsessive compulsive disorder

April, a 35-year-old woman, was referred because gradually over a 2-year period she had developed some unusual habits, beliefs and feelings. With respect to her behaviour, she scrubbed the floors and walls of the kitchen, bathroom and toilet every day. On one occasion she put a full set of new bathroom towels in the dustbin after a student lodger had used them once. On another occasion she put all the crockery from her kitchen and the family's Sunday dinner which she had cooked in the dustbin.

She prevented the children from playing anywhere that they might fall and cut themselves, including the playground. She took an hour to go to bed each night because she had to return downstairs repeatedly to check that the doors were locked and the fire was extinguished. She had been an affectionate person, but now balked if her friends tried to embrace or kiss her.

With respect to her beliefs, she was frightened that she or her children or husband would catch HIV and develop AIDS. She feared that the student lodger, her friends, or germs from the crockery might infect her with the HIV virus. She was also frightened that a burglar might break in if she did not lock up at night, stab her with a needle and infect herself or the children with the HIV virus.

With respect to her mood, she felt anxious much of the time and had difficulty sleeping. She also felt sad and empty. She was embarrassed, because she knew that her extreme fears of HIV infection were unfounded.

Family history

April was brought up by strict parents with whom she continued to have close contact. She had trained as a nurse but now was a homemaker with a caring and successful husband and two healthy children. She devoted herself fully to the welfare of her children and her husband. Before the onset of her problems, in every way she described herself as an exemplary wife and mother.

While on duty as a nurse she pricked her finger with a needle, and this led to her first thought of HIV infection. Her HIV test was negative, but she could not accept this and developed the obsessional belief that she, her children and her husband would get AIDS. The belief became stronger when her husband changed job, her youngest child went to play school and she took in a lodger.

Her family and friends responded to her condition in the following ways. Her husband helped with her cleaning and checking rituals and reinforced them. Her children did not object to over-protection. Her friends were very understanding of her lack of physical affection. Her sisters discussed her fear of AIDS with her regularly in a sympathetic manner.

Formulation

April presented with OCD which was precipitated by her pricking her finger with a hypodermic needle and recent life stresses including her husband's change of jobs, her children starting preschool and taking in a lodger. She was predisposed to developing OCD by two main factors. First, she came from a family where control and cleanliness were valued. Second, because of her nursing training she was highly aware of the risk of possible infection with the HIV virus.

The OCD was maintained in the following way. She found that her compulsions to clean, discard food, over-protect the children, and check the security of the house every night relieved her anxiety, so she repeated these actions compulsively. Her family and friends reinforced her obsessional thoughts and her husband participated in her compulsive behaviour by, for example, checking the security of the house at her request.

There were two protective factors in this case deserving mention. April was very intelligent and able to take on board a formulation of her problem and understand its relevance to treatment. Her husband was prepared to be involved and enlist family help in combating the compulsions. This formulation is diagrammed in Figure 5.4.

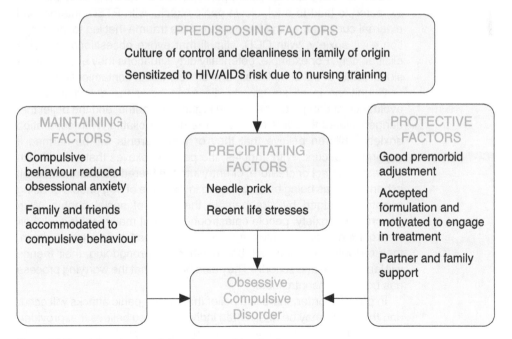

Figure 5.4 Formulation of a case of obsessive compulsive disorder

Treatment

April was treated with a multimodal programme that included anti-depressant medication and a spouse-assisted behaviour therapy programme of exposure and response prevention. She drew up a list of situations that elicited her obsessions, from the least to the most anxiety-provoking. She planned to expose herself to these situations in order of increasing provocativeness and not engage in compulsions while doing so (with her husband's support) until her anxiety abated. For example, she lay in bed, allowed herself to worry about the security of the house, and prevented herself from returning downstairs to check that the doors were locked and the fire extinguished, while her husband talked reassuringly with her, until her anxiety abated. She responded well to treatment, which was carried out over a 3-month period.

Clinical features of anxiety disorders

The clinical features of the six types of anxiety disorder described above are presented in Table 5.1. In the table clinical features are classified into the domains of perception, cognition, affect, arousal, behaviour and interpersonal adjustment. With respect to perception, the disorders differ in the classes of stimuli that elicit anxiety.

With separation anxiety, the stimulus is separation from parents. For phobias it is specific creatures (e.g. animals), events (e.g. injury), or situations (e.g. meeting new people) that elicit anxiety. With generalized anxiety disorder, the person interprets many aspects of their environment as potentially threatening. In panic disorder, somatic sensations of arousal such as tachycardia are perceived as threatening since they are expected to lead to a full-blown panic attack. With PTSD, internal and external cues that remind the person of the trauma that led to the condition elicit anxiety. With OCD, stimuli that evoke obsessional thoughts elicit anxiety. For example, potentially dirty situations may evoke obsessional ideas about cleanliness, and anxiety about contamination.

Cognitions in all six anxiety disorders have the detection and/or avoidance of danger as the central organizing theme, and the belief that danger-related thoughts have become uncontrollable. With separation anxiety, children believe that they or their parents will be harmed if separation occurs. With phobias, the person believes that contact with the feared object or creature, or entry into the feared situation, will result in harm such as being bitten by a dog in the case of dog phobia or being negatively judged by strangers in the case of social phobia. With generalized anxiety, people catastrophize about many features of their environment. For example they may fear that the house will burn down, their car will crash, they will be punished for wrongdoing, their friends will leave them, and so forth. They also believe that the worrying process has become uncontrollable.

In panic disorder, there is a belief that further panic attacks will occur and that these may be fatal. Often individuals also believe that provided they remain within the safety of the home, the panic attacks are less

TABLE 5.1
Clinical features of anxiety disorders

	Separation anxiety disorder	Phobias	Generalized anxiety disorder	Panic disorder	Posttraumatic stress disorder (PTSD)	Obsessive compulsive disorder (OCD)
Perception	• Separation from parents or caregivers is perceived as threatening	• Specific objects, events or situations are perceived as threatening	• The whole environment is perceived as threatening • The person is hyper-vigilant, scanning the environment for threats to well-being	• The recurrence of panic attacks is seen as threatening • Attention is directed inwards and benign somatic sensations are misinterpreted as threatening because they are seen as signalling the onset of a panic attack	• Cues that remind the person of the trauma are perceived as threatening. • Flashbacks, hallucinations or illusions may occur where aspects of the trauma are reperceived	• Specific situations, such as those involving dirt, are perceived as threatening and elicit obsessional thoughts
Cognition	• The child believes that harm to the parent or the self will occur following separation • This belief seems to occur involuntarily and is experienced as uncontrollable	• The person believes that contact with the phobic object or entry into the phobic situation will lead to catastrophe • This belief seems to occur involuntarily and is experienced as uncontrollable	• The person catastrophizes about many minor daily events • There is a belief that the worrying process is uncontrollable	• The person believes that the panic attacks may lead to loss of control, insanity, a heart attack or death	• Recurrent uncontrollable memories of the trauma occur • The person tries to distract themselves from recalling these traumatic memories or to suppress them • A belief in a foreshortened future may develop	• Involuntary, uncontrollable obsessional thoughts, images or impulses elicited by environmental cues intrude into consciousness and may involve themes of contamination, sex or aggression • The person tries to exclude these thoughts from consciousness

(Continued)

TABLE 5.1
(Continued)

	Separation anxiety disorder	Phobias	Generalized anxiety disorder	Panic disorder	Posttraumatic stress disorder (PTSD)	Obsessive compulsive disorder (OCD)
Affect	• Intense fear or anger occurs when separation is anticipated, during separation or following separation	• Intense fear or anger is experienced if contact with the feared object or situation is anticipated or occurs	• A continual moderately high level of fear is experienced – free-floating anxiety	• During panic attacks intense fear occurs and between attacks a moderate level of fear of recurrence is experienced	• Against a background of hyper-arousal, periodic intrusive episodes of intense fear, horror or anger like those that occurred during the trauma are experienced • In chronic cases the person may become emotionally blunted and unable to experience tender emotions • Depression may occur	• The obsessions cause anxiety because they are experienced as uncontrollable and senseless
Arousal	• Episodes of hyper-arousal occur with recurrent abdominal pain, headaches, nausea or vomiting • Sleep problems	• Episodes of hyper-arousal or panic attacks occur when exposed to the feared object or situation • Sleep problems if imminent exposure to the phobic object is anticipated	• Continual hyper-arousal occurs with trembling, dry-sweating, dry-mouth, light-headedness, palpitations, dizziness, and stomach discomfort • Sleep problems	• Episodes of extreme hyper-arousal occur with palpitations, sweating, trembling, shortness of breath, feelings of choking or smothering, chest pain, nausea, dizziness, chills or hot flushes, parasthesias, derealization and depersonalization • Between attacks there is moderate hyper-arousal • Sleep problems	• Episodes of extreme hyper-arousal occur against a background of moderate hyper-arousal with difficulties concentrating and relaxing • Sleep problems	• Ongoing moderate hyper-arousal occurs • Hyper-arousal occurs when cues elicit obsessions and compulsions are resisted

	Separation	Phobias	Generalised worry	Panic/agoraphobia	Post-traumatic stress	Obsessive–compulsive
Behaviour	• Separation is avoided or resisted • The child refuses to go to school • The child refuses to sleep alone • If forced to separate, crying, tantrums, freezing or clinging may occur	• The phobic object or situation is avoided • If exposed to the phobic object or situation, crying, tantrums, freezing or clinging may occur in children	• As worrying intensifies, social activities become restricted	• Secondary agoraphobia may develop where the person avoids public places in case the panic attacks occur away from the safety of home	• Children may cling to parents and refuse to sleep alone • Teenagers and adults may use drugs or alcohol to block the intrusive thoughts and emotions • Suicidal attempts may occur	• Motivated by a wish to reduce the anxiety aroused by obsessional beliefs, individuals engage in compulsive rituals which they believe will prevent a catastrophe from occurring or undo some potentially threatening event that has occurred • These rituals are usually unrealistic or excessive
Interpersonal adjustment	• Peer relationships may deteriorate • Academic performance may deteriorate	• With specific phobias, interpersonal problems are confined to phobic situations • Agoraphobia and social phobia may lead to social isolation	• Peer relationships may deteriorate • Occupational or academic performance may deteriorate	• If agoraphobia develops secondary to the panic attacks, social isolation may occur	• Complete social isolation may occur if the trauma was solitary • Where the trauma was shared, the individual may confine interactions to the group that shared the trauma	• Members of the individual's family or social network may become involved in helping the person perform compulsive rituals and inadvertently reinforce them • Social, educational and occupational functioning may become impaired

Note: Features are based on ICD-10 (World Health Organization, 1992) and DSM-IV-TR (American Psychiatric Association, 2000) descriptions of anxiety disorders.

likely to occur, and so secondary agoraphobia develops. With PTSD, there is a belief that provided the memories of the trauma are excluded from consciousness, the danger of re-experiencing the intense fear, distress and horror associated with the trauma that led to PTSD can be avoided. With OCD, the most common obsessions are with dirt and contamination; catastrophes such as fires, illness or death; symmetry, order and exactness; religious scrupulosity; disgust with bodily wastes or secretions such as urine, stools or saliva; unlucky or lucky numbers; and forbidden sexual thoughts. There is also the belief that engaging in specific rituals will neutralize the threat posed by specific obsession-related stimuli.

In all six of the anxiety disorders listed in Table 5.1 the beliefs about threat and danger are accompanied by affective states, characterized by feelings of tension, restlessness and uneasiness. If one is compelled to approach feared stimuli, or in the case of OCD prevented from executing a compulsive ritual, outbursts of anger may occur. For example, children with separation anxiety may have aggressive tantrums if forced to remain at school without their parents. In PTSD, in addition to the affective experiences of uneasiness and tension, an affective experience of emotional numbing, arising from attempts to exclude all affective material from consciousness, may develop.

The patterning of physiological arousal varies depending on the frequency with which contact with feared stimuli occurs. With separation anxiety, hyper-arousal occurs only when separation is imminently anticipated. With specific phobias it occurs only in the presence of the feared object. With generalized anxiety disorder, there is a pattern of ongoing continual hyper-arousal. With panic disorder and PTSD there is a moderate level of chronic hyper-arousal, punctuated by brief episodes of extreme hyper-arousal. These occur in panic disorder during panic attacks and in PTSD when memories of the traumatic event intrude into consciousness. With OCD, specific obsession-related cues evoke acute and intense episodes of arousal.

The extent to which physiological arousal finds expression in somatic symptoms varies across conditions. For example, recurrent abdominal pain and headaches are especially common in separation anxiety; full-blown panic attacks with sweating, trembling, shortness of breath, feelings of choking or smothering, chest pain, nausea, dizziness, chills or hot flushes, parasthesias, derealization and depersonalization are most common during panic attacks; whereas sleep problems occur in most anxiety disorders.

Avoidance behaviours characterize all anxiety disorders. With specific phobias, avoidance may lead to only a moderate constriction in lifestyle. For example, a person may refuse to engage in sports or athletics or to ride a bicycle because of an injury phobia. However, with separation anxiety, generalized anxiety disorder, panic disorder and PTSD, avoidance behaviour may lead the person to become housebound. With PTSD, individuals may use alcohol or drugs to regulate negative affect and suppress traumatic memories. With OCD, individuals engage in compulsive rituals to regulate anxiety associated with obsessional thoughts. Common compulsions include washing, repeating an action, checking, removing contaminants, touching, ordering and collecting.

Interpersonal relationships are affected by each of the anxiety disorders in different ways. With simple phobias interpersonal difficulties arise only in those situations where the individual refuses to conform or co-operate with normal social activities so as to avoid the feared stimuli. For example, a brief episode of marital conflict may occur if one partner refuses to get in an elevator at a shopping mall because of claustrophobia. Separation anxiety, panic disorder, generalized anxiety and PTSD may prevent young people from attending school or adults from attending work, and in all of these conditions family relationships and friendships may be seriously compromised. With OCD, family members may attempt to reduce the sufferer's anxiety by participating in compulsive rituals or in other instances they may increase anxiety by punishing the individual for his or her compulsive behaviour. In extreme cases, compulsive behaviour may become so frequent and intense that the person's lifestyle becomes constricted.

Epidemiology, risk factors and course

Anxiety disorders are more prevalent than any other category of psychological disorders. The lifetime prevalence rate in adults for all DSM-IV anxiety in the US National Comorbidity Survey Replication was 28.8% (Kessler et al., 2005). Across a wide range of epidemiological studies there is a consensus that phobias are the most prevalent anxiety disorders and that OCD is the least prevalent (Kessler et al., 2009; Furr et al., 2009). Lifetime prevalence estimates for phobias range from 6% to 12%, whereas those for OCD fall below 3%. The lifetime prevalence rate of generalized anxiety disorder is 1–6%, and of panic disorder in adults and separation anxiety in children is 2–5%. The prevalence of PTSD in national representative samples ranges from less than 1% or 2% in western European countries to almost 8% in the US. This wide variability is due to the fact that PTSD rates are dependent on both the prevalence of trauma exposure within specific countries and the vulnerability of populations within these countries to developing PTSD symptoms. In populations exposed to terrorism the prevalence of PTSD is 12–16% (DiMaggio & Galea, 2006).

Comorbidity among anxiety disorders is quite high, and up to a third of people with one anxiety disorder also suffer from another (Kessler et al., 2009). Anxiety disorders may also occur comorbidly with mood disorders in children and adults, substance use disorders in adolescents and adults, and disruptive behaviour disorders in children (Furr et al., 2009; Huppert, 2009; Zahradnik & Stewart, 2009). Where substance misuse occurs, often alcohol or drugs are used for self-medication to manage anxiety.

Comorbidity between anxiety disorders and personality disorders is very common, and the highest level of comorbidity occurs with Cluster

C personality disorders (avoidant, dependent, and obsessive compulsive personality disorders) (Brandes & Bienvenu, 2009). There is a strong association between OCD and eating disorders. A significant proportion of people with eating disorders such as anorexia nervosa also suffer from OCD (Halmi, 2010).

There are clear age and gender differences in the prevalence of anxiety disorders (Antony & Stein, 2009a; Furr et al., 2009; Kessler et al., 2009). Across most available studies, the modal age of onset of separation anxiety disorder and specific phobias is in childhood, whereas that of other anxiety disorders tends to be in adolescence or adulthood. In children and adults more females than males suffer from anxiety disorders. The main exception to this finding is that equal numbers of males and females suffer from OCD.

Anxiety disorders follow a recurring episodic course with a gradual reduction in prevalence over the course of the life cycle (Kessler et al., 2009). While most anxious adults have a history of childhood anxiety disorders, most children with anxiety disorders do not grow up to have anxiety or depression in adulthood (Pine & Klein, 2008).

A number of risk factors are associated with the development of anxiety disorders. These include a family history of anxiety disorders or psychopathology, a behaviourally inhibited temperament, neuroticism, a personal history of psychopathology, a history of over-controlling or critical parenting, a history of family conflict and violence, and a history of stressful life events (Antony & Stein, 2009b; Pine & Klein, 2008). In this context, behaviourally inhibited temperament is the tendency, present from birth, to become nervous and withdraw from unfamiliar stimuli and situations. Neuroticism is a personality trait that develops over the life-span characterized by the tendency to experience negative affect including anxiety, depression and hostility.

For PTSD, additional risk factors include trauma severity, dissociative experiences immediately following the trauma, low social support and high life stress following the trauma, and low socio-economic status, educational level and intelligence (Ehlers, 2009; Ozer et al., 2003). In this context dissociative experiences refer to abnormalities of perception, memory or identity such as derealization (seeing the world as dream-like), depersonalization (viewing the self from an external perspective) or inability to recall important personal information. For children, parental PTSD is also a risk factor for developing the condition (Pine & Klein, 2008).

Aetiological theories

Theoretical explanations for anxiety disorders, related research and interventions have been developed within biological, psychoanalytic, cognitive-behavioural, and family systems traditions. Vulnerability to anxiety disorders has also been studied by temperament and trait theorists, and from an experimental psychopathology perspective to identify information-processing biases associated with anxiety disorders.

Biological theories

Biological theories point to the role of genetic factors and neurobiological abnormalities in the aetiology of anxiety disorders.

Genetics

The genetic hypothesis proposes that anxiety disorders develop where a person with an inherited vulnerability to anxiety is exposed to threatening or stressful environmental stimuli at critical developmental stages when they are primed or prepared to develop fears. Results of twin and family studies of anxiety disorders partially support the genetic hypothesis, with twin studies yielding moderate heritability estimates ranging from about 25% to 60%, with most in the 30–40% range, for phobias, panic disorder, and vulnerability to PTSD and OCD (Afifi et al., 2010; Gelernter & Stein, 2009; Hettema et al., 2001).

There is also support for the proposal that sensitivity to particular classes of stimuli emerges at particular developmental stages (De Silva et al., 1977). For example, it was mentioned in the section on epidemiology that vulnerability to developing specific phobias and separation anxiety is highest during childhood, whereas vulnerability to social phobias, panic disorder, generalized anxiety disorder and OCD more commonly emerges in adolescence.

The genetic hypothesis also entails the view that a dysfunctional biological factor which underpins the process of regulating stress responses is genetically transmitted in families where anxiety disorders occur. Many candidate genes for anxiety disorders have been investigated; few have been identified; and where significant associations between candidate genes and anxiety disorders have been found, very few consistent replication studies are available. The search for candidate genes has focused in large part on those whose products affect neurotransmitters thought to be involved in the aetiology of anxiety disorders. Two candidate genes – which affect the serotonin and dopamine systems – deserve mention because consistent support has been found for a link between them and anxiety disorders.

The short (rather than the long) allele variant of the 5-HTTLPR polymorphism, which regulates expression of the serotonin transporter gene (which is called 5HTT or SLC6A4), is a risk factor for PTSD and significantly increases the chances of developing PTSD following trauma (Xie et al., 2009). In response to stress or trauma, people with the short allele variant of 5-HTTLPR show decreased serotonin reuptake, increased amygdala neuronal activity, and increased hypothalamic–pituitary–adrenal (HPA) axis reactivity. The amygdala is a brain structure within the limbic system (which includes the amygdala, hippocampus, insula and parts of the anterior cingulated cortex) located in the medial temporal lobes that subserves the processing of emotional information and memories. The HPA axis is a major part of the neuroendocrine system involving the hypothalamus, the pituitary gland located below the hypothalamus, and the adrenal glands (located on top of the kidneys), which controls stress reactions and other processes including the immune system, sexuality and digestion.

At a behavioural level, these neurobiological processes associated with the short allele variant of 5-HTTLPR subserve increased attentional bias to threat, enhanced fear conditioning and stress sensitivity (Caspi et al., 2010). However, the short allele variant of 5-HTTLPR seems to be a general vulnerability factor for stress-related psychological disorders, rather than a specific vulnerability factor for PTSD. For example, it is also a vulnerability factor for depression and borderline personality disorder.

A specific allele of the Val158Met polymorphism of the catechol-O-methyltransferase COMT gene is a risk factor for panic disorder (Maron et al., 2010). The COMT gene encodes an enzyme that breaks down dopamine, weakening its signal. People with panic disorder are more likely to have the COMPT allele associated with less efficient dopamine breakdown. The consequent higher levels of dopamine in the limbic systems of such people with panic disorder may subserve their increased sustained attention to salient stimuli, even when these stimuli are anxiety provoking.

Neurobiology

The neurobiological hypothesis is that anxiety disorders are characterized by neuroanatomical, neurotransmitter and neuroendocrine abnormalities. There is considerable support for this hypothesis from neuroimaging, psychophysiological and pharmacological studies, although current knowledge of these abnormalities is incomplete (Britton & Rauch, 2009; Khan et al., 2009; Martin et al., 2009).

However, there is a consensus about certain aspects of the neurobiology of anxiety disorders. With the exception of OCD, which has distinct neurocircuitry mentioned below, anxiety disorders are associated with abnormalities in brain structures that subserve processing information about danger, fear conditioning and fear responses, primarily the limbic system. Within this system, overactivity of the amygdala during exposure to feared stimuli is central to anxiety disorders. Excessive activity in the limbic system which subserves the experience of fear and anxiety is normally inhibited by the orbitofrontal cortex, which subserves impulse control, and the prefrontal cortex, which subserves executive functions such as planning and decision-making. In anxiety disorders, communication between the limbic system and the frontal cortex is impaired and so persistent limbic overactivity occurs when one is exposed to anxiety-provoking stimuli.

There is evidence for dysregulations of neurotransmitters, notably GABA (gamma-amino-butyric-acid) and serotonin, which facilitate communication between the limbic system and the frontal cortex – the brain structures centrally involved in anxiety disorders. The efficiency of both of these neurotransmitter systems is reduced in anxiety disorders, and increased by anti-anxiety drugs (Dent & Bremner, 2009; Mathew & Hoffman, 2009; Pollack & Simon, 2009; Stewart et al., 2009; van Ameringen et al., 2009).

Selective serotonin reuptake inhibitors (SSRIs) such as fluoxetine (Prozac) target the serotonergic neurotranmitter system, and benzodi-azepines such as diazepam (Valium) target the GABA neurotransmitter system. In the normal brain, GABA is usually released once arousal reaches a certain level and decreases the experience of anxiety, but this process is less efficient in people with anxiety disorders. Benzo-diazepines reduce anxiety by binding to GABA neuroreceptors. Unfortunately, benzodiazepines are addictive, and so long-term use for the treatment of anxiety disorders is not regarded as best practice. Dopamine, noradrenaline, glutamate and other neurotransmitter sys-tems may also be dysregulated in anxiety disorders, although their roles are less clearly understood.

Genetic vulnerability to anxiety disorders involves genes whose action affects the efficiency of neurotransmitter systems associated with anxiety, as was noted above in the discussion of genetic factors. Evidence from a small number of neuroimaging studies shows that psychological interventions, such as cognitive behaviour therapy, normalize neurobiological functional abnormalities associated with anxiety disorders (Frewen et al., 2008a).

In anxiety disorders there is evidence for the dysregulation of neuro-peptides in the limbic system, notably corticotropin-releasing factor (CRF). CRF is associated with HPA axis hyperactivity. Such hyperactiv-ity is a central neurobiological feature of anxiety disorders, and is asso-ciated with the release of the stress steroid cortisol which is elevated in people with anxiety disorders (Khan et al., 2009).

The neurobiology of OCD differs from that of other anxiety disorders. With OCD there are abnormalities in the functioning of circuits which link the basal ganglia, the prefrontal cortex (particularly orbitofontal and anterior cingulate regions) and the thalamus, which is referred to as the cortico-striatal–thalamic circuit. Overactivity of the prefrontal cortex and thalamus subserves the initiation and maintenance of obsessional worrying, and overactivity of the basal ganglia subserves stereotyped compulsive behaviour patterns typical of people with OCD. Surgical disruption of the cortico-striatal–thalamic circuit alleviates chronic OCD, although this invasive treatment is used only in cases resistant to psychotherapy or medication (Aouizerate et al., 2006; Stewart et al., 2009; Zohar et al., 2009). SSRIs are the most common pharmacological intervention in both adults and children for OCD because, the condition is associated with inefficient functioning of the serotonin neurotransmitter system (Rapoport & Shaw, 2008; Zohar et al., 2009).

Temperament, traits, cognitive biases and coping strategies

Temperament, traits, cognitive bias and coping strategy theories propose that anxiety disorders develop in people who have specific anxiety-prone dispositions. Temperamental characteristics are biologi-cally based behavioural attributes present from birth. In support of this view there is a substantial body of longitudinal research which shows that infants with a temperament characterized by behavioural inhibition – nervousness and avoidance of unfamiliar stimuli and situations – are at risk for developing anxiety disorders (Kagan, 2010).

Personality traits are cross-situationally stable psychological characteristics determined by both genetic and environmental factors. There is a growing consensus that a five-factor model of personality traits is probably the most parsimonious (John et al., 2008). The 'Big 5' personality traits are neuroticism, extraversion, openness to experience, conscientiousness and agreeableness. In a meta-analysis Kotov et al. (2010) found that all anxiety disorders were strongly associated with the personality trait neuroticism; all disorders except specific phobias were associated with low conscientiousness; and all anxiety disorders except simple phobias and generalized anxiety disorder were associated with high levels of introversion. High neuroticism entails emotional instability and distress; low conscientiousness is the tendency not to follow through on plans; and introversion involves social withdrawal.

A number of lower-order traits have been found to correlate with specific anxiety disorders. These include anxiety sensitivity, fear of negative evaluation, intolerance of uncertainty, perfectionism, thought–action fusion and alexithymia (Starcevic & Berle, 2006). Because correlational evidence on these traits comes from cross-sectional studies, it is not clear whether they are predisposing vulnerability factors or correlates of anxiety disorders. In a meta-analysis, Naragon-Gainey (2010) found that anxiety sensitivity correlated .4–.6 with all anxiety disorders and most strongly with panic disorder. Anxiety sensitivity refers to the tendency to fear somatic, cognitive and social anxiety-related symptoms. Fear of negative evaluation by others in social situations is correlated with social phobia (Weeks et al., 2005). Intolerance of uncertainty is associated most strongly with generalized anxiety disorder (Dugas et al., 2004). People with a high level of intolerance for uncertainty believe uncertainty is undesirable and should be avoided, and have difficulties functioning well in uncertain situations, especially where stressful events may occur. Perfectionism and thought–action fusion are strongly correlated with OCD (Berle & Starcevic, 2005; Egan et al., 2011). Perfectionism is the tendency to adhere to very high standards and experience distress if these standards are not reached. With thought–action fusion, there are beliefs that thoughts and actions are inextricably linked, that immoral thoughts are equivalent to immoral acts, and that that thoughts about specific events increase the likelihood of such events occurring. Alexithymia, which refers to difficulty identifying and labelling feelings, is strongly correlated with PTSD (Frewen et al., 2008b).

Research from experimental psychopathology has consistently shown that people with anxiety disorders show a range of information-processing biases (McNally & Reese, 2009). They have an attentional bias for threatening information, as shown by the tendency to take longer to name the colours of threatening words than the colours of positive or neutral words in the emotional Stroop test. In this test individuals read randomized lists of all three types of words printed in different colours. People with anxiety disorders also show a bias towards threatening interpretations of ambiguous situations in studies where they are asked to write interpretations of descriptions of situations such as 'You are awoken by a noise at night'. People with panic disorder have a memory bias favouring recall of threatening information, in studies where they memorize threatening and non-threatening stimuli. It is still unclear whether these information-processing biases are correlates of anxiety or predispositions that confer vulnerability to anxiety disorders.

Certain coping strategies are associated with anxiety disorders. In a meta-analysis, Aldao et al. (2010) found that anxiety disorders were associated with the use of rumination, avoidance and suppression as coping strategies. They also found negative correlations between anxiety and a number of adaptive coping strategies including problem-solving, acceptance and reappraisal.

Psychoanalytic theories

In anxiety disorders, according to classical psychoanalytic theory, defence mechanisms are used to keep unacceptable sexual or aggressive impulses and moral anxiety about their expression from entering consciousness (Busch et al., 2010). The unacceptable impulses and related moral anxiety become transformed into neurotic anxiety. In phobias, the unacceptable impulse is repressed and the neurotic anxiety into which it is transformed is displaced onto a substitute object which symbolizes the original object about which the unacceptable impulses were felt. The key defence mechanism is displacement. Thus, when people say that they are frightened of a particular object or situation, the psychoanalytic hypothesis is that they are frightened about something else, but have displaced their fear from the original taboo object or event onto a more socially acceptable target. In Freud's original statement of this hypothesis, in the Little Hans case, where the boy had a horse phobia, he argued that the taboo fear was castration anxiety, and this fear of the father was displaced onto horses (Freud, 1909a). In generalized anxiety disorders, the defences break down and the person becomes overwhelmed with anxiety as the unacceptable impulses continually intrude into consciousness and seek expression. Anxiety about taboo objects is displaced onto every available target.

Within psychoanalytic theory it is proposed that the unacceptability of certain impulses, and habitual ways of defending against these, are learned early in childhood in relationships with parents. In adulthood these same defences and habitual ways of interacting with parents tend to be deployed in relationships with significant people in the person's life (including partners, colleagues and therapists), a phenomenon referred to as transference. From a psychoanalytic perspective, OCD is explained as the sequelae of toilet training battles (Freud, 1909b).

According to classical psychoanalytic theory, children evolve through oral, anal and phallic stages of development, with gratification being principally derived from these differing bodily areas as development occurs. During the anal phase of development, according to psycho-analytic theory, children become angry with their parents' insistence that they use the toilet in an appropriate way. Attempts to express these aggressive impulses are met with sanctions from the parents and so the aggression is repressed. When these repressed sexual–aggressive impulses attempt to find expression, this causes anxiety. The aggressive impulses and thoughts are displaced and substituted by less unacceptable thoughts or impulses. When these intrude into consciousness, they are experienced as ego-alien because they have been disowned or isolated. The anxiety is managed by carrying out a compulsive ritual to undo or cancel out the undesirable impulse. Because the source of this tendency towards compulsions is theorized to have arisen during the anal developmental phase, it has become commonplace in popular culture to refer to meticulous people as 'anal'.

In psychoanalytic treatment, the aim is to interpret the defence, the repressed forbidden feelings and the associated neurotic anxiety. These three elements (the defence, the hidden feeling, and the associated anxiety) are referred to as the triangle of conflict (Ezriel, 1952). During psychoanalytic treatment attention is drawn to the parallels between the way in which the person manages current problematic relationships with other significant people in their lives such as their peers, work colleagues or partners; the current relationship with the therapist; and past relationships with the parents. These three sets of relationships are referred to as the triangle of person (Menninger, 1958). Because the tendency to replicate relationship patterns from childhood in adult life with friends, colleagues and therapists is referred to as transference, interpretations that point to these replications, within the triangle of person, are referred to as transference interpretations. The triangle of conflict and the triangle of person are presented in Figure 5.5. Interpretations based on these are offered tentatively, at a stage in the therapy when a strong working alliance has been established, and within the context of a coherent psychodynamic case formulation (Malan, 1995; McCullough-Vaillant, 1997).

The idea of displacement is clinically useful when working with anxious patients. In my clinical experience, people worried about one thing may say that they are worried about another. However, there is no evidence to support the idea that all anxiety disorders represent displacement of anxiety associated with psychosexual developmental conflicts. There is some limited evidence from a small number of controlled trials that short-term psychodynamic therapy is effective for anxiety disorders (Leichsenring, 2009). For example, in a controlled trial, Milrod et al. (2007) found that panic-focused psychodynamic psychotherapy was more effective than applied relaxation training in the treatment of panic disorder, and in another controlled trial Leichsenring et al. (2009) found that short-term psychodynamic psychotherapy was as effective as cognitive-behavioural therapy in the treatment of generalized anxiety disorder.

Ezriel's Triangle of Conflict   Menninger's Triangle of Person

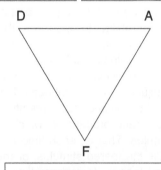
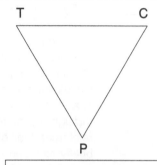

Defence	Anxiety	Therapist	Current Persons
Behaviour patterns, cognitive styles & emotional states to manage conflict between adaptive feelings and anxiety	Guilt and shame due to conflict between adaptive feelings and internal or societal inhibitions		Partner, spouse, children, friends, colleagues, boss, authority figures

D   A   T   C

F   P

Adaptive Feelings	Past Persons
Adaptive forms of anger, sexual desire, attachment, positive feelings about the self, joy, excitement, interest, and grief	Parents, carers, teachers, siblings, significant relatives, close childhood friends

Defences (D) are used to manage conflict between anxieties (A) about expression of adaptive feelings and impulses (F). These D–A–F patterns began with past persons (P), are maintained by interactions with current persons (C), and are re-enacted as transference with the therapist (T).

Figure 5.5 Psychodynamic triangles of conflict and person (based on Ezriel, H. (1952). Notes on psychoanalytic group therapy: II. Interpretation. *Research Psychiatry*, 15, 119. Menninger, K. (1958). *Theory of Psychoanalytic Technique*. London: Imago. Malan, D. (1995). *Individual Psychotherapy and the Science of Psychodynamics*. London: Arnold. McCullough-Vaillant, L. (1997). *Changing Character: Short-Term Anxiety Regulating Psychotherapy for Restructuring Defences, Affects and Attachments*. New York: Basic Books.)

Cognitive-behavioural theories

Theories developed within the cognitive-behavioural tradition (which includes both behavioural and cognitive formulations) point to the importance of conditioning and cognitive learning processes in the development of anxiety disorders.

Behavioural approaches

Behavioural theories of anxiety disorders, such as Mowrer's (1939) two-factor theory, propose that anxiety and associated avoidance of feared objects, situations or memories are learned though the processes of classical and operant conditioning. With classical conditioning, it is proposed that a person becomes frightened of a neutral object, situation or memory that was present during a trauma or exposure to a highly anxiety-provoking stimulus. The classically conditioned fear response to the previously neutral stimulus does not extinguish because the person's avoidant behaviour is negatively reinforced each time the previously neutral stimulus is avoided. In behavioural psychology, negative reinforcement is the term used to describe the strengthening of a response that leads to escaping from an aversive situation, such as the experience of anxiety.

Eysenck (1979) added the concepts of biological preparedness, incubation and constitutional vulnerability to Mowrer's theory. He proposed that as a result of evolutionary processes, people are biologically prepared at specific developmental stages to develop phobias through one-trial classical conditioning to specific classes of stimuli such as snakes, spiders, injuries and natural hazards (De Silva et al., 1977). He also proposed that conditioned fears are strengthened through incubation, a positive feedback process, in which fear itself reinforces fear of the phobic stimulus. That is, each time a person is briefly exposed to or briefly recalls the feared stimulus, or the trauma associated with it, the conditioned fear is strengthened, because the person becomes afraid of the experience of anxiety. This whole process occurs outside of cognitive control. Finally, Eysenck proposed that some people are constitutionally vulnerable to developing anxiety disorders through having high levels of neuroticism and introversion, a hypothesis supported by meta-analytic data from personality trait studies of people with anxiety disorders (Kotov et al., 2010).

Behavioural treatment for anxiety disorders involves exposure to stimuli that elicit anxiety until habituation occurs and the anxiety response is extinguished (Moscovitch et al., 2009). Systematic desensitization and flooding (also referred to as implosion therapy) are two commonly used behavioural procedures. With systematic desensitization, a procedure developed by Joseph Wolpe (1969) in South Africa, clients in a deeply relaxed state are exposed to increasingly anxiety-provoking stimuli, with progression to the next stimulus occurring once habituation to the present one has occurred. With flooding (or implosion), a technique developed by Thomas Stampfl (Stampfl & Levis, 1968), clients are exposed for a prolonged period (often lasting a number of hours) to their most anxiety-provoking stimuli until anxiety responses are extinguished. With these exposure-based behavioural interventions, anxiety-provoking stimuli may be presented *in vivo* (real life), in virtual reality using computer simulations, or using mental imagery where the psychologist invites the client to close their eyes and imagine the feared object or situation.

In all behavioural treatment programmes, prior to exposure clients are given detailed psychoeducation about their anxiety disorder, a formulation which explains how it developed and is maintained, the proposed exposure-based treatment plan, and training in relaxation skills or other coping strategies for use during exposure to help them tolerate exposure to the feared object or situation until their anxiety responses are extinguished, although in Stampfl's original implosion therapy protocol he encouraged clients to feel maximum anxiety (Stampfl & Levis, 1968). For separation anxiety disorders, children are exposed to separation from parents, usually through supported attendance at school. For phobias, exposure is arranged to feared objects or situations. For panic disorder, clients are exposed to physiological sensations of hyper-arousal (interopceptive exposure) by directing attention to their heart rate and respiration. If they have secondary agoraphobia, they are also exposed to public places that they typically avoid. For generalized anxiety disorder, clients are exposed to feared objects and situations and are also helped to plan and practise worrying to desensitize them to their fear of uncontrollable rumination. For PTSD, clients are exposed to cues that evoke flashbacks or to traumatic memories. For OCD, exposure treatment is referred to as exposure and response prevention, because clients are exposed to cues (such as dirt) that elicit obsessions, and are helped to prevent themselves from engaging in their anxiety-reducing compulsions until their anxiety responses extinguish. A large body of research supports the effectiveness of exposure-based treatment programmes for adults and children with anxiety disorders (Moscovitch et al., 2009; Olatunji et al., 2010; Rapee et al., 2009).

Cognitive approaches

According to Aaron T. Beck's cognitive theory, anxiety disorders occur when threatening stressful life events reactivate danger-oriented cognitive schemas. It is proposed that these schemas were formed early in child-hood through exposure to traumatic or adverse experiences and parenting practices that sensitized the individual to threat, danger and personal vulnerability and encouraged avoidant coping (Clark & Beck, 2010a). These threat-oriented schemas contain beliefs, attitudes and assumptions about threat and vulnerability relevant to personal safety such as 'The world is dangerous, so I must continually be on guard' or 'My health is ailing so any uncomfortable somatic sensation must reflect serious ill health'. These threat-oriented schemas also direct the identi-fication, interpretation and evaluation of experience and underpin anxiety-maintaining cognitive distortions such as minimizing safety-related events, maximizing threat-related negative events and catastrophizing about the future. These schemas dominate the biased, threat-sensitive way people with anxiety experience themselves in the world.

Anxious people are more likely to attend to threat-oriented rather than safety-oriented objects, events and situations, and to interpret ambiguous situations in a threatening rather than a positive way (McNally & Reese, 2009). On a moment-to-moment basis this tendency finds expression through the experience of danger-oriented negative automatic thoughts. For example, a person with panic disorder who notices their heartbeat and respiration may have the negative automatic thought 'These are signs that I'm going to have a panic attack, I must be going crazy'; or a person with OCD who notices a speck of dirt on their cutlery may think 'That dirt contains germs, so if I use the cutlery I may become infected and die'. These negative automatic thoughts cause anxious arousal, which in turn motivates avoidant coping that alleviates anxiety and reinforces avoidant coping.

According to cognitive theory, over time, the repetition of these types of micro-event in which ambiguous stimuli evoke threat-oriented negative automatic thoughts that elicit anxiety and motivate avoidance strengthen threat-oriented schemas and weaken personal control over anxiety, particularly the capacity to access more adaptive non-threat-oriented schemas.

Cognitive therapy helps clients challenge their negative automatic thoughts and underlying core beliefs, attitudes and assumptions about the dangerousness of the situations in which they feel anxiety. This involves clients monitoring fluctuations in anxiety levels in threatening situations, accessing the negative automatic thoughts and beliefs that underpin these fluctuations, and challenging these thoughts and beliefs by generating safe rather than danger-oriented interpretations of situations and engaging in 'behavioural experiments' such as exposure to feared situations to check out whether the catastrophes they fear actually occur.

Cognitive therapy, like behaviour therapy, uses exposure procedures to treat anxiety disorders, but explains their effectiveness in terms of their effects on threat-oriented schemas rather than extinction of conditioned responses. Beck's theory is supported by evidence which shows that anxiety is associated with a threat-sensitive cognitive style (McNally & Reese, 2009) and also by the results of treatment outcome studies with adults and children which support the efficacy of cognitive-behavioural approaches to treatment (Olatunji et al., 2010; Rapee et al., 2009).

In a meta-analysis of 108 studies of cognitive behaviour therapy involving all types of anxiety disorder, Norton and Price (2007) found that cognitive restructuring and exposure therapy alone, in combination, or combined with relaxation training were all equally effective treatments for anxiety disorders. Cognitive-behaviour therapy is as effective as medication such as SSRIs in the treatment of anxiety disorders. However, its effects are more enduring (Hollon et al., 2006). These more enduring effects are probably due to significant changes in psychological processes that maintain anxiety disorders such as the extinction of conditioned responses, the preferential accessing of non-threat-oriented schemas and the use of non-avoidant coping strategies.

Attempts have been made to integrate the cognitive theory of anxiety disorders with current knowledge about the neurobiology of anxiety. Clark and Beck (2010b) have proposed that activation of negative cognitive schemas is subserved by amygdala hyperactivity and avoidant coping is subserved by hypoactivity of the frontal cortex. In contrast, the process of challenging negative automatic thoughts and actively coping with anxiety-provoking situations is subserved by increased activity in the frontal cortex and a gradual reduction in amygdala activity. There is some evidence that cognitive therapy gradually normalizes the neurobiological abnormalities that typify anxiety disorders (Frewen et al., 2008a).

Family systems theory

Systemic theories of anxiety disorders propose that family interaction is central to the aetiology of anxiety disorders and that this provides a rationale for family therapy as a treatment for anxiety (e.g., Bloch et al., 1994; Combrinck-Graham, 1986; Dadds et al., 1992; Perlmutter, 1996). According to this position, individuals develop anxiety disorders when they are socialized in families where parents (and other caregivers) elicit, model and inadvertently reinforce anxiety-related beliefs and behaviours. Furthermore, trauma, stressful life events and family life-cycle transitions in either the family of origin or the family of procreation precipitate the onset of anxiety disorders. These disorders are maintained by patterns of family interaction that reinforce anxiety-related beliefs and avoidant behaviour.

Family belief systems that promote anxiety involve ideas such as – unknown situations should be routinely interpreted as dangerous because it's better to be safe than sorry; the future will probably entail many hazards, catastrophes and dangers; inconsequential events in the past will lead to dangerous threatening consequences at unexpected times in the future; fluctuations in autonomic arousal should be interpreted as the onset of full-blown anxiety attacks; minor symptoms are reflective of serious illness; and testing out the validity of any of these beliefs will lead to more negative consequences than continuing to assume that they are true. Through observing parents and other significant family members articulate these types of danger-oriented belief and engaging in family interactions premised on them, individuals come to internalize them and develop danger-saturated belief systems.

Parental modelling of avoidant coping and inadvertent reinforcement of children's danger-saturated beliefs and avoidant behaviour are the main behaviour patterns that promote anxiety. When children observe parents coping with perceived threats by avoiding rather than confronting them, they adopt similar coping strategy themselves. Such anxiety-related beliefs and avoidant coping are inadvertently reinforced when parents acknowledge their validity and do not challenge them.

Family life-cycle transitions, such as starting school, moving house, birth of a sibling, having children, changing jobs and family stresses such as child abuse, marital discord, illness, injury or bereavement may precipitate the onset of anxiety disorders. In such situations, the individual interprets the transition or stress as a major threat and copes by engaging in avoidant behaviour.

Parents (in the case of children) or partners (in the case of adults) may inadvertently maintain an individual's anxiety-related beliefs and avoidant behaviour by sympathizing with their irrational fears, accepting their danger-saturated view of the situation, and condoning their avoidant behaviour as a legitimate coping strategy. Parents' and partners' own danger-saturated belief systems and personal adjustment problems, if such are present, may prevent them from providing the person with the anxiety disorder with opportunities to develop the skills required to confront and master feared situations. So, for example, in families where there are marital problems, parental depression, parental alcohol abuse or some other difficulty, the parents may avoid facing these difficulties and focus their attention instead on reassuring an anxious child or arranging extensive medical investigations for anxiety-related somatic complaints. The patterns of family interaction that evolve in such situations may inadvertently maintain the child's anxiety and reinforce the parents' avoidance of their own marital or personal difficulties.

Commonly, family members are not consciously aware of the secondary gains associated with these problem-maintaining patterns of interaction. Where adults develop anxiety disorders, their partners may become involved in rituals that help them avoid feared situations and this process may allow the couple to avoid dealing with unresolved marital conflicts over issues such as the distribution of power within the marriage.

Family therapy for children with anxiety disorders aims to support parents and children in creating opportunities within which children can develop the skills required to confront and master feared situations. Couples therapy for cases in which one partner has an anxiety disorder involves helping the couple to work as a team and jointly enter situations that are increasingly anxiety-provoking for the person with the anxiety disorder, and remain in these until the anxiety subsides. The non-symptomatic partner's role in such programmes is to provide support and encourage the symptomatic partner to engage in active coping strategies. Family therapy also aims to reduce danger-oriented family cultures by encouraging family members in their conversations and behaviour to focus more on bravery and positive accomplishments and less on danger and avoidance.

There is substantial evidence, mainly from cross-sectional studies, that the parents of most children with anxiety disorders have anxiety disorders or other psychological problems themselves; that modelling plays an important role in the transmission of anxiety patterns from parents to children; that anxiety disorders are associated with an over-controlling parenting style, a negative or critical style and styles that foster insecure attachment, such as not responding to children's distress signals; and that stressful family circumstances, especially child abuse and marital discord, are associated with anxiety (Bögels & Brechman-Toussaint, 2006; Degnan et al., 2010; Hudson & Rapee, 2009; Rapee et al., 2009; van der Bruggen et al., 2008). There is also evidence that in adulthood, anxiety disorders, notably PTSD, can lead to significant relationship difficulties, which in turn may reduce the support available to the partner with the anxiety disorder and thereby maintain it (Taft et al., 2011).

Comparative trials have shown that family-based interventions are effective for childhood anxiety disorders, but are not always more effective than individual CBT (Bögels & Brechman-Toussaint, 2006; Rapee et al., 2009). In a review of 12 studies of couples-based treatment for panic disorder for agoraphobia, Byrne et al. (2004) concluded that couples-based exposure therapy was as effective as individually based CBT.

An integrative perspective

In clinical practice an integrative approach to conceptualizing and treating anxiety disorders is useful. Distinctions may be made between predisposing, precipitating, maintaining and protective factors, and insights and related evidence associated with the various theories reviewed above may be integrated into this formulation framework.

A range of personal and family factors may predispose people to develop anxiety disorders. Personal factors include a genetic vulnerability to anxiety, a behaviourally inhibited temperament, a threat-oriented cognitive bias, attachment insecurity and personality traits such as neuroticism, introversion, low conscientiousness, anxiety sensitivity, fear of negative evaluation, intolerance of uncertainty, perfectionism, thought–action fusion, and alexithymia. Family factors that may predispose people to develop anxiety disorders include growing up in a stressful family with anxious parents who adopt controlling or critical, unsupportive parenting styles and foster a threat-oriented family culture, or families characterized by domestic violence and child abuse. All of these predisposing factors sensitize children to threat, and support the development of avoidant coping.

The onset of anxiety disorders may be precipitated by trauma, life-cycle transitions or stressful life events that threaten the individual's safety or security. Once anxiety disorders occur they may be maintained by a range of processes. These include a threat-oriented cognitive style, hyper-vigilance, and ruminative and avoidant coping strategies and defence mechanisms. Avoidant coping maintains anxiety through the process of negative reinforcement (getting relief from avoiding feared situations), and prevents individuals from testing out danger-oriented beliefs. Anxiety disorders may also be maintained by interacting with family members who support these processes and/or who adopt threat-sensitive belief systems and avoidant coping styles. Protective factors include personal attributes and social relationships that support actively coping with feared stimuli, and challenging danger-saturated belief systems.

Assessment

Through careful clinical interviewing of clients and members of their families, the symptoms of anxiety, situations in which they occur and relevant history are obtained. A diagnosis is given in accordance with the criteria outlined in ICD-10 and DSM-IV-TR. A formulation explaining the symptoms entailed by the diagnosis may be developed in which the relevant predisposing, precipitating, maintaining and protective factors are outlined. A general clinical formulation model for anxiety disorders is given in Figure 5.6.

The best available structured interview for assessing anxiety disorders is the Anxiety Disorders Interview Schedule for DSM-IV, for which both adult and child versions are available (ADIS, Brown et al., 1994; Silverman & Albano, 1996). A range of standardized self-report instruments and rating scales may be used to assess specific anxiety

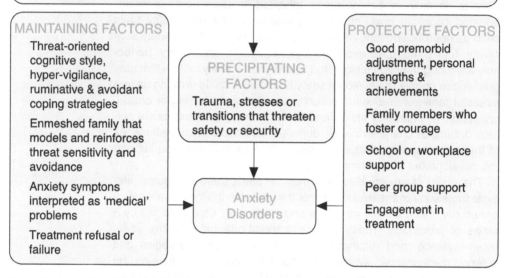

PREDISPOSING FACTORS

Any developmental factors that sensitize a person to danger

Personal factors – Genetic vulnerability to anxiety, inhibited temperament, neuroticism, introversion, low conscientiousness, threat-oriented cognitive bias, anxiety sensitivity, fear of negative evaluation, intolerance of uncertainty, perfectionism, thought-action fusion, alexithymia, attachment insecurity

Family factors – Parental anxiety, over-controlling or critical parenting, family conflict and violence, threat-sensitive family culture

MAINTAINING FACTORS

Threat-oriented cognitive style, hyper-vigilance, ruminative & avoidant coping strategies

Enmeshed family that models and reinforces threat sensitivity and avoidance

Anxiety symptons interpreted as 'medical' problems

Treatment refusal or failure

PRECIPITATING FACTORS

Trauma, stresses or transitions that threaten safety or security

Anxiety Disorders

PROTECTIVE FACTORS

Good premorbid adjustment, personal strengths & achievements

Family members who foster courage

School or workplace support

Peer group support

Engagement in treatment

Figure 5.6 General formulation model for anxiety disorders

disorders or specific traits associated with them in children and adults (Carr, 2006a; Carr & McNulty, 2006; Hunsley & Mash, 2008). During the process of assessment and treatment, patients and family members may be invited to keep daily records of fluctuations in feelings of anxiety, related thoughts, related avoidant behaviours and the circumstances surrounding these fluctuations.

Treatment

The discovery that exposure therapies effectively alleviate anxiety is one of the most important contributions that psychologists have made to the treatment of anxiety disorders. Another important discovery is that briefly exposing patients with anxiety disorders to threatening stimuli sensitizes them to these stimuli and increases anxiety. Thus, non-directive permissive approaches to counselling people with anxiety disorders may actually exacerbate rather than alleviate their anxiety. Many of us who work clinically with people who suffer from anxiety come across clients whose anxiety has worsened as a result of participation in well-intentioned, non-directive counselling.

Current best practice is to take a stepped-care approach to the treatment of anxiety disorders. For people with mild or non-chronic anxiety disorders, guided self-help approaches may be taken. Meta-analyses of controlled trials have shown that both bibliotherapy and computer-based guided self-help are effective for people with anxiety disorders recruited through media advertisements (Andrews et al., 2010; Cuijpers et al., 2010; Salloum, 2010). Fear Fighter is a particularly well researched computer-based programme for the treatment of panic disorder and phobias in adults (www.fearfighter.com).

Psychological treatment may be offered to cases that do not respond to self-help. For all of the anxiety disorders, cognitive-behaviour therapy protocols have been developed and positively evaluated in adults (Barlow et al., 2007; Franklin & Foa, 2007; Najavits, 2007) and children (In-Albon & Schneider, 2007; Watson & Rees, 2008). While the evidence base for CBT anxiety disorder programmes is vast, there is also strong, though less extensive, evidence for the effectiveness of systemic therapy for a number of anxiety disorders including separation anxiety disorder and OCD in children, and panic disorder with agoraphobia in adults (Carr, 2009b, 2009c). There is some evidence from a small number of controlled trials for the effectiveness of psychoanalytic psychotherapy in the treatment of generalized anxiety disorder and panic disorder in adults (Leichsenring, 2009).

Process studies of a range of different types of psychotherapy for anxiety show that a better outcome occurs where there is a strong therapeutic alliance, a structured and intensive approach to treatment that involves psychoeducation, challenging danger-oriented beliefs, exposure to feared situations until habituation occurs, the provision of training in coping strategies, fostering social and family support and good compliance with exposure-based homework assignments between sessions (Stiles & Wolfe, 2006; Woody & Ollendick, 2006). A number of client characteristics influence the outcome of psychotherapy for anxiety disorders (Newman, Crits-Christoph et al., 2006; Newman, Stiles et al., 2006). A poorer outcome is associated with more severe symptoms; comorbid depression, substance use, interpersonal problems and personality disorders; an external locus of control; a history of problematic relationships with parents; low socio-economic status; and low expectations of therapeutic success.

In adults, pharmacological therapy is appropriate where there is limited response to psychotherapy, or where patients express a preference for medication rather than psychological intervention. For most anxiety disorders, SSRIs are the medication of choice. Benzodiazepines, once popular, are not now widely used except on a short-term basis, because of the potential for addiction. For chronic OCD that is unresponsive to both psychological and pharmacological intervention, psychosurgery that disrupts the cortico-striatal–thalamic circuit that subserves OCD symptomatology may be considered, because there is some evidence for its effectiveness (Aouizerate et al., 2006; Stewart et al., 2009; Zohar et al., 2009).

Evidence from meta-analyses supports the effectiveness of SSRIs for childhood anxiety disorders (Bridge et al., 2007). However, because selective serotonin reuptake inhibitors may increase suicide risk, they should be used very cautiously, and only with frequent clinical monitoring in cases where there is no response to psychological intervention (Rudd et al., 2009).

This overall approach to the management of anxiety disorders in children and adults is consistent with international best practice guidelines (American Academy of Child and Adolescent Psychiatry, 2007c, 2009, 2010; American Psychiatric Association, 2004a, 2007, 2009; NICE, 2005a, 2005b, 2006b, 2011).

Controversies

There are many controversies in the scientific study and clinical treatment of anxiety disorders. The medicalization of fear and courage is one deserving particular mention (Breggin, 1991). Within ICD-10 and DSM-IV-TR, anxiety disorders are framed as medical conditions requiring treatment, and in practice in many instances pharmacological treatment is favoured because it is more convenient to offer than non-pharmacological alternatives. An alternative viewpoint is that this way of conceptualizing fundamental human experiences such as fear and courage further disempowers people who are already feeling frightened and powerless. For example, if a person has repeated panic attacks and develops a constricted lifestyle because they are afraid of having a panic attack while away from the safety of their home, it may lead them to believe that they are truly powerless to control their fear if their fear is defined as an illness requiring pharmacological treatment. A further aspect of this argument is that for many years addictive pharmacological treatments, such as diazepam (Valium) or other benzodiazepines, were routinely prescribed for anxiety disorders.

Those who are critical of the medicalization of experiences such as fear and courage would argue that if a person can understand that panic attacks develop from the misinterpretation of bodily sensations and hyperventilation, then they may use this knowledge and their own courage to take control of their fear. In this way they are empowered to be courageous rather than disempowered by being defined as ill. Those who are critical of the medicalization of distress would argue, in the same vein, that a person given a diagnosis of PTSD and prescribed medication to manage the recurrent traumatic memories may also become disempowered. They may develop a belief that they are powerless to control recurrent traumatic memories of experiences such as road traffic accidents, assault with a deadly weapon, or involvement in war or combat. In contrast, if they are helped to understand that traumatic memories of life-threatening events must be repeatedly recalled, processed and integrated into people's overall views of themselves, then this opens up a range of non-pharmacological procedures which trauma survivors may follow to help them take control of recurrent, intrusive distressing memories.

In order to further our understanding of apparently irrational fears, post-traumatic distress and courage, continued scientific study is essential. The use of diagnoses such as PTSD and panic disorder may be valuable in this context. However, it is also valuable to study fear, distress and courage as normal psychological process. It may be fruitful too to study the social processes that underpin the medicalization and the medical treatment of fear in clinical practice and to explore the degree to which these, and alternative conceptualizations of fear, empower clients to be courageous.

Summary

Normal fear is an adaptive response to potential threats to safety while anxiety is a similar non-adaptive response to situations that are not threatening. In DSM-IV-TR and ICD-10 a number of anxiety disorders are defined which differ in the stimuli that elicit anxiety and associated types of avoidant response. With separation anxiety, separation from parents elicits anxiety and is avoided. Consequently school refusal often occurs. For phobias specific creatures, events or situations elicit anxiety and these circumscribed situations are avoided. With generalized anxiety disorder, many aspects of the environment elicit anxiety; the process of apparently uncontrollable worrying also is experienced as anxiety-provoking; and a wide range of situations are avoided. In panic disorder, somatic sensations of arousal are perceived as a threatening prelude to a panic attack, and public situations in which panic attacks previously occurred are avoided, leading to secondary agoraphobia in many cases. With PTSD, cues that trigger flashbacks to traumatic events that precipitated the condition elicit anxiety; these cues are avoided; and recollections of the trauma are suppressed. With OCD, stimuli that evoke obsessional thoughts (such as dirt) elicit anxiety, and compulsive behaviour (such as hand washing) alleviate this anxiety.

At a clinical level anxiety disorders involve selective attention to potential threats, threat-oriented cognition, abnormal levels of physiological arousal, avoidance behaviour, and the disruption of interpersonal relationships so that the individual's lifestyle becomes constricted. In a major US study the lifetime prevalence rate for all anxiety disorders was about 29%. With the exception of OCD, more females than males suffer from anxiety disorders. The typical age of onset of separation anxiety disorder and specific phobias is in childhood, whereas other anxiety disorders typically first occur in adolescence or adulthood. Up to a third of people with one anxiety disorder also suffer from another. There is considerable comorbidity with other disorders, notably substance misuse, disruptive behaviour, and personality and eating disorders. Risk factors for anxiety disorders include a family history of anxiety disorders or psychopathology; a behaviourally inhibited temperament; neuroticism; a personal history of psychopathology; a history of significant family conflict or violence; and a history of stressful life events.

Theoretical explanations for anxiety disorders and related treatments have been developed within biological, trait theory, psychoanalytic, cognitive-behavioural, and family systems traditions. Genetic studies show that anxiety disorders are about 30–40% heritable. Candidate genes that affect the serotonergic and dopaminergic neurotransmitter systems partly explain this genetic vulnerability. With the exception of OCD, anxiety disorders are associated with overactivity within the limbic system, especially the amygdala, which subserves the processing of fear-related information, and inadequate inhibition of this by the frontal cortex, which subserves rational evaluation of potentially threatening situations. In OCD, overactivity of the prefrontal cortex and thalamus subserves the initiation and maintenance of obsessional worrying, and overactivity of the basal ganglia subserves the repetition of compulsive behaviour patterns. In anxiety disorders there is dysregulation of neurotransmitter systems that facilitate communication between brain structures involved in these conditions. Pharmacological treatments such as SSRIs and benzodiazepines aim to rectify these dysregulated neurotransmitter systems. Dysregulation of neuropeptides, notably CRF, also occurs in anxiety disorders and this is associated with HPA axis hyperactivity and the release of the stress steroid, cortisol.

A variety of traits are associated with all anxiety disorders, including the temperamental characteristic behavioural inhibition, neuroticism, conscientiousness and introversion. Associations have been found between specific cognitive traits and specific anxiety disorders including anxiety sensitivity and panic disorder; fear of negative evaluation and social phobia; intolerance of uncertainty and generalized anxiety disorder; perfectionism and OCD; thought–action fusion and OCD; and alexithymia and PTSD. People with anxiety disorders also show information processing biases favouring the detection and recall of threat-oriented material and the interpretation of ambiguous situations as threatening.

Psychoanalytic theories propose that defence mechanisms, such as displacement and undoing, are used to keep unacceptable sexual or aggressive impulses and moral anxiety about their expression from entering consciousness. Treatment involves the interpretation of defences, related neurotic anxiety and repressed unacceptable unconscious impulses. Cognitive-behavioural theories of anxiety point to the role of conditioning, especially negative reinforcement, and cognitive learning processes, especially the development and elaboration of threat-oriented cognitive schemas, in the development of anxiety disorders. CBT for anxiety disorders involves exposure to feared stimuli until extinction of anxiety occurs, cognitive restructuring, and relaxation and coping skills training. Family systems theories highlight the roles of family belief systems and interaction patterns in the development and maintenance of anxiety disorder and the significance of family life-cycle transitions in precipitating the onset of these conditions. Family therapy aims to reduce the danger-oriented family culture and facilitate parents (in the case of anxious children) and partners (in the case of anxious adults) in helping individuals with anxiety disorders enter feared situations and cope with these.

In clinical practice an integrative approach to assessment and treatment of anxiety disorders may be taken. Assessment of anxiety symptoms and relevant personal and family history informs the development of a formulation that explains the aetiology and maintenance of the condition. This formulation guides treatment. A stepped care approach to treatment is considered best practice, with guided self-help being offered in the first instance and progression to evidence-based psychological and/or pharmacological interventions where required. There is a substantial evidence base for the effectiveness of CBT, and a smaller evidence base for the effectiveness of systemic and psychoanalytic approaches for anxiety disorders. SSRIs are the pharmacotherapy of choice for most anxiety disorders and are as effective as psychotherapy in the short term, but their effects are not as enduring as those of psychological intervention. There is controversy about the medicalization of fear and courage.

Questions

- What are the main clinical features of separation anxiety, phobias, generalized anxiety disorder, panic disorder, posttraumatic stress disorder and obsessive compulsive disorder?
- How prevalent are anxiety disorders?
- What are the risk factors for anxiety disorders?
- What are the main biological and psychological theories of anxiety disorders and the main research findings relevant to these theories?
- What are the main evidence-based approaches to assessment and treatment of anxiety disorders?
- Is the medicalization of fear justified?

FURTHER READING

Professional

- Antony, M. & Stein, M. (2009). *Oxford handbook of anxiety and related disorders.* New York: Oxford University Press.
- Carr, A. (2006). *Handbook of child and adolescent clinical psychology: A contextual approach* (second edition). London: Routledge (Chapters 12–13).

- Carr, A. & McNulty, M. (2006). *Handbook of adult clinical psychology: An evidence based practice approach.* London: Brunner-Routledge (Chapters 11–15).
- Clark, D. A. & Beck, A. T. (2010). *Cognitive therapy of anxiety disorders.* New York: Guilford Press.
- Ollendick, T. & March, J. (2003). *Phobic and anxiety disorders in children and adolescents: A clinical guide to effective psychosocial and pharmacological interventions.* Oxford: Oxford University Press.

Self-help

- Antony, M. & Swinson, R. (2000). *The shyness and social anxiety workbook: Proven, step-by-step techniques for overcoming your fear.* Oakland, CA: New Harbinger.
- Antony, M., Craske, M. & Barlow, D. (2006). *Mastering your fears and phobias: Workbook* (second edition). Oxford: Oxford University Press.
- Barlow, D. H. (2006). *Master your anxiety and panic: Workbook* (fourth edition). Oxford: Oxford University Press.
- Craske, M., & Barlow, D. (2006). *Mastery of your anxiety and worry: Workbook* (second edition). Oxford: Oxford University Press.
- Foa, E. B. & Wilson, R. (2001). *Stop obsessing! How to overcome your obsessions and compulsions* (revised edition). New York: Bantam Books.
- Herbert, C. & Wetmore, A. (1999). *Overcoming traumatic stress: A self-help guide using cognitive behavioural techniques.* London: Robinson.
- Last, C. (2006). *Help for worried kids.* New York: Guilford.
- Rapee, R., Spense, S., Cobham, V., & Wignal, A. (2000). *Helping your anxious child: A step-by-step guide for parents.* San Francisco: New Harbinger.

WEBSITES

- American Academy of Child and Adolescent Psychiatry's practice parameters for the treatment of anxiety disorders, PTSC and OCD:
www.aacap.org/cs/root/member_information/practice_information/practice_parameters/practice_parameters
- American Psychiatric Association's practice guidelines for treating panic disorder, PTSD and OCD:
http://psychiatryonline.org/guidelines.aspx
- Anxiety Alliance, UK:
www.anxietyalliance.org.uk
- Anxiety Disorders Association of America:
www.adaa.org
- Anxiety UK:
www.anxietyuk.org.uk
- Fearfighter computer-based CBT programme for anxiety:
www.fearfighter.com
- National Institute for Clinical Excellence guidelines for treating anxiety disorders, PTSD and OCD:
http://guidance.nice.org.uk/topic/mentalhealthbehavioural
- NHS:
www.nhs.uk/Conditions/Anxiety/Pages/Introduction.aspx

Depression

6

Learning objectives

After studying this chapter you will be able to:

- give an account of the main clinical features of depression and distinguish it from normal sadness
- distinguish between major depressive disorder, bipolar disorder, dysthymia and cyclothymia
- summarize the epidemiology of depression
- list the risk factors for depression and for suicide
- outline the main biological and psychological theories of depression
- name the main evidence-based approaches to assessment and treatment of depression
- do the right thing if a friend is suicidal
- give a considered view on antidepressants, electroconvulsive therapy and gender differences in the prevalence of depression.

Introduction

Feelings of happiness and sadness are adaptive. Many behaviour patterns that lead to happiness, such as socializing with others, becoming absorbed in productive work and developing longstanding friendships, are important for the survival of the species. Sadness, which commonly follows loss of valued relationships, skills, personal characteristics, objects and events, may also be adaptive, in that it reminds us to take care of things we value in future so that we don't lose them again. Sadness also signals to others that we require care and elicits support from others, which soothes our emotional pain.

Extreme mood states such as mania and depression are less adaptive. There is no doubt that during periods of mania or hypomania some individuals with bipolar disorder, which is characterized by episodes of mania and depression, produce highly creative work (Silvia & Kaufman, 2010). However, this is done at a high cost. Inevitably people who suffer from bipolar disorder run the risk of dangerous risk-taking, dehydration and exhaustion during manic episodes.

Seasonal affective disorder (or winter depression, as it is colloquially known) may be linked phylogenetically to hibernation and this may have been adaptive for our cave-dwelling ancestors (Montañés et al., 2006). However, nowadays depression seems to fulfil no adaptive function. Despite this, it is a highly prevalent condition, affecting up to 25% of the population (Kessler & Wang, 2009). Because of its prevalence, the main focus in this chapter will be on major depressive disorder, although reference will be made to other mood problems such as bipolar disorder.

From Table 6.1, in which the diagnostic criteria for a depressive episode from DSM-IV-TR (American Psychiatric Association, 2000) and

TABLE 6.1
Criteria for a major depressive episode

DSM-IV-TR	ICD-10

A. Five or more of the following symptoms have been present during the same 2-week period nearly every day and this represents a change from pervious functioning; at least one of the symptoms is either (1) depressed mood or (2) loss of interest or pleasure. Symptoms may be reported or observed.
  1. Depressed mood. In children and adolescents can be irritable mood.
  2. Markedly diminished interest or pleasure in almost all daily activities.
  3. Significant weight loss or gain (of 5% per month) or decrease or increase in appetite. In children consider failure to make expected weight gains.
  4. Insomnia or hypersomnia.
  5. Psychomotor agitation or retardation.
  6. Fatigue or loss of energy.
  7. Feelings of worthlessness, excessive guilt.
  8. Poor concentration and indecisiveness.
  9. Recurrent thoughts of death, suicidal ideation or suicide attempt.
B. Symptoms do not meet criteria for mixed episode of mania and depression.
C. Symptoms cause clinically significant distress or impairment in social occupational, educational or other important areas of functioning.
D. Symptoms not due to the direct effects of a drug or a general medical condition such as hypothyroidism.
E. The symptoms are not better accounted for by uncomplicated bereavement.
	In a typical depressive episode the individual usually suffers, for a period of at least 2 weeks, from depressed mood, loss of interest and enjoyment and reduced energy leading to increased fatiguability and diminished activity. Marked tiredness after only slight effort is common. Other common symptoms are:
	  1. Reduced concentration and attention
	  2. Reduced self-esteem and confidence
	  3. Ideas of guilt and unworthiness
	  4. Bleak and pessimistic views of the future
	  5. Ideas or acts of self-harm or suicide
	  6. Disturbed sleep
	  7. Diminished appetite.
	The lowered mood varies little from day to day, is often unresponsive to circumstances and may show a characteristic diurnal variation as the day goes on.

Note: Adapted from DSM-IV-TR (APA, 2000), ICD-10 (WHO, 1992).

ICD-10 (World Health Organization, 1992) are given, it may be seen that depression is not simply 'feeling sad'. Major depressive disorder is a recurrent condition characterized by episodes of low mood and loss of interest in pleasurable activities along with other symptoms such as poor concentration, fatigue, pessimism, suicidal thoughts, and sleep and appetite disturbance. Depression is a major public health concern because it radically reduces quality of life, has huge economic costs in terms of reduced productivity of the national work force, and has adverse effects on the mental health and adjustment of children of depressed parents (Garber, 2010; Kessler & Wang, 2009). This chapter will consider the clinical features, epidemiology, risk factors, course, theoretical explanations, assessment and treatment of depression. Risk factors for suicide will also be discussed.

Case example of major depression

May, a single woman in her early thirties, was referred for counselling by her family doctor. She insisted on being seen by the psychologist at her house, since she had been bedridden for 2 years. May's first episode of depression occurred in her mid-twenties, after her first and only significant romantic relationship ended. She said that her boyfriend, Rob, had 'broken her heart'. This first depressive episode lasted almost a year. During this time May spent most of her days in bed. She had little energy and no desire to get up and engage with life. Unfortunately, during this depressive episode she lost her job as a teacher.

May lived in a small maritime town about 250 miles from the village where she grew up. Her mother came to stay with her during her first episode of depression. At her family doctor's suggestion, May attended a series of counselling sessions. These helped her to recover. Shortly after her recovery, May's counsellor left the district. After a few months and a series of disappointing and unsuccessful attempts to rekindle old college friendships, May relapsed. She spent most of the next 2 years in bed. Once again, her energy level dropped, she lost interest in all activities, felt very sad and empty, and believed that there was little point in trying to recover. For much of this period, May refused to see anyone except her mother and the family doctor.

Personal and family history

May was born and brought up until the age of 8 in a small rural village. She moved house when she was 8 years old and lost a number of close friends through the change of address. This was particularly stressful for her because she had difficulty making new friends, and felt lonely much of the time afterwards. Before moving house, May had relied on her childhood friends to make living with her parents bearable. When she lost this support, she felt very isolated. May's home life was unbearably stressful because she and her mother were regularly beaten brutally by May's father. Her mother would not talk to her about this, nor would she protect May from the beatings. May lived in this violent family situation until she left home to go to college at the age of 18. During her childhood and teenage years May spent a lot of time studying to distract herself from the unhappy home atmosphere.

On the positive side, May had a good relationship with her cousins and some happy childhood memories of staying at their seaside house. She made a couple of good friends at college with whom she went on holidays to Greece in her early 20s. When May left college, she began work as a teacher and loved her job. She got on well with children and was admired by her colleagues for this.

Within May's extended family there was a history of mood and alcohol problems. Her aunt and a cousin had suffered from depression. She also had an uncle with a drink problem, which may have been related to a difficulty with mood regulation.

Presentation

May presented with profound feelings of sadness and emptiness, a loss of interest in her career and friendships and an inability to experience pleasure. Notable features of her behaviour were the fact that she lived a constricted housebound lifestyle, was unable to concentrate and complained of forgetfulness. May also experienced early morning waking, had diurnal variation of mood, with her mood being worse in the morning, had little appetite and marked weight loss, and refused to take antidepressant medication. From time to time she thought about killing herself, but never planned in a detailed way to end her life and never made a suicide attempt.

She held a distinctly negative view of herself, the world and the future. She talked about herself in self-deprecating ways. For example, she said 'I'm no good as a teacher. I've lost my job because of this illness. I'm no good as a woman. I'll never be married. I'm no good as a person. I'm dirty and worthless and I'm rotting inside. I deserve to be hurt.' She viewed the world as a bleak place. What follows are some of her beliefs about her world: 'My father is no good. He beat me as a child and beat my mother. He is the reason why I am ill. I can't change the past, so I will be ill forever. My mother is no good. I would recover if she were not here looking after me. She interferes in my life and tries to control me. I have no friends so there is no point in recovery. Other people deserve to be hurt. Whatever pleasant things I have experienced were few and far between. For example, my holiday in Greece. I had no control over either the good or bad things that happened to me, so I cannot control my recovery.'

May's view of the future was also dark. For example, she said: 'There is no point in recovery because other people will only take advantage of me. You can't trust anyone because they will abandon you. I have been unfortunate in the past, so I will always be unfortunate. There is no light at the end of the tunnel.'

Formulation

May presented with the symptoms of major depressive disorder: low mood, diurnal variation in mood, loss of interest and pleasure in daily activities, poor concentration, appetite and sleep disturbance, energy loss, worthlessness, pessimism and suicidal ideation. She had experienced two episodes of major depression, each precipitated by the loss of valued relationships. The first episode was triggered by her losing her boyfriend and the second by her failing to renew old friendships, the loss of her counsellor and the loss of work relationships. For other people these types of event might not have led to depression, but for May the losses were particularly stressful because biological and psychological predisposing factors had rendered her especially vulnerable to depression.

May's family history of mood disorders suggested that she might have had a genetic biological vulnerability to developing depression. Her negative childhood experiences of violence and loss of supportive friends after moving house probably rendered her psychologically vulnerable to developing depression, since these led her to view herself, other people and the future in a pessimistic way. Once May's mood dropped, it was maintained by this negative way of interpreting events. In addition to this cognitive maintaining factor, at behavioural and interpersonal levels May's constricted lifestyle also maintained her depression. Her lifestyle reduced opportunities for engaging in pleasant activities, forming relationships, and finding employment. The absence of these opportunities confirmed May's negative view of herself, her world and her future. She was locked into a vicious cycle.

Eventually this had taken its toll on May's appetite, circadian rhythms and activity level. She slept poorly, awoke early, ate little and rarely exercised. These sleeping, eating and activity problems may also have maintained May's depressed mood. However, there were protective factors in this case. May had a history of good premorbid adjustment, and strong support for her recovery from both her mother and her family doctor. This formulation is diagrammed in Figure 6.1.

Intervention

Following assessment, May was helped to understand this formulation. She engaged in a multimodal treatment programme involving cognitive-behavioural interventions, family therapy and antidepressant medication. Behaviour therapy helped her alter her self-defeating patterns of behaviour; engage in regular exercise and pleasant activities; and expand her constricted lifestyle. Cognitive therapy helped her to challenge her pessimistic thinking style and view the world in more positive terms. Family therapy helped May's mother reduce her inappropriate over-involvement with May and her father apologize for the violence to which May had been subjected and exposed to as a child.

Antidepressant medication aimed to normalize the dysregulated serotonergic neurotransmitter system that was presumed to underpin May's depressive symptoms. Over a period of months she increased her activity level, developed a more positive thinking style, achieved greater autonomy from her parents and began to engage in a more normal lifestyle.

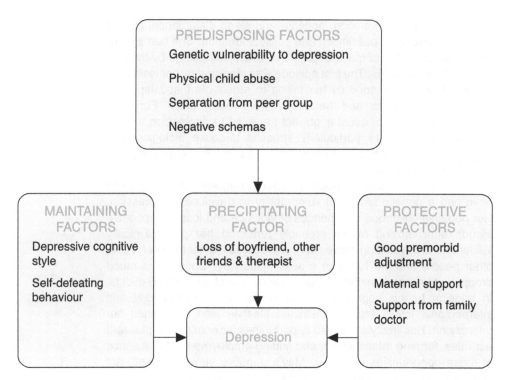

Figure 6.1 Formulation of a case of depression

Major depression is a recurring episodic condition, so May was not 'cured' by this multimodal programme. While she gradually began to enjoy a better quality of life, she continued to struggle to maintain a positive mood state and was vulnerable to relapse when faced with subsequent life stresses, particularly those involving loss of valued relationships.

Clinical features

Table 6.1 gives diagnostic criteria for episodes of major depression from DSM-IV-TR (American Psychiatric Association, 2000) and ICD-10 (World Health Organization, 1992). Within both systems depressive episodes may be classified in terms of severity and with respect to the presence or absence of melancholic or somatic features and psychotic features.

Severity

With regard to symptom severity, episodes of depression may be subclassified as mild, moderate or severe, depending on the number of symptoms present and the degree of impairment.

Melancholia

With regard to melancholic or somatic features, in severe depression where there is a loss of pleasure in all activities (referred to as anhedonia) and a lack of reactivity to pleasant stimuli along with diurnal variation in mood, and sleep and appetite disturbance, the DSM codes such episodes as having melancholic features. In the ICD this presentation is referred to as the somatic syndrome. Historically there was a view that these symptoms reflected an 'endogenous', genetically determined and biologically based form of depression, as distinct from a 'reactive' depression arising from exposure to stressful life events and environmental adversity (Monroe ct al., 2009).

This distinction between endogenous and reactive depression has not been supported by research, which shows that all episodes of depression are preceded by stressful life events, and that in any given case some combination of genetic vulnerability and environmental adversity contributes to the development of depression (Parker, 2009).

Psychotic depression

In both DSM and ICD, if mood-congruent delusions and hallucinations are present, then depressive episodes are described as having psychotic features. Mood-congruent delusions are strongly held, extremely pessimistic beliefs that have no basis in reality, such as the belief of an innocent person that he or she is guilty of many wrongs and so deserves to die. In depression, mood-congruent hallucinations are usually auditory and involve hearing voices in the absence of external stimuli, which say depressing things, such as that the patient is a failure, guilty of wrongdoing, or evil.

A range of clinical features of children, adolescents and adults with major depressive disorders have been identified through research and clinical observation (e.g., Bech, 2009; Brent & Weersing, 2008; Gotlib & Hammen, 2009; Nolen-Hoeksema & Hilt, 2009a). A classification of common clinical features of depression into the domains of perception, cognition, mood, somatic state, behaviour and relationships is given in Table 6.2. When depressive episodes occur, clinical features may be linked by assuming that depressed individuals have usually suffered a loss of some sort: a loss of an important relationship, a loss of some valued attribute such as athletic ability or health, or a loss of status.

Perception

With respect to perception, having suffered a loss, depressed individuals tend to perceive the world as if further losses are probable. Depressed people selectively attend to negative features of the environment. This in turn leads them to engage in depressive cognitions and unrewarding behaviour patterns which further entrench their depressed mood. In severe depression, individuals may report mood-congruent auditory hallucinations. We may assume that this severe perceptual abnormality is present when individuals report hearing voices criticizing them or telling them depressive things, as noted above. Auditory hallucinations also occur in schizophrenia. However, the hallucinations that occur in schizophrenia are not necessarily mood-congruent.

TABLE 6.2
Clinical features of depression

Perception	Perceptual bias towards negative events
	Mood-congruent hallucinations[†]
Cognition	Negative view of self, world and future
	Over-general memory
	Cognitive distortions
	Inability to concentrate
	Indecision
	Suicidal ideation
	Suicidal intention*
	Excessive guilt*
	Mood-congruent delusions[†]
Mood	Depressed mood
	Irritable mood
	Anxiety and apprehension
	Distinct quality of depressed mood*
	Loss of interest in pleasurable activities (anhedonia)*
	Lack of emotional reactivity*
Somatic state	Fatigue
	Diminished activity
	Loss of appetite or overeating
	Aches and pains
	Early morning waking*
	Diurnal variation of mood (worse in morning)*
	Change in weight*
	Loss of interest in sex*
Behaviour	Psychomotor retardation or agitation*
	Depressive stupor[†]
Relationships	Deterioration in family relationships
	Withdrawal from peer relationships
	Poor work or educational performance

*These features are associated with melancholic depression and are referred to as vegetative features or the somatic syndrome. [†]These features occur in psychotic depression.

Cognition

With respect to cognition, depressed individuals describe themselves, the world and the future in negative terms. They evaluate themselves as worthless and are critical of their occupational and social accomplishments. Often this negative self-evaluation is expressed as guilt for not living up to certain standards or letting others down. They see their world, including family, friends and work or school as unrewarding, critical and hostile or apathetic. They describe the future in bleak terms and report little if any hope that things will improve. Where they report extreme hopelessness and this is coupled with excessive guilt for which they believe they should be punished, suicidal ideas or intentions may be reported. Extremely negative thoughts about the self, the world and the future may be woven together in severe cases into depressive delusional systems.

In addition to the content of the depressed individual's thought being bleak, they also display logical errors in their thinking and concentration problems. Errors in reasoning are marked by a tendency to maximize the significance and implications of negative events and minimize the significance of positive events. They also have over-general autobiographical memories. That is, they have difficulty remembering specific happy events in detail (which might lighten their mood), but rather remember both positive and negative past episodes in their lives in global over-general ways. In addition they have concentration, attention and decision-making problems that lead to difficulties managing occupational, academic or leisure activities demanding sustained attention and decisiveness.

Affect

With respect to affect, low mood, diurnal variation in mood and anhedonia are key features of depression. Depressed mood is usually reported as a feeling of sadness, emptiness, loneliness or despair. Diurnal variation in mood is particularly common in severe depression, with mood being worse in the morning. During an episode of major depression as a person moves from mild to moderate to severe depression, the increasing number and intensity of symptoms may lead to intense anxiety. That is, fears are experienced such as 'Will this get worse? Am I stuck in this living hell for ever? Will I ever be myself again? Will I be able to prevent myself from committing suicide to escape?' Irritability may also occur, with the person expressing anger at the source of their loss, for example anger at a deceased loved one for abandoning the grieving person, or anger at health professionals for being unable to alleviate the depression.

Somatic state

Changes in somatic state associated with depression include loss of energy, disturbances of sleep and appetite, weight loss or failure to make age-appropriate weight gain, pain symptoms and loss of interest in sex. Typically, depressed people have difficulty sleeping and eat little due to appetite loss. These symptoms are referred to as vegetative features. With regard to sleep disturbance, depressed people may have difficulty going to sleep, wake frequently during the night, or suffer from early-morning waking. Usually, they report having racing thoughts and engaging in depressive rumination when they can't sleep. In atypical cases of depression people may sleep too much due to constant feelings of exhaustion and eat excessively due to increased appetite or because eating may temporarily reduce their distress.

Headaches and medically unexplained chest, back or abdominal pain are other somatic features of depression. For some patients, these pain symptoms are the first to be reported to their family doctors, and only when medical investigations of these complaints are negative is depression considered as a possible diagnosis. All of the somatic features of depression mentioned above are consistent with research findings, discussed below, that dysregulation of neurobiological, endocrine and immune functions is associated with depression and that sleep architecture is also affected.

Behaviour

At a behavioural level, depressed individuals may show either reduced and slowed activity levels (psychomotor retardation) or increased but ineffective activity (psychomotor agitation). They typically fail to engage in activities that would bring them a sense of achievement or connect-edness to family or friends. Where individuals become immobile, this is referred to as depressive stupor. Fortunately this is rare.

One risky behavioural complication of depression is self-harm. A dis-tinction is made between suicidal behaviour and non-suicidal deliberate self-harm. With suicidal behaviour, self-harm is primarily motivated by the intention to end one's life. With non-suicidal deliberate self-harm, there are other motivations. People may cut or burn themselves to dis-tract themselves from their depressive feelings. They may take non-lethal overdoses to elicit care from family or friends or to gain admission to hospital and remove them from stressful situations.

Relationships

At an interpersonal level, depressed individuals report a deterioration in their relationships with family, friends, colleagues, school teachers and other significant figures in their lives. They describe themselves as lonely and yet unable or unworthy to take steps to make contact with others. Ironically, when depressed people try to overcome their loneli-ness by talking to others, they tend to drive them away through their pessimistic, self-centred talk and depressive behaviour.

Classification

In DSM-IV-TR and ICD-10, mood disorders are primarily classified in terms of polarity (unipolar versus bipolar conditions) and course (episodic versus continuous conditions). Distinctions are made between

- major depressive disorder
- bipolar disorder
- dysthymia
- cyclothymia.

Major depressive disorder and bipolar disorder are episodic conditions, with the former characterized by episodes of low mood, negative cognition, and sleep and appetite disturbance and the latter characterized in addition by episodes of mania in which elation, grandiosity, flight of ideas and expansive behaviour occur. Dysthymia and cyclothymia are less severe non-episodic chronic and continuous conditions, with dysthymia being characterized by depressive symptomatology and cyclothymia being characterized by similar but less extreme mood fluctuations than bipolar disorder.

The distinctions between unipolar and bipolar conditions and between episodic and persistent disorders that are central to the classification of mood disorders in ICD-10 and DSM-IV-TR have subordinated earlier classification systems, which made primary distinctions between psychotic and neurotic, endogenous and reactive, and overt and masked depression (Farmer & McGuffin, 1989; Kendell, 1976; Parker, 2009). With the psychotic/neurotic and endogenous/reactive classification systems, it was assumed that psychotic and endogenous depressions were more severe than neurotic and reactive depressions, with the more severe conditions being due to genetic and biological factors and requiring treatment with medication or electroconvulsive therapy, and the less severe conditions being due to environmental factors and requiring treatment with psychotherapy (Parker, 2009). However, evidence from stressful life-event research shows that all episodes of depression, regardless of quality or severity, are preceded by stressful life events and in that sense are reactive (Monroe et al., 2009). Treatment outcome research has shown that only about two out of three cases of depression respond to available treatments; that symptom type or severity does not always predict which patients will respond to physical or psychological interventions; and that for most patients multimodal therapy involving a combination of medication and psychotherapy is most effective (Paykel & Scott, 2009). The older psychotic/neurotic and endogenous/reactive distinctions have been incorporated into DSM-IV-TR and ICD-10, insofar as depressive episodes may be specified as having either psychotic features or melancholic/somatic features, typical of what formerly was referred to as endogenous depression.

With regard to the overt/masked distinction, this was introduced to take account of adults whose depression was masked by medically unexplained symptoms such as headaches and chest pains (Hoogenhout et al., 2010) or children whose depression was masked by conduct problems (Carlson & Cantwell, 1980). Adult cases that would formerly have been described as having masked depression are classified in DSM-IV-TR and ICD-10 as having a somatoform disorder, a condition characterized by multiple medically unexplained symptoms. What would formerly have been referred to as masked depression in children is classified as comorbid depression and conduct disorder in DSM-IV-TR and as depressive conduct disorder in ICD-10.

Epidemiology, course and risk factors

Major depression is the most common mood disorder, with a lifetime prevalence rate of 6–25% in international community studies (Kessler & Wang, 2009). In the US National Co-morbidity Survey Replication the lifetime prevalence of DSM-IV major depression was 16.6%, whereas the lifetime prevalence of dysthymia was 2.5% and of bipolar disorder was 3.9% (Kessler et al., 2005). Depression is less common among prepubertal children than adolescents and adults (Brent & Weersing, 2008). In children, equal numbers of boys and girls have depression, but this changes in adolescence and by adulthood, compared with men, about twice as many women have depression (Nolen-Hoeksema & Hilt, 2009b).

Comorbid disorders occur in most cases of depression. In the US National Comorbidity Replication Survey, 59% of depressed participants had comorbid anxiety disorders and 24% had comorbid substance use disorders (Kessler & Wang, 2009). In clinical samples of depressed patients, comorbid personality disorders occur in 50–85% of inpatients and 20–50% of outpatients (Klein et al., 2009). The highest level of comorbidity occurs with cluster C personality disorders (avoidant, dependent, and obsessive compulsive personality disorders).

Depression follows a chronic relapsing course, with up to 80% of people having recurring episodes, and in community samples the median duration of episodes is about 5 or 6 weeks (Kessler & Wang, 2009). In clinical samples episodes typically last for 5–6 months; the majority of cases recover from a depressive episode within a year; about half of all patients continue to have fluctuating residual symptoms between episodes; for less than 10% recovery does not occur and chronic depressive symptoms persist; and most cases relapse within 5 years (Angst, 2009; Boland & Keller, 2009).

As more depressive episodes occur, there are decreases in inter-episode intervals and a reduction in the amount of stress required to trigger the onset of further depressive episodes, an issue discussed below under stress theories (Boland & Keller, 2009).

Risk factors for depression include a family history of mood disorders, female gender, low socio-economic status involving economic and educational disadvantage, an adverse early family or institutional environment, a depressive temperament, a negative cognitive style, deficits in self-regulation, high levels of life stress, and low levels of social support from family and friends (Garber, 2010; Hammen et al., 2010).

Risk factors for recurrent major depressive episodes identified in the US Collaborative Depression Study of over 500 patients include a history of three or more prior episodes, comorbid dysthymia (often called double depression), comorbid anxiety and substance use disorders, long duration of individual episodes, poor control of symptoms by antidepressant medication, onset after 60 years of age, a family history of mood disorder, and being a single female (Boland & Keller, 2009).

For a subgroup of people who suffer from depression, deficits in visually processing light and the season of the year are risk factors for depression (Rosenthal, 2009). These people, who experience regularly recurring depressive episodes in the autumn and winter, with remission in the spring and summer, are said to have seasonal affective disorder. They develop symptoms in the absence of adequate light and respond favourably to enhanced environmental lighting, often referred to as 'light therapy' (Golden et al., 2005).

In community samples about 3.4% of people with a major depressive disorder commit suicide; the rate in clinical samples is about 15%; and about 60% of completed suicides (studied by psychological autopsy) are depressed (Berman, 2009).

Aetiological theories

Theoretical explanations for depression and related treatments have been developed within biological, psychoanalytic, cognitive-behavioural and family systems traditions. Much research on depression has been guided by these theories. In addition, research on depression has been informed by psychological constructs such as stress, temperament, personality traits, cognitive biases, coping strategies and interpersonal styles. A number of influential theories, hypotheses and related treatments and research findings from these areas will be briefly reviewed below.

Biological theories

Biological theories of depression point to the role of genetic factors in rendering people vulnerable to the development of mood disorders, and to the role of structural and functional brain abnormalities; dsysregulation of neurotransmitter, neuroendocrine and immune systems; and sleep architecture and circadian rhythm abnormalities in the aetiology of depression. There is considerable support for biological theories from neuroimaging, pharmacological, psychophysiological and other neurobiological studies, although current knowledge of these abnormalities is incomplete (Davidson et al., 2009; Hamilton et al., 2011; Levinson, 2009; Sullivan et al., 2000; Thase, 2009). However, there is a consensus about certain aspects of the neurobiology of depression which will be presented below.

Genetics

The genetic hypothesis proposes that depression develops where a person with an inherited vulnerability to mood disorders is exposed to stressful life events. Results of twin, adoption and family studies show that a predisposition to depression is genetically transmitted. Major depression is about 40% heritable (Sullivan et al., 2000), whereas bipolar disorder is about 70% heritable (Edvardsen et al., 2008). Precisely what biological characteristics are genetically transmitted and the mechanisms of transmission are still largely unknown. However, results of studies on structural and functional brain abnormalities, neurotransmitter dysregulation, endocrine abnormalities, immune system dysfunction, sleep architecture and circadian rhythm abnormalities in some cases suggest that a biological vulnerability to dysregulation of one or more of these systems is probably inherited. It is also probable that the vulnerability is polygenetically transmitted, since the results of family studies cannot easily be accounted for by simpler models of genetic transmission.

Many candidate genes for depression have been investigated; few have been identified; and where significant associations between candidate genes and depression have been found, very few consistent replication studies are available (Levinson, 2009; Shyn & Hamilton, 2010). The search for candidate genes has focused in large part on those whose products affect neurotransmitters thought to be involved in the aetiology of mood disorders, notably serotonin and noradrenaline.

One candidate gene that affects the serotonin system deserves mention because consistent support has been found for the link between it and vulnerability to depression. A common polymorphism (5-HTTLPR) in the promoter region of the serotonin transporter gene (5HTT or SLC6A4) regulates gene expression. In a large meta-analysis, Karg et al. (2011) found that the short (rather than the long) allele variant of the 5-HTTLPR polymorphism increases the risk of developing depression under stress, particularly in the case of child abuse and severe medical problems. This increased stress sensitivity for these types of life event probably occurs because of decreased serotonin re-uptake and increased amygdala neuronal activity in response to stress. The vulner-ability associated with the short allele variant of the 5-HTTLPR polymor-phism is not specific to depression. It also renders people vulnerable to PTSD and borderline personality disorder. This is because the seroton-ergic neurotransmitter system subserves a range of stress-related emo-tional processes including both depression and anxiety.

The limbic system and dorsolateral prefrontal cortex

Depression is associated with abnormalities in the functioning of brain structures that subserve the experience and expression of emotions, primarily the limbic system (which includes the amygdala, hippocampus, insula and parts of the anterior cingulate cortex), and those that subserve self-regulation, primarily the dorsolateral prefrontal cortex. In depressed people the limbic system (especially the amygdala and anterior cingulate cortex) is overactive, while the dorsolateral prefrontal cortex is underactive (Hamilton et al., 2011). The overactive limbic system probably subserves the ongoing experience of intense negative emotions, while the underactive dorsolateral prefrontal cortex probably subserves a deficit in regulating these negative emotional experiences through reappraisal and purposeful problem-solving.

There is some preliminary evidence that successful psychological and pharmacological treatments normalize these abnormalities in dif-ferent ways. Psychological interventions such as cognitive therapy probably ameliorate depression by increasing activity in the prefrontal cortex, whereas antidepressant medication probably alleviates depres-sion by decreasing limbic system overactivity (Clark & Beck, 2010; Thase, 2009).

Neurotransmitters

There is evidence for hypoactivity of the serotonergic and noradrener-gic neurotransmitter systems in neuroanatomical centres associated with depression (Thase, 2009). Originally depletion of serotonin and noradrenaline was thought to cause depression, but now a more com-plex dysregulation of these systems involving a reduction in the sensi-tivity of postsynaptic receptor sites is hypothesized to be the critical difficulty. The efficiency of these neurotransmitter systems is reduced in depression, and increased by antidepressant drugs (Gitlin, 2009).

Four main classes of antidepressant medication have been developed: tricyclic antidepressants (TCAs), monoamine oxidase inhibitors (MAOIs), selective serotonin reuptake inhibitors (SSRIs), and novel or dual action antidepressants (Gitlin, 2009). TCAs such as imipramine (which has the trade name Tofranil) increase the sensitivity of dysfunctional receptor sites to serotonin and noradrenaline. MAOIs such as phenelzine (which has the trade name Nardil) prevent the enzyme – monoamine oxidase – from breaking down neurotransmitters in the synaptic cleft and lead to an increase in neurotransmitter levels.

TCAs and MAOIs were developed in the 1950s and were widely used until the 1980s, when they were largely replaced in clinical practice by SSRIs and novel or dual-action antidepressants. SSRIs such as fluoxetine (which has the trade name Prozac) prevent serotonin from being reabsorbed into the presynaptic membrane and so increase levels of this neurotransmitter. Novel and dual action antidepressants operate in a variety of ways. For example venlafaxine (with the trade name Effexor), which is a dual-action antidepressant, prevents both noradrenaline and serotonin from being reabsorbed into the presynaptic membrane and so increases levels of both of these neurotransmitters.

Results of meta-analyses of controlled trials show that for severe depression the positive effects of antidepressants are substantial, but for mild or moderate depression their effects are negligible (Fournier et al., 2010). Furthermore, there is no evidence that the newer antidepressants, such as the SSRIs, are any more effective than the older ones, such as the TCAs, although some have fewer side-effects (Gitlin, 2009). Antidepressant side-effects are discussed below in the section on controversies. There is consistent evidence that genetic vulnerability to depression involves genes whose action affects the efficiency of the serotonin neurotransmitter system, which is associated with depression, as was noted above in the discussion of genetic factors.

Neuroendocrine and immune systems

Hypothalamic–pituitary–adrenal (HPA) axis overactivity is a central aspect of the stress response. The HPA axis is a major part of the neuroendocrine system3 involving the hypothalamus, the pituitary gland located below the hypothalamus, and the adrenal glands (located on top of the kidneys), which controls stress reactions and other processes including the immune system, sexuality and digestion. The HPA axis is activated by noradrenaline and inhibited by serotonin neurotransmission.

There is evidence for the dysregulation of neuropeptides, notably corticotropin-releasing factor (CRF), in the limbic system of depressed people. CRF is released in response to stress and is associated with HPA axis hyperactivity. CRF release and increased HPA axis activity result in elevated levels of the stress steroid cortisol and disruption of normal cortisol circadian rhythms (Thase, 2009). Elevated cortisol arising from HPA axis overactivity in turn compromises the efficiency of the immune system, rendering depressed patients more susceptible to inflammatory diseases including arthritis and atherosclerosis (Glassman

& Miller, 2007). Such illnesses in turn are additional stresses that may maintain or exacerbate depression.

Sleep architecture and circadian rhythms

Depression is associated with a disruption of sleep architecture and circadian rhythms. Sleep disturbance, which includes difficulty falling asleep, broken sleep and early-morning waking, is a core symptom of depression. Psychophysiological studies show that abnormal sleep architecture underpins depressive sleep disturbance (Thase, 2009). Depressed people spend more time in rapid eye movement (REM) sleep and less time in slow-wave sleep. They also show shorter REM onset latency. Up to 60% of depressed people temporarily recover following sleep deprivation, although they relapse after even a brief sleep (Hemmeter et al., 2010). Antidepressants regularize abnormal sleep architecture, probably by normalizing serotonin and noradrenaline neurotransmitter systems, which are dysregulated in depression and regulate sleep architecture. Light therapy, which artificially extends exposure to daylight during short winter days to the duration of long summer days is an effective treatment for seasonal affective disorder, suggesting that seasonal depression is associated with disrupted circadian rhythms (Monteleone et al., 2010).

In summary, there is considerable support for a neurobiological theory of depression. Major depressive disorder is about 40% heritable. Vulnerability to depression is probably polygenetic, and so far the only candidate gene for which there is consistent evidence is one that affects the efficiency of the serotonegic neurotransmitter system. Dysregulations of this system and the noradrenergic system occur in depression. Both neurotransmitter systems are involved in a range of other neurobiological features of depression including overactivity of the limbic system and underactivity of the dorsolateral prefrontal cortex; HPA axis overactivity, elevated cortisol levels and reduced immune system efficiency; and disturbed sleep architecture characterized by increased REM and reduced slow-wave sleep. These neurobiological abnormalities occur more commonly in severe depression. Antidepressant medication, which is effective for severe but not mild or moderate depression, alleviates depression by increasing the efficiency of serotonergic and noradrenergic neurotransmitter systems.

Stress theories

Stress theories propose that depression develops following exposure to stress. There are variations on this theme, for example diathesis–stress theories propose that depression only follows exposure to stress in people who have specific biological or psychological attributes that render them vulnerable to stressful life events, and the most vulnerable require the least stress for depression to occur (e.g., Joiner & Timmons 2009; Joormann, 2009; Levinson, 2009). Stress-generation theory proposes that people with certain personal attributes inadvertently generate excessive stress, which in turn leads to depression (Liu & Alloy, 2010).

A substantial body of research shows that the onset, course and severity of depression are associated with stress, including acute and chronic stressful life events and recent and early life adversity and loss (Goodman & Brand, 2009; Hammen, 2009; Harkness & Lumley, 2008; McLeod et al., 2007; Monroe et al., 2009). Early life stress such as rejection and hostility, child abuse, parental depression and parental death may cause childhood depression and render people vulnerable to further episodes of depression in adulthood. In adulthood loss of important relationships, roles and resources may precipitate initial episodes of depression and relapse in recovered patients, or may delay recovery during treatment. Higher levels of stress are associated with more severe depressive symptoms.

As the number of episodes of depression increases, the amount of stress required to precipitate a relapse decreases (Boland & Keller, 2009). This may be due to the neurobiological process of kindling (Monroe & Harkness, 2005) and the cognitive process of rumination (McLaughlin & Nolen-Hoeksema, 2011). According to cognitive theory, minor stresses, which might normally lead to small negative mood changes, may give rise to chronic rumination and catastrophizing in people who have previously had depressive episodes, and this rumination and catastrophizing may lead to major negative mood changes and the onset of further episodes of depression. According to kindling theory, multiple episodes of depression probably render the neurobiological systems that maintain depression more vulnerable to depressogenic changes in response to minor stresses.

Depressed people are not passive recipients of environmental stress, but play an active role in stress generation. Available research indicates that those more likely to generate stress leading to depression are female, have been exposed in early life to child abuse or chronic adversity and have depressive cognitive styles (discussed below in the section on cognitive and behavioural theories) (Liu & Alloy, 2010).

Temperament, traits, cognitive biases, coping strategies and interpersonal styles

Hypotheses that variables such as temperament, personality traits, cognitive biases, coping strategies and interpersonal style render people vulnerable to depression when they encounter stress and adversity, or maintain depression, will be considered below.

Temperament

The Temperament and Character Inventory has been used in much of the research on temperament and depression (Cloninger et al., 1993). This instrument includes four dimensions of temperament: harm avoidance, reward dependence, novelty seeking and persistence. The structure of temperament in this model has been inferred from genetic studies of personality. Three of the temperamental dimensions are hypothesized to be related to specific neurotransmitter systems of the brain. It is proposed that harm avoidance is subserved by the serotonin system; reward dependence by the noradrenaline system; and novelty seeking by the dopamine system. In a meta-analysis, Kampman and Poutanen (2011) found that the harm avoidance temperamental dimension was strongly associated with current depressive symptoms, and improvements in harm avoidance occurred in treatment studies of major depressive disorder. This finding is consistent with evidence for the central role of dysregulation of the serotonergic neurotransmitter system in depression.

In Watson and Clark's model of temperament a distinction is made between positive and negative emotionality. They have found that depressed people tend to have high levels of negative emotionality and low levels of positive emotionality (Watson, 2009). In this model negative emotionality is the temperamental dimension that underpins the personality trait neuroticism, whereas the personality trait extraversion is underpinned by the temperamental dimension of positive emotionality. The role of these personality traits in depression will now be considered.

Personality traits

In a major meta-analysis, Kotov et al. (2010) investigated correlations between depression and the 'Big 5' personality traits: neuroticism, extraversion, conscientiousness, openness and agreeableness. They found that neuroticism was the personality trait most strongly associated with major depressive disorder. There were significant but smaller negative correlations between depression and both extraversion and conscientiousness. Thus, the typical personality trait profile of people with major depressive disorder was characterized by a high level of neuroticism (which entails negative emotionality and distress), introversion (which involves social withdrawal and a lack of positive emotionality) and low conscientiousness (where there is a tendency not to follow through on plans). It is not clear whether this personality profile predisposes people to depression, whether it occurs as a result of depression, or whether depression and the personality profile are the result of some independent factor.

Within both the psychoanalytic and cognitive-behavioural traditions there are hypotheses about the association between specific personality dimensions and vulnerability to depression when one is faced with specific types of stressor. Within the psychoanalytic tradition, Blatt (2004) has proposed that distinctions may be made between dependent and self-critical, perfectionistic forms of depression. Within the cognitive-behavioural tradition, Beck et al. (1983) distinguished between sociotropic and autonomous depressives. In these formulations it is proposed that people with high levels of dependence or sociotropy have strong needs for relatedness and so are vulnerable to depression when faced with loss of important relationships, whereas people with high levels of perfectionistic self-criticism or autonomy have strong needs for self-definition through achievement and so are vulnerable to depression when faced with failure. Extensive research has shown that the personality traits of dependence/sociotropy and self-criticism/autonomy are correlated with depression (Klein et al., 2009; Luyten et al., 2005).

A number of lower-order traits have been found to correlate with depression. These include low self-esteem (Orth et al., 2008), perfectionism (Egan et al., 2011), shame and guilt (Kim et al., 2011).

Cognitive biases

Research from experimental psychopathology has consistently found that people with depression show a range of information-processing biases before, during and between depressive episodes at the levels of attention, memory and reasoning that render them vulnerable to depression and maintain low mood during depressive episodes (Joormann, 2009). People with depression are more likely to selectively attend to, and remember, negative information about the self and the world (Peckham et al., 2010; Phillips et al., 2010). Over-general autobiographical memory – the tendency to remember generalities but not specific details of past events – is also a well established characteristic of depression, with greater over-general memory being predictive of more severe future depressive symptoms (Sumner et al., 2010). In depression there is also a bias towards pessimistic interpretations of situations, known as depressive cognitive style (Haeffel et al., 2008). Depressive cognitive style and its relationship to helplessness will be discussed below under cognitive and behavioural theories.

Alongside depression-specific cognitive biases that confer vulnerability to depression, a number of general cognitive deficits arise as a result of depression. In a meta-analysis, McDermott and Ebmeier (2009) found significant correlations between depression severity and a range of cognitive functions including processing speed, episodic memory and executive function, but not semantic or visuo-spatial memory.

Coping strategies

Certain coping strategies are associated with depression. In a meta-analysis, Aldao et al. (2010) found that depression was strongly associated with the use of rumination as a coping strategy. With rumination, depressed people repeatedly recycle negative and depressive thoughts and have difficulty disengaging from them. Depression was also correlated, although less strongly, with the use of avoidance and suppression as coping strategies. Aldao et al. (2010) found negative correlations between depression and a number of adaptive coping strategies including problem-solving, acceptance and reappraisal.

Interpersonal styles

Distinctive interpersonal styles are associated with the development and maintenance of depression. In line with Bowlby's (1980) attachment theory, there is evidence that depression is associated with an insecure attachment style arising from child-rearing experiences that interfered with the development of attachment security, such as parental rejection, child abuse and neglect, and loss of a parent through bereavement (Bakermans-Kranenburg & van IJzendoorn, 2009; Dozier et al., 2008).

Depressed people tend to have higher levels of dependency and sociotropy, both of which are associated with strong needs for interpersonal closeness, as noted above in the section on personality traits (Klein et al., 2009).

Compared with non-depressed people, depressed people have social skills deficits (Joiner & Timmons, 2009). In both quality and content their speech is more negative. They talk more slowly and quietly and with less modulation about more negative things, with a greater focus on the self and a reduced focus on the concerns of others. Their non-verbal behaviour is more negative. They engage in less eye contact, show fewer positive emotional facial expressions and more animated negative facial expressions. They also engage in more reassurance seeking and negative feedback seeking than people without depression. Some of these skills deficits predate the onset of depressive episodes and remain after remission.

The interpersonal style of depressed people has a number of consequences (Joiner & Timmons, 2009). It leads to low mood and distress in others who interact with depressed people (known as the depression contagion effect). This in turn may lead others to avoid them, or act in critical, hostile and blaming ways towards them. This negative response involving criticism and hostility, or responding in an over-involved way towards a depressed family member, is referred to as expressed emotion. Depressed people who live in family situations characterized by high levels of expressed emotion, which is very stressful for the depressed person, have been found to relapse more rapidly than those whose families respond to them in a low-key way (Hooley, 2007).

Psychoanalytic theories

Of the many psychoanalytic theories of depression that have been developed, reference will be made here to Freud's (1917) original position, Bibring's (1965) ego-psychological model and Blatt's (2004) object relations formulation. These theories have been selected because they are illustrative of psychodynamic explanations, and Blatt's model has been singled out for attention because, unlike many psychodynamic theories, considerable effort has gone into empirically testing it.

Freud's classical psychoanalytic theory

In Freud's (1917) psychoanalytic theory he proposed that depression arose from self-directed anger which occurred in response to loss of a valued person or attribute. He argued that following a major loss in adult life such as bereavement (referred to as object loss), regression to the earliest stage of development – the oral stage – occurs. In this regressed state the person functions psychologically like an infant and so a distinction between the self and the lost object is not made. The lost object is introjected and experienced as part of the self. In depression, aggression at the introject of the lost object for bringing about a state of abandonment is experienced as self-directed anger or the self-criticism that characterizes depressed people.

People whose primary caregivers either failed to meet their dependency needs during the oral phase and so neglected them, or were over-indulgent and so did not provide them with opportunities to learn self-sufficiency, are predisposed to developing depression according to this model. When they lose a loved one, they feel the loss more acutely than others and are more likely to regress, introject the lost object and experience retroflexive anger. Freud proposed that the loss of valued personal attributes (such as career status) as well as the loss of valued people could symbolize object loss. In Freud's structural personality theory he distinguished between the unconscious id, which represented sexual and aggressive instincts; the superego, which represented the internalization of societal norms and standards; and the ego, which represented conscious functions that attempted to reconcile and balance the instincts of the id, the standards set by the superego and the demands of day-to-day life.

In depression, the superego is the psychological structure that directs anger at the ego. Because the superego, which is not fully developed in children, is the psychological structure necessary for directing anger at the ego, the traditional psychoanalytic position entails the view that children are unable to experience depression. This view is unsupported by available epidemiological data. However, Freud's position was important in drawing attention to the significance of loss in depression, a hypotheses that has been supported by subsequent research (Goodman & Brand, 2009; Monroe et al., 2009).

There is also good evidence that self-directed anger, in the form of guilt and shame, is strongly associated with depression (Kim et al., 2011). Finally, Freud pointed out the importance of early life experiences in creating a vulnerability to depression, an idea that is central to modern psychodynamic, attachment and cognitive theories of depression, and one that has considerable empirical support (Bakermans-Kranenburg & van IJzendoorn, 2009; Blatt, 2004; Goodman & Brand, 2009; Joormann, 2009).

Bibring's ego-psychology theory

Bibring (1965), a later psychodynamic ego psychologist, explained depression as the outcome of low self-esteem which resulted from perceiving a large discrepancy between the self as it is and the ideal self. Internalization of harsh, critical parental injunctions or perfectionistic parental injunctions during early childhood accounted for the development of a particularly unrealistic ego-ideal, which in psychoanalytic theory is an aspect of the superego. A substantial body of evidence supports the view that low self-esteem is an important correlate and in some instances a precursor of depression, and in some but not all cases this is associated with a history of critical or punitive parenting (Blatt, 2004; Orth et al., 2008).

Blatt's psychoanalytic theory of two types of depression

It was noted in the section on personality traits that Blatt (2004) distinguished between two types of depression associated with two distinct types of early parent–child relationships that engender vulnerability to depression when faced with two distinct types of stress in later life. A vulnerability to stresses involving loss of attachment relationships is central to the anaclitic or dependent type of depression, and this has its roots in early experiences of neglectful parenting or loss of parents. A vulnerability to stresses involving loss of autonomy and control is central to the introjective or self-critical perfectionistic type of depression, and this has its roots in early experiences of critical, punitive parenting.

This distinction between depression associated with disruption of interpersonal relationships and that associated with threats to mastering important achievement-oriented tasks has been made by many theorists, but has found its clearest articulation in Blatt's work. Dependent and self-critical types of depression may be assessed with Blatt's Depressive Experiences Questionnaire. A growing body of evidence using this instrument has shown that in adults, these subtypes of depression are associated with the recall of different childhood experiences, which have led to the development of different types of depressive object-relations that are typically activated in later life by different types of stressful life event, and lead to the use of different types of defence mechanism (Blatt, 2004).

Children who experience either neglectful parenting or the loss of a parent develop internal working models for later life relationships in which expectations of abandonment are a central feature. For such individuals, denial and repression are the most common defence mechanisms employed to deal with perceived threats. These individuals are particularly vulnerable in later life to stressful events that involve the disruption of relationships such as rejection or bereavement. When they develop a mood disorder it is characterized by a preoccupation with the themes of abandonment, helplessness and a desire to find someone who will provide love. On the other hand, children exposed to critical and punitive parenting develop internal working models for relationships in which the constructs of success and failure or blame and responsibility are central organizing features. Projection or reaction formation are the most common defences used by such individuals. In teenage years and adulthood they are particularly vulnerable to experiences of criticism, failure or loss of control. Their mood disorders are characterized by a sense of self-criticism, inferiority, failure, worthlessness, anger and guilt.

Psychodynamic treatment of depression

Short-term psychodynamic psychotherapy and long-term psychoanalysis are the principal treatments that have been developed within the psychoanalytic tradition. In short-term psychodynamic psychotherapy, which may last for about 20 sessions, the focus is on the main depression-maintaining, self-defeating defences and the therapist plays quite an active role in facilitating therapeutic change. In long-term psychoanalysis the focus is less circumscribed, and the therapist takes a less active stance, which encourages the development to transference.

Certain practices are common to most psychoanalytic approaches to depression (Blatt, 2004; McCullough-Vaillant, 1997). Self-defeating defences repeatedly used by patients to regulate anxiety associated with unacceptable unconscious feelings are explored. (The triangle of conflict in Figure 5.5 in Chapter 5 guides the exploration of defences, anxiety and repressed impulses.) Blatt's twin themes of dependency and self-criticism typically emerge as central to these repetitive self-defeating and depression-maintaining patterns.

Therapists point out the parallels between the way patients repeat these patterns which were learned in early parent–child attachment relationships with important people in their current lives and with the therapist. (The triangle of person in Figure 5.5 in Chapter 5 guides the exploration of parallels between relationships with parents, the therapist and significant others.) This process is referred to as transference inter-pretation, because it involves interpreting how patterns learned in one context are transferred to other contexts. Through repeated transfer-ence interpretations patients learn to mentalize – that is, to understand the mental state of themselves and others – in these depression-maintaining repetitive patterns (Allen et al., 2008). The analytic relation-ship also provides patients with a forum within which they can repeatedly work through the intense depressive and angry feelings, and related anxieties that underpin their problematic defences and ways of manag-ing relationships, rooted in their early attachment experiences.

Developing skill at mentalizing and working through previously unac-ceptable unconscious feelings frees patients to explore more adaptive ways of living their lives. This may involve developing more realistic standards for self-evaluation and/or more trusting ways of engaging in relationships.

In a meta-analysis of 23 studies involving over 1300 cases, Driessen et al. (2010) found that short-term psychodynamic psychotherapy was an effective treatment for depression in an outpatient context. It is as effective at one-year follow-up as other therapeutic approaches, includ-ing CBT, which has the largest evidence base and is often popularized as the only effective psychotherapy for depression. In the UK, Lemma et al. (2011) have developed a manual for short-term psychodynamic psychotherapy for depression – dynamic interpersonal therapy (DIT) – which integrates practices used in previous trials that support the effec-tiveness of short-term psychodynamic psychotherapy.

Cognitive and behavioural theories

Of the many behavioural theories of depression, Lewinsohn's (Lewinsohn & Gotlib, 1995) is particularly important because it has led to a consider-able amount of research on the effectiveness of behavioural treatments for depression. Cognitive theories of depression developed by Beck et al. (1979) and Abramson et al. (1978) are among the most important and influential in the field. They have spawned an extraordinary amount of research on psychological processes in depression and the effectiveness of cognitive therapy. For these reasons, the theories of Lewinsohn, Beck and Abramson will be considered in this section.

Lewinsohn's behavioural theory

In Lewinsohn's behavioural theory, he proposes that depression is maintained by a lack of response-contingent positive reinforcement (RCPR) (Lewinsohn & Gotlib, 1995). This occurs because people with depression lack the social skills for eliciting rewarding interactions from others. In the 12-session, group-based Coping with Depression programme based on this model, clients learn social skills necessary for increasing the rate of response-contingent positive reinforcement in their lives. In addition they learn to arrange their lives so that they are more active, engage in more pleasant events and have more opportunities for using social skills to obtain RCPR. The Coping with Depression programme also includes relaxation and coping skills training so that clients are better able to deal with negative emotions arising from stressful events. A meta-analysis of the programme supports its effectiveness with outpatient adolescents and adults (Cuijpers et al., 2009a).

Beck's cognitive theory

According to Beck's cognitive theory, depression occurs when life events involving loss occur and reactivate negative cognitive schemas formed early in childhood as a result of early loss experiences (Beck, 2005, 2008; Beck et al., 1979). These negative schemas entail negative assumptions such as 'I am only worthwhile if everybody likes me'. Negative assumptions may be assessed with the Dysfunctional Attitudes Scale (Weissman & Beck, 1978). When activated, depressive schemas underpin the occurrence of negative automatic thoughts, such as 'No one here likes me', and cognitive distortions, such as 'all-or-nothing thinking'. When a depressed person experiences a drop in mood in a particular situation, according to Beck's theory, this mood change is due not to the situation but to the negative automatic thought that the situation elicited. The low mood and related depressive behaviour that occur in such situations make it more likely that similar situations will recur. These episodes also reinforce depressive schemas. A diagram of Beck's model is presented in Figure 6.2.

Negative schemas have their roots in loss experiences in early childhood, including

- loss of parents or family members through death, illness or separation
- loss of positive parental care through parental rejection, criticism, severe punishment, over-protection, neglect or abuse
- loss of personal health

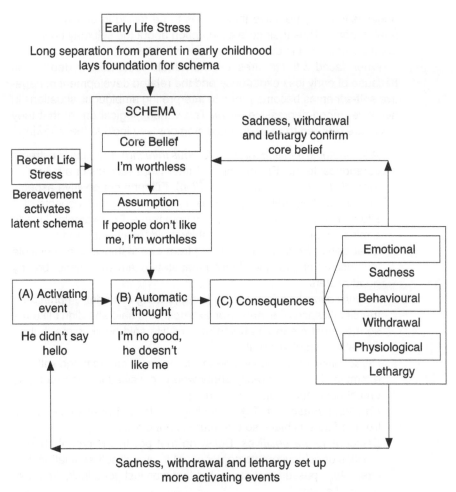

Figure 6.2 Cognitive-behavioural model of depression

- loss of positive peer relationships through bullying or exclusion from peer groups
- the expectation of loss, for example where a parent was expected to die of chronic illness.

According to Beck, two negative schemas that contain latent attitudes about the self, the world and the future are of particular importance in depression. The first relates to interpersonal relationships and the second to personal achievement. He referred to these as sociotropy and autonomy, as mentioned earlier in the section on personality traits. Individuals who have negative self-schemas where sociotropy is the central organizing theme define themselves negatively if they perceive themselves to be failing to maintain positive relationships. Thus their core assumption about the self may be 'If I am not liked by everybody, then I am worthless'. Individuals who have negative self-schemas where autonomy is the central organizing theme define themselves negatively if they perceive themselves to be failing in achieving work-related goals. Thus their core assumption about the self may be 'If I am not a success and in control, then I am worthless'.

When faced with life stresses, individuals vulnerable to depression because of early loss experience and the related development of negative self-schemas become prone to interpreting ambiguous situations in negative, mood-depressing ways. The various logical errors that they make are referred to as cognitive distortions and include the following.

- *All-or-nothing thinking (or dichotomous thinking)*. Thinking in extreme categorical terms. For example, 'Either I'm a success or a failure'.
- *Mental filter (or selective abstraction)*. Filtering out positive aspects of the situation, selectively focusing on the negative aspects of a situation, and drawing conclusions from these. For example, 'I made a mistake earlier today so everything I did today was wrong'.
- *Over-generalization*. Generalizing from one instance to all possible instances. For example, 'I failed that stats exam so I'll never be any good at stats'.
- *Magnification or minimization*. Exaggerating or under-emphasizing the significance of events. For example, 'He said she didn't like me so that must mean she hates me', or 'He said he likes me, but he probably doesn't mean it'.
- *Personalization*. Attributing negative feeling of others to the self. For example, 'He looked really angry when he walked into the room, so I must have done something wrong'.
- *Emotional reasoning*. Taking feelings as facts. For example, 'I feel like the future is black so the future is hopeless'.
- *Discounting the positives*. Believing that positive personal characteristics or achievements do not count in overall self-evaluation. For example. 'I passed that exam, but that was just good luck, I'm really no good at stats'.
- *Mind reading*. Assuming that others are reacting negatively to you without having evidence for this. For example, 'Her silence means that she doesn't like me'.
- *Fortune telling*. Predicting that things will turn out badly without having evidence to support this. For example, 'I will probably not enjoy the party'.
- *Catastrophizing*. Erroneously predicting extreme distress on the basis of limited evidence. For example, 'My heart is racing. I must be going to have a heart attack'.
- *Labelling*. Identifying completely with situational shortcomings. For example, 'I didn't just make a mistake, I proved that I'm a complete fool'.
- *'Should' and 'must' statements*. Making absolute statements about how the self or others ought to be. For example, 'I should always be perfect and he should be loving'.

Depressed individuals interpret situations in terms of their negative cognitive schemas and so their automatic thoughts are characterized by these depressive cognitive distortions. Automatic thoughts are self-statements that occur without apparent volition when an individual attempts to interpret a situation so as to respond to it in a coherent way.

In cognitive therapy, clients learn to monitor situations where negative mood changes occur; to identify negative automatic thoughts that lead to these decreases in mood; to generate alternative positive interpretations of situations in which negative mood changes occur; and to evaluate the validity of these positive and negative views of mood-altering situations. This may involve reflecting on available evidence, or generating evidence by carrying out behavioural tasks and checking the impact of these. For example, attempting to complete successfully a task where failure is expected.

Meta-analyses have shown that with adults, cognitive therapy is as effective as antidepressant medication in alleviating depressive symptoms, and more effective in relapse prevention (Butler et al., 2006; Hollon et al., 2006), and that CBT is effective in treating depressed adolescents (Harrington, 1998; Maag et al., 2009). Meta-analyses also show that CBT self-help programmes involving either bibliotherapy or computer-based interventions are effective for treating mild to moderate depression (Andrews et al., 2010; Gregory et al., 2004).

Beck (2008) has proposed a neurobiological explanation for the effectiveness of CBT. He argues that the generation of negative automatic thoughts is subserved by overactivity in the limbic system, particularly the amygdala, and underactivity of the prefrontal cortex. This pattern of underactivity and overactivity of these brain regions arises from both genetic factors and loss experiences in early life. Cognitive therapy alleviates depression by facilitating an increase in activity in the prefrontal cortex (by encouraging patients to reappraise situations in which they have negative mood changes) which in turn downregulates the overactive limbic system.

Learned helplessness theory

According to learned helpless theory, depression arises when a person repeatedly fails to control the occurrence of aversive stimuli or has repeated experiences of failure at valued tasks and adopts a cognitive style that involves making internal, global, stable attributions for these failures and external, specific, unstable attributions for success (Abramson et al., 1978). For example, saying 'I failed an exam because I've always been useless at school' is an internal, global, stable attribution for failure. On the other hand, saying 'I failed the exam because the questions were unexpected and I was tired that day' involves attributing failure to partially external, specific and unstable factors.

Attributional style is assessed with the Attributional Style Questionnaire (Peterson & Villanova, 1988). The Penn Resiliency Programme, in which young people are trained in learned optimism, is based on the learned helplessness model (Gillham et al., 2008). In this programme, participants learn to attribute success to internal, global, stable factors, and failure to specific, unstable factors that may be changed by using coping and problem-solving skills that are included in the programme curriculum. The Penn Resiliency Programme rests on the assumption that if people can develop an optimistic cognitive style, they will be less vulnerable to depression. A meta-analysis has confirmed the effectiveness of this programme in preventing depression in at-risk young people (Brunwasser et al., 2009).

Family systems theory

Family systems theories of depression highlight the importance of family-based stress, support, belief systems and interaction patterns in the aetiology and maintenance of depression. What follows is one example of such a theory that I have elaborated in greater detail elsewhere (Carr, 2006b). Both genetic and environmental factors contribute to the development of depressive conditions. The amount of stress required to precipitate the onset of an episode of depression is proportional to the genetic vulnerability. That is, little stress may precipitate the onset of an episode in individuals who are genetically vulnerable to the condition, whereas a great deal of stress may be necessary to precipitate the disorder in individuals without a family history of depression.

A variety of family factors may predispose people to developing depression. Both loss experiences and exposure to stresses in early life that prevent needs for safety and security from being met may render individuals vulnerable to developing depression in adolescence and adulthood. Loss experiences include death of a parent, unsupported lengthy separations from parents, and parental psychological absence for extended periods, for example through parental depression. Stresses that prevent needs for safety and security from being met include child abuse, neglect, multiplacement experiences, parental conflict and violence, family disorganization and long-term exposure to a pessimistic family culture.

Episodes of major depression may be precipitated by stressful family life-cycle transitions, such as the birth of children, bereavements or divorce. Loss experiences associated with the disruption of significant relationships or failure to achieve valued goals may precipitate episodes of depression. For example, family relationships may be disrupted through conflict and criticism, threats of separation, violence, infidelity and violations of trust. Failure to achieve valued goals include exam failure, work-related performance difficulties, unemployment, and serious illnesses or injury.

Depression may be maintained by particular types of personal and family belief systems, notably those characterized by a preoccupation with past losses, a negative view of the self as valueless and powerless, and pessimism and hopelessness about the future. Such depressive belief systems may lead to a reduction in activities and an avoidance of participation in relationships that might disprove these depressive beliefs or lead to a sense of pleasure and optimism.

Depression may be maintained by particular patterns of family interaction. Where a teenager becomes depressed, parents may take conflicting positions on how best to respond, with one parent treating the adolescent as an ill child and the other treating the young person as a disobedient teenager, and the parents engaging in repetitive conflicts about how best to deal with their adolescent. This triangulation process prevents parents from jointly supporting their teenager's recovery. Where an adult becomes depressed and behaves in increasingly helpless ways, their partner may respond by increasingly engaging in caretaking, so that the entire relationship becomes dominated by interactions involving helplessness and caregiving. This process disrupts the couple's capacity to meet each other's needs for desired levels of intimacy and autonomy.

This family systems conceptualization of depression is supported by evidence on the role of genetic factors and early life stress in predisposing people to developing depression; recent life stress in precipitating the onset of depressive episodes; and both pessimistic belief systems and negative patterns of family interaction in maintaining depression (Beach et al., 2009; Garber, 2010; Hammen et al., 2010; Joiner & Coyne, 1999; Kaslow et al., 2009).

Effective systemic interventions for depression help family members understand how episodes of depression develop and the role of family belief systems and patterns of family interaction in maintaining depression. They also empower family members to develop more adaptive belief systems and supportive interaction patterns. Systemic interventions include family therapy, where therapists conduct sessions with whole families; couples therapy, where marital or cohabiting partners attend therapy sessions together; and individual interpersonal therapy, where interpersonal issues are the central focus of therapy conducted with depressed individuals. Evidence from controlled trials and metaanalyses support the effectiveness of these various approaches to systemic therapy (Beach et al., 2009; Carr, 2009a, 2009b; Kaslow et al., 2009).

An integrative approach

In clinical practice an integrative approach to conceptualizing depression is useful. Distinctions may be made between predisposing, precipitating, maintaining and protective factors. Insights and related evidence associated with the various theories reviewed above may be integrated into the following formulation framework.

A range of personal, family and community-based factors may predispose people to developing depression. Personal factors include a genetic vulnerability to depression and a depressive temperament; loss and failure experiences and related depressive cognitive schemas, low self-esteem and a depressive cognitive style; attachment insecurity, a depressive interpersonal style and social skills deficits; and personality traits, particularly perfectionism, neuroticism, introversion and low conscientiousness. Family factors that predispose to depression include separations and bereavements, child abuse, excessive parental criticism, family adversity, and growing up in a family where parents suffer from depression or other psychopathology. With respect to the community and the wider social context, socio-economic status and social and educational disadvantage are important predisposing factors for depression. All of these personal, family and community-based predisposing factors sensitize individuals to loss.

The onset of depression may be precipitated by stressful life events, particularly those that involve loss or failure. Once an episode of depression occurs it may be maintained by a range of processes including a depressive cognitive style; self-defeating behaviour and a lifestyle with few opportunities for pleasant events or positive reinforcement; ruminative and avoidant coping; and problematic relationships with family, friends and colleagues. Protective factors in cases of depression include personal attributes and social relationships that support developing a more active and positive lifestyle and challenging pessimistic belief systems.

Assessment

Through careful clinical interviewing of individuals and members of their families, the symptoms of depression and relevant history are obtained. A diagnosis is given in accordance with the criteria outlined in ICD-10 and DSM-IV-TR, and a formulation explaining the symptoms entailed by the diagnosis may be given in which the relevant predisposing, precipitating, maintaining and protective factors are outlined. A general clinical formulation model is given in Figure 6.3.

Validated structured interviews for diagnosing depression that may be used in clinical practice include the mood disorders module of the Structured Clinical Interview for DSM-IV Axis I Disorders (SCID, First et al., 1996) for adults and the depression module of the Development and Well-Being Assessment (DAWBA, Goodman et al., 2000) for children. Depressive symptom severity may be rated with the Hamilton Rating Scale (HRS, Hamilton, 1967) and the Children's Depression Rating Scale (CDRS, Polanski & Mokros, 1999). Self-reported symptom severity may be assessed with the Beck Depression Inventory II (BDI-II, Beck et al., 1996) and the depression scale of the Beck Youth Inventories II (BYI-II, Steer et al., 2005). A range of standardized self-report instruments and rating scales may be used to assess personal characteristics such as cognitive style, and environmental factors such as stressful life events in adults and children (Dougherty et al., 2008; Persons & Fresco, 2008). During the process of assessment and treatment patients and family members may be invited to keep daily records of fluctuations in mood, related thoughts and behaviour, and the circumstances preceding and following these fluctuations.

Suicide risk

A central concern when evaluating depression is the assessment of suicide risk (Hawton & Fortune, 2008; Hawton & Taylor, 2009). This is because depression is one of the most important risk factors for suicide.

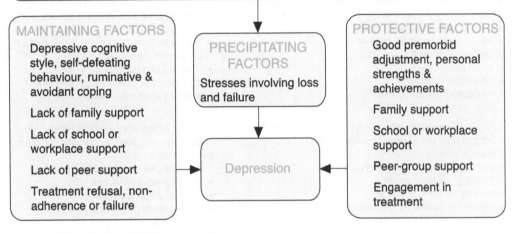

PREDISPOSING FACTORS

Any developmental factors that sensitize a person to loss of significant relationships or esteem

Personal factors – Genetic vulnerability to depression, loss and failure experiences, depressive temperament, neuroticism, introversion, low conscientiousness, depressive cognitive schemas & style, low self-esteem, perfectionism, attachment insecurity, social skills deficits, depressive interpersonal style

Family factors – Separations and bereavements, child abuse, excessive criticism, family adversity, parental depression or psychopathology

Community factors – Low SES, social & educational disadvantage

MAINTAINING FACTORS

Depressive cognitive style, self-defeating behaviour, ruminative & avoidant coping

Lack of family support

Lack of school or workplace support

Lack of peer support

Treatment refusal, non-adherence or failure

PRECIPITATING FACTORS

Stresses involving loss and failure

Depression

PROTECTIVE FACTORS

Good premorbid adjustment, personal strengths & achievements

Family support

School or workplace support

Peer-group support

Engagement in treatment

Figure 6.3 General formulation model for depression

In conducting this type of risk assessment, interviews are conducted with the depressed person and members of their family to develop an understanding of their current circumstances, and the extent to which the risk factors listed in Table 6.3 are present.

A key feature of suicide risk assessment is determining whether the person is actively planning to end their life (referred to as suicidal intention) or alternatively is experiencing thoughts of their own death, without planning how to bring this about (referred to as suicidal ideation). Suicidal intention is the most important risk factor for suicide and may be assessed with the Beck Scale for Suicide Ideation (Beck & Steer, 1991). Where it is judged that a person is at risk of suicide, international best practice guidelines advise that arrangements be made for constant supervision of the person until their level of risk decreases (American Academy of Child and Adolescent Psychiatry, 2001; American Psychiatric Association, 2003; NICE, 2004b). This supervision may be provided by the family in the home or, where that is not possible, in a hospital. If a person judged to be at high risk of suicide refuses to be admitted to hospital (and that is the only viable option for ongoing supervision), then they may be involuntarily admitted to hospital. Legislation and practical procedures for involuntary hospital admission vary from

TABLE 6.3
Risk and protective factors for suicide

Risk factors	Domain	Protective factors
• Suicidal intention • Advanced planning • Precautions against discovery • Lethal method • Absence of help-seeking • A final act	*Suicidal intention and ideation*	• Suicidal ideation (not intention) • Acceptance by adolescent of no-suicide contract • Acceptance by parents and carers of suicide monitoring contract
Availability of lethal methods	*Method lethality*	Absence of lethal methods
• Loss of parents or partner by death, separation or illness • Conflict with parents or partner • Involvement in judicial system • Severe personal illness • Major exam failure • Unwanted pregnancy • Imitation of other suicides	*Precipitating factors*	• Resolution of interpersonal conflict with parents or partner that precipitated attempted suicide • Acceptance and mourning of losses that precipitated attempted suicide • Physical and psychological distancing from peers or others who precipitated imitative attemptive suicide
Suicide attempted to serve the function of: • escaping an unbearable psychological state or situation • gaining revenge by inducing guilt • inflicting self-punishment • gaining care and attention • sacrificing the self for a greater good	*Motivation*	Capacity to develop non-destructive coping styles or engage in treatment to be better able to: • regulate difficult psychological states • modify painful situations • express anger assertively • resolve conflicts productively • mourn losses • manage perfectionistic expectations • solicit care and attention from others • cope with family disorganization
• High level of hopelessness • High level of perfectionism • High level of impulsivity • High levels of hostility and aggression • Inflexible coping style	*Personality-based factors*	• Low level of hopelessness • Low level of perfectionism • Low level of impulsivity • Low levels of hostility and aggression • Flexible coping style
• Depression • Alcohol and drug abuse • Conduct disorder • Antisocial personality disorder • Borderline personality disorder • Epilepsy • Chronic painful illness • Multiple comorbid chronic disorders	*Disorder-related factors*	• Absence of psychological disorders • Absence of physical disorders • Absence of multiple comorbid chronic disorders • Capacity to form therapeutic alliance and engage in treatment for psychological and physical disorders
• Previous suicide attempts • Loss of a parent in early life • Previous psychiatric treatment • Involvement in the juvenile justice system	*Historical factors*	• No history of previous suicide attempts • No history of loss of a parent in early life • No history of previous psychiatric treatment • No history of involvement in the juvenile justice system

Risk factors	Domain	Protective factors
• Family history of suicide attempts • Family history of depression • Family history of drug and alcohol abuse • Family history of assaultive behaviour • Disorganized unsupportive family • Family deny seriousness of suicide attempts • Family has high stress and crowding • Family has low social support and is socially isolated	Family factors	• No family history of suicide attempts • No family history of depression • No family history of drug and alcohol abuse • No family history of assaultive behaviour • Well-organized supportive family • Family has low stress • Family has high social support
• Male • Social class 5 • White (not black) in US • Weak religious commitment • Early summer	Demographic factors	• Female • Social class 2, 3 or 4 • Black (not white) in US • Strong religious commitment

country to country. In the UK and Ireland such admissions are usually made by a psychiatrist.

If you have a friend who you think may be at risk of suicide, the most useful thing you can do is to help them contact their family doctor (or staff at their university health centre) to talk about the things that are bothering them.

Treatment

Research on the psychological treatment of depression has shown that relatively brief structured interventions of up to 20 sessions over 6 months are effective in helping about two-thirds of adolescents and adults recover from a depressive episode (Carr, 2009a). Comparative trials and meta-analyses have shown that CBT, psychodynamic and systemic interventions are equally effective, although both the drop-out rate and the evidence base for CBT are larger (Cuijpers et al., 2008).

The development of a strong therapeutic alliance and the adoption of an approach that modifies depression-maintaining factors underpin effective psychotherapy for depression (Castonguay et al., 2006; Follette & Greenberg, 2006). There is evidence from meta-analyses that guided self-help with books, or computer-based instruction on CBT approaches to mood management and simple interventions that lead to increased activity and physical exercise levels, often referred to as behavioural activation, can effectively reduce depressive symptoms, especially in people with mild to moderate depression (Andrews et al., 2010; Daley et al., 2009; Gregory et al., 2004; Mazzucchelli et al., 2009).

In the short term, psychotherapy and antidepressant medication are equally effective in patients with moderate depression, but in the long term relapse rates are lower for psychotherapy and multimodal pro-grammes that include psychotherapy (Vittengl et al., 2007). This is prob-ably because through psychotherapy people learn relapse prevention skills. Multimodal programmes, which may be offered by multidisciplinary teams including clinical psychologists and physicians, that combine psychotherapy and medication are more effective than either intervention alone (Cuijpers et al., 2009b).

Mindfulness-based cognitive therapy, which combines cognitive behavioural methods with mindfulness meditation, is particularly effective at delaying relapse in people with a history of chronically relapsing depression (Baer, 2003). This is probably because through mindfulness training people learn to 'let go' of negative thoughts and avoid ruminating about them. For patients with seasonal affective disorder, light therapy – where the day is artificially lengthened by placing bright lights in the home – has been shown in a meta-analysis to be effective (Golden et al., 2005). For patients who do not wish to use conventional antidepressants there is some evidence for the effectiveness of St John's wort (*Hypericum*), although meta-analytic results are inconclusive (Linde et al., 2005).

About a third of people with moderate to severe depression do not respond to routine psychological intervention or medication. Evidence for the effectiveness of combining various pharmacological interventions to treat these patients is mixed, although this practice is widespread (Zajecka & Goldstein, 2009). For severe treatment-resistant depression, electroconvulsive therapy (ECT) is widely used, although there is controversy (discussed below) about this because of its negative impact on memory and the relatively brief duration of its effectiveness (Carpenter et al., 2009; Read & Bentall, 2010).

Current best practice is to take a stepped-care approach to the treatment of depression. For people with mild to moderate depression, a guided self-help approach may initially be taken. Brief structured CBT, psychodynamic or systemic psychological treatment may be offered to cases that do not respond to self-help. This may be offered alone or in combination with antidepressants, depending on patient preferences. Fluoxetine may be effective for depression in children and adolescents, although it is less effective in young people than in adults (Bridge et al., 2007). Because SSRIs may increase suicide risk, they should be used very cautiously with young people, and only with frequent clinical monitoring in cases where there is no response to psychological intervention (Rudd et al., 2009). For chronic relapsing depression, mindfulness-based CBT may be offered to delay or prevent relapse. For severe depression, hospitalization may be necessary.

This overall approach to the management of depression in young people and adults is consistent with international best practice guidelines (American Academy of Child and Adolescent Psychiatry, 2007d; American Psychiatric Association, 2010; NICE, 2005c, 2009a).

Controversies

There are many controversies in the scientific study and clinical treatment of mood disorders. Three that deserve mention here concern the use of antidepressants and ECT as well as explanations given for the high rate of depression in women compared with men.

Antidepressants

Antidepressant medication, while widely used, is controversial because of its questionable efficacy and side-effects. Initial enthusiasm for SSRIs as a panacea for depression was tempered by results of Turner et al.'s (2008) meta-analysis, which showed that the high level of effectiveness of antidepressants reported in academic journals was largely the result of journals publishing only trials with positive results and rejecting studies in which antidepressants were shown to be no more effective than placebos. Subsequent meta-analyses showed that compared with placebos, the effects of TCAs and SSRIs were negligible for mild to moderate depression; however, for severe depression their effects are substantial (e.g., Fournier et al., 2010).

Antidepressants may have negative side-effects, some of which are troublesome while others are risky or dangerous. Loss of sexual desire and impotence, weight gain, nausea, sedation or activation, and dizziness are some of the more troublesome, with different types of antidepressant having different side-effect profiles (Gitlin, 2009). For depressed pregnant women, antidepressant treatment may create health risks for their offspring (Udechuku et al., 2010). MAOIs are particularly dangerous antidepressants, and are used only with conscientious patients who can follow strict dietary instructions, because patients on MAOIs develop high blood pressure and suffer hypertensive crises if they do not exclude foods that contain thyramine (such as cheese) from their diets. Antidepressants may increase suicide risk in patients under 25 years, although results of meta-analyses suggest that the benefits may outweigh the risks (Bridge et al., 2007).

Electroconvulsive therapy

ECT is controversial because of the brevity of its antidepressant effects and its negative side-effects on memory functioning. In ECT seizures are induced by briefly passing an electric current through the brain via electrodes applied to the scalp. ECT is conducted under general anaesthetic, and muscle relaxants are used to prevent body spasms. A typical course of ECT involves 6–12 twice-weekly sessions. Low-dose and brief-pulse ECT applied to the non-dominant cerebral hemisphere is sometimes used as an alternative to high-dose bilateral administration to reduce the negative effect of ECT on memory and other cognitive functions.

In a large meta-analysis, Carney et al. (2003) found that ECT was more effective than a placebo (simulated ECT) and antidepressants. They also found that the most effective form was bilateral and high dose rather than unilateral and low dose. However, it was precisely this type of ECT that they found led to greatest memory loss. ECT led to short-term disorientation and temporary loss of memory for recent events (anterograde amnesia) and also for distant autobiographical memories (retrograde amnesia).

A more recent meta-analysis concluded that ECT's effects on cognitive function are not all negative. Semkovska and McLoughlin

(2010) found that after 15 days, processing speed, working memory, anterograde memory, and some aspects of executive function improved beyond baseline levels. The current 'mainstream' position reflected in international best practice guidelines for psychiatrists is that ECT is the treatment of choice for severe depression that does not respond to antidepressants and psychotherapy (American Academy of Child and Adolescent Psychiatry, 2004; American Psychiatric Association, 2001a; NICE, 2009a; Royal College of Psychiatrists, 2005). In deciding on the frequency, dosage, and unilateral or bilateral administration, the benefits in terms of effectiveness must be balanced against the costs in terms of memory impairment.

In contrast to this 'mainstream' position, Read and Bentall (2010) propose that ECT should never be used. They conducted a thorough review of studies on the effectiveness of ECT and its side-effects. They found that ECT is effective only for a brief duration, and then only for some patients when ratings of effectiveness are made by psychiatrists who have a vested interest in showing that ECT is effective. They also found that ECT leads to retrograde and anterograde amnesia and a slight but significant increased risk of death. In view of this cost–benefit analysis of ECT, they concluded that its use cannot be scientifically justified. In a qualitative study of patients' negative experiences of ECT, Johnstone (1999) concluded that for some patients ECT leads to fear, shame and humiliation and reinforces experiences of worthlessness and helplessness associated with depression.

Gender and depression

The finding that twice as many women as men are diagnosed with depression, whereas in childhood the prevalence of depression is the same for boys and girls, has led to a variety of conflicting explanations (Nolen-Hoeksema & Hilt, 2009b). One view is that the higher rate of depression in women arises from the societal inequalities that favour men over women and the oppressive sex-roles into which women fall when they enter long-term heterosexual relationships. A second view is that with the transition to adolescence, females undergo biological changes that render them vulnerable to depression. A third view is that women are more likely than men to acknowledge and report personal distress and so receive a diagnosis of depression.

This controversy about the reasons for high rates of depression in women has led to the development of complex explanations, and a wealth of empirical data, which show that multiple personal and contextual predisposing, precipitating and maintaining factors account for the gender difference in depression (Nolen-Hoeksema & Hilt, 2009b; Shibley-Hyde et al., 2008). Results of twin studies show that different genetic factors render teenage girls vulnerable to depression compared with boys. Also, girls have higher levels of the personality trait – neuroticism – that is a vulnerability factor for depression.

Both biological and environmental factors precipitate the onset of depression in females, and the nature and patterning of these is different for females compared with males. With regard to biological precipitating factors, uniquely female hormonal changes associated with puberty, the menstrual cycle, the postpartum period and the menopause trigger depression in genetically vulnerable women, mainly by affecting oestrogens that in turn affect the serotonin neurotransmitter system which subserves mood regulation. With regard to environmental precipitating factors, females experience more independent stressful life events than males and elicit more stressful life events (such as interpersonal rejection) from others. With regard to maintaining factors, females ruminate more than males and interpret stressful events in a more pessimistic way than males. Also, female social roles within society are more oppressive than male roles and this may maintain depression. Collectively, the aggregation of these factors may partly explain the higher rates of depression in women.

Summary

Major depressive disorder is a recurrent condition, characterized by episodes of low mood and loss of interest in pleasurable activities along with other symptoms such as poor concentration, fatigue, pessimism, suicidal thoughts and sleep and appetite disturbance. Depressive episodes can vary in severity from mild to severe, and melancholic or psychotic symptoms may be present in severe cases.

The clinical features of depression include selective attention to negative features of the environment, a pessimistic cognitive style, low mood, somatic symptoms, psychomotor retardation or agitation and a deterioration in relationships. Loss is often the core theme linking these clinical features: loss of an important relationship, loss of some valued attribute such as health, or loss of status, for example through unemployment. Major depression is distinguished from bipolar disorder, where there are also episodes of elation, and from dysthymia, which is a milder, non-episodic mood disorder.

Depression is a relatively common disorder with a lifetime prevalence of about 17%. More adults than children and more women than men suffer from depression. It follows a chronic relapsing course, with up to 80% of people having recurring episodes. About 3.4% of people with a major depressive disorder commit suicide.

Theoretical explanations for depression and related treatments have been developed within biological, psychoanalytic, cognitive-behavioural and family systems traditions. Biological theories of depression point to the role of genetic factors in rendering people vulnerable to the development of mood disorders, and to the role of structural and functional brain abnormalities; dysregulation of neurotransmitter, neuroendocrine and immune systems; and sleep architecture and circadian rhythm abnormalities in the aetiology of depression. Psychoanalytic theories of depression, from Freud's initial formulation to the present time, point to the role of loss of valued relationships, self-directed anger, self-criticism, and low self-esteem in the aetiology of depression. Behavioural theories propose that a lack of response-contingent positive reinforcement causes depression. Cognitive theories propose that depression arises when stressful life events reactivate depressive schemas that developed as a result of early loss experiences. Systemic theories point to the role of family factors in the aetiology and maintenance of depression.

Research on stress shows that depression develops following exposure to stress and that people with certain personal attributes inadvertently generate excessive stress, which in turn leads to depression. Temperamental characteristics such as harm avoidance, high negative emotionality and low positive emotionality; personality traits such as high neuroticism, low extraversion and low conscientiousness; a pessimistic cognitive style; the use of rumination, avoidance and suppression as coping strategies; and an interpersonal style characterized by limited social skills, attachment insecurity, reassurance seeking and negative feedback seeking all play a role in the aetiology of depression.

Assessment of depression should address depressive symptoms; relevant predisposing, precipitating and maintaining factors; and suicide risk. A stepped-care approach to treatment is usually taken. Patients who do not respond to guided self-help may be offered multimodal programmes by multidisciplinary teams which include antidepressant and psychological therapy. Evidence-based psychodynamic, cognitive-behavioural and system approaches are equally effective. There are controversies about the effectiveness of antidepressants, the use of ECT for severe depression, and the reasons for the large gender differences in depression.

Questions

- Is depression the same as feeling sad?
- What are the main clinical features of depression?
- What are the differences between major depressive disorder, bipolar disorder, dysthymia and cyclothymia?
- How prevalent is depression in men and women?

- What is your view on the controversy about explanations for gender differences in depression?
- What are the risk factors for depression?
- What are the risk factors for suicide?
- What are the main biological and psychological theories of depression and the main research findings relevant to these theories?
- What are the main evidence-based approaches to assessment and treatment of depression?
- What should you do if you think your friend is suicidal?
- Is the use of antidepressants justified in all cases of depression?
- What are the arguments for and against the use of electroconvulsive therapy for treatment-resistant depression?

FURTHER READING

Professional

- Gotlib, H. & Hammen, C. (2009). *Handbook of depression* (second edition). New York: Guilford Press.
- Nolen-Hoeksema, S. & Hilt, L. M. (2009). *Handbook of depression in adolescents*. New York: Routledge.

Self-help

- Burns, D. (1999). *Feeling good: The new mood therapy.* New York: Avon.
- Burns, D. (1999). *The feeling good handbook* (revised edition). New York: Plume.
- Gilbert, P. (2000). *Overcoming depression: A self-help guide using cognitive behavioural techniques* (revised edition). London: Robinson.
- Greenberger, D. & Padesky, C. (1995). *Mind over mood: Changing how you feel by changing the way you think.* New York: Guilford.
- Williams, M., Teasdale, J., Segal, Z. & Kabat-Zinn, J. (2007). *The mindful way through depression: Freeing yourself from chronic unhappiness.* New York: Guilford.

WEBSITES

- American Academy of Child and Adolescent Psychiatry's practice parameters for the treatment of depression, bipolar disorder and suicidal behaviour in young people:
www.aacap.org/cs/root/member_information/practice_information/practice_parameters/practice_parameters
- American Psychiatric Association's practice guidelines for treating depression and bipolar disorder:
http://psychiatryonline.org/guidelines.aspx
- Beating the Blues computer-based CBT programme for depression:
www.beatingtheblues.co.uk
- Depression Alliance (UK):
www.depressionalliance.org

- Depression and Bipolar Support Alliance (USA): www.dbsalliance.org
- NICE. National Institute for Clinical Excellence guidelines for treating depression and bipolar disorder: http://guidance.nice.org.uk/topic/mentalhealthbehavioural

Schizophrenia

7

Introduction

The term schizophrenia refers to a collection of seriously debilitating conditions characterized by positive and negative symptoms and disorganization (Mueser & Jeste, 2008). Hallucinations and delusions are the principal positive symptoms of schizophrenia.

Hallucinations involve experiencing sensations in the absence of external stimuli. For example, with auditory hallucinations – which are the most common type in schizophrenia – people report hearing voices that others cannot hear. Delusions are strongly held, unfounded, culturally alien beliefs. For example, with persecutory delusions, individuals may believe that a group of people are conspiring to harm them.

The negative symptoms of schizophrenia include flattened affect, alogia and avolition. With flattened affect there is limited emotional expression. With alogia there is impoverished thought which is inferred from speech. Brief, concrete replies are given to questions (referred to as poverty of speech), or speech production is normal but it conveys little information due to repetition, or being overly concrete or overly abstract (referred to as poverty of content). With avolition there is a lack of goal-directed behaviour. Negative symptoms typically give rise to a restricted lifestyle involving little activity, little social interaction with others and little emotional expression. In schizophrenia, disorganization may affect both speech and behaviour. Disorganized, illogical, incoherent speech reflects an underlying formal thought disorder. Disorganized catatonic behaviour in schizophrenia includes the virtual absence of spontaneous activity or excessive purposeless activity.

The diagnostic criteria for schizophrenia are given in Table 7.1. From the criteria it is clear that schizophrenia is a debilitating condition that compromises the capacity to carry out normal activities. Schizophrenia is a chronic relapsing disorder with incomplete remission between episodes (Hafner & an der Heiden, 2008). The symptoms of schizophrenia typically first appear in late adolescence or early adulthood, wax and wane over the life course, and have a profound long-term effect on patients and their families.

Schizophrenia is the most debilitating of all psychological disorders, affecting people's capacity to live independently, make and maintain satisfying relationships, engage in family life, parent children effectively, work productively and enjoy leisure activities. Rates of unemployment, homelessness and imprisonment are very high among people with schizophrenia. Although just under 1% of people suffer from schizophrenia, the World Health Organization has ranked it as second only to cardiovascular disease in terms of overall disease burden internationally (Murray & Lopez, 1996).

Despite these gloomy facts, scientific advances in our understanding of schizophrenia, and advances in both pharmacological and psychological approaches to treatment, are making it increasingly possible for people with schizophrenia to live far more productive lives than were previously possible (Mueser & Jeste, 2008). In this chapter there will be a consideration of the clinical features, epidemiology, risk factors, course, theoretical explanations, assessment and treatment of schizophrenia. First, however, let us consider a case example.

Case example of schizophrenia

Julian was referred for assessment and advice by his family doctor. His parents were worried about him because he had been behaving

TABLE 7.1
Diagnostic criteria for schizophrenia

DSM-IV-TR	ICD-10
A. Characteristic symptoms. Two or more of the following, each present for a significant portion of time during a 1-month period (or less if successfully treated): (1) delusions (2) hallucinations (3) disorganized speech (e.g. frequent derailment or incoherence) (4) Grossly disorganized or catatonic behaviour (5) Negative symptoms, affective flattening, alogia or avolition Only one criterion A symptom required if delusions are bizarre or hallucinations consist of a voice keeping up a running commentary on the person's behaviour or thoughts or two or more voices conversing with each other B. Social/occupational dysfunction. For a significant portion of the time since the onset of the disturbance, one or more major areas of functioning such as work, interpersonal relations, or self-care are markedly below the level achieved prior to onset or with children a failure to achieve the expected level of interpersonal, academic or occupational achievement C. Duration. Continuous signs of the disturbance persist for at least *6 months* D. Not due to schizoaffective or mood disorder E. Not due to substance use or general medical condition F. If there is autism or a pervasive developmental disorder, then prominent delusions and hallucinations of 1 month's duration must be present.	A minimum of one very clear symptom (or two or more of less clear-cut) belonging to any one of the groups (a) to (d) and at least two of the symptoms (e) to (h) should have been present most of the time during a period of *1 month* or more. (a) thought echo, thought insertion or withdrawal and **thought broadcasting** (b) delusions of control, influence, or passivity, clearly referred to body or limb movements or specific thoughts (c) hallucinatory voices giving a running commentary on the patient's behaviour, or discussing the patient among themselves, or other types of hallucinatory voice coming from some part of the body (d) persistent delusions of other kinds that are culturally inappropriate and completely impossible, such as religious or political identity, or superhuman powers and abilities (e) persistent hallucinations in any modality, when accompanied either by fleeting or half-formed delusions without clear affective content, or by persistent overvalued ideas, or when occurring every day for weeks or months on end (f) breaks or interpolations in the train of thought, resulting in incoherence or irrelevant speech or neologisms (g) catatonic behaviour, such as excitement, posturing, or waxy flexibility, negativism, mutism or stupor (h) negative symptoms such as marked apathy, paucity of speech, and blunting or incongruity of emotional responses, usually resulting in social withdrawal and lowering of social performance (i) a significant and consistent change in the overall quality of some aspects of personal behaviour, manifest as loss of interest, aimlessness, idleness, a self-absorbed attitude and social withdrawal

Note: Adapted from DSM-IV-TR (APA, 2000) and ICD-10 (WHO, 1992, 1996).

strangely since returning to his rural home after studying in London for a year. Julian had failed his exams and said he came home to 'sort his head out'. Since his return, Julian's parents had noticed that he lacked concentration and his conversation was incoherent much of the time. Also, his behaviour was erratic and unpredictable.

His parents became particularly concerned when he went missing some weeks prior to the referral. After searching for a few hours, they found him 35 miles from their home, exhausted, dehydrated and dressed in only his sports shorts, singlet and running shoes. Apparently Julian believed he had to complete a secret mission in the east. While jogging that morning, he headed eastwards towards the rising sun. He thought he might jump onto the car ferry when he reached the coast, cross the sea to Holland, and continue east towards India on his secret mission. According to the family doctor, Julian's account of this episode was not coherent.

Since the episode, Julian has spent much of the time in his room muttering to himself, often becoming quite distressed. When his parents spoke to him, they found it hard to make sense of what he said.

Family history

Julian was the 19-year-old son of a prominent farmer in a rural English village. The family lived in a large mansion on an extensive estate. Julian's father managed the farm; he had a traditional authoritarian manner and a positive, if distant, relationship with Julian. While he was centrally involved in the search for Julian, once he found his son, Julian's father returned to work and left the care of Julian to his wife.

Julian's mother was an artist. She dressed flamboyantly, behaved in a theatrical manner and held eccentric, unconventional beliefs. For example, she held conspiracy theories about many issues, was interested in eastern mysticism and believed that faith healing and alternative medicine were preferable to traditional western medicine. This personal style affected how she treated Julian after the 'running east' episode. She engaged him in intense conversations about the mystical meaning of the psychotic experiences that led to him trying to make his way to India on foot. Rather than taking Julian to the accident and emergency department of the local hospital for assessment, she brought him to a faith healer and then a homeopathist. It was only after these interventions failed to soothe his distress that she brought Julian to the family doctor, who made the referral to the community mental health team. In the preliminary assessment interview that we conducted with Julian and both of his parents, Julian's mother responded to him with intense emotional overinvolvement (an index of high expressed emotion associated with relapse in schizophrenia; Hooley, 2007).

With regard to the extended family, according to Julian's parents there was no family history of psychological disorder. However, some members of the mother's well-to-do family were odd or eccentric, especially her brother, Sedrick, and her uncle, William Junior. William's eccentricities led him into serious conflict with his father, and Sedrick's odd behaviour underpinned his highly conflictual, childless marriage.

Developmental history

Julian grew up on the family farm and went to school locally. His development was essentially normal. His academic performance at school was above average. He had many friends in his local village, and was a popular child and adolescent. Julian was excellent at cricket. He had no psychological problems before going to university in London at 18.

Julian's first term at college was successful academically and socially. However, the occasional experimental cannabis use that had begun the summer before going to college turned to regular use once Julian moved to London. During his time at university Julian also experimented with LSD on a few occasions. In the final term of his first year at college, Julian developed an intense fear of exam failure. He began to have difficulty studying effectively and often had difficulty sleeping. He stopped attending classes regularly and increasingly spent time alone. Julian was relieved to return home after sitting his exams. His parents described him as quiet and thoughtful during the time he spent at home prior to the 'running east' episode.

Presentation

Julian presented with delusions, hallucinations, disorganized speech and anxiety. He was reluctant to be interviewed because he believed he had urgent business to attend to in Holland and further afield in India. He showed signs of being anxiously distressed throughout the interview. He explained that his path was to the east. He believed he was being called there by an unknown source. He knew this because of the sign he had seen while out jogging on the morning of the 'running east' episode. The way an old cart wheel caught the sunlight and cast a shadow on the red-brick wall of a barn against which it leaned made a distinctive pattern. This pattern was a special sign for him indicating that he should go east, first to Holland and then all the way to India. When he questioned this idea, a clear authoritative voice said that he should leave at once.

At this point in his narrative, he stopped in mid-sentence. He showed thought blocking, and lost the thread of what he was saying. When asked to continue his story, he began to giggle. When asked what was amusing, he said that he could hear someone say something funny. Julian then spoke about a number of unconnected topics in an incoherent way before experiencing thought blocking again.

Later he said that he must go soon because people would try to prevent him. He had heard them talking about him the day before. Julian said they had tried to put bad ideas into his head. He described being frightened by this and by periodic sensations that everything was too loud and too bright and coming at him. He said 'it was like doing acid [LSD] all the time … a really bad trip'.

Formulation

Julian presented with auditory hallucinations, delusions, thought disorder, anxiety and a significant deterioration in social and occupational functioning which had been present for more than a month – symptoms consistent with an ICD-10 diagnosis of schizophrenia. He also showed a complete lack of insight. He was unable to appreciate that the voices he heard were hallucinations and his delusional beliefs were unfounded.

Among the important precipitating factors were the experience of recent exam pressure and Julian's transition from living at home to living in London and attending college. The principal predisposing factors were a possible genetic vulnerability to psychosis and a history of hallucinogenic drug use. We suspected that there was a genetic

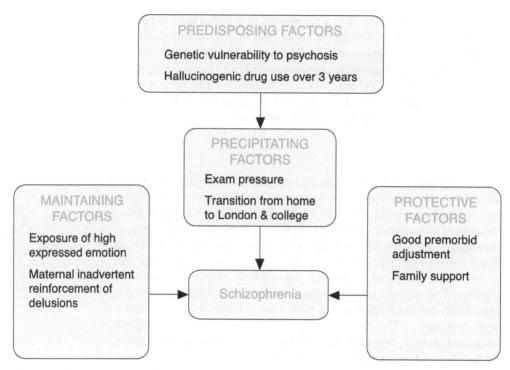

Figure 7.1 Formulation of a case of schizophrenia

vulnerability in this case because of the odd, eccentric behaviour of his mother and uncles, suggestive of a high level of the trait schizotypy (Lenzenweger, 2010).

His condition was maintained, we suspected, by a high level of maternal expressed emotion characterized principally by emotional over-involvement. Also, his mother inadvertently reinforced his delusions through engaging him in long conversations about them. Protective factors in this case were good premorbid adjustment and strong family support. This formulation is diagrammed in Figure 7.1.

Treatment

The treatment plan included antipsychotic medication and family work to reduce parental expressed emotion, with an initial brief period of hospitalization. Julian did recover from this first psychotic episode. With medication, his hallucinations and delusions decreased considerably. Through family psychoeducation, his parents developed an understanding of his condition and of his need for a 'low-key' approach to interacting with him as he recovered.

However, there were obstacles to this multimodal treatment programme being as effective as possible. Julian did not like the side-effects of his medication, especially weight gain and reduced sexual functioning, and so had poor medication adherence. He also became depressed during remission, when he thought about the many losses that followed from his condition. He was unable to continue his university education, and so could not pursue the career in law he had dreamed of. He found it difficult to maintain friendships or to commit to engaging regularly in sports. When he felt low, Julian would smoke cannabis to lift his spirits.

Julian's mother found it difficult to accept his diagnosis, and continued to believe that there was a spiritual or mystical explanation for his psychotic symptoms. She said she sometimes thought he was not an ill young man, but a gifted seer or a 'chosen one'. She often engaged Julian in intense, distressing conversations about these issues. In the years that followed his initial assessment, poor medication adherence, ongoing cannabis use and exposure to high levels of expressed emotion led Julian to relapse more frequently than might otherwise have been the case.

Clinical features

A range of clinical features associated with schizophrenia have been identified through research and clinical observation (Mueser & Jeste, 2008). A classification of these in the domains of perception, cognition, emotion, behaviour, social adjustment and somatic state is given in Table 7.2.

TABLE 7.2
Clinical features of schizophrenia

Perception	• Breakdown in perceptual selectivity • Hallucinations
Cognition	• Delusions • Confused sense of self • Lack of insight • Formal thought disorder • Cognitive impairment (IQ, attention, memory, executive function, psychomotor speed)
Emotion	• Prodromal anxiety and depression • Inappropriate, flattened or blunted affect • Postpsychotic depression
Behaviour	• Prodromal excitation (sleeplessness, impulsivity, overactivity, compulsivity) • Impaired goal-directed behaviour • Excited or retarded catatonic behaviour
Social adjustment	• Poor self-care and hygiene • Poor educational or work performance • Withdrawal from peer relationships • Deterioration in family relationships
Somatic state	• Comorbid substance use • Comorbid health problems (CPOD, obesity, heart disease, HIV/AIDS, Hepatitis B & C) • Unhealthy lifestyle (poor diet, obesity, little exercise, smoking)

Perception

At a perceptual level, individuals with schizophrenia describe a break-down in perceptual selectivity, with difficulties in focusing on essential information or stimuli to the exclusion of accidental details or back-ground noise. Everything seems to be salient, and it is difficult to distin-guish figure from ground. During an acute psychotic state, internal stimuli such as verbal thoughts are experienced as auditory hallucina-tions that have the same sensory quality as the spoken word.

Auditory hallucinations may be experienced as loud thoughts, as thoughts being repeated by another person aloud (thought echo), as voices speaking inside the head or as voices coming from somewhere in the outer environment. Auditory hallucination may occur as a third-person commentary on the patient's action, as a voice speaking in the second person directly to the patient, or as two or more people talking or arguing. Patients may perceive voices to vary along a number of dimensions. Voices may be construed as benign or malevolent, control-ling or impotent, all-knowing or knowing little about the person, and the person may feel compelled to do what the voice says or not.

Hallucinations that are perceived to be malevolent, controlling, all-knowing and which the individual feels compelled to obey are far more distressing than those that are not construed as having these attributes. While auditory hallucinations are the most common in schizophrenia, hallucinations may occur in other sensory modalities. Somatic halluci-nations often occur in schizophrenia, with patients reporting feelings of electricity in their body or things crawling under their skin. These may be given delusional interpretations. For example, a patient reported that the television was activating a transmitter in her pelvis and she could feel the electricity from this causing insects to grow and move around under her skin. Visual hallucinations – seeing visions – are relatively rare in schizophrenia, but common in temporal lobe epilepsy.

Cognition

Delusions are the most prominent cognitive clinical features of schizo-phrenia. Delusions are false, idiosyncratic, illogical and stubbornly maintained erroneous inferences drawn to explain unusual experi-ences, such as hallucinations. For example, a patient with auditory hallucinations in which she heard an authoritative voice giving her commands to gather the children to her inferred that she had been chosen by God to prepare all children for the second coming of Christ.

Delusions may arise not only from hallucinations, but also from un-usual feelings associated with psychosis. Persecutory delusions may develop from feelings of being watched. Delusions of thought insertion or thought withdrawal may develop as explanations for feelings that thoughts are not one's own, or that one's thoughts have suddenly dis-appeared. Factor analyses show that delusions fall into three broad categories: delusions of influence (including thought withdrawal or in-sertion, and beliefs about being controlled); delusions of self-significance (including delusions of grandeur or guilt); and delusions of persecution

(Vahia & Cohen, 2008). Delusions may vary in the degree of conviction with which they are held (from great certainty to little certainty), the degree to which the person is preoccupied with them (the amount of time spent thinking about the belief), and the amount of distress they cause.

Particular sets of delusions may entail a confused sense of self, particularly paranoid delusions where individuals believe that they are being persecuted or punished for misdeeds, or delusions of control where there is a belief that one's actions are controlled by others.

During a psychotic episode there is usually lack of insight and impaired judgement. That is, patients believe that the content of their hallucinations and delusions is legitimate, and they have difficulty entertaining the idea that these experiences and beliefs arise from a clinical condition. Between psychotic episodes, insight may improve and patients may move towards accepting that their hallucinations and delusions are symptoms of schizophrenia.

The speech of patients with schizophrenia is difficult to understand because of abnormalities in the underlying form of thought. Formal thought disorder is characterized by tangentiality, derailment, incoherence, thought blocking, loss of goal and neologisms. With tangentiality, answers given to questions are off the point. With derailment, sentences make sense, but little meaning is conveyed by sequences of sentences because there is a constant jumping from one topic to another, with very loose associations between topics and little logic to what is said. With incoherence, sentences are incorrectly formed so they do not make sense. With thought blocking, the person abruptly stops in mid-sentence and is unable complete their train of thought. With loss of goal there is a difficulty in following a logical train of thought from A to B. With neologisms, new words are made up that have an idiosyncratic meaning for the patient.

Cognitive impairment or deterioration occurs in schizophrenia. This may be either general or specific. With general cognitive deterioration, there is a reduction in overall IQ with many cognitive functions negatively affected. With specific cognitive impairment one or more of the following functions may be impaired: attention, memory, cognitive flexibility, social cognition and executive function, particularly the capacity to follow through on a planned course of action. Cognitive impairment is a better predictor of disability and vocational functioning than positive symptoms.

Emotions

At an emotional level, during the prodromal phase, before an acute psychotic episode, anxiety or depression may occur in response to initial changes in perceptual selectivity and cognitive inefficiency. A key part of relapse prevention is for patients to learn how to identify and manage prodromal changes in affect.

During acute psychotic episodes, anxiety or depression may occur in response to hallucinations, delusions, formal thought disorder and other distressing symptoms. Inappropriate affect may be present particularly in hebephrenic schizophrenia, where the individual responds not to the external social context but to internal stimuli such as auditory hallucinations, for example by laughing wildly. Flattened or blunted affect may occur, particularly in chronic cases. During remission following an episode of psychosis, the sense of loss that comes with increased insight into the reality of the condition may give rise to post-psychotic depression.

Behaviour

At a behavioural level, prodromal excitation may occur prior to an acute psychotic episode, characterized by sleep disturbance, impulsive behaviour, and overactivity which may include compulsive behaviour. During acute psychotic episodes, avolition occurs, with impairment of goal-directed behaviour.

In chronic cases catatonic behaviour may occur, with impairment in the capacity to initiate and organize voluntary movement and posture. Catatonia may be either retarded or excited. Excessive purposeless motor activity is the hallmark of excited catatonia and may include stereotypies (repetitive actions), echolalia (repeating words said by others) or echopraxia (imitating the actions of others). With retarded catatonic behaviour there is a marked reduction in purposeful activity. Patients may show immobility, mutism, adopt unusual postures for long periods of time, and display waxy flexibility (allowing one's limbs to be manipulated like a warm candle) or negativism (resisting attempts to have one's limbs moved).

Social adjustment

In schizophrenia there a marked deterioration in social adjustment. The capacity for self-care, dressing appropriately, grooming and personal hygiene deteriorates, so that people with schizophrenia often look dishevelled and unkempt. A significant decline in performance in educational and work settings occurs. There is a withdrawal from regular socializing with friends and difficulty in making and maintaining new relationships. A deterioration in relationships with family members also occurs. Schizophrenia has a negative impact on parent–child, marital and sibling relationships.

Somatic state

About half of all people with schizophrenia have comorbid substance use disorders and almost three-quarters have significant health problems. The most common health problems include chronic obstructive pulmonary disease (COPT), which is usually due to smoking; heart disease and diabetes due to obesity; HIV/AIDS and hepatitis B and C due to unsafe sex and intravenous drug use. The substance use and medical problems so common in schizophrenia are essentially lifestyle problems. On the positive side, schizophrenia is associated with reduced rates of cancer and rheumatoid arthritis (Tandon et al., 2008a).

Classification

To take account of the marked variability in symptomatology among people with schizophrenia, various subtypes have been defined. Also, a number of psychotic conditions that closely resemble schizophrenia have been identified, and referred to as schizophrenia spectrum disorders. Schizophrenia subtypes and spectrum disorders are considered in this section. In ICD-10 (World Health Organization, 1992) and DSM-IV-TR (American Psychiatric Association, 2000), four main subtypes of schizophrenia are distinguished:

- paranoid
- catatonic
- hebephrenic or disorganized
- undifferentiated.

Where paranoid delusions predominate, a diagnosis of paranoid schizophrenia is given. Cases in which either retarded or excited catatonic behaviour is the principal feature are classified as having catatonic schizophrenia. Cases are classified as hebephrenic in the ICD-10 and disorganized in the DSM-IV-TR when inappropriate or flat affect is the principal feature and where there is disorganized behaviour and speech. In both ICD-10 and DSM-IV-TR, when cases do not fall into any of the three categories just mentioned, they are classified as undifferentiated. While distinctions between the four main subtypes of schizophrenia have been useful for describing different clinical presentations and date back to Emil Kraepelin's (1899) work, research has shown that these subtypes are not consistently differentiated by family history, course, prognosis or treatment response.

In contrast to the lack of success in validating subtypes of schizophrenia, there has been considerable progress in identifying other conditions that share a very similar pattern of family history, course, prognosis and treatment response to schizophrenia. These include disorders that have the same symptomatology as schizophrenia, but are of briefer duration (such as schizophreniform disorder); those with the same symptomatology as schizophrenia in addition to the symptoms of a mood disorder (schizoaffective disorder); and those characterized by chronic mild schizophrenia-like symptoms (such as schizotypal, schizoid and paranoid personality disorders). These conditions, along with schizophrenia, constitute schizophrenia spectrum disorders (Mamah & Barch, 2011).

Research on the shared aetiology, course and treatment response of these disorders and factor analytic studies of their symptomatology suggest that the distribution of psychotic symptoms within the population more closely approximates dimensions than disease-like categories. The three principal dimensions are those involving positive symptoms, negative symptoms and disorganization, mentioned in the opening paragraph of this chapter (Rietkerk et al., 2008).

Epidemiology, course, outcome and risk factors

Reviews of international epidemiological studies allow a number of conclusions to be drawn about the epidemiology of schizophrenia. Under 1% of the population suffer from schizophrenia, and the lifetime risk of this condition is about 0.7% (Saha et al., 2005). More men than women suffer from schizophrenia: the male–female ratio is about 1.4:1 (McGrath et al., 2004). The onset of schizophrenia is earlier in males (20–28 years) than in females (28–32 years) (Murray & Van Os, 1998). The rates of schizophrenia are similar across countries and cultures when similar diagnostic criteria are used (Mueser & Duva, 2011).

Schizophrenia follows a distinctive course although there is considerable variability across cases (Jablensky, 2009; Jobe & Harrow, 2010; Mueser & Duva, 2011, Tandon et al., 2009). The onset of schizophrenia typically occurs in late adolescence or early adulthood and may be acute or insidious. Typically the onset takes place over 5 years, starting with negative and depressive symptoms, followed by cognitive and social impairment and finally positive symptoms. Longitudinal studies suggest that there is an early deterioration phase that extends over 5–10 years, a stabilization phase and a final gradual improvement phase. For 50–70% of cases the condition follows a chronic relapsing course, typically with incomplete remission between episodes. However, up to 40% of patients show one or more periods of complete recovery with good adjustment for at least a year, and 4–20% show complete remission.

Psychotic episodes may last from 1 to 6 months, although some extend to a year. They are usually preceded by a prodromal period of a number of weeks. Psychotic episodes may be shortened and the severity of symptomatology ameliorated through early detection and the use of pharmacological and psychological treatment as outlined below. Inter-episode functioning may vary greatly, and better inter-episode functioning is associated with a better prognosis. The duration of remission between episodes may be lengthened through the use of maintenance medication and psychosocial interventions to reduce stress and improve coping and illness management.

With treatment, usually positive symptoms (hallucinations and delusions) abate between episodes but negative symptoms (blunted affect, alogia and avolition) are relatively enduring and are more likely to persist during remission. In the stabilization phase of schizophrenia positive symptoms becoming less prominent, while negative symptoms and cognitive deficits become more prominent. The lifespan of people with schizophrenia is about 9 years shorter than that of the general population, and this is partly accounted for by the high rate of suicide during the first 10 years of the disorder and the high rate of comorbid medical disorders mentioned earlier. About half of all people with schizophrenia attempt suicide or self-harm, and about 10% commit suicide (Heisel, 2008; Schennach-Wolff et al., 2011).

Risk factors for schizophrenia are listed in Table 7.3 (Lenzenweger, 2010; Murray & Castle, 2009; Tandon et al., 2008b). The greatest risk

TABLE 7.3
Risk factors for schizophrenia

Genetic factors
Positive family history of psychosis

Personality
Schizotypy

Prenatal and perinatal factors
Maternal flu infection or malnutrition in first or second trimester
Father over 35 years
Obstetric complications (low birth weight, prematurity, resuscitation)
Birth in late winter or early spring

Demographic factors
Male
Unmarried
Urban dwelling
Migrant
Low SES

Life history factors
Trauma history
Cannabis use

factor for schizophrenia is a family history of psychosis. This probably finds subclinical expression as schizotypy, a personality trait in which the central feature is a disorganized thinking style similar to (although much milder than) that shown in schizophrenia (Lenzenweger, 2010).

Other risk factors make a small but significant contribution to overall risk within the context of that associated with genetic vulnerability. However, at present there is no consensus on how these risk factors operate. Prenatal and perinatal risk factors, such as maternal flu infection and obstetric complications, probably have a negative direct or indirect effect on the development of the nervous system in line with the neurodevelopmental hypothesis mentioned below, rendering those genetically predisposed even more neurobiologically vulnerable to psychosis (Murray & Lewis, 1987). Trauma exposure and most demographic risk factors (being an unmarried, low-SES urban migrant) are associated with higher levels of stress and lower levels of social support, which increase the risk of psychosis in the genetically vulnerable according to diathesis–stress conceptualizations of the condition (Zubin & Spring, 1977). It is probable that the mechanism by which cannabis use affects schizophrenia is neurobiological rather than social–environmental (Barkus & Murray, 2010).

In the short term, relapse is more likely in cases where there is heavy cannabis use, poor treatment adherence, frequent contact with family members who display high expressed emotion (criticism, hostility and emotional over-involvement) and exposure to acute stressful life events (Jablensky, 2009).

Longitudinal studies show that the risk factors listed in Table 7.4 are associated with poorer outcome (Bota et al., 2011; Jablensky, 2009; Jobe & Harrow, 2010). A poor outcome is associated with substance

TABLE 7.4
Risk factors for a poor outcome in schizophrenia

Early stage
Early age of onset
Insidious onset
Poor premorbid adjustment
Longer duration of untreated psychosis
Substance use
Lack of an identifiable precipitating stressor prior to hospitalization

Personality traits
Trait anxiety (and HPA axis hyperactivity)
External locus of control

Symptom profile
Severe negative symptoms (blunted affect, alogia, avolition)
Severe cognitive impairment
Lack of depressive symptoms

Lifestyle
Poor treatment adherence
Substance use

Social context
Single
Few friends
Stressful life events
Frequent contact with family members who display high expressed emotion
(over-involvement and criticism)
Living in a developing country

use and a longer period of untreated psychosis in people who have poor premorbid adjustment and an early insidious onset with no clear stressful life event preceding their first treated episode. A high level of trait anxiety, which is probably subserved by hypothalamic–pituitary– adrenal (HPA) axis overactivity and an external locus of control, is the main personality trait associated with poor outcome. People with this stress-sensitive profile are more reactive to stressful life-events, including those associated with living in a developing country, and family-based stress associated with high levels of expressed emotion, all of which are also risk factors for poor outcome. A poorer outcome occurs for those who are single and have few friends – factors which suggest low levels of social support. The symptom profile predictive of a poor outcome is marked by severe negative symptoms, cognitive impairment and lack of depressive symptoms.

A favourable outcome in schizophrenia is associated with a range of factors (Bota et al., 2011). These include good premorbid adjustment, and a brief duration of untreated psychosis characterized by an acute onset in response to precipitating stressful life events. A family history of affective disorder (rather than schizophrenia) or little psychopathology and a personal symptom profile in which there are affective as well as psychotic features are also predictive of a good prognosis. A better outcome occurs for those who have a favourable life situation to return to following discharge from hospital.

Aetiological theories

Historically, research on schizophrenia has followed from two principal traditions founded by the German psychiatrist Emile Kraepelin (1899) and the Swiss psychiatrist Eugen Bleuler (1911). Kraepelin defined the condition, which he named 'dementia praecox', as principally characterized by a constellation of observable symptoms (such as delusions, hallucinations and thought disorder) and a chronic course due to an underlying degenerative neurological condition. In contrast, Bleuler, who coined the term 'schizophrenia', conceptualized the condition as a disturbance in a circumscribed set of inferred psychological processes. He speculated that the capacity to associate one thought with another, to associate thoughts with emotions, and to associate the self with reality were impaired or *split*. Hence the term 'schizophrenia' (from the Greek words for *split* and *mind*).

Bleuler proposed that the four primary symptoms of schizophrenia were loosening of *associations* (difficulty in thinking straight), incongruous or flattened *affect*, impaired goal-directed behaviour or *ambivalence* due to conflicting impulses, and *autism* or social withdrawal. The emphasized words in the last sentence are sometimes referred to as Bleuler's 'four As'. Bleuler argued that positive symptoms such as delusions and hallucinations were secondary to these central psychological difficulties. For Bleuler, the symptoms of schizophrenia such as delusions and hallucinations represented the person's attempt to cope with the world despite disruption of central psychological processes. While Kraepelin conceptualized schizophrenia as being distributed within the population as a discrete disease-like category, Bleuler viewed the disturbed psychological processes that he proposed underpinned schizophrenia as on a continuum with normal psychological functioning. These different views were precursors of the modern categorical and dimensional approaches to understanding schizophrenia (Linscott & Van Os, 2010).

Up to the late 1970s, Bleuler's tradition, associated with a broad definition of schizophrenia, predominated in the US whereas in the UK, Ireland and Europe, Kraepelin's narrower definition held sway. Following the landmark US–UK diagnostic study (US–UK Team, 1974) that highlighted the extraordinary differences between the way schizophrenia was defined in America and Britain, there has been a gradual move towards developing an internationally acceptable set of diagnostic criteria. The narrowing of the gap between the North American and European definitions of schizophrenia is reflected in the marked similarity between the diagnostic criteria for the disorder contained in current versions of the ICD and DSM presented in Table 7.1.

Modern research on schizophrenia has also been guided by two broad groups of theories. The first, in the tradition of Kraepelin, has been concerned largely with the role of biological factors in the aetiology and maintenance of the disorder. The second group of theories, in the tradition of Bleuler, has addressed the role of psychological factors in schizophrenia. In the following section, biological theories of schizophrenia and related research findings will be considered. This will be followed by a consideration of the stress-vulnerability or diathesis–stress approaches to conceptualizing schizophrenia and research findings of relevance to this position.

Biological theories

Biological theories of schizophrenia point to the role of genetic and neurodevelopmental factors in rendering people vulnerable to the development of psychosis, and to the role of structural and functional brain abnormalities; dysregulation of neurotransmitter systems; and sleep architecture and eye movement abnormalities in the aetiology of schizophrenia. There is considerable support for biological theories from neuroimaging, pharmacological, psychophysiological and other neurobiological studies, although current knowledge of these abnormalities is incomplete (Bora et al., 2011; Downar & Kapur, 2008; Eyler, 2008; Fatemi & Folsom, 2009; Glatt, 2008; Harrison, 2009; Hollis, 2008; Keshavan et al., 2008; Murray & Castle, 2009; Ritsner & Gottesman, 2011; Stewart & Davis, 2008). However, there is a consensus about certain aspects of the neurobiology of schizophrenia, which will be presented below.

Genetics

The genetic hypothesis proposes that schizophrenia arises primarily from an inherited vulnerability to psychosis. Results of twin, adoption and family studies show that a predisposition to schizophrenia spectrum disorders is genetically transmitted. Schizophrenia is about 80% heritable (Glatt, 2008; Sullivan et al., 2003). The lifetime risk for developing schizophrenia is proportional to the number of shared genes. For monozygotic twins the risk is 48%; for dizygotic twins the risk is 17%; for children of an affected parent the risk is 13%; for grandchildren the risk is 5%; and for members of the general population the risk is about 1% (Ritsner & Gottesman, 2011). It is also probable that the vulnerability is polygenetically transmitted, since the results of family studies cannot easily be accounted for by simpler models of genetic transmission.

Many candidate genes for schizophrenia have been investigated; some have been identified; and where significant associations between candidate genes and schizophrenia have been found, a growing number of consistent replication studies are available (Harrison, 2009; Ritsner & Gottesman, 2011). Candidate genes for which consistent evidence is available affect the growth and organization of neurones in the brain, the development of synapses, and glutamate and dopamine neurotransmission. Candidate genes include neurreulin 1 (NRG1) and disrupted-in-schizophrenia-1 (DISC1), which have multiple roles in brain development, synapse formation and synaptic signalling; catechol-O-methyltransferase (COMT), which regulates dopamine signalling in the frontal cortex; D-amino acid oxidase activator (DAOA) and dysbindin (DTNBP1), which affect glutamate signalling;

regulator of G-protein signalling 4 (RGS4) and calcineurin (PP3CC), which affect dopamine and glutamate neurotransmission. The mechanisms by which candidate genes give rise to the symptoms of schizophrenia through altering the structure and functioning of the nervous system are currently a focus for intensive research internationally (Bertram, 2008).

Despite evidence for the role of genetic factors in schizophrenia, many people who develop schizophrenia have no relatives that suffer from the condition, and some people with a genetic predisposition to schizophrenia do not develop psychotic symptoms. It is therefore likely that environmental factors also contribute to the development of schizophrenia.

Neurodevelopment and neuropathology

The neurodevelopmental hypothesis proposes that prenatal and perinatal factors (often referred to as obstetric complications) interact with a genetic vulnerability to psychosis to give rise to atypical neuroanatomical development initially in infancy, and later in adolescence, and this culminates in the emergence of schizophrenia (Fatemi & Folsom, 2009; McGlashen & Hoffman, 2000; Murray & Lewis, 1987).

In normal development, synaptic connections within the brain increase up to 2 years, decline gradually before puberty and then decrease markedly in adolescence. This sharp decline is due to synaptic pruning, which involves the elimination of superfluous synapses. It coincides with the emergence of sophisticated cognitive skills in early adolescence such as the capacity for abstract reasoning. According to the neurodevelopmental hypothesis, the synaptic pruning process is excessive in schizophrenia, leading to a fragmented brain and consequent psychotic symptoms (McGlashen & Hoffman, 2000). Excessive pruning is expected to have a more profound effect where fewer synapses were formed during early brain development due to an adverse intrauterine environment associated with obstetric complications.

Obstetric complications

A growing body of evidence supports the link between obstetric complications and schizophrenia (Ellman & Cannon, 2008). Obstetric complications that have been investigated with reference to the neurodevelopmental hypothesis include maternal infection with influenza or rubella during early pregnancy, maternal malnutrition during early pregnancy, diabetes mellitus, smoking during pregnancy, bleeding during pregnancy, problematic labour or delivery, anoxia or asphyxia at birth, low birth weight, small head circumference, and congenital malformations. About 20–30% of patients with schizophrenia have a history of obstetric complications, compared with 5–10% of the unaffected population. Lack of oxygen to the foetus – foetal hypoxia – is involved in many obstetric complications associated with psychosis. Cases with a history of obstetric complications show an earlier onset of schizophrenia and more pronounced neuroanatomical abnormalities, as predicted by the neurodevelopmental hypothesis.

Neuroanatomy

In support of the neurodevelopmental hypothesis, five neuroanotomical abnormalities have consistently emerged in neuroimaging and post-mortem studies of schizophrenia (Bora et al., 2011; Keshavan et al., 2008; Stewart & Davis, 2008). The first abnormality is reduced overall brain volume and enlargement of the cerebral ventricles (particularly the left ventricle) associated with brain atrophy. The second abnormality concerns the reduced size of, and activation within, the frontal lobes. The dorsolateral prefrontal cortex is particularly affected, where there is also increased neuronal packing density. This abnormality may underpin cognitive deficits (IQ, executive function, attention and memory). The third abnormality is reduced temporal lobe volume including reductions in the size of the amygdala and hippocampus, structures that subserve emotional processing and memory. The fourth abnormality is decreased thalamic volume, and disorganization of the thalamocortical pathways. The thalamus plays a central role in attention, and in filtering and relaying information to various areas of the brain including the prefrontal cortex. The fifth abnormality is disorganization of white matter tracts and reduced connectivity between many areas of the brain.

A detailed understanding of how these neuroanatomical abnormalities give rise to the symptoms of schizophrenia is a focus of ongoing research. Many of the structural brain abnormalities listed here precede the onset of psychosis, and in some cases they progress over the course of the schizophrenia (Chan et al., 2011).

Psychophysiology

Results of studies which show that schizophrenia is associated with abnormalities in a number of psychophysiological indices reflective of abnormal neurobiological processes also support the neurodevelopmental hypothesis (Javitt et al., 2008; Keshavan et al., 2008). Sleep architecture assessed by electroencephalogram (EEG) is abnormal in schizophrenia. Total sleep time and time during non-rapid eye movement (REM) sleep is reduced, as is REM sleep latency. Evoked potentials, which are detected with scalp electrodes during visual or auditory tasks, are abnormal in schizophrenia, indicating impairments in neurobiological processes subserving visual and auditory perception and information processing. Eye movements, especially those involved in smooth pursuit tracking of a moving target, are abnormal in schizophrenia, indicating impairments in neurobiological processes subserving occulomotor control. These evoked potential and eye movement abnormalities are highly heritable and present prior to the onset of acute psychosis.

Neurotransmitters

Neurotransmitter dysregulation hypotheses attribute psychotic symptoms to neurotransmission problems. Dysregulations of the dopamine and glutamate neurotransmitter systems have been found in schizophrenia (Downar & Kapur, 2008). Genes that affect both of these neurotransmitter systems have been implicated in the aetiology of the condition, as was noted above in the section on genetics.

Dopamine

The dopamine hypothesis arose from observations that medications, such as chlorpromazine, that block dopamine D_2 receptors alleviate psychotic symptoms; and amphetamines, which release dopamine, induce paranoid psychosis (Seeman, 2011). The original dopamine hypothesis, which attributed psychotic symptoms to an excess of dopamine, has inspired extensive research and the development of a range of antipsychotic medications for schizophrenia; over time it has been supplanted by more sophisticated formulations.

Available evidence indicates that overactivity of the mesolimbic dopamine pathway subserves positive symptoms (hallucinations and delusions), and underactivity of the mesocortical dopamine pathway subserves negative symptoms (blunted affect, alogia and avolition) and cognitive impairment (Downar & Kapur, 2008). First-generation anti-psychotic medications such as chlorpromazine, which block dopamine D_2 receptors, alleviate positive symptoms in most cases, but have no effect on negative symptoms. In contrast, newer second-generation anti-psychotic medications, such as clozapine, block dopamine D_2 receptors in the mesolymbic but not the mesocortical pathway, and so alleviate positive symptoms and some negative symptoms.

Downar and Kapur (2008) have proposed the following explanation to link dysregulation of the dopamine system to psychotic symptoms. Dopamine is the neurotransmitter that gives salience to neural networks associated with thoughts or perceptions. Overactivity of the mesolimbic dopamine pathway probably results in many thoughts and perceptions being misinterpreted as highly salient or important. Thus, thoughts are misinterpreted as 'voices', and fleeting ideas that might otherwise be ignored are misinterpreted as being very important and so are developed into delusional belief systems. Antipsychotic medications that block dopamine D_2 receptors reduce this tendency to misinterpret unimportant perceptions and thoughts as highly salient. However, delusions that have already formed may need to be re-evaluated, which is what occurs in cognitive therapy.

In contrast to the overactive mesolymbic dopamine pathway, the underactive mesocortical dopamine pathway reduces the salience with which certain perceptions, thoughts, feelings and motives are experi-enced. This accounts for the negative symptoms (blunted affect, alogia and avolition) and cognitive impairment that occur in schizophrenia.

Glutamate

The glutamate hypothesis proposes that underactivity of N-methyl-D-asparate (NMDA) glutamate receptors underpins the symptoms and cognitive impairment shown in schizophrenia (Downar & Kapur, 2008; Harrison, 2009; Lin et al., 2011). Low glutamate levels have been found in the cerebrospinal fluid of people with schizophrenia. Drugs that reduce the efficiency of NMDA glutamate receptors (such as phencyclidine (PCP) or 'angel dust') induce psychotic symptoms. Drugs that increase the efficiency of NMDA glutamate receptors, such as glycine, alleviate psychotic symptoms, particularly negative symptoms.

Glutamate is the major excitatory neurotransmitter in the central nervous system and NMDA receptors play a central role in attention, perception and cognition. Reduced glutamate activity in the prefrontal cortex may account for negative symptoms and cognitive impairment in schizophrenia. The NMDA glutamate receptor also plays an important role in the development of the nervous system, for example by influencing synaptic pruning, mentioned earlier in the section on neurodevelopment. Thus, dysfunction of NMDA glutamate receptors may account for some of the neuroanatomical abnormalities associated with schizophrenia.

From a theoretical perspective, the dopamine and glutamate theories are not sophisticated enough to account for all of the symptoms of schizophrenia and its response to antipsychotic medication. Contrary to predictions derived from the dopamine and glutamate hypotheses, antipsychotic medication does not immediately reduce symptoms, although it immediately affects neurotransmission. About a third of patients do not respond to antipsychotic medication. No antipsychotic medication eliminates all symptoms. Dopamine-2 antagonists primarily affect positive symptoms and have little impact on negative symptoms. Drugs that increase the efficiency of NMDA glutamate receptors primarily affect negative symptoms.

Current neurotransmitter-based hypotheses will ultimately be replaced by more complex and integrated formulations involving a number of neurotransmitter systems, which can explain the anomalies listed above.

Two-syndrome hypothesis

In an attempt to integrate results from diverse clinical, genetic and neurobiological studies, Crow (1985) proposed the two-syndrome hypothesis. He argued that a distinction may be made between type 1 schizophrenia, which is a genetically inherited disease marked by a dysregulation of the mesolimbic dopamine system and characterized by positive symptoms, and type 2 schizophrenia, which is a neurodevelopmental disorder arising from prenatal or perinatal insults, resulting in neuroanatomical abnormalites and marked by chronic negative symptoms. Type 1 schizophrenia, he proposed, has an acute onset, clear precipitants, predominantly positive symptoms, a good response to antipsychotic medication and good inter-episode adjustment. Type 2 schizophrenia, he argued, is characterized by poor premorbid functioning, an insidious onset, a chronic course, neuropsychological deficits, predominantly negative symptoms and a poor response to medication. The two-syndrome hypothesis fits a good proportion of available data but is probably an oversimplification, since many cases show aspects of both syndromes.

Antipsychotic medication

The most widely used and most effective pharmacological treatments for psychosis are dopamine-2 antagonists. A distinction is made between first- and second-generation, or typical and atypical anti-psychotic medication. Both are dopamine-2 antagonists. Treatment with second-generation antipsychotic medications such as risperidone, olanzapine and clozapine is currently the first-line approach to pharma-cological intervention for psychotic conditions, although clozapine is reserved for treatment-refractory cases due to its problematic side-effects detailed below (Kutscher, 2008; Tandon et al., 2010).

First- and second-generation antipsychotics are equally effective, but they differ in their side-effect profiles (Dolder, 2008). With regard to effectiveness, about half to two-thirds of patients respond to anti-psychotics, and their main effects are on positive symptoms, with limited effects on negative symptoms and cognitive impairment. With regard to side-effects, rates of extrapyramidal side-effects (such as parkinsonism) and tardive dyskinesia (an irreversible neurological movement disorder) are lower for second-generation antipsychotic medication. However, for second-generation antipsychotics, obesity, raised cholesterol and risk of diabetes are more common. In schizo-phrenia, ideally the lowest possible dose of medication should be used in order to reduce side-effects and enhance quality of life.

Clozapine is an extremely effective second-generation antipsychotic, and has a positive impact on suicidal and aggressive behaviour as well as psychotic symptoms (Sajatovic et al., 2008). However, because of its dangerous side-effects, clozapine is reserved for use in treatment-refractory cases or those where there are high risks of suicide or aggression. Clozapine may cause a severe reduction in white blood cell count (agranulocytosis), and this can result in severe infections that may be fatal. For patients on clozapine, routine monitoring of white blood cell count is best practice.

Typically patients with schizophrenia continue to take antipsychotic medication throughout their lives. Where patients show low adherence in taking oral medication daily, they may be administered long-lasting slow-release depot injections (Cunningham-Owens & Johnstone, 2009; Leucht et al., 2011).

Stress-vulnerability theory

Stress-vulnerability or diathesis–stress theories propose that schizo-phrenia occurs when neurobiologically vulnerable individuals are exposed to psychosocial stress (Walker et al., 2008; Zubin & Spring, 1977). Neurobiological vulnerability may be due to genetic and/or pre-natal and perinatal factors that impact on the integrity of the central nervous system.

A substantial body of research shows that the onset, course and severity of schizophrenia are associated with psychosocial stress and trauma (Bebbington & Kuipers, 2008; Phillips et al., 2007; Tandon et al.,

2008b; Walker et al., 2008). Physical and sexual child abuse, family violence and serious injury render people vulnerable to the development of psychosis and there is a dose–response relationship, with greater levels of trauma being predictive of more severe symptoms (Shevlin et al., 2008). Low socio-economic status, migration to a new country and living in an urban rather than a rural setting all confer risk for the development of schizophrenia, and all entail increased stressful demands on coping resources.

The onset of schizophrenia is typically triggered by a build-up of stressful life events (illness, injury, life transitions, loss, etc.). Following the onset of schizophrenia, a number of stresses associated with the experience of psychosis and the response of others to it may compromise recovery. For most patients psychotic symptoms are intrinsically stressful, both as they are occurring and later, during remission, when insight develops and patients realize that their psychotic symptoms were due to a major and often life-long psychological disorder.

Highly emotional family responses to psychosis involving criticism and hostility on one hand or excessive sympathy and emotional over-involvement on the other (referred to as expressed emotion) are very stressful and have been shown in numerous studies to reduce significantly the time to relapse in patients stabilized on antipsychotic medication (Hooley, 2007). Social stresses resulting from psychosis including the loss of friendships, the development of a constricted lifestyle, the experience of stigma and consequent social isolation may all compromise recovery. Occupational impairment due to psychosis may lead to a reduction in financial resources and SES, and recovery may be impeded by these factors. Higher levels of stress are associated with more severe psychotic symptoms.

HPA axis overactivity is a central aspect of the stress response. The HPA axis is a major part of the neuroendocrine system involving the hypothalamus, the pituitary gland located below the hypothalamus, and the adrenal glands (located on top of the kidneys), which controls stress reactions and other processes including the immune system. In schizophrenia, dysregulation of the HPA axis has been found, for example, in studies of cortisol levels (Bradley & Dinan, 2010; Walker et al., 2008). Raised cortisol levels indicative of HPA axis hyperactivity are more common in first-episode psychosis.

Heightened physiological arousal associated with HPA overactivity probably exacerbates psychotic symptoms, particularly positive symptoms such as hallucinations, delusions and thought disorder. Elevated cortisol arising from HPA axis overactivity compromises the efficiency of the immune system and increases vulnerability to cardiovascular and metabolic disease, common in schizophrenia. Such illnesses in turn are additional stresses that may maintain or exacerbate psychosis.

Multimodal interventions

Multimodal interventions based on the stress-vulnerability model involving antipsychotic medication and psychological therapies aim to equip people with schizophrenia and their families with the resources to control psychotic symptoms, reduce environmental stress, enhance social support and work towards recovery. In a large meta-analysis of 106 studies of interventions for schizophrenia, Mojtabai et al. (1998) found that after an average of 17 months, the relapse rate for patients with schizophrenia who received psychological therapy plus medication was 20% lower than that of those who received medication only. The relapse rate in patients treated with medication only was 52% and that for patients treated with medication combined with psychological therapy was 32%.

Family therapy, cognitive-behaviour therapy, cognitive remediation therapy, social skills training and vocational rehabilitation are among the range of evidence-based psychological interventions that have been developed to help people with schizophrenia and their families achieve these aims (Kern et al., 2009; Tandon et al., 2010). Brief descriptions of these are presented below.

Family therapy

About half of medicated clients with schizophrenia relapse, and relapse rates are higher in unsupportive or stressful family environments, characterized by high levels of expressed emotion which involves criticism, hostility or emotional over-involvement (Barrowclough & Lobban, 2008). High levels of expressed emotion arise from family members' appraisals of the controllability of psychotic symptoms. Family members who express high levels of criticism or hostility tend to view patients as having a high degree of control over their psychotic symptoms and therefore hold patients responsible for their difficulties. In contrast, those who express high levels of emotional over-involvement tend to attribute patients' symptoms to uncontrollable factors and so view patients as helpless victims of a psychiatric illness. Low expressed emotion occurs where family members have an accurate understanding of psychosis and skills for managing the condition within a family context.

The aim of psychoeducational family therapy is to reduce family stress and enhance family support so as to delay or prevent relapse and rehospitalization, and also to promote recovery. This is achieved by helping family members understand schizophrenia within a stress-vulnerability framework and develop knowledge and skills to manage the condition. Psychoeducational family therapy may take a number of formats including therapy sessions with single families; therapy sessions with multiple families; group therapy sessions for relatives; or parallel group therapy sessions for relative and patient groups.

Family therapy may be conducted in clinical settings or in patients' homes. It involves psychoeducation based on the stress-vulnerability models of schizophrenia with a view to helping families understand and manage the symptoms of schizophrenia, antipsychotic medication, related stresses and early warning signs of relapse. Psychoeducational family therapy also helps families develop communication and problem-solving skills, reduce destructive expressions of anger and guilt, and promote self-care among non-symptomatic family members (Falloon et al., 1993; Kuipers et al., 2002; McFarlane, 2004).

Meta-analyses have shown that compared with medication alone, multimodal programmes including psychoeducational family therapy and medication lead to lower relapse and rehospitalization rates, and improved medication adherence (Pfammatter et al., 2006). Effective family therapy spans about 9 months, and longer, more intense programmes are more effective.

Cognitive-behaviour therapy (CBT)

Beck has proposed an integrative model to explain the development of symptoms in schizophrenia and then developed a cognitive-behavioural approach to address these symptoms based on this model (Beck et al., 2011). This is diagrammed in Figure 7.2. According to the model, when people with a neurobiological vulnerability to schizophrenia are exposed to stress, this increases their physiological arousal (HPA axis hyperactivity). There is a consequent reduction in their available cognitive resources, which increases their experience of psychotic symptoms.

In early life, exposure to stressful events and trauma contributes to the development of schemas containing dysfunctional attitudes and beliefs, as well as cognitive biases to make inaccurate inferences.

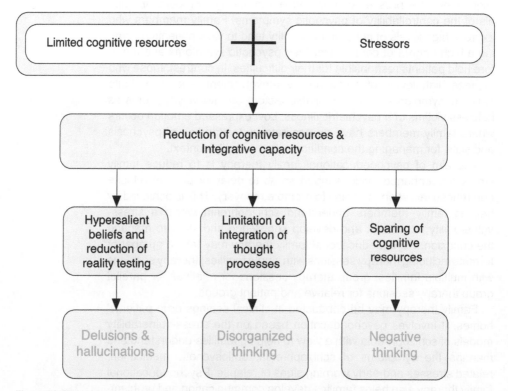

Figure 7.2 Beck's integrated model of schizophrenia for use in CBT (adapted from Beck, A., Rector, N., Stolar, N. & Grant, P. (2011). *Schizophrenia: Cognitive theory, research and therapy*. New York: Guilford)

These are activated by exposure to stress in later life and inform the content of hallucinations and delusions. Exposure to stress and related hyperarousal in adulthood sets the scene for the development of positive symptoms, negative symptoms and disorganization. This is because at these times negative schemas and related cognitive biases are reactivated. Also, limited cognitive resources are available to check out the validity of inferences made about the environment and to manage day-to-day problem-solving.

Within CBT, the symptoms of schizophrenia are viewed as being on a continuum with normal experience. This view is consistent with the finding that normal population surveys show that up to 25% of people have auditory hallucinations, many hold strange, unfounded beliefs (for example about horoscopes and faith healing), and under sufficient stress or exhaustion disorganized thinking and inactivity may occur. Patients are helped to view all of their symptoms as on a continuum with normal experience, as arising within the context of a stress-vulnerability model, and as being controllable through the use of cognitive-behavioural strategies and medication. A fundamental premise of CBT is that activating events give rise to negative automatic thoughts (informed by beliefs in negative schemas), which in turn affect mood, behaviour and the strength of beliefs within negative schemas.

From a CBT perspective, hallucinations are similar to negative automatic thoughts in depression or intrusive thoughts typical of obsessive compulsive disorder. However, they are experienced as loud, external, 'real' and true because people with schizophrenia have a propensity for auditory imagery, a tendency to attribute unusual experiences to external factors (an external bias), and a tendency towards premature closure and deficient reality testing. That is, they hear their negative automatic thoughts as loud, attribute them to an external source, and do not check out the validity of their beliefs against alternatives, for example that these are their own loud thoughts, the content of which may not be valid.

Auditory hallucinations are often incorporated into delusional systems that may maintain them. For example, a patient who hears a critical, omniscient controlling voice may develop paranoid delusions about being persecuted by the owner of the voice, which in turn may raise their arousal level and so make further hallucinations more likely. Patients may try to control voices by engaging in safety behaviours such as isolating themselves. These safety behaviours may reduce hallucinations in the short term, but in the long term may lead to stressful loneliness and this may cause further hallucinations. In CBT patients learn to identify and control stresses that trigger auditory hallucinations, to give up safety behaviours that maintain hallucinations and to reappraise the source of their 'voices' and the content of what they say.

From a CBT perspective, delusions are beliefs or inferences about events or experiences (including hallucinations) that in turn affect mood and behaviour, in the same way that negative automatic thoughts and dysfunctional beliefs affect mood and behaviour in depression and anxiety disorders. However, in schizophrenia, delusions develop within the context of markedly reduced cognitive resources which limit patients' capacity to modify them. The content of delusions is influenced by dysfunctional attitudes and assumptions contained in negative schemas, by hallucinations and by cognitive biases. These include a strong egocentric or self-referential bias, a bias towards external causation of subjective experiences, and a bias towards indiscriminate attribution of extreme positive or negative intentions to others. Thus, a patient who experiences an unusual sensation on the skin may interpret this as due to aliens activating subcutaneous microchips to try to control their behaviour. Delusions are maintained by the belief that they accurately represent reality rather than being testable inferences; by a bias towards focusing on information that confirms the reality of delusions and ignoring disconfirmatory evidence; by engaging in safety-seeking behaviours that prevent the truth of delusions from being tested; and by cognitive resource-sparing strategies such as jumping to conclusions.

In CBT patients are helped to collect evidence to test out the validity of their delusions, starting with the least strongly held ones, and then to test out the validity of the non-delusional schemas that underpin these. In order to test out delusional beliefs, patients are also helped to give up safety behaviours, such as locking the door and disconnecting the phone when strangers are outside their houses, in the case of people with persecutory delusions.

Within CBT, formal thought disorder (characterized by derailment, thought blocking, etc.) is conceptualized as a problematic thinking and speaking pattern that occurs due to limited cognitive capacity arising from stress within the context of a genetic vulnerability to schizophrenia. It is analogous to stuttering. The primary CBT intervention is to help patients recognize thought disorder when it occurs, the stressful situations in which it occurs, and the negative automatic thoughts that give rise to it. They are then helped to challenge these negative automatic thoughts and so reduce the stress associated with thought disorder.

Within CBT, negative symptoms (blunting of affect, alogia and avolition) are conceptualized as ways of coping with the experience of having limited cognitive resources and so limited expectations for success or pleasure, and problematic delusional beliefs or hallucinations. If a patient finds it difficult to think clearly, expects little success or pleasure, believes that his actions are being controlled by others and hears voices telling him that he is useless, then it is understandable that he will be relatively inactive. In CBT behavioural experiments are set up in which patients set goals, engage in activities and monitor their experience of pleasure, success and self-control as they achieve goals.

Controlled trials and meta-analyses show that CBT has a moderate effect, particularly on delusions and hallucinations, in medicated patients whose positive symptoms are not fully controlled by anti-psychotic medication (Pfammatter et al., 2006; Tai & Turkington, 2009; Tandon et al., 2010). Effective CBT spans about 9 months, and longer, more intense programmes are more effective.

Cognitive remediation

Neuropsychological investigations have shown that about three-quarters of people with schizophrenia show significant cognitive deficits (Palmer et al., 2009; Savla et al., 2008). On average the overall IQ of people with schizophrenia is about one standard deviation below the normative mean, although there is considerable heterogeneity between persons and within cases over time.

In schizophrenia most cognitive functions are affected, including attention, memory, processing speed, cognitive flexibility, social cognition and executive function. Episodic memory and processing speed are the areas where greatest deficits occur. While about a quarter of people with schizophrenia show no cognitive deficits, a distinct subgroup show very severe general cognitive deficits (similar to Crow's (1985) type II schizophrenia or Kraepelin's (1899) dementia praecox), and the remainder show variable patterns of specific cognitive deficits (more in keeping with Bleuler's (1911) views on 'loosening of associations' and other specific deficits in schizophrenia).

Many people with schizophrenia show mild premorbid cognitive deficits, followed by a steep decline in cognitive functioning during psychotic episodes, with some amelioration of cognitive deficits during remission and relative stability over the long term. In many cases cognitive deficits have a significant impact on social and occupational adjustment and illness management, and response to psychosocial interventions such as social skills training and supported employment (Kurtz, 2011).

In schizophrenia, cognitive deficits are subserved by the many structural and functional neurobiological abnormalities mentioned in earlier sections. Cognitive rehabilitation therapy is a set of cognitive drills that aim to help patients in remission enhance their attention, memory and executive functions or develop strategies for compensating for their cognitive deficits so that they can better achieve their recovery goals (Tomás et al., 2010). In this type of treatment patients engage in regular computer-based or paper-and-pencil-based training tasks and puzzles a number of times each week over a period of months. Specific tasks are designed to improve specific targeted deficits such as memory. Task difficulty is pitched so that high success rates are achieved or errorless learning occurs. Over time patients build up their cognitive skills or develop strategies for compensating for them.

With compensatory approaches, patients learn strategies or use memory prompts and other devices to make up for their cognitive deficits. Meta-analytic studies of the effectiveness of cognitive remediation report moderate effect sizes on cognitive test performance and indices of daily functioning (Medalia & Choi, 2009; Pfammatter et al., 2006; Tandon et al., 2010).

Social skills training

People with schizophrenia typically show deficits in accurately perceiving social situations, understanding and planning what to do in them, and then responding in a socially appropriate way. This renders them vulnerable to engaging in stressful social interactions, to rejection, to avoidance of further social interaction, and to social isolation (Fett et al., 2011; Walker et al., 2004). The aim of social skills training is to enhance social competence and so prevent social isolation.

Social skills training is usually offered within a group therapy context, and involves the development of communication, conversation, assertiveness, medication management and social problem-solving skills. Modelling, rehearsal, shaping and reinforcement are used during the training process. The main emphasis is on practising skills rather than talking about them (Bellack et al., 2004; Tenhula & Bellack, 2008). Meta-analyses show that compared with medication alone, multimodal programmes that include social skills training and medication lead to significant improvements in social skills in service users with schizophrenia (Kurtz & Mueser, 2008; Pfammatter et al., 2006).

Vocational rehabilitation

Unemployment is a highly prevalent problem in schizophrenia which vocational rehabilitation aims to address (Becker, 2008). Effective vocational rehabilitation involves assessment, job searching, matching available jobs to client preferences, rapid placement in competitive employment (rather than sheltered workshops), and the provision of individualized vocational support and training while service users are in employment (rather than beforehand). Systematic reviews and meta-analyses consistently show that compared with traditional approaches, such as sheltered workshop placement, supported employment doubles the chances of engaging in long-term, paid, competitive employment (Becker, 2008; Cook & Razzano, 2005). Employed service users typically show improved self-esteem and better symptom control.

The recovery model

The recovery movement is being adopted as an overarching framework for mental health services internationally (Roe & Davidson, 2008; Slade, 2009). Kraepelin's (1899) conceptualization of schizophrenia as a neurological disorder with a chronic declining course led to the development of long-term institutional care and a reliance on physical treatments, including medication, as the main interventions for schizophrenia during much of the 20th century. This in turn led to the institutionalization of 'psychiatric patients' and the gradual erosion of their civil rights within institutions. It also led to their stigmatization and marginalization within society. A further consequence of Kraepelin's position was a reduced emphasis on the role of trauma and stress in the aetiology of schizophrenia and the value of psychosocial interventions in its treatment. It was in response to this position that the recovery model emerged at the end of the 20th century and the dawn of the new millennium.

The recovery movement initially arose from service user-groups and mental health professionals involved in rehabilitation, but more recently has become adopted internationally as a best practice framework for service delivery. The model conceptualizes the recovery process as a personal journey, and privileges the concepts of optimism, well-being, personal strengths, supportive relationships, collaboration, personal choice, adaptive coping, developing a meaningful life, civil rights, empowerment and inclusion.

The recovery model has been inspired by longitudinal research which showed that chronic decline in schizophrenia was not inevitable (Häfner & an der Heiden, 2008), that trauma and stress play a role in the aetiology of schizophrenia (Bebbington & Kuipers, 2008), and that psychosocial interventions have an important place in facilitating recovery from psychosis (Mojtabai et al., 1998). The recovery movement embraced these research findings, placing a strong emphasis on professionals working collaboratively with service users to help them achieve their preferred goals. There was a shift in emphasis from institutional to community care, and from remediating patient deficits to fostering service-user strengths. There was also an emphasis on the civil rights of patients to make choices about their preferred treatments and to have an inclusive place in society. The recovery movement has created a context for the development of innovative community-based approaches to mental health service delivery, such as the strengths-based case management model and assertive community treatment.

Strengths-based case management

The strengths-based case management model was developed by Charles Rapp in the Kansas School of Social Welfare (Rapp & Goscha, 2006, 2008). With this model professionals work in partnership with clients to help them recover. Thus, the strengths model falls within the overall framework of the recovery model.

The model is guided by six principles. First, people with schizophrenia can recover and transform their lives. Second, the primary focus of clinical work is on strengths rather than deficits. Third, the community is a source of resources that may facilitate recovery. Fourth, case managers are guided by service users' preferences, and implement plans only with their approval. Fifth, the community is the primary setting for case management. Sixth, a strong therapeutic relationship between the case manager and service user is essential for recovery.

There are four stages in the model: the engagement phase, strengths assessment, creating personal plans and resource acquisition, and disengagement. In the engagement phase the therapist forms a strong and respectful, collaborative therapeutic alliance with the client. Assessment focuses predominantly on evaluating clients' personal strengths, and strengths they can access in their environments. Strengths are identified in domains of the daily living situation, finances, education or work, social support, health, leisure, recreational activities and spiritual or cultural activities. Strengths assessment forms the basis for the client and case manager to set goals and plan an agenda of things clients wish to achieve. To address this agenda, clients are helped to acquire the necessary community resources and supports for implementing their recovery plans which will increase their reintegration into community life. As clients' autonomy increases and is sustained, and as clients come to live more independently in the community, the process of gradual disengagement is negotiated.

A series of empirical evaluations has shown that this strengths model, when implemented with adequate fidelity, is more effective than routine psychiatric services in promoting recovery from schizophrenia (Rapp & Goscha, 2008).

Assertive community treatment

Assertive community treatment was developed by Leonard Stein and Mary Ann Test at the Mendota Mental Health Institute in Madison, Wisconsin to address the challenges of deinstitutionalization. It is an integrated community mental health service delivery model in which hard-to-reach people with schizophrenia receive intensive, continuous individualized treatment, rehabilitation, and support services from community-based multidisciplinary teams in which team members carry small case loads (DeLuca et al., 2008). Assertive community treatment aims to promote rehabilitation and recovery, and to prevent homelessness and unnecessary hospitalization. There is a major focus on helping service users develop the skills to manage everyday problems of living. All therapies and services are provided by team members and are not 'farmed out' to other professionals.

Multimodal treatment in which evidence-based pharmacological and psychosocial therapies are provided in an integrated way is central to this service-delivery model. Thus, evidence-based medication algorithms, adherence programmes, psychoeducational family therapy, cognitive behaviour therapy, supported employment and so forth can be offered within the context of assertive community treatment programmes. Teams help service users to avoid crisis situations, and where necessary provide rapid response crisis intervention on a 24/7 basis to prevent unnecessary hospitalizations. Services are provided to clients in their homes or elsewhere in the community, on a time-unlimited basis. Team composition, training, adherence to assertive community treatment programme fidelity guidelines and ongoing supervision are essential for the effectiveness of this approach to service delivery.

In a meta-analysis of six randomized controlled trials, Coldwell and Bender (2007) found that assertive community treatment led to a 37% reduction in homelessness and a 26% improvement in psychiatric symptom severity compared with standard case management. In a systematic review of 25 randomized controlled trials, Bond et al. (2001) concluded that assertive community treatment substantially reduces psychiatric hospital use, increases housing stability, and moderately improves symptoms and subjective quality of life. It is highly successful in engaging service users in treatment.

Bond et al. (2001) found that the more closely case management programs followed assertive community treatment principles, the better were the outcomes. While assertive community treatment services are costly, these costs are offset by a reduction in hospital use by service users with a history of extensive hospital use. In meta-analysis of 44 studies involving over 6,000 service users, Ziguras and Stuart (2000) found that assertive community treatment was more effective than treatment as usual in reducing care costs and family burden, and in improving family satisfaction with services.

Assessment

The assessment and treatment of schizophrenia is ideally conducted by multidisciplinary teams. The early detection and treatment of psychosis is critical because better outcomes occur in cases where duration of untreated psychosis is brief (Tandon et al., 2008a). For hard-to-reach cases, the adoption of an assertive outreach approach is optimal (DeLuca et al., 2008).

Typically, the preliminary assessment and management of acute psychotic episodes is managed by psychiatrists and psychiatric nurses. Once positive symptoms have been managed with antipsychotic medication, a broader-based assessment is conducted to guide long-term case management. Through careful clinical interviewing of patients and members of their families, the symptoms of schizophrenia and relevant history are obtained. A diagnosis is given in accordance with the criteria outlined in ICD-10 and DSM-IV-TR, given in Table 7.1, and a formulation explaining the symptoms entailed by the diagnosis is developed in which the relevant predisposing, precipitating, maintaining and protective factors are outlined. A general clinical formulation model is given in Figure 7.3.

From Table 7.1 it may be seen that there are differences between DSM and ICD criteria. For a DSM diagnosis, impairment in functioning must have been present for 6 months, whereas for an ICD diagnosis symptoms must have been present for at least a month. The psychotic disorders module of the Structured Clinical Interview for DSM-IV Axis I Disorders is a widely used and well-validated structured interview for diagnosing schizophrenia (SCID, First et al., 1996). Psychotic symptom severity may be initially rated and regularly monitored with the Brief Psychiatric Rating Scale (BPRS, Lukoff et al., 1986) or the Positive and Negative Symptom Scale (PANSS, Kay et al., 1987). With the BPRS and PANSS, the severity of symptoms such as delusions and hallucinations are rated on Likert scales on the basis of observations of patients' behaviour and their responses to questions.

Overall functioning may be monitored periodically with the clinician-rated Global Assessment of Functioning scale (GAF, Luborsky, 1962). On the GAF the patients' overall functioning is rated on a single 100-point rating scale. The social needs of service users indicating the resources required to help them adjust within the community may be assessed with the short version of the Camberwell Assessment of Need (CAN, Slade et al., 1999; Trauer et al., 2008). This covers issues such as mental and physical health, drug use, social relationships, accommodation, transport, budgeting, and activities of daily living. The

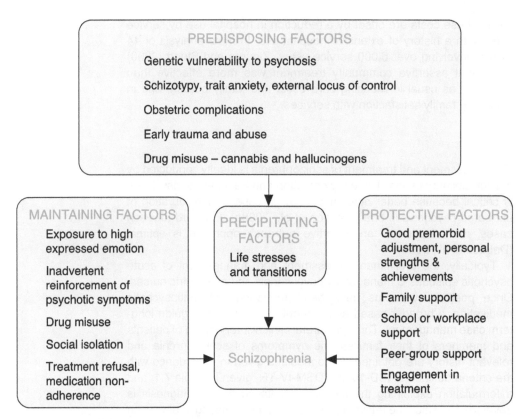

PREDISPOSING FACTORS

Genetic vulnerability to psychosis

Schizotypy, trait anxiety, external locus of control

Obstetric complications

Early trauma and abuse

Drug misuse – cannabis and hallucinogens

MAINTAINING FACTORS

Exposure to high expressed emotion

Inadvertent reinforcement of psychotic symptoms

Drug misuse

Social isolation

Treatment refusal, medication non-adherence

PRECIPITATING FACTORS

Life stresses and transitions

PROTECTIVE FACTORS

Good premorbid adjustment, personal strengths & achievements

Family support

School or workplace support

Peer-group support

Engagement in treatment

Schizophrenia

Figure 7.3 General formulation model for schizophrenia

scale also offers a framework for identifying needs that have and have not been met.

The use of the CAN as a central part of assessment is consistent with Rapp's strengths-based model of case management mentioned earlier (Rapp & Goscha, 2006). In research studies, expressed emotion of family members towards patients, which has an impact on their relapse rates, is assessed by the Camberwell Family Interview (CFI, Leff & Vaughn, 1985). Because this instrument is too cumbersome for use in routine clinical practice, Hooley and Parker (2006) recommend asking patients to rate how critical family members are of them on a 10-point scale, an assessment procedure that correlates highly with expressed emotion assessed by the CFI.

Service users' assessments of their recovery journey may be regularly monitored with the Recovery Assessment Scale (RAS, Corrigan et al., 2004). This self-report instrument assesses hope, meaning of life, quality of life, symptoms and empowerment. During the process of assessment and treatment, patients and family members may be invited to keep daily records of medication adherence, fluctuations in symptoms, distress, beliefs, and the circumstances preceding and following these fluctuations. These idiographic ratings are useful for fine-tuning ongoing family therapy, CBT and other psychosocial interventions.

Treatment

The optimal treatment for schizophrenia is multimodal and includes both antipsychotic medication and psychological therapies (Tandon et al., 2010). Currently second-generation antipsychotic medications are the pharmacological treatments of choice, for reasons stated earlier in this chapter. Evidence-based psychological therapies include family therapy, cognitive-behaviour therapy, cognitive remediation therapy, social skills training and vocational rehabilitation, all of which have been described above.

Treatment programmes should be offered in a carefully planned and co-ordinated way by multidisciplinary teams with adequate training in these evidence-based pharmacological and psychological interventions. Treatment packages should be individually tailored to take account of service users' clinical needs as identified in the case formulation and personal preferences as expressed during assessment, in line with the recovery model orientation. In all cases psychoeducational family therapy to help service users and their families understand schizophrenia and to promote medication adherence is essential, but more intensive family therapy is warranted where family members show high levels of criticism, hostility or emotional overinvolvement. CBT is particularly useful for the management of residual positive symptoms that are not controlled by medication, or to facilitate a reduction in the medication dosage required to control positive symptoms. To be optimally effective, both family therapy and CBT should be offered for about 9 months.

Cognitive remediation therapy and social skills training are appropriate where it is clear that significant cognitive and social skills deficits are present. Vocational rehabilitation is appropriate where service users require employment. Where there is comorbid alcohol or drug misuse or obesity (a side-effect of some antipsychotic medications), evidence-based treatment for these problems should be integrated into the overall treatment package (Kavanagh, 2008).

The development of a strong therapeutic alliance and the adoption of an approach that modifies intrapsychic and interpersonal maintaining factors underpins effective psychosocial interventions for schizophrenia. This overall approach to the management of schizophrenia is broadly consistent with international best practice guidelines (American Psychiatric Association, 2004b; Buchanan et al., 2010; Dixon et al., 2010; NICE, 2009b).

Controversies

There are many controversies surrounding schizophrenia. These centre on issues such as the validity of the schizophrenia construct, the validity of the schizotypy dimensional conceptualization of psychosis, the idea that schizophrenia reflects a split personality, the view that diagnosing schizophrenia is an act of oppression, the role of the family in the aetiology of schizophrenia, and the psychoanalytic treatment of psychosis. These issues will be briefly considered below.

Validity of the schizophrenia construct

There is ongoing controversy about the validity of the construct of schizophrenia. At one extreme schizophrenia is conceptualized as a discrete biomedical disease-like entity – a 'mental illness' – with clearly defined symptoms, arising primarily from genetic and neurobiological factors, and requiring treatment mainly with antipsychotic medication. This is the prevailing position within mainstream psychiatry following the tradition founded by Emil Kraepelin (1899) and currently expressed most authoritatively in works such as the DSM-IV-TR and mainstream psychiatry textbooks.

In the UK, critics of this position include Mary Boyle (2002) and Richard Bentall (2003). They point out that there is scant evidence to support the view that schizophrenia is a biomedical 'mental illness', and marshal many different arguments to support this position. The symptoms that define the illness are not distributed within the population in the way that symptoms of diseases such as cancer or heart disease are. They are distributed as dimensions, not categories. Many so-called normal people have delusions and hallucinations. The supposed biological causes of schizophrenia (genetic vulnerability, structural and functional brain abnormalities, etc.) are not present in all cases or absent in all non-cases. Not all cases of schizophrenia follow a distinct uniform course. Not all cases of schizophrenia respond to biomedical treatment. Some people with psychotic symptoms recover without biomedical intervention either spontaneously or through engaging in psychological therapy. Bentall (2003) and Boyle (2002) support all of these arguments with research evidence (some of which has been covered in this chapter) and conclude that the construct of schizophrenia as a 'mental illness' has no validity.

Schizotypy

There is ongoing controversy about the validity of categorical and dimensional models of psychotic processes (Linscott & van Os, 2010). The schizotypy construct has been proposed by researchers such as Gordon Claridge in the UK and Mark Lenzenweger in the US as a dimensional alternative to the prevailing categorical conceptualization of schizophrenia (Lenzenweger, 2010).

According to the categorical view, which derives from Kraepelin's (1899) work and is enshrined in the ICD and DSM classification systems, schizophrenia is a discrete diagnostic category. Within a population, a proportion of people have schizophrenia and the rest do not. In contrast to this prevailing categorical view is the schizotypy hypothesis. This proposes that anomalous sensory experiences, peculiar beliefs and disorganized thinking are present in an extreme form in schizophrenia as hallucinations, delusions and thought disorder, but these processes are on a continuum with normal experience – a position originally advocated by Bleuler (1911).

A variety of measures of schizotypy have been developed which assess this continuum, and research programmes involving these measures have provided support for the construct (Lenzenweger, 2010). For example, research on schizotypy shows that the continuum may be composed of subdimensions; the continuum extends from normal to psychotic experiences; schizotypy is heritable; and people with high schizotypy scores but who are not psychotic show attentional, eye-movement and other neuropsychological abnormalities associated with schizophrenia.

Schizophrenia and split personality

In popular culture schizophrenia is often used to refer to split personality. For example, in a UK survey of a national random sample Luty et al. (2006) found that 40% of respondents equated split or multiple personality with schizophrenia. However, in psychology, it is clear from this chapter that schizophrenia does not refer to such a condition. The closest scientific equivalent to split personality is a condition referred to as multiple personality disorder (MPD) in ICD-10 and dissociative identity disorder (DID) in DSM-IV-TR. The central feature of MPD or DID is the apparent existence of two or more distinct personalities within the individual, with only one being evident at a time. Each personality (or alter) is distinct, with its own memories, behaviour patterns and interpersonal style. Commonly, the host personality is unaware of the existence of the alters and these vary in their knowledge of each other.

A developmental diathesis–stress model of dissociative identity disorder is now widely accepted (International Society for the Study of Trauma and Dissociation, 2011). Available evidence suggests that the capacity to dissociate is normally distributed within the population. People who have a high degree of this trait, when exposed to extreme trauma (such as repeated severe child abuse) during early childhood may cope by dissociating their consciousness from the experience of trauma. They achieve dissociation by entering a trance-like state.

Where repeated trauma occurs in early childhood, and dissociation is repeatedly used as an effective distress-reducing coping strategy, the process of dissociation is negatively reinforced. That is, the habit of dissociation is strengthened because it brings relief from distress during trauma exposure. Furthermore, the process of dissociation allows the child to preserve relationships with abusive or inadequate caregivers during the periods when traumatic abuse is not occurring. Eventually, sufficient experiences become dissociated to constitute a separate personality. These may be activated in later life at times of stress or trauma or through suggestion in hypnotic psychotherapeutic situations. Psychological treatment commonly involves helping clients integrate the multiple personalities into a single personality and develop non-dissociative strategies for dealing with stress. Unlike schizophrenia, psychotropic medication is of little value in treating the core symptoms of multiple personality disorder.

In the ICD and DSM, MPD and DID are classified with other disso-ciative conditions including dissociative amnesia (inability to recall events following a trauma); dissociative fugue (sudden unexpected travel away from the customary place of activities coupled with confu-sion or amnesia for aspects of one's identity following a trauma); and depersonalization disorder (a sense of being out of one's body following trauma). People who have a strong capacity to dissociate may develop one of the dissociative disorders rather than PTSD following trauma. Dissociative phenomena fall on a continuum, with tip-of-the-tongue experiences being a mild dissociative phenomenon, hypnotic trance states being a more pronounced dissociative condition; depersonaliza-tion disorder and dissociative amnesia and fugue being more extreme forms of dissociation; and MPD or DID being the most extreme form of dissociation. More extreme dissociative conditions develop when the person has a strong capacity to dissociate and is exposed repeatedly to severe trauma.

Diagnosis as oppression

The prevailing professional view within the field of mental health is that a diagnosis of schizophrenia reflects the assignment of a person with an objectively verifiable condition to a valid diagnostic category based on careful and unbiased observation, and that this process is conducted in the patient's best interests. However, an alternative viewpoint most strongly presented by Thomas Szasz (2010) since the early 1960s is that diagnosis is an act of oppression, because it paves the way for involuntary hospitalization and involuntary treatment.

Szasz, a US psychiatrist, argues that the process of diagnosing a person with schizophrenia is a covert, politically oppressive transaction in which a deviant or disadvantaged person is subjected to a process of social control. This is offered as one explanation for the greater rates of schizophrenia among ethnic minorities (particularly African Americans) and people from low socio-economic groups. Furthermore, exponents of this position argue that schizophrenia is not a valid diagnostic category, but an invalid fabrication constructed to exert social control over deviant people who do not conform to societal norms.

Schizophrenia as a sane reaction to an insane situation

R. D. Laing (2009), a Scottish psychiatrist and psychoanalyst, in the 1960s and 1970s strongly opposed the view that schizophrenia was a genetically based medical condition requiring treatment with anti-psychotic medication. He also opposed the prevailing orthodoxy that the contents of delusions and hallucinations were incoherent. Laing proposed that the contents of psychotic symptoms were understand-able as psychological responses to complex, confusing, conflicting and powerful parental injunctions that left no scope for more rational and adaptive attempts at communication. That is, he viewed schizophre-nia as 'a sane reaction to an insane situation'.

For Laing, effective treatment involved creating a context within which insight into the complex family process and the psychotic response to this could be facilitated. The role of the therapist was to understand the content of patients' delusions and hallucinations, and interpret these for the patient as responses to conflicting parental injunctions. The experience of psychosis and recovery was a difficult journey from which the person could emerge with new and valuable insights. Laing advocated drug-free psychotherapeutic treatment for psychosis within the context of a therapeutic community. He founded the Philadelphia Association in the UK, which continues to run therapeutic communities influenced by Laing's ideas.

Laing's view on the exclusive role of the family in the aetiology of schizophrenia and the exclusive use of psychotherapy in its treatment has not been supported by subsequent research. Genetic factors play a major role in the aetiology of schizophrenia, and antipsychotic medication reduces positive symptoms in two-thirds of cases (Ritsner & Gottesman, 2011; Tandon et al., 2010). However, research findings have supported the hypothesis that the family does affect the psychotic process and psychotherapy has a place in the management of psychosis. Personal trauma, including child abuse increases the risk of psychosis, stressful life events including those within the family can precipitate an episode of psychosis, and high levels of family criticism, hostility and emotional overinvolvement increase the risk of relapse (Bebbington & Kuipers, 2008; Hooley, 2007; Shelvin et al., 2008). Family therapy delays relapse in families characterized by high levels of expressed emotion and cognitive behaviour therapy which stresses the idea that psychotic symptoms are understandable and on a continuum with normal experience can help patients control these symptoms (Tandon et al., 2010).

Psychoanalysis and psychosis

There is controversy over the value of psychoanalysis in understanding and treating psychosis. The developers of the influential PORT (Patient Outcomes Research Team) guidelines, on the basis of a literature review, concluded that psychoanalytically based psychotherapy has no place in the treatment of schizophrenia (Lehman & Steinwachs, 1998). In contrast, Gottdiener (2006), in a review of results of controlled trials and meta-analytic results, concluded that psychodynamic psychotherapy was as effective as CBT in the treatment of medicated patients with schizophrenia.

Freud and later psychoanalysts attributed the development of schizophrenia to adverse early family experiences, and many analysts, like Freud, acknowledged that treatment of psychosis with psychoanalytic methods was problematic because psychotic patients did not develop transference to the analyst in the same way that neurotic patients did (Lucas, 2009). Freud never treated a psychotic patient and was pessimistic about the relevance of psychoanalysis to psychosis; this attitude deterred many analysts from attempting to treat schizophrenia.

However, there were exceptions. Frieda Fromm-Reichman in the US and Wilfred Bion in the UK developed supportive psychodynamic psychotherapy approaches to treating psychosis (Lucas, 2009). Currently, despite Gottdiener's (2006) supportive review of psychodynamic treatment outcome studies, psychoanalytically informed interventions are rarely used to treat schizophrenia.

Summary

Schizophrenia refers to a complex group of psychotic disorders that affects about 1% of the population. The condition is marked by positive symptoms such as delusions and hallucinations, negative symptoms such as flattened affect, alogia and avolition, and disorganized speech and behaviour. In the past, a broad definition of schizophrenia was used in North America and a narrow definition used in Europe, but there is now considerable international agreement on a narrow-band definition of schizophrenia. In the DSM and ICD classification systems distinctions are made between four main subtypes of schizophrenia: paranoid, catatonic, hebephrenic or disorganized, and undifferentiated. Schizophrenia, schizophreniform disorder, schizoaffective disorder and schizotypal, schizoid and paranoid personality disorders constitute the schizophrenia spectrum disorders which share a similar genetic aetiology and treatment response.

Schizophrenia typically has its onset in late adolescence or early adulthood and follows a chronic relapsing course, although up to 20% of patients show complete remission. A favourable outcome is associated with good premorbid adjustment, and a brief duration of untreated psychosis characterized by an acute onset in response to precipitating stressful life events, a family history of affective disorder and a favourable life situation to return to following discharge from hospital. The greatest risk factor for schizophrenia is a family history of psychosis.

Currently there is wide acceptance of a stress-vulnerability model of schizophrenia whereby the condition is proposed to arise when a genetically vulnerable individual is exposed to significant life stress. Life stresses include predisposing trauma, precipitating acute stressful life events and maintaining chronic stressful family interactions.

Neurobiological research has identified a number of candidate genes and structural and functional brain abnormalities associated with schizophrenia. The two-syndrome hypothesis offers a simplified way to integrate relevant findings on research into the biological origins of schizophrenia. This hypothesis entails the view that a distinction may be made between type 1 schizophrenia, which is a genetically inherited disease marked by a dysregulation of the dopaminergic system and characterized by positive symptoms, and type 2 schizophrenia, which is a neurodevelopmental disorder arising from prenatal or perinatal insults resulting in neuroanatomical abnormalities marked by chronic negative symptoms.

Comprehensive multidisciplinary assessment and treatment with multimodal evidence-based interventions is internationally accepted as best practice in cases of schizophrenia. Individually tailored multimodal treatment programmes based on the stress-vulnerability model should include both antipsychotic medication and evidence-based psychological therapies such as family therapy, CBT, cognitive rehabilitation, social skills training, and vocational rehabilitation.

Controversies about schizophrenia concern issues such as the validity of the schizophrenia and schizotypy constructs, confusion of schizophrenia with MPD/DID, diagnosis as an oppressive process, family process in the aetiology of schizophrenia, and the psychoanalytic treatment of psychosis.

Questions

- What are the main clinical features of schizophrenia and how is it different from the popular conception of a 'split personality'?
- What are the differences between paranoid, hebephrenic, catatonic and undifferentiated schizophrenia?
- How prevalent is schizophrenia?
- What are the risk factors for schizophrenia?
- What are biological and diathesis–stress theories of schizophrenia, and the main research findings relevant to these theories?
- What are the main evidence-based approaches to assessment and treatment of schizophrenia?
- Which controversial issues concerning schizophrenia interest you most, and why?

FURTHER READING

Professional

- Mueser, K. & Jeste, D. (2008). *Clinical handbook of schizophrenia*. New York: Guilford.
- Rubin, A., Springer, D. & Trawver, K. (2010). *Clinician's guide to evidence-based practice: Psychosocial treatment of schizophrenia*. Hoboken, NJ: Wiley.

Self-help

- Healy, C. (2007). *Understanding your schizophrenia illness: A workbook*. Chichester, UK: Wiley

- Kuipers, E. & Bebbington, P. E. (2005). *Living with mental illness* (third edition). London: Souvenir Press.
- Mueser, K. & Gingerich, S. (2006). *The complete family guide to schizophrenia.* New York: Guilford.

WEBSITES

- American Psychiatric Association's practice guidelines for treating schizophrenia:
  http://psychiatryonline.org/guidelines.aspx
- National Institute for Clinical Excellence guidelines for treating schizophrenia:
  http://guidance.nice.org.uk/topic/mentalhealthbehavioural
- Schizophrenia Patient Outcomes Research Team (PORT) updated treatment recommendations 2009:
  http://schizophreniabulletin.oxfordjournals.org/content/36/1/94.full.pdf+html
- Schizophrenia Research Forum:
  www.schizophreniaforum.org

Personality disorders 8

disorders or personality disorders

Learning objectives

After studying this chapter you will be able to:

- define the concept of personality disorder
- list the main personality disorders in the DSM and ICD classification systems
- distinguish between Cluster A, B and C personality disorders in terms of their main clinical features
- summarize the epidemiology of personality disorders
- outline the diathesis–stress, psychodynamic and cognitive-behavioural theories of personality disorders
- name the main evidence-based approaches to assessment and treatment of personality disorders
- describe some of the controversial issues concerning personality disorders.

Introduction

Often episodes of psychological problems such as anxiety and depression occur against a backdrop of more pervasive and long-standing
personality-based difficulties. To address this, distinctions are made in
ICD-10 (World Health Organization, 1992) and DSM-IV-TR (American
Psychiatric Association, 2000) between episodic psychological disorders

on one hand and persistent personality disorders on the other. In DSM-IV-TR a multiaxial system is used for summarizing diagnostic assessments. The main diagnosis is given on Axis I, and personality disorders are recorded on Axis II. (Comorbid medical conditions are coded on Axis III, psychosocial stressors on Axis IV and current level of functioning on Axis V, although these other axes do not concern us at this point.)

Axis I disorders are characterized by atypical episodes of psychological functioning that deviate from an individual's normal pattern of experience and behaviour. In contrast, Axis II personality disorders are pervasive, enduring, inflexible patterns of behaviour, cognition and affect that differ markedly from prevailing cultural expectations and that lead to distress or impairment.

In clinical practice about 40% of patients present with both classes of disorder (Zimmerman et al., 2008). Personality disorders run a chronic course and are associated with a poor outcome. In the Collaborative Longitudinal Personality Disorders Study, Skodol et al. (2005) found that personality disorders were characterized by functional impairment in personal, social, educational and occupational domains; a poor response to treatment for comorbid depression; a high risk of suicide; and extensive health service usage. Individuals with comorbid Axis I and II disorders have greater service needs than those with Axis I disorders only (Hörz et al., 2010). The economic cost of meeting the treatment needs of patients with personality disorders is therefore significant.

In a Dutch study of 1740 people with comorbid Axis I and II diagnoses treated at six specialist mental health services, Soeteman et al. (2008) found that the average cost in the 12 months prior to attending specialist mental health services was €11,126 per patient. Two-thirds of this was direct medical costs and the remainder was due to productivity losses. The assessment and treatment of personality disorders are an important concern for clinical psychology on both humanitarian and economic grounds.

In this chapter, after considering the clinical features and epidemiology of personality disorders, a number of specific theoretical explanations for personality disorders will be considered, and an outline of their assessment and treatment will be given.

Clinical features and case examples

The defining features of personality disorders described in DSM-IV-TR and ICD-10 include the following:

- an enduring dysfunctional pattern of behaviour and experience
- the pattern begins in adolescence and is consistent across situations
- there are difficulties with cognition, affect, impulse control, behaviour and interpersonal functioning
- recurrent relationship and occupational problems are present
- difficulties in learning from experience or benefiting from psychotherapy occur
- there is usually a history of other psychological disorders and/or criminality.

Personality disorders are characterized by an enduring pattern of behaviour and experience that deviates markedly from cultural expectations. This pattern leads to significant personal distress or significant impairment in social functioning. With personality disorders there are marked difficulties in two or more of the following domains: cognition, affect, impulse control, behaviour, and interpersonal functioning.

With cognition, there may be peculiarities or difficulties in the way self, others and events are interpreted. At an affective level the range, intensity, lability and appropriateness of emotional responses may be out of keeping with cultural expectations. There may be serious difficulties with impulse control leading to highly erratic or impulsive behaviour, markedly inhibited behaviour, or peculiar behaviour. With respect to interpersonal behaviour there are typically serious difficulties in making and maintaining stable and fulfilling interpersonal relationships. Most people find the rigid behavioural patterns of people with personality disorders aversive and so avoid them. In the long term, the social isolation or negative responses of others to people with personality disorders causes them personal distress.

A hallmark of personality disorders is the fact that the cognitive, affective, behavioural and interpersonal difficulties constitute a long-standing and rigid pattern of psychological functioning. Usually personality disorders can be traced back to adolescence or early adulthood. Furthermore, individuals with personality disorders have great difficulty learning from life experiences or therapeutic interventions how to alter their rigid behaviour patterns. They repeatedly make the same mistakes and find it very challenging to learn from their errors. Often they are unaware of the impact of their behaviour on others, and wish to conceal their history of social and psychological difficulties. It is therefore clinically useful to include collateral information from family members when assessing personality disorders.

For some personality disorders, such as antisocial personality disorder, diagnosis is made by reputation rather than presentation. Personality disorders commonly occur in conjunction with other psychological difficulties or criminality. In clinical settings personality disordered patients usually create significant problems for staff and other patients. Staff often describe them as manipulative and as playing one staff member off against another, or as refusing to co-operate with treatment.

In DSM-IV-TR the 10 main personality disorders are subdivided into three clusters on the basis of their cardinal clinical features. The first cluster includes the paranoid, schizoid and schizotypal personality disorders. These are grouped together because they are characterized by odd or eccentric behaviour. It was noted in Chapter 7 that these conditions are schizophrenia spectrum disorders. Their clinical features resemble subclinical psychotic symptoms and they share the same genetic aetiology as schizophrenia.

The second cluster includes the antisocial, borderline, histrionic and narcissistic personality disorders. These are characterized by dramatic, emotional or erratic impulsive behaviour. The third cluster includes the avoidant, dependent and obsessive-compulsive personality disorders, all of which are characterized by anxiety and fear-fulness. A very similar classification system is used in ICD-10. There are, however, some minor differences. The schizotypal syndrome is listed as a psychotic condition along with schizophrenia in ICD-10, and narcissistic personality disorder is omitted. Also, obsessive compulsive personality disorder is referred to as anakastic personality disorder; antisocial personality disorder is referred to as dissocial personality dis-order; and avoidant personality disorder is referred to as anxious avoid-ant personality disorder.

The clinical features of the 10 personality disorders are set out in Table 8.1. The current classification of personality disorders has its roots in the work of the German psychiatrist Kurt Schneider (1923).

Multiple personality disorder (MPD), which was discussed in the closing section of Chapter 7, is not classified with other personality disorders in ICD-10. Nor is dissociative identity disorder (the DSM-IV-TR term for MPD) classified with personality disorders in DSM-IV-TR. Rather, in both classification systems this condition is classified with other disorders where dissociation is the core feature.

Cluster A: The odd, eccentric group

The odd, eccentric group of personality disorders includes:

- paranoid personality disorder
- schizoid personality disorder
- schizotypal personality disorder.

Paranoid personality disorder

Clinical features

People with paranoid personality disorder have a pervasive distrust of others. At a cognitive level, they interpret the motives of others in nega-tive, malevolent, conspiratorial or exploitative terms. They assume, on the basis of minimal or ambiguous evidence, that others intend to harm them, be disloyal to them, exploit them, or use personal information to discredit them. At an affective level they are angry, combative and unforgiving of those whom they view as having harmed them. At a behavioural and interpersonal level, they constantly question the loyalty of close friends, partners or spouses. They may refuse to confide in others in case their confidences are used against them. They may con-stantly check on their spouses' or sexual partners' whereabouts and question their fidelity. They may hold grudges indefinitely if they believe that their friends or partners have harmed, insulted, injured or betrayed them. Kraepelin (1921) and Freud (1911) both gave early accounts of paranoia as a distinct condition.

Case example

Margaret, age 35, had a paranoid personality disorder. She and Brian came for therapy because of extreme marital distress. Brian complained

TABLE 8.1
Main clinical features of major personality disorders

Cluster	Personality disorder	Main clinical feature	Cognition	Affect	Behaviour	Relationships
Cluster A Odd, eccentric group	Paranoid	Mistrust	Paranoid ideas	Aggressive	Secretive	Mistrustful
	Schizoid	Detachment	Odd ideas	Constricted affect	Eccentric	Loner
	Schizotypal*	Eccentricity	Bizarre thoughts Ideas of reference Superstitious Strange speech	Constricted affect Socially anxious	Eccentric	Loner
Cluster B Dramatic, emotional, erratic group	Antisocial	Moral immaturity	No internalized set of moral standards	Aggressive	Violates rights of others Criminality	Multiple exploitative relationships
	Borderline	Impulsivity	Expectation of abandonment Shifts between overvalued and undervalued view of self and others	Impulsive Aggressive Depressed	Fights with others Self-harms	Multiple relationships with frantic unsuccessful attempts to avoid abandonment
	Histrionic	Seductive Attention seeking	Belief in entitlement to attention no matter the cost to others	Shallow	Theatrical, seductive attention seeking	Multiple shallow relationships
	Narcissistic**	Self-importance and grandiosity	Belief in entitlement to VIP treatment because they are better than others	Craves admiration and becomes angry or depressed if this need is frustrated	Admiration seeking	Multiple relationships that fail to meet their high expectations
Cluster C Anxious, fearful group	Avoidant	Shyness	Belief that they will be rejected by others	Fear of rejection	Social withdrawal	Loners
	Dependent	Lack of autonomy	Belief that they cannot function autonomously	Fear of autonomy	Refusal to take responsibility for decision making Clinginess	Multiple relationships in which they are completely dependent on their partners
	Obsessive-compulsive	Perfectionism	Belief that safety and security can be sustained through orderliness	Fear imperfection	Detailed rule following without regard for deadlines or overall goals	Multiple relationships in which their coldness and need for control cause conflict

Note: *Schizotypal syndrome is listed as a psychotic condition with schizophrenia in ICD-10. **Narcissistic personality disorder is not listed in ICD-10.

that he felt like a prisoner in the marriage. Before leaving each morning, Margaret interrogated him about his daily schedule. She phoned him frequently at work and would sometimes visit his office unexpectedly to check up on him. One night he found her checking through his wallet and the memory of his mobile phone to find clues about him having contact with another woman. Margaret complained that Brian had been unfaithful to her recently. He denied this but said that her suspiciousness was making infidelity an attractive option.

Margaret's suspiciousness was a longstanding characteristic. She had a very small circle of friends, whom she had known since childhood, She would not make new friends because she found it hard to trust and confide in others. She also thought that new friends would ridicule her.

She had lost one of her closest female friends, Estelle, over an argument about loyalty. Estelle was ill on an occasion when Margaret had made arrangements for the two of them to go to a James Taylor concert. Margaret believed that she had gone to a party elsewhere on that evening. There was no evidence for this, but Margaret believed that she had been betrayed. She would not forgive Estelle despite the latter's attempts to put the incident to one side and continue the friendship. There were many incidents like this in Margaret's life, dating back to her childhood.

Margaret had grown up in a family where her parents had separated when she was 8 years old. In the time before the parents' separation she often heard them argue about her father's whereabouts. These arguments would often end with her father storming out of the house and her mother shouting and crying. On some of these occasions she would say to Margaret 'You can't trust anyone in this world'.

Margaret was attracted to Brian because of his openness and honesty and his willingness to spend a great deal of time with her. Brian found that after they were married the demands of work prevented himself and Margaret from spending as much time together. As a result of this, Margaret began to accuse him of infidelity. He believed that if she continued to accuse him, despite his innocence, he would seriously consider separation. Margaret interpreted this as evidence of his infidelity.

Schizoid personality disorder

Clinical features

People with schizoid personality disorder show a pervasive pattern of detachment from social relationships. They are loners. At a cognitive level they have a preference for solitary activities and introspection. They have no desire for intimacy and do not wish to have close, confiding relationships with their families, friends or sexual partners. They are indifferent to praise or criticism. At an affective level they have a restricted range of emotions. They are neither depressed, nor do they find that relationships or activities bring them great pleasure, nor are they roused to anger even in extreme circumstances.

At an interpersonal level they have few relationships and others find them cold and indifferent. They have little regard for social conventions, and so are not concerned about being seen to 'do the right thing'. An early account of the schizoid personality was given by Eugen Bleuler (1924).

Case example

Norman, aged 20, had a schizoid personality disorder. He was a mathematics student who came for counselling because he was concerned that his addiction to an international multi-site computer game was interfering with his work. He stayed in a college hall of residence but lived an isolated life. This was the way he had always lived. As a child he was ridiculed for being 'too brainy' and so became immersed in recreational mathematics. At the counselling service he refused to join a social skills group because he said he did not want to form relationships with other students.

Schizotypal personality disorder

Clinical features

People with schizotypal personality disorder have unusual perceptual experiences, eccentric thoughts and speech, inappropriate or constricted affect, peculiar or eccentric behaviour, and a lack of close relationships. At a perceptual level, they may have unusual experiences. For example, they may report sensing the presence of ghosts or spirits, mystical forces or vibrations. They may experience depersonalization and report that sometimes they become an outside observer of themselves in a dream-like state. They may also experience derealization and report that sometimes they perceive the world as dream-like.

At a cognitive level they may have ideas of reference, and believe that routine events have a unique personal significance; for example, that the shape of a cloud means that they must carry out a particular activity. They may also hold paranormal convictions about magic forces, telepathy, aliens and so forth, which are outside the norms of their subculture. They may also hold paranoid ideas and be suspicious of others. Their speech may be unusual, vague, eccentric or peculiar.

At an affective level, people with schizotypal personality disorder show a constricted range of emotions and social anxiety, usually based on paranoid fears. At a behavioural level, people with schizotypal personality disorder are odd, eccentric and peculiar. For example, they may dress in an unfashionable and unkempt way and have unusual mannerisms. At an interpersonal level, people with schizotypal personality disorder are typically socially isolated and find making and maintaining friendships anxiety-provoking, so they avoid others.

Ernst Kretchmer (1936), a German psychiatrist, was among the first to use the term schizotype to describe a character type associated with a constitutional vulnerability to schizophrenia.

Case example

Silver, a man in his late forties, had a schizotypal personality disorder. He was a periodic outpatient at a psychiatric hospital. His appearance was distinctive. His long silver-grey hair and beard accounted for his unusual name. He wore a black overcoat, the hem of which trailed on the ground. He rarely washed and lived alone in a house that had belonged to his parents before they died.

Silver had been referred to the psychiatric hospital by his family doctor years before I met him, for participation in a group programme for people with schizophrenia. He refused to participate in the programme because he was suspicious of other people, but requested periodic individual appointments with the psychologist who directed the group programme. In these outpatient individual sessions he insisted on discussing hypnosis and telepathy. He believed that he could hypnotize others from a distance, that he could see into the future and that he could read minds. He had held these beliefs since adolescence, when he had numerous out-of-body experiences (depersonalization). Otherwise he was in contact with reality and was on no medication.

Cluster B: The dramatic, emotional, erratic group

The dramatic, emotional, erratic group of personality disorders includes:

- antisocial personality disorder
- borderline personality disorder
- histrionic personality disorder
- narcissistic personality disorder.

Antisocial personality disorder

Clinical features

People with antisocial personality disorder show a pervasive disregard for the rights of others and consistently violate these rights. Extreme versions of this pattern are referred to as psychopathy, sociopathy, and dissocial personality disorder.

At a behavioural level, people with antisocial personality disorder are consistently aggressive, destructive and deceitful, and engage in theft and lying. Commonly in clinical practice, antisocial personality disorder is associated with a history of multiple arrests, multiple convictions and imprisonment. At a cognitive level, people with this personality disorder have not internalized rules for moral and ethical behaviour and are motivated by personal profit and pleasure seeking. They believe that aggressiveness, destructiveness, theft, deceit, and lying to achieve personal goals are justified. They develop elaborate rationalizations and cognitive distortions to justify their violations of others' rights.

At an affective level, they are impulsive and reckless, displaying little planning and showing no anxiety even in the most dangerous situations. Their impulsivity and recklessness may find expression in an erratic occupational history, poor financial planning, speeding while driving, substance abuse and other forms of risk-taking which may lead to injury or death in some cases.

People with antisocial personality disorder are aggressive and irritable and frequently become involved in fights. At an interpersonal level they have difficulty maintaining intimate relationships with friends or sexual partners. Commonly they charm people into believing that they wish to pursue a close relationship and then violate the trust the other person has placed in them through irresponsibility, disloyalty, aggression, destruction, theft or deceit. They show little remorse for violating trust in close relationships, and consequently have few if any close friends and typically a history of multiple sexual partners. The diagnosis of antisocial personality disorder is not given until after a person is 18, and commonly it is preceded by conduct disorder.

Antisocial personality was first described in detail by Hervey Cleckley (1941) in his book *The Mask of Sanity* and referred to as psychopathy, although Cleckley's criteria for the condition defined a narrower construct than that in the current DSM classification system. Cleckley emphasized the importance of callousness; lack of empathy, shame, guilt or remorse; and the use of superficial charm, manipulation and violence in violating others' rights to satisfy their needs.

Case example

Tony, who had an antisocial personality disorder, was referred to a psychiatric hospital from a prison for psychological assessment. He was referred because he complained of depression to the visiting psychiatrist at the prison. He had a history of theft and occasional drug abuse.

A thorough clinical interview and a full psychometric evaluation revealed no evidence of a mood disorder or, indeed, any other Axis I psychopathology. During the feedback session when the results of the assessment were presented to him, Tony said he had feigned depression because he wanted to be referred to the psychiatric hospital from the prison for a change of scene. He joked about the fact that he preferred the conditions in the hospital to the prison.

During the psychological assessment he gave a history that drew a picture of himself as a stable, caring man who had fallen on hard times and so had stolen from time to time and unluckily been apprehended for occasional drug abuse. I interviewed his sister and wife to corroborate this essentially normal profile. They offered accounts that were at variance with Tony's. They drew a picture of a man who had grown up in a disorganized family, which his father left when Tony was a baby. His mother had a series of unreliable partners after that.

Tony began rule-breaking and stealing as a child and had continued to do so right up to the present. He also truanted from school and began drinking and drug taking in his teens. He had been married on four occasions and in each marriage had been violent towards his wife for trivial reasons. He had been involved in episodes of serious drug misuse and alcohol binges. Tony had been imprisoned on numerous occasions and participated in a wide range of treatment programmes to help him alter his antisocial and drug-using behaviour patterns. All had been ineffective. He had no close friends, just transient acquaintances. His sister rarely saw him and his present wife (of a year's standing) was considering divorce.

Borderline personality disorder

Clinical features

People with borderline personality disorder are highly impulsive and show a pattern of pervasive instability in interpersonal relationships, self-image and mood. At a cognitive level they have a core belief that within the context of friendships and relationships they will be abandoned. At an affective level, they experience an intense fear of abandonment. They also have a propensity to experience intense uncontrolled aggression towards those whom they perceive as abandoning them.

Their fear of abandonment leads to frantic yet ineffective attempts to make and maintain relationships, particularly with sexual partners. Once in a relationship, their fear of abandonment may lead them to demand continued contact with their partner and continued caregiving and attention. When their partners cannot allay their fear of abandonment or fail to meet their needs for continued caregiving and attention, the person with borderline personality disorder may attempt to reduce the interpersonal distance by either becoming aggressive to their partner or engaging in self-harm. They may rage at their partner for frustrating their need for care and attention. They may then feel shame and guilt and engage in self-harm or self-mutilation to elicit continued caregiving from their partner, or to distract themselves from their internal psychological distress. Their self-harm may involve overdosing, cutting or burning. Sometimes self-mutilation is carried out while in a dissociated state. There may be a link between dissociative disorders such as multiple personality disorder, discussed at the close of Chapter 7, and borderline personality disorder.

Within close personal relationships and therapeutic relationships, beliefs that people with borderline personality disorder hold about themselves and others alternate between extremes of idealization and devaluation. Thus, they may on occasion view themselves or their partners as perfect, kind, caring and highly valued, but on other occasions when their needs to receive care and attention from their partners are frustrated, they may view themselves or their partner as cruel, uncaring and despicable. This alternation between overvalued and undervalued views of the self and others and related changes in affect and behaviour may occur suddenly and unpredictably.

Underlying the belief in the inevitability of abandonment and the related fear and anger is a pervasive sense of emptiness. People with borderline personality disorder may cope with this through impulsive spending, sexual activity, bingeing, drug use, reckless driving or other risk-taking activities. Commonly borderline personality disorder occurs following a history of physical or sexual child abuse, neglect or early parental loss or death. A history of multiple partners and educational and occupational instability is common in cases of borderline personality disorder. The term 'borderline' was first used by the psychoanalyst

Adolf Stern (1938) to describe this personality disorder, which he believed was on the borderline between the neuroses (such as depression and anxiety) and psychoses (such as schizophrenia).

Case example

Mary, aged 24, had a borderline personality disorder. She was referred for a parenting assessment to a child and family psychology service after her child was taken into foster care following a non-accidental injury. Mary had become frustrated with her 10-month-old daughter's continuous crying and bruised her badly by squeezing and shaking her. The parenting assessment showed that Mary had a good knowledge of how to care for her child but little sensitivity to the infant's signals; little understanding that the baby could not intentionally try to annoy her; and little tolerance for managing the routine daily demands of parenting. She also had a very limited social support network and difficulties making and maintaining friendships.

Mary had been involved in several heterosexual relationships. All had ended in violent rows. When these relationships ended she felt deep regret and a sense of being abandoned. Her attempts to rekindle some of these relationships had been unsuccessful and led to further violent or abusive rows. She had a history of episodes of major depression and had frequently engaged in non-suicidal self-harm. She had overdosed on a few occasions and cut her arms. A general feeling of emptiness was occasionally broken by feelings of extreme joy (for example, at the start of a new relationship) and anger. She lacked any coherent life plan.

Mary herself had been in care as a child on two occasions when her parents were unable to cope. She had also been regularly slapped and punched as a child by her father when he came home drunk. In school, she had never fitted in. She had left school at 14 and worked in a variety of casual jobs. She had hoped when she met the baby's father, Kevin, that things would work out. But Kevin left her once she mentioned that she was pregnant. She hoped that her child and her role as a parent would give her happiness and a sense of direction. She was distraught when she found that they had brought her further misery.

Histrionic personality disorder

Clinical features

People with histrionic personality disorder are characterized by a pervasive pattern of dramatic and excessively emotional attention seeking. At a cognitive level there is the underlying belief that they are entitled to be the centre of attention and to have their needs for attention and admiration met, regardless of the cost to others. At an affective level they may feel a hunger for attention that they fear will not be fulfilled. At a behavioural level they routinely create situations in which they are the centre of attention. To do this they may express their views in dramatic and theatrical ways using excessive displays of emotion. However, when questioned in detail about why they hold particular views, typically they have little in the way of well-reasoned arguments or in-depth knowledge to back their assertions. They are highly suggestible and may change their views in response to changes in fads and fashions.

This shallowness that characterizes their views and opinions also characterizes their relationships. They commonly consider their relationships with others (including health professionals) to be far more intimate and deeper than they are. So they may call doctors that they have seen infrequently by their first names and refer to acquaintances as their old friends.

People with this personality disorder may dress and groom themselves so that they become the centre of attention. Often their self-presentation is deliberately seductive. Women with histrionic personality disorder may dress, make themselves up and behave in a way that is erotic, seductive and provocative. Men may dress and behave in a macho manner, drawing attention to their physical appearance, strength, athleticism and sexuality. One of the earliest descriptions of histrionic personality disorder was given by Emil Kraepelin (1913).

Case example

Sarah, aged 18, had a histrionic personality disorder. She was originally referred to a child and family clinic in her final year at secondary school. She was to be excluded from school for instigating fights and disruption. She typically dressed like a film star, spoke like a soap opera character, and demanded everyone's attention. If she didn't get the attention she craved, she threw a tantrum.

She divided her favours between a number of boys at her school and incited them to compete with each other for her affections, promising each an exclusive relationship with her if they defeated the other boys. She was an only child and grew up in a family where her parents, who were involved in the arts, had little time for her. She spent much of her childhood alone and coped with the isolation by watching endless soap operas. She was intelligent but could not apply herself at school or later at college. She changed courses frequently and was led more by her attraction to partners and excitement than by vocational interests.

Narcissistic personality disorder

Clinical features

People with narcissistic personality disorder have a pervasive pattern of grandiosity, a need for admiration, and a lack of empathy for others. At a cognitive level they believe that they are special or better than others and so are entitled to be treated differently. They have an over-inflated view of their own accomplishments and believe that they are entitled to the best of everything and to associate only with people whom they perceive to be special or outstanding like themselves. They are preoccupied with fantasies of success, power and romantic love.

At an affective level, they crave admiration, attention and deferential treatment from others. To confirm this view of themselves, at a behaviour level, they use their charm in social situations or their power in work situations to extract compliments and special treatment from others. Thus they may 'fish for compliments' in social situations and overload their employees in work situations to achieve their own personal goals.

At an interpersonal level they have difficulty sustaining long-term relationships because they have a limited capacity for empathy and so do not appreciate the negative effect that their grandiosity and need for admiration have on others. They also leave many relationships because they fail to meet their high expectations of 'perfect love'. They have difficulties maintaining peer friendships because they are arrogant, patronizing and envious of others' accomplishments and possessions, and expect others to be envious of them.

Occupationally, they may excel at their work or may avoid trying to excel for fear of failure. Furthermore, they are extremely sensitive to criticism and when their partners or others frustrate their need for admiration or are the least bit critical, their self-esteem drops. They feel degraded, humiliated, hollow and empty. This may find expression as range and anger or depression. Detailed psychoanalytic accounts of narcissistic personality disorder and its treatment were first given by Otto Kernberg (1975) and Heinz Kohut (1968).

Case example

Frank, aged 34, had a narcissistic personality disorder. He came for therapy at the insistence of his partner, Maria. She complained that he had become impossible to live with. Since they had met Frank had always depended on her for emotional support and admiration. While she felt that this was appropriate when they were young lovers, she now felt that his demands were immature and excessive.

For example, when he arrived home from work he expected all household routines to cease and Maria and the three children to devote their attention to his accounts of his day's achievements. If they did not meet his expectations he would fly into a rage and verbally abuse them. Later he would be remorseful and if he was not forgiven by Maria he would sink into a cold, detached, depressed state.

The problem had become particularly bad recently when his business partner, Martin, had questioned his judgement in a major deal that went badly wrong and the company made a significant loss. Frank had relied on continued support and admiration from Martin (whom he considered to be a lesser person than himself) and was devastated at his criticism. He had oscillated between threatening to take legal action against Martin for defamation of character and withdrawing completely from frontline business transactions with the company's clients because of his incompetence.

Cluster C: The anxious, fearful group

The anxious, fearful group of personality disorders includes:

- avoidant personality disorder
- dependent personality disorder
- obsessive-compulsive personality disorder.

Avoidant personality disorder

Clinical features

People with avoidant personality disorder show a pervasive pattern of social inhibition and shyness beginning in adolescence or early adulthood. At a cognitive level people with avoidant personality disorder believe that they are inferior to others, unlikable and socially unskilled. They also believe that when they meet new people, there is a high risk that they will be criticized, rejected, ridiculed, shamed or humiliated.

At an affective level they experience intense anxiety in social situations. At a behavioural level they avoid situations, occupations, job promotions and pastimes that involve significant interpersonal contact with unfamiliar people. At an interpersonal level they live a constricted social lifestyle and avoid, or show extreme restraint in, intimate relationships, to avoid humiliation and embarrassment.

Cases with the symptoms of avoidant personality disorder were described by Bleuler (1911) as a variant of schizoid conditions in his work on the schizophrenias.

Case example

Seamus, aged 45, was a bank official with avoidant personality disorder. He was referred to a communications consultancy centre for job interview preparation training. The process involved role-playing, videoing and reviewing the type of job interview in which he was due to participate to achieve promotion. While he was thoughtful and quite coherent during a conversation that preceded the role-play, during it he was virtually incoherent.

In the small rural branch of the bank where he worked he was just about able to tolerate the social anxiety he experienced when dealing with regular customers. He was shy and avoided all social contact outside work. He didn't want to attend our communications consultancy for interview skills training, but the regional personnel manager of his bank said he needed to develop his job interview skills so he could be promoted to Assistant Manager level. He had attended our consultancy so as not to disappoint the personnel manager. However, he would happily have avoided promotion because it would involve increased contact with unfamiliar people.

Dependent personality disorder

Clinical features

People with dependent personality disorder show a pervasive pattern of submissiveness and clinginess. At a cognitive level, they have a belief that they must be taken care of by others (such as parents and partners) and that if separated from others their safety will be jeopardized.

At an affective level, they experience extreme anxiety when separated from parents or partners, whom they view as essential for their safety and security. At a behavioural level, they have difficulty making decisions without asking for and receiving advice and reassurance from others. They have difficulty disagreeing with others, particularly parents or partners, lest this lead to loss of support. They arrange for others to take responsibility for major areas of their lives and rarely initiate projects on their own. They go to great lengths to receive reassurance from others, even when this involves doing very unpleasant tasks. At an interpersonal level, when one intimate relationship ends they quickly seek another, lest they be left to cope and make decisions alone.

One of the first detailed descriptions of dependent personality disorder was given by the psychoanalyst Karl Abraham (1924) and referred to this condition as the oral character type, due to his hypothesis that the seeds of this personality disorder were sown during the oral stage of psychosexual development. This is the earliest stage of development, during which pleasure comes mainly from the process of feeding, hence the term 'oral' and the primary characteristic of dependency.

Case example

Tracy, aged 32, had a dependent personality disorder. She was the wife of a man who phoned a child and family psychology service requesting help with a sexual problem. He initially said that he was attracted to his 15-year-old daughter. It was suspected that sexual abuse had occurred in this case and so a full family assessment was offered. The family assessment revealed that he had had sexual intercourse with the daughter repeatedly for over a year.

We advised that the father leave the home and live separately while a programme of rehabilitation occurred. The programme would involve the mother and daughter strengthening their relationship; the daughter learning self-protection skills; and the father attending group therapy for sex-offenders. Tracy refused to co-operate because she felt unable to make decisions and function without her husband. Thus Tracy was prepared to jeopardize her daughter's safety for her own dependency needs.

Obsessive compulsive personality disorder

Clinical features

People with obsessive compulsive personality disorder show a pervasive pattern of preoccupation with orderliness, perfectionism, ethics, interpersonal control and fiscal economy. At a cognitive level, there is a central belief that for safety and security to be maintained in all areas of life a carefully constructed set of organizational rules must be followed to perfectionistic standards. This belief covers the execution of routine activities of daily living, all areas of occupational responsibility, fairness in dealings with others, co-operating with others in jointly completing tasks, and managing money.

At an emotional level, people with this personality disorder experience anxiety when their set of perfectionistic rules covering all areas of activity is not followed. At a behavioural level, a wide range of problems occur. There is extreme difficulty in finishing tasks on time and meeting deadlines, and in some instances tasks are never finished because perfectionistic standards are never reached. Flexible problem-solving also suffers, because a person with this personality disorder will become so fixed on following the original plan that even when unforeseen obstacles are encountered, the original plan is still followed.

Leisure pursuits and family relationships receive little attention because of devotion to work-related tasks, and this is not accounted for by economic necessity. If a person with obsessive compulsive personality disorder does involve themselves or their children in sports, their dedication to perfectionism makes sporting events unhappy affairs marked by conflict. Practical solutions to problems at work or at home are difficult to find because of ethical scruples, beyond those accounted for by religious or cultural standards.

In work, leisure and family situations, tasks are not delegated because of concerns that others will not do them to a perfectionistic standard. Conflict and eventually social isolation may arise as a result of this. In economic matters, people with obsessive compulsive personality disorder are miserly and hoard money (however abundant) and possessions (however worthless) against possible future times of economic hardship.

At an interpersonal level people with obsessive compulsive personality disorder may become isolated because they place such harsh demands on others to reach high standards and because they have difficulty expressing tender feelings. This is because they can rarely find the perfect way to express their positive feelings for others, and they find it imperative to express their feelings of disappointment when others fail to meet their standards.

Freud (1908) offered a detailed description of the obsessive compulsive personality disorder and referred to it as the 'anal character'. He used this term because his hypothesis was that its seeds were sown during the anal stage of psychosexual development. During this stage there is a psychological focus on the anus as a source of pleasure, and on the capacity to control the sphincter in the process of toilet training. The term 'anal' is now commonly used to describe fussy, perfectionistic, control-oriented people.

Case example

Hank, aged 50, had an obsessive compulsive personality disorder. He was a divorced professor of experimental psychology. He came for therapy because of depression. This was related to the fact that his children and students had refused to have contact with him.

In his home life he had always been meticulous and set the highest standards for family relationships and household routines. It was his anger when these standards were not reached that led to his divorce. However, he continued to have contact with his children. His insistence on punctuality and the critical attitude he took to his children's behaviour had led them to reduce the frequency of their visits with him, and eventually to his wife suggesting that he have very infrequent access to the children.

He was meticulous in his work. He wrote all his own computer programs for conducting his experiments and analysing his data. He insisted that his research students receive daily supervision and follow his guidance to the letter. If they did not meet his standards, he vilified them. His work was internationally known and all of his students had their work published or presented at major conferences. However, students who worked with him found his criticism of tiny errors in their work, his insistence that they follow his guidelines to the letter and his excessive devotion to work to the exclusion of leisure difficult to take. They had complained to the dean about his criticism of them. He took the dean's suggestion that he take a more flexible approach and be less critical with his students very hard. He felt misunderstood and saw it as a personal attack.

Epidemiology and course

Prevalence rates for personality disorders are given in Table 8.2. In the general population the prevalence of personality disorders is about 10%, whereas in samples of mental health service users, the rate is four times that at about 40% (Torgersen, 2009; Zimmerman et al.'s, 2008). The results of the US National Comorbidity Survey Replication showed

TABLE 8.2
Epidemiology of major personality disorders

Cluster	Personality disorder	Prevalence (%) in the community	Prevalence (%) in clinical samples	Gender differences in community studies
	Any personality disorder	10.3	40.5	No differences
	Cluster A	5.7	–	Higher in males
	Cluster B	1.5	–	
	Cluster C	6.0	–	
Cluster A Odd, eccentric group	Paranoid	1.7	4.1	
	Schizoid	0.9	1.1	
	Schizotypal	0.9	4.6	
Cluster B Dramatic, emotional, erratic group	Antisocial	1.1	4.3	Higher in males
	Borderline	1.6	15.8	
	Histrionic	1.5	9.5	
	Narcissistic	0.5	4.5	
Cluster C Anxious, fearful group	Avoidant	1.7	11.4	
	Dependent	0.7	8.0	Higher in females
	Obsessive-compulsive	2.1	5.3	

Note: Community prevalence rates for any personality disorder and individual personality disorders are median rates from 12 community studies summarized in Torgersen (2009). Community prevalence rates for Clusters A, B and C are from Lenzenweger et al.'s (2007) US National Comorbidity Survey Replication. Clinical prevalence rates are median rates from Zimmerman et al.'s (2008) review of 16 clinical studies. Gender differences are from Torgersen (2009).

that in rank order, Cluster C personality disorders were the most prevalent (6.0%); Cluster A were the next most prevalent (5.7%); and Cluster B, the least prevalent (1.5%) types of personality disorders in the general population (Lenzenweger et al., 2007).

For individual types of personality disorder, prevalence rates vary from 0.5% to 2.1% in the general population, with obsessive compulsive personality disorder being the most prevalent. In samples of service users, prevalence rates vary from 1.1% to 15.8%, with borderline personality disorder being far more prevalent than other types. Within the general population the overall rates of personality disorders are similar for males and females. However, Cluster A disorders and antisocial personality disorder have consistently been found to be more prevalent among males, whereas dependent personality disorder has consistently been found to be more prevalent among females (Torgersen, 2009). The high prevalence of borderline personality disorders in females found in clinical practice is not found in general population surveys.

There is considerable comorbidity among personality disorders. Many people who have one personality disorder meet the criteria for a number of others (Lenzenweger et al., 2007). There is also considerable comorbidity of Axis I disorders with Axis II disorders. For example, in a review of 20 large studies, Guzzetta and di Girolamo (2009) found that 57% of people with substance abuse disorders, 49% of people with mood disorders and 40% of people with anxiety disorders also had comorbid personality disorders.

The results of longitudinal studies where the same group of patients is followed up over time and cross-sectional studies where the prevalence of personality disorders in different age groups is examined are fairly consistent. Personality disorders are fairly stable over time, although some improvement does occur, especially among those with Cluster B personality disorders (Grilo & McGlashan, 2009). In midlife people with antisocial and borderline personality disorder begin to mature out of their dysfunctional behaviour patterns. Borderline patients become less impulsive and self-harming and antisocial patients reduce their involvement in criminality. However, for both conditions only a minority establish successful relationships.

People with personality disorders show significant impairment in functioning. They tend to remain single, to have educational, occupational and financial problems that lead them to be of lower SES, and have a lower quality of life (Torgersen, 2009). Between a half and three-quarters of people with personality disorders attempt suicide; attempted and completed suicide rates are highest for borderline and antisocial personality disorder; and about 10% of borderline patients actually commit suicide (Links & Kolla, 2009).

Personality disorders affect the extent to which Axis I disorders respond to treatment. People with mood, anxiety and substance use disorders who also have comorbid personality disorders show less improvement in response to psychotherapy compared with people who have no comorbid personality disorders (Haaga et al., 2006; Newton-Howes et al., 2006; Newman et al., 2006a).

Theories

Diathesis–stress, psychodynamic and cognitive-behavioural theories of personality disorders have been developed and summaries of these are outlined below.

Diathesis–stress theories

Diathesis–stress theories of personality disorders propose that both biological factors and stressful environmental factors, particularly those within the individual's family of origin, contribute to the development of personality disorders. These theories entail the view that people with certain genetically determined temperamental characteristics develop particular personality traits, and that personality disorders emerge when such people are exposed to certain types of psychosocial risk factors within their families or wider social systems (Clark & Watson, 2008; Lenzenweger & Clarkin, 2005; Paris, 1996).

Genetics, temperament and personality traits

The weight of evidence shows that 50% of the variance in major personality traits such as neuroticism, extraversion, openness to experience and conscientiousness may be accounted for by genetic factors (Krueger & Johnson, 2008; Paris, 1996). The mechanisms by which genetic factors influence personality traits are complex. Probably multiple genes determine temperamental characteristics, and these interact with environmental influences in the development of personality traits. There is considerable evidence from longitudinal studies for the link between temperament and personality traits (Clark & Watson, 2008; Rothbart & Bates, 2006).

Children with temperaments characterized by irritability and fearfulness develop high levels of neuroticism in later life. Children with temperaments characterized by high activity levels and positive affect become extraverted as they mature. Children who temperamentally show attentional persistence later develop high levels of conscientiousness. Children with extreme maladaptive temperamental characteristics may be more vulnerable to environmental stressors or they may elicit reactions from parents and others that exacerbate their extreme temperamental characteristics. This in turn may lead them to develop maladaptive personality traits, placing them at risk of developing personality disorders (DePauw & Mervielde, 2010).

Genetics and personality disorders

Genetic studies indicate that personality disorders are moderately heritable, with heritability estimates ranging from about 20% to 70%, and that the extensive comorbidity between personality disorders can be explained by four main genetic factors and three environmental factors (Reichborn-Kjennerud, 2010). The genetic factors include neuroticism (common to most personality disorders), introversion (which mainly affects schizoid and avoidant personality disorder), disagreeableness and impulsivity (which mainly affects antisocial and borderline personality disorder) and conscientiousness or compulsivity, which uniquely affects obsessive compulsive personality disorder. On the other hand, comorbidity within Clusters A, B and C is best explained by three distinct environmental factors. For each of the clusters of personality disorders, research has thrown light on the role neurobiological factors in the aetiology of some specific personality disorders. This will be briefly summarized below.

Neurobiology of schizotypal personality disorder

There is some evidence that neurobiological factors may play a role in the development of schizotypal personality disorder. This disorder forms part of a spectrum of psychotic or psychotic-like disorders that includes schizophrenia. People with schizotypal personality disorder have symptoms similar to those of schizophrenia; they share many of the attentional and information-processing deficits found in people with schizophrenia; and many have been found to have a positive family history for schizophrenia (Mamah & Barch, 2011; Siever & Davis, 1991).

Neurobiological studies have shown that schizotypal personality disorder shares candidate genes, and certain structural and functional brain abnormalities, with schizophrenia (Coccaro & Siever, 2009; Reichborn-Kjennerud, 2010). Candidate genes implicated in the aetiology of schizotypal personality disorder include catechol-O-methyltransferase (COMT), which regulates dopamine signalling in the frontal cortex, and D-amino acid oxidase activator (DAOA) and dysbindin (DTNBP1), which affect glutamate signalling.

Schizotypal personality disorder is associated with less dysregulation of the dopamine neurotransmitter system than that found in schizophrenia, and reduced temporal lobe volumes similar to that present in schizophrenia; but unlike schizophrenia, intact frontal lobes characterize people with schizotypal personality disorder. It is probable that the dopamine system and temporal lobe abnormalities subserve the eccentricities that characterize people with schizotypal personality disorder, but that the less extreme dysregulation of the dopamine system and the normal frontal lobes prevent the emergence of frank psychosis.

Neurobiology of borderline personality disorder

Neurobiological studies have identified candidate genes and structural and functional brain abnormalities associated with borderline personality disorder (Coccaro & Siever, 2009; Reichborn-Kjennerud, 2010). The main candidate gene associated with borderline personality disorder is SLC6A4 or 5-HTT, which affects the efficiency of the serotonin neurotransmitter system. The short allele variant of the 5-HTTLPR polymorphism, which regulates expression of the serotonin transporter gene

(SLC6A4 or 5-HTT), is a risk factor for borderline personality disorder (and is also associated with vulnerability to depression and PTSD, as mentioned in Chapters 5 and 6).

While there is evidence for dysregulation of a range of neurotransmitters in borderline personality disorder, the most robust support is for hypoactivity of the serotonin neurotransmitter system (Coccaro & Siever, 2009). This system affects mood and impulsivity. Neuroimaging studies show that a dysfunction of the frontal and limbic circuitry underpins borderline personality disorder (Schmahl & Bremner, 2006). This network includes the orbitofrontal and dorsolateral prefrontal cortex, the anterior cingulate cortex, the hippocampus and the amygdala. A meta-analysis has shown that people with borderline personality disorder have bilateral decreases in hippocampal and amygdala volumes (Hall et al., 2010). Structural changes and overactivity of the amygdala may underpin enhanced threat perception and the tendency to repeat emotionally charged relationship patterns in borderline personality disorder, while frontal lobe deficits may subserve difficulties in evaluating heightened threat reactions and regulating emotional responses to perceived threats. Reduced hippocampal volume may compromise the capacity for developing coherent adaptive autobiographical narratives as an alternative to repeating destructive, emotionally charged relationship patterns.

It has consistently been found that people with borderline personality disorder have a history of severe trauma including child abuse, particularly child sexual abuse (Johnson et al., 2009). In the emergence of borderline personality disorder, this life stress may both interact with neurobiological vulnerabilities and contribute to their development.

Neurobiology of antisocial personality disorder

Candidate genes for antisocial personality disorder and psychopathy for which there is some support include monoamine oxidase A (MAOA) and the serotonin transporter gene (5-HTT) (Ferguson, 2010; Gunter et al., 2010). Both of these affect the efficiency of the serotonin neurotransmitter system, which in turn affects mood, impulsivity and aggression. Retz et al. (2004) found that a deletion/insertion polymorphism on the 5-HTT gene was a risk factor for violence in male criminals. The MAOA gene has earned the nickname 'warrior gene' because people with low MAOA activity show greater aggression in challenging situations (McDermott et al., 2009). Caspi et al. (2002) found that males with both a low MAOA activity genotype and a history of child abuse were more likely have antisocial behaviour in adulthood than were high MAOA activity genotype males who had been similarly abused.

Neurobiological studies of antisocial personality disorder have led to a distinction between reactive–impulsive aggression (typical of most criminals who engage in opportunistic violence) and proactive–instrumental aggression (which is characteristic of psychopaths who engage in predatory, planned aggression to achieve goals such as money, status and power) (Roth & Buchheim, 2010). With reactive–impulsive aggression, there is hyperarousal to threatening stimuli (subserving increased anger and fear) associated with increased activity in the amygdala and decreased volume and activity in the frontal cortex, notably the orbitofrontal and ventro-medial prefrontal cortex. The increased amygdala activity subserves increased threat perception, while the reduced frontal activity subserves a lack of impulse control. In contrast, with proactive-instrumental aggression, there is hypoarousal to threatening stimuli shown by low heart rate and electrodermal activity (Edens et al., 2007). In some, but not all studies this is associated with decreased activity in the amygdala.

These neurobiological processes subserve low levels of anger or fear. Thus, people with antisocial personality disorders have very low levels of physiological arousal, fail to develop conditioned responses to fear-related stimuli, and are unable to learn from negative experiences. This lack of conditionability reflects a neuropsychological vulnerability to developing antisocial behaviour. However, this vulnerability only leads to antisocial personality disorder when combined with psychosocial risk factors, particularly family disorganization, paternal criminality, maternal psychological difficulties, parental alcoholism, and inconsistent discipline (Kazdin, 1995).

Cluster C personality disorders

Relatively little research has been conducted on the neurobiology of Cluster C personality disorders. An anxious temperament and the personality trait neuroticism (both of which are approximately 50% heritable) probably predispose individuals to developing avoidant and dependent personality disorders (Meyer et al., 2005). However, people with these attributes require exposure to a highly enmeshed family culture in which there is a high degree of parental control and little encouragement for the development of autonomy for the development of avoidant and dependent personality disorders (Paris, 1996). Obsessive compulsive personality disorder has a unique genetic diathesis, which is not shared with other personality disorders (Kendler et al., 2008). There is no evidence to support the link between toilet training (as suggested by Freud's (1908) 'anal character hypothesis') and obsessive compulsive personality disorder (Emmelkamp, 1982).

Stress and personality disorders

In prospective and retrospective studies a wide variety of family-based risk factors have been found to contribute to the development of personality disorders (Bakermans-Kranenburg & van IJzendoorn, 2009; Johnson et al., 2009; Paris, 1996). These include trauma, physical and sexual abuse, neglect, separation from or loss of a parent, parental psychopathology and related impaired parenting, insecure attachment, problematic parent–child relationships, extremely low or high levels of family cohesion, and the absence of social support.

The effectiveness of psychotherapy and medication

Duggan et al. (2007, 2008) reviewed 35 randomized controlled trials (RCTs) of pharmacological studies and 27 RCTs of psychological treatments for personality disorders. They concluded that there was evidence for the effectiveness of specific psychological treatments for certain personality disorders, and for the effectiveness of some pharmacological interventions in managing specific symptoms associated with some Axis II disorders. There was evidence for the effectiveness of cognitive-behaviour therapy and psychodynamic psychotherapy, either alone or in combination with pharmacotherapy. Most studies focused on borderline personality disorder, or heterogeneous groups of patients with various personality disorders. With regard to pharmacological treatments there was evidence for the effectiveness of antipsychotics in reducing cognitive, perceptual and psychotic-like symptoms; mood stabilizers in reducing aggression; and antidepressants in regulating mood.

Psychodynamic approaches

Meta-analyses show that psychodynamic psychotherapy leads to an improvement in the adjustment of people with personality disorders, notably those that fall within Clusters B and C (Leichsenring, 2010). Evidence-based psychodynamic approaches to psychotherapy include transference-focused psychotherapy and mentalization-based treatment for borderline personality disorder (Bateman & Fonagy, 2010a, 2010b; Yeomans and Diamond, 2010) and short-term dynamic psychotherapy for Cluster C personality disorders (Svartberg & McCullough, 2010).

Transference-focused psychotherapy for borderline personality disorder

In modern psychoanalytic practice, Kernberg's approach to understanding borderline personality disorder and an evidence-based practice model derived from it – transference-focused psychotherapy – have been particularly influential (Caligor, 2010; Kernberg & Caligor, 2005; Yeomans & Diamond, 2010). Kernberg's psychoanalytic object relations theory assumes that during the course of early development, individuals evolve through a series of stages. As they mature through these, their internal representations of self and others become increasingly sophisticated. In object relations theory, it is assumed that the children learn about others through their relationships with their mothers or caregivers. 'Object' is the technical term used in object relations theory to refer to others (as distinct from the self) and particularly to the mother during early development.

At a very early stage of development, the infant does not distinguish between representations of the self and the mother. The main distinction that is made is between experiences that make the child feel good or bad. So at the earliest stage the child develops symbiotic fused self–object representations that are 'all good' or 'all bad'. At a second stage of development, the child learns that the self and the mother (or object) are separate. At this stage the child develops representations for an 'all-good self' and an 'all-bad self'; an 'all-good object' and an 'all-bad object'. As the child matures into the third stage of development the 'all-good' and 'all-bad' self-representations are integrated. The child develops a more complete view of the self as having both positive and negative impulses and wishes. Concurrently the 'all-good' and 'all-bad' representations of others (parents, siblings, friends) are integrated. The child develops representations of others as having both positive and negative attributes. When this happens the child becomes capable of having realistic relationships in which ambivalent feelings towards others can be tolerated. So children may feel that they love their parents who are good a lot of the time and a bit annoying some of the time.

In adulthood the way people behave within intimate relationships is predominantly informed and organized by their internal object relations that they learned in childhood; that is, by mental images of how the self and others will function in relationships, and the strong emotions associated with these types of relationship. An image of a bad child-like self, interacting with a threatening, powerful authority figure associated with a strong feeling of fear; or the image of a good child-like self interacting with a good protective authority figure associated with a strong feeling of security, are examples of internal object relations.

Where parents are over-indulgent or overly neglectful, violent or controlling, the child fails to develop mature self–other internal object relations. In their relationships with others, splitting occurs. They view others as 'all-good' idealized rescuers who will meet all their needs or 'all-bad' persecutors who are out to harm them. They also oscillate between viewing the self as 'all-good' or 'all-bad'. These difficulties are the hallmark of all personality disorders. Different types of personality disorder develop depending on the person's temperament, whether the child was over-indulged, neglected or traumatized, the degree to which this occurred, and the specific defence mechanisms that they used to cope with forbidden sexual and aggressive impulses. Cluster A and B personality disorders arise from neglect, rejection or abuse, whereas excessive parental control or over-protection lead to the development of Cluster C personality disorders.

Defences are psychological strategies used to cope with conflict between unacceptable impulses (often unconscious sexual or aggressive urges from the id) and the prohibitions of the conscience (or super-ego). Thus, if a person experiences an unacceptable impulse, anxiety about the consequences of acting on this impulse will be experienced. Defences are used to reduce anxiety. Defences are essential, but some are more adaptive than others. From Table 8.3 it may be seen that the defences of splitting and projection, which typify many personality disorders, particularly borderline personality disorder, are at the most primitive level. Splitting involves reverting to viewing the self and others in 'all-good' or all-bad' terms. Projection involves attributing negative

TABLE 8.3
Defence mechanisms at different levels of maturity

Level	Features of defences	Defence	The individual regulates emotional discomfort associated with conflicting wishes and impulses or external stress by ...
High-adaptive level	Promote an optimal balance among unacceptable impulses and prosocial wishes to maximize gratification and permit conscious awareness of conflicting impulses and wishes	Anticipation	considering emotional reactions and consequences of these before the conflict or stress occurs and exploring the pros and cons of various solutions to these problematic emotional states
		Affiliation	seeking social support from others, sharing problems with them without making them responsible for them or for relieving the distress they entail
		Altruism	dedication to meeting the needs of others and receiving gratification from this (without excessive self-sacrificing)
		Humour	reframing the situation that gives rise to conflict or stress in an ironic or amusing way
		Self-assertion	expressing conflict-related thoughts or feelings in a direct yet non-coercive way
		Self-observation	monitoring how situations lead to conflict or stress and using this new understanding to modify negative affect
		Sublimation	channelling negative emotions arising from conflict or stress into socially acceptable activities such as work or sports
		Suppression	intentionally avoiding thinking about conflict or stress
Mental inhibitions compromise formation level	Keep unacceptable impulses out of awareness	Displacement	transferring negative feelings about one person onto another less threatening person
		Dissociation	experiencing a breakdown in the integrated functions of consciousness, memory, perception, or motor behaviour
		Intellectualization	the excessive use of abstract thinking or generalizations to minimize disturbing feelings arising from conflict
		Isolation of affect	losing touch with the feelings associated with descriptive details of the conflict, trauma or stress
		Reaction formation	substituting acceptable behaviours, thoughts or feelings that are the opposite of unacceptable or unwanted behaviours, thoughts or feelings that arise from a conflict
		Repression	expelling unwanted thoughts, emotions or wishes from awareness
		Undoing	using ritualistic or magical words or behaviour to symbolically negate or make amends for unacceptable impulses

(Continued)

TABLE 8.3
(Continued)

Level	Features of defences	Defence	The individual regulates emotional discomfort associated with conflicting wishes and impulses or external stress by …
Minor image distorting level	Distort image of self and others to regulate self-esteem	Devaluation	attributing exaggerated negative characteristic to the self or others
		Idealization	attributing exaggerated positive characteristics to others
		Omnipotence	attributing exaggerated positive characteristics or special abilities and powers to the self which make oneself superior to others
Disavowal level	Keep unacceptable impulses and ideas out of consciousness with or without misattribution of these to external causes	Denial	refusing to acknowledge the painful features of the situation or experiences which are apparent to others
		Projection	attributing to others one's own unacceptable thoughts, feelings and wishes
		Rationalization	providing an elaborate self-serving or self-justifying explanation to conceal unacceptable thoughts, actions or impulses
Major image distorting level	Gross distortion or misattribution of aspects of the self or others	Autistic fantasy	engaging in excessive daydreaming or wishful thinking as a substitute for using problem-solving or social support to deal with emotional distress
		Projective identification	attributing to others one's own unacceptable aggressive impulses. Then inducing others to feel these by reacting aggressively to them. Then using the other person's aggressive reactions as justification for acting out unacceptable aggressive impulses
		Splitting of self-image or image of others	failing to integrate the positive and negative qualities of self and others and viewing self and others as either all good or all bad
Action level	Action or withdrawal from action	Acting out	acting unacceptably to give expression to the experience of emotional distress associated with conflict or stress
		Apathetic withdrawal	not engaging with others
		Help-rejecting complaining	making repeated requests for help and then rejecting help when offered as a way of expressing unacceptable aggressive impulses
		Passive aggression	unassertively expressing unacceptable aggression towards others in authority by overtly complying with their wishes while covertly resisting these
Level of defensive dysregulation	Failure of defences to regulate conflict-related feelings leading to a breakdown in reality testing	Delusional projection	attributing to others one's own unacceptable thoughts, feelings and wishes to an extreme degree
		Psychotic denial	refusing to acknowledge the painful features of the situation or experiences which are apparent to others to an extreme degree
		Psychotic distortion	viewing reality in an extremely distorted way

Note: Based on American Psychiatric Association (2000) *Diagnostic and statistical manual of mental disorders (fourth edition, text revision, DSM-IV-TR)*. Defensive Functioning Scale (pp. 807–809). Washington, DC: American Psychiatric Association.

aspects of the self to others: for example, attributing extreme anger or spite to another person, and then feeling justified in being hurt and disappointed, because feelings of anger and spite are unacceptable to the self.

Transference-focused psychodynamic psychotherapy for borderline personality disorder is based on Kernberg's model of the development of object relations (Kernberg & Caligor, 2005; Yeomans & Diamond, 2010). With this form of therapy, the therapist initially forms a contact with the patient for twice weekly sessions over a year-long period. In these sessions the therapist creates a safe and secure context within which patients can describe challenging episodes in their lives and express strong emotions, without physically acting these out through violence, self-harm or leaving therapy. For borderline patients these strong emotions typically involve primitive internal object relations dyads where patients experience the self and significant others in their lives (including the therapist) as 'all good' or 'all bad'. The therapist carefully observes the patients' expression of strong affects, the primitive object relations and defences of splitting and projection associated with them, and talks with the patient about these observations in a non-judgemental way.

The main therapeutic interventions are clarification, confrontation and interpretation. With clarification, the therapist invites patients to elaborate on the thoughts, actions and emotions of the self and others (including the therapist) in problematic situations. With confrontation, the therapist points out inconsistencies and contradictions between patients' differing accounts of the self and others at different times, or between patients' accounts, affects and behaviours in a single episode. For example, the therapist may point out that in one instance the therapist–client transference relationship resembles that of a persecuting parent to a frightened and needy child with the client in the role of the child; that at another time the relationship is the same but the roles are reversed, with the client adopting the role of the persecuting parent; while on other occasions the relationship resembles that of a satisfied child and an all-giving mother. With interpretation, the therapist may offer explanations for such inconsistencies by suggesting links between the use of splitting, primitive idealization and projection as defences to reduce anxiety associated with attempting to integrate the all-good and all-bad primitive object relations. For example, the therapist may point out that one reason for viewing people as all-good or all-bad is that it preserves the possibility of having one's needs met by an all-gratifying mother. However, the down-side of using splitting and projection is that it prevents the development of sustainable intimate relationships because it requires denying the existence of frustrating characteristics in people defined as all-good, and positive characteristics of people defined as all-bad. This in turn may involve patients accepting that they have strong unacceptable sexual and aggressive feelings.

As patients repeatedly engage in therapeutic conversations involving clarification, confrontation and interpretation, their capacity for reflection on their own and others' roles in emotionally intense interaction increases. That is, they show increased reflective functioning, which is the capacity to understand the psychological states, motives and intentions of the self and others. They become better able to tolerate painful emotions without resorting to seeing the self and others as 'all-good' or 'all-bad' and acting out their intense emotions in destructive ways.

A series of trials support the effectiveness of transference-focused psychotherapy in improving the functioning of patients with borderline personality disorder on a number of parameters including reflective functioning, mood, self-harm and hospitalization (Yeomans & Diamond, 2010).

Mentalization-based treatment for borderline personality disorder

Mentalization-based treatment is an evidence-based psychodynamic therapy developed by Anthony Bateman and Peter Fonagy in the UK (Bateman & Fonagy, 2010a, 2010b). It aims to improve adjustment in borderline personality disorder by enhancing mentalization skills. Mentalization or mentalizing is the capacity to understand mental states of the self and others, and to conceptualize these states as being separate from behaviour. Mentalizing involves being able to think about thoughts, emotions, wishes, desires, and needs in the self and others; to understand that these internal events may have an impact on actions; but to recognize that they are distinct from those actions. The impulsivity, emotional regulation problems and consequent relationship difficulties that occur in borderline personality disorder arise from a limited capacity to mentalize.

Mentalization develops in early life in the context of caregiver–child attachment relationships within which the child's mental states are understood and 'mirrored' by their caregivers and appropriately responded to. The development of mentalization is compromised where such understanding, mirroring and responsive parenting are absent. Thus, neglectful or abusive parenting and the insecure, and often disorganized, attachment that develops as a consequence inhibits the development of a robust capacity to mentalize within attachment relationships. These processes in combination with the predisposing factors of childhood trauma or abuse and constitutional vulnerability (for example, difficult temperament) lead to the development of borderline personality disorder. In borderline personality disorder a hypersensitive attachment system develops in which there is extreme sensitivity to loss. In situations where loss occurs or is anticipated, the person experiences hyper-arousal. Hyper-arousal radically reduces the capacity to mentalize in such situations. This may occur because hyper-arousal directly reduces the capacity to mentalize, or in cases of child abuse children may defensively inhibit the mentalization process to avoid having to recognize that their attachment figures have intentionally hurt them.

Mentalization-based treatment focuses on facilitating an optimal level of arousal in the context of a secure attachment relationship between patient and therapist which is not too intense or too detached.

Initially the therapist facilitates this optimal level of arousal with techniques such as empathy, support and clarification. These techniques soothe the patient, reduce arousal and create a context that supports mentalization. When patients engage in transference reactions, rather than interpreting these to provide insight, the therapist collaborates with the patient and helps them to mentalize the transference. This involves encouraging patients to think about the current client–therapist relationship with the aim of focusing their attention on another mind – the mind of a therapist – and assisting them to contrast their own perception of themselves with how they are perceived by the therapist.

In this form of treatment, therapists adopt a mentalizing therapeutic stance. This is characterized by humility, curiosity, patience and respect. The therapist humbly adopts a 'not-knowing' position; curiously asks patients in detail about their experiences; patiently takes time to understand these; and legitimizes in a respectful way the differing perspectives of the patient and the therapist. If similarities in patterns of relationships in the therapy and in childhood or currently outside of the therapy are pointed out (following the triangle of person in Figure 5.5), the aim of this is not to provide patients with insight so that they can control this behaviour pattern in future, but to draw attention to other situations that require mentalization. Therapists actively avoid offering transference interpretations in a way that involves them 'thinking for' patients. Rather they stimulate patients to 'mentalize' about transference reactions and reach their own conclusions.

Evidence from trials in which mentalization-based treatment was offered to partially hospitalized patients and to outpatients over periods of 12–18 months shows that it is effective in the short and long terms (Bateman & Fonagy, 2010a, 2010b). In a number of trials it led to improved adjustment of patients with borderline personality disorder, as shown by reduced self-harm and rehospitalization and increased employment.

Short-term psychodynamic psychotherapy for Cluster C personality disorders

Short-term psychodynamic psychotherapy is an evidence-based treatment developed by Leigh McCullough in the US and has been shown in a controlled trail to be effective for Cluster C personality disorders (Svartberg & McCullough, 2010). Within this model (which is diagrammed in Figure 5.5), Cluster C personality disorders are assumed to arise from a dynamic conflict between prohibited adaptive feelings (F) such as anger, grief, attachment or sexual excitement one hand, and inhibiting feelings (A) such as anxiety, guilt and shame on the other. Defences (D) such as social withdrawal, dependency or an excessive concern with order emerge as compromise responses to these conflicts, and as the symptoms of Cluster C personality disorders. For example, a person who is angry (F) may become anxious about reprisals (A) and so may become withdrawn and deferential (D); a person who feels grief due to loss (F) may fear further pain due to loss (A) and so may avoid intimacy by becoming dutiful and orderly (D).

McCullough refers to this process as 'affect phobia' which is a social learning theory way of describing psychodynamic conflict. F–A–D patterns, referred to as the triangle of conflict, are learned in childhood with parents and caregivers (P), and are repeated in adult patients' current lives with partners, friends and colleagues (C) and also in transference relationships with therapists (T). These three contexts, T–C–P, within which the triangle of conflict is replicated are referred to as the triangle of person. In short-term dynamic psychotherapy, through interpretation therapists help patients understand how they repeatedly enact the triangle of conflict in multiple contexts represented by the triangle of person. They then help patients desensitize themselves to their unacceptable feelings (F) by encouraging them to repeatedly experience these hidden feelings in an intense way within therapy sessions, without resorting to the use of defences. This treatment typically involves a year of weekly sessions.

Cognitive-behavioural approaches

Results from a meta-analysis show that cognitive-behavioural approaches and psychodynamic approaches to the treatment of personality disorders are equally effective (Leichsenring & Leibing, 2003). Within the cognitive-behavioural tradition Marsha Linehan's dialectical behaviour therapy for borderline personality disorder is the best validated approach (Stanley & Brodsky, 2009). Aaron T. Beck's cognitive-behavioural conceptualization of personality disorders has also been influential (Beck et al., 2003).

Dialectical behaviour therapy

Dialectical behaviour therapy was developed by Marsha Linehan in the US. Marsha is both an eminent clinical psychologist and a survivor of borderline personality disorder. Dialectical behaviour therapy is based on a biosocial diathesis–stress conceptualization of the aetiology of borderline personality disorder (Stanley & Brodsky, 2009). The theory proposes that the condition arises when individuals with a constitutional vulnerability that compromises their capacity for emotion regulation are chronically exposed to invalidating environments. In such environments, individuals' communications about their inner challenging experiences are repeatedly invalidated, so that eventually they become self-invalidating, which is a central feature of borderline personality disorder. Their moderate displays of emotion are regularly punished, but extreme emotional displays are inadvertently reinforced by family members' expressions of concern or medical care. This results in ongoing emotional inhibition with periodic intense emotional displays characteristic of borderline personality disorder.

Dialectic behaviour therapy aims to decrease suicidal behaviour, posttraumatic symptomatology, behaviours that interfere with engaging in therapy, and behaviours that interfere with quality of life. It also aims to increase behavioural skills for emotion regulation and enhance self-respect. Dialectic behaviour therapy begins with the formation of a therapeutic contract which is typically between 6 months and a year. The cornerstone is a dialectical worldview where polar opposites, or thesis and antithesis, are integrated through synthesis. Clients are helped to acknowledge polarizations in their experiences and work towards a synthesis of these extremes.

For therapists and clients, the overriding dialectic within therapy in between acceptance and change. Dialectical behaviour therapy integrates cognitive-behavioural, change-based interventions with acceptance-based approaches, notably mindfulness meditation derived from Zen practice. It is a multimodal programme that incorporates individual psychotherapy, telephone consultation, group-based skills training, therapists' consultation meetings and ancillary treatments such as medication and acute–inpatient psychiatric services. In group sessions mindfulness meditation, skills for tolerating distress and regulating emotions, and interpersonal effectiveness skills such as assertiveness are acquired. In individual therapy, clients are helped to become motivated to use these skills, and to increase adaptive and decrease maladaptive behaviours by altering the factors that reinforce these behaviours in their day-to-day lives. There is a strong emphasis on validation of clients' experiences and using behavioural analysis to understand factors that promote and inhibit therapeutic progress. In telephone consultations between sessions clients are helped to generalize the skills they have learned to multiple real-life settings and to manage crises. In consultation meetings, liaison with family members and other involved professionals and agencies occurs.

A meta-analysis has shown that dialectical behaviour therapy reduces suicidal and self-injurious behaviour in patients with borderline personality disorder and improves their overall adjustment (Kliem et al., 2010).

Cognitive-behavioural theories

In Aaron T. Beck's cognitive behavioural conceptualization of personality disorders he proposes that people with personality disorders have developed pervasive, self-perpetuating cognitive–interpersonal cycles that are severely dysfunctional (Beck et al., 2003). Early life experiences, including family routines and relationships as well as traumatic events, lead to the formation of assumptions about the world and in particular about interpersonal relationships: for example, 'people are not trustworthy'. In day-to-day interactions, these underlying assumptions lead to automatic thoughts such as 'He's trying to con me'. These in turn lead to emotional reactions such as anger and behavioural reactions such as oppositional and confrontative conversation. This in turn elicits behaviour from others such as secretiveness and avoidance, which reinforces the basic assumption that 'people are not trustworthy'.

For each personality disorder there are predominant mood states and predominant behavioural strategies used to deal with interpersonal situations. Collections of basic assumptions, learned in early life, may be formed into schemas that inform those aspects of the world to which the person attends and how they are apt to interpret most situations. For example, an abuse–mistrust schema may contain a collection of beliefs about the untrustworthiness of others and their potential for abusing or harming the person. In addition to schemas, cognitive distortions such as mind-reading (I just know he's trying to get at me with that remark) or emotional reasoning (I feel angry, so he must be persecuting me) contribute to the way a person reacts to interpersonal situations. Also, predominant mood states may predispose people to attend to particular types of information or to evaluate situations in particular ways. For example, anger may predispose a person to attend to potential threats and to evaluate situations as opportunities for confrontation.

Cognitive therapy aims to break the dysfunctional cognitive–interpersonal cycles that constitute the person's personality disorder using a variety of cognitive and behavioural strategies. These include helping people learn to identify and challenge their automatic thoughts and core assumptions; helping people develop different interpersonal strategies and skills that are less likely to elicit from others behaviour that reinforces dysfunctional beliefs; and helping people engage in activities that will directly alter their mood states. There is some evidence from meta-analyses for the effectiveness of CBT with a range of personality disorders (Leichsenring & Leibing, 2003).

Marital and family therapy

Marital and family therapy interventions for personality disorders focus on helping couples and families recognize and alter current family-based patterns of interaction that maintain the personality disorder. They also help family members identify and challenge the belief systems and narratives that underpin these rigid interaction patters. Finally, in marital and family therapy, family members may be invited to understand how particular personal characteristics or traits and particular family of origin experiences have predisposed them to developing family belief systems and behaviour patterns that maintain personality disorders. Controlled trials of marital and family therapy for personality disorder have not been reported in the literature, but guidelines on current best practice have been published (e.g., Lebow & Uliaszek, 2010).

Risk of violence

The assessment and management of risk of violence is essential in cases of antisocial personality disorder, because of the association between this condition and aggression. In clinical interviews, patients with antisocial personality disorder may not give true accounts of their aggressive impulses. Because of this, the use of validated structured clinical instruments and information from collateral sources such as relatives or other agencies that have had contact with the patient to assess risk violence is important (Scott & Resnick, 2006). Thus, risk management typically involves interviews with the patient and members of their families as well as multidisciplinary and multiagency meetings. Multiagency meetings may involve staff from probation services, since many patients with antisocial personality disorder are on probation.

The Psychopathy Checklist (PCL-R, Hare, 2003) and Historical, Clinical, Risk Management–20 (HCR-20, Douglas et al., 2001) are examples of well-validated and widely used instruments for assessing risk of violence. The HCR-20 consists of 20 items on historical, clinical and risk management issues. The historical items cover previous violence, substance misuse problems, major mental illness, psychopathy and personality disorder. The clinical items are concerned with lack of insight, negative attitudes, active symptoms of mental illness, impulsivity and unresponsiveness to treatment. The risk management items include feasibility of plans, exposure to destabilizing influences, lack of personal support, non-compliance with treatment and stress.

In light of the assessment a formulation of the risk of violence is developed, identifying factors likely to increase or decrease the risk and a plan for managing these. Risk management plans should be directed at crisis resolution, decreasing risk factors and increasing protective factors. Members of the patient's family and other involved professionals such as probation officers and social workers may play a role in risk management plans. Unfortunately, there are no well-validated treatments for antisocial personality disorder, so risk management strategies must focus on using available evidence-based practices to address specific problems such as motivational interviewing for comorbid substance use or training in anger management skills.

Assessment

The assessment of personality disorder occurs within the context of the assessment of the whole person. When assessing patients with personality disorder, typically Axis I disorders such as mood, anxiety, substance use or eating disorders are present, and these are assessed in ways described in Chapters 3–6. In a significant proportion of cases, risky behaviours such as self-harm or violence may also be present. The assessment and management of risk of harm to the patient or others is always prioritized. (Suicide risk assessment has been discussed in Chapter 6.)

Ideally the assessment and treatment of personality disorders is conducted by multidisciplinary teams. Initial screening for personality disorders may be conducted with self-report inventories such as the Millon Clinical Multiaxial Inventory–III (MCMI-III, Millon, 2009), the Schedule for Nonadaptive and Adaptive Personality–II (SNAP-2, Clark et al., 2008) or the personality disorder scales of the Minnesota Multiphasic Personality Inventory–2 (MMPI-2, Colligan et al., 1994).

Where self-report instruments suggest the presence of a personality disorder, a diagnosis may be confirmed through clinical interviewing. A number of structured interviews for the diagnosis of personality disorders are available, such as the Structured Clinical Interview for DSM-IV Personality Disorders (SCID-II, First et al., 1997) and the International Personality Disorder Examination (IPDE, Loranger, 1999). The Revised NEO Personality Inventory (NEO-PI-R, Costa & McCrae, 1992) is the best available instrument for assessing the Big 5 personality factors and their 30 facets, and this may provide a useful profile of personality traits and facets to take into account in formulating the case. (The trait approach to personality disorders is discussed below in the section on controversies.)

The personality disorder diagnosis, along with information from an assessment of personality traits and facets and the clinical history, is used to construct a formulation. The formulation explains the main clinical problems entailed by the personality disorder with reference to predisposing, maintaining and protective factors. Precipitating factors may be included in formulations of personality disorders, to identify events that precipitated referral for treatment or a recent crisis. However, since personality disorders are by definition longstanding patterns of adjustment, factors that precipitated their onset usually are not meaningfully identifiable. During the process of assessment and treatment patients with personality disorders and family members may be invited to keep daily records of fluctuations in symptoms, distress, and beliefs and the circumstances preceding and following these fluctuations. These idiographic ratings are useful for fine-tuning ongoing therapy. Comprehensive reviews of personality disorder assessment instruments are given in Strack (2010) and Widiger (2008).

Treatment

In extensive narrative reviews of the design and delivery of psychotherapy programmes for service users with personality disorders, Bateman and Fonagy (2000) and Linehan et al. (2006) concluded that effective programmes – whether cognitive behavioural or psychodynamic – share a number of common features. They are theoretically coherent (not eclectic), offering an explanation for problematic behaviours and interpersonal styles, and for the role of psychotherapy in offering a solution to these problems. They are well structured and of long duration, usually extending beyond a year. They include procedures for helping clients engage in treatment, maintain therapeutic contact and adhere to therapeutic regimes.

Effective psychotherapy programmes may include sequential or concurrent individual, group and family sessions, following a pre-established coherent pattern. Effective outpatient psychotherapy programmes are offered within the context of broader multimodal, multidisciplinary services in which there are clear policies and practices for inpatient care, use of medication, and crisis management where high-risk behaviour including self-harming, aggression or other crises occurs. Effective programmes have a clear focus on key problem areas such as self-harm, aggression and difficult interpersonal relationships. Effective therapeutic techniques strike a balance between a focus on acceptance of clients' constraints and limitations on one hand, and a focus on behavioural change and developing less problematic ways of living on the other.

Psychotherapists offering effective treatment programmes for personality disorders receive sustained intensive supervision, in which intense countertransference reactions elicited by psychotherapy with these clients are addressed. Positive outcomes are more probable where therapists are patient, flexible and creative in their approach to therapy; are comfortable with long-term, intense therapeutic relationships; are tolerant of their own negative feelings about patients and the therapy process; and have specific training in treating personality disorders (Fernandez-Alderez et al., 2006).

For borderline personality disorder, dialectical behaviour therapy, mentalization-based treatment and transference-focused psychotherapy are well-developed evidence-based treatments. For other personality disorders, either psychodynamic or cognitive behaviour therapy of at least a year's duration may be effective in a proportion of cases. Adjunctive psychopharmacological interventions for symptom management may be integrated into psychological treatment programmes for personality disorders. The central role of psychotherapy in the treatment of personality disorders is consistent with international guidelines for best practice (Alwin et al., 2006; American Psychiatric Association, 2001b; National Institute of Mental Health in England, 2003; NICE, 2009c, 2009d).

Controversies

In the field of personality disorders the main controversies centre on the categorical or dimensional conceptualization of abnormal personality functioning, the validity of the distinction between Axis I and Axis II disorders, and therapeutic communities as an alternative to hospital or outpatient treatment.

Trait theory as an alternative to categorical diagnoses

Within DSM-IV-TR and ICD-10, personality disorders are conceptualized in categorical terms. That is, it is assumed that within a population some people have personality disorders and some do not, and that there are qualitative differences between those that do and do not meet the diagnostic criteria for personality disorders. Trait theories, in contrast, propose that a limited number of dimensions may be used to characterize important aspects of behaviour and experience. Traits are normally distributed within the population. So for any given trait (for example, introversion–extraversion), most people show a moderate level of the trait, but a few people show extremely low or extremely high levels. Within a population, people who fall at the extreme ends of these dimensions may have the sorts of difficulties attributed in DSM-IV-TR and ICD-10 to people with personality disorders. However, these people differ from others only in the degree to which they show particular traits.

Traits are identified by factor-analysing responses of large samples of people to extensive personality questionnaires and rating scales. Factor analysis is a procedure for mathematically clustering questionnaire or rating scale items that correlate with each other into a small set of dimensions.

In recent years trait theory has come to be dominated by the five-factor model of personality (McCrae & Costa, 2008). This model includes the following dimensions: neuroticism, extraversion, openness to experience, agreeableness, and conscientiousness. Neuroticism reflects differences in emotional lability and varies from emotionally stable to unstable. Extraversion reflects differences in sociability and varies from introverted to extraverted. Openness to experience reflects willingness to accept new ideas, feelings and actions and extends from imaginative creativeness to constriction. Agreeableness refers to interpersonal warmth or coldness. Conscientiousness varies from highly dutiful and self-disciplined to irresponsible and undisciplined. Each of the factors within the five-factor model contains six facets, which are listed in Table 8.4. There is evidence

TABLE 8.4
Factors and facets of the five-factor model of personality

Factor	Facet
Neuroticism	Anxiety
	Angry hostility
	Depression
	Self-consciousness
	Impulsiveness
	Vulnerability
Extraversion	Warmth
	Gregariousness
	Assertiveness
	Activity
	Excitement seeking
	Positive emotions
Openness to experience	Fantasy
	Aesthetics
	Feelings
	Actions
	Ideas
	Values
Agreeableness	Trust
	Straightforwardness
	Altruism
	Compliance
	Modesty
	Tender-mindedness
Conscientiousness	Competence
	Order
	Dutifulness
	Achievement striving
	Self-discipline
	Deliberation

for the heritability of all of factors within the Five Factor Model except agreeableness which seems to be predominantly environmentally determined (Costa & Widiger, 1994).

Thomas Widiger has proposed that the five-factor model may be used as an alternative system for describing personality disorders (Widiger & Mullins-Sweatt, 2010). The profiles of major personality disorders on the dimensions of the five-factor model of personality are presented in Table 8.5. These profiles are based on Samuel and Widiger's (2008) meta-analysis of data from 16 studies of 30 facets of the five-factor model of personality in groups of patients with personality disorders.

Widiger argues that trait theory offers a more scientifically useful approach to assessment. Personality questionnaires that have been developed to measure the Big Five personality traits have good psychometric properties (De Raad & Perugini, 2002). They are reliable and valid, and have population norms. The five-factor personality trait theory and related measures assume a demonstrated continuity between normal and abnormal personality. Research on the Big Five personality traits has led to a significant body of knowledge on the genetic and childhood antecedents of normal adult personality, neurobiological correlates of personality traits, and the stability and change in personality traits over the life course. This body of research may inform our understanding of personality disorders, if we base our assessment on the five-factor model. Compared with categorical classification systems, trait models offer a more parsimonious way of describing people with rigid dysfunctional behaviour patterns. This in turn offers a more parsimonious way to conceptualize the development of effective treatments.

Continuity between Axis I and Axis II disorders

A second controversy concerns the validity of the distinction between Axis I and Axis II disorders. There are significant similarities between each of the personality disorders and certain Axis I disorders. However, there are also distinct differences. These are listed in Table 8.6.

Paranoid, schizoid and schizotypal personality disorders each bear a marked resemblance to aspects of schizophrenia. However, people with these three personality disorders do not show frank delusions, hallucinations, thought disorder or negative symptoms. There are clear parallels between antisocial personality disorder and conduct disorder, since both involve moral immaturity and violation of others' rights. About a third of youngsters with conduct disorder, when they reach adulthood, meet the diagnostic criteria for antisocial personality disorder (Kazdin, 1995). Borderline personality disorder resembles depression, insofar as loss and abandonment are central themes and negative affect is a core feature of both conditions.

Hysterical personality disorder and conversion hysteria are similar insofar as in both conditions a caricature of a role is adopted and this is associated with attention seeking and secondary gain. However, with hysterical personality disorder, the role is that of a stereotypically seductive woman or macho male, whereas in conversion hysteria a

TABLE 8.5

Profiles of DSM-IV personality disorders from a meta-analysis of 30 facets of the five-factor model of personality

Cluster	Personality disorder	Neuroticism	Extraversion	Agreeableness	Conscientiousness	Openness	Top three facets
Cluster A Odd, eccentric group	Paranoid	Angry Depressed Self-conscious Anxious	Cold Joyless Aloof	Mistrustful Conflictual Guarded Selfish			Mistrustful Angry Depressed
	Schizoid	Depressed Self-conscious	Cold Joyless Aloof Inactive Submissive Avoids excitement	Mistrustful			Aloof Cold Joyless
	Schizotypal	Depressed Self-conscious Angry Anxious	Cold Aloof	Mistrustful			Depressed Self-conscious Mistrustful
Cluster B Dramatic, emotional, erratic group	Antisocial	Angry Impulsive	Seeks excitement	Guarded Conflictual Selfish Mistrustful	Careless Not dutiful Undisciplined Lacks self-belief		Careless Guarded Conflictual
	Borderline	Depressed Angry Vulnerable Anxious Self-conscious Impulsive	Joyless Cold	Mistrustful Conflictual Guarded	Undisciplined Lacks self-belief Careless Not dutiful		Depressed Angry Anxious
	Histrionic		Gregarious Assertive Excitement seeking Warm Active Joyful				Gregarious Assertive Excitement seeking

					Final column
Narcissistic	Angry		Boastful Guarded Conflictual Selfish Mistrustful		Boastful Guarded Conflictual
Cluster C Anxious, fearful group					
Avoidant	Self-conscious Depressed Anxious Vulnerable Angry	Aloof Submissive Joyless Cold Inactive Avoids excitement	Mistrustful Modest	Lacks self-belief Undisciplined	Avoids new experiences	Self-conscious Depressed Aloof
Dependent	Vulnerable Self-conscious Depressed Angry	Submissive		Lacks self-belief Undisciplined		Vulnerable Self-conscious Depressed
Obsessive-compulsive				Orderly Dutiful Achievement striving Careful Self-disciplined		Orderly Dutiful Achievement striving

Note: Based on Samuel and Widiger's (2008) meta-analysis of data from 16 studies of 30 facets of the five-factor model of personality. For each personality disorder, facets within each factor are listed in order of the size of their correlations with personality disorders. Only facets that had significant correlations ($p < .05$) greater than $r = 0.2$ are listed. In the final column, for each personality disorder the top 3 facets (out of 30) are listed in order of the size of their correlations.

TABLE 8.6
Comparison of personality disorders and Axis I disorders with similar features

Cluster	Personality disorder	Similar Axis 1 disorder	Common clinical features	Differences in clinical features
Cluster A Odd, eccentric group	Paranoid (PPD)	Schizophrenia	Mistrust and suspiciousness	In PPD delusions, hallucinations, thought disorder, and negative symptoms of schizophrenia are absent.
	Schizoid (SDPD)	Schizophrenia	Attachment problems and social isolation	In SDPD delusions, hallucinations, thought disorder, and negative symptoms of schizophrenia are absent.
	Schizotypal (SLPD)	Schizophrenia	Eccentric thoughts, perceptual experiences and speech	In SLD delusions, hallucinations, thought disorder, and negative symptoms of schizophrenia are absent.
Cluster B Dramatic, emotional, erratic group	Antisocial (ALPD)	Conduct disorder	Moral immaturity	For a diagnosis of ALPD the person must be over 18. Conduct disorder applies to children and adolescents.
	Borderline (BPD)	Depression	Impulsivity	In BPD, episodes of low mood are brief and the course of the disorder is lifelong beginning in childhood.
	Histrionic (HPD)	Conversion hysteria	Attention seeking	In HPD attention is gained through adopting seductive or macho role but with hysteria it is gained by adopting a sick-role.
	Narcissistic (NPD)	?		
Cluster C Anxious, fearful group	Avoidant (ATPD)	Social phobia	Shyness	In ATPD people avoid *relationships*, but with social phobia they avoid *situations*
	Dependent (DPD)	Separation anxiety	Lack of autonomy	DPD continues into adulthood and affects all areas of functioning Separation anxiety is a childhood disorder
	Obsessive-compulsive (OCPD)	Obsessive-compulsive disorder	Perfectionism	In OCPD symptoms are accepted but in OCD they are resisted

sick-role is adopted. The symptoms of conversion hysteria, which are not feigned, include deficits in sensory or motor functioning in the absence of an organic illness. Avoidant personality disorder and social phobia are similar insofar as shyness typifies both conditions. However, those with the personality disorder avoid relationships, whereas those with the phobia avoid particular social situations.

Dependent personality disorder and separation anxiety both entail problems with autonomy. Separation anxiety is a childhood disorder, but dependent personality disorder is the adult expression of the same core issues. Obsessive compulsive personality disorder closely resembles obsessive compulsive disorder. However, with the personality disorder the obsession with orderliness and rule-following is fully accepted and embraced as a valued part of the person's lifestyle, whereas with OCD the obsessions and compulsions are resisted.

The similarities between Axis I and Axis II disorders described call into question the validity of the distinctions made between these classes of disorder. For example, it might be more parsimonious to amalgamate diagnoses such as conduct disorder and antisocial personality disorder, and express these difficulties in dimensional terms such as externalizing behaviour problems. This approach is supported by results of genetic studies which show that certain Axis I and Axis II disorders share genetic risk factors (Reichborn-Kjennerud, 2010). These include schizophrenia and Cluster A personality disorders, especially schizotypal personality disorder; borderline personality disorder and depression; avoidant personality disorder and social phobia; and antisocial personality disorder, conduct disorder and substance use disorders.

Therapeutic communities

Therapeutic communities developed as an alternative approach to treating personality disorders, addictions and other severe mental health problems. Traditional inpatient mental health settings were hierarchically organized, and run on authoritarian lines. They encouraged patients to be passive recipients of treatment. Therapeutic communities were run on more democratic lines and encouraged service users to take an active role in their own rehabilitation. Responsibility for the daily running of the community was shared among service users and staff.

In the UK, the radical psychiatrists Maxwell Jones (Jones, 1952) and R. D. Laing (mentioned in Chapter 7 in the section on controversies) were pioneers in the development therapeutic communities. In the US, therapeutic communities were developed mainly for people with addiction problems. Therapeutic communities for people with personality disorders have been run in prisons, hospitals and day hospitals. In these communities there are usually daily meetings of service users and staff, and a predominance of group activities.

The hallmark of therapeutic communities is their democratic, participative approach to decision-making. This creates a context within which service users significantly influence the way their therapeutic communities are run. Complex, participative community processes are the central therapeutic factors of therapeutic communities (Jones, 1952). In a systematic review of 52 outcome studies of the effects of therapeutic communities on people with personality disorders and a meta-analysis of 29 of these, Lees et al. (1999) found that a significant positive effect occurred in 19 of the 29 studies in their meta-analysis. Participants in these trials were young offenders or psychiatric service users with a range of personality disorders. In their narrative review, Lees et al. concluded that for people with personality disorder, long-term treatment in therapeutic communities may lead to improvements in mental health and interpersonal functioning, and that the longer a service user stays in treatment, the better the outcome. They also found that secure therapeutic communities were effective in managing difficult prisoners, and significantly reducing serious prison discipline incidents including fire-setting, violence, self-harm and absconding.

Summary

Personality disorders are characterized by enduring dysfunctional patterns of behaviour and experience that begin in adolescence and are consistent across situations. There are difficulties with cognition, affect, impulse control, behaviour and interpersonal functioning. There are also recurrent relationship problems or occupational problems with a history of other psychological disorders or criminality. People with personality disorders have difficulty learning from experience or benefiting from psychotherapy for their personality disorders or other comorbid Axis I disorders.

In DSM-IV-TR, 10 main personality disorders are subdivided into three clusters on the basis of their cardinal clinical features. The odd, eccentric cluster includes the paranoid, schizoid and schizotypal personality disorders. The dramatic, emotional, erratic cluster includes the antisocial, borderline, histrionic and narcissistic personality disorders. The third cluster includes the avoidant, dependent and obsessive-compulsive personality disorders, all of which are characterized by anxiety and fearfulness. A very similar classification system is used in ICD-10.

The prevalence of personality disorders is approximately 10% in the general population, whereas in samples of mental health service users the rate is about 40%. Many people who have one personality disorder meet the criteria for a number of others. Personality disorders are fairly stable over time, although some improvement does occur, especially among those with Cluster B personality disorders.

Diathesis–stress theories argue that personality disorders emerge when genetically or constitutionally vulnerable individuals are exposed to particular types of environmental stress. Heritability estimates for personality disorders range from 20% to 70% and recent research has begun to discover the neurobiological basis for some personality disorders, especially schizotypal, borderline and antisocial personality disorder. There is evidence for early adversity, problematic parenting, trauma and child abuse in the aetiology of many personality disorders. Psychodynamic and cognitive behavioural theories of personality disorders explain the emergence of personality disorders in diathesis–stress terms, but propose detailed psychological processes to account for symptom aetiology and maintenance. Controlled trials of treatment programmes based on these conceptualizations have been shown them to be effective for some personality disorders, with the strongest evidence base being for dialectical behaviour therapy, transference-focused therapy and mentalization therapy for borderline personality disorder.

With regard to pharmacological treatments there was evidence for the effectiveness of antipsychotics in reducing psychotic-like symptoms, mood stabilizers in reducing aggression, and antidepressants in regulating mood. Patients with personality disorders usually have other Axis I disorders and frequently are at risk of self-harm or violence. The assessment and management of such patients is ideally conducted by multidisciplinary teams and often involves multiagency liaison. The main controversies in the field centre on the categorical or dimensional conceptualization of abnormal personality functioning, the validity of the distinction between Axis I and Axis II disorders and the value of democratic therapeutic communities as an alternative to traditional authoritarian inpatient treatment settings.

Questions

- What is a personality disorder and how does it differ from an Axis I disorder?
- What are the main personality disorders included in the DSM and ICD classification systems?
- What is the main clinical feature of each of the personality disorders?
- How prevalent are personality disorders?
- What are the diathesis–stress, psychodynamic, and cognitive-behavioural theories of personality disorders and the key research findings relevant to these theories?
- What evidence-based approaches have been developed for the assessment and treatment of personality disorders?
- What are the pros and cons of adopting a 'Big 5' dimensional approach to personality disorders as an alternative to the DSM and ICD categorical systems?

FURTHER READING

Professional

- Clarkin, J. & Lenzenweger, M. (2005). *Major theories of personality disorder* (second edition). New York: Guilford.
- Magnavita, J. J. (2010). *Evidence-based treatment of personality dysfunction: Principles, methods, and processes.* Washington, DC: American Psychological Association.
- Oldham, J., Skodol, A. & Bender, D. (2009). *Essentials of personality disorders.* Arlington, VA: American Psychiatric Publishing.

Self-help

- Fusco, G. & Freeman, A. (2004). *Borderline personality disorder: A patient's guide to taking control.* New York: Norton.
- Mason, P. T. & Kreger, R. (1998). *Stop walking on eggshells: Taking your life back when someone you care about has borderline personality disorder.* Oakland, CA: New Harbinger.

WEBSITES

- American Psychiatric Association's practice guidelines for treating borderline personality disorder:
  http://psychiatryonline.org/guidelines.aspx
- National Educational Alliance for Borderline Personality Disorder in the US:
  www.borderlinepersonalitydisorder.com
- National Institute for Clinical Excellence guidelines for treating antisocial and borderline personality disorders:
  http://guidance.nice.org.uk/topic/mentalhealthbehavioural
- PsychNet – Personality Disorders page:
  www.psychnet-uk.com/x_new_site/personality_psychology/a_index_personality_psychology.html
- UK Department of Health Personality Disorder policy documents:
  www.dh.gov.uk/en/publicationsandstatistics/publications/publications policyandguidance/dh_4009546
- UK Personality Disorder site:
  www.personalitydisorder.org.uk

Models that influence the practice of clinical psychology

9

Learning objectives

After studying this chapter you will be able to:

- list the key assumptions of biological, psychodynamic, cognitive-behavioural and family systems models that influence the practice of clinical psychology
- outline the main achievements of the biological, psychodynamic, cognitive-behavioural and family systems models
- critically evaluate the limitations of the biological, psychodynamic, cognitive-behavioural and family systems models
- describe the contributions of the humanistic client-centred tradition, personal construct psychology and positive psychology to the practice of clinical psychology.

Introduction

Explanations and interventions for the various clinical problems described in Chapters 2–8 have arisen from four main models:

- the biological model
- the psychodynamic model
- the cognitive-behavioural model
- the family systems model.

In this chapter the main assumptions of each of these models will be outlined, along with an account of their achievements or strengths and shortcomings or limitations. A summary of these issues is given in Table 9.1. The contribution of a number of other influential approaches to practice will be briefly considered in this chapter, including those based on client-centred humanistic psychology, personal construct psychology and the positive psychology.

Biological model

Assumptions

The biological model of psychological problems is also referred to as the neurobiological, organic, medical or disease model. In this framework it is assumed that the various psychological difficulties that people with a particular syndrome display are symptoms of a specific disease with a discrete neurobiological cause, a unique course and prognosis, and for which a specific physical treatment will ultimately be identified (Nestler & Charney, 2008). This model evolved within the medical tradition where there were numerous examples of physical conditions involving a syndrome of signs and symptoms that could be explained by a discrete cause, such as an infection or metabolic dysfunction.

Syphilis is a good example of a condition where a discrete physical cause (syphilitic infection) leads to a psychological syndrome (general paresis of the insane) and can be treated by a specific physical intervention (inoculation). In 1897 Richard von Krafft-Ebing, a German neurologist, following the work of Louis Pasteur, inoculated patients who had general paresis with pus from syphilitic sores, and this halted the development of the degenerative condition, which typically culminated in insanity. The success of this work gave impetus to the biological model of mental health problems. The model has been championed by psychiatry more than other mental health professions.

Diathesis–stress or stress-vulnerability models are modern variants of the biological model. In these types of model it is assumed that psychological problems or 'psychiatric illnesses' occur when people who are neurobiologically vulnerable to such difficulties are exposed to particular stresses. For example, a diathesis–stress model of schizophrenia was described in Chapter 7 (Walker et al., 2008; Zubin & Spring, 1977).

Achievements

The biological or medical model has led to a number of important achievements. The first of these has been the development of mental health legislation (Bartlett & Sandland, 2007; Gunn & Wheat, 2009). This legislation makes provision for the involuntary detention and treatment of people with psychological disorders whose judgement is severely impaired, especially if they are a danger to themselves or other

TABLE 9.1
Model of abnormal behaviour

	Biological model	Psychoanalytic model	Cognitive behavioural model	Family systems model
Cause of abnormal behaviour	Central nervous system abnormality	Unconscious psychopathology	Learned habits	Dysfunctional family system
Therapy goal	• Rectify CNS abnormality	• Resolve unconscious conflicts	• Learn more adaptive habits	• Alter problem-maintaining family interaction patterns and beliefs
Therapy process	• Pharmacological • ECT • Psychosurgery	• Long-term one-to-one psychoanalysis	• Short-term cognitive behaviour therapy	• Short-term marital or family therapy
Achievements	• Liberation of insane • Mental health legislation • Classification • Scientific method • Medical technology • Pharmacological and physical treatments	• Discovery of unconscious • Makes madness meaningful • Discovery of transference • Legitimized talking cure • Inspired other models of personality and therapy	• Brief and effective • Permits evidence-based practice • Has specific interventions for specific problems • Scientifically rigorous	• Highlighted social context of abnormal behaviour • Brief and cost-effective • Permits evidence-based practice • Permits integration of biological, psychological and social factors • Gives framework for managing complex multi-problem families
Limitations	• Discounts environmental influences • Discounts dimensional models • Side-effects of medications • Discounts socio-political factors • Promotes exclusion • Mental health legislation is abused • Marginalizes non-medics	• Contains untestable hypotheses • Inaccurate account of infantile sexuality • Not cost-effective	• Danger of trivializing problems • Danger of discounting organic factors • Danger of discounting social system factors	• Danger of vagueness • Danger of discounting organic factors • Danger of discounting intrapsychic factors

people. Suicidal behaviour and extremely violent behaviour are recognized within mental health legislation in most countries as possible reflections of impaired judgement and possible grounds for involuntary detention or treatment in a psychiatric treatment centre.

A second important achievement of the biological model has been the development of widely used classification systems. This began with the painstaking work of Kraepelin (1899), who catalogued symptoms characteristic of different groups of patients. Psychological problems are currently classified in the fifth chapter of the World Health Organization's (1992) International Classification of Diseases (now in its 10th edition) and in the American Psychiatric Association's (2000) Diagnostic and Statistical Manual of Mental Disorders (now in its text-revised fourth edition). These two systems – ICD-10 and DSM-IV-TR – are now used widely throughout the world and provide a way for clinicians and researchers to communicate with each other in a relatively unambiguous manner. This was not always the case. In the past there has been wide variation in diagnostic criteria used in different countries. For example, in the US a very broad definition of schizophrenia was typically used until the development of DSM-III in 1980. The extraordinary differences in rates of diagnoses are highlighted by the results of the US–UK project presented in Table 9.2.

The use of scientific methods and quantitative techniques to study psychological problems is a third achievement of the biological model. Case–control studies, longitudinal studies, and randomized controlled trials are three common research designs used in studies conducted within the medical tradition. Case–control studies may be used to determine the unique characteristics associated with a particular psychological disorder. In such studies a group of diagnostically homogeneous cases about which the researcher is trying to find out more information is compared to another group of patients with a known condition or with a normal control group. This was the method Kolvin et al. (1971) used to differentiate between childhood schizophrenia and autism. They found that compared with childhood schizophrenia, autism was associated with an earlier onset, delayed language development, catastrophic reactions to environmental changes, gross stereotypic behaviours, and the absence of delusions and hallucinations.

Longitudinal studies may be used to determine the course of a psychological disorder. In longitudinal studies the researcher obtains information on a group of diagnostically homogeneous cases on a number

TABLE 9.2
Rates of diagnosis of schizophrenia in the US and the UK

	Hospital diagnosis	Project diagnosis
US	61%	29%
UK	34%	35%

Note: N = 192 in US; N = 174 in UK. Adapted from Cooper, J., Kendall, R., Gurland, B., Sharp, L. Copeland, J., & Simon, R. (1972). Psychiatric diagnosis in New York and London. London: Oxford University Press.

of occasions; for example, in childhood and adulthood. This was the research design used by Robins (1966) to establish the course of childhood conduct disorder. He found that about a third of cases developed antisocial personality disorder and a third adjusted well in adulthood. The remaining third had a more variable course.

Randomized controlled trials are used to evaluate the effectiveness of specific treatments. Diagnostically homogeneous cases are randomly assigned to treatment or control conditions. All cases are assessed immediately before and after treatment and then at follow-up some months after treatment has been completed. Standard assessment procedures are used for all cases at all three time points. If the group that receives treatment shows greater improvement than the control group, then the treatment may be said to be effective. This design is typical of studies reviewed in books such as *What Works with Children, Adolescents and Adults?* (Carr, 2009a), *What Works for Whom?* (Roth & Fonagy, 2005) and *A Guide to Treatments That Work* (Nathan & Gorman, 2007).

The development of sophisticated methods for monitoring activity within the central nervous system is a fourth achievement of the biological model. These include brain imaging systems such as the CAT (computerized axial tomography) scan; the PET (positron emission tomography) scan; the SPECT (single photon emission tomography) scan; MRI (magnetic resonance imaging); and fMRI (functional magnetic resonance imaging) (Bremner, 2005). Imaging techniques have thrown light on those areas of the brain associated with particular disorders. For example, Thompson et al. (2001) using MRI scanning have documented extensive grey matter loss in early onset schizophrenia, as shown in Figure 9.1.

A fifth achievement of the biological model is the development of physical treatments for psychological problems. These include psychopharmacological advances such as antipsychotic medication for psychoses; antidepressant medication for unipolar mood disorders; and lithium carbonate for bipolar disorder (Nathan & Gorman, 2007). There is some evidence for the effectiveness of electroconvulsive therapy for major depression that does not respond to medication and psychotherapy (Royal College of Psychiatrists, 2005), although, as was mentioned in Chapter 6, there is considerable controversy about this (Read & Bentall, 2010). Psychosurgery has been found to be effective in extreme cases of OCD (Matthews & Christmas, 2009; Mindus et al., 2001). The development of the physical treatments, particularly psychopharmacological treatments, has depended on hypotheses in which dysregulation of neurotransmitter systems has played a central part; for example, the dopamine theory of schizophrenia (Seeman, 2011).

Limitations

Despite these major achievements, the biological model is not without its limitations. First, psychological problems are not caused exclusively by organic factors. Rather, for conditions such as anxiety, depression and

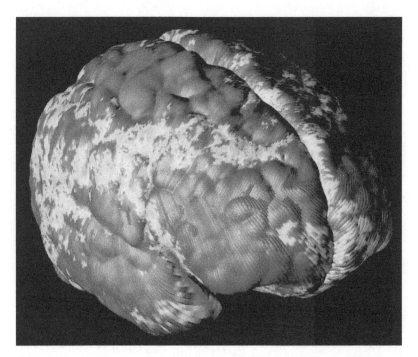

Figure 9.1 MRI image of grey matter loss in very early onset schizophrenia. From Thompson, P., Vidal, C., Giedd, J., Gochman, P. Blumenthal, J., Nicolson, R., Toga, A., & Rapoport, J. (2001). Mapping adolescent brain change reveals dynamic wave of accelerated grey matter loss in very early-onset schizophrenia. *Proceedings of the National Academy of Sciences of the United States of America*, 98, 11650–11655. Copyright (2010) National Academy of Sciences, USA.

schizophrenia, people with a genetic vulnerability to a particular condition develop psychological problems if they are exposed to particular stresses within their environment (Hankin & Abele, 2005). This observation has led people working within the 'medical model' tradition to a move away from a purely biological model to a diathesis–stress conceptualization of psychological problems. Such models acknowledge the importance of psychosocial factors such as family environment, gender, social class and culture in the development of psychological problems. For example, confusing and unsupportive family environments, the societal inequalities that favour men over women, membership of disadvantaged ethnic minorities, or membership of low socio-economic groups may all contribute to the stress experienced by individuals who are biologically vulnerable to psychopathology and who, as a result, develop psychological problems.

Second, many psychological problems are not distributed within the population as a set of discrete syndromes with an underlying biological cause. Boyle (2002) has shown, for example, that schizophrenia does not meet the criteria for a medical syndrome. Furthermore, many psychological problems are normally distributed within the population. Thus, dimensional rather than categorical conceptualizations of specific conditions are probably more valid for many psychological problems

(Helzer et al., 2008). For example, conduct disorder may probably be most validly conceptualized as cases characterized by extreme levels of externalizing behaviour problems, which fall on a continuum, with most children showing moderate levels of these types of difficulty (Walton et al., 2011). This was discussed in Chapter 2. Also, trait conceptualizations of personality disorders are probably more valid than categorical conceptualization (Widiger & Mullins-Sweatt, 2010). This was discussed in Chapter 8.

Third, many psychopharmacological and physical treatments for psychological problems have harmful or unknown side-effects (Breggin, 1991). For example, many widely used antipsychotic medications lead to an irreversible neurological movement disorder known as tardive dyskinesia (Tammenmaa et al., 2004). Electroconvulsive therapy (ECT), which is commonly used to treat major depression that is unresponsive to antidepressant medication, invariably leads to relatively long-term memory loss and confusion, while its therapeutic effects are short-lived (Read & Bentall, 2010). Stimulant therapy with drugs such as Ritalin (methylphenidate), which is widely used to treat ADHD, may adversely affect growth and cardiovascular functioning and its long-term effects in adulthood and old age are unknown (Paykina et al., 2007; Rapport & Moffitt, 2002). Despite the shortcomings of psychoactive medications, the pharmacological treatment of psychological problems has widespread acceptance. This is partly because the development, marketing and sale of psychopharmacological treatments is an influential, lucrative global industry, supported by the medical profession and governments as the mainstay of treatment for psychological problems.

Fourth, in some instances psychological problems are reactions to stresses inherent in family structures such as oppressive, neglectful or abusive patterns of family organization. In others, psychological problems are a reaction to stresses inherent in the structure of society at large such as poverty, injustice, prejudice, racism, sexism, ageism and intolerance for nonconformity. The biological model, with its exclusive emphasis on organic factors in the aetiology of psychological problems and its privileging of physical treatment, draws attention away from important psychosocial and political changes that may be required to alleviate psychological distress and to preserve civil liberties (Laing, 2009; Szasz, 2010). By insisting from the privileged position of a high-status profession that psychological problems are a reflection of mental illness requiring physical treatment, proponents of the biological model prevent society from addressing injustices, stresses and intolerance for nonconformity at a political level.

Fifth, the development of inpatient treatment facilities such as asylums and psychiatric hospitals has led to the exclusion of people with psychological problems from society. This in turn has promoted stigmatization and marginalization of large groups of people with psychological problems, which may further reinforce the difficulties of people with psychological problems and coping difficulties (Rosenhan, 1973).

Sixth, mental health legislation, which emerged within the biological and medical tradition, has been abused so as to limit the freedom of people with psychological problems. Szasz (2010) has argued that imprisoned criminals have more liberty and fewer violations of personal rights than people with psychological problems who are involuntarily detained.

Seventh, because the biological model of psychological problems and practices based on it are championed by biologically oriented psychiatry, non-medical professions, including clinical psychology and psychotherapy, have often been marginalized in the development of mental health services.

Psychoanalytic model

Assumptions

The psychoanalytic or psychodynamic model assumes that psychological problems are symptoms of underlying unconscious conflict or psychopathology (Skelton, 2006). As a child develops, according to classical psychoanalytic theory, primitive sexual and aggressive urges of the unconscious 'id' become gradually controlled by the rational 'ego'. The ego is guided by an internalization of society's standards: the 'superego'. However, intrapsychic conflict is inevitable. Conflict occurs between the sexual and aggressive impulses of the id and societal standards as reflected in the superego.

Such conflict is managed unconsciously by using various defence mechanisms, the function of which is to keep forbidden sexual and aggressive impulses from consciousness. For example, a man who is angry at his boss in work may sing his superior's praises, thereby using the defence of reaction formation. A full list of defences is given in Table 8.3 in Chapter 8. However, defences are compromises between the forces of the id and superego and often carry costly side-effects. For example, the man who is angry at his boss may eventually develop chest pains and anxiety, as a result of repressing rather than acknowledging the anger felt.

Furthermore, the psychoanalytic model proposes that relationship styles learned early in life are transferred in later life to other relationships, notably relationships with authority figures, sexual partners and psychotherapists. These relationship styles or 'transference phenomena', as they are called in psychoanalysis, are coloured in part by feelings aroused and partially resolved during the Oedipus complex phase (for boys) or Electra complex phase (for girls). These developmental phases refer to the psychoanalytic hypothesis that children in early life desire their opposite-sex parent and harbour aggression towards the parent of their own gender. However, these sexual and aggressive impulses are repressed and the child eventually identifies with the parent of the same gender for fear of the consequences of acting them out. In later life patients, such as the man with chest pains referred to earlier, experience feelings towards significant others and deal with them in a manner similar to that which occurred during the Oedipal phase of development. So the man with chest pains experienced aggression towards his boss and later towards his psychotherapist in a similar fashion, and dealt with this using reaction formation in a manner similar to that with which he handled the Oedipal triangle as a child.

Psychoanalysis and psychoanalytic psychotherapy provide a context within which patients can experience transference towards a psychotherapist and then through interpretation gain insight into the transference and related defences that underlie their psychopathology. The analyst or therapist and client meet frequently according to a strict schedule. The patient reports in an uncensored way his or her contents of consciousness. Eventually the client develops transference and the analyst interprets this repeatedly over time until the patient has gained insight into the transference and related defences and worked through related unresolved feelings. Concurrently, the patient's symptoms abate.

In order to be able to practise psychoanalysis, therapists must undergo their own analysis so that they have a first-hand understanding of the process and so that they will recognize transference feelings that they have towards patients (countertransference). Traditionally strict selection criteria are used for psychoanalysis, and typically YAVIS (young, adult, verbal, intelligent and single) patients only have been deemed suitable. However, this has changed in recent years with developments such as object relations approaches to conditions such as borderline personality disorder (discussed in Chapter 8).

Achievements

First, the most outstanding achievement of the psychoanalytic model is the discovery of the unconscious (Ellenberger, 1970). Freud drew together a set of ideas from a wide range of sources and crystallized them in the notion of the unconscious, not as a passive repository of irretrievable memories but as an active set of psychological processes. According to the psychoanalytic model of the unconscious, people can make themselves forget things or keep them outside awareness. Repressed unconscious aggressive and sexual impulses may motivate behaviour.

Second, psychoanalysis gave meaning to apparently meaningless behaviour. For example, Freud (1909a) showed how in phobias, fears of one stimulus (e.g. one's father) could be displaced onto other stimuli (e.g. horses). He also showed how unconscious processes that explained psychological disorders could also explain peculiar everyday behaviour. For example, in his book *The Psychopathology of Everyday Life*, Freud showed how forgetting people's names, slips of the tongue, errors in writing and so forth in some cases are due to repression (Freud, 1901). Such errors or parapraxes have come to be referred to colloquially as 'Freudian slips'. He also showed that apparently meaningless dreams may be interpreted and made coherent to aid self-understanding, a proposition that has been partially supported by subsequent research (Freud, 1900; Siegel, 2010).

Third, psychoanalysis introduced the ideas of transference and countertransference into the practice of psychotherapy. The idea that people have a limited number of relationship-maps which they learn early in life and transfer onto significant others in adulthood has been supported by recent empirical work on continuity in patterns of attachment from childhood to adulthood (Cassidy & Shaver, 2008; Rholes & Simpson, 2004).

Fourth, psychoanalysis established the place of the 'talking cure' in mainstream mental health practice. It also provided a model for the development of both short-term and long-term outpatient treatment of patients with a range of psychological difficulties. In the UK the competencies required for delivering psychodynamic psychotherapy have been delineated by the British Psychological Society's Centre for Outcomes Research and Effectiveness (Lemma et al., 2008).

Fifth, empirical studies of long-term psychoanalysis and short-term psychodynamic psychotherapy show that it is effective with a range of problems including anxiety, mood and personality disorders and complex comorbid presentations (Shedler, 2010; Leichsenring & Rabung, 2008, 2011; Leichsenring et al., 2004).

Finally, Freud provided a model for developing a theory of personality and therapy which spawned a wide range of neo-Freudian derivatives including those of Jung, Adler, Horney, Stack Sullivan, Reich, Fairburn, Klein, Erikson and many others (Schultz & Schultz, 2008).

Limitations

Classical psychoanalysis has many limitations. First, many of its hypotheses were untestable due to the imprecision of the constructs or the imprecision of predictions entailed by psychoanalytic theory. Also, for a considerable time there was little evidence for the effectiveness of psychoanalytic psychotherapy. Recent meta-analyses of treatment outcome studies have addressed this limitation (Shedler, 2010; Leichsenring & Rabung, 2008, 2011; Leichsenring et al., 2004).

Second, Freud's speculations about infantile sexuality were not borne out by subsequent developmental research and in particular by research on child sexual abuse. It is quite likely that many of Freud's patients who reported sexual contact with a parent had in fact been sexually abused and were not simply fantasizing about seducing their parents in Oedipal dramas (Masson, 1984).

Third, as a model for practice, classical psychoanalysis is too time-consuming and expensive. Classical psychoanalysis involves multiple sessions each week for a number of years. It is therefore not sufficiently cost-effective for routine use in a public mental health service where resources are limited. However, in recent times attempts have been made to use psychoanalytic ideas and practices as a basis for brief psychodynamic therapy (Lemma et al., 2010; Leichsenring et al., 2004).

Cognitive-behavioural model

Assumptions

The cognitive-behavioural tradition incorporates a range of psychotherapeutic theories and practices including behaviour therapy, behaviour modification, cognitive therapy and cognitive-behaviour therapy, all of which have their roots in learning theories, both behavioural and cognitive (Freeman et al., 2005). Within the cognitive-behavioural tradition it is assumed that psychological problems are distressing habits that are learned through the same processes as normal behaviour. These processes include operant and classical conditioning, imitation and insight.

Therapy involves helping clients to replace distressing habits of thinking and behaving with more adaptive ones. This process is based on the principles of learning theory. Through careful interviewing and observation, the antecedents that trigger problematic behaviours, beliefs and mood states, and the consequences that reinforce them, are identified. Treatment programmes, based on this type of assessment, include interventions that alter antecedents which signal the onset of psychological problems; interventions that challenge non-adaptive beliefs and styles of information processing that accompany psychological problems; and interventions that change the consequences of behaviour so that normal alternatives to abnormal behaviour patterns are reinforced.

In the behavioural treatment of depression, antecedents of low mood may be altered through inviting clients to schedule pleasant events regularly throughout their day (Lewinsohn & Gotlib, 1995). In the cognitive therapy of depression, anxiety and personality disorders, clients are coached in how to identify and challenge negative automatic thoughts and to identify the use of cognitive distortions (Beck et al., 1979, 2003; Clark & Beck, 2010a). With conduct disordered children, reward programmes are used so that prosocial behavioural targets are routinely reinforced (Forgatch & Patterson, 2010). Modelling, rehearsal, shaping and operant reinforcement procedures may be used to help individuals with skills deficits learn self-regulation, social, communication and problem-solving skills. Skills training is routinely used when working with people who have skills deficits, for example people with schizophrenia who have negative symptoms and limited social skills (Tenhula & Bellack, 2008).

Treatment programmes also include procedures based on classical conditioning. For example, with systematic desensitization for people who have phobias, increasingly threatening stimuli are paired with the experience of relaxation (Head & Gross, 2008). Another example of a classical conditioning based intervention is the use of urine alarm programmes for nocturnal enuresis in which bedwetting is paired with the sound of an alarm (Houts, 2010). Through this procedure, the child learns eventually to awaken when the bladder is full.

Within the cognitive-behavioural tradition, specific treatment programmes are developed for specific symptoms and detailed assessments of the impact of treatment on psychological problems targeted in treatment are routinely made. The tradition has been championed by clinical psychologists.

Achievements

The cognitive-behavioural tradition has made a number of important contributions to the understanding and treatment of psychological difficulties.

First, this tradition has led to the development of brief effective approaches to therapy which are applicable to a wide range of patients (Freeman et al., 2005). Typically cognitive-behaviour therapy is brief, ranging from one to 30 sessions, depending on the nature and severity of the problems.

Second, the cognitive-behavioural tradition has shown empirically that its treatment strategies are effective. It has led the evidence-based practice movement in the mental health field. More than any other approach to treating psychological difficulties, the cognitive-behavioural tradition has generated an enormous volume of empirical research to test the effectiveness of a wide variety of treatment programmes for a broad range of problems in adults and children (Carr, 2009a; Nathan & Gorman, 2007).

Third, the cognitive-behavioural model has led to the development of specific psychological treatment packages for specific types of problem. For example, exposure-based treatments have been developed for anxiety disorders (described in Chapter 5), cognitive therapy has been developed for mood disorders (described in Chapter 6), and cognitive-behavioural approaches have been developed to treat the positive symptoms of schizophrenia (outlined in Chapter 7).

Fourth, compared to other treatment approaches, CBT has been more widely disseminated in books, training videos and brief training programmes that are highly accessible to a range of mental health professionals. In the UK the dissemination of CBT has been mainstreamed within the National Health Service through the Improving Access to Psychological Therapies programme (www.iapt.nhs.uk).

Fifth, methodological and scientific rigour has characterized cognitive-behavioural research on psychological problems and their treatment.

Limitations

The main limitation of the cognitive-behavioural model is the risk it entails of trivializing psychological problems. When people are suffering profound psychological distress, it may seem to them that to construe their difficulties as bad habits does not do justice to the gravity of their distressing life situations.

Two other possible limitations of the cognitive-behavioural model deserve mention. First, there is the danger of disregarding the possible role of organic factors in the aetiology of psychological difficulties. This is problematic because there is extensive evidence for the role of genetic and neurobiological factors in the aetiology of many mental health problems. Second there is the risk of not taking the role of the patient's wider social context into account. Poverty, unemployment, low socio-economic status and stressful family environments may all contribute to the development of psychological problems.

Having noted these two dangers, it should be mentioned that they have been addressed by various members of the cognitive-behavioural tradition at different times. For example, cognitive-behavioural approaches to understanding conditions such as schizophrenia (outlined in Chapter 7) and borderline personality disorder (described Chapter 8) are based on diathesis–stress conceptualizations of their aetiology, which take account of the important role of genetic and neurobiological factors. Also, there is increasing recognition within the cognitive-behavioural tradition for the important role of life stress and immediate family environment in the maintenance and amelioration of psychological problems (Dattilio, 2009).

Family systems model

Assumptions

The family systems model assumes that psychological problems are maintained by patterns of interaction and belief systems within the family and the wider social system of the client. Historical, contextual and constitutional factors may predispose family members to engage in these interaction patterns and adopt these belief systems. The many family therapy schools within this tradition may be classified in terms of their central focus of therapeutic concern and in particular with respect to their emphasis on (1) problem maintaining behaviour patterns; (2) problematic and constraining belief systems; and (3) historical, contextual and constitutional predisposing factors (Carr, 2006b).

With respect to the first theme, some family therapy schools highlight the role of repetitive patterns of family interaction in the maintenance of problem behaviour and advocate practices that aim to disrupt these patterns of interaction. Schools that fall into this category include the MRI brief therapy approach (Segal, 1991), strategic therapy (Robbins et al., 2009), structural therapy (Colapinto, 1991) and functional family therapy (Sexton, 2009).

With respect to the second theme, some schools of family therapy point to the centrality of belief systems and narratives which subserve repetitive interaction patterns that maintain presenting problems. Practices that facilitate the emergence of new belief systems and narratives which liberate family members from problem-maintaining interaction patterns are espoused by these schools. Schools that fall into this category include social constructionist approaches (Anderson, 2003), the Milan school (Campbell et al., 1991), solution-focused family therapy (Cheung, 2009) and narrative therapy (Duvall & Béres, 2011).

With respect to the third theme, a number of family therapy traditions highlight the role of historical, contextual and constitutional factors in predisposing family members to adopt particular belief systems and engage in particular problematic interaction patterns. Such schools advocate using practices that specifically address these historical, contextual and constitutional predisposing factors, including working with members of the extended family and wider social network as well as coaching individuals to manage historical, contextual and constitutional constraints. This category contains transgenerational family therapy (Hargrove, 2009); psychoanalytic family therapy traditions (Magnavita, 2009), attachment theory-based approaches (Diamond, 2005; Johnson & Bradley, 2009), experiential family therapy (Wetchler & Piercey, 1996), multisystemic therapy which includes reference to the wider system (Henggeler et al., 2009) and psychoeducational approaches (McFarlane, 2005).

Elsewhere I have argued that an integrative approach to family therapy may be taken so that for any problem, a formulation may be constructed using ideas from many schools of family therapy in which the pattern of family interaction that maintains the problem is specified, the constraining beliefs and narratives that underpin each family member's role in this pattern are outlined, and the historical and contextual factors that underpin these belief systems and narratives are specified (Carr, 2006b). In parallel with this, a similar formulation may be constructed to explain why the problem does not occur in exceptional circumstances, which, while similar to problematic situations, differ in important key respects.

In light of these formulations, a range of interventions that address factors within each column of the formulations may be considered. Some interventions aim primarily to disrupt problem-maintaining behaviour patterns or amplify exceptional non-problematic patterns. Others aim to help family members change the personal narratives that make them repeat the same problematic behaviour patterns and develop more liberating and flexible belief systems that underpin exceptions to the problem. Still others aim to modify the negative impact of historical, contextual and constitutional factors or to draw on family strengths in these domains.

In family systems therapy, assessment and treatment involves the client and the family participating in multi-person meetings. Multiple perspectives on the problem and related interaction patterns, belief systems and predisposing factors are therefore available to the therapist. Furthermore, there is the possibility of multiple people being involved in therapeutic change. Because of this, it is a fundamental assumption of family systems therapy that a small intervention may lead to a big change. It is therefore not surprising that family therapy is usually brief, with treatment rarely extending beyond 20 sessions. Furthermore, family therapy is dominated neither by clinical psychology nor by psychiatry. Many disciplines are involved, including social work and nursing.

Achievements

Family therapy has made an important contribution to the understanding and treatment of psychological problems. First, in a field dominated by essentially individualistic models of practice, it has highlighted the role of the social context in the aetiology and treatment of psychological difficulties. Second, family therapy is a brief, affordable form of treatment well suited to public health services. It is highly cost-effective (Crane, 2011). Where different family members have problems, they may all be treated by the same therapist or team. Third, empirical research shows that family therapy is effective with a wide range of problems in children and adults (Carr, 2009b, 2009c). Thus, there is a sound foundation for evidence-based practice. Fourth, systems theory can offer an integrative framework for comprehending not just the role of social factors but also those of biological and intrapsychic factors in the understanding and treatment of psychological difficulties. Fifth, in clinical practice, an integrative approach to family therapy is particularly useful in managing complex cases in which multiple family members have multiple problems, since often these are interconnected – a point missed by individualistic conceptualizations of psychological problems.

Limitations

The main limitations of the family systems model are a danger of vagueness, the risk of losing sight of the needs and rights of the individual, and the danger of failing to take account of neurobiological factors.

Other influential models

The four models described above are the most influential in the field of clinical psychology. However, there are many other frameworks that influence the way clinical psychologists conduct their work. These include the client-centred humanistic tradition, personal construct psychology and positive psychology.

Client-centred humanistic psychology

Client-centred humanistic psychotherapy is an overarching term for a tradition that includes a variety of specific approaches to therapy and counselling; for example, Carl Rogers' client-centred therapy, Fritz Perls' gestalt therapy and various experiential therapies (Cain & Seeman, 2001). Within this tradition, it is assumed that avoidance or denial of current feelings, emotions and desires, and deliberate or inadvertent failure to take responsibility for these aspects of experience, prevent self-actualization and give rise to psychological symptoms.

A defining feature of client-centred humanistic psychotherapy is the use of the therapeutic relationship between client and therapist as a resource in promoting self-actualization and personal growth. A second defining feature of this tradition is facilitating personal growth by helping clients to become more aware of their disavowed emotions and desires and to take responsibility for these. Within this tradition, personal growth is the main goal of therapy. Resolving presenting problems is often secondary to this superordinate goal. The practice within clinical psychology of establishing a strong therapeutic alliance with the client reflects the influence of the client-centred humanistic tradition.

Constructivist psychotherapy

Constructivist psychotherapy is based on George Kelly's personal construct psychology (Winter & Viney, 2005). Personal construct psychology holds that people's problems are rooted in the way they construe or interpret the world. Consequently a defining feature of personal construct psychotherapy is the exploration and transformation of clients' unique construct and belief systems. In the UK personal construct psychology and constructivist psychotherapy have had an impact on the practice of clinical psychology through influential clinical psychologists, notably Don Bannister and Fay Francella.

Positive psychology

Remediating deficits and managing disabilities has been a central concern for clinical psychology since its inception. Positive psychology, in contrast, complements this aim by focusing instead on the enhancement of happiness. Positive psychology was founded by Martin Seligman in the US at the turn of the millennium.

While modern positive psychology is a new movement, it draws on a rich intellectual heritage that includes the humanistic tradition. However, the distinguishing features of the modern positive psychology movement are its commitment to the scientific study of positive aspects of human experience, the academic infrastructure that has been established to support this research, and the intellectual leadership provided by the founders of the movement.

Positive psychology focuses on understanding and facilitating (1) happiness and well-being, (2) positive traits and engagement in absorbing activities, and (3) the development of meaningful positive relationships, social systems and institutions (Lopez & Snyder, 2009). Common themes within positive psychology that influence the practice of clinical psychology include resilience, optimism, hope, forgiveness, curiosity, creativity, wisdom, emotional intelligence, self-efficacy, self-determination, self-regulation, humour, mindfulness, therapeutic writing, posttraumatic growth, attachment, empathy and altruism.

The client-centred humanistic, personal construct and positive psychology models, with their emphasis on the quality of the therapeutic alliance, the uniqueness of each client, client strengths and optimism, are common themes in the practice of clinical psychology.

Summary

The biological, psychoanalytic, cognitive-behavioural and family systems models are each based on a unique set of assumptions. Despite limitations, each model has given rise to a unique set of achievements. With the biological model it is assumed that psychological problems may be classified into syndromes. Each syndrome is due to an underlying brain disease for which a discrete cause and physical cure may be ultimately identified. It is also assumed that each condition follows a distinctive course and has a particular prognosis.

The biological model's greatest achievement was the liberation of people with psychological problems and the creation of asylums where those in psychological distress received humane treatment. Mental health legislation, widely used classification systems such as the DSM and ICD, a commitment to scientific study of psychological problems, and the development of psychopharmacological treatments are among the major achievements of the biological model. Its limitations include the facts that many psychological problems are not caused by organic factors, many psychopharmacological treatments have harmful side-effects, asylums have led to social exclusion and mental health legislation has been abused.

The psychoanalytic model assumes that psychological problems are symptoms of underlying psychopathology. Psychotherapy gives insight into the conflicts, defences and transference phenomena that constitute this psychopathology. Achievements of the psychoanalytic model include the discovery of the unconscious, the demonstration of continuity between normality and psychological problems and the establishment of talking therapy as a valid method for treating psychological problems. Classical psychoanalysis, however, is too expensive to be a viable approach for routinely treating people in the public health services. This and the fact that is diagnostically vague, many of its propositions are untestable, and it pathologizes everyone are its major limitations.

The cognitive-behavioural model assumes that symptoms are learned through conditioning, imitation and insight and that therapy involves changing patterns of learned behaviour using specific treatments that have been developed for specific symptoms. The development of brief evidence-based effective approaches to therapy applicable to a wide range of patients is the main achievement of the cognitive-behavioural model. The risk of trivializing psychological problems and of paying insufficient attention to organic or social factors are its principal limitations.

The systems model assumes that psychological problems are maintained by patterns of interaction and belief systems within the family and the wider social system of the patient. Historical, contextual and constitutional factors may predispose family members to engage in these interaction patterns and adopt these belief systems. In family therapy, assessment and treatment involves the client and the family. In terms of achievements, empirical research shows that family therapy is effective with a wide range of problems and that systems theory offers a framework for integrating biological, psychological and social factors. The main limitations of this approach are a danger of vagueness, a risk of losing sight of the individual, and a danger of failing to take account of neurobiological factors.

The biological, psychoanalytic, cognitive-behavioural and family systems models have been the most influential in the field of clinical psychology. Other frameworks that have influenced the practice of clinical psychology include the client-centred humanistic tradition, personal construct psychology and positive psychology.

Questions

- What are the key assumptions, *general* achievements and *general* limitations of the biological, psychodynamic, cognitive-behavioural and family systems models?
- Having read Chapters 2–8, what do you consider to be the top three *specific* achievements of the biological, psychodynamic, cognitive-behavioural and family systems models?
- Why are the client-centred humanistic tradition, personal construct psychology and positive psychology important for the practice of clinical psychology?

FURTHER READING

- Tyrer, P. & Sternberg, D. (2005). *Models of mental disorder: Conceptual models in psychiatry* (fourth edition). Chichester, UK: Wiley.
- Watchel, P. & Messer, S. (1997). *Theories of psychotherapy: Origins and evolution.* Washington, DC: APA. This text includes up-to-date accounts of psychodynamic, cognitive-behavioural and family systems approaches to psychotherapy.

WEBSITES

Psychiatric associations that privilege the neurobiological model

- American Psychiatric Association:
  www.psych.org
- Royal Australian & New Zealand College of Psychiatrists:
  www.ranzcp.org
- Royal College of Psychiatrists:
  www.rcpsych.ac.uk

Psychoanalytic associations

- American Psychoanalytical Association:
  www.apsa.org
- Australian Psychoanalytical Society:
  www.psychoanalysis.asn.au
- British Psychoanalytical Society:
  www.psychoanalysis.org.uk
- International Psychoanalytical Association:
  www.ipa.org.uk

Cognitive-behavioural associations

- Association for Behavioural and Cognitive Therapies (US):
  www.abct.org
- Australian Association for Cognitive and Behaviour Therapy:
  www.aacbtqld.org.au

- British Association of Behavioural & Cognitive Psychotherapies:
www.babcp.com

Family therapy associations

- American Association for Marital and Family Therapy:
www.aamft.org
- Association for Family Therapy (UK):
www.aft.org.uk
- European Family Therapy Association:
www.europeanfamilytherapy.eu
- Family Therapy Association of Ireland:
www.familytherapyireland.com

10 Effectiveness of psychological therapies

Learning objectives

After studying this chapter you will be able to:

- define evidence-based practice in clinical psychology
- explain the hierarchy of evidence that informs evidence-based practice
- summarize the main findings from the evidence base for the effectiveness of psychotherapy
- outline the medical cost offset associated with psychotherapy
- describe the role of common and specific factors in the effectiveness of psychotherapy.

Introduction

One of the main ways in which clinical psychologists help clients is through psychotherapy. Psychotherapy is a contractual process in which trained professionals with expert knowledge of their discipline interact with clients to help them resolve psychological problems and address mental health difficulties. Psychotherapy may be offered to children and adults on an individual, couple, family or group basis.

Often clinical psychologists offer psychotherapy as one element of a multimodal programme provided by a multidisciplinary team. For example, a multidisciplinary adult mental health team may routinely offer a multimodal programme of cognitive behaviour therapy combined with antidepressants for depression, as described in Chapter 6. A multidisciplinary child and adolescent mental health team may routinely offer a multimodal programme for children with attention deficit hyperactivity disorder which includes behavioural parent training, school-based behavioural consultation, child-focused self-instructional and social training and methylphenidate, as outlined in Chapter 2. In this chapter the focus will be on the evidence base for the overall effectiveness of psychotherapy and common factors that underpin effective approaches.

Evidence-based practice

In clinical psychology there has been a gradual move from practice guided exclusively by descriptions of clinical cases to evidence-based practice guided by the results of scientific studies on the effectiveness of psychological interventions. This evolution has occurred as part of the broader movement of evidence-based medicine (Sackett et al., 1996, 2000).

Evidence-based practice in medicine and clinical psychology involves the judicious and compassionate use of the best available scientific evidence to make decisions about patient or client care. In clinical psychology, it involves taking account of available scientific evidence about 'what works' on one hand, and clients' unique problems, needs, rights and preferences on the other, and making balanced, compassionate judgements (APA Presidential Task Force on Evidence Based Practice, 2006; Norcross et al., 2006).

Hierarchy of evidence

When considering scientific evidence for the effectiveness of psychological interventions, it is useful to organize categories of available scientific evidence into a hierarchy, from the least to the most persuasive, as illustrated in Figure 10.1. In this hierarchy, case studies are the least persuasive form of evidence. The most persuasive evidence for the effectiveness of psychotherapy and other psychological interventions comes from meta-analyses of controlled trials.

Case studies and case series

In case studies descriptions and explanations are given of the way therapy was conducted with individual cases and the impact of therapy on clients' problems or symptoms. Such studies offer important insights into the details of how particular types of psychotherapy may be conducted with specific cases. Some examples are sketched in Figure 10.2.

The main limitation of case study evidence is that any observed improvements in clients' problems may be due to the passage of time, idiosyncratic responses of individual cases, or biased observation. Studies of case series provide more convincing evidence for the effectiveness of therapy. In such studies, groups of cases with similar sorts of problem are assessed before and after treatment with a standard set

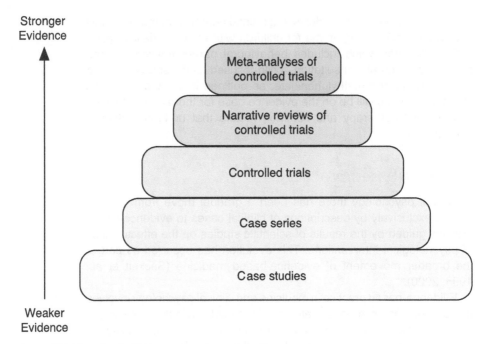

Figure 10.1 Hierarchy of evidence

Sigmund Freud
Psychoanalysis

In Freud's (1909b) case study of the Rat Man (a pseudonym for Ernst Lanzer) he described how he used interpretation of obsessional thoughts and compulsive behaviour to treat obsessive compulsive disorder. He interpreted the symptoms as being related to infantile sexuality and as helping the client avoid making difficult decisions in his adult life.

Aaron T. Beck
Cognitive therapy

Beck (1976) described a series of cases in which he used cognitive therapy to treat depression and anxiety disorders. His approach involved helping people identify and challenge negative automatic thoughts that underpinned their negative mood states. Socratic dialogue, behavioural experiments and other techniques were used to facilitate this process.

Salvador Minuchin
Family therapy

Minuchin and his team (1978) described how he conceptualized anorexia as a process of triangulation within the family. He showed how structural family therapy was used to help an adolescent girl break the cycle of self-starvation and empower the parents to help their daughter recover and maintain normal eating pattern.

Figure 10.2 Case studies

of assessment instruments. Because data are collected on more than one case, case series studies rule out the possibility that improvements reflect idiosyncratic responses of single cases.

The main shortcoming with evidence from case series studies is that they leave open the possibility that improvements in clients' functioning may have been due to the passage of time, rather than the effects of treatment.

Controlled trials

In controlled trials, to rule out the possibility that observed improvements in clients' problems following treatment were due to the passage of time, gains made by treated cases are compared with gains made by a control group (case–control studies). In psychotherapy studies, clients in control groups usually receive routine clinical management of their problems. An example of results from a controlled trial – The London Depression Intervention Trial (Leff et al., 2000) – is given in Figure 10.3. The average score of the group that received couples therapy for chronic depression was lower after treatment than before therapy began, and this gain was maintained at follow-up a year later. This pattern of improvement was better than that for cases treated with antidepressants.

There are many variations of the basic controlled trial, but the gold standard is the randomized controlled trial. In randomized controlled trials, cases are randomly assigned to treatment and control groups, to rule out the possibility that differences in improvement rates are due to responsive and unresponsive cases having been systematically assigned to treatment and control groups. There is a tradition in medical

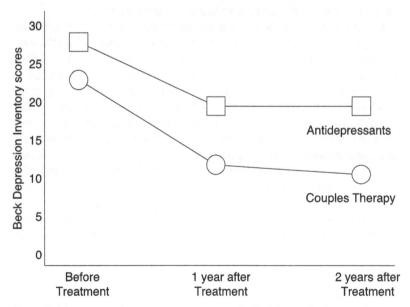

Figure 10.3 Improvement in mean symptom scores on the Beck Depression Inventory for adults with chronic depression receiving systemic couples therapy or antidepressants before treatment, 1 year after treatment and 2 years after treatment. Based on Leff et al. (2000)

randomized controlled trials to use 'sugar pills' as placebos, so patients in the control group do not receive the medicine that is being evaluated, but believe that they are being helped since they are receiving what looks like an active treatment (the placebo sugar pill).

In some psychotherapy treatment outcome studies, clients receive placebo therapy. This usually involves having as much contact with a therapist as those in the treatment group, but receiving some innocuous, though credible, placebo psychotherapy, for example engaging in 'intellectual discussions' about plausible topics. When placebo control groups are included in randomized controlled trials, they rule out the possibility that treatment gains were due simply to therapist contact rather than psychotherapeutic techniques and processes.

Narrative reviews

While an individual trial with positive results provides evidence that in one context, a particular form of treatment was effective for a group of clients with a specific type of problem, narrative reviews provide more convincing evidence because they show the extent to which positive results were replicated across a series of trials. However, the conclusions drawn in narrative reviews are inevitably biased by the conscious and unconscious prejudices of the reviewer.

Meta-analyses

Meta-analysis is a systematic, quantitative approach to reviewing evidence from multiple trials. The impact of reviewer bias inherent in narrative reviews is greatly reduced in meta-analyses because data from many trials are synthesized using statistical methods.

In a meta-analysis effect sizes are calculated for each trial and then averaged across all trials to provide a quantitative index of the effectiveness of a particular form of treatment with a specified population. Effect sizes calculated in meta-analyses express quantitatively the degree to which treated groups improved more than control groups. A graphic explanation of the calculation of an effect size is given in Figure 10.4.

Table 10.1 gives a system for interpreting effect sizes. Using this table, it may be seen that an effect size of .8 is large. If such an effect size were obtained in a meta-analysis it would mean that the average treated case fared better than 79% of cases in the control group. It would also indicate that 69% of cases in the treatment group had a successful outcome compared with 31% of control group cases. Finally, a large effect size of .8 would indicate that 14% of the variance in outcome could validly be attributed to the effects of treatment, rather than other factors.

How effective is psychotherapy?

Mary Smith and Gene Glass published the first major meta-analysis of psychotherapy outcome studies in *American Psychologist* in 1977.

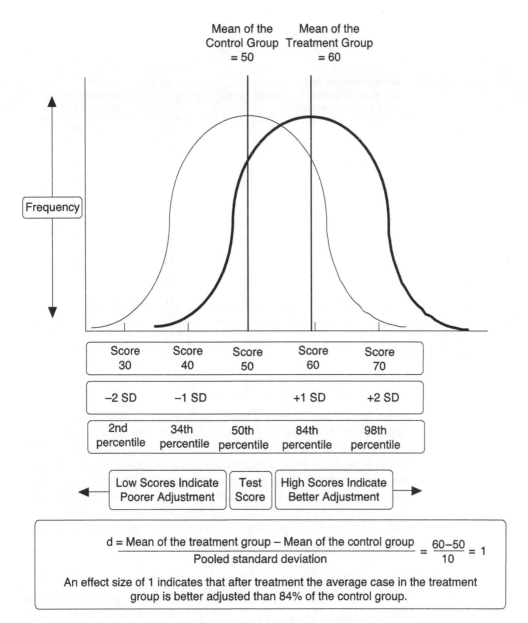

Figure 10.4 Graphic representation of an effect size of 1

They included 375 controlled trials of psychotherapy in their analysis and found an average effect size of .68. They concluded that a typical therapy client was better off than 75% of untreated individuals.

Since that seminal study many meta-analyses have been conducted. In a synthesis of 68 separate meta-analyses of psychotherapy with children, adolescents and adults with a wide range of different psychological problems, Grissom (1996) found an aggregate effect size of .75, indicating that the average treated case fared better than 77% of untreated controls.

TABLE 10.1
Interpretation of effect size

Effect size d	Cohen's designation[1]	Percentage of untreated cases that the average treated case fares better than[2]	Success rate for treated group[3]	Success rate for untreated group[3]	Percentage of outcome variance accounted for by treatment[4]
1.0	Large	84	72	28	20
.9		82	71	29	17
.8		79	69	31	14
.7		76	67	33	11
.6		73	64	36	8
.5	Medium	69	62	38	6
.4		66	60	40	4
.3		62	57	43	2
.2	Small	58	55	45	1
.1		54	53	47	0

Note: Adapted from Wampold (2001, p. 53). 1. From Cohen (1988). 2. From Glass (1976). 3. From Rosenthal and Rubin (1982). Binomial effect size display, assuming overall success rate of .5, success rate for treated cases is .5 + correlation with outcome/2, and success rate for untreated cases is .5 − correlation with outcome/2. 4. From Rosenthal (1994, p. 239), percentage of variance = $d^2/(d^2 + 4)$.

Effects of psychotherapy with adults

While Smith and Glass's (1977) meta-analysis, mentioned above, included mainly studies of psychotherapy with adults, it also included many studies of therapy with children. With a view to determining the effects of psychotherapy for adults with psychological problems, Shapiro and Shapiro (1982) conducted a meta-analysis of 143 studies of psychotherapy exclusively involving adult populations. They found an overall effect size of 1.03, indicating that after treatment the average adult who participated in psychotherapy fared better than 84% of untreated control group cases.

Effectiveness of psychotherapy with children and adolescents

The results of four broad meta-analyses of studies involving children and adolescents under 18 years with a diverse range of psychological problems receiving a variety of forms of psychotherapy provide evidence for the overall effectiveness of psychotherapy with children (Casey & Berman, 1985; Kazdin et al., 1990; Weisz et al., 1987, 1995). These meta-analyses included more than 350 treatment outcome studies. Effect sizes ranged from .71 to .88, with a mean effect size of .77. This indicates that the average treated case fared better than 78% of control group cases.

Efficacy and effectiveness studies

A useful distinction is made between efficacy and effectiveness trials (Cochrane, 1972). In efficacy studies clients with a specific type of problem (and no comorbid difficulties) are randomly assigned to treatment and control groups. The treatment group receives a pure and potent form of a very specific type of psychotherapy from specialist psychotherapists in practice centres of excellence.

Efficacy studies are typically conducted at university-affiliated centres, with carefully selected clients who meet stringent inclusion and exclusion criteria. For example, often patients with comorbid substance abuse and personality disorders or self-harming behaviour are excluded from efficacy studies of treatments for depression. Therapists are highly trained, intensively supervised, have small case loads, and the fidelity with which they offer treatment is scientifically checked by rating the degree to which recordings of therapy sessions conform to treatment protocols specified in therapy manuals.

Effectiveness studies, in contrast, are conducted in routine clinical settings rather than centres of excellence, with typical therapists carrying normal case loads, offering treatment to clients who are representative of typical referrals, and while therapy manuals and supervision are often employed, there is a greater degree of flexibility about their use than in efficacy studies. Efficacy studies tell us how well treatments work under ideal conditions. Information about the impact of treatments under routine conditions is provided by effectiveness studies. It is useful to think of effectiveness and efficacy studies as representing the extremes of a continuum along which a variety of trial designs fall.

One of the criticisms of broad meta-analyses of psychotherapy trials is that many of the studies included in them are efficacy rather than effectiveness trials, and so are not representative of clients who attend typical services. To address this criticism, Shadish et al. (1997) conducted a meta-analysis of 56 effectiveness trials. The studies were conducted in non-university, community settings; included children, adolescents and adults referred for treatment, not solicited by the researcher; and involved experienced professional therapists with normal case loads. The average effect size from these 56 clinically representative studies was .68, which is precisely the effect size found by Smith and Glass in their seminal meta-analysis mentioned above. The results of this meta-analysis show that psychotherapy is effective when conducted under clinically representative conditions.

Psychodynamic psychotherapy

Within the psychodynamic tradition, a distinction is made between short-term psychodynamic psychotherapy and intensive long-term psychoanalysis. The former involves weekly sessions for periods of 6–12 months, while the latter involves two or more sessions per week, usually for periods longer than a year.

Two important broad meta-analyses have been conducted to evaluate the effectiveness of psychodynamic psychotherapy with adult mental health problems (Leichsenring et al., 2004; Leichsenring & Rabung, 2011). In a meta-analysis of 17 studies, Leichsenring et al. (2004) found that short-term psychodynamic psychotherapy yielded an effect size of

.7 for psychiatric symptoms in patients mainly diagnosed with anxiety and mood disorders when therapy was compared with waiting list or minimal intervention control groups. This indicates that after treatment the average treated case fared better than 76% of controls. In this meta-analysis, the outcome for psychodynamic psychotherapy did not differ from that of other forms of psychotherapy in the 14 studies where such comparisons were made.

In a further meta-analysis of 10 studies, Leichsenring and Rabung (2011) found that long-term psychodynamic psychotherapy involving more than 50 sessions over periods longer than a year yielded an effect size of .54 for overall effectiveness for complex cases with severe symptomatology, comorbid diagnoses, or personality disorders, when long-term psychodynamic psychotherapy was compared with a range of other therapies including CBT, dialectical behaviour therapy, family therapy and short-term psychodynamic psychotherapy. This indicates that after treatment the average case treated with long-term psychodynamic psychotherapy fared better than 70% of cases treated with other therapies. Gains made during treatment were sustained at 1–8 years' follow-up.

The results of these two meta-analyses show that short-term psychodynamic psychotherapy is as effective as other widely used forms of psychotherapy, including CBT, for common psychological problems such as anxiety and depression in adults; and that long-term psychodynamic psychotherapy is more effective than some other forms of therapy for adults with complex mental health difficulties.

Client-centred humanistic psychotherapy

Elliott et al. (2004) conducted a meta-analysis of trials of psychotherapy that fall broadly within the client-centred humanistic psychotherapy tradition. Over 90 trials of client-centred, experiential, gestalt and emotionally-focused therapy were included in the analysis. Clients in these studies had a wide variety of psychological problems including anxiety, mood, eating and personality disorders and relationship distress. The average duration of treatment was 22 sessions, reflecting about 6 months of therapy. An effect size of .78 was obtained, indicating that the average treated case fared better than 78% of cases in control groups. These results indicate that client-centred humanistic psychotherapy is an effective form of treatment for a range of common psychological problems in adulthood.

Cognitive-behaviour therapy

In a review of 16 meta-analyses that included 332 studies of the effectiveness of cognitive-behaviour therapy with 16 different disorders or populations, Butler et al. (2006) obtained a mean weighted effect size of .95 for depression and a range of anxiety disorders in children, adolescents and adults. Thus, the average treated case with anxiety and depression fared better than 83% of untreated controls. For marital distress, anger control and chronic pain in adults, and childhood somatic disorders, effect sizes were moderate, with a mean of .62. Thus, the average treated case with these problems fared better than 73% of untreated controls.

For sexual offending the average effect size of .35 was relatively small. However, it was the most effective form of psychotherapy for reducing recidivism in this population. Thus, the average treated sex offender fared better than 64% of untreated controls. There was significant evidence for the long-term effectiveness of cognitive-behaviour therapy, with an average effect size of .79, indicating that the average treated case fared better than 79% of untreated controls at follow-up at least 6 months after therapy.

Systemic therapy

Shadish and Baldwin (2003) reviewed 20 meta-analyses of systemic marital and family interventions for a wide range of child- and adult-focused problems. These included child and adolescent conduct and emotional disorders; drug and alcohol abuse in adolescents and adults; adult anxiety, depression and psychosis; and marital distress. Sixteen of the 20 meta-analyses were of therapy studies and four included marital and family enrichment studies.

For marital and family therapy the average effect size was .65 after therapy and .52 at follow-up 6 months to a year later. These results show that, overall, the average treated couple or family with clinically significant problems fared better after treatment than 75% of untreated controls, and at follow-up fared better than about 71% of cases in control groups. For marital and family enrichment, the effect sizes after therapy and at follow-up were .48 and .32 respectively. These results show that, overall, the average treated couple or family without clinically significant problems fared better after enrichment programmes than 68% of untreated controls, and at follow-up fared better than about 63% of cases in control groups.

Shadish and Baldwin's synthesis of the results of 20 meta-analyses supports the efficacy of systemic therapy for couples and families with a wide range of clinically significant problems, and for couples and families without clinical problems but who want to develop family strengths such as communication and problem-solving skills and greater emotional cohesion.

Summary of the overall effects of psychotherapy

Figure 10.5 summarizes the results of meta-analyses, described above, of the effectiveness of psychotherapy from a range of different traditions with adults and children. In this figure, where appropriate, effect sizes from multiple meta-analyses have been averaged, and graphed as success rates based on the system given in Table 10.1.

From Figure 10.5 it may be seen that meta-analyses of psychotherapy trials yield moderate to large effect sizes that range from .65 to

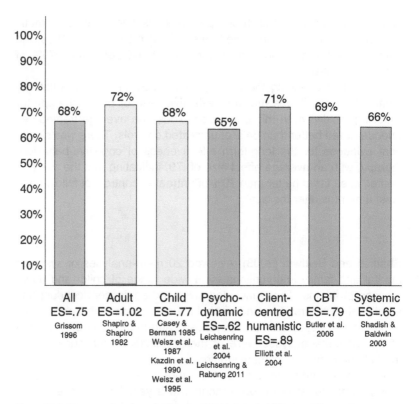

Figure 10.5 Success rates of psychotherapy with adults and children, and therapy from different traditions based on effect sizes from meta-analyses

1.02. When expressed as success rates, the results of meta-analyses indicate that 65–72% of people with psychological problems benefit from psychotherapy. Thus approximately two-thirds to three-quarters of people who engage in psychotherapy find that it leads to improvements in their mental health.

Comparison of the relative effects of psychotherapy and medical procedures

To place the evidence on the overall effectiveness of psychotherapy in a broader context, it is useful to ask: Are the moderate to large effect sizes associated with psychotherapy very different from those associated with the medical and surgical treatment of physical illnesses, diseases and medical conditions?

In a synthesis of 91 meta-analyses of various medical and surgical treatments for a range of medical conditions, Caspi (2004) found an average effect size of .5. This falls in the moderate range of effect sizes (.5–.8) and is not vastly dissimilar to the effect size of .75 from Grissom's (1996) synthesis of 68 meta-analyses of psychotherapy trials mentioned earlier. Thus it may be concluded that the moderate effect sizes associated with psychotherapy are similar to those associated with the treatment of medical conditions.

Deterioration and drop-out

A consistent finding within the psychotherapy research literature is that up to 10% of clients deteriorate following treatment (Lambert and Ogles, 2004; Lilienfeld, 2007). In a review of 46 studies on negative outcome in adult psychotherapy, Mohr (1995) found that deterioration was associated with particular client and therapist characteristics and particular features of psychotherapy. Deterioration was more common among clients with borderline personality disorder, obsessive compulsive disorder, or severe interpersonal difficulties. Lack of motivation and the expectation of benefiting from psychotherapy without personal effort were also associated with deterioration. Deterioration was more common when unskilled therapists lacked empathy and did not collaborate with clients in pursuing agreed goals. Failure to manage counter transference appropriately and frequent transference interpretations were also associated with deterioration.

Dropping out of psychotherapy is a relatively common event. In a meta-analysis of 125 studies, Wierzbicki and Pekarik (1993) found a mean dropout rate of 47%. Dropout rates were higher for minority ethnic groups, less educated clients, and those with lower incomes. Thus, we can conclude that about 1 in 10 clients deteriorate following therapy and that marginalized clients with particularly troublesome disorders and negative attitudes to psychotherapy are vulnerable to dropping out of psychotherapy and deterioration.

Medical cost offset

The evidence reviewed so far shows that psychotherapy is effective for a range of problems and populations. However, an important concern is the financial implications of providing such a psychotherapy service. In this context, two questions are of interest. First: Do clients who avail of psychotherapy services use fewer medical services and so incur reduced medical costs? This saving is referred to as the medical cost offset. The second question is: Is the medical cost offset associated with psychotherapy greater than the cost of providing psychotherapy? If so, we can conclude that psychotherapy has a total cost offset. Findings of meta-analyses and narrative reviews of the cost-offset literature throw light on both of these questions.

In a meta-analysis of 91 studies conducted between 1967 and 1997, Chiles et al. (1999) found that psychotherapy and psychological interventions led to significant medical cost offsets. Participants in reviewed studies included surgery inpatients, high health-service users, and people with psychological and substance use disorders who received psychotherapy or psychological interventions alone or as part of multi-modal programmes. Chiles and his team concluded that medical cost offsets occurred in 90% of studies and ranged from 20% to 30%. In 93% of studies where data were provided, cost offsets exceeded the cost of providing psychotherapy. Greater cost offsets occurred for older inpatients who required surgery, oncology, and cardiac rehabilitation than for outpatients who required care for minor injuries and illnesses. Structured psychological interventions, tailored to patient needs associated with their medical conditions, led to greater medical cost offsets than traditional psychotherapy.

In an earlier set of meta-analytic studies involving Blue Cross and Blue Shield US Federal Employees Plan claim files and 58 controlled studies, Mumford et al. (1984) found that in 85% of studies medical cost offset for psychotherapy occurred. This was due to shorter periods of hospitalization for surgery, cancer, heart disease and diabetes, particularly in patients over 55. In a review of psychological interventions for people with a variety of health-related difficulties, Groth-Marnat and Edkins (1996) found that medical cost offsets occurred when such interventions targeted patients preparing for surgery and patients with difficulty adhering to medical regimens. Medical cost offset also occurred for smoking cessation programmes, rehabilitation programmes, and programmes for patients with chronic pain disorders, cardiovascular disorders and psychosomatic complaints.

Three other important reviews of the medical cost-offset literature, which focused largely on mental health problems in adults rather than adjustment to physical illness, deserve mention. In a review of 30 studies of psychotherapy for psychological disorders and drug and alcohol abuse, Jones and Vischi (1979) found that medical cost offsets occurred in most cases. In a review of eight cost-effectiveness studies for substance abuse, Morgan and Crane (2010) concluded that family-based treatments can be cost-effective and deserve inclusion in health-care delivery systems. In a review of 18 studies of psychotherapy for psychological disorders, Gabbard et al. (1997) found that in more than in 80% of studies, medical cost offsets exceeded the cost of providing psychotherapy. Particularly significant cost offsets occurred for complex problems, notably in studies of psychoeducational family therapy for schizophrenia and dialectical behaviour therapy for personality disorders, by reducing the need for inpatient care and improving occupational adjustment.

From the evidence reviewed here, it is clear that psychotherapeutic interventions have a significant medical cost offset. Those who participate in psychotherapy use fewer other medical services at primary, secondary and tertiary levels and are hospitalized less than those who do not receive psychotherapy.

Common factors and specific psychotherapies

A striking feature of the evidence base for psychotherapy is the similarity in outcomes of diverse approaches with a range of populations and problems, as shown in Figure 10.5. All approaches to psychotherapy, when averaged across different populations, problems and studies, lead to moderate to large effect sizes, and benefits for two-thirds to three-quarters of treated cases. When therapies are compared, differences rarely exceed an effect size of .2, as shown in Figure 10.6, which is based on Grissom's (1996) synthesis of many meta-analyses.

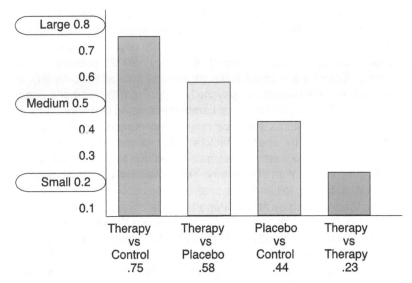

Figure 10.6 The effects of psychotherapy compared with placebo control groups. Based on Grissom (1996)

The hypothesis that different psychotherapies lead to similar improvement rates was first referred to as the Dodo bird verdict by Saul Rosenzweig in 1936. The reference is to a quotation from Lewis Carroll's *Alice in Wonderland* – At last the Dodo said '*Everybody* has won, and *all* must have prizes' – The Dodo's remark was made after a caucus race in which competitors started at different points and ran in different directions for half an hour. This finding that most forms of psychotherapy have similar outcomes has led to the hypothesis that a set of common factors may underpin all effective psychotherapies.

One possibility is that the underlying common factor is the placebo effect. That is, psychotherapy may be no more than a placebo, a psychological sugar pill that gives clients hope and creates the expectation of improvement. It was mentioned above that to evaluate this hypothesis researchers have conducted studies in which a specific form of psychotherapy is compared with a psychological or pharmacological placebo condition. Common psychological placebo conditions involve engaging in intellectual discussion groups, participating in recreational activities, or receiving an inert procedure that is described as providing subliminal treatment.

In Grissom's (1996) synthesis of many meta-analyses summarized in Figure 10.6, the effect size for psychotherapy compared with placebos was .58. Thus, the average treated case fared better than 72% of cases in control groups who received placebos. This shows that psychotherapy is not just a placebo that generates hope, but a set of procedures that actively influences the recovery process. From Figure 10.6 it may also be seen that the effect size for therapy versus waiting list control groups (.75) is larger than the effect size of placebo versus waiting list control groups (.44). This shows that the effects of psychotherapy are nearly double those of placebos.

The results of two important analyses of the relative contribution of common and specific factors to psychotherapy outcome are summarized in Figure 10.7. In a narrative review of over 100 psychotherapy studies Michael Lambert (1992; Lambert & Barley, 2002) estimated that common factors were about twice as important as specific factors in contributing to the outcome of psychotherapy. From the left-hand panel in Figure 10.7, it may be seen that Lambert estimated that about 30% of psychotherapy outcome variance may be accounted for by common factors, and 15% by specific factors; 15% of the remainder of the variance in outcome, Lambert estimated, was due to placebo effects or creating the expectation of recovery. The remaining 40% of variance in outcome, according to Lambert's analysis, was accounted for by factors outside therapy such as social support from family and friends.

The results of an analysis conducted by Bruce Wampold (2001) are presented in the right-hand panel in Figure 10.7. Wampold, like Lambert, concluded that common factors are more important than specific factors in determining the outcome of psychotherapy, but the results of his rigorous analysis led to a far more extreme statement of this position. Wampold (2001) conducted a quantitative review of more than a dozen meta-analyses, and estimated that common factors are nine times more influential than specific factors in determining the outcome of psychotherapy. He concluded that only 13% of the variance of outcome for psychotherapy clients is due to psychotherapy (including common, specific and other factors). This was based on his computation of an overall effect size for psychotherapy of between .7 and .8. He also concluded that only 1% of the variability in outcome for psychotherapy clients was due to specific factors. This was based on an average between-treatment effect size of .2, similar to that shown in Figure 10.6. He estimated that 3% of the variance in outcome was due to unexplained therapy factors, probably client characteristics. The remaining 9% of the variance in outcome, he concluded, was accounted for by common factors.

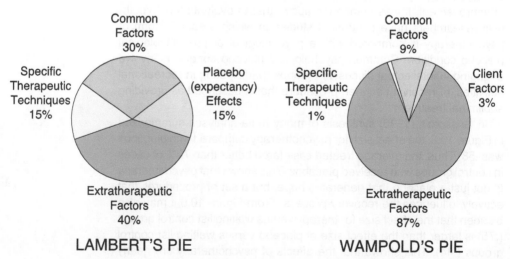

LAMBERT'S PIE — Common Factors 30%; Specific Therapeutic Techniques 15%; Placebo (expectancy) Effects 15%; Extratherapeutic Factors 40%.

WAMPOLD'S PIE — Common Factors 9%; Specific Therapeutic Techniques 1%; Client Factors 3%; Extratherapeutic Factors 87%.

Figure 10.7 Factors that affect the outcome of psychotherapy. Based on Lambert and Barley (2002) and Wampold (2001).

Lambert's and Wampold's analyses share one important conclusion. Common factors have a far greater impact than specific factors in determining whether or not clients benefit from psychotherapy. The major impact of common factors on the outcome of psychotherapy provides a possible explanation for the similarity in outcome of different psychotherapy approaches. However, therapists must engage in specific forms of therapy for common factors to have a medium through which to operate. For example, in family therapy the process of convening family meetings, helping family members view individual problems as part of a pattern of family interaction, and exploring alternative interaction patterns creates a context within which therapists develop good working alliances with clients (which is one of the most important common factors affecting treatment outcome).

Categories of common factor

In considering common factors, it is useful to distinguish between client factors, therapist factors and factors associated with the therapeutic context, including the dose of therapy received, the quality of the therapeutic alliance, and therapeutic procedures. Common factors that contribute to the effectiveness of psychotherapy are listed in Table 10.2.

TABLE 10.2
Therapy, client and therapist 'common factors' that affect positive psychotherapy outcome

Therapeutic context factors	Client factors	Therapist factors
Dose of 20–45 sessions	High personal distress	Personal adjustment
Positive therapeutic alliance	Low symptom severity	Therapeutic competence
Empathy	Low functional impairment	Matching therapy style to patients' needs
Collaboration and goal consensus	Low problem complexity, chronicity and comorbidity	Over-controlled patients – facilitate insight
Positive regard and genuineness	Readiness to change and lack of resistance	Under-controlled patients – build symptom management skills
Relevant feedback and relevant self-disclosure	Early response to therapy	Positive past relationships – facilitate insight
Repair alliance ruptures	Psychological mindedness	Negative past relationships – provide support
Manage transference and countertransference	Ego strength	Compliant clients – use directive interventions
Common procedures	Capacity to make and maintain relationships	Resistant clients – use self-directed interventions
Problem exploration	Social support	Credibility of rationales
Credible rationale	High socio-economic status	Problem-solving creativity
Mobilizing client		Specific training
Support and catharsis		Flexible manual use
Reconceptualizing problem		Supervision and personal therapy
Behavioural change		Feedback on client recovery
Combining psychotherapy and medication		

Client characteristics

A range of client characteristics are associated with a positive response to any type of psychological intervention (Clarkin & Levy, 2004; Lambert, 2005). Distressed clients with circumscribed problems of low severity with little functional impairment who are ready to change, and who show an improvement early in treatment, respond well to psychotherapy. High socio-economic status, social support, the capacity to make and maintain relationships, psychological-mindedness and ego strength are other client attributes associated with a positive response to psychotherapy. Psychologically minded people understand their problems in intrapsychic terms, rather than blaming them on external factors. Ego strength is the capacity to tolerate conflict and distress, while showing flexibility and persistence in pursuing valued goals.

Therapist characteristics

Effective therapists have distinctive profiles (Addis, 2002; Beutler et al., 2004; Lambert et al., 2003; Lambert & Ogles, 1997; Miller et al., 2005; Norcross, 2005; Stein & Lambert, 1995). They are technically competent, credible and creative in their approach to helping clients solve problems. They have engaged in personal therapy, are well adjusted, well trained, use therapy manuals flexibly, and use feedback on client progress to match their therapeutic style to clients' needs.

There is evidence for the effectiveness of three types of matching. For reflective, over-controlled clients, an insight-oriented approach is particularly effective, whereas a symptom-focused, skills-building approach is more effective with impulsive, under-controlled clients. For clients who are resistant to directives, a self-directed approach is most effective, whereas a directive approach is effective with non-resistant clients. For clients with a history of gratifying early relationships, confrontative insight-oriented approaches are effective, whereas supportive approaches are more effective for clients with histories of problematic early relationships.

Therapeutic common factors

For 50–75% of psychotherapy clients to recover, 20–45 sessions of therapy are necessary (Hansen et al., 2002). The therapeutic alliance is the single most important therapeutic common factor and accounts for about 38% of the effectiveness of psychotherapy (Martin et al., 2000; Shirk & Karver, 2003). Strong therapeutic alliances have distinctive features (Norcross, 2002; Orlinsky et al., 2004). For a strong therapeutic alliance, the therapist must be empathic and collaborative, and the client must be co-operative and committed to recovery.

Within the therapy relationship, effective therapists show positive regard, genuineness, and provide clients with both relevant feedback and relevant self-disclosure information. Ruptures in the therapeutic alliance are common. These may be associated with client transference, therapist countertransference or a mismatch between clients' needs and the therapist's way of conducting therapy. Strong therapeutic alliances are maintained by managing such ruptures in therapeutic alliances and customizing therapeutic relationships to take account of clients' needs.

Certain common procedures characterize effective therapy (Frank & Frank, 1991; Hubble et al., 1999; Karasu, 1986; Lambert & Ogles, 2004; Norcross & Goldfried, 2003; Sprenkle & Blow, 2004; Wampold, 2001). Effective therapy involves exploration and reconceptualization of both conscious and unconscious aspects of clients' problems; provision of a credible rationale for conducting therapy; generating hope and the expectation of improvement; and mobilizing clients to engage in problem resolution. This mobilization process may involve helping clients develop more adaptive behaviour patterns and belief systems; more effective ways of regulating their emotions; and more supportive emotional connections with themselves, their family members and their therapists.

There is also a developmental sequence common to most forms of psychotherapy in which interventions that support clients (such as reassurance and facilitating catharsis and emotional expression) precede interventions that promote learning to see problems in new ways (such as reframing and interpretation), and these in turn precede interventions that promote new forms of behaviour such as facing fears, regulating behaviour, interpersonal risk-taking, and practising new skills.

For specific disorders, multimodal programmes in which psychotherapy and psychotropic medication are combined are more effective than either alone (Kazdin, 2004; Thase & Jindal, 2004). For example, in children with attention deficit hyperactivity disorder, the effectiveness of psychotherapy, which includes parent-management training, school intervention, and self-instructional training for the child, can be enhanced by combining this with stimulant therapy as discussed in Chapter 2. In adults being treated with antipsychotic medication for schizophrenia, relapse rates may be reduced by offering psychoeducational family therapy to reduce family stress and cognitive-behaviour therapy to improve symptom management, as discussed in Chapter 7.

Specific factors

Common factors have a profound impact on the effectiveness of psychotherapy. However, therapists must engage in specific forms of therapy for common factors to have a medium through which to operate. In Chapters 2–8, examples of specific evidence-based psychological treatments for particular problems have been given. Comprehensive reviews of the literature on the effectiveness of psychological interventions concur that effective interventions have been developed for a range of problems (Carr, 2009a; Nathan & Gorman, 2007; Roth & Fonagy, 2005). These include mood, anxiety, eating, substance use and sleep disorders in both children and adults; family relationship problems, pain management, adjustment to illnesses such as asthma and diabetes, and adjustment to physical and intellectual disabilities in children and adults; disruptive behaviour disorders and toileting problems in childhood; and personality disorders and psychosis in adults.

Summary

Clinical psychologists provide psychotherapy to children and adults on an individual, couple, family, or group basis, often as one element of a multimodal programme offered by a multidisciplinary team. In doing so, they engage in evidence-based practice by taking account of available scientific evidence about 'what works' on one hand, and clients' unique problems, needs, rights and preferences on the other, and making balanced, compassionate judgements.

Scientific evidence for the effectiveness of psychotherapy ranges in persuasiveness from case studies to meta-analyses of controlled trials. Results of meta-analyses show that approximately two-thirds to three-quarters of people who engage in psychotherapy improve. Similar improvement rates occur for children and adults, individuals and families, and for psychotherapy from a range of different traditions. The moderate effect sizes associated with psychotherapy for mental health problems are similar to those associated with the medical and surgical treatments for physical health problems.

About one in 10 clients deteriorate following psychotherapy. Marginalized clients with particularly troublesome disorders and negative attitudes to psychotherapy are vulnerable to dropping out of psychotherapy and deterioration. Psychotherapy has a significant medical cost offset, and those who participate in psychotherapy use fewer other medical services than those who do not.

Most forms of psychotherapy are equally effective. This is due to the fact that they share common factors that contribute to effectiveness. These common factors include those associated with the client, the therapist and the therapeutic context. Distressed clients with circumscribed problems of low severity and little functional impairment who are ready to change, who show an improvement early in treatment, are of high socio-economic status, have a high level of social support, the capacity to make and maintain relationships, psychological-mindedness and ego strength respond well to psychotherapy.

Particularly effective therapists are technically competent, credible and creative in their approach to helping clients solve problems, have engaged in personal therapy, are well adjusted, well trained, use therapy manuals flexibly, and use feedback on client progress to match their therapeutic style to clients' needs. At least 20 sessions are required for most clients to recover, and the therapeutic alliance is the single most important common therapeutic common factor. For a strong therapeutic alliance, the therapist must be empathic and collaborative, and the client must be co-operative and committed to recovery.

The common procedures that characterize effective therapy include exploration and reconceptualization of conscious and unconscious aspects of problems; provision of a credible rationale for conducting therapy; generating hope and the expectation of improvement; and mobilizing clients to engage in problem resolution. These broad procedures may involve using therapeutic techniques such as providing support and encouraging emotional expression; facilitating new ways of viewing problems; and helping clients to develop new ways of behaving adaptively.

For certain disorders, multimodal programmes in which psychotherapy and pharmacotherapy are combined are more effective than either alone. Therapists must engage in specific forms of therapy for common factors to have a medium through which to operate.

Questions

- What is evidence-based practice in clinical psychology?
- What is the hierarchy of evidence that informs evidence-based practice in clinical psychology?
- What do the results of broad meta-analyses indicate about the overall effectiveness of psychotherapy?
- Is there a medical cost offset associated with psychotherapy?
- What is the 'Dodo bird' verdict?
- How important are common factors in contributing to the effectiveness of psychotherapy?
- What common factors contribute to the effectiveness of psychotherapy?
- How do specific models of practice contribute to the effectiveness of psychotherapy?

FURTHER READING

- Carr, A. (2009a). *What works with children, adolescents and adults? A review of research on the effectiveness of psychotherapy.* London: Routledge.
- Nathan, P. & Gorman, J. (2007). *A guide to treatments that work* (third edition). New York: Oxford University Press.
- Roth, T. & Fonagy, P. (2005). *What works for whom? A critical review of psychotherapy research* (second edition). London: Guilford.

WEBSITE

- Society for Psychotherapy Research: www.psychotherapyresearch.org

Glossary

A-CRA. Adolescent Contingency Reinforcement Approach, an evidence-based therapy for adolescent drug problems in which operant conditioning is the central intervention.

AACAP practice parameters. Clinical guidelines produced by the American Academy of Child and Adolescent Psychiatry, which is the US professional association for child and adolescent psychiatrists. (www.aacap.org/cs/root/member_information/practice_information/practice_parameters/practice_parameters)

AACBT. Australian Association for Cognitive and Behaviour Therapy. (www.aacbtqld.org.au)

AAMFT. American Association for Marital and Family Therapy. (www.aamft.org)

ABCT. Association for Behavioral and Cognitive Therapies (US). (www.abct.org)

ACPA. Australian Clinical Psychology Association. (www.acpa.org.au)

Addictive personality. A profile of personality traits that predisposes a person to addiction.

ADHD. Attention deficit hyperactivity disorder. A syndrome characterized by persistent overactivity, impulsivity and difficulties in sustaining attention. Also known as attention deficit disorder, hyperkinetic disorder, hyperkinesis and minimal brain dysfunction.

ADIS. Anxiety Disorders Interview Schedule, for assessing DSM–IV anxiety disorders. There are adult and child versions.

AFT. Association for Family Therapy (UK) (www.aft.org.uk)

Agoraphobia. A fear of public places, often due to a fear of having panic attacks in public places.

Alogia. Impoverished thought inferred from speech, common in schizophrenia. Brief concrete replies are given to questions (poverty of speech) or a normal amount of speech is produced but conveys little information (poverty of content) due to repetition, being overly concrete or being overly abstract.

Amygdala. An almond-shaped brain structure within the limbic system, located in the medial temporal lobes, that subserves the processing of emotional information and memories. Abnormalities of the amygdala occur in many psychological disorders.

Anaclitic depression. In Blatt's psychoanalytic theory, anaclitic (or dependent) depression is characterized by feelings of abandonment in response to interpersonal loss. It is contrasted with introjective (or self-critical) depression which is characterized by self-criticism in response to perceived failure.

Anakastic personality disorder. See **Obsessive compulsive personality disorder**.

Anomie. A state characterized by normlessness where the social structures provided by family, religion and other institutions become destabilized and leave members of a community feeling alienated. Some disadvantaged communities in which delinquency, drug abuse and suicide occur are characterized by anomie.

Anorexia nervosa. An eating disorder characterized by over-evaluation of weight and shape and their control, and a severe weight loss.

Antisocial personality disorder. A personality disorder characterized by a pervasive disregard for the rights of others and consistent violation of these rights. Has also been referred to as psychopathy, sociopathy and dissocial personality disorder.

APA practice guidelines. Evidence-based clinical practice guidelines produced by the American Psychiatric Association, which is the US professional association for psychiatrists. (www.psychiatryonline.org)

APA. American Psychological Association (www.apa.org); American Psychiatric Association (www.psych.org). American Psychoanalytical Association (www.apsa.org).

APS. Australian Psychological Society (www.psychology.org.au); Australian Psychoanalytical Society (www.psychoanalysis.asn.au).

ASEBA. Achenbach System of Empirically Based Assessment. Parent, teacher and self-report rating scales widely used for assessing internalizing and externalizing behaviour problems in children and adolescents.

Assertive community treatment. An integrated community mental health service delivery model in which hard-to-reach people with psychosis receive intensive, continuous individualized treatment, rehabilitation and support services from community-based multidisciplinary teams.

Assessment. Procedures such as interviewing, psychological testing and behavioural observation used to evaluate individuals with psychological problems.

Assistant Psychologists Ireland Google groups. A forum for discussing issues relevant to getting onto clinical psychology training programmes in Ireland (ap_ireland@googlegroups.com).

AVE (abstinence violation effect). The cognitive process that leads to the experience of loss of control and relapse during recovery from drug problems when a minor slip occurs.

Avoidant personality disorder. A personality disorder characterized by a pervasive pattern of social inhibition and shyness beginning in adolescence or early adulthood.

Avolition. A lack of goal-directed activity common in schizophrenia.

BABCP. British Association for Behavioural & Cognitive Psychotherapies. (www.babcp.com)

Basal ganglia. A subcortical region of the brain which subserves the initiation, control and modulation of voluntary movement. Damage to the basal ganglia may lead to excessive involuntary movement or to a slowing of voluntary movement. Parkinson's disease, Sydenham's chorea and Huntington's chorea all involve damage to the basal ganglia. Dysfunction of the basal ganglia underpins obsessive compulsive disorder and Tourette's syndrome.

BDI-II. Beck Depression Inventory, second edition, a self-report instrument for assessing depression.

Behaviourally inhibited temperament. A temperamental trait involving the tendency to become nervous and withdraw from unfamiliar stimuli and situations.

Biological model. A conceptual framework which assumes that psychological problems are symptoms of 'mental illnesses' each of which has a discrete neurobiological cause, a unique course and prognosis, and for which a specific physical treatment or psychotropic medication will be found. Also referred to as the biomedical, neurobiological, organic, medical or disease model.

Biomedical model. See **Biological model**.

Bipolar disorder. A recurrent mood disorder characterized by episodes of mania and depression, previously known as manic-depression.

BMI. Body mass index. BMI = $W/H2$, where W = weight in kilograms and H = height in metres. The normal range for BMI is 18.5–24.9.

Borderline personality disorder. A personality disorder characterized by fear of abandonment, impulsivity and a pattern of pervasive instability in interpersonal relationships, self-image and mood, often leading to self-harm.

BPRS. Brief Psychiatric Rating Scale, a scale for monitoring psychotic symptom severity.

BPS. British Psychoanalytical Society (www.psychoanalysis.org.uk); British Psychological Society (www.bps.org.uk).

BSFT. Brief strategic family therapy, an evidence-based family therapy intervention for adolescent conduct and drug problems.

Bulimia nervosa. An eating disorder characterized by over-evaluation of weight and shape and their control, and a cycle of bingeing in response to stressful events and compensatory purging.

BYI-II. Beck Youth Inventories, second edition, self-report instruments for assessing depression, anxiety, anger, disruptive behaviour and self-esteem in children and adolescents.

CAN. Camberwell Assessment of Need, a scale for assessing mental health service users' needs in areas such as mental and physical health, drug use, social relationships, accommodation, transport, budgeting, and activities of daily living.

Case–control study. A study design in which a group of diagnostically homogeneous cases about which the researcher is trying to find out more information is compared to another group of patients with a known condition or with a normal control group.

Catatonic behaviour. Behaviour that occurs in some cases of schizophrenia, characterized by a marked reduction or increase in motor activity.

Catatonic schizophrenia. A form of schizophrenia in which catatonic behaviour is the predominant symptom.

CBCL. Child Behaviour Checklist, for screening children for psychological problems. There are parent, teacher and child self-report versions. Also called ASEBA – Achenbach's System for Empirically Based Assessment.

CBT. Cognitive-behaviour therapy, a form of psychotherapy that involves helping people improve their mood and adjustment by directly changing their behaviour and thinking patterns using principles of learning theory and cognitive psychology.

CDRS. Children's Depression Rating Scale, for rating severity of depressive symptoms in children and adolescents.

CFI. Camberwell Family Interview, a structured interview for assessing expressed emotion which includes criticism, hostility and emotional over-involvement.

Classical conditioning. An associative learning process that occurs when two stimuli are regularly paired so that the response originally given to the second stimulus comes to be given to the first.

Clearing House for Postgraduate Courses in Clinical Psychology. A web-based system for applying for UK courses. (www.leeds.ac.uk/chpccp)

Cognitive rehabilitation. A set of cognitive drills that helps patients ameliorate or compensate for cognitive deficits due to neurological conditions.

Common factors. Factors common to many forms of psychotherapy that account for their similar levels of effectiveness.

Comorbid. Having more than one diagnosed psychological disorder or problem at a time.

Compulsions. Repetitive, ritualistic, stereotyped behaviours that people with OCD feel compelled to perform to regulate anxiety caused by obsessions.

Conduct disorder. A pervasive and persistent pattern of antisocial behaviour that extends beyond the family to the school and community and involves serious violations of rules, characterized by defiance of authority, aggression, destructiveness, deceitfulness and cruelty.

Conversion hysteria. A condition characterized by deficits in sensory or motor functioning in the absence of an organic illness, also referred to as conversion disorder.

Counselling psychology. An applied psychology specialism that places a strong emphasis on psychotherapeutic processes in effecting change in people facing a range of normal life challenges as well as psychological disorders.

Countertransference. Therapists' emotional responses to clients.

CPA. Canadian Psychological Association. (www.cpa.ca)

CRS. Conners Rating Scales: parent, teacher and self-report rating scales widely used for assessing the severity of ADHD symptoms and other childhood problems.

Cue exposure treatment. A treatment, based on the classical conditioning model of addiction, in which recovering drug addicts are exposed to cues that elicit craving and concurrently use a variety of coping strategies to tolerate their discomfort and avoid drug-taking.

Cyclothymia. A persistent bipolar disorder characterized by continuous mood swings from elation to sadness.

DAWBA. Development and Well-Being Assessment, a structured interview and set of self-report instruments (the Strengths and Difficulties Scales) for diagnosing childhood psychological disorders.

Defence mechanism. An unconscious psychological strategy for regulating anxiety about unacceptable emotions or impulses such as sex or aggression.

Delusions. Unfounded and culturally alien beliefs.

Dependent personality disorder. A personality disorder characterized by a pervasive pattern of submissiveness and dependence on other people.

Depersonalization. A perceptual distortion in which there is a sense of being detached from the self or observing the self.

Derailment. A speech pattern common in schizophrenia marked by constant jumping from one topic to another, with only very loose associations between topics and little logic to what is said, reflecting an underlying thought disorder.

Derealization. A perceptual distortion in which there is sense of unreality, or being in a dream.

Dialectical behaviour therapy. An evidence-based cognitive-behavioural treatment for borderline personality disorder.

Diathesis–stress theory. A model in which a psychological disorder is proposed to occur when a genetically vulnerable person is exposed to stress.

DID. Dissociative identity disorder, a condition in which two or more distinct personalities exist within the individual, also known as multiple personality disorder.

Disease model. See **Biological model**.

Dissociation. An abnormality of perception, memory or identity that occurs in response to trauma and may include derealization (seeing the world as dream-like), depersonalization (viewing the self from an external perspective) and inability to recall important personal information.

Dizygotic twins. Fraternal twins that come from two separate ova.

Dodo bird verdict. The hypothesis that different forms of psychotherapy have similar effects: refers to a quotation from Lewis Carroll's *Alice in Wonderland* – At last the Dodo said '*Everybody* has won, and *all* must have prizes'.

Dopamine. A neurotransmitter involved in the reward system or mesolimbic dopamine pathway.

DSM-IV-TR. American Psychiatric Association's (2000) *Diagnostic and Statistical Manual of Mental Disorders,* fourth edition, text revision.

Dual diagnosis. A term used to describe cases in which there is a diagnosis of a substance use disorder and another disorder, e.g. an anxiety, mood or psychotic disorder.

Dysthymia. A non-episodic chronic mood disorder characterized by depressive symptomatology.

ECT. Electroconvulsive therapy, an intervention for severe treatment-resistant depression in which seizures are induced by briefly passing an electric current through the brain via electrodes applied to the scalp. ECT is conducted under general anaesthetic and muscle relaxants are used to prevent body spasms.

EDE. Eating Disorder Examination, a detailed interview for assessing anorexia, bulimia and other eating disorders.

EDI. Eating Disorder Inventory, a comprehensive self-report psychological assessment instrument for evaluating eating pathology and related psychological traits such as perfectionism and ineffectiveness.

Educational psychology. An applied psychology specialism concerned with learning problems, and social and emotional problems encountered by young people in educational settings.

EEG. Electroencephalogram, a procedure for assessing electrical activity within the brain. Electrodes placed on the scalp are attached by wires to a machine that records electrical impulses from the brain and displays these as 'brain waves' on a paper printout or a computer screen. Used for assessing seizures, sleep stages and as biofeedback for ADHD.

EFPA. European Foundation for Psychologists and Analysts. (www.efpa.be)

EFTA. European Family Therapy Association. (www.europeanfamilytherapy.eu)

Ego strength. The capacity to tolerate conflict and distress, while showing flexibility and persistence in pursuing valued goals.

Epidemiology. The study of the distribution of disorders and their correlates within populations.

Evidence-based practice. The judicious and compassionate use of the best available scientific evidence to make decisions about patient or client care.

Executive function. Cognitive processes involved in decision making, following through on plans and troubleshooting difficulties without being distracted by irrelevant stimuli or habitual reactions.

Expressed emotion. An attitude of criticism, hostility or emotional over-involvement expressed by family members of mental health service users, assessed with the Camberwell Family Interview, and associated with relapse in mood, and psychotic and other disorders.

Family systems model. A model which assumes that psychological problems are maintained by patterns of interaction and belief systems within the family and the wider social system of the client, and may be resolved by disrupting these processes in family therapy.

Family therapy. A psychosocial intervention where the family is the unit of treatment.

FFT. Functional family therapy, an evidence-based family therapy intervention for adolescent conduct and drug problems.

Five-factor model of personality traits. A theory which proposes that the 'Big 5' personality traits offer the most parsimonious description of personality. The Big 5 are neuroticism, extraversion, openness to experience, conscientiousness and agreeableness.

Flooding. A behavioural treatment for phobias in which clients are exposed for a prolonged period to their most anxiety-provoking stimuli until anxiety responses are extinguished; also called implosion.

Forensic psychology. An applied psychology specialism concerned with the application of psychology to criminal investigation and the assessment and treatment of offending behaviour.

FTAI. Family Therapy Association of Ireland. (www.familytherapyireland.com)

GAF. Global Assessment of Functioning scale, a single 100-point scale for rating the functioning of adult mental health service users.

GAIN. Global Appraisal of Individual Needs, a comprehensive structured interview for assessing drug use severity and personal, family and school-related adjustment problems in adolescents.

Gateway drugs. Nicotine, alcohol and cannabis, which may lead to the use of other drugs such as cocaine and heroin.

Generalized anxiety disorder. Ongoing apprehension that misfortunes of various sorts will occur and anxiety that this worrying process is uncontrollable.

GRE. Graduate Record Examination. (www.ets.org/gre).

Hallucination. Experiencing a sensation in the absence of an external stimulus.

Harm-avoidance. Interventions such as needle exchanges and safe injection sites that reduce the harm caused by drug misuse.

HCR-20. Historical, Clinical, Risk Management–20, a rating scale for assessing risk of violence.

Health psychology. An applied psychology specialism concerned with the application of psychology to address physical health problems.

Hebephrenic schizophrenia. A form of schizophrenia characterized by inappropriate or flat affect and disorganization of behaviour and speech.

Histrionic personality disorder. A condition characterized by pervasive attention-seeking behaviour including inappropriately seductive behaviour and shallow or exaggerated emotions.

HPA axis. Hypothalamic–pituitary–adrenal axis, a major part of the neuro-endocrine system involving the hypothalamus, the pituitary gland located below the hypothalamus, and the adrenal glands (located on top of the kidneys), which controls stress reactions and other processes including the immune system, sexuality and digestion, and is dysregulated in anxiety and mood disorders.

HRS. Hamilton Rating Scale, for rating severity of depressive symptoms in adults.

HSE. Health Service Executive (www.hse.ie), the Irish public health service.

Hull University. The only university in the UK or Ireland that offers an integrated 6-year BSc/DClinPsych (www2.hull.ac.uk).

Humanistic psychotherapy. An overarching term for approaches to explaining psychological problems using the concepts of self-actualization, the self, the ideal self and the organism, and treating such problems with non-directive client-centred therapy.

IAPT. Improving Access to Psychological Therapies (www.iapt.nhs.uk) is an NHS programme to improve access to evidence-based talking therapies through an expansion of the psychological therapy workforce and services.

ICD-10. The World Health Organization's (1992) *International Classification of Diseases – Tenth Edition*. Psychological problems are classified in Chapter 5.

ICP. Irish Council of Psychotherapy. (www.psychotherapy-ireland.com)

Ideas of reference. Incorrect interpretation of events as referring directly to oneself.

Implosion. A behavioural treatment for phobias in which clients are exposed for a prolonged period to their most anxiety-provoking stimuli until anxiety responses are extinguished; also called flooding.

Introjective depression. In Blatt's psychoanalytic theory introjective (or self-critical) depression is characterized by self-criticism in response to perceived failure. It is contrasted with anaclitic (or dependent) depression, which is characterized by feelings of abandonment in response to interpersonal loss.

IPA. International Psychoanalytical Association. (www.ipa.org.uk)

IPDE. International Personality Disorder Examination, a structured interview for the diagnosis of personality disorders.

IPT. Interpersonal therapy, an evidence-based treatment for depression and bulimia in which the focus is on resolving interpersonal difficulties, notably grief, role disputes, role transitions, and interpersonal deficits, which maintain the presenting problem.

IUPsyS. International Union of Psychological Science. (www.iupsys.org)

Learning theory. A theoretical framework which posits that behaviour is learned through the processes of operant and classical conditioning.

Limbic system. A complex of brain structures that subserves the experience and expression of emotions, which includes the amygdala, hippocampus, insula and parts of the anterior cingulated cortex

Longitudinal study. A study design in which a group of cases is assessed on a number of occasions to discover the course of their development over time.

Major depression. A unipolar recurrent episodic mood disorder involving low mood, selective attention to negative features of the environment, a pessimistic belief system, self-defeating behaviour patterns, particularly within intimate relationships, and a disturbance of sleep and appetite.

MAOI. Monoamine oxidase inhibitors, a type of antidepressant, such as phenelzine/Nardil which prevents the enzyme monoamine oxidase from breaking down neurotransmitters in the synaptic cleft and leads to an increase in neurotransmitter levels.

MCMI-III. Millon Clinical Multiaxial Inventory–III, a self-report inventory for assessing personality disorders.

MDFT. Multidimensional family therapy, an evidence-based family therapy intervention for adolescent drug problems.

Medical cost offset. The extent to which clients who avail of psychotherapy services use fewer medical services and so incur reduced medical costs.

Medical model. See **Biological model**.

Mentalization-based treatment. An evidence-based psychodynamic treatment that aims to improve adjustment in borderline personality disorder by enhancing mentalization skills.

Mentalization. The capacity to understand mental states, motives and intentions of the self and others, and to conceptualize these states as being separate from behaviour.

Mesolimbic dopamine pathway. The neurobiological system that underpins reward or reinforcement, involving the ventral tegmental area, the nucleus accumbens and the prefrontal cortex.

Meta-analysis. A systematic, quantitative approach to reviewing evidence from multiple studies in which effect sizes are calculated for each study and then averaged across all studies.

Methadone maintenance. An intervention for opioid dependency involving the prescription of a daily dose of methadone as a substitute for street opioids such as heroin.

Minnesota Model. An approach to treating drug problems that integrates the Narcotics Anonymous/Alcoholics Anonymous 12-step approach with group and family therapy.

MMPI-2. Minnesota Multiphasic Personality Inventory–2, a self-report inventory for assessing personality functioning and psychopathology.

Monozygotic twins. Identical twins that come from a single ovum.

Motivational interviewing. A non-directive intervention that motivates people with drug problems to take steps towards reducing drug use, also called motivational enhancement therapy.

MST. Multisystemic therapy, a comprehensive evidence-based treatment approach to treating conduct disorder in which family therapy is the core intervention but which also involves individual intervention and interventions with the young person's wider social network.

Multidisciplinary team. A team of health professionals from a variety of disciplines such as psychology, medicine and social work.

Multimodal programme. In the mental health field, a programme usually offered by multidisciplinary teams that includes a number of different types of intervention; for example, psychotherapy and psychotropic medication.

Multiple personality disorder. A condition in which two or more distinct personalities exist within the individual, with only one being evident at a time; also known as dissociative identity disorder.

NA. Narcotics Anonymous, a self-help organization for drug addicts involving a 12-step recovery programme like that used in Alcoholics Anonymous.

Narcissistic personality disorder. A personality disorder characterized by a pervasive pattern of grandiosity, a need for admiration, and a lack of empathy for others.

Negative symptoms. Collective term for flattening of affect, poverty of speech and lack of goal-directed behaviour common in schizophrenia.

NEO-PI-R. Revised NEO Personality Inventory, a self-report inventory for assessing the Big 5 personality traits and 30 related facets.

Neologisms. Made-up words that only have meaning for the individual, common in schizophrenia.

Neuroadaptation. A neurobiological process that accompanies drug addiction and accounts for the phenomena of tolerance, dependence, withdrawal, and the high rate of relapse among recovered addicts.

Neurobiological model. See **Biological model**.

Neurodevelopmental hypothesis. The view that prenatal and perinatal adversities interact with a genetic vulnerability to psychosis to give rise to atypical neuroanatomical development initially in infancy, and later in adolescence, to cause schizophrenia.

Neuropsychology. A branch of applied psychology concerned with the assessment and rehabilitation of people with neurological disorders.

Neuroticism. A personality trait characterized by the tendency to experience negative affect including anxiety, depression and hostility.

Neurotransmitters. Chemicals released into synapses between neurons which permit messages to be transmitted from one neuron to the next. Dysregulations of neurotransmitters may occur in certain conditions. For example, there is dysregulation of the dopamine system in schizophrenia, and the serotonin system in depression.

NHS. National Health Service (www.nhs.uk): the UK public health service.

NICE Guidelines. Evidence-based guidelines for the treatment of mental and physical health problems produced by the National Institute for Clinical Excellence. (http://guidance.nice.org.uk/topic/mentalhealthbehavioural)

NUIG. National University of Ireland Galway (www.nuigalway.ie), which runs one of the five clinical psychology training programmes in Ireland.

NZPS. New Zealand Psychological Society. (www.psychology.org.nz)

Obsessions. Involuntary, recurrent, persistent and stereotyped thoughts, images or impulses that concern issues such as danger, violence and obscenity.

Obsessive compulsive personality disorder. A personality disorder characterized by a pervasive pattern of preoccupation with orderliness, perfectionism, ethics, interpersonal control, and fiscal economy, also referred to as anakastic personality disorder.

OCD. Obsessive compulsive disorder, a condition characterized by distressing obsessions on one hand and compulsive rituals which reduce the anxiety associated with the obsessions on the other.

Operant conditioning. A learning process in which responses are strengthened by reinforcement.

Oppositional defiant disorder. A disorder of conduct confined to the home and characterized by difficulties with rule-following.

Organic model. See **Biological model**.

Panic disorder. A condition in which there are recurrent unexpected panic attacks and an ongoing fear of further attacks, often accompanied by agoraphobia.

PANSS. Positive and Negative Symptom Scale, a scale for monitoring psychotic symptom severity.

Paranoid personality disorder. A personality disorder characterized by a pervasive distrust of others.

Paranoid schizophrenia. A form of schizophrenia in which paranoid delusions are the predominant feature.

PCL-R. The Psychopathy Checklist, a rating scale for assessing antisocial personality disorder and risk of violence.

PEI. Personal Experience Inventory, a comprehensive questionnaire for assessing drug use severity and personal, family and school-related adjustment problems.

Personality disorder. Conditions characterized by pervasive, enduring, inflexible patterns of behaviour and experience that deviate markedly from cultural expectations and that lead to significant personal distress or significant impairment in social functioning.

PESQ. Personal Experience Screening Questionnaire, a brief screening instrument for adolescent drug problems.

Phobia. An anxiety disorder characterized by intense fear which occurs when faced with an object, event or situation from a clearly defined class of stimuli that is out of proportion to the danger posed by the stimulus.

Positive symptoms. Collective term for delusions and hallucinations common in schizophrenia.

PRIME theory. PRIME represents plans, responses, impulses and inhibitory forces (felt as urges), motives (felt as wants or needs), and evaluative beliefs – the five components of the motivational system in the PRIME or synthetic theory of motivation and addiction.

Prodromal phase. The period before the onset of a disorder during which individuals may show subclinical symptoms.

PsSI. Psychological Society of Ireland (www.psihq.ie)

Psychiatry. A medical specialty concerned with the assessment and treatment of psychological disorders using both physical and psychological treatments.

Psychoanalytic model. A conceptual framework which assumes that psychological problems are symptoms of underlying unconscious conflict, which may be treated with psychoanalytically informed interventions derived from Sigmund Freud's psychoanalysis, also referred to as the psychodynamic model.

Psychological-mindedness. The capacity to understand problems in intrapsychic terms, rather than inaccurately explaining them in terms of external or physical factors.

Psychotherapy. A contractual process in which trained professionals with expert knowledge of their discipline interact with clients to help them resolve psychological problems.

Psyclick. A website giving information about getting onto UK clinical psychology training programmes (www.psyclick.org.uk)

PTSD. Posttraumatic stress disorder, an anxiety disorder which occurs in response to a catastrophic trauma perceived to be potentially life-threatening, characterized by recurrent intrusive memories of the trauma that lead to intense anxiety coupled with attempts to avoid this by suppressing the memories and avoiding situations that remind the individual of the trauma.

QUB. Queen's University Belfast (www.qub.ac.uk), which runs one of the five clinical psychology training programmes in Ireland.

RANZCP. The Royal Australian & New Zealand College of Psychiatry (www.ranzcp.org)

RAS. Recovery Assessment Scale: assesses hope, meaning of life, quality of life, symptoms and empowerment.

RCPsych. Royal College of Psychiatrists (www.rcpsych.ac.uk)

RCT. Randomized controlled trial: an experimental design for evaluating the effectiveness of a treatment programme, in which cases are randomly assigned to treatment and control groups and evaluated with pre-tests and post-tests.

Recovery model. A rehabilitation model that privileges the concepts of optimism, well-being, personal strengths, supportive relationships, collaboration, personal choice, adaptive coping, developing a meaningful life, civil rights, empowerment and inclusion.

Reward system. The mesolimbic dopamine pathway, which involves the ventral tegmental area, the nucleus accumbens and the prefrontal cortex, and is activated by drug use and reinforcement.

Schizoid personality disorder. A personality disorder characterized by a pervasive pattern of detachment from social relationships.

Schizophrenia. A set of conditions characterized by positive symptoms (delusions and hallucinations), negative symptoms (lack of goal-directed activity, flattening of affect, poverty of speech) and disorganized speech (frequent incoherence and derailment or loosening of associations).

Schizotypal personality disorder. A personality disorder characterized by unusual perceptual experiences, eccentric thoughts and speech, inappropriate or constricted affect, peculiar or eccentric behaviour, and a lack of close relationships.

Schizotypy. A personality structure or set of traits conferring vulnerability to schizophrenia, characterized primarily by disorganized thinking similar to (though less extreme than) that shown in schizophrenia.

SCID-I. Structured Clinical Interview for DSM-IV Axis I Disorders.

SCID-II. Structured Clinical Interview for DSM-IV Personality Disorders.

SDQ. Strengths and Difficulties Questionnaire: brief parent, teacher and self-report rating scales widely used in the UK for assessing emotional and behaviour problems in children and adolescents.

Seasonal affective disorder. A unipolar mood disorder in which episodes of depression occur during the winter months.

Self-medication. The use of street drugs to alleviate negative affective states.

Separation anxiety disorder. An anxiety disorder that occurs most commonly in children, characterized by a recurrent and persistent fear when separation from parents, or other important attachment figures, is anticipated. Headaches, stomach aches and school refusal may occur.

Serotonin. 5-Hydroxytryptamine or 5-HT, a neurotransmitter involved in the regulation of mood and appetite. Dysregulation of the serotonin system in the brain subserves depression and eating disorders.

SNAP-2. Schedule for Nonadaptive and Adaptive Personality–II, a self-report inventory for assessing personality disorders.

Sociotropy. In Beck's cognitive theory of depression, sociotropy is a depressive schema characterized by interpersonal dependency and is contrasted with the autonomy schema, which is characterized by perfectionism and self-criticism.

SSRIs. Selective serotonin reuptake inhibitors (e.g., fluoxetine/Prozac), a type of antidepressant that prevents serotonin from being reabsorbed into the presynaptic membrane and so increases the efficiency of this neurotransmitter system. Used for the treatment of depression, anxiety and eating disorders.

Stepped care. A service delivery model in which more intensive interventions are preceded by less intensive interventions.

Systematic desensitization. A behavioural treatment for phobias in which a client in a deeply relaxed state is exposed to increasingly anxiety-provoking stimuli, with progression to the next stimulus occurring once habituation to the previous one has occurred.

Systemic model. An overarching term for approaches to explaining psychological problems using ideas from general systems theory and treating such problems with couples and family therapy.

TCAs. Tricyclic antidepressants (e.g., imipramine/Tofranil), a type of antidepressant that increases efficiency neurotransmitter systems, which are dysregulated in depression. They were developed and widely used before the advent of SSRIs.

TCD. Trinity College Dublin (www.tcd.ie), which runs one of the five clinical psychology training programmes in Ireland.

Therapeutic community. Residential treatment programme in which a democratic, participative approach to decision-making is used to facilitate recovery of people with addictions and chronic, complex mental health problems.

Thought broadcasting. The feeling that one's thoughts are known by others.

Thought disorder. Confused thinking common in schizophrenia, characterized by disorganized and illogical speech.

Thought echo. A form of auditory hallucination in which thoughts are heard spoken aloud, as they are being thought or a moment or two afterwards.

Thought insertion. The feeling that thoughts in one's mind are not one's own, 'explained' by the delusion that they have been inserted by an outside agency.

Thought withdrawal. The feeling that thoughts are missing from one's mind, 'explained' by the delusion that they have been withdrawn by an outside agency.

Token economy. A therapeutic system used in residential or inpatient settings, based on learning theory, in which tokens are used as secondary reinforcers to encourage patients to engage in positive behaviours and to use adaptive skills. Tokens earned for completing positive behaviours or using adaptive skills may be exchanged for privileges or valued items.

Transference-focused psychotherapy. An evidence-based psychodynamic treatment for borderline personality disorder.

Transference. The unconscious repetition in significant adult relationships of relationship patterns that occurred in childhood with parents. People unconsciously transfer feelings that they had towards their parents onto their partners, friends, colleagues and psychotherapists. In psychoanalytic practice, interpreting transference is a central aspect of therapy.

Transtheoretical stages of change model. An integrative model, widely influential in the field of drug use and health behaviour, which proposes that therapeutic change involves movement through the stages of pre-contemplation, contemplation, preparation, action and maintenance, and that interventions must be designed to suit the client's stage of change.

UCD. University College Dublin (www.ucd.ie), which runs one of the five clinical psychology training programmes in Ireland.

UKCP. UK Council for Psychotherapy (www.psychotherapy.org.uk)

UL. University of Limerick (www.ul.ie), which runs one of the five clinical psychology training programmes in Ireland.

Unconscious. In psychoanalytic theory, a set of processes, of which the individual is unaware, that motivate behaviour.

WIAT. Wechsler Individual Achievement Test, a widely used set of attainment tests for school-aged children. It is now in its third revision. It is designed to be interpreted in conjunction with the WISC.

Wilderness/adventure therapy. A psychotherapeutic treatment for drug problems and antisocial behaviour where adolescents are challenged to take risks and master skills by doing outdoor activities in a 'wilderness' location away form their home community.

WISC. Wechsler Intelligence Scale for Children, the most widely used intelligence test for school-aged children in the world. It is now in its fourth revision. It is a downward extension of the WAIS.

WPPSI. Wechsler Preschool and Primary Scale of Intelligence, a widely used intelligence test for preschoolers. It is now in its third revision. It is a downward extension of the WISC.

References

Abraham, K. (1924). The influence of oral eroticism on character formation. In C. Bryan & A. Strachey (Ed. & trans.), *Selected papers on psychoanalysis* (pp. 393–406). London: Hogarth Press.

Abramson, L., Seligman, M., & Teasdale, J. (1978). Learned helplessness in humans: Critique and reformulation. *Journal of Abnormal Psychology*, 87, 49–74.

Achenbach, T. M. (2009). *ASEBA: Development, findings, theory, and applications*. Burlington, VT: University of Vermont Research Centre for Children, Youth and Families.

Achenbach, T. M., & Rescorla, L. A. (2000). *Manual for ASEBA preschool forms & profiles*. Burlington, VT: University of Vermont, Research Centre for Children, Youth, & Families.

Achenbach, T. M., & Rescorla, L. A. (2001). *Manual for ASEBA school-age forms & profiles*. Burlington, VT: University of Vermont, Research Centre for Children, Youth, & Families.

Addis, M. (2002). Methods for disseminating research products and increasing evidence-based practice: Promises, obstacles, and future directions. *Clinical Psychology: Science and Practice*, 9, 367–378.

Afifi, T. O., Asmundson, G. H., Taylor, S., & Jang, K. L. (2010). The role of genes and environment on trauma exposure and posttraumatic stress disorder symptoms: A review of twin studies. *Clinical Psychology Review*, 30, 101–112.

Agras, W. (2010). *The Oxford handbook of eating disorders*. New York: Oxford University Press.

Aichorn, A. (1935). *Wayward youth*. New York: Viking Press.

Aldao, A., Nolen-Hoeksema, S., & Schweizer, S. (2010). Emotion-regulation strategies across psychopathology: A meta-analytic review. *Clinical Psychology Review*, 30, 217–237.

Allen, J., Fonagy, P., & Bateman, A. (2008). *Mentalizing in clinical practice*. Washington, DC: American Psychiatric Press.

Alwin, N., Blackburn, R., Davidson, K., Hilton, M., Logan, C., & Shine, J. (2006). *Understanding personality disorder: A report by the British Psychological Society*. Leicester, UK: British Psychological Society.

American Academy of Child and Adolescent Psychiatry (2001). Practice parameter for the assessment and treatment of children and adolescents with suicidal behaviour. *Journal of the American Academy of Child and Adolescent Psychiatry*, 40 (7 Supplement), 24S–51S.

American Academy of Child and Adolescent Psychiatry (2004). Practice parameters for use of electroconvulsive therapy with adolescents. *Journal of the American Academy of Child and Adolescent Psychiatry*, 43(12), 1521–1539.

American Academy of Child and Adolescent Psychiatry (2005). Practice parameters for the assessment and treatment of children and adolescents with substance use disorders. *American Academy of Child and Adolescent Psychiatry*, 44(6), 609–621.

American Academy of Child and Adolescent Psychiatry (2007a). Practice parameters for the assessment and treatment of children, adolescents, and adults with attention-deficit/hyperactivity disorder. *Journal of the American Academy of Child and Adolescent Psychiatry*, 46, 894–921.

American Academy of Child and Adolescent Psychiatry (2007b). Practice parameters for the assessment and treatment of children and adolescents with oppositional defiant disorder. *Journal of the American Academy of Child and Adolescent Psychiatry*, 46, 126–141.

American Academy of Child and Adolescent Psychiatry (2007c). Practice parameters for the assessment and treatment of children and adolescents with anxiety disorders. *Journal of the American Academy of Child and Adolescent Psychiatry*, 36, 267–283.

American Academy of Child and Adolescent Psychiatry (2007d). Practice parameters for the assessment and treatment of children and adolescents with depressive disorders. *Journal of the American Academy of Child and Adolescent Psychiatry*, 46, 1503–1526.

American Academy of Child and Adolescent Psychiatry (2009). Practice parameters on the use of psychotropic medication in children and adolescents. *Journal of the American Academy of Child & Adolescent Psychiatry*, 48, 961–973.

American Academy of Child and Adolescent Psychiatry (2010). Practice parameters for the assessment and treatment of children and adolescents with posttraumatic stress disorder. *Journal of the American Academy of Child and Adolescent Psychiatry*, 49, 414–430.

American Academy of Paediatrics (2001). Clinical practice guideline: Treatment of the school-aged child with attention-deficit/hyperactivity disorder. *Paediatrics*, 108(4), 1033–1104.

American Psychiatric Association (2000). *Diagnostic and Statistical Manual of the Mental Disorders* (fourth edition, text revision, DSM-IV-TR). Washington, DC: APA.

American Psychiatric Association (2001a). *Task force report of the American Psychiatric Association on the practice of electroconvulsive therapy: Recommendations for treatment, training, and privileging* (second edition). Washington, DC: American Psychiatric Press.

American Psychiatric Association (2001b). *American Psychiatric Association practice guideline for the treatment of patients with borderline personality disorder* (second edition). Washington, DC: American Psychiatric Association.

American Psychiatric Association (2003). *American Psychiatric Association practice guideline for the assessment and treatment of suicidal behaviour*. Washington, DC: American Psychiatric Association.

American Psychiatric Association (2004a). *American Psychiatric Association practice guideline for the treatment of patients with acute stress disorder and posttraumatic stress disorder*. Washington, DC: American Psychiatric Association.

American Psychiatric Association (2004b). *American Psychiatric Association practice guideline for the treatment of patients with schizophrenia* (second edition). Washington, DC: American Psychiatric Association.

American Psychiatric Association (2006). *American Psychiatric Association practice guidelines for the treatment of eating disorders* (third revision). Washington, DC: APA.

American Psychiatric Association (2007). *American Psychiatric Association practice guideline for the treatment of patients with obsessive-compulsive disorder*. Washington, DC: American Psychiatric Association.

American Psychiatric Association (2009). *American Psychiatric Association practice guideline for the treatment of patients with panic disorder* (second edition). Washington, DC: APA.

American Psychiatric Association (2010). *American Psychiatric Association practice guideline for the treatment of patients with major depressive disorder* (third edition). Washington, DC: American Psychiatric Association.

American Psychological Association (2007). *Getting in: A step-by-step plan for gaining admission to graduate school in psychology* (second edition). Washington, DC: American Psychological Association.

American Psychological Association Presidential Task Force on Evidence Based Practice (2006). Evidence-based practice in psychology. *American Psychologist*, 61, 271–285.

Anastopoulos, A., Barkley, R., & Shelton, T. (2005). Family based treatment: Psychosocial intervention for children and adolescents with attention deficit hyperactivity disorder. In E. Hibbs & P. Jensen (eds.), *Psychosocial treatments for child and adolescent disorders. Empirically based strategies for clinical practice* (second edition, pp. 327–350). Washington, DC: APA.

Anderson, D. A., & Murray, A. D. (2010). Psychological assessment of the eating disorders. In W. S. Agras (Ed.), *The Oxford handbook of eating disorders* (pp. 249–258). New York: Oxford University Press.

Anderson, H. (2003). *Postmodern social construction therapies*. In T. Sexton, G. Weeks, & M. Robbins (Eds.), *Handbook of family therapy: The science and practice of working with families and couples* (pp. 125–146). New York: Brunner-Routledge.

Andrews, G., Cuijpers, P., Craske, M. G., McEvoy, P., & Titov, N. (2010). Computer therapy for the anxiety and depressive disorders is effective, acceptable and practical health care: A meta-analysis. *PLoS ONE*, 5(10), e13196.

Andrews, J. A., & Hops, H. (2010). The influence of peers on substance use. In L. Scheier (Ed.), *Handbook of drug use aetiology: Theory, methods, and empirical findings* (pp. 403–420). Washington, DC: American Psychological Association.

Angst, J. (2009). Course and prognosis of mood disorders. In M. Gelder et al. (Eds.), *New Oxford textbook of psychiatry* (second edition, Vol. 1, pp. 665–669). Oxford: Oxford University Press.

Antony, M., & Stein, M. (2009a). *Oxford handbook of anxiety and related disorders*. New York: Oxford University Press.

Antony, M., & Stein, M. (2009b). Future directions in anxiety disorders research. In M. M. Antony & M. B. Stein (Eds.), *Oxford handbook of anxiety and related disorders* (pp. 667–677). New York: Oxford University Press.

Aouizerate, B., Rotge, J.-Y., & Martin-Guehl, C. (2006). A systematic review of psychosurgical treatments for obsessive-compulsive disorder: Does deep brain stimulation represent the future trend in psychosurgery? *Clinical Neuropsychiatry*, 3, 391–403.

Arnett, J. J. (2005). The developmental context of substance use in emerging adulthood. *Journal of Drug Issues*, 35, 235–254.

Baer, R. (2003). Mindfulness training as a clinical intervention: A conceptual and empirical review. *Clinical Psychology Science and Practice*, 10, 125–143.

Bakermans-Kranenburg, M. J., & van IJzendoorn, M. H. (2009). The first 10,000 Adult Attachment Interviews: Distributions of adult attachment representations in non-clinical and clinical groups. *Attachment and Human Development*, 11, 223–263.

Ballenger, J. (2009). Panic disorder and agoraphobia. In M. Gelder et al. (Eds.), *New Oxford textbook of psychiatry* (second edition, Vol. 1, pp. 750–765). Oxford: Oxford University Press.

Bandura, A., & Walters, R. (1959). *Adolescent aggression.* New York: Ronald Press.

Barkley, R. (2003). Attention deficit hyperactivity disorder. In E. Mash & R. Barkley (Eds.), *Child psychopathology* (second edition, pp. 75–143). New York: Guilford.

Barkley, R. (2005). *Attention deficit hyperactivity disorder: A handbook for diagnosis and treatment* (third edition). New York: Guilford.

Barkley, R., Guevremont, A., Anastopoulas, A., & Fletcher, K. (1992). A comparison of three family therapy programs for treating family conflicts in adolescents with attention deficit hyperactivity disorder. *Journal of Consulting and Clinical Psychology*, 60, 450–462.

Barkus, E., & Murray, R. M. (2010). Substance use in adolescence and psychosis: Clarifying the relationship. *Annual Review of Clinical Psychology*, 6, 365–389.

Barlow, D. H., Allen, L. B., & Basden, S. L. (2007). Psychological treatments for panic disorders, phobias, and generalized anxiety disorder. In P. E. Nathan & J. M. Gorman (Eds.), *A guide to treatments that work* (third edition, pp. 351–394). New York: Oxford University Press.

Barron (2009a). *Barron's GRE* (18th edition). New York: Barron's Educational Series.

Barron (2009b). *Barron's GRE psychology: Barron's how to prepare for the GRE psychology graduate record examination in psychology* (sixth edition). New York: Barron's Educational Series.

Barrowclough, C., & Lobban, F. (2008). Family intervention. In K. Mueser & D. Jeste (Eds.). *Clinical handbook of schizophrenia* (pp. 214–225). New York: Guilford Press.

Bartlett, P. & Sandland, R. (2007). *Mental health law: Policy and practice* (third edition). Oxford: Oxford University Press.

Bateman, A., & Fonagy, P. (2000). Effectiveness of psychotherapeutic treatment of personality disorder. *British Journal of Psychiatry*, 177, 138–143.

Bateman, A. & Fonagy, P. (2010a). Mentalization-based treatment and borderline personality disorder. In J. Clarkin, O. Fonagy & G. Gabbard (Eds.). *Psychodynamic psychotherapy for personality disorders: A clinical handbook* (pp. 187–208). Arlington, VA: American Psychiatric Publishing.

Bateman, A., & Fonagy, P. (2010b). Mentalization based treatment for borderline personality disorder. *World Psychiatry*, 9, 11–15.

Beach, S. R. H., Jones, D. J., & Franklin, K. J. (2009). *Marital, family, and interpersonal therapies for depression in adults.* In H. Gotlib & C. Hammen (Eds.), *Handbook of depression* (second edition, pp. 624–641). New York: Guilford Press.

Bebbington, P., & Kuipers, E. (2008). Psychosocial factors. In K. Mueser & D. Jeste (Eds.). *Clinical handbook of schizophrenia* (pp. 74–81). New York: Guilford Press.

Bech, P. (2009). Clinical features of mood disorders and mania. In M. Gelder et al. (Eds.), *New Oxford textbook of psychiatry* (second edition, Vol. 1, pp. 632–637). Oxford: Oxford University Press.

Beck, A. (1976). *Cognitive therapy and the emotional disorders.* New York: Meridian.

Beck, A. (2005). The current state of cognitive therapy: A 40-year retrospective. *Archives of General Psychiatry*, 62, 953–959.

Beck, A. (2008). The evolution of the cognitive model of depression and its neurobiological correlates. *American Journal of Psychiatry*, 165, 969–977.

Beck, A., Epstein, N., Harrison, R. P., & Emery, G. (1983). *Development of the Sociotropy-Autonomy Scale: A measure of personality factors in psychopathology*. Unpublished manuscript, University of Pennsylvania, Philadelphia.

Beck, A., Freeman, A., & Davis, D. (2003). *Cognitive therapy of personality disorders* (second edition). New York: Guilford Press.

Beck, A. Rector, N., Stolar, N., & Grant, P. (2011). *Schizophrenia: Cognitive theory, research and therapy*. New York: Guilford.

Beck, A., Rush, A., Shaw, B., & Emery, G. (1979). *Cognitive therapy of depression*. New York: Guilford Press.

Beck, A., & Steer, R. (1991). *Beck Scale for Suicide Ideation*. San Antonio, TX: Psychological Corporation.

Beck, A., Steer, R., & Brown, G. (1996). *Beck Depression Inventory – Second edition* (BDI-II). San Antonio, TX: Psychological Corporation.

Becker, D. R. (2008). Vocational rehabilitation. In K. Mueser & D. Jeste (Eds.), *Clinical handbook of schizophrenia* (pp. 261–267). New York: Guilford Press.

Becker, S. P. (2010). Wilderness therapy: Ethical considerations for mental health professionals. *Child & Youth Care Forum*, 39, 47–61.

Beinart, H., Kennedy, P., & Llewelyn, S. (2009). *Clinical psychology in practice*. London: British Psychological Society–Blackwell.

Bellack, A., Mueser, K., Gingerich, S., & Agresta, J. (2004). *Social skill training for schizophrenia: A step-by-step guide* (second edition). New York: Guilford.

Benjamin, L. T., Jr. (2005). A history of clinical psychology as a profession in America (and a glimpse at its future). *Annual Review of Clinical Psychology*, 1(1), 1–30.

Bentall, R. (2003). *Madness explained: Psychosis and human nature*. London: Penguin.

Berle, D., & Starcevic, V. (2005). Thought–action fusion: Review of the literature and future directions. *Clinical Psychology Review*, 25, 263–284.

Berman, A. (2009). Depression and suicide. In H. Gotlib & C. Hammen (Eds.), *Handbook of depression* (second edition, pp. 510–533). New York: Guilford Press.

Bertram, L. (2008). Genetic research in schizophrenia: New tools and future perspectives. *Schizophrenia Bulletin*, 34, 806–812.

Beutler, L., Malik, M., Alimohamed, S., Harwood, T., Talebi, H., Noble, S., et al. (2004). Therapist variables. In M. Lambert (Ed.), *Bergin and Garfield's handbook of psychotherapy and behaviour change* (fifth Edition, pp. 227–306). New York: Wiley.

Bibring, E. (1965). The mechanism of depression. In P. Greenacre (Ed.), *Affective Disorders* (pp. 13–48). New York: International Universities Press.

Bitran, S., Barlow, D., & Spiegel, D. (2009). Generalized anxiety disorders. In M. Gelder et al. (Eds.), *New Oxford textbook of psychiatry* (second edition, Vol. 1, pp. 729–739). Oxford: Oxford University Press.

Blackmore, M., Erwin, B., Heimberg, R., Magee, L., & Fresco, D. (2009). Social anxiety disorder and specific phobias. In M. Gelder et al. (Eds.), *New Oxford textbook of psychiatry* (second edition, Vol. 1, pp. 739–750). Oxford: Oxford University Press.

Blatt, S. (2004). *Experiences of depression: Theoretical, clinical and research perspectives*. Washington, DC: American Psychological Association.

Bleuler, E. (1911). *Dementia praecox or the group of schizophrenias.* New York: International University Press.

Bleuler, E. (1924). *Textbook of psychiatry.* New York: Macmillan.

Bloch, S., Hanfer, J., Harari, E., & Szmukler, G. (1994). *The family in clinical psychiatry.* Oxford: Oxford University Press.

Bögels, S. M., & Brechman-Toussaint, M. L. (2006). Family issues in child anxiety: Attachment, family functioning, parental rearing and beliefs. *Clinical Psychology Review*, 26, 834–856.

Boland, R. J., & Keller, M. B. (2009). *Course and outcome of depression.* In H. Gotlib & C. Hammen (Eds.), *Handbook of depression* (second edition, pp. 23–43). New York: Guilford Press.

Bond, G., Drake, R., Mueser, K., & Latimer, E. (2001). Assertive community treatment for people with severe mental illness. Critical ingredients and impact on patients. *Disease Management & Health Outcomes*, 9(3), 141–159.

Bora, E., Fornito, A., Radua, J., Walterfang, M., Seal, M., Wood, S. J., et al. (2011). Neuroanatomical abnormalities in schizophrenia: A multimodal voxelwise meta-analysis and meta-regression analysis. *Schizophrenia Research*, 127, 46–57.

Bota, R., Munro, S., Nguyen, C., & Preda, A. (2011). The course of schizophrenia: What has been learned from longitudinal studies? In M. Ritsner (Ed.), *Handbook of schizophrenia spectrum disorders, Volume II. Phenotypic and endophenotypic presentations* (pp. 281–300). New York: Springer.

Bowlby, J. (1944). Forty-four juvenile lives: Their characters and homelife. *International Journal of Psychoanalysis*, 25, 1–57.

Bowlby, J. (1980). *Attachment and loss, Volume 3. Loss, sadness and depression.* New York: Basic Books.

Boyle, M. (2002). *Schizophrenia: A scientific delusion* (second Edition). London: Routledge.

Bradley, A. J., & Dinan, T. G. (2010). A systematic review of hypothalamic–pituitary–adrenal axis function in schizophrenia: Implications for mortality. *Journal of Psychopharmacology*, 24, 91–118.

Bradley, C. (1937). The behaviour of children receiving Benzedrine. *American Journal of Psychiatry*, 94, 577–585.

Brandes, M., & Bienvenu, O. J. (2009). Anxiety disorders and personality disorders comorbidity. In M. M. Antony & M. B. Stein (Eds.), *Oxford handbook of anxiety and related disorders* (pp. 587–595). New York: Oxford University Press.

Breggin, P. (1991). *Toxic psychiatry.* London: Harper Collins.

Breggin, P. (2001). *Talking back to Ritalin: What doctors aren't telling you about stimulants and ADHD.* New York: Da Capo Press

Bremner, D. (2005). *Brain imaging handbook.* New York: Norton.

Brent, D., & Weersing, R. (2008). Depressive disorders in childhood and adolescence. In M. Rutter et al. (Eds.), *Rutter's child and adolescent psychiatry* (fifth edition, pp. 587–612). London: Blackwell.

Bridge, J. A., Iyengar, S., & Salary, C. B. (2007). Clinical response and risk for reported suicidal ideation and suicide attempts in paediatric antidepressant treatment: A meta-analysis of randomized controlled trials. *Journal of the American Medical Association*, 297, 1683–1696.

Britton, J. C., & Rauch, S. L. (2009). Neuroanatomy and neuroimaging of anxiety disorders. In M. M. Antony & M. B. Stein (Eds.), *Oxford handbook of anxiety and related disorders* (pp. 97–110). New York: Oxford University Press.

Bronfenbrenner, U., & Morris, P. A. (2006). The bioecological model of human development. In R. M. Lerner (Ed.), *Handbook of child psychology, Volume*

1: Theoretical models of human development (sixth Edition, pp. 793–828). Hoboken, NJ: Wiley.

Brown, T. (2009). *ADHD comorbidities: Handbook for ADHD complications in children and adults.* Arlington, VA: American Psychiatric Publishing.

Brown, T., DiNardo, P., & Barlow, D. (1994). *Anxiety Disorders Interview Schedule for DSM-IV. (ADIS-IV).* New York: Oxford University Press.

Bruch, H. (1973). *Eating disorders.* New York: Basic Books.

Bruch, H. (1978). *The golden cage: The enigma of anorexia nervosa.* Cambridge, MA: Harvard University Press.

Brunwasser, S. M., Gillham, J. E., & Kim, E. S. (2009). A meta-analytic review of the Penn Resiliency Program's effect on depressive symptoms. *Journal of Consulting and Clinical Psychology, 77*(6), 1042–1054.

Buchanan, R. W., Kreyenbuhl, J., Kelly, D. L., Noel, J. M., Boggs, D. L., & Fischer, B. A. (2010). The 2009 schizophrenia PORT psychopharmacological treatment recommendations and summary statements. *Schizophrenia Bulletin, 36,* 71–93.

Busch, F. N., Milrod, B. L., & Shear, K. (2010). Psychodynamic concepts of anxiety. In D. J. Stein, E. Hollander, & B. O. Rothbaum (Eds.), *Textbook of anxiety disorders* (second edition, pp. 117–128). Arlington, VA: American Psychiatric Publishing.

Butler, A., Chapman, J., Forman, E., & Beck, A. (2006). The empirical status of cognitive-behavioural therapy: A review of meta-analyses. *Clinical Psychology Review, 36,* 17–31.

Byrne, M., Carr, A., & Clarke, M. (2004). The efficacy of couples based interventions for panic disorder with agoraphobia. *Journal of Family Therapy, 26*(2), 105–125.

Cain, D., & Seeman, J. (2001). *Humanistic psychotherapies: Handbook of research and practice.* Washington, DC: American Psychological Association.

Caligor, E. (2010). An object relations model of personality and personality pathology. In J. Clarkin, O. Fonagy, & G. Gabbard (Eds.), *Psychodynamic psychotherapy for personality disorders: A clinical handbook* (pp. 3–36). Arlington, VA: American Psychiatric Publishing.

Campbell, D., Draper, R., & Crutchley, E. (1991). The Milan systemic approach to family therapy. In A. Gurman & D. Kniskern (Eds.), *Handbook of family therapy* (Vol. II, pp. 325–362). New York: Brunner Mazel.

Carlson, G. A., & Cantwell, D. P. (1980). Unmasking masked depression in children and adolescents. *American Journal of Psychiatry, 137*(4), 445–449.

Carney, S., Cowen, P., Geddes, J., Goodwin, G., Rogers, R., Dearness, K., et al. (2003). Efficacy and safety of electroconvulsive therapy in depressive disorders: A systematic review and meta-analysis. *Lancet, 361*(9360), 799–808.

Carpenter, L., Philip, N., & O'Riordan, J. (2009). Advances in neurostimulation for depression: Electroconvulsive therapy, transcranial magnetic stimulation, vagus nerve stimulation and deep brain stimulation. In T. L. Schwartz & T. J. Petersen (Eds.), *Depression: Treatment strategies and management* (second edition, pp. 166–185). London: Inform Healthcare

Carr, A. (2000). *Clinical psychology in Ireland, Volume 1: Empirical studies of professional practice.* Lampeter, UK: Edwin Mellen Press.

Carr, A. (2006a). *Handbook of child and adolescent clinical psychology: A contextual approach* (second edition). London: Routledge.

Carr, A. (2006b). *Family therapy: Concepts, process and practice* (second edition). Chichester, UK: Wiley.

Carr, A. (2009a). *What works with children, adolescents and adults? A review of research on the effectiveness of psychotherapy.* London: Routledge.

Carr, A. (2009b). The effectiveness of family therapy and systemic interventions for child-focused problems. *Journal of Family Therapy*, 31, 3–45.

Carr, A. (2009c). The effectiveness of family therapy and systemic interventions for adult-focused problems. *Journal of Family Therapy*, 31, 46–74.

Carr, A. (2011). *Positive psychology: The science of happiness and human strengths* (second edition). London: Routledge.

Carr, A., & McNulty, M. (2006). *Handbook of adult clinical psychology: An evidence based practice approach.* London: Brunner-Routledge.

Carr, A., O'Reilly, G., Walsh, P., & McEvoy, J. (2007). *Handbook of intellectual disability and clinical psychology practice.* London; Brunner-Routledge.

Casey, R. J., & Berman, J. S. (1985). The outcome of psychotherapy with children. *Psychological Bulletin*, 98, 388–400.

Caspi, A., Hariri, A., Holmes, A., Uher, R., & Moffitt, T. (2010). Genetic sensitivity to the environment: The case of the serotonin transporter gene and its implications for studying complex diseases and traits. *American Journal of Psychiatry*, 167, 509–527.

Caspi, A., McClay, J., Moffitt, T., Mill, J., Martin, J., Craig, I., et al. (2002). Role of genotype in the cycle of violence in maltreated children. *Science*, 297, 851–854.

Caspi, O. (2004). How good are we? A meta-analytic study of effect sizes in medicine. *Dissertation Abstracts International, Section B: The Sciences and Engineering*, 65(5-B), 2607.

Cassidy, J., & Shaver, P. (2008). *Handbook of attachment* (second edition). New York: Guilford.

Cassin, S., & von Ranson, K. M. (2005). Personality and eating disorders: A decade in review. *Clinical Psychology Review*, 25, 895–916.

Castonguay, L., Grosse Holtforth, M., Coombs, M., Beberman, R., Kakouros, A., Boswell, J., et al. (2006). Relationship factors in treating dysphoric disorders. In L. Castonguay & L. Beutler (Eds.), *Principles of therapeutic change that work* (pp. 65–82). Oxford: Oxford University Press.

Catalano, R. F., Haggerty, K. P., Hawkins, J. D., & Elgin, J. (2011). Prevention of substance use and substance use disorders: Role of risk and protective factors. In Y. Kaminer & K. C. Winters (Eds.), *Clinical manual of adolescent substance abuse treatment* (pp. 25–63). Arlington, VA: American Psychiatric Publishing.

Chambers, R. A., Taylor, J. R., & Potenza, M. N. (2003). Developmental neurocircuitry of motivation in adolescence: A critical period of addiction vulnerability. *American Journal of Psychiatry*, 160, 1041–1052.

Chan, R., Di, X., McAlonan, G. M., & Gong, Q. (2011). Brain anatomical abnormalities in high-risk individuals, first-episode, and chronic schizophrenia: An activation likelihood estimation meta-analysis of illness progression. *Schizophrenia Bulletin*, 37, 177–188.

Cherkasova, M. V., & Hechtman, L. (2009). Neuroimaging in attention-deficit hyperactivity disorder: Beyond the frontostriatal circuitry. *Canadian Journal of Psychiatry*, 54(10), 651–664.

Cheshire, K., & Pilgrim, D. (2004). *A short introduction to clinical psychology.* London: Sage.

Chess, S., & Thomas, A. (1995). *Temperament in clinical practice.* New York: Guilford.

Cheung, S. (2009). Solution-focused brief therapy. In J. Bray & M. Stanton (Eds.), *The Wiley–Blackwell handbook of family psychology* (pp. 212–225). Chichester, UK: Wiley–Blackwell.

Chiles, J., Lambert, M., & Hatch, A. (1999). The impact of psychological interventions on medical cost offset: A meta-analytic review. *Clinical Psychology: Science and Practice*, 6, 204–220.

Chung, T., & Martin, C. S. (2011). Prevalence and clinical course of adolescent substance use and substance use disorders. In Y. Kaminer & K. C. Winters (Eds.), *Clinical manual of adolescent substance abuse treatment* (pp. 1–23). Arlington, VA: American Psychiatric Publishing.

Clare, L. (1995). Successful applicants for clinical training: A descriptive profile of one trainee cohort. *Clinical Psychology Forum*, 77, 31–34.

Clark, D., & Beck, A. (2010). Cognitive theory and therapy of anxiety and depression: Convergence with neurobiological findings. *Trends in Cognitive Sciences*, 14(9), 418–424.

Clark, D. A., & Beck, A. T. (2010a). *Cognitive therapy of anxiety disorders*. New York: Guilford Press.

Clark, D. A., & Beck, A. T. (2010b). Cognitive theory and therapy of anxiety and depression: Convergence with neurobiological findings. *Trends in Cognitive Sciences*, 14(9), 418–424.

Clark, L. A., Simms, L. J., Wu, K. D., & Casillas, A. (2008). *Schedule for Nonadaptive and Adaptive Personality – Second edition*. Minneapolis: University of Minnesota Press.

Clark, L. A., & Watson, D. (2008). Temperament: An organizing paradigm for trait psychology. In O. John, R. Robins & L. Pervin (Eds.), *Handbook of personality psychology: Theory and research* (third edition, pp. 265–286). New York: Guilford Press.

Clarkin, J., & Levy, K. (2004). The influence of client variables on psychotherapy. In M. Lambert (Ed.), *Bergin and Garfield's handbook of psychotherapy and behaviour change* (fifth edition, pp. 194–226). New York: Wiley.

Cleckley, H. (1941). *The mask of sanity*. St Louis, MO: Mosby Medical Library.

Cloninger, C., Svrakic, D. & Przybeck, T. (1993). A psychobiological model of temperament and character. *Archives of General Psychiatry*, 50, 975–990.

Cloward, R., & Ohlin, L. (1960). *Delinquency and opportunity*. Glencoe, IL: Free Press.

Coccaro, E. F., & Siever, L. J. (2009). Neurobiology. In J. Oldham, A. Skodol, & D. Bender (Eds.), *Essentials of personality disorders* (pp. 103–122). Arlington, VA: American Psychiatric Publishing.

Cochrane, A. (1972). *Effectiveness and efficiency: Random reflections on health services*. London: Nuffield Provincial Hospitals Trust.

Cohen, J. (1988). *Statistical power analysis for the behavioural sciences* (second edition). Hillsdale, NJ: Lawrence Erlbaum Associates.

Colapinto, J. (1991). Structural family therapy. In A. Gurman & D. Kniskern (Eds.), *Handbook of family therapy* (Vol. II, pp. 417–443). New York: Brunner/Mazel.

Coldwell, C., & Bender, W. (2007). The effectiveness of assertive community treatment for homeless populations with severe mental illness: A meta-analysis. *American Journal of Psychiatry*, 164, 393–399.

Collier, D., & Treasure, J. (2004). The aetiology of eating disorders. *British Journal of Psychiatry*, 185, 363–365.

Colligan, R., Morey, L., & Offord, K. (1994). MMPI/MMPI-2 personality disorder scales: Contemporary norms for adults and adolescents. *Journal of Clinical Psychology*, 50, 168–200.

Combrinck-Graham, L. (1986). Family treatment for childhood anxiety disorders. *Family Therapy Collections*, 18, 22–30.

Conklin, C. A., & Tiffany, S. T. (2002). Applying extinction research and theory to cue-exposure addiction treatments. *Addiction*, 97, 155–167.

Conners, C. (1997). *Conners' Rating Scales: Revised Technical Manual.* North Tonawanda, NY: Multihealth Systems.

Consensus Development Panel (2000). National Institutes of Health Consensus Development Conference statement: Diagnosis and treatment of attention-deficit/hyperactivity disorder (ADHD). *Journal of the American Academy of Child and Adolescent Psychiatry*, 39(2), 182–193.

Cook, J., & Razzano, L. (2005). Evidence-based practices in supported employment. In C. Stout & R. Hayes (Eds.), *The evidence-based practice: Methods, models, and tools for mental health professionals* (pp. 10–30). Hoboken, NJ: Wiley.

Cooper, J., Kendall, R., Gurland, B., Sharp, L., Copeland, J., & Simon, R. (1972). *Psychiatric diagnosis in New York and London.* Maudsley Monograph Series No. 20. London: Oxford University Press.

Corrigan, P. W., Salzer, M., Ralph, R. O., Sangster, Y., & Keck, L. (2004). Examining the factor structure of the Recovery Assessment Scale. *Schizophrenia Bulletin*, 30, 1035–1041.

Costa, P. & Widiger, T. (1994). *Personality disorders and the five factor model of personality.* Washington, DC: APA.

Costa, P. T., Jr., & McCrae, R. R. (1992). *Revised NEO Personality Inventory (NEOPI-R) and NEO Five-Factor Inventory (NEO-FFI) professional manual.* Odessa, FL: Psychological Assessment Resources.

Costello, E. J., Mustillo, S., Keeler, G., & Angold, A. (2004). Prevalence of psychiatric disorders in childhood and adolescence. In B. L. Levin, J. Petrila, & K. D. Hennessy (Eds.), *Mental health services: A public health perspective* (second edition, pp. 111–128). New York: Oxford University Press.

Crane, D. R. (2011). Does family therapy reduce health care costs for more than the identified patient? *Clinical Child Psychology and Psychiatry*, 16, 3–4.

Crick, N., & Dodge, K. (1994). A review and reformulation of social information processing mechanisms in children's social adjustment. *Psychological Bulletin*, 115, 74–101.

Crisp, A. (1983). Anorexia nervosa. *British Medical Journal*, 287, 855–858.

Crome, I., Ghodse, H., Gilvarry, E., & McArdle, P. (2004). *Young people and substance misuse.* London: Gaskell.

Crosnoe, R., & Cavanagh, S. E. (2010). Families with children and adolescents: A review, critique, and future agenda. *Journal of Marriage and Family*, 72(3), 594–611.

Crow, T. (1985). The two syndrome concept: Origins and current status. *Schizophrenia Bulletin*, 9, 471–486.

Cuijpers, P., Donker, T., van Straten, A., Li, J., & Andersson, G. (2010). Is guided self-help as effective as face-to-face psychotherapy for depression and anxiety disorders? A systematic review and meta-analysis of comparative outcome studies. *Psychological Medicine*, 40(12), 1943–1957.

Cuijpers, P., Muñoz, R. F., Clarke, G. N., & Lewinsohn, P. M. (2009a). Psychoeducational treatment and prevention of depression: The "coping with depression" course thirty years later. *Clinical Psychology Review*, 29, 449–458.

Cuijpers, P., van Straten, A., Andersson, G., & van Oppen, P. (2008). Psychotherapy for depression in adults: A meta-analysis of comparative outcome studies. *Journal of Consulting and Clinical Psychology*, 76, 909–922.

Cuijpers, P., van Straten, A., Warmerdam, L., & Andersson, G. (2009b). Psychotherapy versus the combination of psychotherapy and pharmacotherapy in the treatment of depression: A meta-analysis. *Depression and Anxiety*, 26, 279–288.

Cunningham-Owens, D., & Johnstone, E. (2009). Treatment and management of schizophrenia. In M. Gelder et al. (Eds.), *New Oxford textbook of psychiatry* (second edition, Vol. 1, pp. 578–595). Oxford: Oxford University Press.

Currin, L., Schmidt, U., Treasure, J., & Jick, H. (2005). Time trends in eating disorder incidence. *British Journal of Psychiatry*, 186, 132–135.

Dadds, M., Heard, P., & Rapee, R. (1992). The role of family intervention in the treatment of child anxiety disorders: Some preliminary findings. *Behaviour Change*, 9, 171–177.

Dakof, G. A., Godley, S. H., & Smith, J. E. (2011). The adolescent community reinforcement approach and multidimensional family therapy: Addressing relapse during treatment. In Y. Kaminer & K. C. Winters (Eds.), *Clinical manual of adolescent substance abuse treatment* (pp. 239–268). Arlington, VA: American Psychiatric Publishing.

Daley, A., Jolly, K., & MacArthur, C. (2009). The effectiveness of exercise in the management of post-natal depression: Systematic review and meta-analysis. *Family Practice*, 26, 154–162.

Dare, C. (1985). The family therapy of anorexia nervosa. *Journal of Psychiatric Research*, 19, 435–453.

Dattilio, F. (2009). *Cognitive-behavioural therapy with couples and families: A comprehensive guide for clinicians.* New York: Guilford.

Davidson, R. J., Pizzagalli, D. A., & Nitschke, J. B. (2009). *Representation and regulation of emotion in depression: Perspectives from affective neuroscience.* In H. Gotlib & C. Hammen (Eds.), *Handbook of depression* (second edition, pp. 218–248). New York: Guilford Press.

Dawson, G., Ashman, S. B., & Carver, L. J. (2000). The role of early experience in shaping behavioural and brain development and its implications for social policy. *Development and Psychopathology*, 12, 695–712.

Deault, L. C. (2010). A systematic review of parenting in relation to the development of comorbidities and functional impairments in children with attention-deficit/hyperactivity disorder (ADHD). *Child Psychiatry and Human Development*, 41(2), 168–192.

Degnan, K. A., Almas, A. N., & Fox, N. A. (2010). Temperament and the environment in the etiology of childhood anxiety. *Journal of Child Psychology and Psychiatry*, 51, 497–517.

DeLuca, N. L., Moser, L. L., & Bond, G. R. (2008). Assertive community treatment. In K. Mueser & D. Jeste (Eds.). *Clinical handbook of schizophrenia* (pp. 329–338). New York: Guilford Press.

Dennis, M. (1998), *Global Appraisal of Individual Needs (GAIN) manual: Administration, scoring and interpretation.* Bloomington, IL: Lighthouse Publications.

Dent, M. F., & Bremner, J. D. (2009). Pharmacotherapy for posttraumatic stress disorder and other trauma-related disorders. In M. M. Antony & M. B. Stein (Eds.), *Oxford handbook of anxiety and related disorders* (pp. 405–416). New York: Oxford University Press.

Department of Health (2007). *Drug misuse and dependence: UK guidelines on clinical management.* London: Department of Health.

DePauw, S., & Mervielde, I. (2010). Temperament, personality and developmental psychopathology: A review based on the conceptual dimensions underlying childhood traits. *Child Psychiatry and Human Development*, 41, 313–329.

De Raad, B., & Perugini, M. (2002). *Big five assessment.* Bern, Switzerland: Hogrefe & Huber.

DeSilva, P., Rachman, S., & Seligman, M. (1977). Prepared phobias and obsessions: Therapeutic outcome. *Behaviour Research and Therapy*, 15, 65–77.

Diamond, G. (2005). Attachment-based family therapy for depressed and anxious adolescents. In J. Lebow (Ed.), *Handbook of clinical family therapy* (pp. 17–41). Hoboken, NJ: Wiley.

DiClemente, C. (2003). *Addiction and change.* New York: Guilford.

DiMaggio, C., & Galea, S. (2006). The behavioural consequences of terrorism: A meta-analysis. *Academy of Emergency Medicine*, 13, 559–566.

Dishion, T., & Dodge, K. (2005). Peer contagion in interventions for children and adolescents: Moving towards an understanding of the ecology and dynamics of change. *Journal of Abnormal Child Psychology*, 33, 395–400.

Dixon, L. B., Dickerson, F., Bellack, A. S., Bennett, M., Dickinson, D., & Goldberg, R. (2010). The 2009 schizophrenia PORT psychosocial treatment recommendations and summary statements. *Schizophrenia Bulletin*, 36, 48–70.

Dodge, K. (2011). Social information processing patterns as mediators of the interaction between genetic factors and life experiences in the development of aggressive behaviour. In P. Shaver & M. Mikulincer (Eds.), *Human aggression and violence: Causes, manifestations, and consequences* (pp. 165–185). Washington, DC: American Psychological Association.

Dodge, K., Coie, J., & Lynam, D. (2006). Aggression and antisocial behaviour in youth. In N. Eisenberg (Ed.), *Handbook of child psychology, Volume 3: Social, emotional and personality development* (sixth edition, pp. 719–788). Hoboken, NJ: Wiley.

Dodge, K. A., & Pettit, G. S. (2003). A biopsychosocial model of the development of chronic conduct problems in adolescence. *Developmental Psychology*, 39, 349–371.

Dolder, C. R. (2008). Side effects of antipsychotics. In K. Mueser & D. Jeste (Eds.), *Clinical handbook of schizophrenia* (pp. 168–177). New York: Guilford Press.

Dougherty, L. R., Klein, D. N., Olino, T. M., & Laptook, R. S. (2008). Depression in children and adolescents. In J. Hunsley & E. J. Mash (Eds.), *A guide to assessments that work* (pp. 69–95). New York: Oxford University Press.

Douglas, K. S., Webster, C. D., Hart, S. D., Eaves, D., & Ogloff, J. R. P. (Eds.) (2001). *HCR-20: Violence risk management companion guide.* Vancouver, Canada/Tampa, FL: Mental Health, Law, and Policy Institute, Simon Fraser University/Department of Mental Health Law & Policy, University of South Florida.

Douglas, V. (1983). Attention and cognitive problems. In M. Rutter (Ed.), *Developmental neuropsychiatry* (pp. 280–329). New York: Guilford.

Downar, J., & Kapur, S. (2008). Biological theories. In K. Mueser & D. Jeste (Eds.), *Clinical handbook of schizophrenia* (pp. 25–34). New York: Guilford Press.

Dozier, M., Stovall-McClough, K., & Albus, K. (2008). Attachment and psychopathology in adulthood. In J. Cassidy & P. Shaver (Eds.), *Handbook of attachment* (second edition, pp. 718–744). New York: Guilford.

Driessen, E., Cuijpers, P., de Maat, S., Abbass, A. A., de Jonghe, F. & Dekker, J. (2010). The efficacy of short-term psychodynamic psychotherapy for depression: A meta-analysis. *Clinical Psychology Review*, 30, 25–36.

Drummond, D., Tiffany, S., Glautier, S. & Remingron, B. (1995). *Addictive behaviour: Cue exposure theory and practice.* Chichester, UK: Wiley.

Dugas, M. J., Buhr, K., & Ladoucer, R. (2004). The role of intolerance of uncertainty in etiology and maintenance. In R. Heimberg, C. Turk, & D. Mennin (Eds), *Generalized anxiety disorder: Advances in research and practice* (pp. 143–163). New York: Guilford Press.

Duggan, C., Huband, N., & Smailagic, N. (2008). The use of pharmacological treatments for people with personality disorder: A systematic review of randomized controlled trials. *Personality and Mental Health*, 2, 119–170.

Duggan, C., Huband, N., Smailagic, N., Ferriter, M., & Adams, C. (2007). The use of psychological treatments for people with personality disorder: A systematic review of randomized controlled trials. *Personality and Mental Health*, 1, 95–125.

Duvall, J., & Béres, L. (2011). *Innovations in narrative therapy: Connecting practice, training, and research.* New York: Norton.

Edens, J. F., Campbell, J. S., & Weir, J. M. (2007). Youth psychopathy and criminal recidivism: A meta-analysis of the psychopathy checklist measures. *Law and Human Behaviour*, *31*(1), 53–75.

Edvardsen, J., Torgersen, S., Røysamb, E., Lygren, S., Skre, I., Onstad, S., et al. (2008). Heritability of bipolar spectrum disorders. Unity or heterogeneity? *Journal of Affective Disorders*, 106, 229–240.

Egan, S. J., Wade, T. D., & Shafran, R. (2011). Perfectionism as a transdiagnostic process: A clinical review. *Clinical Psychology Review*, 31, 203–212.

Egger, J., Carter, C., Graham, P., Gumley, D., & Soothill, J. (1985). Controlled trial of oligoantigenic treatment in the hyperkinetic syndrome. *Lancet*, i, 540–545.

Ehlers, A. (2009). Post-traumatic stress disorder. In M. Gelder et al. (Eds.), *New Oxford textbook of psychiatry* (second edition, Vol. 1, pp. 700–713). Oxford: Oxford University Press.

Eisler, I. (2005). The empirical and theoretical base of family therapy and multiple family day therapy for adolescent anorexia nervosa. *Journal of Family Therapy*, 27, 104–113.

Ellenberger, H. (1970). *The discovery of the unconscious.* New York: Basic Books.

Elliott, R., Greenberg, L., & Lietaer, G. (2004). Research on experiential psychotherapies. In M. Lambert (Ed.), *Bergin and Garfield's handbook of psychotherapy and behaviour change* (fifth edition, pp. 493–539). New York: Wiley.

Ellman, L. M., & Cannon, T. D. (2008). Environmental pre- and perinatal influences in aetiology. In K. Mueser & D. Jeste (Eds.), *Clinical handbook of schizophrenia* (pp. 65–73). New York: Guilford Press.

Emmelkamp, P. (1982). *Phobic and obsessive compulsive disorder.* New York: Plenum.

Erikson, E. (1950). *Childhood and society.* New York: Norton.

Erikson, E. (1968). *Identity, youth and crisis.* New York: Norton.

Eyler, L. T. (2008). Brain imaging. In K. Mueser & D. Jeste (Eds.), *Clinical handbook of schizophrenia* (pp. 35–43). New York: Guilford Press.

Eysenck, H. (1979). The conditioning model of neurosis. *Behavioural and Brain Sciences*, 2, 155–199.

Ezriel, H. (1952). Notes on psychoanalytic group therapy: II. Interpretation. *Research Psychiatry*, 15, 119.

Fairburn, C. (2008). *Cogntive behaviour therapy and eating disorders.* London: Guilford.

Fairburn, C., Cooper, Z., & O'Connor, E. (2008). The Eating Disorder Examination (Edition 16.0D). In C. Fairburn (Ed.), *Cognitive behaviour therapy and eating disorders* (pp. 265–308). London: Guilford.

Falloon, I., Laporta, M., Fadden, G., & Graham-Hole, V. (1993). *Managing stress in families.* London: Routledge.

Faraone, S., Biederman, J., & Mick, E. (2006). The age dependent decline of attention deficit hyperactivity disorder: A meta-analysis of follow-up studies. *Psychological Medicine*, 36, 159–165.

Farmer, A., & McGuffin, P. (1989). The classification of depressions: Contemporary confusions revisited. *British Journal of Psychiatry*, 155, 437–443.

Farrington, D. (1995). The twelfth Jack Tizard Memorial Lecture. The development of offending and antisocial behaviour from childhood: Key findings of the Cambridge Study of Delinquent Development. *Journal of Child Psychology and Psychiatry*, 36, 929–964.

Fatemi, S. H., & Folsom, T. D. (2009). The neurodevelopmental hypothesis of schizophrenia, revisited. *Schizophrenia Bulletin*, 35, 528–548.

Feingold, B. (1975). Hyperkinesis and learning difficulties linked to artificial food flavours and colours. *American Journal of Nursing*, 75, 797–803.

Ferguson, C. (2010). Genetic contributions to antisocial personality and behaviour: A meta-analytic review from an evolutionary perspective. *Journal of Social Psychology*, 150, 160–180.

Fernandez-Alderez, H., Clarkin, J., delCarmen Salgueiro, M., & Critchfield, K. (2006). Participant factors in treating personality disorders. In L. Castonguay & L. Beutler (Eds.), *Principles of therapeutic change that work* (pp. 203–218). Oxford: Oxford University Press.

Fett, A. J., Viechtbauer, W., Dominguez, M., Penn, D. L., van Os, J., & Krabbendam, L. (2011). The relationship between neurocognition and social cognition with functional outcomes in schizophrenia: A meta-analysis. *Neuroscience and Biobehavioural Reviews*, 35, 573–588.

First, M., Spitzer, R., Gibbon, M., & Williams, J. (1996). *Structured Clinical Interview for DSM-IV Axis I Disorders, Clinician Version (SCID-CV)*. Washington, DC: American Psychiatric Press.

First, M., Spitzer, R., Gibbon M., & Williams, J. (1997). *Structured Clinical Interview for DSM-IV Personality Disorders (SCID-II)*. Washington, DC: American Psychiatric Press.

Fleming, I. & Steen, L. (2004). *Supervision in clinical psychology: Theory, practice and perspectives*. London: Brunner Routledge.

Follette, W., & Greenberg, L. (2006). Technique factors in treating dysphoric disorders. In L. Castonguay & L. Beutler (Eds.), *Principles of therapeutic change that work* (pp. 83–110). Oxford: Oxford University Press.

Fonagy, P., & Target, M. (1994). The efficacy of psychoanalysis for children with disruptive disorders. *Journal of the American Academy for Child and Adolescent Psychiatry*, 33, 45–55.

Forgatch, M. S., & Patterson, G. R. (2010). Parent management training—Oregon model: An intervention for antisocial behaviour in children and adolescents. In J. R. Weisz & A. E. Kazdin (Eds.), *Evidence-based psychotherapies for children and adolescents* (second edition, pp. 159–177). New York: Guilford Press.

Fournier, J., DeRubeis, R., Hollon, S., Dimidjian, S., Amsterdam, J., & Shelton, R. (2010). Antidepressant drug effects and depression severity. *Journal of the American Medical Association*, 303, 47–53.

Frank, J., & Frank, J. (1991). *Persuasion and healing: A comparative study of psychotherapy* (third edition). Baltimore: Johns Hopkins University Press.

Franklin, M. E., & Foa, E. B. (2007). Cognitive behavioural treatment of obsessive-compulsive disorder. In P. E. Nathan & J. M. Gorman (Eds.), *A guide to treatments that work* (third edition, pp. 431–446). New York: Oxford University Press.

Franko, D. L., & Keel, P. K. (2006). Suicidality in eating disorders: Occurrence, correlates, and clinical implications. *Clinical Psychology Review*, 26(6), 769–782.

Freeman, A., Felgoise, S., Nezu, A., Nezu, C., & Reinecke, M. (2005). *Encyclopaedia of cognitive behaviour therapy*. New York: Plenum.

Freud, S. (1900). *The interpretation of dreams* (trans. J. Strachey). London: Hogarth Press.

Freud, S. (1901). *Psychopathology of everyday life* (trans. A. Brill). London: Fisher Unwin.

Freud, S. (1908). Character and anal eroticism. In J. Strachey (Ed. & trans.), *The standard edition of the complete psychological works of Sigmund Freud* (Vol. 9, pp. 167–175). London: Hogarth Press.

Freud, S. (1909a). The analysis of a phobia in a five year old boy. In J. Strachey (Ed. & trans.). *The standard edition of the complete works of Sigmund Freud* (Vol. 10, pp. 1–147). London: Hogarth Press.

Freud, S. (1909b). Notes upon a case of obsessional neurosis. In J. Strachey (Ed. & trans). *The standard edition of the complete works of Sigmund Freud* (Vol. 10, pp. 151–220). London: Hogarth Press.

Freud, S. (1911). Psycho-analytic notes on an autobiographical account of a case of paranoia (dementia paranoides). In J. Strachey (Ed. & trans.), *The standard edition of the complete psychological works of Sigmund Freud* (Vol. 12, pp. 1–82). London: Hogarth Press.

Freud, S. (1917). Mourning and melancholia. In J. Strachey (Ed & trans.). *The standard edition of the complete works of Sigmund Freud* (Vol. 14, pp. 237–258). London: Hogarth Press.

Frewen, P. A., Dozois, D. J. A., & Lanius, R. A. (2008a). Neuroimaging studies of psychological interventions for mood and anxiety disorders: Empirical and methodological review. *Clinical Psychology Review*, 28, 228–246.

Frewen, P. A., Dozois, D. A., Neufeld, R. W. J., & Lanius, R. A. (2008b). Meta-analysis of alexithymia in posttraumatic stress disorder. *Journal of Trauma and Stress*, 21, 243–246.

Frichter, M., & Pirke, K. (1995). Starvation models and eating disorders. In G. Szmukler, C. Dare, & J. Treasure (Eds.), *Handbook of eating disorders* (pp. 83–108). Chichester, UK: Wiley.

Friedman, M. J. (2009). Phenomenology of posttraumatic stress disorder and acute stress disorder. In M. M. Antony & M. B. Stein (Eds.), *Oxford handbook of anxiety and related disorders* (pp. 65–72). New York: Oxford University Press.

Frischer, M., McArdle, P., & Crome, I. (2004). The epidemiology of substance misuse in young people. In I. Crome et al. (Eds.), *Young people and substance misuse* (pp. 31–50). London: Gaskell.

Furr, J. M., Tiwari, S., Suveg, C., & Kendall, P. C. (2009). Anxiety disorders in children and adolescents. In M. M. Antony & M. B. Stein (Eds.), *Oxford handbook of anxiety and related disorders* (pp. 636–656). New York: Oxford University Press.

Gabbard, G. O., Lazar, S. G., Hornberger, J., & Spiegel, D. (1997). The economic impact of psychotherapy: A review. *American Journal of Psychiatry*, 154, 147–155.

Garber, J. (2010). Vulnerability to depression in childhood and adolescence. In R. Ingram and J. Price (Eds.), *Vulnerability to psychopathology: Risk across the lifespan* (second edition, pp. 189–247). New York: Guilford Press.

Gardner, M., Barajas, R. G., & Brooks-Gunn, J. (2010). Neighborhood influences on substance use etiology: Is where you live important? In L. Scheier (Ed.), *Handbook of drug use etiology: Theory, methods, and empirical findings* (pp. 423–441). Washington, DC: American Psychological Association.

Garner, D. (2005). *Eating Disorder Inventory, third edition (EDI-3)*. Odessa, FL: Psychological Assessment Resources.

Gelernter, J., & Stein, M. B. (2009). Heritability and genetics of anxiety disorders. In M. M. Antony & M. B. Stein (Eds.), *Oxford handbook of anxiety and related disorders* (pp. 87–96). New York: Oxford University Press.

Gillham, J. E., Brunwasser, S. M., Freres, D. R., Abela, J. R. Z., & Hankin, B. L. (2008). Preventing depression in early adolescence: The Penn Resiliency Program. In J. Abela & B. Hankin (eds.), *Handbook of depression in children and adolescents* (pp. 309–322). New York: Guilford.

Gitlin, M. (2009). Pharmcotherapy and other somatic treatments for depression. In H. Gotlib & C. Hammen (Eds.), *Handbook of depression* (second edition, pp. 554–585). New York: Guilford Press.

Glass, V. (1976). Primary, secondary and meta-analysis of research. *Educational Researcher*, 5, 3–8.

Glassman, A. H., & Miller, G. E. (2007). Where there is depression, there is inflammation… sometimes! *Biological Psychiatry*, 62, 280–281.

Glatt, S. J. (2008). Genetics. In K. Mueser & D. Jeste (Eds.), *Clinical handbook of schizophrenia* (pp. 55–64). New York: Guilford Press.

Godley, S. H., Meyers, R. J., Smith, J. E., Karvinen, T., Titus, J. C., Godley, M. D., et al. (2006). *The adolescent community reinforcement approach for adolescent cannabis users*. Cannabis Youth Treatment Series, Vol. 4. Rockville, MD: Center for Substance Abuse Treatment, Substance Abuse and Mental Health Services Administration.

Golden, T., Gaynes, B., Ekstrom, D., Hamer, R., Jacobsen, F., Suppes, T., et al. (2005). The efficacy of light therapy in the treatment of mood disorders: A review and meta-analysis of the evidence. *American Journal of Psychiatry*, 162, 656–662.

Goodman, R. (2001). Psychometric properties of the Strengths and Difficulties Questionnaire (SDQ). *Journal of the American Academy of Child and Adolescent Psychiatry*, 40, 1337–1345.

Goodman, R., Ford, T., Richards, H., Gatward, R., & Meltzer, H. (2000). The Development and Well-Being Assessment: Description and initial validation of an integrated assessment of child and adolescent psychopathology. *Journal of Child Psychology and Psychiatry*, 41, 645–655.

Goodman, S. H., & Brand, S. R. (2009). Depression and early adverse experiences. In H. Gotlib & C. Hammen (Eds.), *Handbook of depression* (second edition, pp. 249–274). New York: Guilford Press.

Gotlib, H., & Hammen, C. (2009). *Handbook of depression* (second edition). New York: Guilford Press.

Gottdiener, W. (2006). Individual psychodynamic psychotherapy of schizophrenia: Empirical evidence for the practicing clinician. *Psychoanalytic Psychology*, 23, 583–589.

Gregory, R. J., Schwer Canning, S., Lee, T. W., & Wise, J. C. (2004). Cognitive bibliotherapy for depression: A meta-analysis. *Professional Psychology: Research and Practice*, 35, 275–280.

Griffin, K. W. (2010). The epidemiology of substance use among adolescents and young adults: A developmental perspective. In L. Scheier (Ed.), *Handbook of drug use etiology: Theory, methods, and empirical findings* (pp. 73–92). Washington, DC: American Psychological Association.

Griffin, K. W., & Botvin, G. J. (2010). Evidence-based interventions for preventing substance use disorders in adolescents. *Child and Adolescent Psychiatric Clinics of North America*, 19(3), 505–526.

Grilo, C. M., & McGlashan, T. H. (2009). Course and outcome. In J. Oldham, A. Skodol, & D. Bender (Eds.), *Essentials of personality disorders* (pp. 63–82). Arlington, VA: American Psychiatric Publishing.

Grissom, R. (1996). The magical number. 7 ± .2: Meta-meta-analysis of the probability of superior outcome in comparisons involving therapy, placebo, and control. *Journal of Consulting and Clinical Psychology*, 64, 973–982.

Groth-Marnat, G., & Edkins, G. (1996). Professional psychologists in general health care settings: A review of financial efficacy of direct treatment interventions. *Professional Psychology: Research and Practice*, 27, 161–174.

Grunberg, N. E., Berger, S. S., & Hamilton, K. R. (2011). Stress and drug use. In R. J. Contrada & A. Baum (Eds.), *The handbook of stress science: Biology, psychology, and health* (pp. 287–300). New York: Springer.

Gull, W. (1874). Anorexia nervosa (apesia hysterica, anorexia hysterica). *Transactions of the Clinical Society of London*, 7, 22–28.

Gunn, M., & Wheat, K. (2009). General principles of law relating to people with mental disorder. In M. Gelder et al. (Eds.), *New Oxford textbook of psychiatry* (second edition, Vol. 2, pp. 1895–1908). Oxford: Oxford University Press.

Gunter, T. D., Vaughn, M. G., & Philibert, R. A. (2010). Behavioural genetics in antisocial spectrum disorders and psychopathy: A review of the recent literature. *Behavioural Sciences & the Law, 28,* 148–173.

Guzzetta, F., & di Girolamo, G. (2009). Epidemiology of personality disorders. In M. Gelder et al. (Eds.), *New Oxford textbook of psychiatry* (second edition, Vol. 1, pp. 881–886). Oxford: Oxford University Press.

Haaga, D., Hall, S., & Haas, A. (2006). Participant factors in treating substance use disorders. In L. Castonguay & L. Beutler (Eds.), *Principles of therapeutic change that work* (pp. 275–292). Oxford: Oxford University Press.

Haeffel, G., Gibb, B., Metalsky, G., Alloy, L., Abramson, L., & Hankin, B. (2008). Measuring cognitive vulnerability to depression: Development and validation of the cognitive style questionnaire. *Clinical Psychology Review, 28*(5), 824–836.

Häfner, H., & an der Heiden, W. (2008). Course and outcome. In K. Mueser & D. Jeste (Eds.), *Clinical handbook of schizophrenia* (pp. 100–116). New York: Guilford Press.

Hall, J., & Llewelyn, S. (2006). *What is clinical psychology?* (fourth edition). Oxford: Oxford University Press.

Hall, J., Olabi, B., Lawrie, S. M., & McIntosh, A. M. (2010). Hippocampal and amygdala volumes in borderline personality disorder: A meta-analysis of magnetic resonance imaging studies. *Personality and Mental Health*, 4, 172–179.

Halmi, K. A. (2010). Psychological comorbidity of eating disorders. In W. S. Agras (Ed.), *The Oxford handbook of eating disorders* (pp. 292–303). New York: Oxford University Press.

Hamilton, J. P., Furman, D. J., & Gotlib, I. H. (2011). The neural foundations of major depression: Classical approaches and new frontiers. In F. F. Lopez-Munoz & C. Alamo (Eds.), *Neurobiology of depression.* Boca Raton, FL: CRC Press.

Hamilton, M. (1967). Development of a rating scale for primary depressive illness. *British Journal of Social and Clinical Psychology*, 6, 278–296.

Hammen, C. (2009). Children of depressed parents. In H. Gotlib & C. Hammen (Eds.), *Handbook of depression* (second edition, pp. 275–297). New York: Guilford Press.

Hammen, C., Bistricky, S., & Ingram, R. (2010). *Vulnerability to depression in adulthood.* In R. Ingram and J. Price (Eds.), *Vulnerability to psychopathology: Risk across the lifespan* (second edition, pp. 248–281). New York: Guilford Press.

Hankin, B., & Abele, J. (2005). *Developmental psychopathology: A vulnerability–stress perspective.* Thousand Oaks, CA: Sage.

Hansen, N., Lambert, M., & Forman, E. (2002). The psychotherapy dose–response effect and its implications for treatment delivery services. *Clinical Psychology Science and Practice*, 9, 329–343.

Hare, R. D. (2003). *Manual for the Revised Psychopathy Checklist* (second edition). Toronto, Canada: Multi-Health Systems.

Hargrove, D. S. (2009). *Psychotherapy based on Bowen family systems theory.* In J. Bray & M. Stanton (Eds.), *The Wiley–Blackwell handbook of family psychology* (pp. 286–299). Chichester, UK: Wiley–Blackwell.

Harkness, K. L., & Lumley, M. N. (2008). Child abuse and neglect and the development of depression in children and adolescents. In J. Abela & B. Hankin (Eds.), *Handbook of depression in children and adolescents* (pp. 466–488). New York: Guilford Press.

Harrington, R., Campbell, F., Shoebridge, P., & Whittaker, J. (1998). Meta-analysis of CBT for depression in adolescents. *Journal of the American Academy of Child & Adolescent Psychiatry*, 37, 1005–1006.

Harrison, P. (2009). The neurobiology of schizophrenia. In M. Gelder et al. (Eds.), *New Oxford textbook of psychiatry* (Vol. 1, second edition, pp. 561–568). Oxford: Oxford University Press.

Hasin, D. S., & Katz, H. (2010). Genetic and environmental factors in substance use, abuse, and dependence. In L. Scheier (Ed.), *Handbook of drug use etiology: Theory, methods, and empirical findings* (pp. 247–267). Washington, DC: American Psychological Association.

Hauser, P., Zametkin, A., Martinez, P., Vitietllo, B., Matochik, J., Mixon, A. et al. (1993). Attention deficit hyperactivity disorder in people with generalized resistance to thyroid hormone. *New England Journal of Medicine*, 328, 997–1001.

Hawton, K., & Fortune, S. (2008). Suicidal behaviour and deliberate self-harm. In M. Rutter et al. (Eds.), *Rutter's child and adolescent psychiatry* (fifth edition, pp. 648–669). London: Blackwell.

Hawton, K. & Taylor, T. (2009). Treatment of suicide attempters and prevention of suicide and attempted suicide. In M. Gelder et al. (Eds.), *New Oxford textbook of psychiatry* (second edition, Vol. 1, pp. 669–679). Oxford: Oxford University Press.

Hay, P. J., & Claudino, A. de M. (2010). Evidence-based treatment for the eating disorders. In W. S. Agras (Ed.), *The Oxford Handbook of eating disorders* (pp. 452–479). New York: Oxford University Press.

Hazlett-Stevens, H., Pruitt, L. D., & Collins, A. (2009). Phenomenology of generalized anxiety disorder. In M. M. Antony & M. B. Stein (Eds.), *Oxford handbook of anxiety and related disorders* (pp. 47–55). New York: Oxford University Press.

Head, L., & Gross, A. (2008). *Systematic desensitization.* In W. O'Donohue & J. Fisher (Eds.), *Cognitive behaviour therapy: Applying empirically supported techniques in your practice* (second edition, pp. 542–549). Hoboken, NJ: Wiley.

Heath, A., Lynskey, M., & Waldron, M. (2008). Substance use and substance use disorders. In M. Rutter et al. (Eds.), *Rutter's child and adolescent psychiatry* (fifth edition, pp. 565–586). London: Blackwell.

Heisel, M. J. (2008). Suicide. In K. Mueser & D. Jeste (Eds.), *Clinical handbook of schizophrenia* (pp. 491–506). New York: Guilford Press.

Helzer, J., Kraemer, H., Krueger, R., Wittchen, H., Sirovatka, P., & Regier, D. (2008). *Dimensional approaches to diagnostic classification: A critical appraisal.* Arlington, VA: American Psychiatric Association.

Hemmeter, U., Hemmeter-Spernal, J., & Krieg, J. (2010). Sleep deprivation in depression. *Expert Review of Neurotherapeutics*, 10, 1101–1115.

Hemmings, R., & Simpson, J. (2008). *Investigating the predictive validity of the Lancaster DClinPsy written shortlisting test on subsequent trainee performance*. Final Report to the Clearing House. Retrieved 24 January 2011 from www.lancs.ac.uk/shm/dhr/courses/dclinpsy/admissions/selection ProcessReport.pdf

Henggeler, S. W., & Schaeffer, C. (2010). Treating serious antisocial behaviour using multisystemic therapy. In J. R. Weisz & A. E. Kazdin (Eds.), *Evidence-based psychotherapies for children and adolescents* (second edition, pp. 259–276). New York: Guilford Press.

Henggeler, S. W., Sheidow, A. J., & Lee, T. (2009). *Multisystemic therapy (MST)*. In J. Bray & M. Stanton (Eds.), *The Wiley–Blackwell handbook of family psychology* (pp. 370–387). Chichester, UK: Wiley–Blackwell.

Hettema, J. M., Neale, M. C., & Kendler, K. S. (2001). A review and meta-analysis of the genetic epidemiology of anxiety disorders. *American Journal of Psychiatry*, 158, 1568–1578.

Hinshaw, S. (1994). *Attention deficits and hyperactivity in children*. Thousand Oaks, CA: Sage.

Hinshaw, S., Klein, R. & Abikoff, H. (2007). Childhood attention-deficit hyperactivity disorder: Nonpharmacological treatments and their combination with medication. In P. Nathan & J. Gorman (Eds.), *A guide to treatments that work* (third edition, pp. 3–28). New York: Oxford University Press.

Hoek, H. W. (2006). Incidence, prevalence and mortality of anorexia nervosa and other eating disorders. *Current Opinion in Psychiatry*, 19, 389–394.

Hofmann, S. G., Alpers, G. W., & Pauli, P. (2009). Phenomenology of panic and phobic disorders. In M. M. Antony & M. B. Stein (Eds.), *Oxford handbook of anxiety and related disorders* (pp. 34–46). New York: Oxford University Press.

Hollis, C. (2008). Schizophrenia and allied disorders. In M. Rutter et al. (Eds.), *Rutter's child and adolescent psychiatry* (fifth edition, pp. 737–758). London: Blackwell.

Hollon, S., Stewart, M., & Strunk, D. (2006). Enduring effects for cognitive behaviour therapy in the treatment of depression and anxiety. *Annual Review of Psychology*, 57, 285–315.

Hoogenhout, E., van der Elst, W., de Groot, R., van Boxtel, M., & Jolles, J. (2010). The neurovegetative complaints questionnaire in the Maastricht aging study: Psychometric properties and normative data. *Aging & Mental Health*, 14, 613–623.

Hooley, J. (2007). Expressed emotion and relapse of psychopathology. *Annual Review of Clinical Psychology*, 3, 329–352.

Hooley, J. M., & Parker, H. A. (2006). Measuring expressed emotion: An evaluation of the shortcuts. *Journal of Family Psychology*, 20(3), 386–396.

Hörz, S., Zanarini, M. C., Frankenburg, F. R., Reich, D. B., & Fitzmaurice, G. (2010). Ten-year use of mental health services by patients with borderline personality disorder and with other axis II disorders. *Psychiatric Services*, 61, 612–616.

Houts, A. (2010). Behavioural treatment for enuresis. In J. Weisz & A. Kazdin (Eds.), *Evidence-based psychotherapies for children and adolescents* (second edition, pp. 359–374). New York: Guilford Press.

Hubble, M., Duncan, B., & Miller, S. (1999). *The heart and soul of change: What works in therapy*. Washington, DC: The American Psychological Association.

Hudson, J. L., & Rapee, R. M. (2009). Familial and social environments in the etiology and maintenance of anxiety disorders. In A. Martin & M. Stein (Eds.), *Handbook of anxiety and anxiety disorders* (pp. 173–189). New York: Oxford University Press.

Hughes, A., & Byrne, A. (2011). Clinical psychology trainee perceptions of what facilitates a good placement start. *Clinical Psychology Forum*, 226 (October), 42–47.

Hughes, J., & Youngson, S. (2009). *Personal development and clinical psychology.* Oxford: BPS-Blackwell.

Huizink, A. C., Mulder, E. J. H., & Buitelaar, J. K. (2004). Prenatal stress and risk for psychopathology: Specific effects or induction of general susceptibility. *Psychological Bulletin, 130,* 115–142.

Hunsley, J., & Lee, C. (2009). *Introduction to clinical psychology* (second edition). Mississauga, CA: Wiley.

Hunsley, J., & Mash, E. (2008). *A guide to assessments that work.* New York: Oxford University Press.

Huppert, J. D. (2009). Anxiety disorders and depression comorbidity. In M. M. Antony & M. B. Stein (Eds.), *Oxford handbook of anxiety and related disorders* (pp. 576–586). New York: Oxford University Press.

Hutchison, K. E. (2010). Substance use disorders: Realizing the promise of pharmacogenomics and personalized medicine. *Annual Review of Clinical Psychology,* 6, 577–589.

In-Albon, T., & Schneider, S. (2007). Psychotherapy of childhood anxiety disorders: A meta-analysis. *Psychotherapy and Psychosomatics,* 76(1), 15–24.

International Society for the Study of Trauma and Dissociation. (2011). Guidelines for treating dissociative identity disorder in adults, third revision. *Journal of Trauma & Dissociation,* 12, 115–187.

Jablensky, A. (2009). Course and outcome of schizophrenia and their prediction. In M. Gelder et al. (Eds.), *New Oxford textbook of psychiatry* (second edition, Vol. 1, pp. 568–578). Oxford: Oxford University Press.

Jacobi, C., & Fittig, E. (2010). Psychosocial risk factors for eating disorders. In W. S. Agras (Ed.), *The Oxford handbook of eating disorders* (pp. 123–136). New York: Oxford University Press.

Jacobi, C., Hayward, C., de Zwaan, M., Kraemer, H. C., & Agras, W. S. (2004). Coming to terms with risk factors for eating disorders: Application of risk terminology and suggestions for a general taxonomy. *Psychological Bulletin,* 130, 19–65.

Jacobson, M., & Schardt, D. (1999). *Diet, ADHD and behaviour: A quarter century review.* Washington, DC: Centre for Science in the Public Interest.

Jaffe, S. L., & Kelly, J. F. (2011). Twelve-step mutual-help programs for adolescents. In Y. Kaminer & K. C. Winters (Eds.), *Clinical manual of adolescent substance abuse treatment* (pp. 269–282). Arlington, VA: American Psychiatric Publishing.

Javitt, D., Spencer, S., Thaker, G., Winterer, G., & Hajos, M. (2008). Neurophysiological biomarkers for drug development in schizophrenia. *Nature Reviews Drug Discovery,* 7, 1–17.

Jessor, R., & Jessor, S. (1977). *Problem behaviour and psychosocial development.* New York: Academic Press.

Jobe, T. H., & Harrow, M. (2010). Schizophrenia course, long-term outcome, recovery, and prognosis. *Current Directions in Psychological Science,* 19, 220–225.

Jochman, K. A., & Fromme, K. (2010). Maturing out of substance use: The other side of etiology. In L. Scheier (Ed.), *Handbook of drug use etiology: Theory, methods, and empirical findings* (pp. 565–578). Washington, DC: American Psychological Association.

John, O., Naumann, L. P., & Soto, C. J. (2008). Paradigm shift to the integrative big-five trait taxonomy: History, measurement, and conceptual issues. In

O. P. John, R. W. Robins, & L. A. Pervin (Eds.), *Handbook of personality: Theory and research* (third edition, pp. 114–158). New York: Guilford Press.

Johnson, J. G., Bromley, E., & McGeoch, P. G. (2009). Childhood experiences and development of maladaptive and adaptive personality traits. In J. Oldham, A. Skodol, & D. Bender (Eds.), *Essentials of personality disorders* (pp. 143–160). Arlington, VA: American Psychiatric Publishing.

Johnson, S., & Bradley, B. (2009). *Emotionally focused couple therapy: Creating loving relationships.* In J. Bray & M. Stanton (Eds.), *The Wiley–Blackwell handbook of family psychology* (pp. 402–415). Chichester, UK: Wiley–Blackwell.

Johnston, C., & Mash, E. (2001). Families of children with attention-deficit/hyperactivity disorder: review and recommendations for future research. *Clinical Child and Family Psychology Review*, 4(3), 183–207.

Johnstone, L. (1999). Adverse psychological effects of ECT. *Journal of Mental Health*, 8, 69–85.

Joiner, T., & Coyne, J. (1999). *The interactional nature of depression.* Washington, DC: APA.

Joiner, T., & Timmons, K. A. (2009). Depression in its interpersonal context. In H. Gotlib & C. Hammen (Eds.), *Handbook of depression* (second edition, pp. 322–339). New York: Guilford Press.

Jones, K., & Vischi, T. (1979). The impact of alcohol, drug abuse, and mental health treatment on medical care utilization: A review of the research literature. *Medical Care*, 17 (Suppl. 12), 43–131.

Jones, M. (1952). *A study of therapeutic communities.* London: Tavistock.

Joormann, J. (2009). Cognitive aspects of depression. In H. Gotlib & C. Hammen (Eds.), *Handbook of depression* (second edition, pp. 298–321). New York: Guilford Press.

Kagan, J. (2010). *The temperament thread.* New York: Dana Press.

Kaminer, Y., Ford, J. D., & Clark, D. (2011a). Assessment and treatment of internalizing disorders: Depression, anxiety disorders, and posttraumatic stress disorder. In Y. Kaminer & K. C. Winters (Eds.), *Clinical manual of adolescent substance abuse treatment* (pp. 307–347). Arlington, VA: American Psychiatric Publishing.

Kaminer, Y., & Marsch, L. A. (2011). Pharmacotherapy of adolescent substance use disorders. In Y. Kaminer & K. C. Winters (Eds.), *Clinical manual of adolescent substance abuse treatment* (pp. 163–186). Arlington, VA: American Psychiatric Publishing.

Kaminer, Y., Spirito, A., & Lewander, W. (2011b). Brief motivational interventions, cognitive-behavioural therapy, and contingency management for youth substance use disorders. In Y. Kaminer & K. C. Winters (Eds.), *Clinical manual of adolescent substance abuse treatment* (pp. 213–237). Arlington, VA: American Psychiatric Publishing.

Kaminer, Y., & Winters, K. (2011). *Clinical manual of adolescent substance abuse treatment.* Arlington, VA: American Psychiatric Publishing.

Kampman, O., & Poutanen, O. (2011). Can onset and recovery in depression be predicted by temperament? A systematic review and meta-analysis. *Journal of Affective Disorders*, 135, 20–27.

Kaplan (2010a). *Kaplan GRE subject test: Psychology* (fifth edition). New York: Kaplan.

Kaplan (2010b). *Kaplan GRE 2011 premier with CD-ROM.* New York: Kaplan.

Karasu, T. B. (1986). The specificity versus nonspecificity dilemma: Toward identifying therapeutic change agents. *American Journal of Psychiatry*, 143, 687–695.

Karg, K., Burmeister, K., Shedden, K., & Sen, S. (2011). The serotonin transporter promoter variant (5-HTTLPR), stress, and depression meta-analysis revisited: Evidence of genetic moderation. *Archives of General Psychiatry*, 68, 444–454.

Kaslow, N. J., Broth, M. R., Arnette, N. C., & Collins, M. H. (2009). Family-based treatment for adolescent depression. In S. Nolen-Hoeksema & L. Hilt (Eds.), *Handbook of depression in adolescents* (pp. 531–570). New York: Routledge.

Katzman, D. K., Kanbur, N. O., & Steinegger, C. M. (2010). Medical screening and management of eating disorders in adolescents. In W. S. Agras (Ed.), *The Oxford handbook of eating disorders* (pp. 267–291). New York: Oxford University Press.

Kavanagh, D. J. (2008). Management of co-occurring substance use disorders. In K. Mueser & D. Jeste (Eds.), *Clinical handbook of schizophrenia* (pp. 459–470). New York: Guilford Press.

Kay, S. R., Opler, L. A., & Fiszbein, A. (1987). The Positive and Negative Syndrome Scale (PANSS) for schizophrenia. *Schizophrenia Bulletin*, 13, 261–276.

Kaye, W. (2008). Neurobiology of anorexia and bulimia nervosa. *Physiology & Behaviour*, 94(1), 121–135.

Kazdin, A. (1995). *Conduct disorders in childhood and adolescence* (second edition). Thousand Oaks, CA: Sage.

Kazdin, A. (2004). Psychotherapy for children and adolescents. In M. Lambert (Ed.), *Bergin and Garfield's handbook of psychotherapy and behaviour change* (fifth edition, pp. 543–589). New York: Wiley.

Kazdin, A. (2010). Problem-solving skills training and parent management training for oppositional defiant disorder and conduct disorder. In J. R. Weisz & A. E. Kazdin (Eds.), *Evidence-based psychotherapies for children and adolescents* (second edition, pp. 211–226). New York: Guilford Press.

Kazdin, A., Bass, D., Ayers, W., & Rodgers, A. (1990). Empirical and clinical focus of child and adolescent psychotherapy research. *Journal of Consulting and Clinical Psychology*, 58, 729–740.

Keel, P. K. (2010). Epidemiology and course of eating disorders. In W. S. Agras (Ed.), *The Oxford handbook of eating disorders* (pp. 25–32). New York: Oxford University Press.

Kendell, R. (1976). The classification of depressions: A review of contemporary confusion. *British Journal of Psychiatry*, 129, 15–88.

Kendler, K., Aggen, S., Czajkowski, N., Røysamb, E., Tambs, K., & Torgersen, S. (2008). The structure of genetic and environmental risk factors for personality disorders: A multivariate twin study. *Archives of General Psychiatry*, 65, 1438–1446.

Kern, R. S., Glynn, S. M., Horan, W. P., & Marder, S. R. (2009). Psychosocial treatments to promote functional recovery in schizophrenia. *Schizophrenia Bulletin*, 35, 347–361.

Kernberg, O. (1975). *Borderline conditions and pathological narcissism*. New York: Jason Aronson.

Kernberg, O. F., & Caligor, E. (2005). A psychoanalytic theory of personality disorders. In J. Clarkin & M. Lenzenweger (Eds.), *Major theories of personality disorder* (second edition, pp. 114–156). New York: Guilford.

Kernberg, P., & Chazan, S. (1991). *Children with conduct disorders: A psychotherapy manual*. New York: Basic Books.

Keshavan, M. S., Tandon, R., Boutros, N. N., & Nasrallah, H. A. (2008). Schizophrenia, "just the facts": What we know in 2008: Part 3: Neurobiology. *Schizophrenia Research*, 106, 89–107.

Kessler, R., Berglund, P., Demler, O., Jin, R., Merikangas, K., & Walters, E. (2005). Lifetime prevalence and age-of-onset distributions of DSM-IV disorders in the National Comorbidity Survey Replication. *Archives of General Psychiatry*, 62, 593–602.

Kessler, R., Ruscio, A. M., Shear, K., & Wittchen, H. (2009). Epidemiology of anxiety disorders. In M. M. Antony & M. B. Stein (Eds.), *Oxford handbook of anxiety and related disorders* (pp. 19–33). New York: Oxford University Press.

Kessler, R., & Wang, P. S. (2009). Epidemiology of depression. In H. Gotlib & C. Hammen (Eds.), *Handbook of depression* (second edition, pp. 5–22). New York: Guilford Press.

Khan, S., King, A. P., Abelson, J. L., & Liberzon, I. (2009). Neuroendocrinology of anxiety disorders. In M. M. Antony & M. B. Stein (Eds.), *Oxford handbook of anxiety and related disorders* (pp. 111–122). New York: Oxford University Press.

Khantzian, E. J. (2003). The self-medication hypothesis revisited: The dually diagnosed patient. *Primary Psychiatry*, 10, 47–48, 53–54.

Kim-Cohen, J., Caspi, A., Taylor, A., Williams, B., Newcombe, R. & Craig, I. W. (2006). MAOA, maltreatment, and gene–environment interaction predicting children's mental health: New evidence and a meta-analysis. *Molecular Psychiatry*, 11, 903–913.

Kim, S., Thibodeau, R., & Jorgensen, R. S. (2011). Shame, guilt, and depressive symptoms: A meta-analytic review. *Psychological Bulletin*, 137, 68–96.

Klein, D. N., Durbin, C. E., & Shankman, S. A. (2009). Personality and mood disorders. In H. Gotlib & C. Hammen (Eds.), *Handbook of depression* (second edition, pp. 93–112). New York: Guilford Press.

Kliem, S., Kroger, C., & Kosfelder, J. (2010). Dialectical behaviour therapy for borderline personality disorder: A meta-analysis using mixed-effects modelling. *Journal of Consulting and Clinical Psychology*, 78, 936–951.

Kliewer, W. (2010). Family processes in drug use etiology. In L. Scheier (Ed.), *Handbook of drug use etiology: Theory, methods, and empirical findings* (pp. 365–381). Washington, DC: American Psychological Association.

Klump, K. L., Bulik, C. M., Kaye, W. H., Treasure, J., & Tyson, E. (2009). Academy for eating disorders position paper: Eating disorders are serious mental illnesses. *International Journal of Eating Disorders*, 42, 97–103.

Knight, A. (2002). *How to become a clinical psychologist: Getting a foot in the door*. London: Routledge.

Kohut, H. (1968). The psychoanalytic treatment of narcissistic personality disorders: Outline of a systematic approach. *Psychoanalytic Study of the Child*, 23, 86–113.

Kolvin, I., Oustend, C., Humphrey, M., & McNay, A. (1971). Studies of childhood psychoses. II. Phenomenology of childhood psychoses. *British Journal of Psychiatry*, 118, 385–394.

Kotov, R., Gamez, W., Schmidt, F. & Watson, D. (2010). Linking "big" personality traits to anxiety, depressive, and substance use disorders: A meta-analysis. *Psychological Bulletin*, 136(5), 768–821.

Kraepelin, E. (1899). *Psychiatrie* (sixth edition). Leipzig, Germany: Barth.

Kraepelin, E. (1913). Hysterical insanity. In E. Kraepelin (Ed.), *Lectures on clinical psychiatry* (trans. T. Johnstone, pp. 249–258). New York: William Wood.

Kraepelin, E. (1921). *Manic-depressive insanity and paranoia*. Edinburgh: Livingstone.

Kretchmer, E. (1936). Physique and character. London: Kegan Paul, Trench & Trubner.

Krueger, R. F., & Johnson, W. (2008). Behavioural genetics and personality. In L. A. Pervin, O. P. John, & R. W. Robins (Eds.), *Handbook of personality: Theory and research* (third edition, pp. 287–310). New York: Guilford.

Kuipers, E., Leff, J., & Lam, D. (2002). *Family work for schizophrenia* (second edition). London: Gaskell.

Kurtz, M. M. (2011). Neurocognition as a predictor of response to evidence-based psychosocial interventions in schizophrenia: What is the state of the evidence? *Clinical Psychology Review*, 31, 663–672.

Kurtz, M. M., & Mueser, K. T. (2008). A meta-analysis of controlled research on social skills training for schizophrenia. *Journal of Consulting and Clinical Psychology*, 76(3), 491–504.

Kutcher, S., Aman, M., & Brooks, S. (2004). International consensus statement on attention-deficit/hyperactivity disorder (ADHD) and disruptive behaviour disorders (DBDs): Clinical implications and treatment practice suggestions. *European Neuropsychopharmacology*, 14(1), 11–28.

Kutchins, H. & Kirk, S. (1999). *Making us crazy: DSM – The psychiatric bible and the creation of mental disorders.* New York: Constable.

Kutscher, E. C. (2008). Antipsychotics. In K. Mueser & D. Jeste (Eds.), *Clinical handbook of schizophrenia* (pp. 159–167). New York: Guilford Press.

Laing, R. D. (2009). *Selected works of R. D. Laing, Volumes 1–7. (Vol. 1. The divided self. Vol. 2. Self and others. Vol. 3. Reason and violence. Vol 4. Sanity and madness in the family. Vol. 5. The politics of the family. Vol. 6. Interpersonal perception. Vol. 7. Knots.)* London: Routledge.

Lambert, M. (1992). Psychotherapy outcome research: Implications for integrative and eclectic therapists. In J. Norcross & M. Goldfried (Eds.), *Handbook of psychotherapy integration* (pp. 94–129). New York: Basic.

Lambert, M. (2005). Early response in psychotherapy: Further evidence for the importance of common factors rather than "placebo effects". *Journal of Clinical Psychology*, 61, 855–869.

Lambert, M., & Barley, D. (2002). Research summary on the therapeutic relationship and psychotherapy outcome. In J. Norcross (Ed.), *Relationships that work* (pp. 17–36). Oxford: Oxford University Press.

Lambert, M., & Ogles, B. (1997). The effectiveness of psychotherapy supervision. In C. E. Watkins Jr. (Ed.), *Handbook of psychotherapy supervision* (pp. 421–446). New York: Wiley.

Lambert, M., & Ogles, B. (2004). The efficacy and effectiveness of psychotherapy. In M. J. Lambert (Ed.), *Bergin and Garfield's handbook of psychotherapy and behaviour change* (fifth edition, pp. 139–193). New York: Wiley.

Lambert, M., Whipple, J., & Hawkins, E. (2003). Is it time for clinicians to routinely track patient outcome? A meta-analysis. *Clinical Psychology: Science and Practice*, 10, 288–301.

Lasègue, E. (1873). De l'anorexie hysterique. *Archives Generales de Medicine*, 21, 385–403.

Lebow, J. L., & Uliaszek, A. A. (2010). Couples and family therapy for personality disorders. In J. J. Magnavita (Ed.), *Evidence-based treatment of personality dysfunction: Principles, methods, and processes* (pp. 193–221). Washington, DC: American Psychological Association.

Lees, J., Manning, N., & Rawlings, B. (1999). *Therapeutic community effectiveness: A systematic international review of therapeutic community treatment for people with personality disorders and mentally disordered offenders.* York, UK: University of York, NHS Centre for Reviews and Dissemination.

Leff, J., & Vaughn, C. (1985). *Expressed emotion in families.* New York: Guilford.

Leff, J., Vearnals, S., Brewin, C., Wolff, G., Alexander, B., Asen, E., et al. (2000). The London Depression Intervention Trial: Randomised controlled trial of antidepressants versus couple therapy in the treatment and maintenance of people with depression living with a partner: Clinical outcomes and costs. *British Journal of Psychiatry*, 177, 95–100.

le Grange, D. & Rienecke Hoste, R. (2010). Family therapy. In W. S. Agras (Ed.), *The Oxford handbook of eating disorders* (pp. 373–385). New York: Oxford University Press.

Lehman, A., & Steinwachs, D. (1998). At issue: Translating research into practice: The Schizophrenia Patient Outcomes Research Team (PORT) treatment recommendations. *Schizophrenia Bulletin*, 24, 1–10.

Leichsenring, F. (2009). Applications of psychodynamic psychotherapy to specific disorders: Efficacy and indications. In G. O. Gabbard (Ed.), *Textbook of psychotherapeutic treatments* (pp. 97–132). Arlington, VA: American Psychiatric Publishing.

Leichsenring, F. (2010). Evidence for psychodynamic psychotherapy in personality disorders: A review. In J. Clarkin, O. Fonagy, & G. Gabbard (Eds.), *Psychodynamic psychotherapy for personality disorders: A clinical handbook* (pp. 421–438). Arlington, VA: American Psychiatric Publishing.

Leichsenring, F., & Leibing, E. (2003). The effectiveness of psychodynamic therapy and cognitive behaviour therapy in the treatment of personality disorders: A meta-analysis. *American Journal of Psychiatry*, 160, 1223–1232.

Leichsenring, F., & Rabung, S. (2008). Effectiveness of long-term psychodynamic psychotherapy: A meta-analysis. *Journal of the American Medical Association*, 300, 1551–1565.

Leichsenring, F., & Rabung, S. (2011). Long-term psychodynamic psychotherapy in complex mental disorders: A meta-analysis. *British Journal of Psychiatry*, 199, 15–22.

Leichsenring, F., Rabung, S., & Leibing, E. (2004). The efficacy of short-term psychodynamic psychotherapy in specific psychiatric disorders: A meta-analysis. *Archives of General Psychiatry*, 61, 1208–1216.

Leichsenring, F., Salzer, S., Jaeger, U., Kächele, H., Kreische, R., & Leweke, F. (2009). Short-term psychodynamic psychotherapy and cognitive-behavioural therapy in generalized anxiety disorder: A randomized, controlled trial. *American Journal of Psychiatry*, 166, 875–881.

Lemma, A., Roth, A., & Pilling, S. (2008). The competences required to deliver effective psychoanalytic/psychodynamic therapy. London: Centre for Outcomes Research & Effectiveness.

Lemma, A., Target, M., & Fonagy, P. (2010). The development of a brief psychodynamic protocol for depression: Dynamic interpersonal therapy (DIT). *Psychoanalytic Psychotherapy*, 24, 329–346.

Lemma, A., Target, M., & Fonagy, P. (2011). *Brief dynamic interpersonal therapy: A clinician's guide.* Oxford: Oxford University Press.

Lenzenweger, M. (2010). *Schizotypy and schizophrenia.* New York: Guilford.

Lenzenweger, M. F., & Clarkin, J. F. (2005). The personality disorders: History, classification, and research issues. In J. Clarkin & M. Lenzenweger (Eds.), *Major theories of personality disorder* (second edition, pp. 1–42). New York: Guilford.

Lenzenweger, M., Lane, M., Loranger, A., & Kessler, R. (2007). DSM IV personality disorders in the national comorbidity survey replication. *Biological Psychiatry*, 62, 533–564.

Leshner, A. (2008). By now, "harm reduction" harms both science and the public health. *Clinical Pharmacology & Therapeutics*, 83(4), 513–514.

Leucht, C., Heres, S., Kane, J. M., Kissling, W., Davis, J. M., & Leucht, S. (2011). Oral versus depot antipsychotic drugs for schizophrenia—A critical systematic review and meta-analysis of randomised long-term trials. *Schizophrenia Research*, 127, 83–92.

Levine, M. P., & Murnen, S. K. (2009). "Everybody knows that mass media are/ are not a cause of eating disorders": A critical review of evidence for a causal link between media, negative body image, and disordered eating in females. *Journal of Social and Clinical Psychology*, 28, 9–42.

Levine, M. P., & Smolak, L. (2010). Cultural influences on body image and the eating disorders. In W. S. Agras (Ed.), *The Oxford handbook of eating disorders* (pp. 223–246). New York: Oxford University Press.

Levinson, D. F. (2009). *Genetics of major depression*. In H. Gotlib & C. Hammen (Eds.), *Handbook of depression* (second edition, pp. 165–186). New York: Guilford Press.

Lewinsohn, P., & Gotlib, I. (1995). Behavioural theory and treatment of depression. In E. Becker & W. Leber (Eds.), *Handbook of depression* (pp. 352–375). New York: Guilford.

Lezak, M., Howieson, D., & Loring, D. (2004). *Neuropsychological assessment* (fourth edition). Oxford: Oxford University Press.

Liddle, H. A. (2010). Treating adolescent substance abuse using multidimensional family therapy. In J. R. Weisz & A. E. Kazdin (Eds.), *Evidence-based psychotherapies for children and adolescents* (second edition, pp. 416–432). New York: Guilford Press.

Lilienfeld, S. (2007). Psychological treatments that cause harm. *Perspectives on Psychological Science*, 2, 53–70.

Lin, C., Lane, H., & Tsai, G. E. (2011). Glutamate signaling in the pathophysiology and therapy of schizophrenia. *Pharmacology, Biochemistry and Behaviour*. Advance oinline publication. doi:10.1016/j.pbb.2011.03.023

Linde, K., Berner, M., & Egger, M. (2005). St John's wort for depression – Meta-analysis of randomised controlled trials. *British Journal of Psychiatry*, 86, 99–107.

Linehan, M., Davison, G., Lynch, T., & Sanderson, G. (2006). Technique factors in treating personality disorders. In L. Castonguay & L. Beutler (Eds.), *Principles of therapeutic change that work* (pp. 239–252). Oxford: Oxford University Press.

Links, P. S., & Kolla, N. (2009). Assessing and managing suicide risk. In J. Oldham, A. Skodol, & D. Bender (Eds.), *Essentials of personality disorders* (pp. 343–360). Arlington, VA: American Psychiatric Publishing.

Linscott, R. J., & van Os, J. (2010). Systematic reviews of categorical versus continuum models in psychosis: Evidence for discontinuous subpopulations underlying a psychometric continuum: Implications for DSM-V, DSM-VI, and DSM-VII. *Annual Review of Clinical Psychology*, 6, 391–419.

Lipsey, M. W. (2009). The primary factors that characterize effective interventions with juvenile offenders: A meta-analytic overview. *Victims & Offenders*, 4(2), 124–147.

Liu, R. T., & Alloy, L. B. (2010). Stress generation in depression: A systematic review of the empirical literature and recommendations for future study. *Clinical Psychology Review*, 30, 582–593.

Lochman, J. E., Boxmeyer, C. L., Powell, N. P., Barry, T. D., & Pardini, D. A. (2010). Anger control training for aggressive youths. In J. R. Weisz & A. E. Kazdin (Eds.), *Evidence-based psychotherapies for children and adolescents* (second edition, pp. 227–242). New York: Guilford Press.

Lock, J., Le Grange, D., Agras, W., & Dare, C. (2001). *Treatment manual for anorexia nervosa: A family based approach*. New York: Guilford.

Lopez, S., & Snyder, C. (2009). *Oxford handbook of positive psychology* (second edition). New York: Oxford University Press.

Loranger, A. W. (1999). *International Personality Disorder Examination*. Odessa, FL: Psychological Assessment Resources.

Lorber, M. F. (2004). The psychophysiology of aggression, psychopathy, and conduct problems: A meta-analysis. *Psychological Bulletin*, 130, 531–552.

Losel, F., & Beelmann, A. (2005). Social problem-solving programs for preventing antisocial behaviour in children and youth. In M. McMurran & J. McGuire (Eds.), *Social problem solving and offending: Evidence, evaluation and evolution* (pp. 127–143). Chichester, UK: Wiley.

Lubman, D., & Yücel, M. (2008). Drugs, mental health and the adolescent brain: Implications for early intervention. *Early Intervention in Psychiatry*, 2, 63–66.

Luborsky, L. (1962). Clinicians' judgements of mental health. *Archives of General Psychiatry*, 7, 407–417.

Lucas, R. (2009). *Psychotic wavelength: A psychoanalytic perspective for psychiatry*. London: Routledge.

Lukoff, D., Nuechterlein, K., & Ventura, J. (1986). Manual for expanded Brief Psychiatric Rating Scale (BRS). *Schizophrenia Bulletin*, 12, 594–602.

Lunt, I. (2008). Psychologist qualifications in Europe: Common standard for quality and mobility. *Australian Psychologist*, 43(4), 222–230.

Luty, J., Fekadu, D., & Dhandayudham, A. (2006). Understanding of the term 'schizophrenia' by the British public. *Psychiatric Bulletin*, 30, 435–435.

Luyten, P., Corveleyn, J., & Blatt, S. J. (2005). The convergence among psychodynamic and cognitive-behavioural theories of depression: A critical overview of empirical research. In J. Corveleyn, P. Luyten, & S. J. Blatt (Eds.), *The theory and treatment of depression: Towards a dynamic interactionism model* (pp. 107–147). Leuven, Belgium/Mahwah, NJ: Leuven University Press/Lawrence Erlbaum Associates.

Maag, J. W., Swearer, S. M., & Toland, M. D. (2009). Cognitive-behavioural interventions for depression in children and adolescents: Meta-analysis, promising programs, and implications for school personnel. In M. J. Mayer, J. E. Lochman, & R. Van Acker (Eds.), *Cognitive-behavioural interventions for emotional and behavioural disorders: School-based practice* (pp. 235–265). New York: Guilford Press.

Macgowan, M. J., & Engle, B. (2010). Evidence for optimism: Behavior therapies and motivational interviewing in adolescent substance abuse treatment. *Child and Adolescent Psychiatric Clinics of North America*, 19, 527–545.

Magnavita, J. J. (2009). Psychodynamic family psychotherapy: Toward unified relational systematics. In J. Bray & M. Stanton (Eds.). *The Wiley–Blackwell handbook of family psychology* (pp. 240–257). Chichester, UK: Wiley-Blackwell.

Maine, M. & Bunnell, D. (2010). A perfect biopsychosocial storm: Gender, culture, and eating disorders. In M. Maine, B. McGilley, & D. Bunnell (Eds.), *Treatment of eating disorders: Bridging the research–practice gap* (pp. 3–16). San Diego, CA: Elsevier.

Makris, N., Biederman, J., Monuteaux, M. C., & Seidman, L. J. (2009). Towards conceptualizing a neural systems-based anatomy of attention-deficit/hyperactivity disorder. *Developmental Neuroscience*, 31, 36–49.

Malan, D. (1995). *Individual psychotherapy and the science of psychodynamics* (second edition). London: Butterworth-Heinemann.

Mamah, D., & Barch, D. (2011). Diagnosis and classification of the schizophrenia spectrum disorders. In M. Ritsner (Ed.), *Handbook of schizophrenia spectrum disorders, Volume I: Conceptual issues and neurobiological advances* (pp. 45–83). New York: Springer.

Marlatt, G. A., & Witkiewitz, K. (2010). Update on harm-reduction policy and intervention research. *Annual Review of Clinical Psychology*, 6, 591–606.

Maron, E., Hettema, J. M., & Shlik, J. (2010). Advances in molecular genetics of panic disorder. *Molecular Psychiatry*, *15*(7), 681–701.

Martin, D., Graske, J., & Davis, M. (2000). Relation of the therapeutic alliance with outcome and other variables: A meta-analytic review. *Journal of Consulting & Clinical Psychology*, 68, 438–450.

Martin, E. I., Ressler, K. J., Binder, E., & Nemeroff, C. B. (2009). The neurobiology of anxiety disorders: Brain imaging, genetics, and psychoneuroendocrinology. *Psychiatric Clinics of North America*, 32(3), 549–575.

Mason, M. J. (2010). Mental health, school problems, and social networks: Modeling urban adolescent substance use. *Journal of Primary Prevention*, 31, 321–331.

Masson, J. (1984). *Freud's suppression of seduction theory.* New York: Farrar, Straus, & Giroux.

Mathew, S. J., & Hoffman, E. J. (2009). Pharmacotherapy for generalized anxiety disorder. In M. M. Antony & M. B. Stein (Eds.), *Oxford handbook of anxiety and related disorders* (pp. 350–363). New York: Oxford University Press.

Mathews, C. A. (2009). Phenomenology of obsessive-compulsive disorder. In M. M. Antony & M. B. Stein (Eds.), *Oxford handbook of anxiety and related disorders* (pp. 56–64). New York: Oxford University Press.

Matthews, K., & Christmas, D. (2009). Neurosurgery for psychiatric disorders. In M. Gelder, et al. (Eds.), *New Oxford textbook of psychiatry* (second edition, Vol. 2, pp. 1266–1272). Oxford: Oxford University Press.

Mazzeo, S. E., & Bulik, C. M. (2009). Environmental and genetic risk factors for eating disorders: What the clinician needs to know. *Child and Adolescent Psychiatric Clinics of North America*, 18(1), 67–82.

Mazzucchelli, T., Kane, R., & Rees, C. (2009). Behavioural activation treatments for depression in adults: A meta-analysis and review. *Clinical Psychology: Science and Practice*, 16, 383–411.

McCart, M., Priester, P., Davies, W., & Azen, R. (2006). Differential effectiveness of cognitive-behavioural therapy and behavioural parent-training for antisocial youth: A meta-analysis. *Journal of Abnormal Child Psychology*, 34(4), 527–543.

McCrae, R. R., & Costa, P. T., Jr. (2008). The five-factor theory of personality. In O. P. John, R. W. Robins, & L. A. Pervin (Eds.), *Handbook of personality: Theory and research* (third edition, pp. 159–181). New York: Guilford Press.

McCullough-Vaillant, L. (1997). *Changing character: Short-term anxiety regulating psychotherapy for restructuring defences, affects and attachments.* New York: Basic Books.

McDermott, L. M., & Ebmeier, K. P. (2009). A meta-analysis of depression severity and cognitive function. *Journal of Affective Disorders*, 119, 1–8.

McDermott, R., Tingley, D., Cowden, J., Frazzetto, G., & Johnson, D. D. P. (2009). Monoamine oxidase A gene (MAOA) predicts behavioural aggression following provocation. *Proceedings of the National Academy of Sciences of the United States of America*, 106, 2118–2123.

McElroy, S. L., Guerdjikova, A. I., O'Melia, A. M., Mori, N., Keck, P. E., Jr. (2010). Pharmacotherapy of the eating disorders. In W. S. Agras (Ed.), *The Oxford Handbook of eating disorders* (pp. 417–451). New York: Oxford University Press.

McFall, R. M. (2006). Doctoral training in clinical psychology. *Annual Review of Clinical Psychology, 2*, 21–49.

McFarlane, W. (2004). *Multifamily groups in the treatment of severe psychiatric disorders.* New York: Guilford.

McFarlane, W. R. (2005). Psychoeducational multifamily groups for families with persons with severe mental illness. In J. Lebow (Ed.), *Handbook of clinical family therapy* (pp. 195–227). Hoboken, NJ: Wiley.

McGlashen, T., & Hoffman, R. (2000). Schizophrenia as a disorder of developmentally reduced synaptic connectivity. *Archives of General Psychiatry, 57*, 637–648.

McGrath, J., Saha, S., Welham, J., Saadi, O., MacCauley, C., & Chant, D. (2004). A systematic review of the incidence of schizophrenia: The distribution of rates and the influence of sex, urbanicity, migrant status and methodology. *BMC Medicine, 2*, 13.

McLaughlin, K. A., & Nolen-Hoeksema, S. (2011). Rumination as a transdiagnostic factor in depression and anxiety. *Behaviour Research and Therapy, 49*, 186–193.

McLeod, B. D., Weisz, J. R., & Wood, J. J. (2007). Examining the association between parenting and childhood depression: A meta-analysis. *Clinical Psychology Review, 27*, 986–1003.

McMahon, R. J., Witkiewitz, K., Kotler, J. S., & The Conduct Problems Prevention Research Group. (2010). Predictive validity of callous–unemotional traits measured in early adolescence with respect to multiple antisocial outcomes. *Journal of Abnormal Psychology, 119*(4), 752–763.

McNally, R. F. & Reese, H. E. (2009). Information-processing approaches to understanding anxiety disorders. In M. M. Antony & M. B. Stein (Eds.), *Oxford handbook of anxiety and related disorders* (pp. 136–152). New York: Oxford University Press.

Medalia, A., & Choi, J. (2009). Cognitive remediation in schizophrenia. *Neuropsychology Review, 19*, 353–364.

Meltzer, H., Gatward, R., Goodman, R., & Ford, T. (2000). *The Mental Health of Children and Adolescents in Great Britain: The report of a survey carried out in 1999 by Social Survey Division of the Office for National Statistics on behalf of the Department of Health, the Scottish Health Executive and the National Assembly for Wales.* London: The Stationery Office.

Menninger, K. (1958). *Theory of psychoanalytic technique.* London: Imago.

Meyer, B., Ajchenbrenner, M., & Bowles, D. P. (2005). Sensory sensitivity, attachment experiences, and rejection responses among adults with borderline and avoidant features. *Journal of Personality Disorders, 19*, 641–658.

Miller, S., Duncan, B., Sorrell, R., & Brown, G. (2005). The partners for change outcome management system. *Journal of Clinical Psychology, 61*, 199–208.

Miller, W., & Rollnick, S. (2002). *Motivational interviewing. Preparing people for change* (second edition). New York: Guilford.

Millon, T. (2009). *Millon Clinical Multiaxial Inventory–III manual* (fourth edition). Minneapolis, MN: National Computer Systems.

Milne, D. (2009). *Evidence-based clinical supervision: Principles and practice.* Oxford: BPS-Blackwell.

Milrod, B., Leon, A., Busch, F., Rudden, M., Schwalberg, M., Clarkin J., et al. (2007). A randomized controlled clinical trial of psychoanalytic psychotherapy for panic disorder. *American Journal of Psychiatry, 164*, 265–272.

Mindus, P., Rasmussen, S. A., Lindquist, C., & Noren, G. (2001). *Neurosurgical treatment for refractory obsessive-compulsive disorder: Implications for understanding frontal lobe function*. Arlington, VA: American Psychiatric Publishing.

Minuchin, S., Rosman, B., & Baker, L. (1978). *Psychosomatic families: Anorexia nervosa in context*. Cambridge, MA: Harvard University Press.

Mitchell, J. E., & Crow, S. J. (2010). Medical comorbidities of eating disorders. In W. S. Agras (Ed.), *The Oxford handbook of eating disorders* (pp. 259–266). New York: Oxford University Press.

Moffitt, T. (2005). The new look of behavioural genetics in developmental psychopathology: Gene–environment interplay in antisocial behaviours. *Psychological Bulletin*, 131, 533–554.

Moffitt, T., & Scott, S. (2008). Disorders of attention and activity. In M. Rutter et al. (Eds.), *Rutter's child and adolescent psychiatry* (fifth edition, pp. 543–564). London: Blackwell.

Mohr, D. (1995). Negative outcome in psychotherapy: A critical review. *Clinical Psychology: Science and Practice*, 2, 1–27.

Mojtabai, R., Nicholson, R., & Carpenter, B. (1998). Role of psychosocial treatments in management of schizophrenia: A meta-analysis review of controlled outcome studies. *Schizophrenia Bulletin*, 24, 569–587.

Monroe, S., & Harkness, K. (2005). Life stress, the "kindling" hypothesis, and the recurrence of depression: Considerations from a life stress perspective. *Psychological Review*, 112, 417–445.

Monroe, S., Slavich, G. M., & Georgiades, K. (2009). The social environment and life stress in depression. In H. Gotlib & C. Hammen (Eds.), *Handbook of depression* (second edition, pp. 340–360). New York: Guilford Press.

Montañés, F., & de Lucas Taracena, M. T. (2006). Evolutionary aspects of affective disorders, critical review and proposal of a new model. *Actas Españolas De Psiquiatría*, 34, 264–276.

Monteleone, P., Martiadis, V., & Maj, M. (2010). Circadian rhythms and treatment implications in depression. *Progress in Neuropsychopharmacology & Biological Psychiatry*, 35, 1569–1574.

Morgan, T. B., & Crane, D. R. (2010). Cost-effectiveness of family-based substance abuse treatment. *Journal of Marital and Family Therapy*, 36, 486–498.

Moscovitch, D. A., Antony, M. M., & Swinson, R. P. (2009). Exposure-based treatments for anxiety disorders: Theory and process. In M. M. Antony & M. B. Stein (Eds.), *Oxford handbook of anxiety and related disorders* (pp. 461–475). New York: Oxford University Press.

Moss, E. S., Nicole, C. C., Dubois-Comtois, K., Mazzarello, T., & Berthiaume, C. (2006). Attachment and behaviour problems in middle childhood as reported by adult and child informants. *Development and Psychopathology*, 18(2), 425–444.

Mowrer, O. (1939). A stimulus response analysis of anxiety and its role as a reinforcing agent. *Psychological Review*, 46, 553–565.

Mueser, K. & Duva, S. (2011). Schizophrenia. In D. Barlow (Ed.), *The Oxford handbook of clinical psychology* (pp. 469–503). New York: Oxford University Press.

Mueser, K., & Jeste, D. (2008). *Clinical handbook of schizophrenia*. New York: Guilford Press.

Mumford, E., Schlesinger, H., Glass, G., Patrick, C., & Cuerdon, T. (1984). A new look at evidence about reduced cost of medical utilization following mental health treatment. *American Journal of Psychiatry*, 141, 1145–1158.

Murray, C., & Lopez, A. (1996). *The global burden of disease: A comprehensive assessment of mortality and disability from diseases, injuries and risk factors in 1990 and projected to 2020*. Cambridge, MA: Harvard University Press.

Murray, R., & Castle, D. (2009). Genetic and environmental risk factors for schizophrenia. In M. Gelder et al. (Eds.), *New Oxford textbook of psychiatry* (second edition, Vol. 1, pp. 553–561). Oxford: Oxford University Press.

Murray, R., & Lewis, S. (1987). Is schizophrenia a neurodevelopmental disorder? *British Medical Journal*, 295, 681–682.

Murray, R., & Van Os, J. (1998). Predictors of outcome in schizophrenia. *Journal of Clinical Psychopharmacology*, 18, 25–45.

Najavits, L. M. (2007). Psychosocial treatments for posttraumatic stress disorder. In P. E. Nathan & J. M. Gorman (Eds.), *A guide to treatments that work* (third edition, pp. 513–530). New York: Oxford University Press.

Naragon-Gainey, K. (2010). Meta-analysis of the relations of anxiety sensitivity to the depressive and anxiety disorders. *Psychological Bulletin*, 136(1), 128–150.

Narcotics Anonymous (2008). *Narcotics Anonymous* (sixth edition). Chatsworth, CA: Narcotics Anonymous World Services.

Nasser, M., & Katzman, N. (2003). Sociocultural theories of eating disorders. In J. Treasure, U. Schmidt, & E. van Furth (Eds.), *Handbook of eating disorders* (second edition, pp. 139–150). Chichester, UK: Wiley.

Nathan, P., & Gorman, J. (2007), *A guide to treatments that work* (third edition). New York: Oxford University Press.

National Advisory Committee on Drugs and the Drug and Alcohol Information and Research Unit (2004). *Drug use in Ireland and Northern Ireland 2003/2003 Drug Prevalence Survey*. Dublin, Ireland and Belfast, UK: Health Board (Ireland) and Social Service Board (Northern Ireland).

National Centre for Social Research and the National Foundation for Educational Research (2002). *Drug use, smoking and drinking among young people in England in 2001*. London: NCSR and NFER.

National Institute of Mental Health in England (2003). *Personality disorder: No longer a diagnosis of exclusion*. Leeds, UK: National Institute of Mental Health in England.

Nestler, E., & Charney, D. (2008). *Neurobiology of mental illness* (third edition). Oxford: Oxford University Press.

Newman, M., Crits-Christoph, P., Connoly Gibbons, M., & Erickson, T. (2006a). Participant factors in treating anxiety disorders. In L. Castonguay & L. Beutler (Eds.), *Principles of therapeutic change that work* (pp. 121–154). Oxford: Oxford University Press.

Newman, M., Stiles, W., Woody, S. & Janeck, A. (2006b). Integration of therapeutic factors in anxiety disorders. In L. Castonguay & L. Beutler (Eds.), *Principles of therapeutic change that work* (pp. 187–202). Oxford: Oxford University Press.

Newton-Howes, G., Tyrer, P., & Johnson, T. (2006). Personality disorder and the outcome of depression: Meta-analysis of published studies. *British Journal of Psychiatry*, 188, 13–20.

NICE (2004a). *Eating disorders: Core interventions in the treatment and management of anorexia nervosa, bulimia nervosa and related disorders*. London: National Institute for Clinical Excellence.

NICE (2004b). *Self-harm: The short-term physical and psychological management and secondary prevention of self-harm in primary and secondary care (Clinical guideline 16)*. London: National Institute of Clinical Excellence.

NICE (2005a). *Post-traumatic stress disorder: The management of PTSD in adults and children in primary and secondary care (Clinical guideline 26)*. London: National Institute of Clinical Excellence.

NICE (2005b). *Obsessive compulsive disorder: Core interventions in the treatment of obsessive compulsive disorder and body dysmorphic disorder (Clinical guideline 31)*. London: National Institute for Clinical Excellence.

NICE (2005c). *Depression in children and young people: Identification and management in primary, community and secondary care (Clinical guideline 28)*. London: National Institute of Clinical Excellence.

NICE (2006a). *Parent-training/education programmes in the management of children with conduct disorders. NICE technology appraisal guidance 102*. London: National Institute of Clinical Excellence.

NICE (2006b). *Computerized cognitive behaviour therapy for depression and anxiety (Technology appraisal 97)*. London: NICE.

NICE (2008a). *Attention deficit hyperactivity disorder. Diagnosis and management of ADHD in children, young people and adults. NICE guideline 72*. London: National Institute of Clinical Excellence.

NICE (2008b). *Drug misuse: Psychosocial interventions. National clinical practice guideline 51*. London: British Psychological Society and the Royal College of Psychiatrists.

NICE (2009a). *Depression: The treatment and management of depression in adults (update) (Clinical guideline 90)*. London: National Institute of Clinical Excellence.

NICE (2009b). *Core interventions in the treatment and management of schizophrenia in primary and secondary care (update). (Clinical guideline 82)*. London: National Institute of Clinical Excellence.

NICE (2009c). *Antisocial personality disorder: Treatment, management and prevention (Clinical guideline 77)*. London: National Institute of Clinical Excellence.

NICE (2009d). *Borderline personality disorder: Treatment and management (Clinical guideline 78)*. London: National Institute of Clinical Excellence.

NICE (2011). *Generalized anxiety disorder and panic disorder, with and without agoraphobia. Management in primary, secondary and community care (Clinical guideline 113)*. London: National Institute of Clinical Excellence.

Nigg, J. (2001). Is ADHD an inhibitory disorder. *Psychological Bulletin*, 125, 571–596.

Nigg, J. (2005). Neuropsychologic theory and findings in attention-deficit/hyperactivity disorder: The state of the field and salient challenges for the coming decade. *Biological Psychiatry*, 57, 1424–1435.

Nigg, J., & Huang-Pollock, C. L. (2003). An early onset model of the role of executive functions and intelligence in conduct disorder/delinquency. In B. B. Lahey, T. Moffitt, & A. Caspi (Eds.), *The causes of conduct disorder and serious juvenile delinquency* (pp. 227–253). New York: Guilford.

Nolen-Hoeksema, S., & Hilt, L. M. (2009a). *Handbook of depression in adolescents*. New York: Routledge.

Nolen-Hoeksema, S., & Hilt, L. M. (2009b). Gender differences in depression. In H. Gotlib & C. Hammen (Eds.), *Handbook of depression* (second edition, pp. 386–404). New York: Guilford Press.

Norcross, J. (2002). *Psychotherapy relationships that work*. Oxford: Oxford University Press.

Norcross, J. (2005). The psychotherapist's own psychotherapy: Educating and developing psychologists. *American Psychologist*, 60(8), 840–850.

Norcross, J., Beutler, L., & Levant, R. (2006). *Evidence-based practices in mental health: Debate and dialogue on the fundamental questions*. Washington, DC: American Psychological Association.

Norcross, J. C., Ellis, J. L., & Sayette, M. A. (2010). Getting in and getting money: A comparative analysis of admission standards, acceptance rates, and financial assistance across the research–practice continuum in clinical psychology programs. *Training and Education in Professional Psychology*, 4(2), 99–104.

Norcross, J., & Goldfried, M. (Eds.) (2003). *Handbook of psychotherapy integration* (second edition). New York: Basic Books.

Norton, P., & Price, E. (2007). A meta-analytic review of adult cognitive-behavioural treatment outcome across the anxiety disorders. *Journal of Nervous and Mental Disease*, 195(6), 521–531.

Nunez-Smith, M., Wolf, E., Huang, H. M., Chen, P. G., Lee, L., Emanuel, E. J., et al. (2010). Media exposure and tobacco, illicit drugs, and alcohol use among children and adolescents: A systematic review. *Substance Abuse*, 31, 174–192.

O'Brien, C., Childress, A., McLellan, A., & Ehrman, R. (1992). A learning model of addiction. *Research Publication of the Association of Research on Nervous and Mental Diseases*, 70, 157–177.

Olatunji, B. O., Cisler, J. M., & Deacon, B. J. (2010). Efficacy of cognitive behavioural therapy for anxiety disorders: A review of meta-analytic findings. *Psychiatric Clinics of North America*, 33(3), 557–577.

Orlinsky, D., Tonnestad, M., & Willutzki, U. (2004). Fifty years of psychotherapy process–outcome research: Continuity and change. In M. Lambert (Ed.), *Bergin and Garfield's handbook of psychotherapy and behaviour change* (fifth edition, pp. 307–389). New York: Wiley.

Orth, U., Robins, R. W., & Roberts, B. W. (2008). Low self-esteem prospectively predicts depression in adolescence and young adulthood. *Journal of Personality and Social Psychology*, 95, 695–708.

O'Shea, G., & Byrne, M. (2010). In pursuit of clinical training. *Irish Psychologist*, 36(4), 79–81.

O'Shea, G., & Byrne, M. (2011a). A profile of entrants to Irish clinical training programmes. *Irish Psychologist*, 37(5), 118–123.

O'Shea, G., & Byrne, M. (2011b). Entrants' experiences of the clinical psychology programme selection process. *Irish Psychologist*, 37(6), 150–157.

Ozer, E., Best, S., Lipsey, T., & Weiss, D. (2003). Predictors of posttraumatic stress disorder and symptoms in adults: A meta-analysis. *Psychological Bulletin*, 129, 52–73.

Pachana, N., O'Donovan, A., & Helmes, E. (2006). Australian clinical psychology training program directors survey. *Australian Psychologist*, 41(3), 168–178.

Pachana, N., Sofronoff, K., & O'Brien, M. (2008). Focus on clinical psychology postgraduate training: Taking the curriculum into the next decade. *Australian Psychologist*, 43(4), 219–221.

Page, A. & Stritzke, W. (2006). *Clinical psychology for trainees*. Cambridge, UK: Cambridge University Press.

Palmer, B. W., Dawes, S. E., & Heaton, R. K. (2009). What do we know about neuropsychological aspects of schizophrenia? *Neuropsychology Review*, 19, 365–384.

Papworth, M. (2004). Getting on clinical psychology training courses: Responses to frequently asked questions. *Clinical Psychology*, 42, 32–36.

Papworth, M. (2007). Getting on clinical psychology training courses: Responses to frequently asked questions (part 2). *Clinical Psychology Forum*, 177, 37–41.

Pardini, D. A., Frick, P. J., & Moffitt, T. E. (2010). Building an evidence base for DSM-V conceptualizations of oppositional defiant disorder and conduct disorder: Introduction to the special section. *Journal of Abnormal Psychology*, *119*(4), 683–688.

Paris, J. (1996). *Social factors in the personality disorders: A biopsychosocial approach to etiology and treatment*. New York: Cambridge University Press.

Parker, G. (2009). Diagnosis, classification and differential diagnosis of the mood disorders. In M. Gelder et al. (Eds.) *New Oxford textbook of psychiatry* (second edition, Vol. 1, pp. 637–645). Oxford: Oxford University Press.

Patterson, G. (1982). *Coercive family process*. Eugene, OR: Castalia.

Paykel, E., & Scott, J. (2009). Treatment of mood disorders. In M. Gelder et al. (Eds.), *New Oxford textbook of psychiatry* (second edition, Vol. 1, pp. 6669–6680). Oxford: Oxford University Press.

Paykina, N., Greenhill, L., & Gorman, J. (2007). Pharmacological treatments for attention-deficit hyperactivity disorder. In P. Nathan & J. Gorman (Eds.), *A guide to treatments that work* (third edition, pp. 29–70). New York: Oxford University Press.

Peckham, A. D., McHugh, R. K., & Otto, M. W. (2010). A meta-analysis of the magnitude of biased attention in depression. *Depression and Anxiety*, *27*, 1135–1142.

Perlmutter, R. (1996). *A family approach to psychiatric disorders*. Washington, DC: American Psychiatric Press.

Persons, J. B., & Fresco, D. M. (2008). Adult depression. In J. Hunsley & E. J. Mash (Eds.), *A guide to assessments that work* (pp. 96–120). New York: Oxford University Press.

Peterson, C., & Villanova, P. (1988). An expanded Attributional Style Questionnaire. *Journal of Abnormal Psychology*, *97*, 87–89.

Pfammatter, M., Junghan, U., & Brenner, H. (2006). Efficacy of psychological therapy in schizophrenia: Conclusions from meta-analyses. *Schizophrenia Bulletin*, *32*(Suppl. 1), S64–S80.

Phillips, A., Hatton, C., & Gray, I. (2001). Which selection methods do clinical psychology courses use? *Clinical Psychology*, *8*, 19–23.

Phillips, A., Hatton, C., & Gray, I. (2004). Factors predicting the short-listing and selection of trainee clinical psychologists: A prospective national cohort study. *Clinical Psychology and Psychotherapy*, *11*, 111–125.

Phillips, L. J., Francey, S. M., Edwards, J., & McMurray, N. (2007). Stress and psychosis: Towards the development of new models of investigation. *Clinical Psychology Review*, *27*, 307–317.

Phillips, P., McKeown, O., & Sandford, T. (2010). *Dual diagnosis: Practice in context*. Oxford: Wiley–Blackwell.

Phillips, W. J., Hine, D. W., & Thorsteinsson, E. B. (2010). Implicit cognition and depression: A meta-analysis. *Clinical Psychology Review*, *30*, 691–709.

Pine, D. & Klein, R. (2008). Anxiety disorders. In M. Rutter et al. (Eds.), *Rutter's child and adolescent psychiatry* (fifth edition, pp. 628–647). London: Blackwell.

Plante, T. (2009). *Contemporary clinical psychology* (third edition). Hoboken, NJ: Wiley.

Pliszka, S. R. (2007). Pharmacologic treatment of attention-deficit/hyperactivity disorder: Efficacy, safety and mechanisms of action. *Neuropsychology Review*, *17*(1), 61–72.

Polanski, E., & Mokros, H. (1999). *Children's Depression Rating Scale – Revised*. Los Angeles: Western Psychological Services.

Pollack, M. H., & Simon, N. M. (2009). Pharmacotherapy for panic disorder and agoraphobia. In M. M. Antony & M. B. Stein (Eds.), *Oxford handbook of anxiety and related disorders* (pp. 295–307). New York: Oxford University Press.

Princeton Review (2010a). *Cracking the GRE 2011 edition.* Framingham, MA: Princeton Review.

Princeton Review (2010b). *Cracking the GRE psychology subject test* (eighth edition). Framingham, MA: Princeton Review.

Prochaska, J., DiClemente, C., & Norcross, J. (1992). In search of how people change: Applications to addictive behaviours. *American Psychologist, 47,* 1102–1114.

Raine, A. (1996). Autonomic nervous system activity and violence. In D. M. Stoff & R. B. Cairns (Eds.), *Aggression and violence: Genetic, neurobiological and biological perspectives* (pp. 145–168). Mahwah, NJ: Lawrence Erlbaum Associates.

Raine, A., & Yang, Y. (2006). Neural foundations to moral reasoning and antisocial behaviour. *Social, Cognitive, and Affective Neuroscience, 1,* 203–213.

Rapee, R. M., Schniering, C. A., & Hudson, J. L. (2009). Anxiety disorders during childhood and adolescence: Origins and treatment. *Annual Review of Clinical Psychology, 5,* 311–341.

Rapoport, J., & Shaw, P. (2008). Obsessive compulsive disorders. In M. Rutter et al. (Eds.), *Rutter's child and adolescent psychiatry* (fifth edition, pp. 698–718). London: Blackwell.

Rapp, C., & Goscha, R. (2006). *The strengths model: Case management with people with psychiatric disabilities* (second edition). New York: Oxford University Press.

Rapp, C., & Goscha, R. (2008). Strengths-based case management. In K. Mueser & D. Jeste (Eds.), *Clinical handbook of schizophrenia* (pp. 319–328). New York: Guilford Press.

Rapport, M. & Moffitt, C. (2002). Attention deficit/hyperactivity disorder and methylphenidate: A review of height/weight, cardiovascular, and somatic complaint side effects. *Clinical Psychology Review, 22,* 1107–1131.

Read, J., & Bentall, R. (2010). The effectiveness of electroconvulsive therapy: A literature review. *Epidemiologia e Psichiatria Sociale, 19,* 333–347.

Reichborn-Kjennerud, T. (2010). The genetic epidemiology of personality disorders. *Dialogues in Clinical Neuroscience, 12,* 103–114.

Retz, W., Retz-Junginger, P., Supprian, T., Thome, J., & Rosler, M. (2004). Association of serotonin transporter promoter gene polymorphism with violence: Relation with personality disorders, impulsivity and childhood ADHD psychopathology. *Behavioural Sciences and the Law, 22,* 415–425.

Rholes, S., & Simpson, J. (2004). *Adult attachment: Theory, research, and clinical implications.* New York: Guilford.

Rietkerk, T., Boks, M. P. M., Sommer, I. E., Liddle, P. F., Ophoff, R. A., & Kahn, R. S. (2008). The genetics of symptom dimensions of schizophrenia: Review and meta-analysis. *Schizophrenia Research, 102,* 197–205.

Ritsner, M., & Gottesman, I. (2011). The schizophrenia construct after 100 years of challenges. In M. Ritsner (Ed.), *Handbook of schizophrenia spectrum disorders, Volume I: Conceptual issues and neurobiological advances* (pp. 1–44). New York: Springer.

Robbins, M. S., Horigian, V., Szapocznik, J., & Ucha, J. (2010). Treating Hispanic youths using brief strategic family therapy. In J. R. Weisz & A. E. Kazdin (Eds.), *Evidence-based psychotherapies for children and adolescents* (second edition, pp. 375–390). New York: Guilford Press.

Robbins, M. S., Szapocznik, J., & Horigian, V. E. (2009). *Brief strategic family therapy for adolescents with behaviour problems.* In J. Bray & M. Stanton (Eds.), *The Wiley–Blackwell handbook of family psychology* (pp. 416–430). Chichester, UK: Wiley-Blackwell.

Robins, L. (1966). *Deviant children growing up.* Baltimore: Williams and Wilkins.

Roe, D., & Davidson, L. (2008). Recovery. In K. Mueser & D. Jeste (Eds.), *Clinical handbook of schizophrenia* (pp. 566–574). New York: Guilford Press.

Rosenhan, D. (1973). On being sane in insane places. *Science*, 179, 250–258.

Rosenthal, N. E. (2009). Issues for DSM-V: Seasonal affective disorder and seasonality. *American Journal of Psychiatry*, 166, 852–853.

Rosenthal, R. (1994). Parametric measures of effect size. In H. Cooper and L. Hedges (Eds.), *The handbook of research synthesis* (pp. 231–260). New York: Sage.

Rosenthal., R., & Rubin, D. (1982). A simple, general purpose display of magnitude of experimental effect. *Journal of Educational Psychology*, 74, 166–196.

Rosenzweig, S. (1936). Some implicit common factors in diverse methods of psychotherapy: "At last the Dodo bird said, 'Everybody has won and all must have prizes.'" *American Journal of Orthopsychiatry*, 6, 412–415.

Roth, G., & Buchheim, A. (2010). Neurobiology of personality disorders. In J. Clarkin, O. Fonagy, & G. Gabbard (Eds.). *Psychodynamic psychotherapy for personality disorders: A clinical handbook* (pp. 89–124). Arlington, VA: American Psychiatric Publishing.

Roth, T. (1998). Getting on clinical training courses. *The Psychologist*, 11(12), 589–592.

Roth, T. & Fonagy, P. (2005). *What works for whom? A critical review of psychotherapy research* (second edition). London: Guilford.

Roth, T., & Leiper, R. (1995). Selecting for clinical training. *The Psychologist*, 8(1), 25–28.

Rothbart, M. K., & Bates, J. E. (2006). Temperament. In W. Damon & R. M. Lerner (Series Eds.) & N. Eisenberg (Volume Ed.), *Handbook of child psychology, Volume 3: Social, emotional, and personality development* (sixth edition, pp. 99–166). New York: Wiley.

Rowe, D. L., Robinson, P. A., Lazzaro, I. L., Powles, R. C., Gordon, E., & Williams, L. M. (2005). Biophysical modeling of tonic cortical electrical activity in attention deficit hyperactivity disorder. *International Journal of Neuroscience*, 115(9), 1273–1305.

Royal College of Psychiatrists (2005). *The ECT handbook (second edition): The third report of the Royal College of Psychiatrists' Special Committee on ECT* (Council Report CR128). London: Royal College of Psychiatrists.

Rudd, D. N., Cordero, L., & Bryan, C. J. (2009). What every psychologist should know about the Food and Drug Administration's black box warning label for antidepressants. *Professional Psychology: Research and Practice*, 40, 321–326.

Russell, G. (1979). Bulimia nervosa: An ominous variant of anorexia nervosa? *Psychological Medicine*, 9, 429–448.

Sackett, D., Rosenberg, W., Gray, J., Haynes, R., & Richardson, W. (1996). Evidence-based medicine: What it is and what it isn't. *British Medical Journal*, 312, 71–72.

Sackett, D., Straus, S., Richardson, W., Rosenberg, W., & Haynes, R. (2000). *Evidence based medicine: How to practice and teach EBM* (second edition). London: Churchill Livingstone.

Saha, S., Chant, D., Welham, J., & McGrath, J. (2005). A systematic review of the prevalence of schizophrenia. *PLoS Medicine*, 2, 413–433.

Sajatovic, M., Madhusoodanan, S., & Fuller, M. A. (2008). Clozapine. In K. Mueser & D. Jeste (Eds.), *Clinical handbook of schizophrenia* (pp. 178–185). New York: Guilford Press.

Salloum, A. (2010). Minimal therapist-assisted cognitive-behavioural therapy interventions in stepped care for childhood anxiety. *Professional Psychology: Research and Practice*, 41(1), 41–47.

Sammons, M., Paige, R., & Levant, R. (2003). *Prescriptive authority for psychologists: A history and guide*. Washington, DC: American Psychological Association.

Samuel, D. B., & Widiger, T. A. (2008). A meta-analytic review of the relationships between the five-factor model and personality disorders: A facet level analysis. *Clinical Psychology Review*, 28, 1326–1342.

Savla, G. N., Moore, D. J., & Palmer, B. W. (2008). Cognitive functioning. In K. Mueser & D. Jeste (Eds.), *Clinical handbook of schizophrenia* (pp. 91–99). New York: Guilford Press.

Sayette, M., Mayne, T., & Norcross, J. (2010). *Insider's guide to graduate programs in clinical and counseling psychology: 2010/2011* (seventh edition). New York: Guilford.

Scaife, J. (2010). *Supervising the reflective practitioner: An essential guide to theory and practice*. London: Brunner-Routledge.

Schachar, R. (1991). Childhood hyperactivity. *Journal of Child Psychology and Psychiatry*, 32, 155–191.

Scheier, L. (2010). *Handbook of drug use etiology: Theory, methods, and empirical findings*. Washington, DC: American Psychological Association.

Schennach-Wolff, R., Seemuller, F., Musil, R., Spellmann, I. Holler, H., & Riedel, M. (2011). Suicidality and the outcome of schizophrenia. In M. Ritsner (Ed.), *Handbook of schizophrenia spectrum disorders, Volume III: Therapeutic approaches, comorbidity and outcome* (pp. 365–382). New York: Springer.

Scherag, S., Hebebrand, J., & Hinney, A. (2010). Eating disorders: The current status of molecular genetic research. *European Child & Adolescent Psychiatry*, 19, 211–226.

Schmahl, C., & Bremner, J. D. (2006). Neuroimaging in borderline personality disorder. *Journal of Psychiatric Research*, 40, 419–427.

Schneider, K. (1923). *Die Psychopathischen Persönlichkeiten*. Berlin: Springer.

Schuckit, M. (1994). Low level of response to alcohol as a predictor of future alcoholism. *American Journal of Psychiatry*, 151, 184–189.

Schulteis, G., & Koob, G. (1996). Reinforcement processes in opiate addiction: A homeostatic model. *Neurochemical Research*, 21, 1437–1454.

Schultz, D., & Schultz, S. (2008). *Theories of personality* (ninth edition). Belmont, CA: Wadsworth.

Schwartz, S. J., Forthun, L. F., Ravert, R. D., Zamboanga, B. L., Umaña-Taylor, A. J., & Filton, B. J. (2010). Identity consolidation and health risk behaviours in college students. *American Journal of Health Behaviour*, 34, 214–224.

Scior, K., Gray, J., Halsey, R., & Roth, A. (2007). Selection for clinical psychology training: Is there evidence of any bias against applicants from ethnic minorities? *Clinical Psychology Forum*, 175, 7–11.

Scott, C. L., & Resnick, P. J. (2006). Violence risk assessment in persons with mental illness. *Aggression and Violent Behaviour*, 11, 598–611.

Scott, S. (2009). Conduct disorders in childhood and adolescence. In M. Gelder et al. (Eds.), *New Oxford textbook of psychiatry* (second edition, Vol. 2, pp. 1654–1664). Oxford: Oxford University Press.

Seeman, P. (2011). All roads to schizophrenia lead to dopamine supersensitivity and elevated dopamine D2 receptors. *CNS Neuroscience & Therapeutics*, 17, 118–132.

Segal, L. (1991). Brief therapy: The MRI approach. In A. Gurman & D. Kniskern (Eds.), *Handbook of family therapy* (Vol. 2, pp. 17–199). New York: Brunner/ Mazel.

Selvini Palazzoli, S. (1988). *The work of Mara Selvini Palazzoli.* New York: Jason Aronson

Semkovska, M., & McLoughlin, D. M. (2010). Objective cognitive performance associated with electroconvulsive therapy for depression: A systematic review and meta-analysis. *Biological Psychiatry*, 68, 568–577.

Serpell, L., & Troup, N. (2003). Sociocultural theories of eating disorders. In J. Treasure, U. Schmidt, & E. van Furth (Eds.), *Handbook of eating disorders* (second edition, pp. 151–167). Chichester, UK: Wiley.

Sexton, T. L. (2009). *Functional family therapy: Traditional theory to evidence-based practice.* In J. Bray & M. Stanton (Eds.), *The Wiley–Blackwell handbook of family psychology* (pp. 327–340). Chichester, UK: Wiley-Blackwell.

Sexton, T., & Alexander, J. (2003). Functional family therapy: A mature clinical model for working with at-risk adolescents and their families. In T. Sexton, G. Weeks, & M. Robbins (Eds.), *Handbook of family therapy* (third edition, pp. 323–350). New York: Brunner-Routledge.

Shadish, W., & Baldwin, S. (2003). Meta-analysis of MFT interventions. *Journal of Marital and Family Therapy*, 29, 547–570.

Shadish, W., Matt, G., Navarro, A., Siegle, G., Crits-Cristoph, P., Hazelrigg, H., et al. (1997). Evidence that therapy works in clinically representative conditions. *Journal of Consulting Psychology*, 65, 355–365.

Shaham, Y., & Hope, B. (2005). The role of neuroadaptations in relapse to drug seeking. *Nature Neuroscience*, 8, 1437–1439.

Shapiro, D. A., & Shapiro, D. (1982). Meta-analysis of comparative therapy outcome studies: A replication and refinement. *Psychological Bulletin*, 92, 581–604.

Shaw, P. (2010). The shape of things to come in attention deficit hyperactivity disorder. *American Journal of Psychiatry*, 167(4), 363–365.

Shedler, J. (2010). The efficacy of psychodynamic psychotherapy. *American Psychologist*, 65, 98–109.

Sherlin, L., Arns, M., Lubar, J., & Sokhadze, E. (2010). A position paper on neurofeedback for the treatment of ADHD. *Journal of Neurotherapy*, 14(2), 66–78.

Shevlin, M., Houston, J. E., Dorahy, M. J., & Adamson, G. (2008). Cumulative traumas and psychosis: An analysis of the national comorbidity survey and the British psychiatric morbidity survey. *Schizophrenia Bulletin*, 34, 193–199.

Shibley-Hyde, J., Mezulis, A., & Abramson, L. (2008). The ABCs of depression: Integrating affective, biological, and cognitive models to explain the emergence of the gender difference in depression. *Psychological Review*, 115, 291–313

Shirk, S., & Karver, M. (2003). Prediction of treatment outcome from relationship variables in child and adolescent therapy: A meta-analytic review. *Journal of Consulting and Clinical Psychology*, 71, 452–464.

Shyn, S. I., & Hamilton, S. P. (2010). The genetics of major depression: Moving beyond the monoamine hypothesis. *Psychiatric Clinics of North America*, 33, 125–140.

Siegel, A. B. (2010). Dream interpretation in clinical practice: A century after Freud. *Sleep Medicine Clinics*, 5(2), 299–313.

Siever, L., & Davis, L. (1991). A psychobiological perspective on the personality disorders. *American Journal of Psychiatry*, 148, 1647–1658.

Silverman, W. K., & Albano, A. M. (1996). *The Anxiety Disorder Interview Schedule for Children–IV–Child and Parent Version.* Boulder, CO: Graywind.

Silvia, P. J., & Kaufman, J. C. (2010). Creativity and mental illness. In J. Kaufman & R. Sternberg (Eds.), *The Cambridge handbook of creativity* (pp. 381–394). New York: Cambridge University Press.

Singh, A. (2002). Recent and conceptualized basic research activities for eating disorder: A review and future directions. *International Medical Journal*, 9, 83–85.

Skelton, R. (2006). *The Edinburgh international encyclopaedia of psychoanalysis.* Edinburgh: Edinburgh University Press.

Skodol, A. E., Gunderson, J. G., Shea, M. T., McGlashan, T. H., Morey, L. C., Sanislow, C. A., et al. (2005). The Collaborative Longitudinal Personality Disorders Study (CLPS). *Journal of Personality Disorders*, 19, 487–504.

Slade, M. (2009). *Personal recovery and mental illness: A guide for mental health professional.* Cambridge, UK: Cambridge University Press.

Slade, M., Loftus, L., Phelan, M., Thornicroft, G., & Wykes, T. (1999). *The Camberwell Assessment of Need.* London: Gaskell.

Smith, D. K., & Chamberlain, P. (2010). Multidimensional treatment foster care for adolescents: Processes and outcomes. In J. R. Weisz & A. E. Kazdin (Eds.), *Evidence-based psychotherapies for children and adolescents* (second edition, pp. 243–258). New York: Guilford Press.

Smith, L., Gates, S., & Foxcroft, D. (2006). Therapeutic communities for substance related disorder. *Cochrane Database of Systematic Reviews*, Issue 1, Art. No. CD005338. Published inline. doi:10.1002/14651858.CD005338.pub2

Smith, M., & Glass, G. (1977). Meta-analysis of psychotherapy outcome studies. *American Psychologist*, 32, 752–760.

Snyder, L. B., & Nadorff, P. G. (2010). Youth substance use and the media. In L. Scheier (Ed.), *Handbook of drug use etiology: Theory, methods, and empirical findings* (pp. 475–491). Washington, DC: American Psychological Association.

Soeteman, D., Hakkaart-van Roijen, L., Verheul, R., & Busschbach, J. (2008). The economic burden of personality disorders in mental health care. *Journal of Clinical Psychiatry*, 69, 259–265.

Solanto, M. (1998). Neuropsychopharmacological mechanisms of stimulant drug action in attention-deficit hyperactivity disorder: A review and integration. *Behavioural Brain Research*, 94, 127–152.

Spoont, M. R. (1992). Modulatory role of serotonin in neural information processing: Implications for human psychopathology. *Psychological Bulletin*, 112, 330–350.

Sprenkle, D., & Blow, A. (2004). Common factors and our sacred models. *Journal of Marital and Family Therapy*, 30, 113–130.

Stampfl, T. G., & Levis, D. J. (1968). Implosive therapy—A behavioural therapy. *Behaviour Research and Therapy*, 6, 31–36.

Stanley, B., & Brodsky, B. S. (2009). Dialectical behaviour therapy. In J. Oldham, A. Skodol, & D. Bender (Eds.), *Essentials of personality disorders* (pp. 235–252). Arlington, VA: American Psychiatric Publishing.

Starcevic, V., & Berle, D. (2006). Cognitive specificity of anxiety disorders: A review of selected key constructs. *Depression and Anxiety*, 23, 51–61.

Steer, R., Beck, J., Beck, A., & Jolly, J. (2005). *Beck Youth Inventories for Children and Adolescents* (second edition) (BYI-II). San Antonio, TX: Psychological Corporation.

Stein, D., & Lambert, M. (1995). Graduate training in psychotherapy: Are therapy outcomes enhanced? *Journal of Consulting & Clinical Psychology*, 63, 182–196.

Steinhausen, J. (2002). The outcome of anorexia nervosa in the 20th century. *American Journal of Psychiatry*, 159, 1284–1293.

Stern, A. (1938). Psychoanalytic investigation of and therapy in the borderline group of neuroses. *Psychoanalytic Quarterly*, 7, 467–489.

Stevenson, J. (2010). Recent research on food additives: Implications for CAMH. *Child and Adolescent Mental Health*, 15(3), 130–133.

Stewart, D. G., & Davis, K. L. (2008). Neuropathology. In K. Mueser & D. Jeste (Eds.), *Clinical handbook of schizophrenia* (pp. 44–54). New York: Guilford Press.

Stewart, S. E., Jenike, E., & Jenike, M. A. (2009). Biological treatment for obsessive-compulsive disorder. In M. M. Antony & M. B. Stein (Eds.), *Oxford handbook of anxiety and related disorders* (pp. 375–390). New York: Oxford University Press.

Stice, E. (2002). Risk and maintenance factors for eating pathology: A meta-analytic review. *Psychological Bulletin*, 825–848.

Stice, E., Agras, S., & Hammer, L. (1999). Risk factors for the development of childhood eating disturbances: A five year prospective study. *International Journal of Eating Disorders*, 25, 375–387.

Stiles, W., & Wolfe, B. (2006). Relationship factors in treating anxiety disorders. In L. Castonguay & L. Beutler (Eds.), *Principles of therapeutic change that work* (pp. 155–166). Oxford: Oxford University Press.

Still, G. (1902). The Coulstonian lectures on some abnormal physical conditions in children, *Lancet i*, 1008–1012, 1077–1082, 1163–1169.

Strack, S. (2010). Evidence-based assessment and instrumentation for personality disorders. In J. J. Magnavita (Ed.), *Evidence-based treatment of personality dysfunction: Principles, methods, and processes* (pp. 19–48). Washington, DC: American Psychological Association.

Strauss, A. & Lehtinen, L. (1947). *Psychopathology and education of the brain-injured child.* New York: Grune & Stratton.

Striegel-Moore, R. H., & Bulik, C. M. (2007). Risk factors for eating disorders. *American Psychologist* (Special Issue: Eating Disorders), 62(3), 181–198.

Sullivan, H. S. (1953). *The interpersonal theory of psychiatry.* New York: Norton.

Sullivan, P., Kendler, K., & Neale, M. (2003). Schizophrenia as a complex trait—Evidence from a meta-analysis of twin studies. *Archives of General Psychiatry*, 60, 1187–1192.

Sullivan, P., Neale, M., & Kendler, K. (2000). Genetic epidemiology of major depression: Review and meta-analysis. *American Journal of Psychiatry*, 157, 1552–1562.

Sumner, J. A., Griffith, J., & Mineka, S. (2010). Overgeneral autobiographical memory as a predictor of the course of depression: A meta-analysis. *Behaviour Research and Therapy*, 48, 614–625.

Susman, E. J. (2006). Psychobiology of persistent antisocial behaviour: Stress, early vulnerabilities and the attenuation hypothesis. *Neuroscience and Biobehavioural Reviews*, 30, 376–389.

Svartberg, M., & McCullough, L. (2010). Cluster C personality disorders: Prevalence, phenomenology, treatment effects, and principles of treatment. In J. Clarkin, O. Fonagy, & G. Gabbard (Eds.), *Psychodynamic psychotherapy for personality disorders: A clinical handbook* (pp. 337–368). Arlington, VA: American Psychiatric Publishing.

Swanson, J. M., & Volkow, N. D. (2009). Psychopharmacology: Concepts and opinions about the use of stimulant medications. *Journal of Child Psychology and Psychiatry*, 50(1–2), 180–193.

Szasz, T. (2010). Psychiatry, anti-psychiatry, critical psychiatry: What do these terms mean? *Philosophy, Psychiatry, & Psychology*, 17, 229–232.

Taft, C. T., Watkins, L. E., Stafford, J., Street, A. E., & Monson, C. M. (2011). Posttraumatic stress disorder and intimate relationship problems: A meta-analysis. *Journal of Consulting and Clinical Psychology*, 79, 22–33.

Tai, S., & Turkington, D. (2009). The evolution of cognitive behaviour therapy for schizophrenia: Current practice and recent developments. *Schizophrenia Bulletin*, 35, 865–873.

Tammenmaa, I. A., Sailas, E., McGrath, J. J., Soares-Weiser, K., & Wahlbeck, K. (2004). Systematic review of cholinergic drugs for neuroleptic-induced tardive dyskinesia: A meta-analysis of randomized controlled trials. *Progress in Neuro-Psychopharmacology & Biological Psychiatry*, 28(7), 1099–1107.

Tandon, R., Keshavan, M. S., & Nasrallah, H. A. (2008a). Schizophrenia, "just the facts": What we know in 2008. Part 1: Overview. *Schizophrenia Research*, 100, 4–19.

Tandon, R., Keshavan, M. S., & Nasrallah, H. A. (2008b). Schizophrenia, "just the facts": What we know in 2008. Part 2: Epidemiology and aetiology. *Schizophrenia Research*, 102, 1–18.

Tandon, R., Nasrallah, H. A., & Keshavan, M. S. (2009). Schizophrenia, "just the facts" 4. Clinical features and conceptualization. *Schizophrenia Research*, 110, 1–23.

Tandon, R., Nasrallah, H. A., & Keshavan, M. S. (2010). Schizophrenia, "just the facts" 5. Treatment and prevention past, present and future. *Schizophrenia Research*, 122, 1–23.

Tanofsky-Kraff, M., & Wilfley, D. E. (2010). Interpersonal psychotherapy for the treatment of eating disorders. In W. S. Agras (Ed.), *The Oxford handbook of eating disorders* (pp. 348–372). New York: Oxford University Press.

Taylor, E. (2008). Disorders of attention and activity. In M. Rutter et al. (Eds.), *Rutter's child and adolescent psychiatry* (fifth edition, pp. 521–542). London: Blackwell.

Taylor, E., & Rogers, J. W. (2005). Practitioner review: Early adversity and developmental disorders. *Journal of Child Psychology and Psychiatry*, 46(5), 451–467.

Teichner, G., & Golden, C. J. (2000). The relationship of neuropsychological impairment to conduct disorder in adolescence: A conceptual review. *Aggression and Violent Behaviour*, 5, 509–528.

Tenhula, W. N., & Bellack, A. S. (2008). Social skills training. In K. Mueser & D. Jeste (Eds.), *Clinical handbook of schizophrenia* (pp. 240–248). New York: Guilford Press.

Tevyaw, T., & Monti, P. (2004). Motivational enhancement and other brief interventions for adolescent substance abuse: Foundations, applications and evaluations. *Addiction*, 99, 63–75.

Thapar, A., & Scourfield, J. (2002). Childhood disorders. In P. McGuffin, M. Owen, & I. Gottesman (Eds.), *Psychiatric genetics and genomics* (pp. 147–180). Oxford: Oxford University Press.

Thapar, A., & Stergiakouli, E. (2008). An overview on the genetics of ADHD. *Acta Psychologica Sinica* (Special Issue: Behavioural Genetics), 40(10), 1088–1098.

Thase, M. (2009). *Neurobiological aspects of depression*. In H. Gotlib & C. Hammen (Eds.), *Handbook of depression* (second edition, pp. 187–217). New York: Guilford Press.

Thase, M., & Jindal, R. (2004). Combining psychotherapy and pharmacotherapy for treatment of mental disorders. In M. Lambert (Ed.), *Bergin and Garfield's handbook of psychotherapy and behaviour change* (fifth edition, pp. 743–766). New York: Wiley.

Thompson, P., Vidal, C., Giedd, J., Gochman, P. Blumenthal, J., Nicolson, R., et al. (2001). Mapping adolescent brain change reveals dynamic wave of accelerated gray matter loss in very early-onset schizophrenia. *Proceedings* of the *National Academy of Sciences of the United States of America*, 98, 11650–11655.

Thompson-Brenner, H., Glass, S., & Westen, D. (2003). A multidimensional meta-analysis of psychotherapy for bulimia nervosa. *Clinical Psychology: Science and Practice*, 10, 268–287.

Thompson-Brenner, H., Weingeroff, J., & Westen, D. (2009). Empirical support for psychodynamic psychotherapy for eating disorders. In R. A. Levy & J. S. Ablon (Eds.), *Handbook of evidence-based psychodynamic psychotherapy: Bridging the gap between science and practice* (pp. 67–92). Totowa, NJ: Humana Press.

Tomás, P., Fuentes, I., Roder, V., & Ruiz, J. (2010). Cognitive rehabilitation programs in schizophrenia: Current status and perspectives international. *Journal of Psychology and Psychological Therapy*, 10, 191–204.

Toplak, M. E., Connors, L., Shuster, J., Knezevic, B., & Parks, S. (2008). Review of cognitive, cognitive-behavioural, and neural-based interventions for attention-deficit/hyperactivity disorder (ADHD). *Clinical Psychology Review*, 28(5), 801–823.

Torgersen, S. (2009). Prevalence, sociodemographics, and functional impairment. In J. Oldham, A. Skodol, & D. Bender (Eds.), *Essentials of personality disorders* (pp. 83–102). Arlington, VA: American Psychiatric Publishing.

Toumbourou, J. W., Stockwell, T., Neighbors, C., Marlatt, G. A., Sturge, J., & Rehm, J. (2007). Interventions to reduce harm associated with adolescent substance use. *The Lancet*, 369(9570), 1391–1401.

Trauer, T., Tobias, G., & Slade, M. (2008). Development and evaluation of a patient-rated version of the Camberwell Assessment of Need Short Appraisal Schedule (CANSAS-P). *Community Mental Health Journal*, 44, 113–124.

Turner, E. H., Matthews, A. M., Linardatos, E., Tell, R. A., & Rosenthal, R. (2008). Selective publication of antidepressant trials and its influence on apparent efficacy. *New England Journal of Medicine*, 358, 252–260.

Udechuku, A., Nguyen, T., Hill, R., & Szego, K. (2010). Antidepressants in pregnancy: A systematic review. *Australian and New Zealand Journal of Psychiatry*, 44, 978–996.

US–UK Team (1974). The diagnosis and psychopathology of schizophrenia in New York and London. *Schizophrenia Bulletin*, 1, 80–102.

Vahia, I. V., & Cohen, C. I. (2008). Psychopathology. In K. Mueser & D. Jeste (Eds.), *Clinical handbook of schizophrenia* (pp. 82–90). New York: Guilford Press.

Van Ameringen, M., Mancini, C., & Patterson, B. (2009). Pharmacotherapy for social anxiety disorder and specific phobia. In M. M. Antony & M. B. Stein (Eds.), *Oxford handbook of anxiety and related disorders* (pp. 321–333). New York: Oxford University Press.

van Goozen, S. H. M., Fairchild, G., & Harold, G. T. (2008). The role of neurobiological deficits in childhood antisocial behaviour. *Current Directions in Psychological Science*, 17(3), 224–228.

van Goozen, S. H. M., Fairchild, G., Snoek, H., & Harold, G. T. (2007). The evidence for a neurobiological model of childhood antisocial behaviour. *Psychological Bulletin*, 133(1), 149–182.

Vittengl, J., Clark, L., Dunn, T., & Jarrett, R. (2007). Reducing relapse and recurrence in unipolar depression: A comparative meta-analysis of cognitive-behavioural therapy. *Journal of Consulting and Clinical Psychology*, 75, 475–488.

Vögele, C., & Gibson, E. L. (2010). Mood, emotions, and eating disorders. In W. S. Agras (Ed.), *The Oxford handbook of eating disorders* (pp. 180–205). New York: Oxford University Press.

Wade, T. D. (2010). Genetic influences on eating and the eating disorders. In W. S. Agras (Ed.), *The Oxford handbook of eating disorders* (pp. 103–122). New York: Oxford University Press.

Waldron, H. B., & Brody, J. L. (2010). Functional family therapy for adolescent substance use disorders. In J. R. Weisz & A. E. Kazdin (Eds.), *Evidence-based psychotherapies for children and adolescents* (second edition, pp. 401–415). New York: Guilford Press.

Waldron, H. B., & Turner, C. W. (2008). Evidence-based psychosocial treatments for adolescent substance abuse. *Journal of Clinical Child and Adolescent Psychology* (Special Issue: Evidence-Based Psychosocial Treatments for Children and Adolescents: A Ten Year Update), 37, 238–261.

Walker, E., Kestler, L. & Bollini, A. (2004). Schizophrenia: Aetiology and course. *Annual Review of Psychology*, 55, 401–430.

Walker, E., Mittal, V., & Tessner, K. (2008). Stress and the hypothalamic pituitary adrenal axis in the developmental course of schizophrenia. *Annual Review of Clinical Psychology*, 4, 189–216.

Walton, K. E., Ormel, J., & Krueger, R. F. (2011). The dimensional nature of externalizing behaviours in adolescence: Evidence from a direct comparison of categorical, dimensional, and hybrid models. *Journal of Abnormal Child Psychology*, 39, 553–561.

Wampold, B. (2001). *The great psychotherapy debate: Models, methods, and findings.* Mahwah, NJ: Lawrence Erlbaum Associates.

Watson, D. (2009). Differentiating the mood and anxiety disorders: A quadripartite model. *Annual Review of Clinical Psychology*, 5, 221–247.

Watson, H. J., & Rees, C. S. (2008). Meta-analysis of randomized, controlled treatment trials for pediatric obsessive-compulsive disorder. *Journal of Child Psychology and Psychiatry*, 49(5), 489–498.

Webster-Stratton, C., & Reid, M. J. (2010). The Incredible Years parents, teachers, and children training series: A multifaceted treatment approach for young children with conduct disorders. In J. R. Weisz & A. E. Kazdin (Eds.), *Evidence-based psychotherapies for children and adolescents* (second edition, pp. 194–210). New York: Guilford Press.

Wechsler, D. (2004a). *Wechsler Intelligence Scale for Children. Fourth Edition UK (WISC-IV[uk]).* San Antonio, TX: Psychological Corporation.

Wechsler, D. (2004b). *Wechsler Preschool and Primary Scale of Intelligence–III UK (WPPSI-III[uk]).* San Antonio, TX: Psychological Corporation.

Wechsler, D. (2005). *Wechsler Individual Achievement Test–II UK (WIAT-II[uk].* San Antonio, TX: Psychological Corporation.

Wechsler, D. (2009). *Wechsler Adult Intelligence Scale–Fourth Edition UK (WAIS-IV[uk]).* San Antonio, TX: Psychological Corporation.

Weeks, J. W., Heimberg, R. G., Fresco, D. M., Hart, T. A., Turk, C. L., Schnieier, F. R., et al. (2005). Empirical validation and psychometric evaluation of the Brief Fear of Negative Evaluation Scale in patients with social anxiety disorder. *Psychological Assessment*, 17, 179–190.

Weinberg, W., Harper, C., & Brumback, R. (2002). Substance use and abuse: Epidemiology, pharmacological considerations, identification and suggestions towards management. In M. Rutter & E. Taylor (Eds.), *Child and adolescent psychiatry* (fourth edition, pp. 437–454). Oxford: Blackwell.

Weissman, A., & Beck, A. (1978). *Development and validation of the Dysfunctional Attitudes Scale.* Paper presented at AABT, Chicago. Scale is on pp. 100–104 of Williams, M. (1992). *The Psychological treatment of depression* (second edition). London: Routledge.

Weisz, J., Weiss, B., Alicke, M., & Klotz, M. (1987). Effectiveness of psychotherapy with children and adolescents: A meta-analysis for clinicians. *Journal of Consulting and Clinical Psychology*, 55, 542–549.

Weisz, J., Weiss, B., Han, S. & Granger, D. (1995). Effects of psychotherapy with children and adolescents revisited: A meta-analysis of treatment outcome studies. *Psychological Bulletin*, 117, 450–468.

West, R. (2006). *Theory of addiction*. Oxford: Blackwell.

Wetchler, J., & Piercy, F. (1996). Experiential family therapies. In F. Piercy et al. (Eds.), *Family therapy sourcebook* (second edition, pp. 79–105). New York: Guilford.

Widiger, T. A. (2008). Personality disorders. In J. Hunsley & E. J. Mash (Eds.), *A guide to assessments that work* (pp. 413–435). New York: Oxford University Press.

Widiger, T. A., & Mullins-Sweatt, S. N. (2010). Clinical utility of a dimensional model of personality disorder. *Professional Psychology: Research and Practice*, 41, 488–494.

Wieder, H. & Kaplan, E. (1969). Drug use in adolescents: Psychodynamic meaning and pharmacological effect. *Psychoanalytic Study of the Child*, 24, 399.

Wierzbicki, M., & Pekarik, G. (1993). A meta-analysis of psychotherapy dropout. *Professional Psychology: Research & Practice*, 24, 190–195.

Wikler, A. (1973). Dynamics of drug dependence. *Archives of General Psychiatry*, 28, 611–616.

Williams, R. & Chang, S. (2000). A comprehensive and comparative review of adolescent substance abuse treatment outcome. *Clinical Psychology: Science and Practice*, 7, 138–166.

Williams, W. (2001). Relevant experience. *The Psychologist*, 14(4), 188–189.

Wills, T. A., & Ainette, M. G. (2010). Temperament, self-control, and adolescent substance use: A two-factor model of etiological processes. In L. Scheier (Ed.), *Handbook of drug use etiology: Theory, methods, and empirical findings* (pp. 127–146). Washington, DC: American Psychological Association.

Wilson, G. (2010). Cognitive behavioural therapy for eating disorders. In W. S. Agras (Ed.), *The Oxford handbook of eating disorders* (pp. 331–347). New York: Oxford University Press.

Wilson, G., & Fairburn, C. (2007). Treatments for eating disorders. In P. Nathan & J. Gorman (Eds.), *A guide to treatments that work* (third edition, pp. 579–609). New York: Oxford University Press.

Winkelmann, K., Stefini, A., Hartmann, M., Geiser-Elze, A., Kromüller, A., Schenkenbach, C., et al. (2005). Efficacy of psychodynamic short-term psychotherapy for children and adolescents with behavioural disorders. *Praxis der Kinderpsychologie und Kinderpsychiatrie*, 54, 598–614.

Winter, D., & Viney, L. (2005). *Personal construct psychotherapy: Advances in theory, practice and research*. London: Whurr.

Winters, K. (1991). *Personal Experience Screening Questionnaire*. Los Angeles: Western Psychological Services.

Winters, K., & Henly, G. (1989). *Personal Experience Inventory*. Los Angeles: Western Psychological Services.

Winters, K. C., Stinchfield, R. D., Opland, E., Weller, C., & Latimer, W. W. (2000). The effectiveness of the Minnesota Model approach in the treatment of adolescent drug abusers. *Addiction*, 95, 601–612.

Witkiewitz, K., & Marlatt, G. A. (2004). Relapse prevention for alcohol and drug problems: That was zen, this is tao. *American Psychologist*, 59, 224–235.

Wolpe, J. (1969). *The practice of behaviour therapy*. New York: Pergamon Press.

Woods, R., & Clare, L. (2008). *Handbook of the clinical psychology of ageing* (second edition). Chichester, UK: Wiley.

Woody, S., & Ollendick, T. (2006). Technique factors in treating anxiety disorders. In L. Castonguay & L. Beutler (Eds.), *Principles of therapeutic change that work* (pp. 167–186). Oxford: Oxford University Press.

World Health Organization (1992). *The ICD-10 Classification of Mental and Behavioural Disorders.* Geneva, Switzerland: WHO.

Xie, P., Kranzler, H., Poling, J., Stein, M., Anton, R., Brady, K., et al. (2009). Interactive effect of stressful life events and the serotonin transporter 5-HTTLPR genotype on posttraumatic stress disorder diagnosis in 2 independent populations. *Archives of General Psychiatry*, 66, 1201–1209.

Yeomans, F. E., & Diamond, D. (2010). Transference-focused psychotherapy and borderline personality disorder. In J. Clarkin, O. Fonagy, & G. Gabbard (Eds.), *Psychodynamic psychotherapy for personality disorders: A clinical handbook* (pp. 209–238). Arlington, VA: American Psychiatric Publishing.

Young, S., & Amarasinghe, J. M. (2010). Practitioner review: Non-pharmacological treatments for ADHD: A lifespan approach. *Journal of Child Psychology and Psychiatry*, 51(2), 116–133.

Zahradnik, M., & Stewart, S. H. (2009). Anxiety disorders and substance use disorder comorbidity. In M. M. Antony & M. B. Stein (Eds.), *Oxford handbook of anxiety and related disorders* (pp. 565–575). New York: Oxford University Press.

Zajecka, J., & Goldstein, C. (2009). Combining medications to achieve remission. In T. L. Schwartz & T. J. Petersen (Eds.), *Depression: Treatment strategies and management* (second edition, pp. 54–100). London: Inform Healthcare.

Zgierska, A., Rabago, D., Chawla, N., Kushner, K., Koehler, R., & Marlatt, A. (2009). Mindfulness meditation for substance use disorders: A systematic review. *Substance Abuse*, 30, 266–294.

Ziguras, S., & Stuart, G. (2000). A meta-analysis of the effectiveness of mental health case management over 20 years. *Psychiatric Services*, 51, 1410–1421.

Zimmerman, M., Chelminski, I., & Young, D. (2008). The frequency of personality disorders in psychiatric patients. *Psychiatric Clinics of North America*, 31, 405–420.

Zohar, J., Fostick, L. & Juven-Wetzler, E. (2009). Obsessive-compulsive disorder. In M. Gelder et al. (Eds.), *New Oxford textbook of psychiatry* (second edition, Vol. 1, pp. 765–774). Oxford: Oxford University Press.

Zubin, J., & Spring, B. (1977). Vulnerability: A new view of schizophrenia. *Journal of Abnormal Psychology*, 86, 103–126.

Zuckerman, M. (2007). *Sensation seeking and risky behaviour.* Washington, DC: American Psychological Association.

Index